P9-DHK-323

Rick Steves ®

SCANDINAVIA

CONTENTS

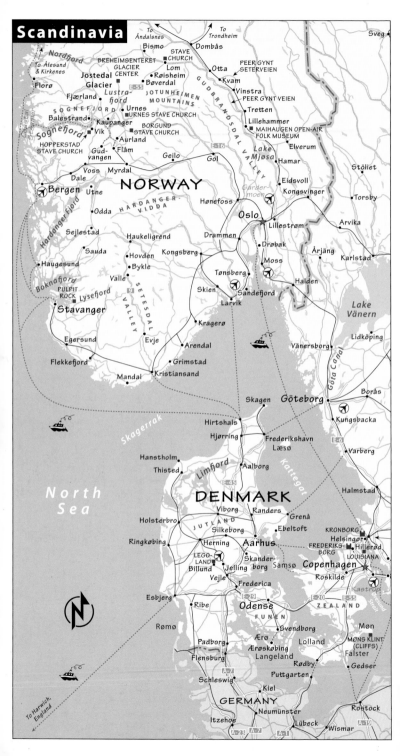

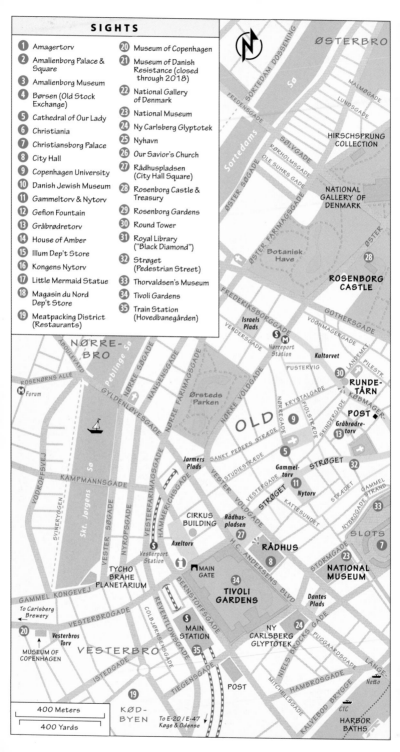

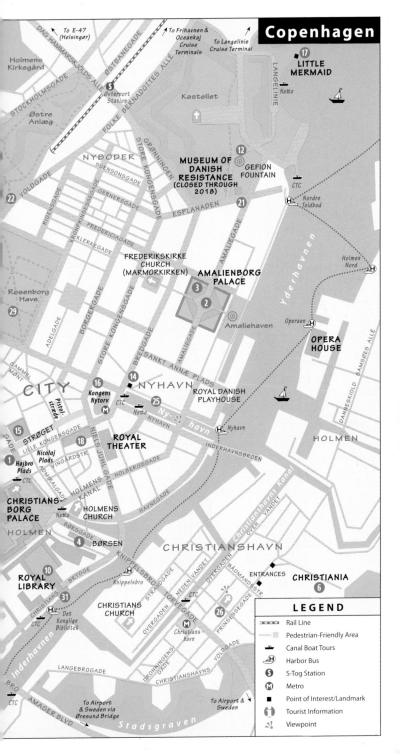

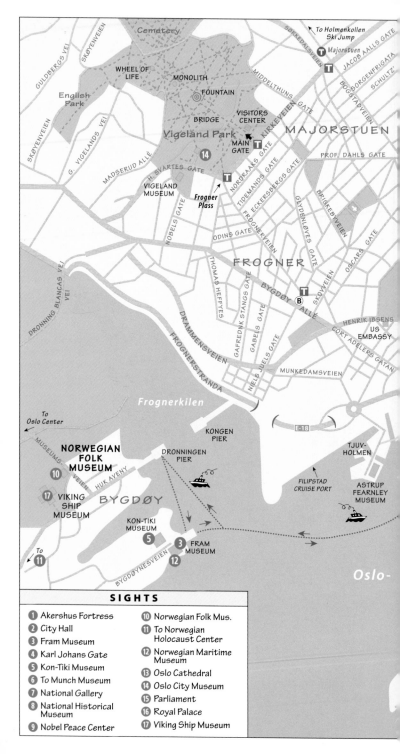

SIGHTS

1. Akershus Fortress
2. City Hall
3. Fram Museum
4. Karl Johans Gate
5. Kon-Tiki Museum
6. To Munch Museum
7. National Gallery
8. National Historical Museum
9. Nobel Peace Center
10. Norwegian Folk Mus.
11. To Norwegian Holocaust Center
12. Norwegian Maritime Museum
13. Oslo Cathedral
14. Oslo City Museum
15. Parliament
16. Royal Palace
17. Viking Ship Museum

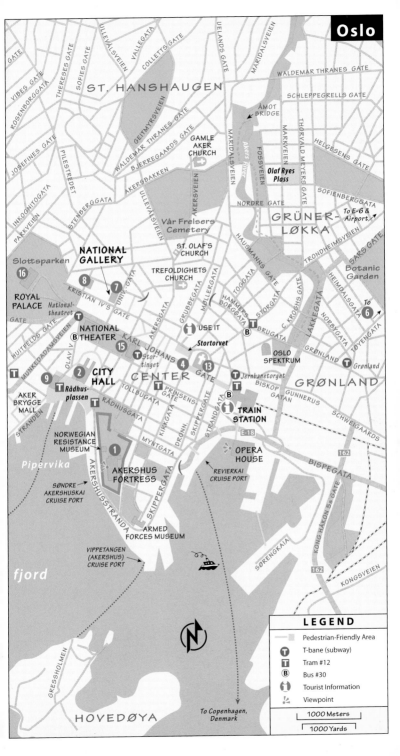

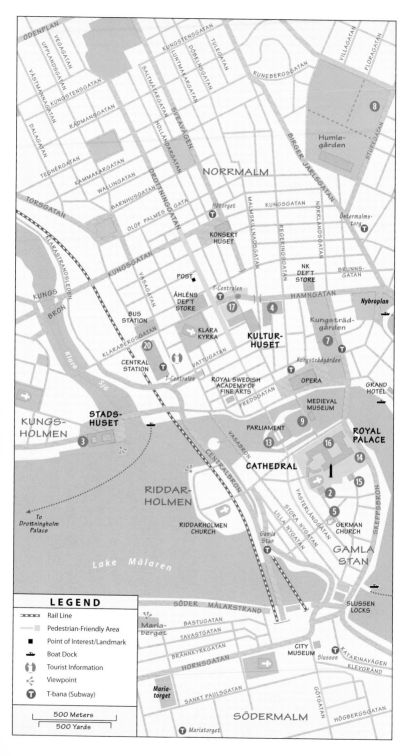

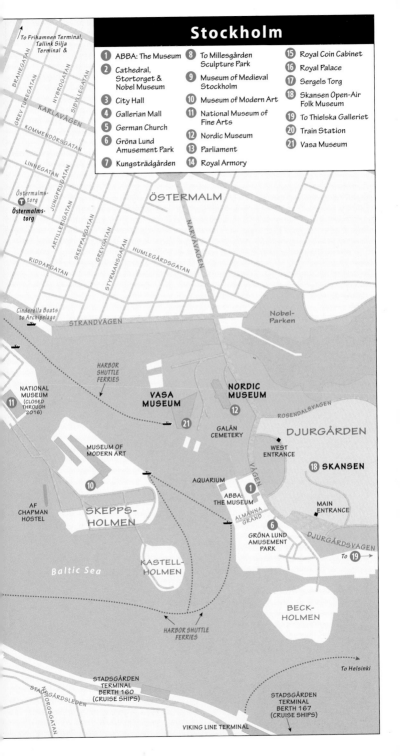

Stockholm

1. ABBA: The Museum
2. Cathedral, Stortorget & Nobel Museum
3. City Hall
4. Gallerian Mall
5. German Church
6. Gröna Lund Amusement Park
7. Kungsträdgården
8. To Millesgården Sculpture Park
9. Museum of Medieval Stockholm
10. Museum of Modern Art
11. National Museum of Fine Arts
12. Nordic Museum
13. Parliament
14. Royal Armory
15. Royal Coin Cabinet
16. Royal Palace
17. Sergels Torg
18. Skansen Open-Air Folk Museum
19. To Thielska Galleriet
20. Train Station
21. Vasa Museum

To Frihamnen Terminal, Tallink Silja Terminal &

BRAHEGATAN
GREV TUREGATAN
NYBROGATAN
SIBYLLEGATAN
KARLAVÄGEN
KOMMENDÖRSGATAN
LINNÉGATAN

Östermalms-torg

ÖSTERMALM

ARTILLERIGATAN
SKEPPARGATAN
GREVGATAN
STYRMANSGATAN
JUNGFRUGATAN
HUMLEGÅRDSGATAN
NARVAVÄGEN
RIDDARGATAN

Cinderella Boats to Archipelago

STRANDVÄGEN

Nobel-Parken

HARBOR SHUTTLE FERRIES

NATIONAL MUSEUM (CLOSED THROUGH 2016)

VASA MUSEUM

NORDIC MUSEUM

ROSENDALSVÄGEN

DJURGÅRDEN

GALÄN CEMETERY

WEST ENTRANCE

SKANSEN

MUSEUM OF MODERN ART

AQUARIUM

ABBA: THE MUSEUM

MAIN ENTRANCE

AF CHAPMAN HOSTEL

SKEPPS-HOLMEN

ALMÄNNA GRAND

GRÖNA LUND AMUSEMENT PARK

DJURGÅRDSVÄGEN

To 19 →

Baltic Sea

KASTELL-HOLMEN

BECK-HOLMEN

HARBOR SHUTTLE FERRIES

STADSGÅRDEN TERMINAL BERTH 160 (CRUISE SHIPS)

STADSGÅRDSLEDEN

STADSGÅRDEN TERMINAL BERTH 167 (CRUISE SHIPS)

To Helsinki

VIKING LINE TERMINAL

Bergen

SKOLTEN CRUISE TERMINAL

SKOLTEGRUNNS-KAIEN

INTERNATIONAL FERRIES

B

SKUTEVIKSTORGET

E85

BERGENHUS FORTRESS

2

HÅKON'S HALL

9

FESTNINGS-KAIEN

Harbor

ROSEN-KRANTZ TOWER

NORDNES

AQUARIUM

1

STRANDGATEN

C. SUNDTS GATE

HARBOR FERRIES

POOL

HAUGEVEIEN

SWIMMING BEACH

Nordnesparken

STRANDSIDEN

NORDNESVEIEN

NYKIRKEN

C. SUNDTS GATE

STRANDGATEN

Puddefjorden

HAUGEVEIEN

HOLBERGSALLM.

KLOSTERGATEN

SKOTTEGATEN

NØSTEGATEN

ENGEN

HURTIGRUTE TERMINAL (COASTAL STEAMERS)

NØSTEGATTEN

555

TORBORG NEDREAASGATE

JEKTEVIKEN/DOKKEN CRUISE PORT

SIGHTS

1. Aquarium
2. Bergenhus Fortress
3. Bryggens Museum
4. Cathedral
5. Fish Market
6. Fløibanen Funicular
7. Fortress Museum
8. To Gamle Bergen
9. Håkon's Hall
10. Hanseatic Quarter & Museum
11. Kode Art Museums of Bergen
12. Leprosy Museum
13. Ole Bulls Plass
14. Rosenkrantz Tower
15. St. Mary's Church
16. Theta Museum
17. Torgallmenningen (Main Square)
18. Bus to Ulriken643 Cable Car
19. Tram to Troldhaugen & Fantoft Stave Church

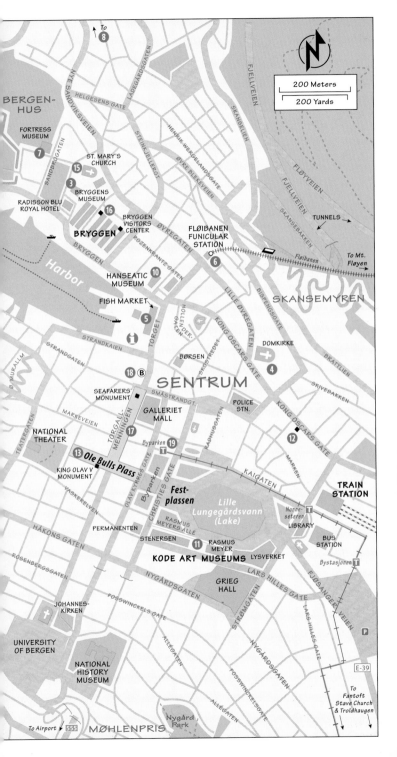

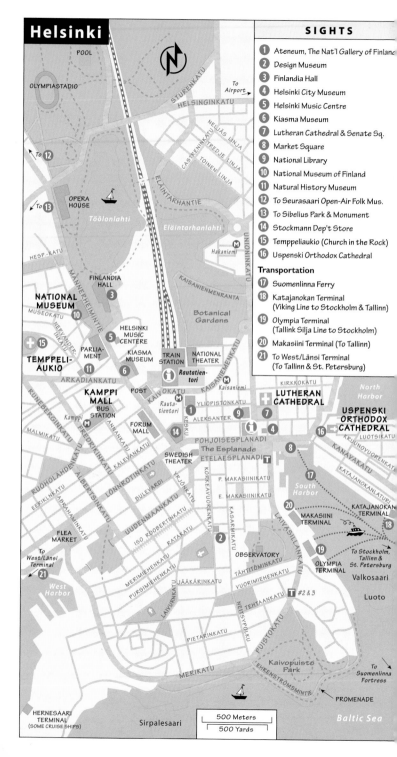

Helsinki

POOL

OLYMPIASTADIO

To Airport

STURENKATU

HELSINGINKATU

NELJÄS LINJA

CASTRENINKATU / TREDJE LINJA

TOINEN LINJA

ELÄINTARHANTIE

OPERA HOUSE

To 12

To 13

Töölönlahti

Eläintarhanlahti

HESP-KATU

Hakaniemi

FINLANDIA HALL

KAISANIEMENRANTA

UNIONINKATU

NATIONAL MUSEUM

MUSEOKATU

MANNERHEIMINTIE

Botanical Gardens

NEXANDER- INKATU

HELSINKI MUSIC CENTERE

TEMPPELI- AUKIO

PARLIA- MENT

KIASMA MUSEUM

TRAIN STATION

NATIONAL THEATER

ARKADIANKATU

Rautatien- tori

KAISANIEMENKATU

KIRKKOKATU

Kaisaniemi

North Harbor

RUNEBERGINKATU

KAMPPI MALL

POST

KAIVOKATU

Rautatien- tori

YLIOPISTONKATU

LUTHERAN CATHEDRAL

USPENSKI ORTHODOX CATHEDRAL

BUS STATION

Kamppi

FORUM MALL

ALEKSANTER.

LUOTSIKATU

MALMIKATU

FREDRIKINKATU

ANNANKATU

KALEVANKATU

SWEDISH THEATER

POHJOISESPLANADI

The Esplanade ETELÄESPLANADI

KRUUNUVUORENKATE

KANAVAKATU

EERIKINKATU

ABRAHAMINKATU

ALBERTINKATU

LÖNNROTINKATU

YRJÖNKATU

KORKEAVUORENKATU

P. MAKASIINIKATU

E. MAKASIINIKATU

South Harbor

KANAVAKATU

KATAJANOKANLAITURI

KATAJANOKAN TERMINAL

RUOHOLAHDENKATU

BULEVARDI

UUDENMAANKATU

ISO ROOBERTINKATU

RATAKATU

KASARMIKATU

MAKASIINI TERMINAL

FLEA MARKET

To West/Länsi Terminal

MERIMIEHENKATU

PURSIMIEHENKATU

JÄÄKÄRINKATU

LAIVURINKATU

OBSERVATORY

TÄHTITORNINKATU

VUORIMIEHENKATU

LAIVASILLANKATU

OLYMPIA TERMINAL

To Stockholm, Tallinn & St. Petersburg

Valkosaari

Luoto

West Harbor

#2 & 3

NEITSYPOLKU

TEHTAANKATU

PIETARINKATU

PUISTOKATU

To Suomenlinna Fortress

MERIKATU

EHRENSTRÖMSMINTIE

Kaivopuisto Park

PROMENADE

HERNESAARI TERMINAL (SOME CRUISE SHIPS)

Sirpalesaari

500 Meters

500 Yards

Baltic Sea

SIGHTS

1. Ateneum, The Nat'l Gallery of Finland
2. Design Museum
3. Finlandia Hall
4. Helsinki City Museum
5. Helsinki Music Centre
6. Kiasma Museum
7. Lutheran Cathedral & Senate Sq.
8. Market Square
9. National Library
10. National Museum of Finland
11. Natural History Museum
12. To Seurasaari Open-Air Folk Mus.
13. To Sibelius Park & Monument
14. Stockmann Dep't Store
15. Temppeliaukio (Church in the Rock)
16. Uspenski Orthodox Cathedral

Transportation

17. Suomenlinna Ferry
18. Katajanokan Terminal (Viking Line to Stockholm & Tallinn)
19. Olympia Terminal (Tallink Silja Line to Stockholm)
20. Makasiini Terminal (To Tallinn)
21. To West/Länsi Terminal (To Tallinn & St. Petersburg)

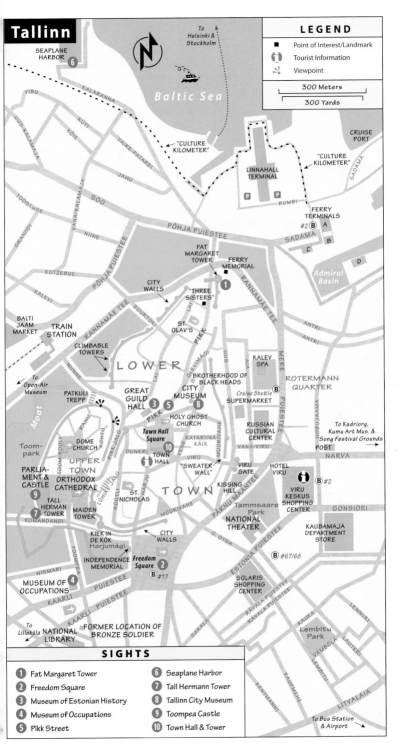

Tallinn

LEGEND

- ■ Point of Interest/Landmark
- 🛈 Tourist Information
- 📷 Viewpoint

300 Meters

300 Yards

To Helsinki & Stockholm

Baltic Sea

CRUISE PORT

SADAMA

"CULTURE KILOMETER"

"CULTURE KILOMETER"

LINNAHALL TERMINAL

P   P

RUMBI

FERRY TERMINALS

Ⓑ #2   A

SADAMA   B

C   B

Admiral Basin

D

PÕHJA PUIESTEE

VIBU

UUS-KALAMAJA

KÜTI

VAIKE-PATAREI

KALARANNA

JAHU

SOO

VANA-KALAMAJA

NIINE

TOOSTUSE

GRANIIDI

KOTZEBUE

KALEVI

BALTI JAAM MARKET

TRAIN STATION

RANNAMÄE TEE

SUURTÜKI

CITY WALLS

FAT MARGARET TOWER

FERRY MEMORIAL

❶

"THREE SISTERS"

ST. OLAV'S

PIKK

OLEVIMÄGI

SUUR

AIA

RANNAMÄE TEE

AHTRI

AHTRI

KALEV SPA

MERE PUIESTEE

ROTERMANN QUARTER

CLIMBABLE TOWERS

L O W E R

NUNNE

LAI

PIKK

BROTHERHOOD OF BLACK HEADS

CITY MUSEUM ❽

Cruise Shuttle SUPERMARKET

RUSSIAN CULTURAL CENTER

To Open-Air Museum

PATKULI TREPP

Moat

RATU

KOHTU

GREAT GUILD HALL

PIKK ❸ ❺

HOLY GHOST CHURCH

Town Hall Square

DUNKRI

❿

KATARIINA KÄIK

MÜÜRIVAHE

VANA-VIRU

OBUJAAMA

To Kadriorg, Kumu Art Mus. & Song Festival Grounds

POST

NARVA

Toom-park

TOOM-KOOLI

DOME CHURCH

UPPER TOWN

PARLIA-MENT & CASTLE ❾

ORTHODOX CATHEDRAL

TOOM-RÜÜTLI

PIISKOPI

ST. NICHOLAS

LÜHIKE JALG

RÜÜTLI

HARJU

DUNKRI

TOWN HALL 🛈

VIRU

"SWEATER WALL"

VIRU GATE

T O W N

PÄRNU MAANTEE

KISSING HILL

VIRU HOTEL VIRU

🛈 Ⓑ #2

VIRU KESKUS SHOPPING CENTER

GONSIORI

TALL HERMAN TOWER ❼

MAIDEN TOWER

KOMANDANDI

KIEK IN DE KÖK

Harjumägi

CITY WALLS

MÜÜRIVAHE

Tammsaare Park

NATIONAL THEATER

KAUBAMAJA DEPARTMENT STORE

TOOMPEA

INDEPENDENCE MEMORIAL

Freedom Square ❷

Ⓑ #17

G. OTSA

ESTONIA PUIESTEE

Ⓑ #67/68

SOLARIS SHOPPING CENTER

RAVALA PUIESTEE

KAUKA

LENNUKI

Lembitu Park

WISMARI

MUSEUM OF OCCUPATIONS ❹

KAARLI

KAARLI PUIESTEE

PUIESTEE

SAKALA

RAVALA PUIESTEE

YAMBOLA

LAUTERI

LEMBITU

To Lilleküla

NATIONAL LIBRARY

FORMER LOCATION OF BRONZE SOLDIER

KAUPMEHE

KENTMANNI

To Bus Station & Airport

LITYALALA

SIGHTS

❶ Fat Margaret Tower
❷ Freedom Square
❸ Museum of Estonian History
❹ Museum of Occupations
❺ Pikk Street

❻ Seaplane Harbor
❼ Tall Hermann Tower
❽ Tallinn City Museum
❾ Toompea Castle
❿ Town Hall & Tower

SEAPLANE HARBOR ❻

Join in the Viking fun

Helsinki harbor, Finland

Gamla Stan, Stockholm, Sweden

Rick Steves

SCANDINAVIA

INTRODUCTION

Scandinavia—known for its stunning natural beauty, fun-loving cities, trend-setting design, progressive politics, high latitudes, and even higher taxes—is one of Europe's most enjoyable and most interesting corners. A visit here connects you with immigrant roots, modern European values, and the great outdoors like nowhere else. You'll gasp at breathtaking fjords, glide on a cruise ship among picturesque islands, and marvel at the efficiency and livability of its big cities. Yes, Scandinavia is expensive. But, delightfully, the best time to visit—summer—is also the best time to get great deals on the fancier hotels.

This book breaks Scandinavia into its top big-city, small-town, and rural attractions. It gives you all the information and opinions necessary to wring the maximum value out of your limited time and money. If you plan to visit for a month or less in Scandinavia, this book has all the information you'll need.

Experiencing the culture, people, and natural wonders of Scandinavia economically and hassle-free has been my life-long goal as a traveler, tour guide, and travel writer. With this book, I pass on to you the lessons I've learned.

This book is balanced to include a comfortable mix of exciting capital cities and cozy small towns. It covers the predictable biggies and mixes in a healthy dose of Back Door intimacy. Along with seeing Tivoli Gardens, Hans Christian Andersen's house, and *The Little Mermaid,* you'll take a bike tour of a sleepy, remote Danish isle, dock at a time-passed fjord village, and wander among eerie, prehistoric monoliths in Sweden. And for an exciting Baltic side trip, I've added my vote for the most interesting city in this corner of Europe—Tallinn, Estonia.

The best is, of course, only my opinion. But after spending half of my adult life exploring and researching Europe, I've developed a

INTRODUCTION

Map Legend

⅃	Viewpoint	✈	Airport	)⎯⎯⎯(	Tunnel
↑	Entrance	Ⓣ	T-Bana Stop		Pedestrian Zone
⊖	Tourist Info	Ⓣ	Tram Stop	------	Railway
WC	Restroom	Ⓜ	Metro Stop	....	Ferry/Boat Route
🏰	Castle	Ⓑ	Bus Stop	├─┼─┤	Tram
⛪	Church	Ⓢ	S-Tog Station	▦▦▦▦	Stairs
▪	Statue/Point of Interest	Ⓗ	Harbor Bus	. . . . .	Walk/Tour Route
	Park	Ⓟ	Parking	-------	Trail
		)(	Mtn. Pass		

Use this legend to help you navigate the maps in this book.

sixth sense for what travelers enjoy. Just thinking about the places featured in this book makes me want to belly up to a *smörgåsbord*.

ABOUT THIS BOOK

Rick Steves Scandinavia is your smiling Swede, your Nordic navigator, and a personal tour guide in your pocket. This book is organized by destination. Each is a mini-vacation on its own, filled with exciting sights, strollable neighborhoods, affordable places to stay, memorable places to eat, and handy survival phrases.

In the following chapters, you'll find these sections:

Planning Your Time suggests a schedule for how to best use your limited time.

Orientation includes specifics on public transportation, helpful hints, local tour options, easy-to-read maps, and tourist information.

Sights describes the top attractions and includes their cost and hours.

Self-Guided Walks take you through interesting neighborhoods, pointing out sights and fun stops.

Sleeping describes my favorite hotels, from good-value deals to cushy splurges.

Eating serves up a range of options, from inexpensive eateries to fancy restaurants.

Connections outlines your options for traveling to destinations by bus, train, plane, and boat. In car-friendly regions, I've also included route tips for drivers.

Country introductions give you an overview of each country's culture, customs, money, history, current events, cuisine, language, and other useful practicalities.

The **Scandinavian History** chapter introduces you to some

Key to This Book

Updates

This book is updated regularly—but things change. For the latest, visit www.ricksteves.com/update.

Abbreviations and Times

I use the following symbols and abbreviations in this book:

Sights are rated:

▲▲▲	Don't miss
▲▲	Try hard to see
▲	Worthwhile if you can make it
No rating	Worth knowing about

Tourist information offices are abbreviated as **TI,** and bathrooms are **WCs.** To categorize accommodations, I use a **Sleep Code** (described on page 724).

Like Europe, this book uses the **24-hour clock.** It's the same through 12:00 noon, then keeps going: 13:00, 14:00, and so on. For anything over 12, subtract 12 and add p.m. (14:00 is 2:00 p.m.).

When giving **opening times,** I include both peak season and off-season hours if they differ. So, if a museum is listed as "May-Oct daily 9:00-16:00," it should be open from 9 a.m. until 4 p.m. from the first day of May until the last day of October (but expect exceptions).

For **transit** or **tour departures,** I first list the frequency, then the duration. So, a train connection listed as "2/hour, 1.5 hours" departs twice each hour and the journey lasts an hour and a half.

key people and events in these nations' complicated pasts, making your sightseeing that much more meaningful.

Practicalities is a traveler's tool kit, with my best travel tips and advice about money, sightseeing, sleeping, eating, staying connected, and transportation (trains, buses, boats, car rentals, driving, and flights). There's also a list of recommended books and films.

The **appendix** has nuts-and-bolts information, including useful phone numbers and websites, a festival list, a climate chart, and a handy packing checklist.

Browse through this book, choose your favorite destinations, and link them up. Then have a great trip! Traveling like a temporary local, you'll get the absolute most out of every mile, minute, and dollar. As you visit places I know and love, I'm happy that you'll be meeting some of my favorite Scandinavian people.

Please Tear Up This Book!

There's no point in hauling around a big chapter on Norway for a day in Stockholm. That's why I hope you'll rip this book apart. Before your trip, attack this book with a utility knife to create an army of pocket-sized mini-guidebooks—one for each area you visit.

I love the ritual of trimming down the size of the guidebooks I'll be using: Fold the pages back until you break the spine, neatly slice apart the sections you want with a utility knife, then pull them out with the gummy edge intact. If you want, finish each one off with some clear, heavy-duty packing tape to smooth and reinforce the spine, or use a heavy-duty stapler along the edge to prevent the first and last pages from coming loose.

To make things even easier, I've created a line of laminated covers with slide-on binders. Every evening, you can make a habit of swapping out today's pages for tomorrow's. (For more on these binders, see www.ricksteves.com.)

While you may be tempted to keep this book intact as a souvenir of your travels, you'll appreciate even more the footloose freedom of traveling light.

Planning

This section will help you get started on planning your trip—with advice on trip costs, when to go, and what you should know before you take off.

TRAVEL SMART

Your trip to Scandinavia is like a complex play—it's easier to follow and really appreciate on a second viewing. While no one does the same trip twice to gain that advantage, reading this book in its entirety before your trip accomplishes much the same thing.

Design an itinerary that enables you to visit sights at the best possible times. Note holidays, festivals, specifics on sights, and days when sights are closed or most crowded (all covered in this book). To get between destinations smoothly, read the tips in the Practicalities chapter on taking trains, buses, and boats, or renting a car and driving. A smart trip is a puzzle—a fun, doable, and worthwhile challenge.

When you're plotting your itinerary, strive for a mix of intense and relaxed stretches. To maximize rootedness, minimize one-night stands. It's worth taking a long drive after dinner (or a train ride with a dinner picnic) to get settled in a town for two nights. Hotels are more likely to give a good price to someone staying more than one night. Every trip—and every traveler—needs slack time (laundry, picnics, people-watching, and so on). Pace yourself. Assume you will return.

Reread this book as you travel, and visit local tourist information offices (abbreviated as TI in this book). Upon arrival in a new town, lay the groundwork for a smooth departure; get the schedule for the train, bus, or boat that you'll take when you depart. Drivers can figure out the best route to their next destination.

Update your plans as you travel. You can carry a small mobile device (phone, tablet, laptop) to find out tourist information, learn the latest on sights (special events, tour schedule, etc.), book tickets and tours, make reservations, reconfirm hotels, research transportation connections, and keep in touch with your loved ones. If you don't want to bring a pricey device, you can use guest computers at hotels and make phone calls from landlines.

Enjoy the friendliness of the Scandinavian people. Connect with the culture. Set up your own quest for the best *kringle*, stave church, or *smörgåsbord*. Slow down and be open to unexpected experiences. Ask questions—most locals are eager to point you in their idea of the right direction. Keep a notepad in your pocket for noting directions, organizing your thoughts, and confirming prices. Wear your money belt, learn the currency, and figure out how to estimate prices in dollars. Those who expect to travel smart, do.

TRIP COSTS

Five components make up your trip costs: airfare, surface transportation, room and board, sightseeing and entertainment, and shopping and miscellany.

Airfare: A basic round-trip flight from the US to Copenhagen can cost $1,000-2,000, depending on where you fly from and when (cheaper in winter). Consider saving time and money in Scandinavia by flying into one city and out of another; for instance, into Copenhagen and out of Bergen. Overall, Kayak.com is the best place to start searching for flights on a combination of mainstream and budget carriers.

Surface Transportation: For a three-week whirlwind trip of my recommended destinations by public transportation, allow $650 per person. This pays for a second-class Scandinavia Eurail pass (4-country, 10 days in 2 months; offers a 20-40 percent discount on Stockholm-Helsinki or Helsinki-Tallinn boat fares), and the extra boat rides that aren't discounted by the pass (such as Tallinn-Stockholm). Train passes normally must be purchased outside Europe but aren't necessarily your best option—you may save money by simply buying tickets as you go. For more on public transportation and car rental, see "Transportation" in the Practicalities chapter.

Budget Tips

While Scandinavia is expensive, transportation passes, groceries, alternative accommodations, and admissions are affordable (about what you'd pay in England or Italy). Being aware of your budget options will save you money.

Even though it's still possible to find midsummer hotel discounts, these discounts are generally offered only by the more expensive hotels. You'll save much more by staying in hostels like the Scandinavians do (many hostels have double rooms and great breakfasts).

The breakfasts offered at your lodgings are all-you-can-eat, and so hearty that you'll need only a sandwich for lunch. If you'd prefer more of a meal, the good news is that many restaurants offer lunch specials under $20. At most restaurants, tap water is served free (except in Denmark), as are seconds on potatoes (so even if a restaurant's entrées cost $25, one entrée can easily make a complete dinner). Beer is very expensive, and wine is even more so (quench your thirst in Denmark, where alcohol isn't quite as pricey as it is farther north). Convenience and grocery stores offer a broad array of affordable to-go dishes, rescuing those shell-shocked by restaurant prices. You're never too far from a picnic-friendly park.

A Scandinavia rail pass can make train travel one of your smaller expenses; bus travel is even cheaper—and sometimes faster. At sights, ask about discounted admission costs, as many aren't posted.

The great scenery is free. When things are pricey, remind yourself you're not getting less for your travel dollar. Up here there simply aren't any lousy or cheap alternatives to classy, cozy, sleek Scandinavia. Even youth-hostel toilets are flushed by electronic sensors.

This book will help you save a shipload of money and days of headaches. Read it carefully. Many of the skills and tricks that are effective in Copenhagen work in Oslo and Stockholm as well.

If you'll be renting a car, allow roughly $300 per week, not including tolls, gas, and supplemental insurance; add about $180 per person for the round-trip boat fare between Stockholm and Helsinki. Ferrying to and from Tallinn adds another $130. If you'll be keeping the car for three weeks or more, look into leasing, which can save you money on insurance and taxes for trips of this length. Car rentals and leases are cheapest if arranged from the US.

Don't hesitate to consider flying, as budget airlines can be cheaper than taking the train (check www.skyscanner.com for intra-European flights).

Room and Board: You can manage comfortably in Scandinavia on an average of $140 a day per person for room and board. This allows $20 for lunch, $30 for dinner, and $90 for lodging (based on two people splitting the cost of a $180 double room that includes breakfast). Students and tightwads can enjoy Scandinavia for as little as $65 a day ($35 per hostel bed, $30 for groceries and snacks).

Sightseeing and Entertainment: In big cities, figure $10-20 per major sight (Oslo's Kon-Tiki Museum-$15, Copenhagen's Tivoli Gardens-$17), $5 for minor ones (climbing towers), and $30-40 for splurge experiences (such as folk concerts, bus tours, and fjord cruises). The major cities have cards giving you a 24-hour free run of the public transit system and entrance to many sights for about $50-60/day.

An overall average of $45 per day works for most people. Don't skimp here. After all, this category is the driving force behind your trip—you came to sightsee, enjoy, and experience Scandinavia.

Shopping and Miscellany: Shopping can vary in cost from nearly nothing to a small fortune. Good budget travelers find that this category has little to do with assembling a trip full of lifelong and wonderful memories.

SIGHTSEEING PRIORITIES

So much to see, so little time. How to choose? Depending on the length of your trip, and taking geographical proximity into account, here are my recommended priorities:

4 days:	Copenhagen, Stockholm (connected by a 5.5-hour express train)
6 days, add:	Oslo
8 days, add:	Norway in a Nutshell fjord trip, Bergen
10 days, add:	Overnight cruise from Stockholm to Helsinki
14 days, add:	Ærø, Odense, Roskilde, Frederiksborg (all in Denmark)
17 days, add:	Aarhus (Denmark), Kalmar (Sweden)
21 days, add:	Tallinn (Estonia) and more time in capitals
24 days, add:	More Norwegian countryside or Stockholm's archipelago

The map on page 9 and the three-week itinerary on page 8 include most of the stops in the first 21 days.

WHEN TO GO

Summer is a great time to go. Scandinavia bustles and glistens under the July and August sun; it's the height of the tourist season, when all the sightseeing attractions are open and in full swing. In many cases, things don't kick into gear until midsummer—about June 20—when Scandinavian schools let out. Most local industries take July off, and the British and southern Europeans tend to visit Scandinavia in August. You'll notice crowds during these times, but up here "crowds" mean fun and action rather than congestion.

Scandinavia's Best
Three-Week Trip by Car

Day	Plan	Sleep in
1	Arrive in Copenhagen	Copenhagen
2	Copenhagen	Copenhagen
3	Copenhagen	Copenhagen
4	Sights near Copenhagen, into Sweden	Växjö
5	Växjö, Glass Country, Kalmar	Kalmar
6	Kalmar to Stockholm	Stockholm
7	Stockholm	Stockholm
8	Stockholm	Boat to Helsinki
9	Helsinki	Boat to Stockholm
10	Uppsala to Oslo	Oslo
11	Oslo	Oslo
12	Oslo	Oslo
13	Lillehammer, Gudbrandsdal Valley	Jotunheimen area
14	Jotunheimen Country	Lustrafjord area or Aurland
15	Sognefjord, Norway in a Nutshell	Bergen
16	Bergen	Bergen
17	Long drive south, Setesdal Valley	Kristiansand
18	Jutland, Aarhus, maybe Legoland	Aarhus (maybe Billund)
19	Jutland to Odense en route to Ærø	Ærøskøbing
20	Ærø	Ærøskøbing
21	Roskilde on the way into Copenhagen	Copenhagen

At these northern latitudes, the days are long—on June 21 the sun comes up around 4:00 in Oslo and sets around 23:00. Things really quiet down when the local kids go back to school, around August 20.

"Shoulder-season" travel—in late May, early June, and September—lacks the vitality of summer but offers occasional good weather and minimal crowds. Norway in particular can be good from late May to mid-June, when the days are long but the tourist lines are short.

Flying into Copenhagen and out of Bergen (with a likely transfer in Copenhagen) can be wonderfully efficient; if you opt for this, you can see Jutland and Ærø sights near Copenhagen at the beginning of your trip.

Winter is a bad time to explore Scandinavia unless winter sports are high on your agenda. Like a bear, Scandinavia's metabolism slows down, and many sights and accommodations are closed or open on a limited schedule (especially in remote fjord towns). Business travelers drive hotel prices way up. Winter weather can be cold and dreary. Days are short, and nighttime will draw the shades on your sightseeing well before dinner. Christmastime activities (such as colorful markets and Copenhagen's festively decorated

Scandinavia's Best Three-Week Trip by Train and Boat

Day	Plan	Sleep in
1	Arrive in Copenhagen	Copenhagen
2	Copenhagen	Copenhagen
3	Copenhagen	Copenhagen
4	Roskilde, Odense, Ærø	Ærøskøbing
5	Ærø	Ærøskøbing
6	Ærø to Kalmar	Kalmar
7	Kalmar	Kalmar
8	Kalmar, early train to Stockholm	Stockholm
9	Stockholm	Stockholm
10	Stockholm, night boat to Helsinki	Boat
11	Helsinki	Helsinki
12	Helsinki, afternoon boat to Tallinn	Tallinn
13	Tallinn, night boat to Stockholm	Boat
14	Stockholm, afternoon train to Oslo	Oslo
15	Oslo	Oslo
16	Oslo	Oslo
17	Train and boat to Aurland	Aurland
18	Aurland to Bergen via fjord cruise	Bergen
19	Bergen	Bergen
20	Free day: more fjords, resting, or whatever	
21	Trip over	

If you want to see Legoland (near Billund) and the "bog man" (in Aarhus), visit these from Odense (closer) or Copenhagen. You could save lots of time by flying from Tallinn to Oslo.

Tivoli Gardens) offer a brief interlude of warmth at this chilly time of year.

KNOW BEFORE YOU GO

Your trip is more likely to go smoothly if you plan ahead. Check this list of things to arrange while you're still at home.

You need a **passport**—but no visa or shots—to travel in Scandinavia. You may be denied entry into certain European countries if your passport is due to expire within three months of your ticketed date of return. Get it renewed if you'll be cutting it close. It can take up to six weeks to get or renew a passport (for more on passports, see www.travel.state.gov). Pack a photocopy of your passport in your luggage in case the original is lost or stolen.

Book rooms well in advance if you'll be traveling during peak season (July and Aug) or any major holidays (see page 766). Try to schedule visits to the capitals outside of convention season, when hotels can be hard to find.

Call your **debit- and credit-card companies** to let them know the countries you'll be visiting, to ask about fees, request your PIN code (it will be mailed to you), and more. See page 716 for details.

Do your homework if you want to buy **travel insurance.** Compare the cost of the insurance to the likelihood of your using it and your potential loss if something goes wrong. Also, check whether your existing insurance (health, homeowners, or renters) covers you and your possessions overseas. For more tips, see www.ricksteves. com/insurance.

Consider buying a **rail pass** after researching your options (see page 748 and www.ricksteves.com/rail for all the specifics).

If you plan to take an **overnight boat** between major Scandinavian cities in summer or on weekends, book it in advance (Copenhagen to Oslo, page 120; Stockholm to Helsinki, page 634; Stockholm to Tallinn, page 697). If you're doing the Norway in a Nutshell in July or August, make reservations for the Oslo-Myrdal train, and consider reservations for the Myrdal-Flåm train (see page 296).

Border crossings between Norway, Sweden, Denmark, Finland, and Estonia are a wave-through (there are typically no border formalities at all). When you change countries, you change money (except between Finland and Estonia, which both use the euro), phone cards, and postage stamps.

If you plan to hire a **local guide,** reserve ahead by email. Popular guides can get booked up.

If you're bringing a **mobile device,** download any apps you might want to use on the road, such as translators, maps, and transit schedules. Check out **Rick Steves Audio Europe,** featuring hours of travel interviews and other audio content about Scandinavia (via the free Rick Steves Audio Europe app, www.ricksteves. com/audioeurope, iTunes, or Google Play; for details, see page 756).

Check the **Rick Steves guidebook updates** page for any recent changes to this book (www.ricksteves.com/update).

Because **airline carry-on restrictions** are always changing, visit the Transportation Security Administration's website (www. tsa.gov) for a list of what you can bring on the plane and for the

Scandinavia at a Glance

Denmark

▲▲▲**Copenhagen** Vibrant Danish capital city, with *The Little Mermaid*, old-time Tivoli Gardens amusement park, excellent National Museum, Renaissance King Christian IV's Rosenborg Castle, delightful pedestrian Strøget, and eye-opening hippie enclave at Christiania.

▲**Near Copenhagen** Great day-trip options: West to the Viking Ship Museum and Royal Cathedral at Roskilde, and north to Frederiksborg Castle—the "Danish Versailles"—in Hillerød, the Louisiana Art Museum in Humlebæk, and Kronborg Castle in Helsingør.

▲▲**Central Denmark** Peaceful isle of Ærø—perfect for a loop tour by bike or car—and home to Denmark's best-preserved 18th-century village—Ærøskøbing; and the busy town of Odense, with the Hans Christian Andersen Hus and the nearby Funen Village open-air folk museum.

▲**Jutland** Family-friendly region with Legoland kids' adventure park; the tiny village of Jelling with historic rune stones; and Denmark's second-largest city, Aarhus, with its strollable pedestrian center, ARoS art museum, and Den Gamle By open-air folk museum.

Norway

▲▲**Oslo** Norway's sharp capital city, with its historic and walkable core, mural-lined City Hall, sculptures at Vigeland Park, and inspiring Nobel Peace Center, while the nearby Bygdøy district hosts museums dedicated to ships (Viking, *Fram*, and *Kon-Tiki*), the Holocaust, and traditional folk life.

▲▲▲**Norway in a Nutshell** A combination train, bus, and ferry trip to and through Norway's most spectacularly beautiful fjords—the Sognefjord and Nærøyfjord—passing pristine waterfalls, verdant forests, and take-your-breath-away scenery.

▲**More on the Sognefjord** Fjordside hamlet of Balestrand, a cozy home base for exploring nearby sights (including a medieval stave church), plus the serene Lustrafjord, with another stave church and a glacier you can walk on.

▲**Gudbrandsdal Valley and Jotunheimen Mountains** Lush green valley connecting northern and southern Norway, with touristy Lillehammer, the excellent Maihaugen Open-Air Folk Museum, and a rugged mountain range with some of this country's finest hikes and drives.

▲▲**Bergen** Salty port town and medieval capital of Norway, with lively fish market, colorful Hanseatic quarter (Bryggen), and a funicular to the top of Mount Fløyen with great views.

▲**South Norway** Harborside Stavanger—with its Petroleum Museum and Pulpit Rock; time-passed and remote Setesdal Valley; and the resort town of Kristiansand with ferry connections to Denmark.

Sweden
▲▲▲**Stockholm** Bustling capital of Sweden, with its charming island core of Gamla Stan, Europe's original—and unsurpassed—Skansen open-air folk museum, the *Vasa* museum (17th-century warship), and the Nordic Museum's look at five centuries of Swedish lifestyles.

▲**Near Stockholm** Good day-trip options: Drottningholm Palace, the lavish royal residence with nearby Baroque-era theater; Sigtuna, Sweden's oldest town with many rune stones and 18th-century buildings; and the university town of Uppsala, with its cathedral and Linnaeus Museum.

▲**Stockholm's Archipelago** Sweden's rocky garden of more than 30,000 islands, best seen on a boat trip from Stockholm.

▲**Southeast Sweden** Växjö, with a first-rate emigration museum and the Smålands Museum of glass-making; Kalmar, with its massive 12th-century Kalmar Castle and nearby holiday island of Öland; and the touristy "Kingdom of Crystal" Glass Country.

Finland
▲▲**Helsinki** Finland's capital city—an architectural delight for its Neoclassical and Art Nouveau buildings and churches—with the stirring "Chapel in the Rock," fine National Museum of Finland, and island fortress and open-air folk museum.

Estonia
▲▲**Tallinn** Russian-influenced, full-of-life capital of Estonia, with quaint Old Town center, remarkably intact medieval walls, and stirringly patriotic sights (Estonian art museum and the historic Song Festival Grounds).

How Was Your Trip?

Were your travels fun, smooth, and meaningful? If you'd like to share your tips, concerns, and discoveries, please fill out the survey at www.ricksteves.com/feedback. To check out readers' hotel and restaurant reviews—or leave one yourself—visit my travel forum at www.ricksteves.com/travel-forum. I value your feedback. Thanks in advance—it helps a lot.

latest security measures (including screening of electronic devices, which you may be asked to power up).

Traveling as a Temporary Local

We travel all the way to Scandinavia to enjoy differences—to become temporary locals. You'll experience frustrations. Certain truths that we find "God-given" or "self-evident," such as cold beer, ice in drinks, bottomless cups of coffee, and bigger being better, are suddenly not so true. One of the benefits of travel is the eye-opening realization that there are logical, civil, and even better alternatives.

While the materialistic culture of the US is sneaking into these countries, simplicity has yet to become subversive. Scandi-

navians are into "sustainable affluence." They have experimented aggressively in the area of social welfare—with mixed results. Travel in high-tax/high-government-service Scandinavia can rattle capitalist Americans. The people seem so happy and the society seems so genteel. Fit in, don't look for things American on the other side of the Atlantic, and you're sure to enjoy some thought-provoking stimulation and a full dose of Scandinavian hospitality.

Europeans generally like Americans. But if there is a negative aspect to the Scandinavian image of Americans, it is that we are loud, wasteful, ethnocentric, too informal (which can seem disrespectful), and a bit naive. While Scandinavians look bemusedly at some of our Yankee excesses—and worriedly at others—they nearly always afford us individual travelers all the warmth we deserve.

Judging from all the happy feedback I receive from travelers who have used this book, it's safe to assume you'll enjoy a great, affordable vacation—with the finesse of an independent, experienced traveler.

Thanks, and happy travels!

Rick Steves

Back Door Travel Philosophy

From *Rick Steves Europe Through the Back Door*

Travel is intensified living—maximum thrills per minute and one of the last great sources of legal adventure. Travel is freedom. It's recess, and we need it.

Experiencing the real Europe requires catching it by surprise, going casual..."through the Back Door."

Affording travel is a matter of priorities. (Make do with the old car.) You can eat and sleep—simply, safely, and enjoyably—anywhere in Europe for $125 a day plus transportation costs. In many ways, spending more money only builds a thicker wall between you and what you traveled so far to see. Europe is a cultural carnival, and time after time, you'll find that its best acts are free and the best seats are the cheap ones.

A tight budget forces you to travel close to the ground, meeting and communicating with the people. Never sacrifice sleep, nutrition, safety, or cleanliness to save money. Simply enjoy the local-style alternatives to expensive hotels and restaurants.

Connecting with people carbonates your experience. Extroverts have more fun. If your trip is low on magic moments, kick yourself and make things happen. If you don't enjoy a place, maybe you don't know enough about it. Seek the truth. Recognize tourist traps. Give a culture the benefit of your open mind. See things as different, but not better or worse. Any culture has plenty to share.

Of course, travel, like the world, is a series of hills and valleys. Be fanatically positive and militantly optimistic. If something's not to your liking, change your liking.

Travel can make you a happier American, as well as a citizen of the world. Our Earth is home to seven billion equally precious people. It's humbling to travel and find that other people don't have the "American Dream"—they have their own dreams. Europeans like us, but with all due respect, they wouldn't trade passports.

Thoughtful travel engages us with the world. In tough economic times, it reminds us what is truly important. By broadening perspectives, travel teaches new ways to measure quality of life.

Globetrotting destroys ethnocentricity, helping us understand and appreciate other cultures. Rather than fear the diversity on this planet, celebrate it. Among your most prized souvenirs will be the strands of different cultures you choose to knit into your own character. The world is a cultural yarn shop, and Back Door travelers are weaving the ultimate tapestry. Join in!

SCANDINAVIA

SCANDINAVIA

Scandinavia is Western Europe's least populated, most literate, most prosperous, most demographically homogeneous, most highly taxed, most socialistic, and least churchgoing corner. For the visitor, it's a land of Viking ships, brooding castles, salty harbors, deep green fjords, stave churches, and farmhouses—juxtaposed with the sleek modernism of its people-friendly cities.

Denmark, Norway, and Sweden are Scandinavia's core. They share a common linguistic heritage with Iceland, and a common history, religion, and culture with Finland and the Baltic nation of Estonia (both former Swedish colonies).

Emerging only slowly from under the glacial ice sheets, Scandinavia was the last part of Europe to be settled (its land mass is still rising from the ocean, rebounding from the press of the glaciers). Later, it was almost the last part of Europe to accept Christianity, and it's never quite forgotten its pagan roots, which live on in literature, place names, and the ancient runic alphabet. (For more background, see the Scandinavian History chapter.)

Scandinavia is blessed with natural beauty. The cavernous fjords of Norway's west coast are famous. Much of the region has mountains, lakes, green forests, and waterfalls. By contrast, low-lying Denmark has its rugged islands, salty harbors, and windswept, sandy coasts.

Climate-wise, Scandinavia has four distinct seasons. With Alaska-like latitudes, it's the "land of the midnight sun" in summer (18 hours of daylight) and of mid-afternoon darkness in winter (when there are just six hours between sunrise and sunset).

Most of Scandinavia is sparsely populated and very big. Sweden is the size of California, but has only a quarter the people (9.5 million). Just over five million Norwegians stretch out in Norway, where Oslo is as far from the northern tip of the country as it is from Rome. The exception is Denmark, which packs 5.5 million fun-loving Danes into a flat land the size of Switzerland.

Though each of the Scandinavian countries has its own language, there are some common threads. Danes and Norwegians can read each other's newspapers and can converse somewhat (but with difficulty because of thick accents). Swedes (whose written language is different) have a hard time with printed Danish and Norwegian, but can carry on simple conversations in those languages. Finns (whose language is not related at all) learn Swedish in school, thanks to Sweden's long historical presence in Finland. Estonian is similar to Finnish. Despite these common denominators, communication can be difficult due to one more factor—national pride. A Dane may simply pretend not to understand a Swede's request, and vice versa. If there's ever a language barrier, though, most Scandinavians can easily revert to their common second language—English.

It's not easy (and probably unwise) to make sweeping generalizations about a region's people, but here goes: In general, Scandinavians are confident, happy, healthy, and tall. They speak their minds frankly, even about taboo subjects like sex. They're strong individualists who cut others slack for their own eccentricities. They don't fawn on the rich and famous or look down on the down and out. At work, they're efficient and conscientious. They don't take cuts in line. They're well-educated, well-traveled, and worldly. Though reserved and super-polite at first, they have a good sense of humor and don't take life or themselves too seriously.

Scandinavians work hard, but they guard their leisure time fiercely. They like the out-of-doors, perhaps in keeping with the still-rural landscape they live in. For many, a weekend with the family at a (well-furnished) country cottage is all they need. Cycling, boating, and fishing are popular. Internationally, they're known for skiing, speed skating, hockey, and other winter sports. And, as with the rest of Europe, they're wild about football (soccer).

The region is a leader in progressive lifestyles, including recognizing same-sex partnerships. More than half the heterosexual couples in Denmark are "married" only because they've lived together for so long and have children. Wives and mothers generally have a job outside the home. While the state religion is Lutheran, only a small percentage of Scandinavians actually attend church

Scandi-hoovians You Might Know

Famous Danes

Hans Christian Andersen, writer of *The Ugly Duckling*, *The Little Mermaid*.

Søren Kierkegaard, proto-existentialist philosopher

Bertel Thorvaldsen, sculptor

Karen Blixen, who wrote *Out of Africa* under pen name Isak Dinesen

Niels Bohr, physicist who described the atom as a tiny planetary system

Victor Borge, classical-music comedian

Arne Jacobsen, architect

Lars Ulrich, drummer for rock band Metallica

Brigitte Nielsen and Viggo Mortensen (half-Danish), movie actors

Carl Nielsen, composer

Lars von Trier, movie director

Morten Andersen, NFL placekicker and all-time leading scorer

Famous Norwegians

Eric the Red, first European settler in Greenland and father of Icelander Leif Eriksson, the Viking who discovered America

Edvard Grieg, Romantic composer

Edvard Munch, *The Scream* painter

Henrik Ibsen, playwright

Roald Amundsen, Arctic and Antarctic explorer

Gustav Vigeland, sculptor

Knute Rockne, football player and coach at University of Notre Dame

Sonja Henie, figure skater and movie actress

Thor Heyerdahl, explorer of *Kon-Tiki* fame

Jan Stenerud, NFL placekicker

other than at Easter or Christmas. Most are either indifferent or assertively secular.

Scandinavia is rich, with a very high standard of living (as American tourists learn the hard way). Norway has been blessed with offshore oil, Denmark with farmland, and Sweden and Finland with lush forests. They are all rich in fish. Alternative energy sources are important, especially hydroelectric and wind power. Given such pristine natural surroundings, the Scandinavians are environmentalists, committed to preserving their resources for future generations (except for the Norwegians' stubborn appetite for whaling).

Liv Ullmann, movie actress and director

Jo Nesbø, author of crime series featuring Oslo detective Harry Hole

Rick Steves, travel writer

Famous Swedes

Anders Celsius, inventor of the temperature scale

Carolus Linnaeus, botanist who developed taxonomic naming system

August Strindberg, playwright

Alfred Nobel, inventor of dynamite and the Nobel Peace Prize

Carl Milles, sculptor

Astrid Lindgren, children's author who created *Pippi Longstocking*

Ingmar Bergman, movie director

Greta Garbo and Noomi Rapace, actresses

Max von Sydow and Stellan Skarsgård, actors

Dag Hammarskjöld, UN secretary general

Björn Borg and Stefan Edberg, tennis players

Hans Blix, UN weapons inspector

Annika Sörenstam and Jesper Parnevik, golfers

ABBA, pop-rock supergroup

Stieg Larsson, author of the *Millennium* trilogy

Famous Finns

Jean Sibelius, Romantic composer

Alvar Aalto, Modernist architect

Eliel Saarinen and son Eero, Modernist architects (the father known for his work in Finland, the son for his work in the US)

Esa-Pekka Salonen, classical conductor

Tove Jansson, author of the *Moomin* books

Linus Torvalds, creator of the Linux operating system

Scandinavian society, carefully organized to maximize prosperity and happiness for everyone, is the home of cradle-to-grave security. Residents pay hefty taxes but get a hefty return. Children are educated. The old and sick are cared for. Cities are carefully planned to be clean, green, crime-free, and built on a human scale—with parks, fountains, public art, and pedestrian zones.

Generally speaking, citizens willingly share the burden for the common good. High taxes mean there's less of a gap between the very rich and the very poor, resulting in a less class-oriented society. Scandinavians are proud of this. If they seem a bit smug, you can't fault them, because statistics verify that they live longer, healthier, happier lives.

Scandinavia is also on the high-tech edge of the global economy. They practice a mix of free-market capitalism and enlightened socialism. In international business, they make their mark with telecommunications (Nokia from Finland, Ericsson from Sweden), Ikea furniture (originally from Sweden), Electrolux appliances (Sweden), and Lego toys (Denmark).

Politically, Denmark, Norway, and Sweden are constitutional monarchies with a figurehead monarch who cuts ribbons, works with parliament and a prime minister, and tries to stay out of the tabloids. Finland and Estonia have democratically elected presidents. The Scandinavian nations maintain close ties with each other. To some degree or other, they all participate in the European Union (though Norway is not a member, and only Finland and Estonia use the euro). Every election brings another debate about how closely they want to tie themselves to the rest of Europe. The Scandinavian nations have a reputation for international cooperation, exemplified by their leading role in the United Nations, and Sweden and Norway's Nobel Peace Prize.

All of Scandinavia's monarchs are descended from Oscar I, King of Sweden and Norway (and son of King Karl Johan XIV), through the House of Bernadotte: Denmark's Queen Margrethe II and Crown Prince Frederik (b. 1968), Sweden's King Carl XVI Gustaf and Crown Princess Victoria (b. 1977), and Norway's King Harald V and Crown Prince Håkon (b. 1973).

Artistically, Scandinavia is known for its serious playwrights (Henrik Ibsen and August Strindberg), brooding filmmakers (Ingmar Bergman), and gloomy painters (Edvard Munch), and more recently for its popular crime-thriller authors, Stieg Larsson and Jo Nesbø. Nordic mythology is familiar to the English-speaking world for its *Lord of the Rings*-style roots.

Hans Christian Andersen, Astrid Lindgren, and Tove Jansson brought us children's tales. Less familiar are Scandinavia's people-friendly sculptors—Bertel Thorvaldsen, Gustav Vigeland, and Carl Milles—whose noble, realistic statues evoke the human spirit. Architecturally, Scandinavia continues to lead the way, with sleek modern buildings that fit in with the natural landscape. Late-20th-century Modernism (or Functionalism) had several Scandinavian champions, including Eero Saarinen and Alvar Aalto (Finland) and Arne Jacobsen (Denmark). Musically, Scandinavia is known for classical composers like Grieg (Norway) and Sibelius (Finland) who celebrate the region's nature and folk tunes. Scandinavia's cities have thriving jazz scenes that rival America's. Oh yes, and then there's Scandinavia's biggest musical export—the '70s pop band from Sweden named ABBA.

The Scandinavian flair for art shines best in the design of everyday objects. They fashion chairs, lamps, and coffeemakers to be both functional and beautiful: sleek, with no frills, where the "beauty" comes from how well it works. In their homes, Scandinavians strive for a coziness that mixes modern practicality with

traditional designs—carved wood and old flower-and-vine patterns.

Despite its ultra-modern, progressive outlook, Scandinavia still honors its traditions. Parents tell kids the old folk tales about grumpy, clever trolls, and gardeners dot their yards with friendly garden gnomes. At midsummer, you'll see locals in traditional clothes dancing around a maypole to the tunes of a folk

band. At winter solstice and Christmas, they enjoy Yule cakes and winter beer. Scandinavia is sailing into the high-tech future on the hardy ship of its Viking past.

DENMARK

DENMARK

Danmark

Denmark is by far the smallest of the Scandinavian countries, but in the 16th century, it was the largest—at one time, Denmark ruled all of Norway and the three southern provinces of Sweden. Danes are proud of their mighty history and are the first to remind you that they were a lot bigger and a lot stronger in the good old days. And yet, they're a remarkably mellow, well-adjusted lot—organized without being uptight, and easygoing with a delightfully wry sense of humor.

In the 10th century, before its heyday as a Scan-superpower, Denmark was, like Norway and Sweden, home to the Vikings. More than anything else, these fierce warriors were known for their great shipbuilding, which enabled them to travel far. Denmark's Vikings journeyed west to Great Britain and Ireland (where they founded Dublin) and brought back various influences, including Christianity.

Denmark is composed of many islands, a peninsula (Jutland) that juts up from northern Germany, Greenland, and the Faroe Islands.

The two main islands are Zealand (Sjælland in Danish), where Copenhagen is located, and Funen (Fyn in Danish), where Hans Christian Andersen (or, as Danes call him, simply "H. C.") was born. Out of the hundreds of smaller islands, ship-in-bottle-cute Æro is my favorite. The Danish landscape is gentle compared with the dramatic fjords, mountains, and vast lakes of other Scandinavian nations. Danes (not to mention Swedes and Norwegians) like to joke about the flat Danish landscape, saying that you can stand on a case of beer and see from one end of the country to the other. Denmark's highest point in Jutland is only 560 feet above sea level, and no part of the country is more than 30 miles from the sea.

In contrast to the rest of Scandinavia, much of Denmark is arable. The landscape consists of rolling hills, small thatched-roof farmhouses, beech forests, and whitewashed churches with characteristic stairstep gables. Red brick, which was a favorite material of the nation-building King Christian IV, is everywhere—especially in major civic buildings such as city halls and train stations.

Like the other Scandinavian countries, Denmark is predominantly Lutheran, but only a small minority attend church regularly. The majority are ethnic Danes, and many (but certainly not all) of them have the stereotypical blond hair and blue eyes. Two out of three Danes have last names ending in "-sen." The assimilation of ethnic groups into this homogeneous society, which began in earnest in the 1980s, is a source of some controversy. But in general, most Danes have a live-and-let-live attitude and enjoy one of the highest standards of living in the world. Taxes are high in this wel-

Denmark Almanac

Official Name: Kongeriget Danmark—the Kingdom of Denmark— or simply Denmark.

Population: Denmark's 5.5 million people are mainly of Scandinavian descent, with immigrants—mostly German, Turkish, Iranian, and Somali—making up 12 percent of the population. Greenland is home to the indigenous Inuit, and the Faroe Islands to people of Nordic heritage. Most Danes speak both Danish and English, with a small minority speaking German, Inuit, or Faroese. The population is 80 percent Protestant (mostly Evangelical Lutheran), 4 percent Muslim, and 16 percent "other."

Latitude and Longitude: 56°N and 10°E, similar latitude to northern Alberta, Canada.

Area: 16,600 square miles, roughly twice the size of Massachusetts.

Geography: Denmark includes the Jutland peninsula in northern Europe. Situated between the North Sea and the Baltic Sea, it shares a 42-mile border with Germany. In addition to Greenland and the Faroe Islands, Denmark also encompasses over 400 islands (78 of which are inhabited). Altogether Denmark has 4,544 miles of coastline. The mainland is mostly flat, and nearly two-thirds of the land is cultivated.

Biggest Cities: Denmark's capital city, Copenhagen (pop. 1.2 million), is located on the island of Zealand (Sjælland). Aarhus (on the mainland) has 310,000, and Odense (on Funen/Fyn) has 170,000.

fare state, but education is free and medical care highly subsidized. Generous parental leave extends to both men and women.

Denmark, one of the most environmentally conscious European countries, is a front-runner in renewable energy, recycling, and organic farming. You'll see lots of modern windmills dotting the countryside. Wind power accounts for nearly 30 percent of Denmark's energy today, with a goal of 50 percent by 2020. By 2050, the country hopes to free itself completely from its dependence on fossil fuels. About 60 percent of waste is recycled. In grocery stores, organic products are shelved right alongside nonorganic ones—for the same price.

Denmark's Queen Margrethe II is a very popular and talented woman who, along with her royal duties, has designed coins, stamps, and book illustrations. Danes gather around the TV on New Year's Eve

Economy: Denmark's modern economy is holding its own, with a Gross Domestic Product of just over $210 billion. Denmark's top exports include pharmaceuticals, oil, machinery, and food products. It is also one of the world's leaders in exports of wind turbine technology. The GDP per capita is about $37,800.

Currency: 6 Danish kroner (kr, officially DKK) = about $1.

Government: Denmark is a constitutional monarchy. Queen Margrethe II is the head of state, but the head of government is the prime minister, a post held since October 2011 by Helle Thorning-Schmidt. The 179-member parliament (Folketinget) is elected every four years.

Flag: The Danish flag is red with a white cross.

The Average Dane: He or she is 41 years old, has 1.7 children, and will live to be 79. About 74 percent of Danish women are employed outside the home, and about 53 percent of Danes own a home or apartment. De-

spite the cozy lifestyle, no European nation consumes more antidepressants per capita except Iceland.

to hear her annual speech to the nation and flock to the Royal Palace in Copenhagen on April 16 to sing her "Happy Birthday." Her son, Crown Prince Frederik, married Australian Mary Donaldson in 2004. Their son Christian's birth in 2005 was cause for a national celebration (the couple now have four children).

The Danes are proud of their royal family and of the flag, a white cross on a red background. Legend says it fell from the sky during a 13th-century battle in Estonia, making it Europe's oldest continuously used flag. You'll see it everywhere—decorating cakes, on clothing, or fluttering in the breeze atop government buildings. It's as much a decorative symbol as a patriotic one.

You'll also notice that the Danes have an odd fixation on two animals: elephants and polar bears, both of which are symbols of national (especially royal) pride. The Order of the Elephant is the highest honor that the Danish monarch can bestow on someone; if you see an emblematic elephant, you know somebody very important is involved. And the polar bear represents the Danish protectorate of Greenland—a welcome reminder to Danes that their nation is more than just Jutland and a bunch of flat little islands.

From an early age, Danes develop a passion for soccer. You may see red-and-white-clad fans singing on their way to a match.

Despite the country's small size, the Danish national team does well in international competition. Other popular sports include sailing, cycling, badminton, and team handball.

The Danish language, with its three extra vowels (Æ, Ø, and Å), is notoriously difficult for foreigners to pronounce. Even seemingly predictable consonants can be tricky. For example, the letter "d" is often dropped, so the word *gade* (street)—which you'll see, hear, and say constantly—is pronounced "gah-eh." Luckily for us, most Danes also speak English and are patient with thick-tongued foreigners. Danes have playful fun teasing tourists who make the brave attempt to say Danish words. The hardest phrase, *rød grød med fløde* (a delightful red fruit porridge topped with cream), is nearly impossible for a non-Dane to pronounce. Ask a local to help you.

Sample Denmark's sweet treats at one of the many bakeries you'll see. The pastries that we call "Danish" in the US are called *wienerbrød* in Denmark. Bakeries line their display cases with several varieties of *wienerbrød* and other delectable sweets. Try *kringle, snegle,* or *Napoleonshatte,* or find your own favorite. (Chances are it will be easier to enjoy than to pronounce.)

For a selection of useful Danish survival phrases, see the following pages. Two important words to know are *skål* ("cheers," a ritual always done with serious eye contact) and *hyggelig* (pronounced HEW-geh-lee), meaning warm and cozy. Danes treat their home like a sanctuary and spend a great deal of time improving their gardens and houses—inside and out. Cozying up one's personal space (a national obsession) is something the Danes do best. If you have the opportunity, have some Danes adopt you during your visit so you can enjoy their warm hospitality.

Heaven to a Dane is returning home after a walk in a beloved beech forest to enjoy open-faced sandwiches washed down with beer among good friends. Around the *hyggelig* candlelit table, there will be a spirited discussion of the issues of the day, plenty of laughter, and probably a few good-natured jokes about the Swedes or Norwegians. *Skål!*

Danish Survival Phrases

The Danes tend to say words quickly and clipped. In fact, many short vowels end in a "glottal stop"—a very brief vocal break immediately following the vowel. While I haven't tried to indicate these in the phonetics, you can listen for them in Denmark...and (try to) imitate.

Three unique Danish vowels are æ (sounds like the e in "egg"), ø (sounds like the German ö—purse your lips and say "oh"), and å (sounds like the o in "bowl"). The letter r is not rolled—it's pronounced farther back in the throat, almost like a w. A d at the end of a word sounds almost like our th; for example, mad (food) sounds like "math." In the phonetics, ī sounds like the long i sound in "light," and bolded syllables are stressed.

English	Danish	Pronunciation
Hello. (formal)	Goddag.	goh-**day**
Hi. / Bye. (informal)	Hej. / Hej-hej.	hī / hī-hī
Do you speak English?	Taler du engelsk?	**tay**-lehr doo **eng**-elsk
Yes. / No.	Ja. / Nej.	yah / nī
Please. (May I?)*	Kan jeg?	kahn yī
Please. (Can you?)*	Kan du?	kahn doo
Please. (Would you?)*	Vil du?	veel doo
Thank you (very much).	(Tusind) tak.	(**too**-sin) tack
You're welcome.	Selv tak.	sehl tack
Can I help (you)?	Kan jeg hjælpe (dig)?	kahn yī **yehl**-peh (dī)
Excuse me. (to pass)	Undskyld mig.	**oon**-skewl mī
Excuse me. (Can you help me?)	Kan du hjælpe mig?	kahn doo **yehl**-peh mī
(Very) good.	(Meget) godt.	(**mī**-ehl) goht
Goodbye.	Farvel.	fah-**vehl**
one / two	en / to	een / toh
three / four	tre / fire	tray / feer
five / six	fem / seks	fehm / sehks
seven / eight	syv / otte	syew / **oh**-deh
nine / ten	ni / ti	nee / tee
hundred	hundred	**hoo**-nuh
thousand	tusind	**too**-sin
How much?	Hvor meget?	vor **mī**-ehl
local currency: (Danish) crown	(Danske) kroner	(**dahn**-skeh) **kroh**-nah
Where is...?	Hvor er...?	vor ehr
...the toilet	...toilettet	toy-**leh**-teht
men	herrer	**hehr**-ah
women	damer	**day**-mah
water / coffee	vand / kaffe	van / **kah**-feh
beer / wine	øl / vin	uhl / veen
Cheers!	Skål!	skohl
Can I have the bill?	Kan jeg få regningen?	kahn yī foh **rī**-ning-ehn

*Because Danish has no single word for "please," they approximate that sentiment by asking "May I?", "Can you?", or "Would you?", depending on the context.

COPENHAGEN

København

Copenhagen, Denmark's capital, is the gateway to Scandinavia. It's an improbable combination of corny Danish clichés, well-dressed executives having a business lunch amid cutting-edge contemporary architecture, and some of the funkiest counterculture in Europe. And yet, it all just works so tidily together. With the Øresund Bridge connecting Sweden and Denmark (creating the region's largest metropolitan area), Copenhagen is energized and ready to dethrone Stockholm as Scandinavia's powerhouse city.

A busy day cruising the canals, wandering through the palace, and taking an old-town walk will give you your historical bearings. Then, after another day strolling the Strøget (STROY-et, Europe's first and greatest pedestrian shopping mall), biking the canals, and sampling the Danish good life (including a gooey "Danish" pastry), you'll feel right at home. Live it up in Scandinavia's cheapest and most fun-loving capital.

PLANNING YOUR TIME

A first visit deserves a minimum of two days. Note that many sights are closed on Monday year-round or in the off-season.

Day 1: Catch a 9:30 city walking tour with Richard Karpen (Mon-Sat mid-May-mid-Sept). After lunch, catch the relaxing canal-boat tour out to *The Little Mermaid* and back. Enjoy the rest of the afternoon tracing Denmark's cultural roots in the National

The Story of Copenhagen

If you study your map carefully, you can read the history of Copenhagen in today's street plan. København (literally, "Merchants' Harbor") was born on the little island of Slotsholmen—today home to Christiansborg Palace—in 1167. What was Copenhagen's medieval moat is now a string of pleasant lakes and parks, including Tivoli Gardens. You can still make out some of the zigzag pattern of the moats and ramparts in the city's greenbelt.

Many of these fortifications—and several other landmarks—were built by Denmark's most memorable king. You need to remember only one character in Copenhagen's history: Christian IV. Ruling from 1588 to 1648, he was Denmark's Renaissance king and a royal party animal (see the "King Christian IV" sidebar, later). The personal energy of this "Builder King" sparked a Golden Age when Copenhagen prospered and many of the city's grandest buildings were erected. In the 17th century, Christian IV extended the city fortifications to the north, doubling the size of the city, while adding a grid plan of streets and his Rosenborg Castle. This "new town" was the district around the Amalienborg Palace.

In 1850, Copenhagen's 140,000 residents all lived within this defensive system. Building in the no-man's-land outside the walls was only allowed with the understanding that in the event of an attack, you'd burn your dwellings to clear the way for a good defense.

Most of the city's historic buildings still in existence were built within the medieval walls, but conditions became too crowded, and outbreaks of disease forced Copenhagen to spread outside the walls. Ultimately those walls were torn down and replaced with "rampart streets" that define today's city center: Vestervoldgade (literally, "West Rampart Street"), Nørrevoldgade ("North"), and Østervoldgade ("East"). The fourth side is the harbor and the island of Slotsholmen, where København was born.

Museum and visiting the Ny Carlsberg Glyptotek art gallery (Impressionists and Danish artists). Spend the evening following my "Copenhagen City Walk" and strolling with Copenhageners at the same time.

Day 2: At 10:00, go Neoclassical at Thorvaldsen's Museum, and tour the royal reception rooms at the adjacent Christiansborg Palace. After a *smørrebrød* lunch, spend the afternoon seeing

Rosenborg Castle, with Denmark's crown jewels. Spend the evening at Tivoli Gardens.

Christiania—the hippie squatters' community—is not for everyone. But it's worth considering if you're intrigued by alternative lifestyles, or simply want a break from museums. During a busy trip, Christiania fits best in the evening.

Budget Itinerary Tip: Remember the efficiency and cost-effectiveness of sleeping while traveling in and out of town (saving time and hotel costs). Consider taking a night train to Sweden with connections to Stockholm, or cruise up to Oslo on a night boat. Kamikaze sightseers on tight budgets see Copenhagen as a useful Scandinavian bottleneck. They sleep heading into town on a train, tour the city during the day, and sleep on a boat or train as they travel north to their next destination. At the end of their Scandinavian travels, they do the same thing in reverse. The result is two days and no nights in Copenhagen (you can check your bag and take a shower at the train station). Considering the joy of Oslo and Stockholm, this isn't all that crazy if you have limited time and can sleep on a moving train or boat.

Orientation to Copenhagen

Copenhagen is huge (with 1.2 million people), but for most visitors, the walkable core is the diagonal axis formed by the train station, Tivoli Gardens, Rådhuspladsen (City Hall Square), and the Strøget pedestrian street, ending at the colorful old Nyhavn sailors' harbor. Bubbling with street life, colorful pedestrian zones, and most of the city's sightseeing, the Strøget is fun. But also be sure to get off the main drag and explore. By doing things by bike or on foot, you'll stumble upon some charming bits of Copenhagen that many travelers miss. The city feels pretty torn up, as they are deep into a multiyear Metro expansion project, which will add 17 stations to their already impressive system.

Outside of the old city center are three areas of interest to tourists:

• To the north are Rosenborg Castle and Amalienborg Palace, with *The Little Mermaid* nearby.

• To the east, across the harbor, are Christianshavn (Copenhagen's "Little Amsterdam" district) and the alternative enclave of Christiania.

• To the west (behind the train station) is Vesterbro, a young and trendy part of town with lots of cafés, bars, and boutiques; the hip Meatpacking District (Kødbyen); and the Carlsberg Brewery (plus the picnic-friendly Frederiksberg Park).

All of these sights are walkable from the Strøget, but taking a bike, bus, or taxi is more efficient. I rent a bike for my entire visit

COPENHAGEN

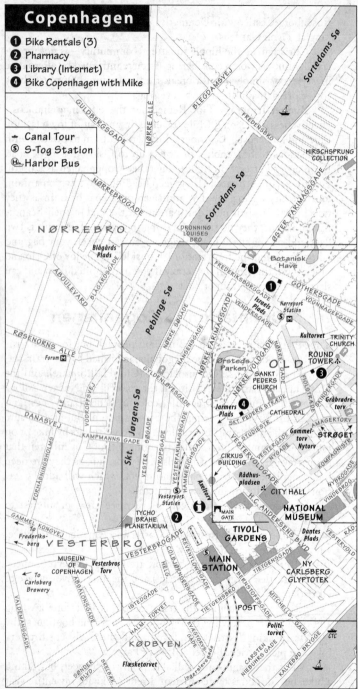

Copenhagen

1. Bike Rentals (3)
2. Pharmacy
3. Library (Internet)
4. Bike Copenhagen with Mike

- Canal Tour
- S S-Tog Station
- Harbor Bus

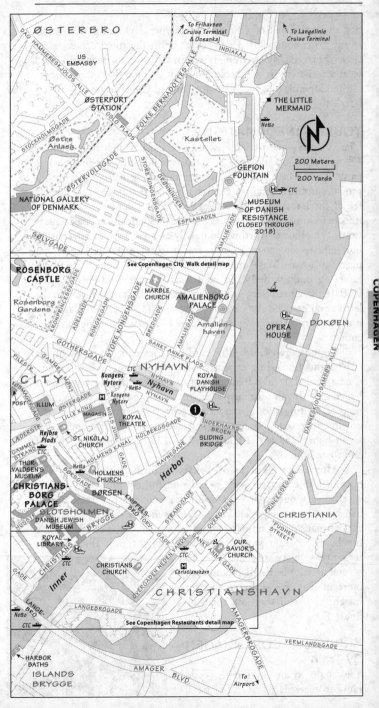

ØSTERBRO

DAG HAMMERSKJOLDS ALLE

US EMBASSY

To Frihavnen Cruise Terminal & Oceankaj

INDIAKAJ

To Langelinie Cruise Terminal

ØSTERPORT STATION

Oslo Plads

STOCKHOLMSGADE

Østre Anlaeg

FOLKE BERNADOTTES ALLE

Kastellet

THE LITTLE MERMAID

Netto

200 Meters
200 Yards

ØSTERVOLDGADE

STORE KONGENSGADE

GRØNNINGEN

GEFION FOUNTAIN

NATIONAL GALLERY OF DENMARK

ESPLANADEN

AMALIEGADE

CTC

MUSEUM OF DANISH RESISTANCE (CLOSED THROUGH 2018)

SØLVGADE

See Copenhagen City Walk detail map

ROSENBORG CASTLE

Rosenborg Gardens

KRONPRINSESSEGADE

ADELGADE

BORGERGADE

STORE KONGENSGADE

MARBLE CHURCH

BREDGADE

AMALIENBORG PALACE

AMALIEGADE

Amalien-haven

OPERA HOUSE

DOKØEN

PILESTR.

GAMMEL MØNT

GOTHERSGADE

CITY

KOMPAGNISTR.

POST

ILLUM

Kongens Nytorv

Netto

SANKT ANNÆ PLADS

NYHAVN

CTC

NYHAVN
Nyhavn
NYHAVN

ROYAL DANISH PLAYHOUSE

DANNESKIOLD-SAMSØES ALLE

ØSTERGADE

Kongens Nytorv

LILLE KONG.

MAGASIN

NIELS JUELS GADE

ROYAL THEATER

HOLBERGSGADE

HAVNEGADE

INDERHAVNS-BROEN

SLIDING BRIDGE

LEDERSTR.

Højbro Plads

ST. NIKOLAJ CHURCH

HOLMENS KANAL

GAMMEL STRAND

CTC

THOR-VALDSEN'S MUSEUM

BORSGADE

Netto

HOLMENS CHURCH

Harbor

CHRISTIANS-BORG PALACE

HUSSTR.

SLOTSHOLMEN

BØRSEN

KNIPPELS-BRO TORV

STRANDGADE

OVERGADEN

CHRISTIANIA

"PUSHER STREET"

DANISH JEWISH MUSEUM

CHRISTIANS BRYGGE

ROYAL LIBRARY

CTC

CHRISTIANS CHURCH

OVERGADEN NEDEN VANDET

SANKT ANNÆ GADE

CTC

OUR SAVIOR'S CHURCH

Christianshavn

Inner

LANGE-BRO

Netto

CTC

LANGEBROGADE

CHRISTIANSHAVN

See Copenhagen Restaurants detail map

AMAGERBROGADE

VERMLANDSGADE

HARBOR BATHS

ISLANDS BRYGGE

AMAGER BLVD.

To Airport

COPENHAGEN

COPENHAGEN

(for about the cost of a single cab ride per day) and park it safely in my hotel courtyard. I get anywhere in the town center faster than by taxi (nearly anything is within a 10-minute pedal). In good weather, the city is an absolute delight by bike (for more on biking in Copenhagen, see "Getting Around Copenhagen: By Bike," later).

TOURIST INFORMATION

Copenhagen's questionable excuse for a TI, which bills itself as "Wonderful Copenhagen," is actually a blatantly for-profit company. As in a (sadly) increasing number of big European cities, it provides information only about businesses that pay a hefty display fee of thousands of dollars each year. This colors the advice and information the office provides. While they can answer basic questions, the office is worthwhile mostly as a big rack of advertising brochures—you can pick up the free map at many hotels and other places in town (May-June Mon-Sat 9:00-18:00, Sun 9:00-14:00; July-Aug daily 9:00-19:00; Sept-April Mon-Fri 9:00-16:00, Sat 9:00-14:00, closed Sun; just up the street from train station—to the left as you exit the station—at Vesterbrogade 4A, good Lagkagehuset bakery in building, tel. 70 22 24 42, www.visitcopenhagen.com).

Copenhagen Card: This card includes entry to many of the city's sights (including expensive ones, like Tivoli and Rosenborg Castle) and all local transportation throughout the greater Copenhagen area. It can save busy sightseers some money; if you're planning on visiting a lot of attractions with steep entry prices, do the arithmetic to see if buying this pass adds up (339 kr/24 hours, 469 kr/48 hours, 559 kr/72 hours, 779 kr/120 hours—sold at the TI and some hotels).

Alternative Sources of Tourist Information: As the TI's bottom line competes with its mission to help tourists, you may want to seek out other ways to inform yourself. The weekly English-language newspaper, *The Copenhagen Post*, has good articles about what's going on in town (often available free at TI or some hotels, or buy it at a newsstand, www.cphpost.dk). The witty alternative website, www.aok.dk, has several articles in English (and many more in Danish—readable and very insightful if you translate them online).

ARRIVAL IN COPENHAGEN
By Train

The main train station is called Hovedbanegården (HOETH-bahngorn; look for *København H* on signs and schedules). It's a temple of travel and a hive of travel-related activity (and 24-hour thievery). Kiosks and fast-food eateries cluster in the middle of the main arrivals hall. The **ticket office** is on the left (as you face the front of the hall), and a **train information** kiosk is right in the middle of the hall.

Within the station, you'll find **baggage storage** (go down stairs at back of station marked *Bagagebokse;* lockers and check-room/*garderobe* both open long hours daily); pay **WCs** (right side of station, near ticket offices); a **post office** (back of station, Mon-Fri 9:00-19:00, Sat-Sun 12:00-16:00); a branch of the recommended **Lagkagehuset** bakery (front of station); and lots more. At both the front and the back of the station, you'll find **ATMs** and **Forex** exchange desks (the least expensive place in town to change money, daily 8:00-21:00).

The tracks at the back of the station (tracks 9-10 and 11-12) are for the suburban train (S-tog). The military music you may hear playing at the back end of the station is to keep the street riff-raff from hanging out in that area (they can't handle march music).

Tickets: While you're in the station, you can plan for your departure by reserving your overnight train seat or *couchette* at the *Billetsalg* office (Mon-Fri 7:00-20:00, Sat-Sun 8:00-18:00). Some international rides and high-speed InterCity trains require reservations (usually 25-55 kr), but rail-pass holders can ride any Danish train without a reservation.

Getting into Town: If you want to get right to sightseeing, you're within easy walking distance of downtown. Just walk out the front door and you'll run into one of the entrances for Tivoli amusement park; if you go around its left side and up a couple of blocks, you'll be at Rådhuspladsen, where my "Copenhagen City Walk" begins.

Hotels are scattered far and wide around town. It's best to get arrival instructions from your hotelier, but if you're on your own, here are some tips:

To reach hotels **behind the station,** slip out the back door—just go down the stairs at the back of the station marked *Reventlowsgade*.

For hotels **near Nørreport** (Ibsens and Jørgensen), ride the S-tog from the station two stops to Nørreport, within about a 10-minute walk of the hotels. Bus #14 also runs from near the train station to Nørreport.

For hotels **near Nyhavn** (71 Nyhavn and Bethel Sømandshjem), you can take the S-tog to Nørreport, then transfer to the Metro one stop to Kongens Nytorv, within a 10-minute walk of Nyhavn. Or you can take bus #11A (or #26 from around the corner) to Kongens Nytorv.

Note: If you're staying near Nørreport (or near Nyhavn, an easy Metro connection from Nørreport), check the train schedule carefully; many local trains (such as some from Roskilde and those from the airport) continue through the main train station to Nørreport Station, saving you an extra step.

By Plane

Copenhagen Airport (Kastrup)

Copenhagen's international airport is a traveler's dream, with a TI, baggage check, bank, ATMs, post office, shopping mall, grocery store, bakery, and more (airport code: CPH, airport info tel. 32 31 32 31, www.cph.dk). The three check-in terminals are within walking distance of each other (departures screens tell you which terminal to go to). On arrival, all flights feed into one big lobby in Terminal 3. When you pop out here, a TI kiosk is on your left, taxis are out the door on your right, trains are straight ahead, and shops and eateries fill the atrium above you. You can use dollars or euros at the airport, but you'll get change back in kroner.

Getting Between the Airport and Downtown: Your options include the Metro, trains, and taxis. There are also buses into town, but the train/Metro is generally better.

The **Metro** runs directly from the airport to Christianshavn, Kongens Nytorv (near Nyhavn), and Nørreport, making it the best choice for getting into town if you're staying in any of these areas (36-kr three-zone ticket, yellow M2 line, direction: Vanløse, 4-10/hour, 11 minutes to Christianshavn). The Metro station is located at the end of Terminal 3 and is covered by the roof of the terminal.

Convenient **trains** also connect the airport with downtown (36-kr three-zone ticket, covered by rail pass, 4/hour, 12 minutes). Buy your ticket from the ground-level ticket booth (look for *DSB: Tickets for Train, Metro & Bus* signs) before riding the escalator down to the tracks. Track 2 has trains going into the city (track 1 is for trains going east, to Sweden). Trains into town stop at the main train station (signed *København H;* handy if you're sleeping at my recommended hotels behind the train station), as well as the Nørreport and Østerport stations. At Nørreport, you can connect to the Metro for Kongens Nytorv (near Nyhavn) and Christianshavn.

With the train/Metro trip being so quick, frequent, and cheap, I see no reason to take a taxi. But if you do, **taxis** are fast, civil, accept credit cards, and charge about 250-300 kr for a ride to the town center.

By Boat or Cruise Ship

For information on Copenhagen's cruise terminals, see the end of this chapter.

HELPFUL HINTS

Emergencies: Dial 112 and specify fire, police, or ambulance. Emergency calls from public phones are free.

Pharmacy: Steno Apotek is across from the train station (open 24 hours, Vesterbrogade 6C—see map on page 36, tel. 33 14 82 66).

Blue Monday: As you plan, remember that most sights close on Monday, but these attractions remain open: Amalienborg Museum (closed Mon Nov-April), Christiansborg Palace (closed Mon Oct-April), City Hall, Museum of Copenhagen, Rosenborg Castle (closed Mon Nov-April), Round Tower, Royal Library, Our Savior's Church, Tivoli Gardens (generally closed late Sept-mid-April), Harbor Baths, and all of the various tours (canal, bus, walking, and bike). You can explore Christiania, but Monday is its rest day so it's unusually quiet and some restaurants are closed.

Internet Access: Wi-Fi is easy to find in Copenhagen (available free at virtually all hotels and many cafés). If you need a terminal with Internet access, you can get online for free at the **Copenhagen Central Library** (Mon-Fri 10:00-19:00, Sat 10:00-14:00, closed Sun, midway between Nørreport and the Strøget at Krystalgade 15—see map on page 36) and **"Black Diamond" library** (see page 77). The **Telestation** call shop behind the train station offers pay Internet terminals (kitty-corner from TI, Mon-Fri 10:00-19:30, Sat 10:00-16:30, closed Sun, Banegårdspladsen 1, tel. 33 93 00 02).

Laundry: Pams Møntvask is a good coin-op laundry near Nørreport (wash-31 kr/load, soap-6 kr, dry-2 kr/minute, daily 6:00-21:00, 50 yards from Ibsens Hotel at 86 Nansensgade). **Tre Stjernet Møntvask** ("Three Star Laundry") is several blocks past the Meatpacking District (wash-27 kr/load, soap-5 kr, dry-1 kr/1.5 minutes, daily 6:00-21:00, Sønder Boulevard 97). For both locations, see the map on page 36. *Vaskel* is wash, *torring* is dry, and *sæbe* is soap.

Ferries: While in Copenhagen, book any ferries that you plan to take in Scandinavia. Visit a travel agent or book directly with the ferry company. For the Copenhagen-Oslo overnight ferry, contact **DFDS** or visit the **DSB Rejsebureau** at the main train station (see page 120 for details). For boats between Stockholm and Helsinki, see page 634. For the boat from Helsinki to St. Petersburg, see page 640.

Jazz Festival: The Copenhagen Jazz Festival—10 days in early July—puts the town in a rollicking slide-trombone mood. The Danes are Europe's jazz enthusiasts, and this music festival fills the town with happiness. The TI prints up an extensive listing of each year's festival events, or get the latest at www. jazz.dk. There's also a winter jazz festival in February.

Updates to This Book: For updates to this book, check www. ricksteves.com/update.

GETTING AROUND COPENHAGEN
By Public Transit

It's easy to navigate Copenhagen, with its fine buses, Metro, and S-tog (a suburban train system with stops in the city; rail passes valid on S-tog). For a helpful website that covers public-transport options (nationwide) in English, consult www.rejseplanen.dk.

Tickets: The same tickets are used throughout the system. A 24-kr, **two-zone ticket** gets you an hour's travel within the center—pay as you board buses, or buy from station ticket offices, convenience stores, or vending machines for the Metro. (Ticket machines may not accept American credit cards, but I was able to use an American debit card with a PIN, and most machines also take Danish cash; if you want to use your credit card and the machine won't take it, find a cashier.) Assume you'll be within the middle two zones unless traveling to or from the airport, which requires a **three-zone ticket** (36 kr).

One handy option is the blue, two-zone *klippekort,* which can be shared—for example, two people can take five rides each (150 kr for 10 rides, insert it in the validation box each time you board a train and it'll snip off one of your rides).

If you're traveling exclusively in central Copenhagen, the **City Pass** is a good value (80 kr/24 hours, 200 kr/72 hours, covers travel within zones 1-4, including the airport). To travel throughout the greater Copenhagen region—including side-trips to Roskilde, Frederiksborg Castle, Louisiana Art Museum, and Kronborg Castle—you'll need to pay more for a **"24-hour ticket"** (130 kr) or a **"7-day FlexCard"** (245 kr—can be a good value even for less

than a week). All passes are sold at stations, the TI, 7-Elevens, and other kiosks. Validate any all-day or multi-day ticket by stamping it in the yellow machine on the bus or at the station.

Buses: While the train system is slick (Metro and S-tog, described later), its usefulness is limited for the typical tourist—but buses serve all of the major sights in town every five to eight minutes during daytime hours. If you're not riding a bike everywhere, get comfortable with the buses. Bus drivers are patient, have change, and speak English. City maps list bus routes. Locals are usually friendly and helpful. There's also a floating "Harbor Bus" (described on page 44).

Bus lines that end with "A" (such as #1A) use quiet, eco-friendly, electric buses that are smaller than normal buses, allowing access into the narrower streets of the old town. Designed for tourists, these provide an easy overview to the city center. Among these, the following are particularly useful:

Bus **#1A** loops from the train station up to Kongens Nytorv (near Nyhavn) and then farther north, to Østerport.

Bus **#2A** goes from Christianshavn to the city center, then onward to points west.

Bus **#5A** connects the station more or less directly to Nørreport.

Bus **#6A** also connects the station to Nørreport, but on a much more roundabout route that twists through the central core (with several sightseeing-handy stops).

Bus **#11A** does a big loop from the train station through the core of town up to Nørreport, then down to Nyhavn before retracing its steps back via Nørreport to the train station.

Other, non-"A" buses, which are bigger and tend to be more direct, can be faster for some trips:

Bus **#14** runs from Nørreport (and near my recommended hotels) down to the city center, stopping near the Strøget, and eventually going near the main train station.

Bus **#26** runs a handy route right through the main tourist zone: train station/Tivoli to Slotsholmen Island to Kongens Nytorv (near Nyhavn) to the Amalienborg Palace/*Little Mermaid* area. It continues even farther north to the city's three main cruise ports, but the line splits, so check with the driver to make sure you're on the right bus.

Bus **#66** goes from Nyhavn to Slotsholmen Island to Tivoli.

Metro: Copenhagen's Metro line, while simple, is super-futuristic and growing. For most tourists' purposes, only the airport and three consecutive stops within the city matter: Nørreport (connected every few minutes by the S-tog to the main train station), Kongens Nytorv (near Nyhavn and the Strøget's north end), and Christianshavn. Nearly all recommended hotels are within walking distance of the main train station or these three stops.

The city is busy at work on the new Cityringen (City Circle) Metro line. When it opens in 2018, the Metro will instantly become far handier for tourists—linking the train station, Rådhuspladsen, Gammel Strand (near Slotsholmen Island), and Kongens Nytorv (near Nyhavn). In the meantime, expect to see massive construction zones at each of those locations. Eventually the Metro will also extend to Ørestad, the industrial and business center created after the Øresund Bridge was built between Denmark and Sweden (for the latest on the Metro, see www.m.dk).

S-tog Train: The S-tog is basically a commuter line that links stations on the main train line through Copenhagen; for those visiting the city, the most important stops are the main train station and Nørreport (where it ties into the Metro system). The S-tog is very handy for reaching many of the outlying sights described in the Near Copenhagen chapter.

By Boat

The hop-on, hop-off "Harbor Bus" (Havnebus) boat stops at the "Black Diamond" library, Christianshavn (near Knippels Bridge),

Nyhavn, the Opera House, and Nordre Toldbod, which is a short walk from *The Little Mermaid* site. The boat is part of the city bus system (lines #991 and #992) and covered by the tickets described earlier. Taking a long ride on this boat, from the library to the end of the line, is the "poor man's cruise"—without commentary, of course (runs 6:00-19:00). Or, for a true sightseeing trip, consider a guided harbor cruise (described later, under "Tours in Copenhagen").

By Taxi

Taxis are plentiful, easy to call or flag down, and pricey (35-kr pickup charge and then 15 kr/kilometer). For a short ride, four people spend about the same by taxi as by bus. Calling 35 35 35 35 will get you a taxi within minutes...with the meter already well on its way.

By Bike

Cyclists see more, save time and money, and really feel like locals. With a bike, you have Copenhagen at your command. I'd rather have a bike than a car and driver at my disposal. Virtually every street has a dedicated bike lane (complete with bike signal lights). Warning: Police routinely issue 500-kr tickets to anyone riding on sidewalks or through pedestrian zones. Note also that bikes can't be parked just anywhere. Observe others and park your bike among other bikes. The simple built-in lock that binds the back tire is adequate.

Renting a Bike: Your best bet for renting a bike is to ask your hotelier first. Many rent (or loan) decent bikes at reasonable rates to guests.

For an (often) better-quality bike and advice from someone with cycle expertise, consider one of these rental outfits in or near the city center (see map on page 36 for locations).

• **Københavens Cyklebørs,** near Nørreport Station, has a good selection of three-gear bikes (75 kr/1 day, 140 kr/2 days, 200 kr/3 days, 350 kr/week; Mon-Fri 9:00-17:30, Sat-Sun 10:00-14:00 & 18:00-20:00, closed Sat evening and all day Sun in off-season; Gothersgade 157, tel. 33 14 07 17, www.cykelborsen.dk).

• **Cykelbasen,** even closer to Nørreport, rents three- and seven-gear bikes (80 kr/day, 400 kr/week, includes lock; Mon-Fri 9:00-17:30, Sat 9:00-14:30, closed Sun; Gothersgade 137, tel. 22 18 06 42, www.cykel-basen.dk, click on "Info").

• **Copenhagen Bicycles,** at the entrance to Nyhavn by the Inderhavnsbroen pedestrian/bicycle bridge, rents basic three-gear bikes (70 kr/3 hours, 80 kr/6 hours, 110 kr/24 hours, includes lock, helmet-40 kr, daily 8:30-17:30, Nyhavn 44, tel. 33 93 04 04, http://www.copenhagenbicycles.dk/). They also offer guided tours in English and Danish (100 kr, mid-April-Sept daily at 11:00, 2.5-3 hours).

Using City Bikes: The city's public bike-rental program, called **Bycyklen,** lets you ride shiny-white, three-gear "smart bikes" (with

built-in GPS and an electric motor, should you need a boost) for 25 kr/hour. You'll find them parked in racks near the train station, on either side of City Hall, and at many other locations around town. Use the touchscreen on the handlebars to create an account, enter your credit card info, and off you go (but be sure to return the bike to a Bycyklen docking station or face a 200-kr fine). At their website (http://bycyklen.dk), you can locate docking stations, reserve a bike at a specific station, and create an account in advance. I'd use the bikes for a one-way pedal here or there, but for more than a couple of hours, it's more cost-efficient to rent a regular bicycle.

Tours in Copenhagen

ON FOOT

Copenhagen is an ideal city to get to know by foot. You have several good options:

▲▲Hans Christian Andersen Tours by Richard Karpen

Once upon a time, American Richard Karpen visited Copenhagen and fell in love with the city. Now, dressed as Hans Christian An-

dersen in a 19th-century top hat and long coat, he leads 1.5-hour tours that wander in and out of buildings, courtyards, back streets, and unusual parts of the old town. Along the one-mile route, he gives insightful and humorous background on the history, culture, and contemporary life of Denmark, Copenhagen, and the Danes (100 kr, kids under 12 free; departs from the TI, up the street from the main train station at Vesterbrogade 4A—at the corner with Bernstorffsgade; mid-May-mid-Sept Mon-Sat at 9:30, none on Sun; Richard departs promptly—if you miss him try to catch up with the tour at the next stop on Rådhuspladsen).

Richard also gives excellent one-hour tours of **Rosenborg Castle,** playing the role of a dapper Renaissance "Sir Richard" (90 kr, doesn't include castle entry, mid-May-mid-Sept Mon and Thu at 12:00, meet outside castle ticket office). No reservations are needed for any of Richard's scheduled tours—just show up.

You can also hire Richard for private tours of the city or of Rosenborg Castle (1,000 kr/1.5 hours, June-Aug, mobile 91 61 95 02, www.copenhagenwalks.com, copenhagenwalks@yahoo.com).

▲Daily City Walks by Red Badge Guides

Five local female guides work together, giving two-hour English-language city tours. Their walks mix the city's highlights, back lanes, history, and contemporary social issues, and finish at Amalienborg Palace at noon for the changing of the guard (100 kr, daily mid-April-Sept at 10:00, departs from TI, just show up, pay direct, no minimum, tel. 20 92 23 87, www.redbadgeguides.dk, redbadgeguides@gmail.com). They also offer private guided tours upon request.

▲▲Copenhagen History Tours

Christian Donatzky, a charming young Dane with a master's degree in history, runs a walking tour on Saturday mornings. In April and May, the theme is "Reformed Copenhagen" (covering the period from 1400-1600); in June and July, "King's Copenhagen" (1600-1800); and in August and September, "Hans Christian Andersen's Copenhagen" (1800-present). Those with a serious interest in Danish history will find these tours time well spent (80 kr, Sat at 10:00, approximately 1.5 hours, small groups of 5-15 people, tours depart from statue of Bishop Absalon on Højbro Plads between the Strøget and Christiansborg Palace, English only, no reservations necessary—just show up, tel. 28 49 44 35, www.historytours.dk, info@historytours.dk).

BY BOAT

For many, the best way to experience the city's canals and harbor is by canal boat. Two companies offer essentially the same live, three-language, one-hour cruises. Both boats leave at least twice an hour from Nyhavn and Christiansborg Palace, cruise around the palace and Christianshavn area, and then proceed into the wide-open harbor. Best on a sunny day, it's a relaxing way to see *The Little Mermaid* and munch on a lazy picnic during the slow-moving narration.

▲Netto-Bådene

These inexpensive cruises cost about half the price of their rival, Canal Tours Copenhagen. Go with Netto; there's no reason to pay nearly double (40 kr, mid-March-mid-Oct daily 10:00-17:00, runs later in summer, shorter hours in winter, sign at dock shows next departure, generally every 30 minutes, dress warmly—boats are open-top until Sept, tel. 32 54 41 02, www.havnerundfart.dk). Netto boats often make two stops where passengers can get off, then hop back on a later boat—at the bridge near *The Little Mermaid*, and at the Langebro bridge near Danhostel. Not every boat makes these stops; check the clock on the bridges for the next departure time.

Don't confuse the cheaper Netto and pricier Canal Tours Copenhagen boats: At Nyhavn, the Netto dock is midway down the canal (on the city side), while the Canal Tours Copenhagen dock is at the head of the canal. Near Christiansborg Palace, the Netto boats leave from Holmen's Bridge in front of the palace, while Canal Tours Copenhagen boats depart from Gammel Strand, 200

Hans Christian Andersen (1805-1875)

The author of such classic fairy tales as *The Ugly Duckling* was an ugly duckling himself—a misfit who blossomed. Hans Christian Andersen (called H. C., pronounced "hoe see" by the Danes) was born to a poor shoemaker in Odense. As a child he was gangly, high-strung, and effeminate. He avoided school because the kids laughed at him, so he spent his time in a fantasy world of books and plays. When his father died, the 11-year-old was on his own, forced into manual labor. He loved playing with a marionette theater that his father had made for him, sparking a lifelong love affair with the theater. In 1819, at the age of 14, he moved to Copenhagen to pursue an acting career and worked as a boy soprano for the Royal Theater. When his voice changed, the director encouraged him to return to school. He dutifully attended—a teenager among boys—and eventually went on to the university. As rejections piled up for his acting aspirations, Andersen began to shift his theatrical ambitions to playwriting.

After graduation, Andersen won a two-year scholarship to travel around Europe, the first of many trips he'd make and write about. His experiences abroad were highly formative, providing inspiration for many of his tales. Still in his 20s, he published an obviously autobiographical novel, *The Improvisatore*, about a poor young man who comes into his own while traveling in Italy. The novel launched his writing career, and soon he was hobnobbing with the international crowd—Charles Dickens, Victor Hugo, Franz Liszt, Richard Wagner, Henrik Ibsen, and Edvard Grieg.

yards away. Boats leaving from Christiansborg are generally less crowded than those leaving from Nyhavn.

Canal Tours Copenhagen

This more expensive option does the same cruise as Netto for 75 kr (daily March-late Oct 9:30-18:00, runs later in summer, shorter hours in winter, no tours Jan-Feb, boats are sometimes covered if it's raining, tel. 32 96 30 00, www.stromma.dk).

In summer, Canal Tours Copenhagen also runs audioguided hop-on, hop-off **"water bus"** tours (95 kr/24 hours, daily late May-mid-Sept 9:30-19:00) and 1.5-hour evening **jazz cruises** (see "Nightlife in Copenhagen," page 97).

Despite his many famous friends, Andersen remained a lonely soul who never married. He had very close male friendships and journaled about unrequited love affairs with several women, including the famous opera star of the day, Jenny Lind, the "Swedish Nightingale." Without a family of his own, he became very close with the children of his friends—and, through his fairy tales, with a vast extended family of kids around the world.

Though he wrote novels, plays, and travel literature, it was his fairy tales, including *The Ugly Duckling*, *The Emperor's New Clothes*, *The Princess and the Pea*, *The Little Mermaid*, *The Snow Queen*, and *The Red Shoes*, that made him famous in Denmark and abroad. They made him Denmark's best-known author, the "Danish Charles Dickens." Some stories are based on earlier folk tales, and others came straight from his inventive mind, all written in an informal, conversational style that was considered unusual and even surprising at the time.

Andersen's compelling tales appeal to children and adults alike. They're full of magic and touch on strong, universal emotions—the pain of being different, the joy of self-discovery, and the struggle to fit in. The ugly duckling, for example, is teased by his fellow ducks before he finally discovers his true identity as a beautiful swan. In *The Emperor's New Clothes*, a boy is derided by everyone for speaking the simple, self-evident truth that the emperor is fooling himself. J. K. Rowling recently said, "The indelible characters he created are so deeply implanted in our subconscious that we sometimes forget that we were not born with the stories." (For more on Andersen's famous story *The Little Mermaid*—and what it might tell us about his life—see page 65.)

By the time of his death, the poor shoemaker's son was wealthy, cultured, and had been knighted. His rise through traditional class barriers mirrors the social progress of the 19th century.

BY BUS
Hop-On, Hop-Off Bus Tours

Several buses with recorded narration circle the city for a basic 1.25- to 1.5-hour orientation, allowing you to get on and off as you like at the following stops: Tivoli Gardens, Gammel Strand near Christiansborg Palace, *The Little Mermaid*, Rosenborg Castle, Nyhavn sailors' quarter, and more. Cruise passengers arriving at the Langelinie Pier can catch a hop-on, hop-off bus there; those arriving at other ports can take their cruise shuttle to *The Little Mermaid*, where you can pick up a hop-on, hop-off bus.

The same company runs **City Sightseeing**'s red buses and **Open Top Tours**' green buses. Both offer a Mermaid route for 175 kr and Carlsberg Brewery and Christiania routes for 195 kr (tickets good for 24 hours, pay driver, 2/hour, May-mid-Sept daily 9:30-18:00, shorter hours off-season, buses depart near the TI at the Radisson Blu Royal Hotel and at many other stops throughout city, tel. 25 55 66 88, www.city-sightseeing.dk). Open Top Tours also offers a 225-kr ticket that includes all tour routes and a cruise on their hop-on, hop-off canal boat.

Another operation—called **Red Blue Bus Tours**—does a similar route but runs a little less frequently (every 45 minutes in summer, hourly in winter; 190 kr/1 day, 230 kr/2 days, www.sightseeing-cph.dk).

BY BIKE
▲Bike Copenhagen with Mike
Mike Sommerville offers three-hour guided bike tours of the city. A Copenhagen native, Mike enjoys showing off his city to visitors, offering both historic background and contemporary cultural insights along the way (April-Sept daily at 10:00, second departure Wed and Sat at 14:00; 300 kr includes bike rental, price same with or without a bike, 50-kr discount with this book—maximum 2 discounts per book and must have book with you, cash only). All tours are in English and depart from his bike shop at Sankt Peders Straede 47, in the Latin Quarter (see map on page 36). Mike also offers evening tours (19:00, 2.5 hours) and private tours; see the details at www.bikecopenhagenwithmike.dk.

Copenhagen City Walk

This self-guided walk takes about two hours. It starts at Rådhuspladsen (City Hall Square) and heads along the pedestrian street, the Strøget, through the old city, onto "Castle Island" (home of Christiansborg Palace), along the harbor promenade, and through Nyhavn, the sailors' quarter with the city's iconic canalfront houses. The walk officially ends at Kongens Nytorv ("King's New Square"), though you can continue another 10 minutes to Amalienborg Palace and then another 15 minutes beyond that to *The Little Mermaid*.

❶ Rådhuspladsen
Start from Rådhuspladsen (City Hall Square), the bustling heart of Copenhagen, dominated by the tower of the City Hall. Today this square always seems to be hosting some lively community event, but it was once Copenhagen's fortified west end. For 700 years, Copenhagen was contained within its city walls. By the

mid-1800s, 140,000 people were packed inside. The overcrowding led to hygiene problems. (A cholera outbreak killed 5,000.) It was clear: The walls needed to come down...and they did. Those formidable town walls survive today only in echoes—a circular series of roads and the remnants of moats, which are now people-friendly city lakes (see the sidebar on page 34).

• Stand 50 yards in front of City Hall and turn clockwise for a...

Rådhuspladsen Spin-Tour: The **City Hall,** or Rådhus, is worth a visit (described on page 68). Old **Hans Christian Andersen** sits to the right of City Hall, almost begging to be in another photo (as he used to in real life). Climb onto his well-worn knee. (While up there, you might take off your shirt for a racy photo, as many Danes enjoy doing.)

He's looking at ❷ **Tivoli Gardens** (across the street), which he loved and which inspired him when writing some of his stories. Tivoli Gardens was founded in 1843, when magazine publisher Georg Carstensen convinced the king to let him build a pleasure garden outside the walls of crowded Copenhagen. The king quickly agreed, knowing that happy people care less about fighting for democracy. Tivoli became Europe's first great public amusement park. When the train lines came, the station was placed just beyond Tivoli.

The big, glassy building with the *DI* sign is filled with the offices of Danish Industry—a collection of Danish companies whose logos you can see in the windows (plus the Irma grocery store at street level).

The big, broad boulevard is **Vesterbrogade** ("Western Way"), which led to the western gate of the medieval city (behind you, where the pedestrian boulevard begins). Here, in the traffic hub of this huge city, you'll notice...not many cars. Denmark's 180 percent tax on car purchases makes the bus, Metro, or bike a sweeter option. In fact, the construction messing up this square is part of a huge expansion of the Metro system.

Down Vesterbrogade towers the **Radisson Blu Royal Hotel** (formerly the SAS building), Copenhagen's only skyscraper. Locals say it seems so tall because the clouds hang so low. When it was built in 1960, Copenhageners took one look and decided—that's enough of a skyline. Notice there are no other buildings taller than the five-story limit in the old center.

The golden ❸ **weather girls** (on the corner, high above Vesterbrogade) indicate the weather: on a bike (fair weather) or with an umbrella (foul). These two have been called the only women in Copenhagen you can trust, but for years they've been stuck in the almost-sunny mode...with the bike just peeking out. Notice that the red temperature dots max out at 28° Celsius (that's 82° Fahrenheit...a good memory aid: transpose 28 to get 82).

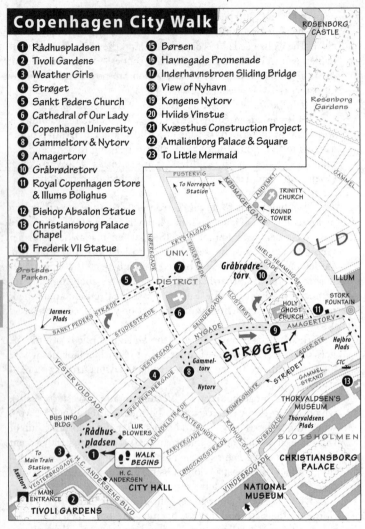

Copenhagen City Walk

1. Rådhuspladsen
2. Tivoli Gardens
3. Weather Girls
4. Strøget
5. Sankt Peders Church
6. Cathedral of Our Lady
7. Copenhagen University
8. Gammeltorv & Nytorv
9. Amagertorv
10. Gråbrødretorv
11. Royal Copenhagen Store & Illums Bolighus
12. Bishop Absalon Statue
13. Christiansborg Palace Chapel
14. Frederik VII Statue
15. Børsen
16. Havnegade Promenade
17. Inderhavnsbroen Sliding Bridge
18. View of Nyhavn
19. Kongens Nytorv
20. Hviids Vinstue
21. Kvæsthus Construction Project
22. Amalienborg Palace & Square
23. To Little Mermaid

To the right, just down the street, is the Tiger Store (a popular local "dollar store"...nearly everything is under 50 kr). The next street (once the local Fleet Street, with the big newspapers) still has the offices for *Politiken* (the leading Danish newspaper) and the best bookstore in town, Boghallen.

As you spin farther right, three fast-food joints stand at the entry to the Strøget (STROY-et), Copenhagen's grand pedestrian boulevard—where we're heading next. Just beyond that and the Art Deco-style Palace Hotel (with a tower to serve as a sister to the City Hall) is the *Lur Blowers* **sculpture,** which honors the earliest

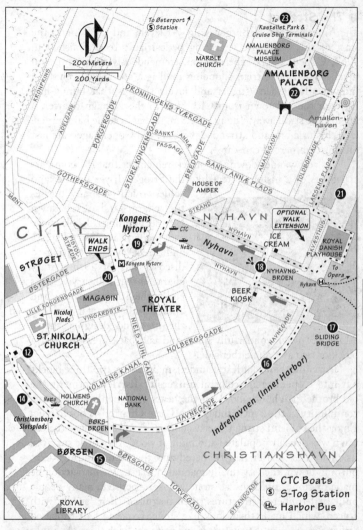

warrior Danes. The *lur* is a curvy, trombone-sounding horn that was used to call soldiers to battle or to accompany pagan religious processions. The earliest bronze *lurs* date as far back as 3,500 years ago. Later, the Vikings used a wood version of the *lur*. The ancient originals, which still play, are displayed in the National Museum.

• *Now head down the pedestrian boulevard (pickpocket alert).*

❹ The Strøget

The American trio of Burger King, 7-Eleven, and KFC marks the start of this otherwise charming pedestrian street. Finished in 1962, Copenhagen's experimental, tremendously successful, and much-copied pedestrian shopping mall is a string of lively (and individually named) streets and lovely squares that bunny-hop through the old town from City Hall to the Nyhavn quarter, a 20-minute stroll away. Though the Strøget has become hamburger-ized, historic bits and attractive pieces of old Copenhagen are just off this commercial can-can.

COPENHAGEN

As you wander down this street, remember that the commercial focus of a historic street like the Strøget drives up the land

value, which generally trashes the charm and tears down the old buildings. Look above the modern window displays and street-level advertising to discover bits of 19th-century character that still survive. This end of the Strøget is young and cheap, while the far end has the high-end designer shops. Along the way, wonderfully quiet and laid-back areas are just a block or two away on either side.

After one block (at Kattesundet), make a side-trip three blocks left into Copenhagen's colorful **university district.** Formerly the old brothel neighborhood, later the heart of Copenhagen's hippie community in the 1960s, today this "Latin Quarter" is SoHo chic. Enjoy the colorful string of artsy shops and cafés. Because the old town was densely populated and built of wood, very little survived its many fires. After half-timbered and thatched buildings kept burning down, the city finally mandated that new construction be made of stone. But because stone was so expensive, many people built half-timbered structures, then disguised their facades with stucco, which made them look like stone. Exposed half-timbered structures are seen in courtyards and from the back sides. At Sankt Peders Stræde, turn right and walk to the end of the street. Notice the old guild signs (a baker, a key maker, and so on) identifying the original businesses here.

Along the way, look for large mansions that once circled expansive **courtyards.** As the population grew, the city walls constricted Copenhagen's physical size. The courtyards were gradually filled with higgledy-piggledy secondary buildings. Today throughout the old center, you can step off a busy pedestrian mall and back in time in these characteristic, half-timbered, time-warp courtyards. Replace the parked car with a tired horse and the bikes with a line of outhouses, and you're in 19th-century Copenhagen. If you see an open courtyard door, you're welcome to discreetly wander in and look around.

You'll also pass funky shops and the big brick ❺ **Sankt Peders Church**—the old German merchant community's church, which still holds services in German. Its fine 17th-century brick grave chapel (filling a ground-floor building out back due to the boggy nature of the soil) is filled with fancy German tombs (25 kr to enter).

• *When Sankt Peders Stræde intersects with Nørregade, look right to find the big, Neoclassical...*

❻ Cathedral of Our Lady (Vor Frue Kirche)

The obelisk-like **Reformation Memorial** across the street from the cathedral celebrates Denmark's break from the Roman Catho-

lic Church to become Lutheran in 1536. Walk around and study the reliefs of great Danish reformers protesting from their pulpits. The relief facing the church shows King Christian III presiding over the pivotal town council meeting when they decided to break away from Rome. As a young man, Prince Christian had traveled to Germany, where he was influenced by Martin Luther. He returned to take the Danish throne by force, despite Catholic opposition. Realizing the advantages of being the head of his own state church, Christian confiscated church property and established the state Lutheran Church. King Christian was crowned in-

side this cathedral. Because of the reforms of 1536, there's no Mary in the Cathedral of Our Lady. The other reliefs show the popular religious uprising, with people taking control of the word of God by translating the Bible from Latin into their own language.

Like much of this part of town, the church burned down in the British bombardment of 1807 and was rebuilt in the Neoclassical style. The cathedral's **facade** looks like a Greek temple. (Two blocks to the right, in the distance, notice more Neoclassicism— the law courts.) You can see why Golden Age Copenhagen (early 1800s) fancied itself a Nordic Athens. Old Testament figures (King David and Moses) flank the cathedral's entryway. Above, John the Baptist stands where you'd expect to see Greek gods. He invites you in...into the New Testament.

The **interior** is a world of Neoclassical serenity (free, open daily 8:00-17:00). It feels like a pagan temple that now houses

Christianity. The nave is lined by the 12 apostles, clad in classical robes—masterpieces by the great Danish sculptor Bertel Thorvaldsen (see sidebar, page 76). Each strikes a meditative pose, carrying his identifying symbol: Peter with keys, Andrew with the X-shaped cross of his execution, Matthew and John writing their books, and so on. They lead to a statue of the *Risen Christ* (see photo), standing where the statue of Zeus would have been: inside a temple-like niche, flanked by columns and topped with a pediment. Rather than wearing a royal robe, Jesus wears his burial shroud, opens his arms wide, and says, "Come to me." (Mormons will recognize this statue—a rep-

lica stands in the visitors center at Salt Lake City's Temple Square and is often reproduced in church publications.) The marvelous acoustics are demonstrated in free organ concerts Saturdays in July and August at noon. Notice how, in good Protestant style, only the front half of the pews are "reversible," allowing the congregation to flip around and face the pulpit (in the middle of the church) to better hear the sermon.

• *Head back outside. If you face the church's facade and look to the left (across the square called Frue Plads), you'll see...*

❼ Copenhagen University

Now home to 30,000 students, this university was founded by the king in the 15th century to stop the Danish brain drain to Paris. Today tuition is free (but room, board, and beer are not). Locals say it's easy to get in, but given the wonderful student lifestyle, very hard to get out.

Step up the middle steps of the university's big building; if the doors are open, enter a colorful lobby, starring Athena and Apollo. The frescoes celebrate high thinking, with themes such as the triumph of wisdom over barbarism. Notice how harmoniously the architecture, sculpture, and painting work together.

Outside, busts honor great minds from the faculty, including (at the end) Niels Bohr, a professor who won the 1922 Nobel Prize for theoretical physics. He evaded the clutches of the Nazi science labs by fleeing to America in 1943, where he helped develop the atomic bomb.

• *Rejoin the Strøget (one block downhill from the Reformation Memorial to the black-and-gold fountain) at the twin squares called...*

❽ Gammeltorv and Nytorv

This was the old town center. In Gammeltorv ("Old Square"), the Fountain of Charity (Caritas) is named for the figure of Charity on top. It has provided drinking water to locals since the early 1600s. Featuring a pregnant woman squirting water from her breasts next to a boy urinating, this was just too much for people of the Victorian Age. They corked both figures and raised the statue to what they hoped would be out of view. The exotic-looking kiosk was one of the city's first community telephone centers from the days before phones were privately owned. Look at the reliefs ringing its top: an airplane with bird wings (c. 1900) and two women talking on a newfangled telephonic device. (It was thought business would popularize the telephone, but actually it was women.)

While Gammeltorv was a place of happiness and merriment, Nytorv ("New Square") was a place of severity and judgment. Walk

to the small raised area 20 yards in front of the old ancient-Greek-style former City Hall and courthouse. Do a 360. The square is Neoclassical (built mostly after the 1807 British bombardment). Read the old Danish on the City Hall facade: "With Law Shall Man Build the Land." Look down at the pavement and read the plaque: "Here stood the town's *Kag* (whipping post) until 1780."

• *Now walk down the next stretch of the Strøget—called Nygade—to reach...*

❾ Amagertorv

This is prime real estate for talented street entertainers. Walk to the stately brick Holy Ghost church (Helligåndskirken). The fine spire is typical of old Danish churches. Under the stepped gable was a medieval hospital run by monks (one of the oldest buildings in town, dating from the 12th century). Today the hospital is an antiques hall. In summer the pleasant courtyard is shared by a group of charities selling light bites and coffee.

Walk behind the church, down Valkendorfsgade—the street just before the church—and through a passage under the rust-colored building at #32 (if locked, loop back and go down Klosterstræde);

Copenhagen at a Glance

▲▲▲Tivoli Gardens Copenhagen's classic amusement park, with rides, music, food, and other fun. **Hours:** Mid-April-late Sept daily 11:00-23:00, Fri-Sat until 24:00, also open daily 11:00-22:00 for a week in mid-Oct and mid-Nov-New Year's Day. See page 66.

▲▲▲National Museum History of Danish civilization with tourable 19th-century Victorian Apartment. **Hours:** Museum—Tue-Sun 10:00-17:00, closed Mon; Victorian Apartment—English tours June-Sept Sat at 14:00, Danish tours Sat-Sun at 11:00, 12:00, and 13:00 year-round. See page 70.

▲▲▲Rosenborg Castle and Treasury Renaissance castle of larger-than-life "warrior king" Christian IV. **Hours:** June-Aug daily 10:00-17:00; May and Sept-Oct daily 10:00-16:00; Nov-Dec Tue-Sun 11:00-14:00 (treasury until 16:00), closed Mon; Jan-April Tue-Sun 11:00-16:00, closed Mon. See page 80.

▲▲▲Christiania Colorful counterculture squatters' colony. **Hours:** Always open; guided tours at 15:00 (daily late June-Aug, only Sat-Sun rest of year). See page 89.

▲▲Christiansborg Palace Royal reception rooms with dazzling tapestries. **Hours:** Reception rooms, castle ruins, and stables open daily except closed Mon in Oct-April. Hours vary by sight: Reception rooms 9:00-17:00 (may close for royal events), ruins 10:00-17:00, stables 13:30-16:00 except 10:00-17:00 in July. See page 73.

▲▲Thorvaldsen's Museum Works of the Danish Neoclassical sculptor. **Hours:** Tue-Sun 10:00-17:00, closed Mon. See page 75.

▲City Hall Copenhagen's landmark, packed with Danish history

here you'll find the leafy and beer-stained ❿ **Gråbrødretorv.** Surrounded by fine old buildings, this "Grey Friars' Square"—a monastic square until the Reformation made it a people's square—is a popular place for an outdoor meal or drink in the summer. At the end of the square, the street called Niels Hemmingsens Gade returns (past the recommended Copenhagen Jazz House, a good place for live music nightly) to the Strøget.

and symbolism and topped with a tower. **Hours:** Mon-Fri 8:30-16:00, some Sat 10:00-13:00, closed Sun. See page 68.

▲**Ny Carlsberg Glyptotek** Scandinavia's top art gallery, featuring Egyptians, Greeks, Etruscans, French, and Danes. **Hours:** Tue-Sun 11:00-17:00, closed Mon. See page 69.

▲**Museum of Copenhagen** The story of Copenhagen, displayed in an old house. **Hours:** Daily 10:00-17:00. See page 73.

▲**Danish Jewish Museum** Exhibit tracing the 400-year history of Danish Jews, in a unique building by American architect Daniel Libeskind. **Hours:** June-Aug Tue-Sun 10:00-17:00; Sept-May Tue-Fri 13:00-16:00, Sat-Sun 12:00-17:00; closed Mon year-round. See page 78.

▲**Amalienborg Museum** Quick and intimate look at Denmark's royal family. **Hours:** May-Oct daily 10:00-16:00; Nov-April Tue-Sun 11:00-16:00, closed Mon. See page 79.

▲**Rosenborg Gardens** Park surrounding Rosenborg Castle, filled with statues and statuesque Danes. **Hours:** Always open. See page 86.

▲**National Gallery of Denmark** Good Danish and Modernist collections. **Hours:** Tue-Sun 10:00-17:00, Wed until 20:00, closed Mon. See page 86.

▲**Our Savior's Church** Spiral-spired church with bright Baroque interior. **Hours:** Church—daily 11:00-15:30 but may close for special services; tower—July-mid-Sept Mon-Sat 10:00-19:00, Sun 10:30-19:00; April-June and mid-Sept-Nov daily until 16:00, closed Dec-March and in bad weather. See page 88.

Once back on busy Strøget, turn left and continue down Amagertorv, with its fine inlaid Italian granite stonework, to the next square with the "stork" fountain (actually three herons). The Victorian WCs here (free, steps down from fountain) are a delight.

This square, Amagertorv, is a highlight for shoppers, with the ⓫ **Royal Copenhagen store**—stacked with three floors of porcelain—and **Illums Bolighus**—a fine place to ogle modern Danish design (see "Shopping in Copenhagen," later). A block toward the canal—running parallel to the Strøget—starts Strædet, which is a "second Strøget" featuring cafés and antique shops.

North of Amagertorv, a broad pedestrian mall called **Køb-**

magergade leads past a fine modern bakery (Holm's Bager) to Christian IV's Round Tower and the Latin Quarter (university district). The recommended Café Norden overlooks the fountain—a good place for a meal or coffee with a view. The second floor offers the best vantage point.

• *Looking downhill from the fountain, about halfway to an imposing palace in the distance, you'll see a great man on a horse. Walk here to view this statue of Copenhagen's founder,* **⓬ Bishop Absalon,** *shown in his Warrior Absalon get-up.*

From the bishop, you'll continue across a bridge toward the palace and the next statue—a king on a horse. As you cross the bridge, look right to see the City Hall tower, where this walk started. (A couple of the city's competing sightseeing boat tours depart from near here—see page 47.)

Christiansborg Palace and the Birthplace of Copenhagen

You're stepping onto the island of Slotsholmen (or Castle Island), the easy-to-defend birthplace of Copenhagen in the 12th century. It's dominated by the royal palace complex. Christiansborg Palace (with its "three crowns" spire)—the imposing former residence of kings—is now the Parliament building.

Ahead of you, the Neoclassical Lutheran church with the low dome is the **⓭ Christiansborg Palace Chapel,** site of 350 years of royal weddings and funerals (free, only open Sun 10:00-17:00).

Walk to the next green copper equestrian statue. **⓮ Frederik VII** was crowned in 1848, just months before Denmark got its constitution on June 5, 1849. (Constitution Day is celebrated with typical Danish understatement—stores are closed and workers get the day off.) Frederik, who then ruled as a constitutional monarch, stands in front of **Christiansborg Palace,** which Denmark's royal family now shares with its people's assembly (queen's wing on right, Parliament on left; for information on visiting the palace, see page 73). This palace, the seat of Danish government today, is considered the birthplace of Copenhagen. It stands upon the ruins of Absalon's 12th-century castle (literally under your feet). The big stones between the statue and the street were put in for security after the 2011 terror attacks in Norway (in which 77 people were murdered, most of them teens and young adults). While Danes strive to keep government accessible, security measures like this are today's reality.

This is Denmark's power island, with the Parliament, Supreme Court, Ministry of Finance (to the left), and **⓯ Børsen**—the historic stock exchange (farther to the left, with the fanciful dragon-tail spire; not open to tourists). The eye-catching red-brick stock exchange was inspired by the Dutch Renaissance, like much of 17th-century Copenhagen. Built to promote the mercantile ambitions of Denmark in the 1600s, it was the "World Trade Center" of Scandinavia. The facade reads, "For the profitable use of buyer and seller." The dragon-tail spire with three crowns represents the Danish aspiration to rule a united Scandinavia—or at least be its commercial capital.

Notice Copenhagen's distinctive green copper spires all around you. Beyond the old stock exchange lies the island of **Christianshavn,** with its own distinct spire. It tops the Church of Our Savior and features an external spiral staircase winding to the top for an amazing view. While political power resided here on Slotsholmen, commercial power was in the merchant's district, Christianshavn (neighborhood and church described later, under "Sights in Copenhagen"). The Børsen symbolically connected Christianshavn with the rest of the city, in an age when trade was a very big deal.

• *Walk along the old stock exchange toward Christianshavn, but turn left at the crosswalk with the signal before you reach the end of the building. After crossing the street, go over the canal and turn right to walk along the harborfront promenade, enjoying views of Christianshavn across the water to your right.*

COPENHAGEN

⑯ Havnegade Promenade

The Havnegade promenade to Nyhavn is a delightful people zone with trampolines, harborview benches (a good place to stop, look across the water, and ponder the trendy apartments and old-warehouses-turned-modern-office-blocks), and an ice-cream-licking ambience. Stroll several blocks from here toward the new ⑰ **Inderhavnsbroen sliding bridge** for pedestrians and bikes. This "Kissing Bridge" (it's called that because the two sliding, or retractable, sections "kiss" when they come together) is designed to link the town center with Christianshavn and to make the new Opera House (ahead on the right, across the water) more accessible to downtown. Walk until you hit the Nyhavn canal.

Across the way, at the end of Nyhavn canal, stands the glassy Royal Danish Theatre's Playhouse. While this walk finishes on

Kongens Nytorv, the square at the head of this canal, you could extend it by continuing north along the harbor from the playhouse.

• *For now, turn left and walk to the center of the bridge over the canal for a...*

⑱ View of Nyhavn

Established in the 1670s along with Kongens Nytorv, Nyhavn ("New Harbor") is a recently gentrified sailors' quarter. (Hong Kong is the last of the nasty bars from the rough old days.) With its trendy cafés, jazz clubs, and tattoo shops (pop into Tattoo Ole at #17—fun photos, very traditional), Nyhavn is a wonderful place to hang out. The canal is filled with glamorous old sailboats of all sizes. Historic sloops are welcome to moor here in Copenhagen's ever-changing boat museum. Hans Christian Andersen lived and wrote his first stories here (in the red double-gabled building at #20).

From the bridge, take a few steps left to the cheap **beer kiosk** (on Holbergsgade, open daily until late). At this mini-market, let friendly manager Nagib give you a little lesson in Danish beer, and then buy a bottle or can. Choose from Carlsberg (standard lager, 5 percent alcohol), Carlsberg Elephant (strong, 7.2 percent), Tuborg Grøn (standard lager, 4.6 percent), Tuborg Gold (stronger, 5.8 percent), and Tuborg Classic (dark beer, 4.6 percent). The cost? About 10-15 kr depending on

the alcohol level. Take your beer out to the canal and feel like a local. A note about all the public beer-drinking here: There's no more beer consumption here than in the US; it's just out in public. Many young Danes can't afford to drink in a bar, so they "picnic drink" their beers in squares and along canals, at a quarter of the price for a bottle.

If you crave **ice cream** instead, cross the bridge, where you'll find a popular place with freshly made waffle cones facing the canal (Vaffelbageren).

Now wander the quay, enjoying the frat-party parade of tattoos (hotter weather reveals more tattoos). Celtic and Nordic mythological designs are in (as is bodybuilding, by the looks of things). The place thrives—with the cheap-beer drinkers dockside and the richer and older ones looking on from comfier cafés.

• *Make your way to the head of the canal, where you'll find a minuscule amber museum, above the House of Amber (see "Shopping in Copenhagen," page 96). Just beyond the head of Nyhavn canal sprawls the huge and stately King's New Square. Check it out.*

⓬ Kongens Nytorv

The "King's New Square" is home to the National Theater, French embassy, and venerable Hotel d'Angleterre, where VIPs and pop stars stay. In the mid-1600s the city expanded, pushing its wall farther east. The equestrian statue in the middle of the square celebrates Christian V, who made

this square the city's geographical and cultural center. In 1676, King Christian rode off to reconquer the southern tip of Sweden and reclaim Denmark's dominance. He returned empty-handed and broke. Denmark became a second-rate power, but Copenhagen prospered. In the winter this square becomes a popular ice-skating rink.

Across the square on the left, small glass pyramids mark the Metro. The **Metro** that runs underground here features state-of-the-art technology (automated cars, no driver...sit in front to watch the tracks coming at you). As the cars come and go without drivers, compare this system to the public transit in your town.

Wander into ❷⓪ **Hviids Vinstue**, the town's oldest wine cellar (from 1723, just beyond the Metro station, at #19, under an Indian restaurant) to check out its characteristic interior and fascinating old Copenhagen photos. It's a colorful spot for an open-face sandwich and a beer (three sandwiches and a beer for 70 kr at lunchtime). Their wintertime *gløgg* (hot spiced wine) is legendary. Across the street, towering above the Metro station, is Magasin du Nord, the grandest old department store in town.

• *You've reached the end of this walk. But if you'd like to extend it by heading out to Amalienborg Palace and* The Little Mermaid, *retrace your steps to the far side of Nyhavn canal.*

Nyhavn to Amalienborg

Stroll along the canal to the Royal Danish Theatre's Playhouse and follow the harborfront promenade from there left through the big ❷⓵ **Kvæsthus construction project.** The Kvæsthus project's exhibition pavilion shows the vision for enhancing this waterfront area. You'll then stroll a delightful promenade to the modern fountain of Amaliehaven Park, immediately across the harbor from Copenhagen's slick Opera House. The Opera House is bigger than it looks—of its 14 floors, five are below sea level. Its striking design is controversial. Completed in 2005 by Henning Larsen, it was a $400 million gift to the nation from an oil-shipping magnate.

• *A block inland (behind the fountain) is the orderly...*

❷⓶ Amalienborg Palace and Square

Queen Margrethe II and her husband live in the mansion to your immediate left as you enter the square from the harborside. (If the flag's flying, she's home.) The mansion across the street (on the right as you enter) is where her son and heir to the throne, Crown

Prince Frederik, lives with his wife, Australian businesswoman Mary Donaldson, and their four children. The royal guesthouse palace is on the far left. And the palace on the far right is the **Amalienborg Museum,** which offers an intimate look at royal living (described on page 79).

Though the guards change daily at noon, they do it with royal fanfare only when the queen is in residence (see page 79 for details). The royal guard often has a police escort when it marches through town on special occasions—leading locals to joke that theirs is "the only army in the world that needs police protection."

The equestrian statue of Frederik V is a reminder that this square was the centerpiece of a planned town he envisioned in 1750. It was named for him—Frederikstaden. During the 18th century, Denmark's population grew and the country thrived (as trade flourished and its neutrality kept it out of the costly wars impoverishing much of Europe). Frederikstaden, with its strong architectural harmony, was designed as a luxury neighborhood for the city's business elite. Nobility and other big shots moved in, but the king came here only after his other palace burned down in a 1794 fire.

Just inland, the striking Frederikskirke—better known as the **Marble Church**—was designed to fit this ritzy new quarter. If it's open, step inside to bask in its vast, serene, Pantheon-esque atmosphere (free, Mon-Thu 10:00-17:00, Fri-Sun 12:00-17:00).

• *From the square, Amaliegade leads two blocks north to...*

Kastellet Park

In this park, you'll find some worthwhile sightseeing. The 1908 **Gefion Fountain** illustrates the myth of the goddess who was

given one night to carve a hunk out of Sweden to make into Denmark's main island, Sjælland (or "Zealand" in English), which you're on. Gefion transformed her four sons into oxen to do the job, and the chunk she removed from Sweden is supposedly Vänern, Sweden's largest lake. If you look at a map showing Sweden and Denmark, the island and the lake are, in fact, roughly the same shape. Next to the fountain is an Anglican church built of flint.

• *Climb up the stairs by the fountain and continue along the top of the rampart about five minutes to reach the harborfront site of the overrated, overfondled, and overphotographed symbol of Copenhagen,* Den Lille Havfrue, *or...*

The Little Mermaid and Hans Christian Andersen

"Far out in the ocean, where the water is as blue as a cornflower, as clear as crystal, and very, very deep..." there lived a

young mermaid. So begins one of Hans Christian Andersen's best-known stories. The plot line starts much like the Disney movie, but it's spiced with poetic description and philosophical dialogue about the immortal soul.

The mermaid's story goes like this: One day, a young mermaid spies a passing ship and falls in love with a handsome human prince. The ship is wrecked in a storm, and she saves the prince's life. To be with the prince, the mermaid asks a sea witch to give her human legs. In exchange, she agrees to give up her voice and the chance of ever returning to the sea. And, the witch tells her, if the prince doesn't marry her, she will immediately die heartbroken and without an immortal soul. The mermaid agrees, and her fish tail becomes a pair of beautiful but painful legs. She woos the prince—who loves her in return—but he eventually marries another. Heartbroken, the mermaid prepares to die. She's given one last chance to save herself: She must kill the prince on his wedding night. She sneaks into the bedchamber with a knife...but can't bear to kill the man she loves. The mermaid throws herself into the sea to die. Suddenly, she's miraculously carried up by the mermaids of the air, who give her an immortal soul as a reward for her long-suffering love.

The tale of unrequited love mirrors Andersen's own sad love life. He had two major crushes—one of them for the famous opera singer, Jenny Lind—but he was turned down both times, and he never married. He had plenty of interest in sex but likely died a virgin. He had close brotherly and motherly relations with women but stayed single, had time to travel and write, and maintained a child-like wonder about the world to his dying days.

㉓*The Little Mermaid*

The Little Mermaid statue was a gift to the city of Copenhagen in 1909 from brewing magnate Carl Jacobsen (whose art collection forms the basis of the Ny Carlsberg Glyptotek). Inspired by a ballet performance of Andersen's story, Jacobsen hired the young sculptor Edvard Eriksen to immortalize the mermaid as a statue. Eriksen used his wife Eline as the model. The statue sat unappreciated for

40 years until Danny Kaye sang "Wonderful Copenhagen" in the movie *Hans Christian Andersen*, and the tourist board decided to use the mermaid as a marketing symbol for the city. For the non-Disneyfied *Little Mermaid* story—and insights into Hans Christian Andersen—see the sidebar. For more on his life, see page 48.

• *This is the end of our extended wonderful, wonderful "Copenhagen City Walk." From here you can get back downtown on foot, by taxi, on bus #1A from Store Kongensgade on the other side of Kastellet Park, or bus #26 from farther north, along Folke Bernadottes Allé.*

Sights in Copenhagen

NEAR THE TRAIN STATION

Copenhagen's great train station, the Hovedbanegården, is a fascinating mesh of Scandinavian culture and transportation efficiency. From the station, delightful sights fan out into the old city. The following attractions are listed roughly in order from the train station to Slotsholmen Island (except for the Museum of Copenhagen, which is several blocks from the station, in the opposite direction).

▲▲▲Tivoli Gardens

The world's grand old amusement park—since 1843—is 20 acres, 110,000 lanterns, and countless ice cream cones of fun. You pay one admission price and find yourself lost in a Hans Christian Andersen wonderland of rides, restaurants, games, marching bands, roulette wheels, and funny mirrors. A roller coaster screams through the middle of a tranquil Asian food court, and the Small World-inspired Den Flyvende Kuffert ride floats through Hans Christian Andersen fairy tales. It's a children's fantasyland midday, but it becomes more adult-oriented later on. With or without kids, this place is a true magic kingdom. Tivoli doesn't try to be Disney. It's wonderfully and happily Danish. (Many locals appreciate the lovingly tended gardens.) I find it worth the admission just to see Danes—young and old—at play.

As you stroll the grounds, imagine the place in the mid-1800s, when it was new. Built on the site of the old town fortifications (today's lake was part of the old moat), Tivoli was an attempt to introduce provincial Danes to the world (for example, with the Asian Pavilion) and to bring people of all classes together.

Cost: 99 kr, free for kids under 8. To go on rides, you must buy ride tickets (from booth or machine, 25 kr/ticket, color-coded rides cost 1, 2, or 3 tickets apiece); or you can buy a multi-ride pass for 199 kr. If you'll be using at least eight tickets, buy the ride pass instead. To leave and come back later, you'll have

to buy a 25-kr re-entry ticket before you exit. Tel. 33 15 10 01, www.tivoli.dk.

Hours: Mid-April-late Sept daily 11:00-23:00, Fri-Sat until 24:00. In winter, Tivoli opens daily 11:00-22:00 for a week in mid-Oct for Halloween, then again from mid-Nov to New Year's Day for a Christmas market with *gløgg* (hot spiced wine) and ice-skating on Tivoli Lake. Dress warm for chilly evenings any time of year. There are lockers by each entrance.

Getting There: Tivoli is across Bernstoffsgade from the train station. If you're catching an overnight train, this is *the* place to spend your last Copenhagen hours.

Entertainment at Tivoli: Upon arrival (through main entrance, on left in the service center), pick up a map and look for the events schedule. Take a moment to sit down and plan your entertainment for the evening. Events are generally spread between 15:00 and 23:00; the 19:30 concert in the concert hall can be as little as 50 kr or as much as 1,200 kr, depending on the performer (box office tel. 33 15 10 12). If the Tivoli Symphony is playing, it's worth paying for. The ticket box office is outside, just to the left of the main entrance (daily 10:00-20:00; if you buy a concert ticket you get into Tivoli for free).

Free concerts, pantomime theater, ballet, acrobats, puppets, and other shows pop up all over the park, and a well-organized

visitor can enjoy an exciting evening of entertainment without spending a single krone beyond the entry fee. Friday evenings feature a (usually free) rock or pop show at 22:00. People gather around the lake 45 minutes before closing time for the "Tivoli Illuminations." Fireworks blast a few nights each summer. The park is particularly romantic at dusk, when the lights go on.

Eating at Tivoli: Inside the park, expect to pay amusement-park prices for amusement-park-quality food. Still, a meal here is part of the fun. **Søcafeen** serves only traditional open-face sandwiches in a fun beer garden with lakeside ambience.

They allow picnics if you buy a drink (and will rent you plates and silverware for 10 kr/person). The *pølse* (sausage) stands are cheap, and a bagel sandwich place is in the amusements corner. **Færgekroen** offers a quiet, classy lakeside escape from the amusement-park intensity, with traditional dishes washed down by its own microbrew (200-300-kr hearty pub grub). They host live piano on Friday, as well as Saturday evenings from 20:00, often resulting in an impromptu sing-along with a bunch of very happy Danes. **Wagamama,** a modern pan-Asian slurpathon from the UK, serves healthy noodle dishes (at the far back side of the park, also possible to enter from outside, 100-175-kr meals). **Nimb Terrasse** offers a simple selection of seasonal meat and fish dishes in a garden setting (200-300-kr dishes). **Café Georg,** to the left of the concert hall, has tasty 85-kr sandwiches and a lake view (also 100-kr salads and omelets). The kid-pleasing **Piratiriet** lets you dine on a pirate ship (150-180-kr main dishes).

For something more upscale, consider the complex of Nimb restaurants, in the big Taj Mahal-like pavilion near the entrance facing the train station. For dinner, **Nimb Bar'n' Grill** is a definite splurge, with sophisticated 95-500-kr starters (such as veal tartare and caviar) and 220-600-kr meat dishes. **Nimb Brasserie,** sharing the same lobby, serves French classics (230-300-kr main dishes).

If it's chilly, you'll find plenty of **Mamma Mokka** coffee take-away stands. If you get a drink "to go," you'll pay an extra 5-kr deposit for the cup, which you can recoup by returning it to a machine (marked on maps).

▲City Hall (Rådhus)

This city landmark, between the train station/Tivoli and the Strøget, is free and open to the public (including a public WC). You can wander throughout the building and into the peaceful garden out back. It also offers private tours and trips up its 345-foot-tall tower.

Cost and Hours: Free to enter building, Mon-Fri 8:30-16:00; you can usually slip in Sat 10:00-13:00 when weddings are going on, or join the Sat tour; closed Sun. Guided English-language tours—30 kr, 45 minutes, gets you into more private, official rooms; Mon-Fri at 13:00, Sat at 10:00. Tower by escort only—20 kr, 300 steps for the best aerial view of Copenhagen, Mon-Fri at 11:00 and 14:00, Sat at 12:00, closed Sun. Tel. 33 66 33 66.

Visiting City Hall: It's draped, inside and out, in Danish symbolism. The city's founder, Bishop Absalon, stands over the door. Absalon (c.

1128-1201)—bishop, soldier, and foreign-policy wonk—was King Valdemar I's right-hand man. In Copenhagen, he drove out pirates and built a fort to guard the harbor, turning a miserable fishing village into a humming Baltic seaport. The polar bears climbing on the rooftop symbolize the giant Danish protectorate of Greenland. Six night watchmen flank the city's gold-and-green seal under the Danish flag.

Step inside. The info desk (on the left as you enter) has racks of tourist information (city maps and other brochures). The building and its huge tower were inspired by the city hall in Siena, Italy (with the necessary bad-weather addition of a glass roof). Enormous functions fill this grand hall (the iron grate in the center of the floor is an elevator for bringing up 1,200 chairs), while the marble busts of four illustrious local boys—fairy-tale writer Hans Christian Andersen, sculptor Bertel Thorvaldsen, physicist Niels Bohr, and the building's architect, Martin Nyrop—look on. Underneath the floor are national archives dating back to 1275, popular with Danes researching their family roots.

As you leave, pop into the amazing clock opposite the info desk. Jens Olsen's World Clock, built in 1943-1955, was the mother of all astronomical clocks in precision and function. And it came with something new: tracking the exact time across the world's time zones. One of its gears does a complete rotation only every 25,753 years.

▲Ny Carlsberg Glyptotek

Scandinavia's top art gallery is an impressive example of what beer money can do. Brewer Carl Jacobsen (son of J. C. Jacobsen, who

funded the Museum of National History at Frederiksborg Castle) was an avid collector and patron of the arts. (Carl also donated *The Little Mermaid* statue to the city.) His namesake museum has intoxicating artifacts from the ancient world, along with some fine art from our own times. The next time you sip a Carlsberg beer, drink a toast to Carl Jacobsen and his marvelous collection. *Skål!*

Cost and Hours: 75 kr, free on Sun; open Tue-Sun 11:00-17:00, closed Mon; behind Tivoli at Dantes Plads 7, tel. 33 41 81 41, www.glyptoteket.com. It has a classy cafeteria under palms, as well as a rooftop terrace with snacks, drinks, and city views.

Visiting the Museum: Pick up a floor plan as you enter to help navigate the confusing layout. For a chronological swing, start with Egypt (mummy coffins and sarcophagi, a 5,000-year-old hippo statue), Greece (red-and-black painted vases, statues), the

Etruscan world (Greek-looking vases), and Rome (grittily realistic statues and portrait busts).

The sober realism of 19th-century Danish Golden Age painting reflects the introspection of a once-powerful nation reduced to second-class status—and ultimately embracing what made it unique. The "French Wing" (just inside the front door) has Rodin statues. A heady, if small, exhibit of 19th-century French paintings (in a modern building within the back courtyard) shows how Realism morphed into Impressionism and Post-Impressionism, and includes a couple of canvases apiece by Géricault, Delacroix, Monet, Manet, Millet, Courbet, Degas, Pissarro, Cézanne, Van Gogh, Picasso, Renoir, and Toulouse-Lautrec. Look for art by Gauguin—from before Tahiti (when he lived in Copenhagen with his Danish wife and their five children) and after Tahiti. There's also a fine collection of modern (post-Thorvaldsen) Danish sculpture.

Linger with marble gods under the palm leaves and glass dome of the very soothing winter garden. Designers, figuring Danes would be more interested in a lush garden than in classical art, used this wonderful space as leafy bait to cleverly introduce locals to a few Greek and Roman statues. (It works for tourists, too.) One of the original *Thinker* sculptures by Rodin (wondering how to scale the Tivoli fence?) is in the museum's backyard.

▲▲▲National Museum

Focus on this museum's excellent and curiously enjoyable Danish collection, which traces this civilization from its ancient beginnings. Its prehistoric collection is the best of its kind in Scandinavia. Exhibits are laid out chronologically and are eloquently described in English.

Cost and Hours: Free, Tue-Sun 10:00-17:00, closed Mon, mandatory lockers, enter at Ny Vestergade 10, tel. 33 13 44 11, www.natmus.dk. The café overlooking the entry hall serves coffee, pastries, and lunch (90-145 kr).

Visiting the Museum: Pick up the museum map as you enter, and head for the Danish history exhibit. It fills three floors, from the bottom up: prehistory, the Middle Ages and Renaissance, and modern times (1660-2000).

Danish Prehistory: Start before history did, in the Danish Prehistory exhibit (on the right side of the main entrance hall). Follow the room numbers in order, working counterclockwise around the courtyard and through the millennia.

In the Stone Age section, you'll see primitive tools and still-clothed skeletons of Scandinavia's reindeer hunters. The oak coffins were originally covered by burial mounds (called "barrows"). People put valuable items into the coffins with the dead, such as a folding chair (which, back then, was a real status symbol). In the

farming section, ogle the ceremonial axes and amber necklaces.

The Bronze Age brought the sword (several are on display). The "Chariot of the Sun"—a small statue of a horse pulling the sun across the sky—likely had religious significance for early Scandinavians (whose descendants continue to celebrate the solstice with fervor). In the

same room are those iconic horned helmets. Contrary to popular belief (and countless tourist shops), these helmets were not worn by the Vikings, but by their predecessors—for ceremonial purposes, centuries earlier. In the next room are huge cases filled with still-playable *lur* horns (see page 50). Another room shows off a bitchin' collection of well-translated rune stones proclaiming heroic deeds.

This leads to the Iron Age and an object that's neither Iron nor Danish: the 2,000-year-old Gundestrup Cauldron of art-textbook

fame. This 20-pound, soup-kitchen-size bowl made of silver was found in a Danish bog, but its symbolism suggests it was originally from either Thrace (in northeast Greece) or Celtic Ireland. On the sides, hunters slay bulls, and gods cavort with stags, horses, dogs, and dragons. It's both mysterious and fascinating.

Prehistoric Danes were fascinated by bogs. To make iron, you need ore—and Denmark's many bogs provided that critical material in abundance, leading people to believe that the gods dwelled there. These Danes appeased the gods by sacrificing valuable items (and even people) into bogs. Fortunately for modern archaeologists, bogs happen to be an ideal environment for preserving fragile objects. One bog alone—the Nydam bog—has yielded thousands of items, including three whole ships.

COPENHAGEN

No longer bogged down in prehistory, the people of Scandinavia came into contact with Roman civilization. At about this time, the Viking culture rose; you'll see the remains of an old warship. The Vikings, so feared in most of Europe, are still thought of fondly here in their homeland. You'll notice the descriptions straining to defend them: Sure, they'd pillage, rape, and plunder. But they also founded thriving, wealthy, and cultured trade towns. Love the Vikings or hate them, it's impossible to deny their massive reach—Norse Vikings even carved runes into the walls of the Hagia Sophia church (in today's Istanbul).

Middle Ages and Renaissance: Next, go upstairs and follow signs to Room 101 to start this section. You'll walk through the

Middle Ages, where you'll find lots of bits and pieces of old churches, such as golden altars and *aquamaniles*, pitchers used for ritual handwashing. The Dagmar Cross is the prototype for a popular form of crucifix worn by many Danes (Room 102, small glass display case—with colorful enamel paintings). Another cross in this case (the Roskilde Cross, studded with gemstones) was found inside the wooden head of Christ displayed high on the opposite wall. There are also exhibits on tools and trade, weapons, drinking horns, and fine, wood-carved winged altarpieces. Carry on to find

a fascinating room on the Norse settlers of Greenland, material on the Reformation, and an exhibit on everyday town life in the 16th and 17th centuries.

Modern Times: The next floor takes you through the last few centuries, with historic toys and a slice-of-Danish-life (1660-2000)

gallery where you'll see everything from rifles and old bras to early jukeboxes. You'll learn that the Danish Golden Age (which dominates most art museums in Denmark) captured the everyday pastoral beauty of the countryside, celebrated Denmark's smallness and peace-loving nature, and mixed in some Nordic mythology. With industrialization came the

labor movement and trade unions. After delving into the World Wars, Baby Boomers, creation of the postwar welfare state, and the

"Depressed Decade" of the 1980s (when Denmark suffered high unemployment), the collection is capped off by a stall that, until recently, was used for selling marijuana in the squatters' community of Christiania.

The Rest of the Museum: If you're eager for more, there's plenty left to see. The National Museum also has exhibits on the history of this building (the Prince's Palace), a large ethnology collection, antiquities, coins and medallions, temporary exhibits, and a good children's museum. The floor plan will lead you to what you want to see.

▲National Museum's Victorian Apartment

The National Museum inherited an incredible Victorian apartment just around the corner. The wealthy Christensen family managed to keep its plush living quarters a 19th-century time capsule until the granddaughters passed away in 1963. Since then, it's been part of the National Museum, with all but two of its rooms looking just as they did around 1890.

Cost and Hours: 50 kr, required one-hour tours leave from the National Museum reception desk (in Danish Sat-Sun at 11:00, 12:00, and 13:00 year-round; in English, June-Sept Sat only at 14:00).

▲Museum of Copenhagen (Københavns Museum)

This fine old house is filled with an entertaining and creative exhibit telling the story of Copenhagen. The ground floor covers the city's origins, the upper floor is dedicated to the 19th century, and the top floor includes a fun year-by-year walk through Copenhagen's 20th century, with lots of fun insights into contemporary culture.

Cost and Hours: 40 kr, daily 10:00-17:00, about 6 blocks past the train station at Vesterbrogade 59, tel. 33 21 07 72, www. copenhagen.dk.

ON SLOTSHOLMEN ISLAND

This island, where Copenhagen began in the 12th century, is a short walk from the train station and Tivoli, just across the bridge from the National Museum. It's dominated by Christiansborg Palace and several other royal and governmental buildings. Note that my "Copenhagen City Walk" (earlier) cuts right through Slotsholmen and covers other landmarks on the island (see page 60).

▲▲Christiansborg Palace

A complex of government buildings stands on the ruins of Copenhagen's original 12th-century fortress: the Parliament, Supreme Court, prime minister's office, royal reception rooms, royal library, several museums, and royal stables. Although the current palace dates only from 1928 and the royal family moved out 200 years ago, this building—the sixth to stand here in 800 years—is rich with tradition.

Three palace sights (the reception rooms, old castle ruins, and stables) are open to the public, giving us commoners a glimpse of the royal life.

Cost and Hours: Reception rooms-80 kr, castle ruins-40 kr, stables-40 kr, combo-ticket for all three-110 kr. All three sights are open daily (except in Oct-April, when they're closed on Mon) but have different hours: reception rooms 9:00-17:00 (may close at any time for royal events), ruins 10:00-17:00, stables and carriage museum 13:30-16:00 except July, when they're open 10:00-17:00. Tel. 33 92 64 92, www.christiansborg.dk.

Visiting the Palace: From the equestrian statue in front, go through the wooden door; the entrance to the ruins is in the corridor on the right, and the door to the reception rooms is out in the next courtyard, also on the right.

Royal Reception Rooms: While these don't rank among Europe's best palace rooms, they're worth a look. This is still the place where Queen Margrethe II impresses visiting dignitaries. The information-packed, hour-long English tours of the rooms are excellent (included in ticket, daily at 15:00). At other times, you'll wander the rooms on your own in a one-way route, reading the sparse English descriptions. As you slip-slide on protect-the-floor slippers through 22 rooms, you'll gain a good feel for Danish history, royalty, and politics. Here are a few highlights:

After the Queen's Library you'll soon enter the grand Great Hall, lined with boldly colorful (almost gaudy) tapestries. The palace highlight is this dazzling set of modern tapestries—Danish-designed but Gobelin-made in Paris. This gift, given to the queen on her 60th birthday in 2000, celebrates 1,000 years of Danish history, from the Viking age to our chaotic times...and into the future. Borrow the laminated descriptions for blow-by-blow explanations of the whole epic saga. The Velvet Room is where royals privately greet VIP guests before big functions.

In the corner room on the left, don't miss the family portrait of King Christian IX, which illustrates why he's called the "father-in-law of Europe"—his children eventually became, or married into, royalty in Denmark, Russia, Greece, Britain, France, Germany, and Norway.

In the Throne Room you'll see the balcony where new monarchs are proclaimed (most recently in 1972). And at the end, in the Hall of Giants (where you take off your booties among heroic figures supporting the building), you'll see a striking painting of Queen Margrethe II from 2010 on her 70th birthday. The three playful lions, made of Norwegian silver, once guarded the throne and symbolize absolute power—long gone since 1849, when Denmark embraced the notion of a constitutional monarch.

Castle Ruins: An exhibit in the scant remains of the first fortress built by Bishop Absalon, the 12th-century founder of Copenhagen, lies under the palace. A long passage connects to another set of ruins, from the 14th-century Copenhagen Castle. There's precious little to see, but it is, um, old and well-described. A video covers more recent palace history.

Royal Stables and Carriages Museum: This facility is still home to the horses that pull the queen's carriage on festive days, as well as a collection of historic carriages. While they're down from 250 horses to about a dozen, the royal stables are part of a strong tradition and, as the little video shows, will live on.

▲▲Thorvaldsen's Museum

This museum, which has some of the best swoon-worthy art you'll see anywhere, tells the story and shows the monumental work of the great Danish Neoclassical sculptor Bertel Thorvaldsen (see sidebar). Considered Canova's equal among Neoclassical sculptors, Thorvaldsen spent 40 years in Rome. He was lured home to Copenhagen with the promise to showcase his work in a fine museum, which opened in the revolutionary year of 1848 as Denmark's first public art gallery. Of the 500 or so sculptures Thorvaldsen completed in his life—including 90 major statues—this museum has most of them, in one form or another (the plaster model used to make the original or a copy done in marble or bronze).

Cost and Hours: 40 kr, free on Wed, Tue-Sun 10:00-17:00, closed Mon, includes excellent English audioguide on request, located in Neoclassical building with colorful walls next to Christiansborg Palace, tel. 33 32 15 32, www.thorvaldsensmuseum.dk.

Visiting the Museum: The ground floor showcases his statues. After buying your ticket, go straight in and ask to borrow a free audioguide at the desk. This provides a wonderful statue-by-statue narration of the museum's key works.

Just before the audioguide desk, turn left into the Great Hall, which was the original entryway of the museum. It's filled with

Bertel Thorvaldsen (1770-1844)

Bertel Thorvaldsen was born, raised, educated, and buried in Copenhagen, but his most productive years were spent in Rome. There he soaked up the prevailing style of the time: Neoclassical. He studied ancient Greek and Roman statues, copying their balance, grace, and impassive beauty. The simple-but-noble style suited the patriotism of the era, and Thorvaldsen got rich off it. Public squares throughout Europe are dotted with his works, celebrating local rulers, patriots, and historical figures looking like Greek heroes or Roman conquerors.

In 1819, at the height of his fame and power, Thorvaldsen returned to Copenhagen. He was asked to decorate the most important parts of the recently bombed, newly rebuilt Cathedral of Our Lady: the main altar and nave. His *Risen Christ* on the altar (along with the 12 apostles lining the nave) became his most famous and reproduced work—without even realizing it, most people imagine the caring features of Thorvaldsen's Christ when picturing what Jesus looked like.

The prolific Thorvaldsen depicted a range of subjects. His grand statues of historical figures (Copernicus in Warsaw, Maximilian I in Munich) were intended for public squares. Portrait busts of his contemporaries were usually done in the style of Roman emperors. Thorvaldsen carved the Lion Monument, depicting a weeping lion, into a cliff in Luzern, Switzerland. He did religious statues, like the *Risen Christ*. Thorvaldsen's most accessible works are from Greek mythology—*The Three Graces*, naked *Jason with the Golden Fleece*, or Ganymede crouching down to feed the eagle Jupiter.

Though many of his statues are of gleaming white marble, Thorvaldsen was not a chiseler of stone. Like Rodin and Canova, Thorvaldsen left the grunt work to others. He fashioned a life-sized model in plaster, which could then be reproduced in marble or bronze by his assistants. Multiple copies were often made, even in his lifetime.

Thorvaldsen epitomized the Neoclassical style. His statues assume perfectly balanced poses—maybe even a bit stiff, say critics. They don't flail their arms dramatically or emote passionately. As you look into their faces, they seem lost in thought, as though contemplating deep spiritual truths.

In Copenhagen, catch Thorvaldsen's *Risen Christ* at the Cathedral of Our Lady, his portrait bust at City Hall, and the full range of his long career at the Thorvaldsen's Museum.

replicas of some of Thorvaldsen's biggest and grandest statues—national heroes who still stand in the prominent squares of their major cities (Munich, Warsaw, the Vatican, and others). Two great equestrian statues stare each other down from across the hall; while they both take the classic, self-assured pose of looking one way while pointing another (think Babe Ruth calling his home run), one of them (Jozef Poniatowski) is modeled after the ancient Roman general Marcus Aurelius, while the other (Bavaria's Maximilian I) wears modern garb.

Then take a spin through the smaller rooms that ring the central courtyard. Each of these is dominated by one big work—mostly classical subjects drawn from mythology. At the far end of the building stand the plaster models for the iconic *Risen Christ* and the 12 Apostles (the final marble versions stand in the Cathedral of Our Lady—see page 55). Peek into the central courtyard to see the

planter-box tomb of Thorvaldsen himself (who died in 1844). Continue into the next row of rooms: In the far corner room look for Thorvaldsen's (very flattering) self-portrait, leaning buffly against a partially finished sculpture.

Downstairs you'll find a collection of plaster casts (mostly ancient Roman statues that inspired Thorvaldsen) and a video about his career.

Upstairs, get into the mind of the artist by perusing his personal possessions and the private collection of paintings from which he drew inspiration.

Royal Library

Copenhagen's "Black Diamond" (Den Sorte Diamant) library is a striking, supermodern building made of shiny black granite, leaning over the harbor at the edge of the palace complex. From the inviting lounge chairs, you can ponder this stretch of harborfront, which serves as a showcase for architects. Inside, wander through the old and new sections, catch the fine view from the "G" level, read a magazine, use the free computers (in the skyway lobby over the street nearest the harbor), and enjoy a classy—and pricey—lunch.

COPENHAGEN

Cost and Hours: Free, special exhibits generally 30 kr; different parts of the library have varying hours but reading room generally open July-Aug Mon-Fri 8:00-19:00, Sat 10:00-16:00, longer hours rest of the year, closed Sun year-round; tel. 33 47 47 47, www.kb.dk.

▲Danish Jewish Museum (Dansk Jødisk Museum)

This museum, which opened in 2004 in a striking building by American architect Daniel Libeskind, offers a very small but well-exhibited display of 400 years of the life and impact of Jews in Denmark.

Cost and Hours: 50 kr; June-Aug Tue-Sun 10:00-17:00; Sept-May Tue-Fri 13:00-16:00, Sat-Sun 12:00-17:00; closed Mon year-round; behind "Black Diamond" library at Proviantpassagen 6—enter from the courtyard behind the red-brick, ivy-covered building; tel. 33 11 22 18, www.jewmus.dk.

Visiting the Museum: Frankly, the architecture overshadows the humble exhibits. Libeskind—who created the equally conceptual Jewish Museum in Berlin, and whose design is the basis for the redevelopment of the World Trade Center site in New York City—has literally written Jewish culture into this building. The floor plan, a seemingly random squiggle, is actually in the shape of the Hebrew characters for *Mitzvah*, which loosely translated means "act of kindness."

Be sure to watch the two introductory films about the Jews' migration to Denmark, and about the architect Libeskind (12-minute loop total, English subtitles, plays continuously). As you tour the collection, the uneven floors and asymmetrical walls give you the feeling that what lies around the corner is completely unknown... much like the life and history of Danish Jews. Another interpretation might be that the uneven floors give you the sense of motion, like waves on the sea—a reminder that despite Nazi occupation in 1943, nearly 7,000 Danish Jews were ferried across the waves by fishermen to safety in neutral Sweden.

NEAR THE STRØGET
Round Tower

Built in 1642 by Christian IV, the tower connects a church, library, and observatory (the oldest functioning observatory in Europe) with a ramp that spirals up to a fine view of Copenhagen (though the view from atop Our Savior's Church is far better—see page 88).

Cost and Hours: 25 kr, nothing to see inside but the ramp and the view; tower—daily mid-May-mid-Sept 10:00-20:00, off-season until 18:00; observatory—summer Sun 13:00-16:00, mid-Oct-mid-March Tue-Wed 19:00-22:00; just off the Strøget on Købmagergade.

AMALIENBORG PALACE AND NEARBY

For more information on this palace and nearby attractions, including the famous *Little Mermaid* statue, see the end of my "Copenhagen City Walk" (page 65).

▲Amalienborg Museum (Amalienborgmuseet)

While Queen Margrethe II and her husband live quite privately in one of the four mansions that make up the palace complex, another mansion has been open to the public since 1994. It displays the private studies of four kings of the House of Glucksborg, who ruled from 1863-1972 (the immediate predecessors of today's queen). Your visit is short—six or eight rooms on one floor—but it affords an intimate and unique peek into Denmark's royal family. You'll see the private study of each of the last four kings of Denmark. They feel particularly lived-in—with cluttered pipe collections and bookcases jammed with family pictures—because they were. It's easy to imagine these blue-blooded folks just hanging out here, even today. The earliest study, Frederik VIII's (c. 1869), feels much older and more "royal"—with Renaissance gilded walls, heavy drapes, and a polar bear rug. With a little luck, the upstairs gala hall will be open during your visit.

Cost and Hours: 70 kr (90 kr on Sat), 130-kr combo-ticket also includes Rosenborg Palace; May-Oct daily 10:00-16:00; Nov-April Tue-Sun 11:00-16:00, closed Mon; with your back to the harbor, the entrance is at the far end of the square on the right; tel. 33 15 32 86, www.dkks.dk.

Amalienborg Palace Changing of the Guard

This noontime event is boring in the summer, when the queen is not in residence—the guards just change places. (This goes on for

quite a long time—no need to rush here at the stroke of noon, or to crowd in during the first few minutes; you'll have plenty of good photo ops.) If the queen's at home (indicated by a flag flying above her home), the changing of the guard is accompanied by a military band.

Museum of Danish Resistance (Frihedsmuseet)

This museum, which tells the story of Denmark's heroic Nazi-resistance struggle (1940-1945), is closed through 2018 for reconstruction.

ROSENBORG CASTLE AND NEARBY
▲▲▲Rosenborg Castle (Rosenborg Slot) and Treasury

This finely furnished Dutch Renaissance-style castle was built by King Christian IV in the early 1600s as a summer residence.

Rosenborg was his favorite residence and where he chose to die. Open to the public since 1838, it houses the Danish crown jewels and 500 years of royal knickknacks. While the old palace interior is a bit dark and not as immediately impressive as many of Europe's later Baroque masterpieces, it has a certain lived-in charm. It oozes the personality of the fascinating Christian IV and has one of the finest treasury collections in Europe. For more on Christian, read the sidebar on page 81.

Cost and Hours: 90 kr, 130-kr ticket also includes Amalienborg Museum; June-Aug daily 10:00-17:00; May and Sept-Oct daily 10:00-16:00; Nov-Dec Tue-Sun 11:00-14:00 (treasury until 16:00), closed Mon; Jan-April Tue-Sun 11:00-16:00, closed Mon; mandatory lockers take 20-kr coin, which will be returned; Metro or S-tog: Nørreport, then 5-minute walk on Østervoldgade and through park; tel. 33 15 32 86, www.dkks.dk.

Tours: Richard Karpen leads fascinating one-hour tours in princely garb (90 kr plus entry fee, mid-May-mid-Sept Mon and Thu at 12:00, meet outside castle ticket office; see listing on page 46, under "Tours in Copenhagen"). Or take the following self-guided tour that I've woven together from the highlights of Richard's walk. You can also use your mobile device to take advantage of the palace's free Wi-Fi signal, which is intended to let you follow the "Konge Connect" step-by-step tour through the palace highlights (with audio/video/text explanations for your smartphone or tablet—bring earphones; instructional brochure at the ticket desk).

❷ Self-Guided Tour: Buy your ticket, then head back out and look for the *castle* sign. You'll tour the ground floor room by room, then climb to the third floor for the big throne room. After a quick sweep of the middle floor, finish in the basement (enter from outside) for the jewels.

• *Begin the tour on the palace's ground floor (turn right as you enter), in the Winter Room.*

King Christian IV:
A Lover and a Fighter

King Christian IV (1577-1648) inherited Denmark at the peak of its power, lived his life with the exuberance of the age, and

went to his grave with the country in decline. His legacy is obvious to every tourist—Rosenborg Castle, Frederiksborg Palace, the Round Tower, Christianshavn, and on and on. Look for his logo adorning many buildings: the letter "C" with a "4" inside it and a crown on top. Thanks to both his place in history and his passionate personality, Danes today regard Christian IV as one of their greatest monarchs.

During his 50-year reign, Christian IV reformed the government, rebuilt the army, established a trading post in India, and tried to expand Denmark's territory. He took Kalmar from Sweden and captured strategic points in northern Germany. The king was a large man who also lived large. A skilled horseman and avid hunter, he could drink his companions under the table. He spoke several languages and gained a reputation as outgoing and humorous. His lavish banquets were legendary, and his romantic affairs were numerous.

But Christian's appetite for war proved destructive. In 1626, Denmark again attacked northern Germany, but was beaten back. In late 1643, Sweden launched a sneak attack, and despite Christian's personal bravery (he lost an eye), the war went badly. By the end of his life, Christian was tired and bitter, and Denmark was drained.

The heroics of Christian and his sailors live on in the Danish national anthem, "King Christian Stood by the Lofty Mast."

COPENHAGEN

Ground Floor: Here in the wood-paneled **Winter Room,** all eyes were on King Christian IV. Today, your eyes should be on him, too. Take a close look at his bust by the fireplace (if it's not here, look for it out in the corridor by the ticket taker). Check this guy out—fashionable braid, hard drinker, hard lover, energetic statesman, and warrior king. Christian IV was dynamism in the flesh, wearing a toga: a true Renaissance guy. During his reign, Copenhagen doubled in size. You're surrounded by Dutch paintings (the Dutch had a huge influence on 17th-century Denmark). Note the smaller statue of the 19-year-old king, showing him jousting jauntily on his coronation day. In another case, the golden astronomical clock—with musical works and moving figures—did everything you can imagine. Flanking the fireplace (opposite where you entered), beneath the windows, look for the panels in the tile floor that could be removed to let the music performed by the band in the basement waft in. (Who wants the actual musicians in the dining room?) The audio holes were also used to call servants.

The **study** (or "writing closet," nearest where you entered) was small (and easy to heat). Kings did a lot of corresponding. We know

a lot about Christian because 3,000 of his handwritten letters survive. The painting on the right wall shows Christian at age eight. Three years later, his father died, and little Christian technically ascended the throne, though Denmark was actually ruled by a regency until Christian was 19. A portrait of his mother hangs above the boy, and opposite is a portrait of Christian in his prime—having just conquered Sweden—standing alongside the incredible coronation crown you'll see later.

Going back through the Winter Room, head for the door to Christian's **bedroom.** Before entering, notice the little peephole

in the door (used by the king to spy on those in this room—well-camouflaged by the painting, and more easily seen from the other side), and the big cabinet doors for Christian's clothes and accessories, flanking the bedroom door (notice the hinges and keyholes). Heading into the bedroom, you'll see paintings showing the king as an old man...and as a dead man. (Christian died in this room.) In the case are the clothes he wore at his finest hour. During a naval battle against Sweden (1644), Christian stood directing the action when an explosion ripped across the deck, sending him sprawling and riddling him with shrapnel. Unfazed, the 67-year-old monarch bounced right back up and kept going, inspiring his men to carry on the fight. Christian's stubborn determination during this battle is commemorated in Denmark's national anthem. Shrapnel put out Christian's eye. No problem: The warrior king with a knack for heroic publicity stunts had the shrapnel bits removed from his eye and forehead and made into earrings as a gift for his mistress. The earrings hang in the case with his blood-stained clothes (easy to miss, right side). Christian lived to be 70 and fathered 25 children (with two wives and three mistresses). Before moving on, you can peek into Christian's private bathroom—elegantly tiled with Delft porcelain.

Proceed into the **Dark Room.** Here you'll see wax casts of royal figures. This was the way famous and important people were portrayed back then. The chair is a forerunner of the whoopee cushion. When you sat on it, metal cuffs pinned your arms down, allowing the prankster to pour water down the back of the chair (see hole)—making you "wet your pants." When you stood up, the chair made embarrassing tooting sounds.

The **Marble Room** has a particularly impressive inlaid marble floor. Imagine the king meeting emissaries here in the center, with the emblems of Norway (right), Denmark (center), and Sweden (left) behind him.

The end room, called the **King's Chamber,** was used by Christian's first mistress. Notice the ceiling painting, with an orchestra looking down on you as they play.

The long **stone passage** leading to the staircase exhibits an intriguing painting (by the door to the King's Chamber) show-

ing the crowds at the coronation of Christian's son, Frederik III. After Christian's death, a weakened Denmark was invaded, occupied, and humiliated by Sweden (Treaty of Roskilde, 1658). Copenhagen alone held out through the long winter of 1658-1659 (the Siege of Copenhagen), and Sweden eventually had to withdraw from the country. During the siege, Frederik III distinguished himself with his bravery. He seized upon the resulting surge of popularity as his chance to be anointed an absolute, divinely ordained monarch (1660). This painting marks that event— study it closely for slice-of-life details. Next, near the ticket taker, a sprawling family tree makes it perfectly clear that Christian IV comes from good stock. Notice the tree is labeled in German—the second language of the realm.

• *The queen had a hand-pulled elevator, but you'll need to hike up two flights of stairs to the throne room.*

Throne Room (Third Floor): The **Long Hall**—considered one of the best-preserved Baroque rooms in Europe—was great

for banquets. The decor trumpets the accomplishments of Denmark's great kings. The four corners of the ceiling feature the four continents known at the time. (America—at the far-right end of the hall as you enter— was still considered

pretty untamed; notice the decapitated head with the arrow sticking out of it.) In the center, of course, is the proud seal of the Danish Royal Family. The tapestries, designed for this room, are from the late 1600s. Effective propaganda, they show the Danes defeating their Swedish rivals on land and at sea. The king's throne—still more propaganda for two centuries of "absolute" monarchs—was made of "unicorn horn" (actually narwhal tusk from Greenland). Believed to bring protection from evil and poison, the horn was the most precious material in its day. The queen's throne is of hammered silver. The 150-pound lions are 300 years old.

The small room to the left holds a delightful **royal porcelain** display with Chinese, French, German, and Danish examples of the "white gold." For five centuries, Europeans couldn't figure out how the Chinese made this stuff. The difficulty in just getting it back to Europe in one piece made it precious. The Danish pieces, called "Flora Danica" (on the left as you enter), are from a huge royal set showing off the herbs and vegetables of the realm.

• *Heading back down, pause at the middle floor, which is worth a look.*

Middle Floor: Circling counterclockwise, you'll see more fine clocks, fancy furniture, and royal portraits. The queen enjoyed her royal lathe (with candleholders for lighting and pedals to spin it hidden away below; in the Christian VI Room). The small mirror room (up the stairs from the main hall) was where the king played Hugh Hefner—using mirrors on the floor to see what was under those hoop skirts. In hidden cupboards, he had a fold-out bed and a handy escape staircase.

• *Back outside, turn right and find the stairs leading down to the...*

Royal Danish Treasury (Castle Basement): The palace was a royal residence for a century and has been the royal vault right up until today. As you enter, first head to the right, into the **wine cellar,** with thousand-liter barrels and some fine treasury items. The first room has a vast army of tiny golden soldiers, and a wall lined with fancy rifles. Heading into the next room, you'll see fine items of amber (petrified tree resin, 30-50 million years old) and ivory. Study the large box made of amber (in a freestanding case, just to the right as you enter)—the tiny figures show a healthy interest in sex.

Now head back past the ticket taker and into the main part of the treasury, where you can browse through exquisite royal knickknacks.

The diamond- and pearl-studded **saddles** were Christian IV's—the first for his coronation, the second for his son's wedding. When his kingdom was nearly bankrupt, Christian had these constructed lavishly—complete with solid-gold spurs—to impress visiting dignitaries and bolster Denmark's credit rating.

The next case displays **tankards.** Danes were always big drinkers, and to drink in the top style, a king had narwhal steins (#4030). Note the fancy Greenland Inuit (Eskimo) on the lid (#4023). The case is filled with exquisitely carved ivory. On the other side of that case, what's with the mooning snuffbox (#4063)? Also, check out the amorous whistle (#4064).

Drop by the case on the wall in the back-left of the room: The 17th century was the age of **brooches.** Many of these are made of freshwater pearls. Find the fancy combination toothpick and ear spoon (#4140). Look for #4146: A queen was caught having an affair after 22 years of royal marriage. Her king gave her a special present: a golden ring—showing the hand of his promiscuous queen shaking hands with a penis.

Step downstairs, away from all this silliness. Passing through the serious vault door, you come face-to-face with a big, jeweled **sword.** The tall, two-handed, 16th-century coronation sword was drawn by the new king, who cut crosses in the air in four directions, symbolically promising to defend the realm from all attacks. The cases surrounding the sword contain everyday items used by the king (all solid gold, of course). What looks like a trophy case of gold records is actually a collection of dinner plates with amber centers (#5032).

Go down the steps. In the center case is Christian IV's **coronation crown** (from 1596, seven pounds of gold and precious stones, #5124), which some consider to be the finest Renaissance crown in Europe. Its six tallest gables radiate symbolism. Find the symbols of justice (sword and scales), fortitude (a woman on a lion with a sword), and charity (a nursing woman— meaning the king will love God and his people as a mother loves her child). The pelican,  which according to medieval legend pecks its own flesh to feed its young, symbolizes God sacrificing his son, just as the king would make great sacrifices for his people. Climb the footstool to look inside—it's as exquisite as the outside. The shields of various Danish provinces remind the king that he's surrounded by his realms.

Circling the cases along the wall (right to left), notice the fine enameled lady's goblet with traits of a good woman spelled out in Latin (#5128) and above that, an exquisite prayer book (with handwritten favorite prayers, #5134). In the fifth window, the big solid-gold baptismal basin (#5262) hangs above tiny oval silver boxes that contained the royal children's umbilical cords (handy for protection later in life, #5272); two cases over are royal writing sets with wax, seals, pens, and ink (#5320).

Go down a few more steps into the lowest level of the treasury and last room. The two **crowns** in the center cases are more modern (from 1670), lighter, and more practical—just gold and diamonds without all the symbolism. The king's crown is only four pounds, the queen's a mere two.

The cases along the walls show off the **crown jewels.** These were made in 1840 of diamonds, emeralds, rubies, and pearls from earlier royal jewelry. The saber (#5540) shows emblems of the realm's 19 provinces. The sumptuous pendant features a 19-carat diamond cut (like its neighbors) in the 58-facet "brilliant" style for maximum reflection (far-left case, #5560). Imagine these on the dance floor. The painting shows the anointing of King Christian V at the Frederiksborg Castle Chapel in 1671. The crown jewels are still worn by the queen on special occasions several times a year.

▲Rosenborg Gardens

Rosenborg Castle is surrounded by the royal pleasure gardens and, on sunny days, a minefield of sunbathing Danish beauties and picnickers. While "ethnic Danes" grab the shade, the rest of the Danes worship the sun. When the royal family is in residence, there's a daily changing-of-the-guard mini-parade from the Royal Guard's barracks adjoining Rosenborg Castle (at 11:30) to Amalienborg Palace (at 12:00). The Queen's Rose Garden (across the moat from the palace) is a royal place for a picnic. The fine statue of Hans Christian Andersen in the park—erected while he was still alive (and approved by him)—is meant to symbolize how his stories had a message even for adults.

▲National Gallery of Denmark (Statens Museum for Kunst)

This museum fills a stately building with Danish and European paintings from the 14th century through today. It's particularly worthwhile for the chance to be immersed in great art by the Danes, and to see its good collection of French Modernists, all well-described in English.

Cost and Hours: Permanent collection-free, special exhibits-110 kr, Tue-Sun 10:00-17:00, Wed until 20:00, closed Mon, Sølvgade 48, tel. 33 74 84 94, www.smk.dk.

Visiting the Museum: The ground floor holds special exhibits; the second floor has collections of Danish and Nordic artists from 1750 to 1900, and European art from 1300 to 1800; and the

Danish and International Art after 1900 is spread between the second and third floors.

Head first to the Danish and Nordic artists section, and pick up the excellent floor plan that suggests a twisting route through the collection. Take the time to read the descriptions in each room, which put the paintings into historical context. In addition to Romantic works by well-known, non-Danish artists (such as the Norwegian J. C. Dahl and the German Caspar David Friedrich), this is a chance to learn about some very

talented Danish painters not well known outside their native land. Make a point to meet the "Skagen Painters," including Anna Ancher, Michael Ancher, Peder Severin Krøyer, and others (find them in the section called "The Modern Breakthrough I-II"). This group, with echoes of the French Impressionists, gathered in the fishing village of Skagen on the northern tip of Denmark, surrounded by the sea and strong light, and painted heroic folk-fishermen themes in the late 1800s. Also worth seeking out are the canvases of Laurits Andersen Ring, who portrayed traditional peasant scenes with modern style; and Jens Ferdinand Willumsen, who pioneered "Vitalism" (celebrating man in nature). Other exhibits are cleverly organized by theme, such as gender or the body.

In the 20th-century section, the collection of early French Modernism is particularly impressive (with works by Matisse, Picasso, Braque, and more). This is complemented with works by Danish artists, who, inspired by the French avant-garde, introduced new, radical forms and colors to Scandinavian art.

CHRISTIANSHAVN

Across the harbor from the old town, Christianshavn—the former merchant's district—is one of the most delightful neighborhoods in town to explore. It offers pleasant canalside walks and trendy restaurants, along with two things to see: Our Savior's Church (with its fanciful tower) and Christiania, a colorful alternative-living community. Before visiting, make sure to read the background on Christianshavn, which helps explain what you'll see (see sidebar).

Your first look at the island will likely be its main square. Christianshavns Torv has a Metro stop, an early Copenhagen phone kiosk (from 1896), a fine bakery across the street (Lagkagehuset), and three statues celebrating Greenland. A Danish protectorate since 1721, Greenland, with 56,000 people, is represented by two members in the Danish Parliament. The square has long been a

Christianshavn: Then and Now

Christianshavn—Copenhagen's planned port—was vital to Danish power in the 17th and 18th centuries. Denmark had always been second to Sweden when it came to possession of natural resources, so the Danes tried to make up for it by acquiring resource-rich overseas colonies. They built Christianshavn (with Amsterdam's engineering help) to run the resulting trade business—giving this neighborhood a "little Amsterdam" vibe today.

Since Denmark's economy was so dependent on trade, the port town was the natural target of enemies. When the Danes didn't support Britain against Napoleon in 1807, the Brits bombarded Christianshavn. In this "blackest year in Danish history," Christianshavn burned down. That's why today there's hardly a building here that dates from before that time.

Christianshavn remained Copenhagen's commercial center until the 1920s, when a modern harbor was built. Suddenly, Christianshavn's economy collapsed and it became a slum. Cheap prices attracted artsy types, giving it a bohemian flavor. In 1971, squatters set up shop in an old military camp in Christianshavn and created their own community called Christiania, which still survives today (see page 89).

Over the past few decades, Christianshavn has had a resurgence, and these days, prices are driven up by wealthy locals (who pay about 60 percent of their income in taxes) spending too much for apartments, renting them cheaply to their kids, and writing off the loss. Demand for property is huge. Today the neighborhood is inhabited mostly by rich students and young professionals, living in some of the priciest real estate in town.

hangout for Greenlanders, who appreciate the cheap beer and long hours of the big supermarket fronting the square.

▲Our Savior's Church (Vor Frelsers Kirke)

Following a recent restoration, the church gleams inside and out. Its bright Baroque interior (1696) is shaped like a giant cube. The magnificent pipe organ is supported by elephants (a royal symbol of the prestigious Order of the Elephant). Looking up to the ceiling, notice elephants also sculpted into the stucco of the dome, and a little one hanging from the main chandelier. Best of all, you can climb the unique spiral spire (with an outdoor stair-

case winding up to its top—398 stairs in all) for great views of the city and of the Christiania commune below.

Cost and Hours: Church interior—free, open daily 11:00-15:30 but may close for special services; church tower—40 kr; July-mid-Sept Mon-Sat 10:00-19:00, Sun 10:30-19:00; April-June and mid-Sept-Nov daily until 16:00; closed Dec-March and in bad weather; bus #2A, #19, or Metro: Christianshavn, Sankt Annægade 29, tel. 41 66 63 57, www.vorfrelserskirke.dk.

⊙ Spin-Tour from the Top of Our Savior's Church: Climb up until you run out of stairs. As you wind back down, look for these landmarks:

The modern windmills are a reminder that Denmark generates 20 percent of its power from wind. Below the windmills is a great aerial view of the Christiania commune. Beyond the windmills, across Øresund (the strait that separates Denmark and Sweden), stands a shuttered Swedish nuclear power plant. The lone skyscraper in the distance—the first and tallest skyscraper in Scandinavia—is in Malmö, Sweden. The Øresund Bridge made Malmö an easy 35-minute bus or train ride from Copenhagen (it's become a bedroom community, with much cheaper apartments making the commute worthwhile).

Farther to the right, the big red-roof zone is Amager Island. Five hundred years as the city's dumping grounds earned Amager the nickname "Crap Island." Circling on, you come to the towering Radisson Blu Royal Hotel. The area beyond it is slated to become a forest of skyscrapers—the center of Europe's biomedical industry.

Downtown Copenhagen is decorated with several striking towers and spires. The tower capped by the golden ball is a ride in Tivoli Gardens. Next is City Hall's pointy brick tower. The biggest building, with the three-crown tower, is Christiansborg Palace. The Børsen (old stock exchange) is just beyond, with its unique dragon-tail tower. Behind that is Nyhavn. Just across from that and the Royal Danish Theatre's Playhouse is the dramatic Opera House (with the flat roof and big, grassy front yard).

▲▲▲Christiania

In 1971, the original 700 Christianians established squatters' rights in an abandoned military barracks just a 10-minute walk from

Christiania

To Holmen & Opera House

BRØBERGSGADE

MAIN ENTRANCE GATE

To Christianshavns Canal

OVERGADEN

PRINSESSE GADE

OTHER ENTRANCE

BÅDMANDSSTRÆDE

To Our Savior's Church

SANKT ANNÆ GADE

To Airport

REFSHALEVEJ

THE GRAY HALL

CHRISTIANIA

Peaceful walk to residential areas

"PUSHER STREET"

LANGGADEN

PATH

OTHER ENTRANCE

ULRIKS-BASTION RAMPARTS

Stadsgraven (former moat)

Rabbit Island

100 Meters
100 Yards

❶ Carl Madsens Plads
❷ Green Hall
❸ Nemoland
❹ Månefiskeren Café
❺ Morgenstedet Vegetarian Café
❻ Spiseloppen Restaurant
❼ Tour Departure Point

the Danish Parliament building. Two generations later, this "free city" still stands—an ultra-human mishmash of idealists, hippies, potheads, non-materialists, and happy children (600 adults, 200 kids, 200 cats, 200 dogs, 2 parrots, and 17 horses). There are even a handful of Willie Nelson-type seniors among the 180 remaining here from the original takeover. And an amazing thing has happened: The place has become the second-most-visited sight among tourists in Copenhagen, behind Tivoli Gardens. Move over, *Little Mermaid*.

"Pusher Street" (named for the sale of soft drugs here) is Christiania's main drag. Get beyond this touristy side of Christiania, and you'll find a fascinating, ramshackle world of moats and earthen ramparts, alternative housing, cozy tea houses, carpenter shops, hippie villas, children's playgrounds, peaceful lanes, and people who believe that "to be normal is to be in a straitjacket." A local slogan claims, *"Kun døde fisk flyder med strømmen"* ("Only dead fish swim with the current").

Hours and Tours: Christiania is open all the time but quiet (and some restaurants closed) on Mondays, which is its rest day (though "resting" from what, I'm not sure). Guided tours leave from the main entrance at 15:00 (just show up, 40 kr, 1.5 hours, daily late June-Aug, only Sat-Sun rest of year, in English and Danish, info tel. 32 95 65 07, www.rundvisergruppen.dk). You're welcome to snap photos, except on Pusher Street (but ask residents before you photograph them).

The Community: Christiania is broken into 14 administrative neighborhoods on a former military base. Most of the land, once owned by Denmark's Ministry of Defense, has been purchased by the Christiania community; the rest of it is leased from the state (see the sidebar for details). Locals build their homes but don't own them—individuals can't buy or sell property. When someone moves out, the community decides who will be invited in to replace that person. A third of the adult population works on the outside, a third works on the inside, and a third doesn't work much at all.

There are nine rules: no cars, no hard drugs, no guns, no explosives, and so on. The Christiania flag is red and yellow because when the original hippies took over, they found a lot of red and yellow paint onsite. The three yellow dots in the flag are from the three "i"s in Christiania (or, some claim, the "o"s in "Love, Love, Love").

The community pays the city about $1 million a year for utilities and has about $1 million a year more to run its local affairs. A few "luxury hippies" have oil heat, but most use wood or gas. The ground here was poisoned by its days as a military base, so nothing is grown in Christiania. There's little industry within the commune (Christiania Cykler, which builds fine bikes, is an exception—www.pedersen-bike.dk). A phone chain provides a system of communal security (they have had bad experiences calling the police). Each September 26, the day the first squatters took over the barracks in 1971, Christiania has a big birthday bash.

Tourists are entirely welcome here, because they've become a major part of the economy. Visitors react in very different ways to the place. Some see dogs, dirt, and dazed people. Others see a haven of peace, freedom, and no taboos. Locals will remind judgmental Americans (whose country incarcerates more than a quarter of the world's prison inmates) that a society must make the choice: Allow for alternative lifestyles...or build more prisons.

Visiting Christiania: The main entrance is down Prinsessegade, behind the Our Savior's Church spiral tower. Passing under the gate, take Pusher Street directly into the community. The first square—a kind of market square (souvenirs and marijuana-related stuff)—is named Carl Madsens Plads, honoring the lawyer who took the squatters' case to the Danish supreme court in 1976 and won. Beyond that is Nemoland (a food circus, on the right). A huge warehouse called the Green Hall (Den Gronne Hal) is a recycling center and hardware store (where people get most of their building materials) that does double duty at night as a concert

The Fight for Christiania

Ever since several hundred squatters took over an unused military camp in 1971, Christiania has been a political hot potato. No one in the Danish establishment wanted it. And no one had the nerve to mash it.

Part of Christiania's history has been ongoing government attempts to shut the place down. At first, city officials looked the other way because back then, no one cared about the land. But

skyrocketing Christianshavn land values brought pressure to open Christiania to market forces. By the 1980s, the neighborhood had become gentrified, and both the city and developers were eyeing the land Christiania's hippies were squatting on. And when Denmark's conservative government took over in 2001, they vowed to "normalize" Christiania (with pressure from the US), with police regularly conducting raids on pot sellers.

Things were looking grim for the Christianians until 2012, when the Danish government offered to sell most of the land to

hall and as a place where children work on crafts. If you go up the stairs between Nemoland and the Green Hall, you'll climb up to the ramparts that overlook the canal. As you wander, be careful to distinguish between real Christianians and Christiania's motley guests—drunks (mostly from other countries) who hang out here in the summer for the freedom. Part of the original charter guaranteed that the community would stay open to the public.

On the left beyond the Green Hall, a lane leads to the Månefiskeren café, and beyond that, to the Morgenstedet vegetarian restaurant (the best place for a simple, friendly meal; see "Eating in Christiania," later). Beyond these

recommended restaurants, you'll find yourself lost in the totally untouristy, truly local residential parts of Christiania, where kids play in the street and the old folks sit out on the front stoop—just like any other neighborhood. Just as St. Mark's Square isn't the "real Venice," the hippie-druggie scene on Pusher Street isn't the "real Christiania"—you can't say you've experienced Christiania until you've strolled these back streets.

A walk or bike ride through Christiania is a great way to see

the residents at below the market rate, and offered guaranteed loans. In exchange, the Christianians had to promise to upgrade and maintain water, sewage, and electrical services, and preserve rights of way and "rural" areas. Accepting the offer, Christianians formed a foundation—Freetown Christiania—to purchase and control the property. The parts of Christiania that were not sold are leased to the residents and are still owned by the state.

For many Christianians, it's an ironic, capitalistic twist that they now own property, albeit collectively. They even sell symbolic Christiania "shares" to help pay for the land. And, every adult over age 18 now owes a monthly rent that goes toward paying off the loans and to support services. But on the flip side, this is the greatest degree of security Christiania has ever experienced in its four-plus decades of existence. Even so, mistrust of the establishment is by no means dead, and there are still those who wonder what the government might be up to next.

how this community lives. When you leave, look up—the sign above the gate says, "You are entering the EU."

Smoking Marijuana: Pusher Street was once lined with stalls selling marijuana, joints, and hash. Residents intentionally destroyed the stalls in 2004 to reduce the risk of Christiania being disbanded by the government. (One stall was spared and is on display at the National Museum.) Walking along Pusher Street today, you may witness policemen or deals being made—but never at the same time. You may also notice wafts of marijuana smoke and whispered offers of "hash" during your visit. And, in fact, on my last visit there was a small stretch of Pusher Street dubbed the "Green Light District" where pot was being openly sold (signs acknowledged that this activity was still illegal, and announced three rules here: 1. Have fun; 2. No photos; and 3. No running—"because it makes people nervous"). However, purchasing and smoking may buy you more time in Denmark than you'd planned—possession of marijuana is illegal.

About hard drugs: For the first few years, junkies were tolerated. But that led to violence and polluted the mellow ambience residents envisioned. In 1979, the junkies were expelled—an epic confrontation in the community's folk history now—and since then the symbol of a fist breaking a syringe is as prevalent as the leafy marijuana icon. Hard drugs are emphatically forbidden in Christiania.

Eating in Christiania: The people of Christiania appreciate good food and count on tourism as a big part of their economy. Consequently, there are plenty of decent eateries. Most of the restaurants are closed on Monday (the community's weekly holiday). **Pusher Street** has a few grungy but tasty falafel stands, as well as a popular burger bar. **Nemoland** is the hangout zone—a fun collection of stands peddling Thai food, burgers, *shawarma,* and other fast hippie food with great, tented outdoor seating (30-110-kr meals). Its stay-a-while atmosphere comes with backgammon, foosball, bakery goods, and fine views from the ramparts. **Månefiskeren** ("Moonfisher Bar") looks like a modern-day Brueghel painting, with billiards, chess, snacks, and drinks (Tue-Sun 10:00-23:00, closed Mon). **Morgenstedet** ("Morning Place") is a good, cheap vegetarian café with a mellow, woody interior and a rustic patio outside (50-100-kr meals, Tue-Sun 12:00-21:00, closed Mon, left after Pusher Street). **Spiseloppen** is *the* classy, good-enough-for-Republicans restaurant in the community (closed Mon, described on page 113). While there are lots of public concerts at the open-air Nemoland stage, for a music club experience, consider **Musik Loppen** (which has live music almost nightly, under the Spiseloppen restaurant).

GREATER COPENHAGEN
Harbor Baths
Swimming in the middle of a large city is unthinkable in most of the world, yet the enterprising Danes have made it happen. On a warm summer day there's no better way to see Copenhageners at play than to visit the Harbor Baths, a former-industrial-area-turned-bathing-complex located at Islands Brygge, across the Inner Harbor from the main train station and Kødbyen (the Meatpacking District).

Cost and Hours: Free, open long hours June-Aug, tel. 30 89 04 69, http://kulturogfritid.kk.dk/havnebadet-islands-brygge.

Getting There: From Kødbyen, head east on Dybbølsbro, across the train tracks to the Fisketorvet Mall. Passing through the mall you'll come to Bryggebroen—a pedestrian/cyclists' bridge that spans the Inner Harbor. After crossing the bridge, follow the waterside promenade north to the baths. From the main train station, head east over Langebro bridge, then head south—you can't miss the baths. From Christianshavn, follow the ramparts west to where they meet the Inner Harbor. Pass under Langebro bridge, and you'll see the baths.

Visiting the Baths: Designed in 2003, the baths were an early project by Danish "starchitect" Bjarke Ingels, who now has buildings around the world featuring his unique signature. (One of his recent efforts is an artificial ski slope located near the airport and built around an incinerator smokestack; visit www.big.dk to see samples of his work.)

The Harbor Baths consist of a large barge moored to the shore, with five swimming pools (two suitable for kids) and a prow-shaped diving platform offering three- and five-meter leaps into the refreshing water. How refreshing? This is not Hawaii: Water temperatures peak at 65 degrees in August, which should be no problem for those with Viking blood. Though located in a former industrial area, the water has been cleaned up, and the quality is as good as what you'll find at the pristine beaches around Copenhagen. Plus, water quality is constantly monitored, and on the rare occasions it dips below acceptable levels, the baths are closed.

The shore is one big cobbled promenade backed by a grassy area that's great for sunbathing, barbecues, and people-watching. The area hums with life in summer, and even in the winter it's open to hardy members of a local polar bear club. Plans are under way for a sauna and thermal pools to encourage more off-season use.

Carlsberg Brewery
Denmark's beloved source of legal intoxicants is Carlsberg. About 1.5 miles west of Rådhuspladsen (City Hall Square), Carlsberg welcomes you to its visitors center for a self-guided tour and a couple of beers.

Cost and Hours: 80 kr, daily 10:00-17:00, last entry 30 minutes before closing; catch the local train to Enghave, or bus #18, #26, or #6A; enter at Gamle Carlsbergvej 11 around corner from brewery entrance, tel. 33 27 12 82, www.visitcarlsberg.dk.

Nearby: The manicured gardens of the sprawling Frederiksberg Park (Frederiksberg Have) and adjacent Southern Field (Søndermarken) make a lovely setting for a picnic.

Open-Air Folk Museum (Frilandsmuseet)
This park, located north of Copenhagen in the suburb of Lyngby, is part of the National Museum. It's filled with traditional Danish architecture and folk culture, farm animals, and gardens. Bring a picnic or dine at the on-site restaurant.

Cost and Hours: Free; May-mid-Oct Tue-Sun 10:00-16:00, July-mid-Aug until 17:00, closed Mon and off-season; S-tog: Sorgenfri and 10-minute walk to Kongevejen 100 in Lyngby (see map on page 123); tel. 41 20 64 55, http://natmus.dk.

Bakken

Danes gather at Copenhagen's *other* great amusement park, Bakken, situated in the Dyrehaven forest about a 10-minute drive north of the city.

Cost and Hours: Free entry, 250 kr for all-ride pass; late June-mid-Aug daily 12:00-24:00, shorter hours April-late June and mid-Aug-mid-Sept, closed mid-Sept-March; S-tog: Klampenborg, then walk 10 minutes through the woods (see map on page 123); tel. 39 63 73 00, www.bakken.dk.

Dragør

If you don't have time to get to the idyllic island of Ærø (see the Central Denmark chapter), consider the eight-mile trip south of Copenhagen to the fishing village of Dragør, near the airport (bus #350S from Nørreport). For information, see www.visit-dragoer.dk.

Shopping in Copenhagen

Shops are generally open Monday through Friday from 10:00 to 19:00 and Saturday from 9:00 to 16:00 (closed Sun). While big department stores dominate the scene, many locals favor the characteristic, small artisan shops and boutiques.

Uniquely Danish souvenirs to look for include intricate paper cuttings with idyllic motifs of swans, flowers, or Christmas themes; mobiles with everything from bicycles to Viking ships (look for the quality Flensted brand); and the colorful artwork of Danish artist Bo Bendixen (posters, postcards, T-shirts, and more). Jewelry lovers look for amber, known as the "gold of the North." Globs of this petrified sap wash up on the shores of all the Baltic countries.

If you buy anything substantial (minimum 300 kr, about $50) from a shop displaying the **Danish Tax-Free Shopping** emblem, you can get a refund of the Value-Added Tax, roughly 20 to 25 percent of the purchase price (VAT is "MOMS" in Danish). If you have your purchase mailed, the tax can be deducted from your bill. For details, see "Getting a VAT Refund" on page 719.

WHERE TO SHOP

Consider the following stores, markets, and neighborhoods:

For a street's worth of shops selling **"Scantiques,"** wander down Ravnsborggade from Nørrebrogade.

Copenhagen's colorful **flea markets** are small but feisty and surprisingly cheap (May-Nov Sat 8:00-14:00 at Israels Plads; May-Sept Fri and Sat 8:00-17:00 along Gammel Strand and on Kongens Nytorv). For other street markets, ask at the TI.

The city's top **department stores** (Illum at Østergade 52, and Magasin du Nord at Kongens Nytorv 13) offer a good, if expensive, look at today's Denmark. Both are on the Strøget and have fine cafeterias on their top floors. The department stores and the Politiken Bookstore on Rådhuspladsen have a good selection of maps and English travel guides.

The section of the Strøget called **Amagertorv** is a highlight for shoppers. The **Royal Copenhagen** store here sells porcelain on three floors (Mon-Fri 10:00-19:00, Sat 10:00-18:00, Sun 12:00-17:00). The first floor up features figurines and collectibles. The second floor has a second-quality department for discounts, proving that "even the best painter can miss a stroke." Next door, **Illums Bolighus** shows off three floors of modern Danish design (Mon-Fri 10:00-19:00, Sat 10:00-18:00, Sun 11:00-18:00).

House of Amber, which has a shop and a tiny two-room museum with about 50 examples of prehistoric insects trapped in the amber (remember *Jurassic Park*?) under magnifying glasses. You'll also see remarkable items made of amber, from necklaces and chests to Viking ships and chess sets (25 kr, daily May-Aug 10:00-19:00, Sept-April 10:00-18:00, at the top of Nyhavn at Kongens Nytorv 2). If you're visiting Rosenborg Castle, you'll see the ultimate examples of amber craftsmanship in its treasury.

Nightlife in Copenhagen

For the latest event and live music listings, check at the TI and pick up *The Copenhagen Post* (comes out weekly, free at TI and some hotels, also sold at newsstands, www.cphpost.dk).

Nightlife Neighborhoods: The **Meatpacking District,** which I've listed for its restaurants (see page 116), is also one of the city's most up-and-coming destinations for bars and nightlife. On warm evenings, **Nyhavn** canal becomes a virtual nightclub, with packs of young people hanging out along the water, sipping beers. **Christiania** always seems to have something musical going on after dark. **Tivoli** has evening entertainment daily from mid-April through late September (see page 66).

Music Venues: Copenhagen Jazz House is a good bet for live jazz (two stages, 50-300 kr cover, closed Mon, Niels Hemmingsensgade 10, tel. 33 15 26 00, check website for schedule, www.jazzhouse.dk). For blues, try the **Mojo Blues Bar** (70 kr Fri-Sat, otherwise no cover, nightly 20:00-late, music starts at 21:30, Løngangsstræde 21c, tel. 33 11 64 53, schedule in Danish on website, www.mojo.dk). For locations, see the map on page 108.

Jazz Cruises: Canal Tours Copenhagen offers 1.5-hour jazz cruises along the canals of Copenhagen. You can bring a picnic dinner and drinks on board and enjoy a lively night on the water surrounded by Danes (150 kr, mid-May-Aug Thu and Sun at 19:00, Sept-Dec and April-mid-May only Sun at 15:00, no tours Jan-March, departs from Canal Tours Copenhagen dock at Nyhavn, tel. 32 96 30 00). Call to reserve on July and August evenings; otherwise try arriving 20 to 30 minutes in advance.

Sleeping in Copenhagen

I've listed a few big business-class hotels, the best budget hotels in the center, cheap rooms in private homes in great neighborhoods an easy bus ride from the station, and a few backpacker dorm options.

Big Copenhagen hotels have an exasperating pricing policy. Their high rack rates are actually charged only about 20 or 30 days a year (unless you book in advance and don't know better). As hotels are swamped at certain times, they like to keep their gouging options open. Therefore, you'll need to check their website for deals or be bold enough to simply show up and use the TI's booking service to find yourself a room on their push list (ask at their desk, 100-kr fee). The TI swears that, except for maybe 10 days a year, you can land yourself a deeply discounted room in a three- or four-star business-class hotel in the center. That means a 1,400-kr double with American-style comfort for about 900 kr, including a big buffet breakfast.

HOTELS IN CENTRAL COPENHAGEN
Prices include breakfast unless noted otherwise. All of these hotels are big and modern, with elevators and non-smoking rooms, and all accept credit cards. Beware: Many hotels have rip-off phone rates even for local calls.

Near Nørreport
$$$ Ibsens Hotel is a stylish 118-room hotel in a charming neighborhood away from the main train station commotion and a short walk from the old center (on average Sb-1,145-1,245 kr, Db-1,145-1,445 kr, very slushy rates flex with demand—ask about discounts when booking or check website; higher prices are for larger rooms, third bed-400 kr, great bikes-150 kr/24 hours, guest computer, Wi-Fi, parking-185 kr/day, Vendersgade 23, S-tog: Nørreport, tel. 33 13 19 13, www.ibsenshotel.dk, hotel@ibsenshotel.dk).

$$ Hotel Jørgensen is a friendly little 30-room hotel in a great location just off Nørreport, kitty-corner from the bustling

Sleep Code

Abbreviations   **(6 kr = about $1, country code: 45)**
S = Single, **D** = Double/Twin, **T** = Triple, **Q** = Quad, **b** = bathroom
Price Rankings
  $$$ **Higher Priced**—Most rooms 1,000 kr or more.
   $$ **Moderately Priced**—Most rooms 600-1,000 kr.
    $ **Lower Priced**—Most rooms 600 kr or less.
Unless otherwise noted, English is spoken, credit cards are accepted, and Wi-Fi is generally free. Breakfast is generally included at hotels (unless you get a deeply discounted room rate), but not at private rooms or hostels. Prices change; verify current rates online or by email. For the best prices, always book directly with the hotel.

TorvehallerneKBH food market. With some cheap, grungy rooms and some good-value, nicer rooms, it's a fine budget option, though a bit worn around the edges. While the lounge is welcoming, the halls are a narrow, tangled maze (basic S-475-525 kr, Sb-675-725 kr, very basic D-750-800 kr, nicer Db-875-950 kr, cheaper off-season, extra bed-200 kr, Wi-Fi, Rømersgade 11, tel. 33 13 81 86, www.hoteljoergensen.dk, hoteljoergensen@mail.dk). They also rent 175-200-kr dorm beds to those under 35 (4-12 beds per room, sheets-30 kr, breakfast-45 kr).

Near Nyhavn

$$$ 71 Nyhavn has 150 smallish, rustic, but very classy rooms in a pair of beautifully restored, early-19th-century brick warehouses located at the far end of the colorful Nyhavn canal. With a professional, polite staff, lots of old brick and heavy timbers, and plenty of style, it's a worthwhile splurge (Sb-1,000-1,500 kr, Db-1,200-1,700 kr, 200 kr more for canal-view "superior" rooms, 200 kr more for larger "executive" rooms, rates vary depending on demand, some rates include breakfast—otherwise 170 kr, air-con in one of the buildings, guest computer, Wi-Fi, next to the Playhouse at Nyhavn 71, tel. 33 43 62 00, www.71nyhavnhotel.dk, 71nyhavnhotel@arp-hansen.dk).

  $$ Hotel Bethel Sømandshjem ("Seamen's Home"), run by a Lutheran association, is a calm and stately former seamen's hotel facing the boisterous Nyhavn canal and offering 29 tired but cozy rooms at the most reasonable rack rates in town. While the decor is college-dorm-inspired, the hotel boasts a kind, welcoming staff and feels surprisingly comfortable once you settle in. Plus, the colorful Nyhavn neighborhood is a great place to "come home" to after a busy day of sightseeing. Book long in advance (Sb-745 kr, large Sb-845 kr, Db-945 kr, larger "view" Db-1,045 kr, biggest corner

COPENHAGEN

Copenhagen Hotels

1 Ibsens Hotel
2 Hotel Jørgensen
3 71 Nyhavn Hotel
4 Hotel Bethel Sømandshjem
5 Axel Hotel
6 Carlton Hotel
7 Star Hotel
8 Hotel Nebo
9 Wake Up Copenhagen

10 Cab-Inn City
11 Cab-Inn Copenhagen Express
12 Cab-Inn Scandinavia
13 To Cab-Inn Metro & Danhostel Copenhagen Amager
14 Danhostel Copenhagen City
15 Copenhagen Downtown
16 City Public Hostel
17 Laundry (2)

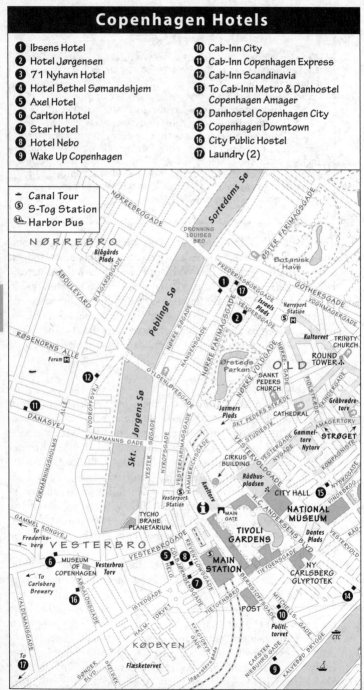

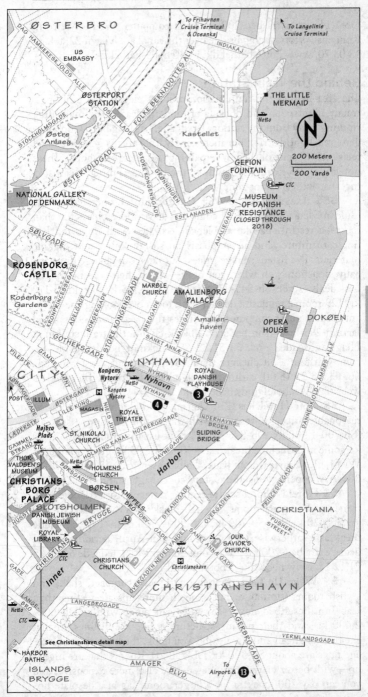

ØSTERBRO

To Frihavnen Cruise Terminal & Oceankaj

To Langelinie Cruise Terminal

US EMBASSY

DAG HAMMERSKJOLDS ALLE

ØSTERPORT STATION

FOLKE BERNADOTTES ALLE

INDIAKAJ

THE LITTLE MERMAID

Netto

Østre Anlaeg

STOCKHOLMSGADE

OSLO PLADS

Kastellet

GEFION FOUNTAIN

ØSTERVOLDGADE

ØSTERVOLDGADE

STORE KONGENSGADE

GRØNNINGEN

ESPLANADEN

CTC

MUSEUM OF DANISH RESISTANCE (CLOSED THROUGH 2018)

NATIONAL GALLERY OF DENMARK

SØLVGADE

AMALIEGADE

ROSENBORG CASTLE

Rosenborg Gardens

KRONPRINCESSEGADE

ADELGADE

BORGERGADE

STORE KONGENSGADE

MARBLE CHURCH

BREDGADE

AMALIENBORG PALACE

Amalien-haven

OPERA HOUSE

DOKØEN

GOTHERSGADE

SANKT ANNÆ PLADS

AMALIEGADE

DANNESKIOLD-SAMSØES ALLE

PILESTR.

GAMMEL

NYHAVN

NYHAVN

ROYAL DANISH PLAYHOUSE

❸

CITY

Kongens Nytorv

Netto

Nyhavn

NYHAVN

POST

KOMPAGNISTR.

ØSTERGADE

ILLUM

TILLE KONG

NIELS JUELSGADE

Kongens Nytorv

MAGASIN

❹

ROYAL THEATER

HOLBERGSGADE

INDERHAVNS-BROEN

LEDERSTR.

Højbro Plads

ST. NIKOLAJ CHURCH

HOLMENS KANAL

H

SLIDING BRIDGE

GAMMEL STRAND

CTC

HAVNEGADE

THOR-VALDSEN'S MUSEUM

Netto

BORGGADE

HOLMENS CHURCH

Harbor

CHRISTIANS-BORG PALACE

BØRSEN

KNIPPELS BRO

STRANDGADE

OVERGADEN

CHRISTIANIA

SLOTSHOLMEN

DANISH JEWISH MUSEUM

BRO TORV

GADE

"PUSHER STREET"

PRINSESSEGADE

ROYAL LIBRARY

H

SANKT ANNÆ GADE

OUR SAVIOR'S CHURCH

CHRISTIANS GADE

CTC

CHRISTIANS CHURCH

OVERGADEN NEDEN VANDET

M

Christianshavn

Inner

LANGE BRO

Netto

CTC

LANGEBROGADE

CHRISTIANSHAVN

AMAGERBROGADE

VERMLANDSGADE

HARBOR BATHS

See Christianshavn detail map

AMAGER BLVD.

ISLANDS BRYGGE

To Airport & ⓭

N

200 Meters

200 Yards

COPENHAGEN

Db-1,145 kr, extra bed-200 kr, guest computer, Wi-Fi, Metro to Kongens Nytorv, facing bridge over the canal at Nyhavn 22, tel. 33 13 03 70, www.hotel-bethel.dk, info@hotel-bethel.dk).

Behind the Train Station

The area behind the train station mingles elegant old buildings, trendy nightspots, and pockets of modern sleaze. The main drag running away from the station, Istedgade, has long been Copenhagen's red-light district; but increasingly, this area is gentrified and feels safe (in spite of the few remaining, harmless sex shops). These hotels are also extremely handy to the up-and-coming Meatpacking District restaurant zone.

$$$ **Axel Hotel** and $$$ **Carlton Hotel,** operated by the Guldsmeden ("Dragonfly") company, have more character than most—a restful spa-like ambience decorated with imported Balinese furniture, and an emphasis on sustainability and organic materials. I've listed average prices, but rates can change dramatically, depending on when you book—check their website for the best deals (Axel: Sb-845-975 kr, Db-985-1,145 kr, breakfast-170 kr, 129 rooms, request a quieter back room overlooking the pleasant garden, guest computer, Wi-Fi, restful spa area with sauna and Jacuzzi-295 kr/person per stay, a block behind the train station at Helgolandsgade 7, tel. 33 31 32 66, booking@hotelguldsmeden. com; Carlton: a bit cheaper than Axel, 64 rooms, Vesterbrogade 66, tel. 33 22 15 00, carlton@hotelguldsmeden.com). They share a website: www.hotelguldsmeden.com.

$$ **Star Hotel** has 134 charmless, cookie-cutter rooms at reasonable prices. Rates vary with the season and online specials (Sb-700-1,300 kr, Db-875-1,555 kr but usually around 950-1,000 kr, some rates include breakfast—otherwise 85 kr, guest computer, Wi-Fi, nice courtyard out back, Colbjørnsensgade 13, tel. 33 22 11 00, www.copenhagenstar.dk, star@copenhagenstar.dk).

$$ **Hotel Nebo,** a secure-feeling refuge with a friendly welcome and 84 comfy rooms, is a half-block from the station (S-420 kr, Sb-620 kr, D-650-700 kr, Db-900-950 kr, most rates include breakfast—otherwise 65 kr, cheaper Oct-April, periodic online deals, extra bed-200 kr, guest computer, Wi-Fi, Istedgade 6, tel. 33 21 12 17, www.nebo.dk, nebo@nebo.dk).

$$ **Wake Up Copenhagen** offers new, compact, slick, and stylish rooms (similar to but a notch more upscale-feeling than Cab-Inn, described next). The rates can range wildly (Db-600-2,400 kr), and their pricing structure is like the airlines' in that the further ahead and less flexibly you book, the less you pay (average rates are about Sb-500 kr, Db-750 kr). Rooms that are higher up—with better views and quieter—are also more expensive, and you can pay 200 kr extra for a larger room. It's in a desolate no-

man's-land behind the station, between the train tracks and the harbor—about a 15-minute walk from the station or Tivoli, but ideal for biking (breakfast-70 kr, Wi-Fi, bike rental, Carsten Niebuhrs Gade 11, tel. 44 80 00 00, www.wakeupcopenhagen. com, wakeupcopenhagen@arp-hansen.dk).

A DANISH MOTEL 6

$$ Cab-Inn is a radical innovation and a great value, with several locations in Copenhagen (as well as Odense, Aarhus, and elsewhere): identical, mostly collapsible, tiny but comfy, cruise-

ship-type staterooms, all bright, molded, and shiny, with TV, coffeepot, shower, and toilet. Each room has a single bed that expands into a twin-bedded room with one or two fold-down bunks on the walls. It's tough to argue with this kind of efficiency (general rates: teensy "economy" Sb-495 kr, Db-625 kr; still small "standard" Sb-545 kr, Db-675 kr, flip-down bunk Tb-805 kr; larger "commodore" Sb-645 kr, Db-775 kr; relatively gigantic "captain's" Sb-745 kr, Db-875 kr; larger family rooms also available, breakfast-70 kr, easy parking-60 kr, guest computer, Wi-Fi, www.cabinn.com). The best of the bunch is **Cab-Inn City,** with 350 rooms and a great central location (a short walk south of the main train station and Tivoli at Mitchellsgade 14, tel. 33 46 16 16, city@cabinn.com). Two more, nearly identical Cab-Inns are a 15-minute walk northwest of the station: **Cab-Inn Copenhagen Express** (86 rooms, Danasvej 32, tel. 33 21 04 00, express@cabinn.com) and **Cab-Inn Scandinavia** (201 rooms, some quads, Vodroffsvej 55, tel. 35 36 11 11, scandinavia@cabinn.com). The newest and largest is **Cab-Inn Metro,** near the Ørestad Metro station (710 rooms, some quads, on the airport side of town at Arne Jakobsens Allé 2, tel. 32 46 57 00, metro@cabinn.com).

ROOMS IN PRIVATE HOMES

At about 650 kr or so per double, staying in a private home can be a great value. While these accommodations offer a fine peek into Danish domestic life, the experience can be as private or as social as you want it to be. Hosts generally speak English, and you'll get a key and can come and go as you like. Rooms generally have no sink, and the bathroom's down the hall. They usually don't include breakfast, but you'll have access to the kitchen. I've listed an agency with a website that represents scores of fine places and—if you'd rather book direct—a couple of good B&Bs in Christianshavn.

Christianshavn

① Sankt Annæ B&B
② Esben Juhl Rooms
③ Ravelinen Restaurant
④ Bastionen & Løven Rest.
⑤ Lagkagehuset Bakery
⑥ Spicy Kitchen Indian
⑦ Spiseloppen Restaurant

$$ Sankt Annæ B&B, centrally located near my favorite Christianshavn sights, offers five clean, comfortable rooms with two shared bathrooms in a 250-year-old townhouse (S-600 kr, D-800 kr, larger D-1,000 kr, lower prices off-season, breakfast-80 kr at choice of three neighborhood cafés, single faces street so expect some noise, no elevator, Wi-Fi, communal kitchen, peaceful courtyard in back, Sankt Annæ Gade 10, Metro: Christianshavn, tel. 20 73 39 15, www.sabnb.dk, info@sabnb.dk).

$ Bed & Breakfast Denmark has served as a clearinghouse for local B&Bs since 1992. Peter Eberth and his staff take a 20-30 percent cut (the "deposit" you pay) but monitor quality. Given the high cost of hostels and hotels and the way local B&B hosts come and go, this is a fine and worthwhile service. Peter's website lets you choose the type and location of place best for you and gives you the necessary details when you pay. He has piles of good local rooms in central apartments (D-500 kr, Db-550-700 kr). He's located near the station at Sankt Peders Stræde 41, but there's no reason to visit his office (tel. 39 61 04 05, www.bbdk.dk).

$ Esben Juhl rents two spic-and-span, bright rooms in his beautiful Christianshavn apartment, close to the harbor and canal. You'll be sharing Esben's bathroom, and if he books both rooms, he'll actually be sleeping out in the living room; if these sound like too-close quarters, look elsewhere. But Esben is soft-spoken and kind, and enjoys treating his guests like houseguests, making this a good opportunity to connect with a local (S-400 kr, D-500 kr, extra bed-150 kr, includes light breakfast, cash only, Wi-Fi, David Balfours Gade 5, Metro: Christianshavn, tel. 32 57 39 08, mobile 27 40 12 15, mail@esju.dk).

HOSTELS

$ Danhostel Copenhagen City, an official HI hostel, is the hostel of the future. This huge harborside skyscraper (1,004 beds on 16 stories) is clean, modern, non-smoking, and a 10-minute walk from the train station and Tivoli. Some rooms on higher floors have pan-

oramic views over the city (available on a first-come, first-served basis). This is your best bet for a clean, basic, and inexpensive room in the city center (dorm beds in 6-bed rooms with bathrooms-135-225 kr, some co-ed, some separate; Sb/Db/Qb-650-775 kr, price depends on demand—check online for deals, sheets and towel-60 kr, breakfast-74 kr, nonmembers pay 60 kr/night extra, elevator, lockers, kitchen, self-service laundry, pay guest computer, Wi-Fi, rental bikes, H. C. Andersens Boulevard 50, tel. 33 11 85 85, www. danhostelcopenhagencity.dk, copenhagencity@danhostel.dk).

$ Copenhagen Downtown is beautifully located on a pleasant street right in the city center, a few steps from Slotsholmen Island and two blocks from the Strøget. Its 300 beds are a bit institutional, but it promises free dinner and comes with a guest kitchen and a colorful, fun hangout bar, which doubles as the reception (rates vary with demand, bunk in 4- to 10-bed dorm-165-250 kr, D-500-750 kr, 100 kr more for a private bathroom, includes sheets, breakfast-65 kr, laundry facilities, Wi-Fi, Vand-kunsten 5, tel. 70 23 21 10, www.copenhagendowntown.com, info@copenhagendowntown.com).

$ City Public Hostel houses travelers late May through August; the rest of the year, it's a latchkey program for local kids. It's well-run, welcomes people of all ages, and has a great location behind the Copenhagen City Museum on Vesterbrogade. With its sprawling grassy front yard, you can even forget you're in the middle of a big city (140 kr/bed in massive 66-bed room, 150 kr/bed in 32- or 22-bed dorm, 160 kr/bed in 12-bed dorm, 170 kr/bed in 10- or 6-bed dorm, sheets-60 kr, no breakfast, relaxing lounge, 10-minute walk behind main train station at Absalonsgade 8, tel. 36 98 11 66, www.citypublichostel.dk, info@citypublichostel.dk).

$ Danhostel Copenhagen Amager, an official HI hostel,

is on the edge of town (dorm bed-160 kr, S-390 kr, Sb-490 kr, D-430 kr, Db-530 kr, T-530 kr, Tb-630 kr, Q-690 kr, Qb-750 kr, members save about 35 kr, sheets-45 kr, breakfast-60 kr, family rooms, no curfew, excellent facilities, pay guest computer, Wi-Fi, self-serve laundry, Vejlands Allé 200, tel. 32 52 29 08, www.danhostelcopenhagen.dk, copenhagen@danhostel.dk). To get from downtown to the hostel, take the Metro (Metro: Bella Center, then 10-minute walk).

Eating in Copenhagen

CHEAP MEALS

For a quick lunch, try a *smørrebrød,* a *pølse,* or a picnic. Finish it off with a pastry.

Smørrebrød

Denmark's 300-year-old tradition of open-face sandwiches survives. Find a *smørrebrød* takeout shop and choose two or three that look good (about 25 kr each). You'll get them wrapped and ready for a park bench. Add a cold drink, and you have a fine, quick, and very Danish lunch. Tradition calls for three sandwich courses: herring first, then meat, and then cheese. Downtown, you'll find these handy local alternatives to Yankee fast-food chains. They range from splurges to quick stop-offs.

Between Copenhagen University and Rosenborg Castle

My three favorite *smørrebrød* places are particularly handy when connecting your sightseeing between the downtown Strøget core and Rosenborg Castle.

Restaurant Schønnemann is the foodies' choice—it has been written up in international magazines and frequently wins awards for "Best Lunch in Copenhagen." It's a cozy cellar restaurant crammed with small tables—according to the history on the menu, people "gather here in intense togetherness." The sand on the  floor evokes a bygone era when passing traders would leave their horses out on the square while they lunched here. You'll need to reserve to get a table, and you'll pay a premium for their *smørrebrød* (70-170 kr, two lunch seatings Mon-Sat: 11:30-14:00 & 14:14-17:00, closed Sun, no dinner, Hauser Plads 16, tel. 33 12 07 85, www.restaurantschonnemann.dk).

Café Halvvejen is a small mom-and-pop place serving traditional lunches and open-face sandwiches in a woody and smoke-stained café, lined with portraits of Danish royalty. You can eat inside or at an outside table in good weather (50-70-kr *smørrebrød*, 80-110-kr main dishes, food served Mon-Sat 12:00-15:00, closed Sun, next to public library at Krystalgade 11, tel. 33 11 91 12). In the evening, it becomes a hip and smoky student hangout, though no food is served.

Slagteren ved Kultorvet, a few blocks northwest of the university, is a small butcher shop with bowler-hatted clerks selling good, inexpensive sandwiches to go for about 35 kr. Choose from ham, beef, or pork (Mon-Thu 8:00-17:30, Fri 8:00-18:00, Sat 8:00-15:00, closed Sun, just off Kultorvet square at #4 Frederiksborggade, look for gold bull's head hanging outside).

Near Christiansborg Palace

These eateries are good choices when sightseeing on Slotsholmen.

Kanal Caféen, on Frederiksholms Kanal across from Christiansborg Palace, serves lunch only and is a nice place for a traditional open-face sandwich. Inside, you'll rub elbows with locals in what feels like the cozy confines of a low-ceilinged old sailing ship; outside you can dine right above the canal and watch the tour boats go by (60-90-kr sandwiches, Mon-Fri 11:30-17:00, Sat 11:30-15:00, closed Sun, Frederiksholms Kanal 18, tel. 33 11 57 70).

Café Diamanten serves open-face sandwiches, warm dishes, and salads—and pours microbrews from the tap. Take a seat inside the comfy café or under the parasols out front, with a view across the square to Thorvaldsen's Museum (65-95-kr sandwiches, Mon-Fri 10:00-20:30, Sat-Sun 10:00-19:00, Gammel Strand 50, tel. 33 93 55 45).

Burgers: **Cock's & Cows** is a trendy burger-and-cocktail bar with a happy, young vibe on an elegant street. Eat inside the brick-walled restaurant or in the courtyard out back (90-130-kr burgers—some piled almost ridiculously high, Sun-Thu 12:00-21:30, Fri-Sat 12:00-22:30, Gammel Strand 34, tel. 69 69 60 00).

Near Gammeltorv/Nytorv

Café Nytorv has pleasant outdoor seating on Nytorv (with cozy indoor tables available nearby) and a great deal on a *smørrebrød* sampler for about 200 kr—perfect for two people to share (if you smile, they'll serve it for dinner even though it's only on the lunch menu). This "Copenhagen City Plate" gives you a selection of the traditional sandwiches and extra bread on request (daily 9:00-22:00, Nytorv 15, tel. 33 11 77 06).

Sorgenfri offers a local experience in a dark, woody spot just off the Strøget (80-100 kr, Mon-Sat 11:00-20:45, Sun 12:00-18:00, Brolæggerstræde 8, tel. 33 11 58 80).

Or duck (literally) into **Kronborg Dansk Restaurant,** across the street from Sorgenfri, for finer-quality *smørrebrød* in a wood-

COPENHAGEN

Copenhagen Restaurants

- 🚢 Canal Tour
- Ⓢ S-Tog Station
- Ⓗ Harbor Bus

1. Restaurant Schønnemann
2. Café Halvvejen
3. Slagteren ved Kultorvet
4. Kanal Caféen
5. Café Diamanten
6. Cock's & Cows
7. Café Nytorv
8. Sorgenfri
9. Kronborg Dansk Rest.
10. Domhusets Smørrebrød
11. Andersen Bakery
12. Lagekagehuset Bakeries (4)
13. Nansens Bakery
14. Konditori La Glace
15. Det Lille Apotek
16. Café Sommersko
17. Riz-Raz Veg. Buffet (2)
18. Tight Restaurant
19. Café Norden

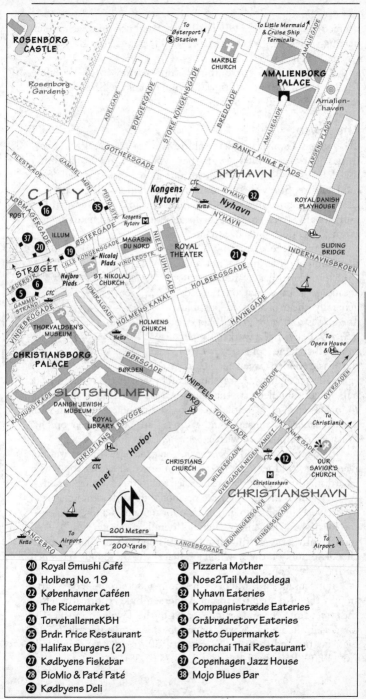

COPENHAGEN

20 Royal Smushi Café
21 Holberg No. 19
22 Københavner Caféen
23 The Ricemarket
24 TorvehallerneKBH
25 Brdr. Price Restaurant
26 Halifax Burgers (2)
27 Kødbyens Fiskebar
28 BioMio & Paté Paté
29 Kødbyens Deli

30 Pizzeria Mother
31 Nose2Tail Madbodega
32 Nyhavn Eateries
33 Kompagnistræde Eateries
34 Gråbrødretorv Eateries
35 Netto Supermarket
36 Poonchai Thai Restaurant
37 Copenhagen Jazz House
38 Mojo Blues Bar

beamed nautical setting (90-110-kr meat and fish sandwiches plus herring specialties, Mon-Sat 11:00-17:00, closed Sun, Brolægger-stræde 12, tel. 33 13 07 08).

Another option is **Domhusets Smørrebrød** (Mon-Fri 8:00-15:00, closed Sat-Sun, off the City Hall end of the Strøget at Kat-tesundet 18, tel. 33 15 98 98).

The *Pølse*

The famous Danish hot dog, sold in *pølsevogne* (sausage wagons) throughout the country, is another typically Danish institution that has resisted the onslaught of our global, prepackaged, fast-food culture. Study the photo menu for variations. These are fast, cheap, tasty, and, like their American cousins, almost worthless nutritionally. Even so, what the locals call the "dead man's finger" is the dog Danish kids love to bite.

There's more to getting a *pølse* than simply ordering a "hot dog" (which in Copenhagen simply means a sausage with a bun on the side, generally the worst bread possible). The best is a *ristet* (or grilled) hot dog *med det hele* (with the works). Employ these other handy phrases: *rød* (red, the basic boiled weenie), *medister* (spicy, better quality), *knæk* (short, stubby, tastier than *rød*), *brød* (a bun, usually smaller than the sausage), *svøb* ("swaddled" in bacon), *Fransk* (French style, buried in a long skinny hole in the bun with sauce). *Sennep* is mustard and *ristet løg* are crispy, fried onions. Wash everything down with a *sodavand* (soda pop).

By hanging around a *pølsevogn*, you can study this institution. Denmark's "cold feet cafés" are a form of social care: People who have difficulty finding jobs are licensed to run these wiener-mobiles. As they gain seniority, they are promoted to work at more central locations. Danes like to gather here for munchies and *pølsesnak*— the local slang for empty chatter (literally, "sausage talk"). And traditionally, after getting drunk, guys stop here for a hot dog and chocolate milk on the way home—that's why the stands stay open until the wee hours.

For sausages a cut above (and from a storefront—not a cart), stop by the little grill restaurant **Andersen Bakery,** directly across the street from the train station (next to the Tivoli entrance). The menu is limited—either pork or veal/beef—but the ingredients are high-quality and the weenies are tasty (50-kr gourmet dogs, daily 7:00-19:00, Bernstorffsgade 5, tel. 33 75 07 35).

Picnics

Throughout Copenhagen, small delis *(viktualiehandler)* sell fresh bread, tasty pastries, juice, milk, cheese, and yogurt (drinkable, in tall liter boxes). Two of the largest supermarket chains are **Irma** (in the glassy DI—Danish Industry—building on Vesterbrogade next to Tivoli) and **Super Brugsen. Netto** is a cut-rate outfit with the cheapest prices and a good bakery section. And, of course, there's the ever-present **7-Eleven** chain, with branches seemingly on every corner; while you'll pay a bit more here, there's a reason they're called "convenience" stores—and they also serve pastries and hot dogs.

Pastry

The golden pretzel sign hanging over the door or windows is the Danes' age-old symbol for a bakery. Danish pastries, called *wienerbrød* ("Vienna bread") in Denmark, are named for the Viennese bakers who brought the art of pastry-making to Denmark, where the Danes say they perfected it. Try these bakeries: **Lagkagehuset** (multiple locations around town; the handiest options include one right in the train station, another nearby inside the TI, one along the Strøget at Frederiksborggade 21, and another on Torvegade just across from the Metro station in Christianshavn) and **Nansens** (on corner of Nansensgade and Ahlefeldtsgade, near Ibsens Hotel). **Emmerys,** a trendy, gluten-free, Starbucks-like organic bakery and café, has more than 20 branches around Copenhagen, and sells good pastries and sandwiches. For a genteel bit of high-class 1870s Copenhagen, pay a lot for a coffee and a fresh Danish at **Konditori La Glace,** just off the Strøget at Skoubogade 3.

RESTAURANTS

I've listed restaurants in four areas: the downtown core, the funky Christianshavn neighborhood across the harbor, near Nørreport, and in the trendy Meatpacking District behind the main train station.

In the Downtown Core

Det Lille Apotek ("The Little Pharmacy") is a reasonable, candlelit place. It's been popular with locals for 200 years, and today it's a hit with tourists. Their specialty is "Stone Beef," a big slab of tender, raw steak plopped down and cooked in front of you on a scalding-hot soapstone. Cut it into smaller pieces and it's cooked within minutes (traditional dinners for 125-190 kr, nightly from 17:30, just off the Strøget, between Frue Church and Round Tower at Store Kannikestræde 15, tel. 33 12 56 06).

    Café Sommersko is a venerable eatery serving French-inspired Danish dishes in an elegant setting (125-165-kr lunches, 145-230-kr

Dine with the Danes

For a unique experience and a great opportunity to meet locals in their homes, consider having this organization arrange a dinner for you with a Danish family. You get a homey two-course meal with lots of conversation. Some effort is made to match your age, interests, and occupations. Book online at least two weeks in advance (420 kr/person, www.facebook.com/DineWithTheDanes, dinewiththedanes@msn.com). Fill out an online questionnaire, and you'll soon be contacted via Facebook or by email.

main courses, 300-kr three-course dinner, daily 11:00-22:30, Kronprinsensgade 6, tel. 33 14 81 89).

Riz-Raz Vegetarian Buffet has two locations in Copenhagen: around the corner from the canal boat rides at Kompagnistræde 20 (tel. 33 15 05 75) and across from Det Lille Apotek at Store Kannikestræde 19 (tel. 33 32 33 45). At both places, you'll find a healthy all-you-can-eat Middle Eastern/Mediterranean/vegetarian buffet lunch for 80 kr (cheese but no meat, great falafel, daily 11:30-16:00) and a bigger dinner buffet for 100 kr (16:00-24:00). Use lots of plates and return to the buffet as many times as you like. Tap water is 11 kr per jug.

Tight resembles a trendy gastropub, serving an eclectic international array of food and drink (Canadian, Aussie, French, and burgers, with Danish microbrews) in a split-level maze of hip rooms that mix old timbers and brick with bright colors (150-200-kr main courses, 140-kr burgers, daily 17:00-22:00, just off the Strøget at Hyskenstræde 10, tel. 33 11 09 00).

Café Norden, very Danish with modern "world cuisine," good light meals, and fine pastries, is a big, venerable institution overlooking Amagertorv by the heron fountain. It's family-friendly, with good seats outside on the square, in the busy ground-floor interior, or with more space and better views upstairs (great people-watching from the window seats). Order at the bar—it's the same price upstairs or down. Consider their 185-kr Nordic tapa plate or their 170-kr "triple salad" (120-170-kr sandwiches and salads, 150-kr main courses, huge splittable portions, daily 9:00-24:00, Østergade 61, tel. 33 11 77 91).

Royal Smushi Café is a hit with dainty people who like the idea of small, gourmet, open-face sandwiches served on Royal Copenhagen porcelain. You can sit in their modern chandeliered interior or the quiet courtyard (3 little "smushi" sandwiches for 135 kr, Mon-Sat 10:00-19:00, Sun 10:00-18:00, next to Royal Copenhagen porcelain store at Amagertorv 6, tel. 33 12 11 22).

Holberg No. 19, a cozy American-run café with classic ambience, sits just a block off the tourist crush of the Nyhavn canal. With a loose, friendly, low-key vibe, it offers more personality and lower prices than the tourist traps along Nyhavn (no real kitchen but 65-95-kr salads and sandwiches, selection of wines and beers, order at the bar, Mon-Fri 8:00-22:00, Sat 10:00-20:00, Sun 10:00-18:00, Holberg 19, tel. 33 14 01 90).

Københavner Caféen, cozy and a bit tired, feels like a ship captain's dining room. The staff is enthusiastically traditional, serving local dishes and elegant open-face sandwiches for a good value. Lunch specials (80-100 kr) are served until 17:00, when the more expensive dinner menu kicks in (plates for 120-200 kr, daily, kitchen closes at 22:00, at Badstuestræde 10, tel. 33 32 80 81).

The Ricemarket, an unpretentious Asian fusion bistro, is buried in a modern cellar between the Strøget and Rosenborg Castle. It's a casual, more affordable side-eatery of a popular local restaurant, and offers a flavorful break from Danish food (65-95-kr small dishes, 115-185-kr big dishes, seven-dish family-style meal for 285 kr, daily 12:00-22:00, Hausergade 38 near Kultorvet, tel. 35 35 75 30).

Illum and **Magasin du Nord** department stores serve cheery, reasonable meals in their cafeterias. At Illum, eat outside at tables along the Strøget, or head to the elegant glass-domed top floor (Østergade 52). Magasin du Nord (Kongens Nytorv 13) also has a great grocery and deli in the basement.

Also try **Café Nytorv** at Nytorv 15 or **Sorgenfri** at Brolæggerstræde 8 (both are described under *"Smørrebrød,"* earlier).

In Christianshavn

This neighborhood is so cool, it's worth combining an evening wander with dinner. It's a 10-minute walk across the bridge from the old center, or a 3-minute ride on the Metro. Choose one of my listings (for locations, see map on page 104), or simply wander the blocks between Christianshavns Torv, the main square, and the Christianshavn Canal—you'll find a number of lively neighborhood pubs and cafés.

Ravelinen Restaurant, on a tiny island on the big road 100 yards south of Christianshavn, serves traditional Danish food at reasonable prices to happy local crowds. Dine indoors or on the lovely lakeside terrace (which is tented and heated, so it's comfortable even on blustery evenings). This is like Tivoli without the kitsch and tourists. They offer a shareable "Cold Table" meal for 200 kr at lunch only (80-130-kr lunch dishes, 180-280-kr dinners, mid-April-late Dec daily 11:30-21:00, closed off-season, Torvegade 79, tel. 32 96 20 45).

Bastionen & Løven, at the little windmill (Lille Mølle),

A Culinary Phe-noma-non

Foodies visiting Denmark probably already know that Copenhagen is home to the planet's top-rated restaurant. *Restaurant* magazine has named noma the "Best Restaurant in the World" for several years, making it *the* reservation to get in the foodie universe. Chef René Redzepi is a pioneer in the burgeoning "New Nordic" school of cooking, which combines modern nouvelle cuisine and molecular gastronomy techniques with locally sourced (and, in some cases, foraged) ingredients from Denmark and other Nordic lands. So, while they use sophisticated cooking methods, they replace the predictable French and Mediterranean ingredients with Nordic ones. The restaurant's name comes from the phrase *nordisk mad* (Nordic food).

But noma, which is located at the northern edge of the trendy Christianshavn district (Strandgade 93, tel. 32 96 32 97), is not cheap. The seven-course menu runs 1,600 kr; accompanying wines add 1,200 kr to the bill. A couple going for the whole shebang is looking at spending more than $800. And even if you're willing to take the plunge, you have to plan ahead—noma is booked up around three months in advance. Check their website (www.noma.dk) for the latest procedure; you'll likely need to call on a specific date, at 10:00 in the morning Copenhagen time, about three months before your desired reservation...and hope you get through. You can also put your name on their waiting list, using their online form.

If you can't commit that far out (or don't want to spend that much), many of the top restaurants in Copenhagen (including Kødbyens Fiskebar, listed on page 116) are run by former chefs from noma—giving you at least a taste of culinary greatness.

serves gourmet Danish nouveau cuisine with a French inspiration from a small but fresh menu, on a Renoir terrace or in its Rembrandt interior. The classiest, dressiest, and most gourmet of all my listings, this restaurant fills a classic old mansion. Reservations for indoor dining are required; they don't take reservations for outdoor seating, as weather is unpredictable (95-175-kr lunches, 200-kr dinners, 375-kr three-course meal; Tue-Sat 11:00-23:00, Sun 11:00-18:00, closed Mon; walk to end of Torvegade and follow ramparts up to restaurant, at south end of Christianshavn, Christianshavn Voldgade 50, tel. 31 34 09 40, www.bastionenloven.dk).

Lagkagehuset is everybody's favorite bakery in Christianshavn. With a big selection of pastries, sandwiches, excellent fresh-baked bread, and award-winning strawberry tarts, it's a great place for breakfast or picnic fixings (pastries for less than 20 kr, take-out coffee for 30 kr, daily 6:00-19:00, Torvegade 45). For other locations closer to the town center, see page 111 under "Pastry."

Ethnic Strip on Christianshavn's Main Drag: Torvegade, which is within a few minutes' walk of the Christianshavn Metro station, is lined with appealing and inexpensive ethnic eateries, including Italian, cheap kebabs, Thai, Chinese, and more. **Spicy Kitchen** serves cheap and good Indian food—tight and cozy, it's a hit with locals (80-kr plates, daily 17:00-23:00, Torvegade 56).

In Christiania: Spiseloppen ("The Flea Eats") is a wonderfully classy place in Christiania. It serves great 140-kr vegetarian meals and 175-250-kr meaty ones by candlelight. It's gourmet anarchy—a good fit for Christiania, the free city/squatter town (Tue-Sun 17:00-22:00, kitchen closes at 21:00, closed Mon, reservations often necessary Fri-Sat; 3 blocks behind spiral spire of Our Savior's Church, on top floor of old brick warehouse, turn right just inside Christiania's main gate, enter the wildly empty warehouse, and climb the graffiti-riddled stairs; tel. 32 57 95 58, http://spiseloppen. dk). Other, less-expensive Christiania eateries are listed on page 89.

Near Nørreport

TorvehallerneKBH is in a pair of modern, glassy market halls right on Israel Plads. Survey both halls and the stalls on the square before settling in. In addition to produce, fish, and meat stalls, it has several inviting food counters where you can sit to eat a meal, or grab something to go. I can't think of a more enjoyable place in Copenhagen to browse for a meal than this upscale food court (pricey but fun, with quality food; Tue-Thu 10:00-19:00, Fri 10:00-20:00, Sat 9:00-17:00, Sun 10:00-15:00, most places closed Mon; Frederiksborggade 21).

Brdr. Price Restaurant—an elegant, highly regarded bistro serving creative Danish and international meals just across from Rosenborg Castle—is good for a dressy splurge (150-250-kr main courses, daily 12:00-22:00, Rosenborggade 15, tel. 38 41 10 20, www.brdr-price.dk). They have a more formal, classic French-Danish restaurant downstairs.

Halifax, part of a small local chain, serves up "build-your-own" burgers, where you select a patty, a side dish, and a dipping sauce for your fries (120-135 kr, daily 12:00-22:00, Sun until 21:00, Frederiksborggade 35, tel. 33 32 77 11). They have another location just off the Strøget (at Larsbjørnsstræde 9).

In the Meatpacking District (Kødbyen)

Literally "Meat Town," Kødbyen is an old warehouse zone huddled up against the train tracks behind the main station. Danes raise about 25 million pigs a year (five per person), so there's long been lots of "meatpacking." Today, much of the meatpacking action is diners chowing down.

There are three color-coded sectors in the district—brown, gray, and white—and each one is a cluster of old industrial buildings. At the far end is the white zone (Den Hvide Kødby), which has been overtaken by some of the city's most trendy and enjoyable eateries, which mingle with the surviving offices and warehouses of the local meatpacking industry. All of the places I list here are within a few steps of each other (except for the Mother pizzeria, a block away).

The curb appeal of this area is zilch (it looks like, well, a meatpacking district), but inside, these restaurants are bursting with life, creativity, and flavor. While youthful and trendy, this scene is also very accessible. Most of these eateries are in buildings with old white tile; this, combined with the considerable popularity of this area, can make the dining rooms quite loud. These places can fill up, especially on weekend evenings, when it's smart to reserve ahead.

It's a short stroll from the station: If you go south on the bridge called Tietgens Bro, which crosses the tracks just south of the station, and carry on for about 10 minutes, you'll run right into the area. Those sleeping in the hotels behind the station just stroll five minutes south. Or you can ride the S-tog to the Dybbølsbro stop.

Kødbyens Fiskebar ("Fish Bar") is one of the first and still the most acclaimed restaurant in the Meatpacking District. Focusing on small, thoughtfully composed plates of modern Nordic seafood, the Fiskebar has a stripped-down white interior with a big fish tank and a long cocktail bar surrounded by smaller tables. It's extremely popular (reservations are essential), and feels a bit too trendy for its own good. While the prices are high, so is the quality; diners are paying for a taste of the "New Nordic" style of cooking that's so in vogue here (100-145-kr small plates, 200-245-kr main courses; open in summer daily from 18:00, in winter generally closed Sat-Sun; Flæsketorvet 100, tel. 32 15 56 56, http://fiskebaren.dk).

BioMio, in the old Bosch building, serves rustic Danish, vegan, and vegetarian dishes, plus meat and fish. It's 100-percent organic, and the young boss, Rune, actually serves diners (200-kr plates, daily 12:00-22:00, Halmtorvet 19, tel. 33 31 20 00, http://biomio.dk).

Paté Paté, next door to BioMio, is a tight, rollicking bistro in a former pâté factory. While a wine bar at heart—with a good selection of wines by the glass—it has a fun and accessible menu of creative modern dishes and a cozy atmosphere rare in

the Meatpacking District. Ideally diners choose about three dishes per person and share (Mon-Sat from 17:30, closed Sun, Slagterboderne 1, tel. 39 69 55 57, www.patepate.dk).

Kødbyens Deli is this district's budget fast-food joint, serving chili, fish-and-chips, and burgers. You can take it away or eat there on humble tables (70-kr plates, daily 17:00-21:00, facing Paté Paté at Slagterboderne 8, tel. 24 84 09 82).

Pizzeria Mother is named for the way the sourdough for their crust must be "fed" and cared for to flourish. You can taste that care in the pizza, which has a delicious tangy crust. Out front are comfortable picnic benches, while the interior curls around the busy pizza oven with chefs working globs of dough that will soon be the basis for your pizza (75-150-kr pizzas, daily 11:00-23:00, a block beyond the other restaurants listed here at Høkerboderne 9, tel. 22 27 58 98).

Nose2Tail Madbodega (*mad* means "food") prides itself on locally sourced, sustainable cooking, using the entire animal for your meal (hence the name). You'll climb down some stairs into an unpretentious white-tiled cellar (50-kr small plates, 70-180-kr large plates, Mon-Sat 18:00-24:00, closed Sun, Flæsketorvet 13A, tel. 33 93 50 45, http://nose2tail.dk).

Other Central Neighborhoods to Explore

To find a good restaurant, try simply window-shopping in one of these inviting districts.

Nyhavn's harbor canal is lined with a touristy strip of restaurants set alongside its classic sailboats. Here thriving crowds are served mediocre, overpriced food in a great setting. On any sunny day, if you want steak and fries (120 kr) and a 50-kr beer, this can be fun. On Friday and Saturday, the strip becomes the longest bar in the world.

Kompagnistræde is home to a changing cast of great little eateries. Running parallel to the Strøget, this street has fewer tourists and lower rent, and encourages places to compete creatively for the patronage of local diners.

Gråbrødretorv ("Grey Friars' Square") is perhaps the most popular square in the old center for a meal. It's like a food court, especially in good weather. Choose from Italian, French, or Danish. Two steakhouses are **Jensen's Bøfhus**, a kid-friendly chain (100-kr burgers, 120-220-kr main dishes), and the pricier but better **Bøf & Ost** (170-250-kr main dishes). **Skildpadden** ("The Turtle") is a student hit, with make-it-yourself sandwiches (70 kr, choose the type of bread, salami, and cheese you want) and a 60-kr salad bar, plus draft beer. It's in a cozy cellar with three little tables on the lively square (daily 10:00-20:00, Gråbrødretorv 9, tel. 33 13 05 06).

Istedgade and the surrounding streets behind the train station (just above the Meatpacking District) are home to an assortment of inexpensive ethnic restaurants. You will find numerous places serving kebabs, pizza, Chinese, and Thai (including tasty 65-130-kr meals at **Poonchai Thai Restaurant**—across the street from Hotel Nebo at Istedgade 1). The area can be a bit seedy, especially right behind the station, but walk a few blocks away to take your pick of inexpensive, ethnic eateries frequented by locals.

Copenhagen Connections

BY PUBLIC TRANSPORTATION

From Copenhagen by Train to: Hillerød/Frederiksborg Castle (6/hour, 40 minutes on S-tog), **Roskilde** (5/hour, 30 minutes), **Humlebæk/Louisiana Art Museum** (3/hour, 30 minutes), **Helsingør** (3/hour, 45 minutes), **Odense** (3/hour, 1.5 hours), **Ærøskøbing** (2/hour Mon-Sat, hourly on Sun, 2.5 hours to Svendborg with a transfer in Odense, then 1.25-hour ferry crossing to Ærøskøbing—see page 167 for info on ferry), **Billund/Legoland** (2/hour, 2-2.5 hours to Vejle, then bus to Billund—see page 198, allow 3.5 hours total), **Aarhus** (2/hour, 3 hours), **Malmö** (3-5/hour, 35 minutes), **Stockholm** (almost hourly, 5-6 hours on high-speed train, some with a transfer at Malmö or Lund, reservation required; overnight service available but requires a change in Hässleholm or Lund), **Växjö** (hourly, 2.5 hours), **Kalmar** (hourly, 3.5-4 hours, most direct, some transfer in Alvesta), **Oslo** (3/day, 8.5-9.5 hours, transfer at Göteborg and Halden; also overnight boat option, described later), **Berlin** (4/day, 7 hours, reservation required, one direct, others change in Hamburg), **Amsterdam** (3/day with two changes, 11 hours, more with multiple changes), and **Frankfurt/Rhine** (4/day, 8.5-11 hours, most change in Hamburg, more with multiple stops). Train info tel. 70 13 14 15 (for English, press 1 for general information and tickets, and 2 for international trains). DSB (or Danske Statsbaner) is Denmark's national railway, www.rejseplanen.dk.

By Bus: Taking the bus to **Stockholm** is cheaper but more time-consuming than taking the train (2/day, 9.5 hours, longer for overnight trips, www.swebus.se).

BY CRUISE SHIP

More than half a million people visit Copenhagen via cruise ship each year. For a wealth of online information for cruise-ship passengers, see www.cruisecopenhagen.com. For more in-depth cruising information, pick up my *Rick Steves Northern European Cruise Ports* guidebook.

Most cruise ships use one of three terminals, all north of downtown—**Oceankaj**, the farthest port from town; **Frihavnen**

("Freeport"), about three miles from the city center; and **Langelinie Pier,** about a mile closer to downtown.

Getting Downtown: Bus #26 is a handy way to connect any of the cruise ports to various points in downtown Copenha-

gen, including Kongens Nytorv (big square near Nyhavn); Holmenskirke (church facing Slotsholmen Island and starting point for harbor cruises); Christiansborg Palace; Nationalmuseet (National Museum); Rådhuspladsen (City Hall Square); and Hoevdbanegården (main train station,

across the street from Tivoli). It runs about every 10 minutes from stops near the ports, and the ride downtown takes about 20 minutes (be sure to take a bus going in the direction of Ålholm Plads). Note that on Saturday and Sunday, bus #26 runs as a "Cruise Ship Shuttle" from these ports to the Østerport train station and back. At Østerport you can either catch the S-tog into the city center or board a regular bus #26 for the rest of the trip into town—be sure to ask for a transfer when you get on the #26 shuttle. The bus costs 24 kr (or 80 kr for a 24-hour pass). The driver takes credit cards (you'll need your PIN) and euros (figure about €3 for a simple ticket; you'll get change back in Danish kroner). If taking bus #26 back to your ship, make sure you get on the right bus, as the line splits to go to either Langelinie Pier or the other two cruise ports (ask driver).

Langelinie and Frihavnen are both about a 10- to 15-minute walk from a **train** station on Copenhagen's S-tog suburban rail line, from which you can hop on a train headed downtown, with stops at Nørreport (near Rosenborg Palace); København H (main train station); and Rådhuspladsen (City Hall Square). From Frihavnen or Oceankaj, many cruise lines offer a **shuttle bus** straight to Kongens Nytorv and/or Rådhuspladsen, generally for a fee. From Langelinie, you can **walk** or take a **hop-on, hop-off** bus into town. Taking a **taxi** to downtown is easy but expensive from any port (around 160 kr from Langelinie, 200 kr or more from the others).

Port Details: There are no ATMs at the piers. You'll need to head into town to draw out money.

Langelinie Pier, jutting out from the north end of Kastellet Park, has two berths for big ships, a pier-front road with stops for taxis and hop-on, hop-off buses, and a row of cruise-oriented shops (duty-free, outlet stores). You can ride bus #26 (stops near the entrance to the pier, to the right of the roundabout on Indiakaj street); hop on a hop-on, hop-off bus; or walk. Head to the base of the pier, cross to the mainland, then either bear left to find *The Little Mermaid* (*Den Lille Havfrue;* about a 10-minute walk), or right to circle around Kastellet Fortress and find Østerport train station for a speedy train downtown.

Frihavnen, a bit farther out, is a sprawling industrial zone with several cruise piers (called Sundkaj, Orientkaj, Fortkaj, and—farther to the north—Levantkaj). The first three piers are within an easy 5- to 10-minute walk of the port gate (just follow the thick blue line painted on the sidewalk); from Levantkaj, the cruise line offers a free shuttle bus to the gate. Exiting the port gate, bear right to find the stop for bus #26. To reach the Nordhavn train station, cross the highway called Kalkbrænderihavnsgade and go under the railway underpass, then immediately turn left (on Østbanegade). Walk along this residential street, with the elevated train tracks on your left, until you reach the station.

Oceankaj has three terminals. If your ship docks at Terminal 1, it's a short walk across the street past a cluster of kiosks and down the main road leading away from the cruise port to the stop for bus #26. If your ship arrives at the more distant Terminals 2 or 3, it's a 10- to 15-minute walk along the harborfront road to Terminal 1, where you'll turn right at the kiosks and go a short distance down the main road to the bus #26 stop.

BY OVERNIGHT BOAT TO OSLO

Luxurious DFDS Seaways cruise ships leave daily from Copenhagen at 16:30 and arrive in Oslo at 9:45 the next day (17-hour sailing). They also depart from Oslo at 16:30 for the return to Copenhagen, allowing you to spend about seven hours in Norway's capital if doing it as a day trip (see page 287 for info on departing from Oslo).

Cruise Costs: Cabins vary dramatically in price depending on the day and season (most expensive on weekends and late June-mid-Aug; cheapest on weekdays and Oct-April). For example, a bed in a four-berth "Seaways" shoehorn economy cabin starts at 410 kr/person one-way for four people traveling together (500 kr with a window); a luxurious double "Commodore class" cabin higher on the ship starts at 950 kr/person one-way (and includes a TV, minibar, and free breakfast buffet). A "mini-cruise" round-trip with a day in Oslo and no meals starts at 600 kr/person in an economy double cabin. All cabins have private bathrooms inside.

Onboard Services: DFDS Seaways operates two ships on this route—the MS *Pearl of Scandinavia* and the MS *Crown of Scandinavia*. Both offer all the cruise-ship luxuries: big buffets for breakfast (160 kr) and dinner (300 kr), gourmet restaurants (370-kr three-course meals), a kids' playroom, pool (indoor on the *Crown*, indoor and outdoor on the *Pearl*), sauna, nightclubs, pay Wi-Fi, satellite phone, and tax-free shopping. There are no ATMs on board. Cash advances are available at the shipboard exchange desk. All shops and restaurants accept credit cards as well as euros, dollars, and Danish, Swedish, and Norwegian currency.

Reservations: Reservations are smart in summer and on weekends. Advance bookings get the best prices. Book online or call DFDS Seaway's Danish office (Mon-Fri 9:00-16:30, closed Sat-Sun, tel. 33 42 30 10, www.dfdsseaways.us) or visit the **DSB Rejsebureau** at the main train station.

Port Details: The **Copenhagen Ferry Terminal** (a.k.a. DFDS Terminalen) is a short walk north of *The Little Mermaid*. The terminal is open daily 9:00-17:00 (luggage lockers available).

Getting Downtown: Shuttle bus #20E meets arriving ships from Oslo (daily 9:30-10:15). It goes first to Østerport Station (far from downtown but on the S-tog line—easy connection to the main train station, with some recommended hotels and the start of my "Copenhagen City Walk"), then to Kongens Nytorv (on the Metro line and near Nyhavn and other recommended hotels); from either stop, you can connect to Nørreport Station (with additional recommended hotels).

To reach the ferry terminal *from* the city center, catch bus #20E at Kongens Nytorv (free for cruise passengers, coordinated with sailing schedule; daily 14:00-16:00, departs every 10-30 minutes, arrives at the terminal 11 minutes later). Or take the S-tog from downtown in the direction of Hellerup or Hillerød to the Nordhavn Station. Exit the station, cross under the tracks, and hike toward the water; you'll see the ship on your right.

NEAR COPENHAGEN

Roskilde • Frederiksborg Castle • Louisiana Art Museum • Kronborg Castle

Copenhagen's the star, but there are several worthwhile sights nearby on its island (called Zealand), and the public transportation system makes side-tripping a joy. Visit Roskilde's great Viking ships and royal cathedral. Tour Frederiksborg, Denmark's most spectacular castle, and slide along the cutting edge at Louisiana Art Museum—a superb collection with a coastal setting as striking as its art. At Helsingør, do the dungeons of Kronborg Castle before heading on to Sweden.

PLANNING YOUR TIME

The area's essential sights are Roskilde's cathedral (with the tombs of Danish royalty) and its Viking ships, along with Frederiksborg Castle. Each destination takes a half-day, and each one is an easy commute from Copenhagen in different directions (30- or 40-minute train ride, then a 20-minute walk or short bus ride). If you're really fast and well-organized, you could visit both Roskilde and Frederiksborg with public transportation in a day (see "The Zealand Blitz," later).

If you're choosing between castles, Frederiksborg is the beautiful showpiece with the opulent interior, and Kronborg—darker and danker—is more typical of the way most castles really were. Both are dramatic from the outside, but Kronborg—overlooking the raging sea channel to Sweden—has a more scenic setting. Castle collectors can hit both in a day (see the two-castle day plan, later).

Drivers can visit these sights on the way into or out of Copenhagen. By train, do day trips from Copenhagen, then sleep while traveling to and from Copenhagen to Oslo (by boat, or by train

via Malmö, Sweden) or Stockholm (by train via Malmö). Consider getting a Copenhagen Card (see page 38), which covers your transportation to all of the destinations in this chapter, as well as admission to Roskilde Cathedral, Frederiksborg Castle, Kronborg Castle, and Louisiana Art Museum (but not the Roskilde Viking Ship Museum). Each train ride is just long enough for a relaxed picnic.

The Zealand Blitz—Roskilde Cathedral, Viking Ship Museum, and Frederiksborg Castle in a Day: If you have limited time and are well-organized, you can see the highlights of Zealand in one exciting day. Here's the plan (all times are rough, train connections take about 30-40 minutes, trains depart about every 10 minutes): Leave Copenhagen by train at 8:00, arrive in Roskilde at 8:30, wander through the town and be at the cathedral when it opens at 9:00 (opens later on Sun and in off-season). At 10:00, after an hour in the cathedral, stroll down to the harborfront to tour the Viking Ship Museum. They can call a taxi for you to return to the station for a 13:00 train back to Copenhagen. Buy a picnic lunch at Roskilde's station and munch your lunch on the train. Catch a 14:00 train from Copenhagen to Hillerød; there you'll catch the bus to Frederiksborg Castle, arriving at 15:00. This gives you two hours to enjoy the castle before it closes at 17:00 (earlier in off-season). Browse through Hillerød before catching a train at 18:00 to return to Copenhagen. You'll be back at your hotel by 19:00.

A Two-Castle Day (plus Louisiana) by Public Transportation: You can see both Frederiksborg and Kronborg castles, plus Louisiana Art Museum, in one busy day. (This works best on Tue-Fri, when Louisiana is open until 22:00.) Take the train from Copenhagen to Hillerød (leaving about 9:00), then hop on the awaiting bus to Frederiksborg Castle; you'll hear the 10:00 bells and be the first tourist inside. Linger in the sumptuous interior for a couple of hours, but get back to the station in time for a midday train (about 12:30 or 13:00) to Helsingør, a 15-minute walk from Kronborg Castle. Either munch your picnic lunch on the train, or—if it's a nice day—save it for the ramparts of Kronborg Castle. If you're castled out, skip the interior (saving the ticket price, and more time for Louisiana) and simply enjoy the Kronborg grounds and Øresund views before catching a train south toward Copenhagen. Hop off at Humlebæk for Louisiana.

GETTING AROUND

All of these sights except Roskilde are served by Copenhagen's excellent commuter-train (S-tog) system (covered by Eurail Pass; Copenhagen Card; and "24-hour ticket" and "7-day FlexCard"—both of which include greater Copenhagen; not covered by City Pass, which includes only zones 1-4—see page 42). All of the train connections (including the line to Roskilde) depart from the main train station; but be aware that most lines also stop at other Copenhagen stations, which may be closer to your hotel (for example, the Nørreport Station near the recommended Ibsens and Jørgensen hotels). Check schedules carefully to avoid needlessly going to the main train station.

At the main train station, S-tog lines do not appear on the overhead schedule screens (which are for longer-distance destinations); simply report to tracks 9-10 to wait for your train (there's a schedule at the head of those tracks).

If renting a car, see "Route Tips for Drivers," at the end of the chapter, for more information.

Roskilde

Denmark's roots, both Viking and royal, are on display in Roskilde (ROSS-killa), a pleasant town 18 miles west of Copenhagen. The town was the seat of the bishop and the residence of Danish royalty until 1450, when it shifted to Copenhagen. In its day, it was the second biggest city in the country. Today the town that introduced Christianity to Denmark in A.D. 980 is much smaller, except for the week of its famous rock/jazz/folk festival—northern Europe's largest—when 100,000 fans pack the place and it becomes one of Denmark's biggest cities again (early July, www. roskilde-festival.dk). Wednesday and Saturday are flower/flea/produce market days (8:00-14:00).

GETTING THERE

Roskilde is an easy side-trip from Copenhagen by train (5/hour, 30 minutes). Trains headed to Ringsted, Nykøbing, or Lindholm may not stop in Roskilde (which is an intermediate stop you won't see listed on departure boards)—confirm in advance. Returning to Copenhagen, hop on any train in the direction of Østerport or København H.

Orientation to Roskilde

TOURIST INFORMATION

Roskilde's helpful TI is on the main square, next to the cathedral (Mon-Fri 10:00-17:00, Sat 10:00-13:00, closed Sun; Stændertorvet 1, tel. 46 31 65 65, www.visitroskilde.com).

ARRIVAL IN ROSKILDE

There are no lockers at the train station (or nearby), but the TI—about a five-minute walk away—will take your bags for a few hours if you ask nicely.

From the train station, consider this circular route: First you'll head to the TI, then the cathedral, and finally down to the harborfront museum. Exit straight out from the station, and walk down to the bottom of the square. Turn left (at the Kvickly supermarket) on the pedestrianized shopping street, Algade (literally "the street for all"). After walking down this main drag about four blocks, you emerge into the main square, Stændertorvet, with the TI and the cathedral. After visiting the cathedral, you'll head about 10 minutes downhill (through a pleasant park) to the Viking Ship Museum: Facing the cathedral facade, turn left and head down the tree-lined path through the park. When you emerge at the roundabout (avoiding the temptation to eat a "Viking Pizza"), continue straight through it to reach the museum.

If you want to go directly from the station to the Viking Ship Museum, you can ride a bus; see page 130.

Sights in Roskilde

▲▲Roskilde Cathedral

Roskilde's imposing 12th-century, twin-spired cathedral houses the tombs of nearly all of the Danish kings and queens (39 royals in all; pick up the included guidebook as you enter). If you're a fan of Danish royalty or of evolving architectural styles, it's thrilling; even if you're neither, Denmark's "Westminster Abbey" is still interesting. It's a stately, modern-looking old church with great marble work, paintings, wood carvings, and an engaged congregation that makes the place feel very alive (particularly here in largely unchurched Scandinavia). A big museum and welcome center are in the works.

Cost and Hours: 60 kr; April-Sept Mon-Sat 9:00-17:00, Sun 12:30-17:00; Oct-March Tue-Sat 10:00-16:00, Sun 12:30-16:00, closed Mon; often closed for funerals and on Sat-Sun afternoons for baptisms and weddings; free organ concerts offered July-Aug Thu at 20:00; tel. 46 35 16 24, www.roskildedomkirke.dk.

◑ Self-Guided Tour: Begun in the 1170s by Bishop Absalom (and completed in 1280), Roskilde Cathedral was cleared of its side chapels and altars by the Reformation iconoclasts—leaving a blank slate for Danish royals to fill with their tombs. The highlight here is slowly strolling through a half-millennium's worth of royal chapels, representing a veritable textbook's worth of architectural styles.

• *Before entering, walk around the outside of the cathedral.*

Exterior, King's Door, and Tomb of Frederik IX: Notice the big bricks, which date from the 12th century, and how the cathe-

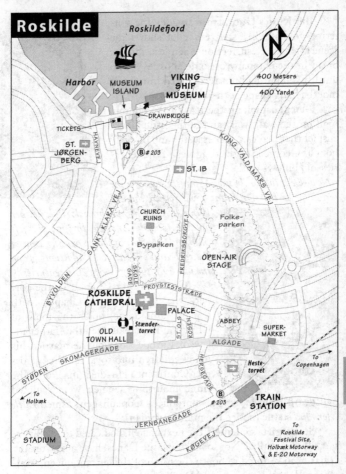

dral is built on the highest ground in town. Face the towering west facade. The main door—called the King's Door—was installed in 2010 and depicts scenes from the ministry of Jesus. This door is used by the congregation only to leave special services; the only people who may enter through this door are members of the royal family.

Find the freestanding brick chapel to the left. This holds the remains of Denmark's last king, Frederik IX (1899-1972), and his wife Ingrid (parents of the current queen, born in 1940). While all of the other monarchs are inside, Frederik—who was an avid sailor in his youth—requested to be buried here, with a view of the harbor.

• *Now go around the right side, buy a ticket, and go inside. First, head to the middle of the nave to look at...*

The King's Door, from Inside: The glittering-gold, highly stylized relief shows the scene after the Resurrection when Jesus breaks bread in the company of some apostles—who until this point had not recognized him (their mouths hang agape at their realization).

Glockenspiel: In the rear of the church, high on the wall, you can see the little glockenspiel that makes a racket at the top of every hour as George kills the dragon and the centuries-old billows wail.

• *Now we'll take a clockwise spin through the interior to see the significant royal burial chapels.*

While this tour is not chronological, neither are the tombs. Continue through the left aisle and into the big chapel housing some of the cathedral's most recent additions (from the late 19th through early 20th centuries).

Glücksburger Chapel: In the corner, the Glücksburger Chapel, with a plain light dome, holds the tomb of Christian IX, nicknamed the "father-in-law of Europe" for how he married his many children into royal families across the Continent. He died in 1906. The three mourning women were sculpted by Edvard Eriksen, who also produced Copenhagen's famed *Little Mermaid* statue (notice the middle woman).

St. Birgitta's Chapel: The next chapel, dedicated to St. Birgitta, will eventually ("Not soon," hope the Danes) have a new tenant: It has been restored to house the tomb of the current queen, Margrethe II, and her husband Henrik. She teamed up with an artist to design her own tomb (there's a model on display). Her body will reside in the stepped area at the bottom, upon which stand three columns representing the far-flung Danish holdings: one made of basalt from the Faroe Islands, another of marble from Greenland, and the third of stone from Denmark proper. Topping the columns are elephants (symbols of Danish royalty) and a semitransparent glass tomb, symbolizing the unpredictability of life and how death, like a seed, is a new beginning.

St. Andrew's Chapel: The next chapel, a modern addition to the church, is dedicated to St. Andrew and has a glittering mosaic over the altar. But pre-Reformation frescoes (1511) peek through the Protestant whitewash. Standing in front of this chapel, look across the nave to see the gorgeous 16th-century Baroque organ.

Christian IV Chapel: The next, larger chapel (up the stairs behind the small wooden organ) dates from the era of Christian IV, the larger-than-life 17th-century king who created modern Denmark. Christian also left his mark on Roskilde Cathedral, building the altarpiece, pulpit, distinctive twin towers...and this chapel. Walk around the stately yet humble tombs, marvel at the painting, and consider the huge personality of the greatest king in Danish history. In here you'll see a fine statue of the king, by Bertel Thorvaldsen; a large 3-D painting with Christian IV wearing his trademark eye patch, after losing his eye in battle; and his rather austere tomb (black with silver trim, surrounded by several others). Great he was...until his many wars impoverished his once mighty country.

• *Head into the nave and climb up the stairs into the choir area.*

The Nave, Choir, and High Altar: Take in the gorgeous gilded altarpiece and finely carved stalls. The three-winged altarpiece, carved in 1560 in Antwerp, shows scenes from Christ's last week. The fine carvings above the chairs in the choir feature scenes from the Old Testament on one side and the New Testament on the other.

Tomb of Margrethe I: Behind the altar is the ornately decorated tomb of Margrethe I, the Danish queen who added Nor-

way to her holdings by marrying Norwegian King Håkon VI in 1363. Legend holds that buried in a nearby brick pilaster are the supposed remains of Harold (read the Latin: *Haraldus*) Bluetooth, who ruled more than a millennium ago (r. 958-985 or 986), made Roskilde the capital of his realm, and converted his subjects to Christianity.

• *Now explore the apse (the area behind the altar).*

Apse: Go down the stairs, walk over the well-worn tombs of 500-year-old aristocrats who had the money to buy prime tomb space, and go through the little door. Circle around the apse, noticing more fine tombs behind Margrethe's.

• *Hooking back around toward the front, dip into the many more chapels you'll pass, including...*

Frederik V's Chapel: The grand, textbook Neoclassical tomb of Frederik V has white pillars, gold trim, and mourning maidens—representing Norway and Denmark—in ancient Greek gowns. You'll also pass a room housing elaborate, canopied Baroque tombs. Imagine: Each king or queen commissioned a tomb that suited his or her time—so different, yet all so grand.

Christian I's Chapel: The next chapel, with the tomb of Christian I, has a stone column marking the heights of visiting monarchs such as Prince Charles. The *P* is for the giant Russian czar Peter the Great—clearly the tallest.

• Leaving the cathedral, turn right and walk downhill for 10 minutes along a peaceful tree-lined lane that will eventually take you to the harbor and the Viking Ship Museum.

▲▲▲Viking Ship Museum (Vikingeskibsmuseet)

Vik literally means "shallow inlet," and "Vikings" were the people who lived along those inlets. Roskilde—and this award-winning museum—are strategically located along one such inlet. (They call it a "fjord," but it's surrounded by much flatter terrain than the Norwegian fjords.) Centuries before Europe's Age of Exploration, Viking sailors navigated their sleek, sturdy ships as far away as the Mediterranean, the Black Sea, the Persian Gulf, and the

Americas. This museum displays five different Viking ships, which were discovered in the Roskilde fjord and painstakingly excavated, preserved, and pieced back together beginning in the 1960s. The ships aren't as intact or as ornate as those in Oslo (see page 256), but this museum does a better job of explaining shipbuilding. The outdoor area (on "Museum Island") continues the experience, with a chance to see modern-day Vikings creating replica ships, chat with an old-time rope maker, and learn more about the excavation. The English descriptions are excellent—it's the kind of museum where you want to read everything.

Cost and Hours: 115 kr, daily mid-June-Aug 10:00-17:00, Sept-mid-June 10:00-16:00, tel. 46 30 02 00, www.vikingeskibsmuseet.dk.

Tours: Free 45-minute tours in English run mid-June-Aug daily at 12:00 and 15:00; May-mid-June and Sept Sat-Sun at 12:00; none off-season.

Boat Ride: The museum's workshop has re-created working replicas of all five of the ships on display here, plus others. For an extra 90 kr, you can go for a fun hour-long sail around Roskilde's fjord in one of these replica Viking vessels (you'll row, set sail, and row again; frequent departures—up to 7/day—in summer, fewer off-season, ask about schedule when you arrive or call ahead).

Eating: Café Knarr serves salads, sandwiches, and "planks" of Viking tapas with ingredients the Vikings knew (decent prices, open daily 11:00-16:00).

Getting There: It's on the harbor at Vindeboder 12. From the train station, catch bus #203 toward Boserup (2/hour, 7-minute ride). From the cathedral, it's a 10-minute downhill walk. The museum desk can call a taxi (100 kr) when you want go back to the station.

Visiting the Museum: The museum has two parts: the Viking Ship Hall, with the remains of the five ships; and, across the drawbridge, Museum Island with workshops, replica ships, a café, and more exhibits. There are ticket offices at each location; it's best to start with the Viking Ship Hall.

As you enter the **Viking Ship Hall,** check the board for the day's activities and demonstrations (including shipbuilding, weaving, blacksmithing, and minting). Consider buying the 20-kr guidebook and request the 14-minute English movie shown in the lobby's cinema.

Your visit is a one-way walk. You'll first see the five ships, then go through the preservation exhibit, the kids' zone with a video about the modern voyage of the *Sea Stallion*, and finally the popular shop.

The core of the exhibit is the remains of five ships, which were deliberately sunk a thousand years ago to block an easy channel into this harbor (leaving open only the most challenging approach—virtually impossible for anyone but a local to navigate). The ships, which are named for the place where they were found (Skuldelev), represent an impressively wide range of Viking shipbuilding technology. *Skuldelev 1* is a big, sail-powered ocean-going trade ship made in Norway, with a crew of six to eight men and room for lots of cargo; it's like the ship Leif Eriksson took to America 1,000 years ago. *Skuldelev 2* is a 100-foot-long, 60-oar longship made in the Viking city of Dublin; loaded with 65 or 70 bloodthirsty warriors, it struck fear into the hearts of foes. It's similar to the ones depicted in the Bayeux Tapestry in Normandy, France. *Skuldelev 3* is a modest coastal trader that stayed closer to home (wind-powered with oar backup, similar to #1 in design and also made in Norway). *Skuldelev 5* is a smaller longship—carrying about 30 warriors, it's the little sibling of #2. And *Skuldelev 6* is a small fishing vessel—a row/sail hybrid that was used for whaling and hunting seals. (There's no #4 because they originally thought #2 was two different ships...and the original names stuck.)

Exhibits in the surrounding rooms show the 25-year process of excavating and preserving the ships, explain a step-by-step attack and defense of the harbor, and give you a chance to climb aboard a couple of replica ships for a fun photo op. You'll also see displays describing the re-creation of the *Sea Stallion*, a replica of the big longship (#2) constructed by modern shipbuilders using ancient techniques. A crew of 65 rowed this ship to Dublin in 2007 and then back to Roskilde in the summer of 2008. You can watch a 20-minute film of their odyssey.

Leaving the hall, cross the drawbridge to **Museum Island.** Replicas of all five ships—and others—bob in the harbor; you can

actually climb on board the largest, the *Sea Stallion* (if in port). At the boatyard, watch modern craftsmen re-create millennium-old ships using the original methods and materials. Poke into the various workshops, with exhibits on tools and methods. The little square called *Tunet* ("Gathering Place") is ringed by traditional craft shops—basket maker, rope maker, blacksmith, wood carver—which are sometimes staffed by workers doing demonstrations. In the archaeological workshop, exhibits explain how they excavated and preserved the precious timbers of those five ships.

Frederiksborg Castle

Frederiksborg Castle, rated ▲▲, sits on an island in the middle of a lake in the cute town of Hillerød. This grandest castle in Scandinavia is often called the "Danish Versailles." Built from 1602 to 1620, Frederiksborg was the castle of Denmark's King Christian IV. Much of it was reconstructed after an 1859 fire, with the normal Victorian over-the-top flair, by the brewer J. C. Jacobsen and his Carlsberg Foundation.

You'll still enjoy some of the magnificent spaces of the castle's heyday: The breathtaking grounds and courtyards, the sumptuous chapel, and the regalia-laden Great Hall. But most of the place was turned into a fine museum in 1878. Today it's the Museum of National History, taking you on a chronological walk through the story of Denmark from 1500 until today (the third/top floor covers modern times). The countless musty paintings are a fascinating scrapbook of Danish history—it's a veritable national portrait gallery, with images of great Danes from each historical period of the last half-millennium.

A fine path leads around the lake, with ever-changing views of the castle. The traffic-free center of Hillerød is also worth a wander.

Tourist Information: Hillerød's TI, with a good town map and brochures for the entire North Zealand region, is in the free-standing white house next to the castle parking lot (to the left as you face the main castle gate; May-Sept Mon-Fri 9:30-16:00, closed Sat-Sun except open Sat in July 9:30-13:30, closed Oct-April, Frederiksværksgade 2A, tel. 48 24 26 26, www.visitnordsjaelland. com). Because the TI is inside an art gallery, if the TI is "closed" while the gallery is open, you can still slip inside and pick up a town map and brochures.

GETTING THERE

By Train: From Copenhagen, take the S-tog to Hillerød (line E, 6/hour, 40 minutes, bikes go free on S-tog trains).

From the Hillerød station, you can enjoy a pleasant 20-minute walk to the castle, or catch **bus** #301 or #302 (free with S-tog ticket or Copenhagen Card, buses are to the right as you exit station, ride three stops to Frederiksborg Slot bus stop; as buses go in two directions from here, confirm direction with driver).

If **walking,** just follow the signs to the castle. Bear left down the busy road (Jernbanegade) until the first big intersection, where you'll turn right. After a couple of blocks, where the road curves to the left, keep going straight; from here, bear left and downhill to the pleasant square Torvet, with great views of the castle and a café pavilion. At this square, turn left and walk through the pedestrian-ized shopping zone directly to the castle gate.

Linking to Other Sights: If continuing directly to Helsingør (with Kronborg Castle), hop on the regional train (departs from track 16 at Hillerød station, Mon-Fri 2/hour, Sat-Sun 1/hour, 30 minutes). From Helsingør, it's a quick trip on the train to the town of Humlebæk (where you'll find Louisiana Art Museum).

By Car: Drivers will find easy parking at the castle (for driving directions, see "Route Tips for Drivers" at the end of this chapter).

ORIENTATION TO FREDERIKSBORG CASTLE

Cost and Hours: 75 kr, daily April-Oct 10:00-17:00, Nov-March 11:00-15:00.

Tours: Take advantage of the free, informative, one-hour iPod audioguide; ask for it when you buy your ticket. My self-guided tour zooms in on the highlights, but the audioguide is more extensive. There are also posted explanations and/or borrow-able English descriptions in many rooms. Daily English-language, 30-minute highlights tours leave at 14:00 (included in admission).

Information: Tel. 48 26 04 39, www.dnm.dk.

NEAR COPENHAGEN

Eating: You can picnic in the castle's moat park or enjoy the **Spis-estedet Leonora** at the moat's edge (70-90-kr *smørrebrød* and sandwiches, 100-kr salads, 145-kr hot dishes, open daily 10:00-17:00, slow service). Or, better, walk into the town center near the bus stop.

❍ SELF-GUIDED TOUR

The castle's included audio tour is excellent, and you can almost follow it in real time for a one-hour blitz of the palace's highlights. Use my self-guided tour to supplement the audioguide.

The Castle Approach

From the entrance of the castle complex, it's an appropriately regal approach to the king's residence. You can almost hear the clopping of royal hooves as you walk over the moat and through the first island (which housed the stables and small businesses needed to support a royal residence). Then walk down the winding (and therefore easy-to-defend) lane to the second island, which was home to the domestic and foreign ministries. Finally, cross over the last moat to the main palace, where the king lived.

Fountain of Neptune Courtyard

Survey the castle exterior from the Fountain of Neptune. Christian IV imported Dutch architects to create this "Christian IV

style," which you'll see all over Copenhagen. The brickwork and sandstone are products of the local clay and sandy soil. The building, with its horizontal lines, triangles, and squares, is generally in Renaissance style, but notice how this is interrupted by a few token Gothic elements on the church's facade. Some say this homey touch was to let the villagers know the king was "one of them."

• *Step over the last moat, through the ornate gate, and into the castle grounds. Go in the door in the middle of the courtyard to buy your ticket, pick up your free audioguide, and put your bag in a locker (mandatory). Pick up a free floor plan; room numbers will help orient you on this tour. You'll enter the Knights' Parlor, also called The Rose, a long room decorated as it was during the palace's peak of power. Go up the stairs on the left side of this hall to the...*

Royal Chapel

Christian IV wanted to have the grandest royal chapel in Europe. For 200 years the coronation place of Danish kings, this chapel

is still used for royal weddings (and is extremely popular for commoner weddings—book long in advance). The chapel is nearly all original, dating back to 1620. As you walk around the upper level, notice the graffiti scratched on the windowpanes by the diamond rings of royal kids visiting for the summer back in the 1600s. Most of the coats of arms show off noble lineage—with a few exceptions we'll get to soon. At the far end of the chapel, the wooden organ is from 1620, with its original hand-powered bellows. (Hymns play on the old carillon at the top of each hour.)

Scan the hundreds of coats of arms lining the walls. These belong to people who have received royal orders from the Dan-

ish crown (similar to Britain's knighthoods). While most are obscure princesses and dukes, a few interesting (and more familiar) names show up just past the organ. In the first window bay after the organ, look for the distinctive red, blue, black, and green shield of South Africa—marking Nelson Mandela's coat of arms. (Notice he was awarded the highly prestigious Order of the Elephant, usually reserved for royalty.) Around the side of the same column (facing the chapel interior), find the coats of arms for Dwight D. Eisenhower (with the blue anvil and the motto "Peace through understanding"), Winston Churchill (who already came from a noble line), and Field Marshal Bernard "Monty" Montgomery. Around the far side of this column is the coat of arms for France's wartime leader, Charles de Gaulle.

Leaving the chapel, you step into the king's private oratory, with evocative Neo-Romantic paintings (restored after a fire) from the mid-19th century.

• *You'll emerge from the chapel into the museum collection. But before seeing that, pay a visit to the Audience Room: Go through the door in the left corner marked* Audienssalen, *and proceed through the little room to the long passageway (easy to miss).*

Audience Room

Here, where formal meetings took place, a grand painting shows the king as a Roman emperor firmly in command (with his two

sons prominent for extra political stability). This family is flanked by Christian IV (on the left) and Frederik III (on the right). Christian's military victories line the walls, and the four great continents—Europe, North America, Asia, and Africa—circle the false cupola (notice it's just an attic). Look for the odd trapdoor in one corner with a plush chair on it. This was where they could majestically lower the king to the exit.

• Now go back to the museum section, and proceed through the numbered rooms.

Museum Collection

Spanning three floors and five centuries, this exhaustive collection juxtaposes portraits, paintings of historical events, furniture, and other objects from the same time period, all combining to paint a picture of a moment in Danish history. While fascinating, the collection is huge, so I've selected only the most interesting items to linger over.

First Floor: Proceed to **Room 26,** which is focused on the Reformation. The case in the middle of the room holds the first Bible translated into Danish (from 1550—access to the word of God was a big part of the Reformation). Over the door to the next room is the image of a monk, Hans Tausen, invited by the king to preach the new thinking of the Reformation...sort of the "Danish Martin Luther." Also note the effort noble families put into legitimizing themselves with family trees and family seals.

Pass through Rooms 27, 28, and 29, and into **Room 30**—with paintings telling the story of Christian IV (for more on this dy-

namic Renaissance king, who built this castle and so much more, see page 81). Directly across from the door you entered is a painting of the chancellor on his deathbed, handing over the keys to the kingdom to a still-wet-behind-the-ears young Christian IV—the beginning of a long and fruitful career. On the right wall is a painting of Christian's coronation (the bearded gentleman looking out the window in the upper-left corner is Carlsberg brewer and castle benefactor J. C. Jacobsen—who, some 300 years before his birth, was probably not actually in attendance). Room 31 covers the royal family of Charles IV, while the smaller, darkened corner Room 32 displays the various Danish orders; find the most prestigious, the Order of the Elephant.

• *Hook back through Room 30, go outside on the little passage, and climb up the stairs.*

Second Floor: Go to the corner **Room 39,** which has a fascinating golden globe designed to illustrate Polish astronomer Nicolaus Copernicus' bold new heliocentric theory (that the sun, not the earth, was the center of our world). Look past the constellations to see the tiny model of the solar system at the very center, with a brass ball for the sun and little figures holding up symbols for each of the planets. The mechanical gears could actually make this model move to make the illustration more vivid.

Continue into one of the castle's most jaw-dropping rooms, the **Great Hall** (Room 38). The walls are lined with tapestries and

royal portraits (including some modern ones, near the door). The remarkable wood-carved ceilings include panels illustrating various industries. The elevated platform on the left was a gallery where musicians could play without getting in the way of the revelry.

Head back out and walk back along the left side of the hall. You can go quickly through the rooms numbered in the 40s and 50s (though pause partway down the long hallway; on the left, find the optical-illusion portrait that shows King Frederik V when viewed from one angle, and his wife when viewed from another). At the far end of this section, Room 57 has a portrait of Hans Christian Andersen. Notice that fashion styles have gotten much more modern...suits and ties instead of tights and powdered wigs. It's time to head into the modern world.

• *Find the modern spiral staircase nearby. Downstairs are late-19th-century exhibits—which are skippable. Instead, head up to the top floor.*

Third Floor: This staircase puts you right in the middle of the modern collection. From here, the museum's focus shifts, focusing more on the art and less on the history. Highlights include:

The Art Critics, showing four past-their-prime, once-rambunctious artists themselves, now happily entrenched in the art institution, leaning back to critique a younger artist's work.

A room focusing on Denmark's far-flung protectorate of Greenland, with a porcelain polar bear and portraits of explorers.

A room of distinctive Impressionist/Post-Impressionist paintings, with a Danish spin.

The *Ninth of April, 1940,* showing the (ultimately unsuccessful) Danish defense against Nazi invaders on that fateful date.

A room focusing on the royal family, with a life-size, photo-realistic portrait of the beloved Queen Margrethe II. Facing her is her daughter-in-law, Mary Donaldson—who, in this portrait at least, bears a striking resemblance to another young European royal.

Peter Carlsen's *Denmark 2009*—a brilliant parody of Eugène Delacroix's famous painting *Liberty Leading the People* (a copy of

the inspiration is on the facing wall). Carlsen has replaced the stirring imagery of the original with some dubious markers of contemporary Danish life: football flags, beer gut, shopping bags, tabloids, bikini babes, even a Christiania flag. It's a delightfully offbeat (and oh-so-Danish) note to end our visit to this seriously impressive palace.

NEAR THE CASTLE: HILLERØD TOWN

While there's not much here, the pedestrianized commercial zone is pleasant enough. It's best visited from the castle. Slotsgade, the main street, leads away from the castle bus stop toward the train station and is lined with shops and cafés. An inviting Scandinavian sweater shop is right at the bus stop. And if you feel like a little (very little) cruise, a tiny ferry leaves from a pier next to the castle and stops at the castle garden across the lake (30 kr, free with Copenhagen Card, 2/hour, 30 minutes).

Louisiana Art Museum

This is Scandinavia's most-raved-about modern-art museum. Located in the town of Humlebæk, beautifully situated on the coast 18 miles north of Copenhagen, Louisiana is a holistic place that masterfully mixes its art, architecture, and landscape.

GETTING THERE

Take the train from **Copenhagen** toward Helsingør, and get off at Humlebæk (3/hour, 30 minutes). It's a pleasant 10-minute walk (partly through a forest) to the museum: Exit the station and immediately go left onto Hejreskor Allé, a residential street; when the road curves right, continue straight along the narrow footpath through the trees. After you exit the trail, the museum is just ahead and across the street (at Gammel Strandvej 13).

If you're arriving by train from **Helsingør,** take the pedestrian underpass beneath the tracks, then follow the directions above. Louisiana is also connected to Helsingør by bus #388 (runs hourly, stops right at museum as well as at Humlebæk).

If you're coming from **Frederiksborg Castle,** you have two options: You can catch the Lille Nord train from Hillerød to Helsingør, then change there to a regional train heading south to Humlebæk (1-2/hour, 30 minutes). Alternately, you can take the S-tog toward Copenhagen and Køge, get off at Hellerup, then catch a regional train north toward Helsingør to reach Humlebæk (6/hour, 30 minutes).

ORIENTATION TO LOUISIANA ART MUSEUM

Cost: 110 kr, included in a special 200-kr round-trip tour ticket from Copenhagen—ask at any train station. Tel. 49 19 07 19, www.louisiana.dk.

Hours: Tue-Fri 11:00-22:00, Sat-Sun 11:00-18:00, closed Mon.

Cuisine Art: The cafeteria, with indoor and outdoor seating, is reasonable and welcomes picnickers who buy a drink (80-kr sandwiches at lunch, 120-kr lunch buffet, 150-kr dinner buffet, 30-40-kr cakes).

VISITING THE MUSEUM

Wander from famous Chagalls and Picassos to more obscure art (everything is post-1945). Poets spend days here nourishing their creative souls with new angles, ideas, and perspectives. Even those who don't think they're art lovers can get sucked into a thought-provoking exhibit and lose track of time. There's no permanent exhibit; they constantly organize their substantial collection into ever-changing arrangements, augmented with borrowed and special exhibits (check www.louisiana.dk for the latest). An Andy Warhol *Marilyn Monroe* you see on one visit may not be there the next. (One favorite item, French sculptor César's *The Big Thumb*—which is simply a six-foot-tall bronze thumb—isn't going anywhere, since

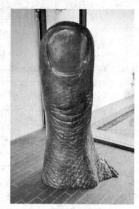

any time they move it, patrons complain.) There's no audioguide, but everything is labeled in English.

Outside, a delightful sculpture garden sprawls through the grounds, downhill toward the sea. The views over the Øresund, one of the busiest passages in the nautical world, are nearly as inspiring as the art. The museum's floor plan is a big loop, and the seaward side is underground—so as not to block the grand views. It's fun to explore the grounds, peppered with sculptures and made accessible by bridges and steps. There are sculptures by Alexander Calder, Jean Dubuffet, Joan Miró, and others.

Taken as a whole, the museum is a joy to explore. What you see from the inside draws you out, and what you see from the outside draws you in. The place can't be rushed. Linger and enjoy.

Kronborg Castle

Kronborg Castle is located in Helsingør, a pleasant, salty Danish seaside town that's often confused with its Swedish sister, Helsingborg, just two miles across the

channel. Kronborg Castle (also called Elsinore, the Anglicized version of Helsingør) is a ▲▲ sight famous for its tenuous (but profitable) ties to Shakespeare. Most of the "Hamlet" castle you'll see today—a darling of every big-bus tour and travelogue—was built long after the historical Hamlet died (more than a thousand years ago), and Shakespeare never saw the place. But this Renaissance castle existed when a troupe of English actors performed here in Shakespeare's time (Shakespeare may have known them). These days, various Shakespearean companies from around the world perform *Hamlet* in Kronborg's courtyard each August. Among the actors who've donned tights here in the title role are Laurence Olivier, Christopher Plummer, Kenneth Branagh, and Jude Law.

To see or not to see? The castle is most impressive from the outside. The free grounds between the walls and sea are great for picnics, with a close-up view of the strait between Denmark and Sweden. If you're heading to Sweden, Kalmar Castle (described in the Southeast Sweden chapter) is a better medieval castle. And in Denmark, Frederiksborg (described earlier), which was built as an upgrade to this one, is far more opulent inside. But if Kronborg is handy to your itinerary—or you never met a castle you didn't like—it's worth a visit...even if just for a short romp across the ramparts (no ticket required). Many big-bus tours in the region stop both here and at Frederiksborg (you'll recognize some of the same fellow tourists at both places)—not a bad plan if you're a castle completist.

Tourist Information: The town of Helsingør has a TI (Mon-Fri 10:00-16:00, until 17:00 in late June-early Aug, closed Sat-Sun except in summer, when it can be open 10:00-14:00; tel. 49 21 13 33, www.visithelsingor.dk), a medieval center, the ferry to Sweden, and lots of Swedes who come over for the lower-priced alcohol.

GETTING THERE

Helsingør is a 45-minute train ride from Copenhagen (3/hour). Exit the station out the front door: The TI is on the little square to your left, and the castle is dead ahead along the coast (about a 15-minute walk). Between the station and the castle, you'll pass through a harborfront zone with the town's cultural center and maritime museum (described later).

ORIENTATION TO KRONBORG CASTLE

Cost: The wonderful grounds are free, but you'll need a ticket to enter the courtyard and the main buildings—80 kr covers royal apartments and casements; 160-kr combo-ticket also includes maritime museum; 40 kr to visit just the casements.

Hours: The whole complex is open June-Aug daily 10:00-17:30, Sept-May daily 11:00-16:00 except closed Mon in Nov-March.

Tours: Free 30-minute **tours** in English are offered of the casements and of the royal apartments (1-2/day; call or check online for times: tel. 33 95 42 00, www.kronborg.dk). You can download a free **audioguide** to your mobile device. Dry English descriptions are posted throughout the castle. The equally arid 20-kr printed **guide** (sold at the ticket counter) tries to inject some life into the rooms.

VISITING THE CASTLE

Approaching the castle, pretend you're an old foe of the king, kept away by many layers of earthen ramparts and moats—just when you think you're actually at the castle, you find there's another gateway or waterway to pass. On the way in, you'll pass a small model of the complex to help get your bearings. On a sunny day, you could have an enjoyable visit to Kronborg just walking around these grounds and playing "king of the castle," without buying a ticket. Many do.

Follow the signs into the ticket desk, buy your ticket, stick your bag in a locker (insert a 20-kr coin, which will be returned), and head upstairs. You'll pop out at the beginning of the royal apartments.

Royal Apartments

Visitors are able to walk through one and a half floors of the complex. The first few rooms are filled with high-tech exhibits, using touchscreens and projected videos to explain the history of the place. You'll learn how, in the 1420s, Danish King Eric of Pomerania built a fortress here to allow for the collection of "Sound Dues," levied on any passing ship hoping to enter the sound of Øresund. This proved hugely lucrative, eventually providing up to two-thirds of Denmark's entire income. By the time of Shakespeare, Kronborg was well-known both for its profitable ability to levy these dues, and for its famously lavish banquets—what better setting for a tale of a royal family unraveling?

Continuing into the apartments themselves, you'll find that the interior is a shadow of its former self; while the structure was rebuilt by Christian IV after a 1629 fire, its rooms were never returned to their former grandeur, making it feel like something of an empty shell. And yet, there are still some fine pieces of furniture and art to see. Frederik II ruled Denmark from the king's chamber in the 1570s; a model shows how it likely looked back in its

heyday. After passing through two smaller rooms, you come to the queen's chamber; from there, stairs lead up to the queen's gallery, custom-built for Queen Sophie to be able to quickly walk directly from her chambers to the ballroom or chapel. Follow her footsteps into the ballroom, a vast hall of epic proportions decorated by a

Øresund Region

When the Øresund (UH-ra-soond) Bridge, which connects Denmark and Sweden, opened in July of 2000, it created a dynamic new metropolitan area. Almost overnight, the link forged an economic power with the 12th-largest gross domestic product in Europe. The Øresund region has surpassed Stockholm as the largest metro area in Scandinavia. Now 3.7 million Danes and Swedes—a highly trained and highly technical workforce—are within a quick commute of each other.

The bridge opens up new questions of borders. Historically, southern Sweden (the area across from Copenhagen, called Skåne) had Danish blood. It was Danish for a thousand years before Sweden took it in 1658. Notice how Copenhagen is the capital on the fringe of its realm—at one time it was in the center.

The 10-mile-long link, which has a motorway for cars (the toll is about 350 kr) and a two-track train line, ties together the main islands of Denmark with Europe and Sweden. The $4 billion project consisted of a 2.5-mile-long tunnel, an artificial island called Peberholm, and a 5-mile-long bridge. With speedy connecting trains, Malmö in Sweden is now an easy half-day side-trip from Copenhagen (about 120 kr each way, 3-5/hour, 35 minutes). The train drops you at the "Malmö C" (central) station right in the heart of Malmö, and all the important sights are within a short walk.

series of paintings commissioned by Christian IV (explained by the board near the entry). At the far end, a model (enlivened by seemingly holographic figures) illustrates how this incredible space must have looked in all its original finery. Beyond the ballroom, the "Little Hall" is decorated with a fine series of tapestries depicting Danish monarchs. Then wind through several more royal halls, chambers, and bedrooms on your way back down into the courtyard. Once there, go straight across and enter the chapel. The enclosed gallery at the upper-left was the private pew of the royal family.

Casements

You'll enter the underground part of the castle through a door on the main courtyard (diagonally across from the chapel). While not particularly tight, these passages are very dark and intentionally not very well-lit; a vending machine at the entrance sells 20-kr flashlights (bring yours—or, at least, a bright mobile phone). This extensive network of dank cellars is a double-decker substructure that once teemed with activity. The upper level, which you'll see first, was used as servants' quarters, a stable, and a storehouse. The lower level was used to train and barrack soldiers during wartime (an efficient use of so much prime, fortified space). As you explore this creepy, labyrinthine, nearly pitch-black zone (just follow the arrows), imagine the miserably claustrophobic conditions the soldiers lived in, waiting to see some action.

The most famous "resident" of the Kronborg casements was Holger Danske ("Ogier the Dane"), a mythical Viking hero revered by Danish children. The story goes that if the nation is ever in danger, this Danish superman will awaken and restore peace and security to the land (like King Arthur to the English, Barbarossa to the Germans, and Wenceslas to the Czechs). While this legend has been around for many centuries, Holger's connection to Kronborg was cemented by a Hans Christian Andersen tale, so now everybody just assumes he lives here. In one of the first rooms, you'll see a famous, giant statue of this sleeping Viking...just waiting for things to get *really* bad.

NEAR THE CASTLE: MARITIME MUSEUM OF DENMARK

Fans of nautical history and modern architecture should consider a visit to this museum, built within the old dry docks adjacent to the castle and designed by noted Danish firm BIG (Bjarke Ingels Group). Cutting-edge exhibits journey through Denmark's rich seafaring tradition, from the days of tall-masted sailing ships to the container-ship revolution, in which Danish shipping company Maersk is a world leader. Topics include life on board, wartime challenges, the globalization of trade, navigation, and maritime traditions (including tattoos!) in popular culture.

Cost and Hours: 110 kr, free for those under age 18, 160-kr combo-ticket also includes Kronborg Castle, pricey admission covered by Copenhagen Card; July-Aug daily 10:00-17:00, Sept-June Tue-Sun 11:00-17:00, closed Mon; café, tel. 49 21 06 85, www.mfs.dk.

Near Copenhagen Connections

ROUTE TIPS FOR DRIVERS

Copenhagen to Hillerød (45 minutes) to Helsingør (30 minutes): Just follow the town-name signs. Leave Copenhagen following signs for *E-47* and *Helsingør*. The freeway is great. *Hillerød* signs lead to the Frederiksborg Castle (not to be confused with the nearby Fredensborg Palace) in the pleasant town of Hillerød. Follow signs to *Hillerød C* (for "center"), then *slot* (for "castle"). Though the E-47 freeway is the fastest, the Strandvejen coastal road (152) is pleasant, passing some of Denmark's grandest mansions (including that of author Karen Blixen of *Out of Africa* fame).

Copenhagen to Sweden: The 10-mile Øresund Bridge linking Denmark with Sweden (€46 toll, or about 350 kr) lets drivers and train travelers skip nonstop from Copenhagen to Malmö, Sweden (see sidebar, earlier).

If you're heading to Sweden from Kronborg Castle—or if you're simply nostalgic for the pre-bridge days—the Helsingør-Helsingborg ferry putters across the Øresund Channel (follow signs to *Helsingborg, Sweden*—freeway leads to dock). Buy your ticket as you roll on board (about 350 kr one-way for car, driver, and up to nine passengers). Reservations are free but not usually necessary, as ferries depart frequently (2-4/hour; tel. 33 15 15 15, or book online at www.scandlines.dk; also see www.hhferries.se). If you arrive early, you can probably drive onto any ferry. The 20-minute Helsingør-Helsingborg ferry ride gives you just enough time to enjoy the view of the Kronborg "Hamlet" castle, be impressed by the narrowness of this very strategic channel, and exchange any leftover Danish kroner into Swedish kronor (the ferry exchange desk's rate is decent).

In Helsingborg, follow signs for *E-4* and *Stockholm*. The road is good, traffic is light, and towns are all clearly signposted. At Ljungby, road 25 takes you to Växjö and Kalmar. Entering Växjö, skip the first Växjö exit and follow the freeway into *Centrum*, where it ends. It takes about four hours total to drive from Copenhagen to Kalmar.

CENTRAL DENMARK

Ærø • Odense

The sleepy isle of Ærø is the cuddle after the climax. It's the perfect time-passed world in which to wind down, enjoy the seagulls, and take a day off. Wander the unadulterated cobbled lanes of Denmark's best-preserved 18th-century town. Get Ærø-dynamic and pedal a rented bike into the essence of Denmark. Settle into a world of sailors, who, after the invention of steam-driven boat propellers, decided that building ships in bottles was more their style.

Between Ærø and Copenhagen, drop by bustling Odense, home of Hans Christian Andersen. Its Hans Christian Andersen House is excellent, and with more time, you can also enjoy its other museums (town history, trains, folk) and stroll the car-free streets of its downtown.

PLANNING YOUR TIME

Allow four hours to get from Copenhagen to Ærø (not counting a possible stopover in Odense). All trains stop in Roskilde (with its Viking Ship Museum—see previous chapter) and Odense (see the end of this chapter). On a quick trip, you can leave Copenhagen in the morning and do justice to both towns en route to Ærø. (With just one day, Odense and Roskilde together make a long but do-able day trip from Copenhagen.)

While out of the way, Ærø is worth the journey. Once there, you'll want two nights

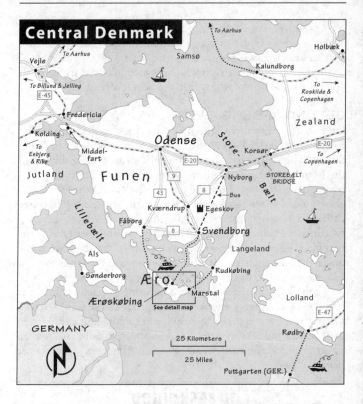

Central Denmark

and a day to properly enjoy it (for details, see "Planning Your Time" for Ærøskøbing, later).

Ærø

This small (22 by 6 miles) island on the south edge of Denmark is as salty and sleepy as can be. A typical tombstone reads: "Here lies Christian Hansen at anchor with his wife. He'll not weigh until he stands before God." It's the kind of island where baskets of strawberries sit in front of houses—for sale on the honor system.

Ærø statistics: 7,000 residents, 500,000 visitors and 80,000 boaters annually, 350 deer, seven priests, no crosswalks, and three police officers. The three big industries are farming (wheat and dairy), shipping, and tourism—in that order. Twenty percent of the Danish fleet still resides on Ærø, in the town of Marstal. But jobs are scarce, the population is slowly dropping, and family farms are consolidating into larger units.

Ærø, home to several windmills and one of the world's largest solar power plants, is going "green." They hope to become completely wind- and solar-powered. Currently, nearly half the island's heat and electricity is provided by renewable sources, and most of its produce is organically grown. New technology is expected to bring Ærø closer to its goal within the next few years.

GETTING AROUND ÆRØ

On a short visit, you won't need to leave Ærøskøbing, except for a countryside bike ride—everything is within walking or pedaling distance. But if you have more time or want to explore the rest of the island, you can take advantage of Ærø's **bus** network. Buses leave from a stop just above the ferry dock (leaving the ferry, walk up about a block and look right). Ærø's main bus line, #790, is free (Mon-Fri hourly until about 19:00; Sat-Sun 3-4/day). There are two different branches—one going to Marstal at the east end of the island, and the other to Søby in the west (look for the town name under the bus number). The main reason to take the bus is to go to Marstal on a rainy day to visit its maritime museum (see page 161).

You can also take a subsidized **taxi** ride to points around the island—but it requires some planning ahead. To use this "Telebus" system, you have to make the trip between 5:00 and 22:00 (from 7:00 on Sat-Sun). At least two hours in advance, call FynBus at 63 11 22 55 to reserve; a ride to anywhere on Ærø costs just 60 kr per person.

Ærøskøbing

Ærøskøbing is Ærø's village in a bottle. It's small enough to be cute, but just big enough to feel real. The government, recognizing the value of this amazingly preserved little town, prohibits modern building anywhere in the center. It's the only town in Denmark protected in this way. Drop into the 1680s, when Ærøskøbing was the wealthy home port of a hundred windjammers. The many Danes and Germans who come here for the tranquility—washing up the cobbled main drag in waves with

the landing of each boat—call it the fairy-tale town. The Danish word for "cozy," *hyggelig*, describes Ærøskøbing perfectly.

Ærøskøbing is simply a pleasant place to wander. Stubby little porthole-type houses, with their birth dates displayed in proud decorative rebar, lean on each other like drunk, sleeping sailors. Wander under flickering old-time lamps. Snoop around town. It's OK. Peek into living rooms (if people want privacy, they shut their drapes). Notice the many "snooping mirrors" on the houses—antique locals are following your every move. The harbor now caters to holiday yachts, and on midnight low tides you can almost hear the crabs playing cards.

The town economy, once rich with the windjammer trade, hit the rocks in modern times. Kids 15 to 18 years old go to a boarding school in Svendborg; many don't return. It's an interesting discussion: Should the island folk pickle their culture in tourism, or forget about the cuteness and get modern?

PLANNING YOUR TIME

You'll regret not setting aside a minimum of two nights for your Ærøskøbing visit. In a busy day you can "do" everything you like—except relax. If ever a place was right for recreating, this is it. I'd arrive in time for an evening stroll and dinner (and, if it's running, the Night Watchman's tour—see page 162). The next morning, do the island bike tour, returning by midafternoon. You can see the town's three museums in less than two hours (but note that they all close early—by 15:00 or 16:00), then browse the rest of your daylight away. Your second evening is filled with options: Stroll out to the summer huts for sunset, watch the classic sailing ships come in to moor for the evening (mostly Dutch and German boats crewed by vacationers), watch a movie in the pint-sized town cinema, go bowling with local teens, or check out live music in the pub.

Note that during the off-season (basically Sept-May), the town is quite dead and may not be worth a visit. Several shops and restaurants are closed, and bad weather can make a bike ride unpleasant.

Orientation to Ærøskøbing

Ærøskøbing is tiny. Everything's just a few cobbles from the ferry landing.

TOURIST INFORMATION

The TI, which faces the ferry landing, is a clearinghouse for brochures promoting sights and activities on the island, has info on other Danish destinations, can help check for room availability, and offers free Wi-Fi (late-June-mid-Aug Mon-Fri 9:00-18:00, Sat 10:00-18:00, Sun 10:00-15:00; off-season Mon-Fri 10:00-16:00, closed Sat-Sun; tel. 62 52 13 00, www.aeroe.dk).

HELPFUL HINTS

Money: The town's only ATM is at the blue building by the ferry dock, facing the TI.

Internet Access: Try the library on Torvet Square, in the old City

Hall (sketchy hours). Or for free Wi-Fi, visit the TI (steady hours).

Laundry: You'll find limited self-service laundry facilities at Ærøskøbing's marinas, on either side of the ferry dock.

Ferries: See "Ærøskøbing Connections" on page 167.

Bike Rental: Pilebækkens Cykler rents bikes year-round at the gas station at the top of town. Manager Janne loans readers of

this book the 25-kr island *cykel* map so they won't get lost (seven-speed bikes-75 kr/24 hours, 140 kr/2 days; Mon-Fri 9:00-16:30, Sat 9:00-12:00, closed Sun except July-Aug—when it's open 9:00-12:30; from Torvet Square, go through green door at Søndergade end of square, past garden to next road, in the gas station at Pilebækken 7; tel. 62 52 11 10). The recommended **Hotel Ærøhus** rents seven-speed bikes (75 kr/24 hours, 200-kr deposit, open long hours). The campground also rents bikes (see "Sleeping in Ærøskøbing," later). Most people on Ærø don't bother locking up their bikes—if your rental doesn't have a lock, don't fret.

Shopping: The town is speckled with cute little shops, including a funky flea market shop next to the bakery. Each July, local artisans show their creations in a warehouse facing the ferry landing.

Ærøskøbing Walk

This self-guided stroll, rated ▲▲▲, is ideal when the sun is low, the shadows long, and the colors rich. Start at the harbor.

Harbor: Loiter around the harbor a bit first. German and Dutch vacationers on grand old sailboats come into port each evening. Because Ærø is only nine miles across the water from Germany, the island is popular with Germans who regularly return to this peaceful retreat.

• *From the harbor and TI, walk up the main street a block and go left on...*

Smedegade: This is the poorest street in town, with the most architectural and higgledy-piggledy charm. Have a close look at the "street spies" on the houses—clever mirrors letting old women inside keep an eye on what's going on outside. The ship-in-a-bottle Bottle Peter Museum is

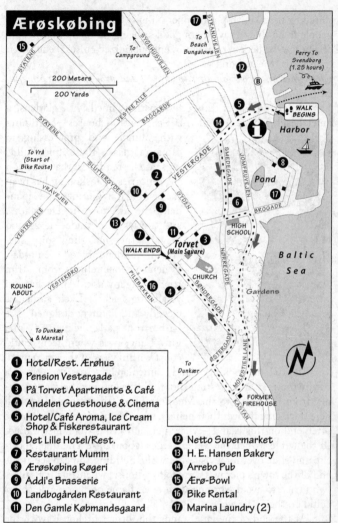

Ærøskøbing

❶ Hotel/Rest. Ærøhus
❷ Pension Vestergade
❸ På Torvet Apartments & Café
❹ Andelen Guesthouse & Cinema
❺ Hotel/Café Aroma, Ice Cream Shop & Fiskerestaurant
❻ Det Lille Hotel/Rest.
❼ Restaurant Mumm
❽ Ærøskøbing Røgeri
❾ Addi's Brasserie
❿ Landbogården Restaurant
⓫ Den Gamle Købmandsgaard

⓬ Netto Supermarket
⓭ H. E. Hansen Bakery
⓮ Arrebo Pub
⓯ Ærø-Bowl
⓰ Bike Rental
⓱ Marina Laundry (2)

on the right (described later, under "Sights in Ærøskøbing"). Notice the gutters—some protect only the doorway. Locals find the rounded modern drainpipes less charming than the old-school ones with hard angles. Appreciate the finely carved old doors. Each is proudly unique—try to find two the same. Number 37 (on the left, after Det Lille Hotel), from the 18th century, is Ærøskøbing's cutest house. Its tiny dormer is from some old ship's poop deck. The plants above the door have a traditional purpose—to keep this part of the house damp and slow to burn in case of fire.

Smedegade ends at the Folkehøjskole (folk high school). Inspired by the Danish philosopher Nikolaj Gruntvig—who wanted people to be able to say, "I am good at being me"—it offers people of any age the benefit of government-subsidized cultural education (music, art, theater, and so on).

• *Jog left, then turn right after the school, and stroll along the peaceful, harborside...*

Molestien Lane: This gravel path is lined with gardens, a quiet beach, and a row of small-is-beautiful houses—beginning

with humble and progressing to captain's class. These fine buildings are a reminder that through the centuries, Ærøskøbing has been the last town in Germany, independent, the first town in Denmark... and always into trade—legal and illegal. (The smuggling spirit survives in residents' blood even today. When someone returns from a trip, friends eagerly ask, "And what did you bring back?") Each garden is cleverly and lovingly designed. The harborfront path, nicknamed "Virgin's Lane," was where teens could court within view of their parents.

The dreamy-looking island immediately across the way is a nature preserve and a resting spot for birds making their long journey from the north to the Mediterranean. There's one lucky bull here (farmers raft over their heifers, who return as cows). Rainbows often end on this island—where plague victims were once buried. In the winter, when the water freezes (about once a decade), locals slip and slide over for a visit. The white building you can see at the end of the town's pier was the cooking house, where visiting sailors (who tried to avoid working with open flame on flammable ships) could do their baking.

At the end of the lane stands the former firehouse (with the tall brick tower, now a place for the high school garage band to practice). Twenty yards before the firehouse, a trail cuts left about 100 yards along the shore to a place the town provides for fishermen to launch and store their boats and tidy up their nets. A bench is strategically placed to enjoy the view.

• *Follow the rutted lane inland, back past the firehouse. Turn right and walk a block toward town. At the first intersection, take a right onto...*

Østergade: This was Ærøskøbing's east gate. In the days of German control, all island trade was legal only within the town. All who passed this point would pay various duties and taxes at a tollbooth that once stood here.

As you walk past the traditional houses, peer into living rooms. Catch snatches of Danish life. (After the bend, you can see right through the windows to the sea.) Ponder the beauty of a society with such a keen sense of civic responsibility that fishing permits entrust you "to catch only what you need." You're welcome to pick berries where you like...but "no more than what would fit in your hat."

The wood on these old houses prefers organic coverings to modern paint. Tar painted on beams as a preservative blisters in the sun. An old-fashioned paint of chalk, lime, and clay lets old houses breathe and feel more alive. (It gets darker with the rain and leaves a little color on your fingers.) Modern chemical paint has much less personality.

The first square (actually a triangle, at #55) was the old goose market. Ærøskøbing—born in the 13th century, burned in the 17th, and rebuilt in the 18th—claims (believably) to be the best-preserved town from that era in Denmark. The original plan, with 12 streets laid out by its founder, survives.

• *Leaving the square, stay left on...*

Søndergade: Look for wrought-iron girders on the walls, added to hold together bulging houses. (On the first corner, at #55, notice the nuts that could be tightened like a corset to keep the house from sagging.) Ærøskøbing's oldest houses (check out the dates)—the only ones that survived a fire during a war with Sweden—are #36 and #32. At #32, the hatch upstairs was where masts and sails were stored for the winter. These houses also have some of the finest doors in town (and in Ærøskøbing, that's really saying something). The red on #32's door is the original paint job—ox blood, which, when combined with the tannin in the wood, really lasts. The courtyard behind #18 was a parking lot in pre-car days. Farmers, in town for their shopping chores, would leave their horses here. Even today, the wide-open fields are just beyond.

• *Wander down to Ærøskøbing's main square.*

Torvet Square: Notice the two hand pumps, which still work. Until 1951, townspeople came here for their water. The linden tree is the town symbol. The rocks around it celebrate the reunion of a big chunk of southern Denmark (including this island), which was ruled by Germany from 1864 to 1920. See the town seal featuring a linden tree, over the door of the old City Hall (now the library, with Internet stations in former prison cells). Read the Danish on the wall: "With law shall man a country build."

• *Our walk is over. Continue straight (popping into recommended Restaurant Mumm, the best place in town, to make a reservation for dinner). You'll return to the main street (Vestergade) and—just when you need it—the town bakery (to the left). But, if you're ready to launch right into a bike ride, instead go through the green door to the right of City Hall to reach the town's bike-rental place (listed earlier, under "Helpful Hints").*

Sights in Ærøskøbing

MUSEUMS

Ærøskøbing's three tiny museums cluster within a few doors of each other just off Torvet Square. While quirky and fun (and with sketchy English handouts), these museums would be much more interesting and worthwhile if they translated their Danish descriptions for the rare person on this planet who doesn't speak *Dansk*. (Your gentle encouragement might help get results.) In July, they organize daily chatty tours.

Tickets and Information: You can buy individual tickets (see "Cost and Hours" for each), but if visiting all three, buy the 85-kr **combo-ticket** at your first stop (note the limited hours for the Hammerich House before committing), tel. 62 52 29 50, www. arremus.dk.

Ærø Museum (Ærøskøbing Bymuseum)

This museum fills two floors of an old house with the island's history, from seafaring to farming. On the ground floor, you'll see household objects (such as pottery, kitchenware, and tools), paintings, a loom from 1683, and a fun diorama showing an aerial view of Ærøskøbing in 1862—notice the big gardens behind nearly every house. (This museum carries on the tradition with its own garden out back—be sure to go out and explore it before you leave.) Upstairs are 19th-century outfits, lots more paintings, an 18th-century peasant's living room with colorful furniture, and the gear from a 100-year-old pharmacy.

Cost and Hours: 30 kr; July-Aug Mon-Fri 10:00-16:00, Sat-Sun 11:00-15:00; mid-April-June and Sept-mid-Oct Mon-Sat

11:00-15:00, closed Sun; shorter hours and closed Sat-Sun off-season; Brogade 3-5.

▲Bottle Peter Museum (Flaske-Peters Samling)

This fascinating house has 750 different bottled ships. Old Peter Jacobsen, who made his first bottle at 16 and his last at 85, created some 1,700 total ships-in-bottles in his lifetime. He bragged that he drank the contents of each bottle...except

those containing milk. This museum opened in 1943, when the mayor of Ærøskøbing offered Peter and his wife a humble home in exchange for the right to display his works. Bottle Peter died in 1960 (and is most likely buried in a glass bottle), leaving a lifetime of tedious little creations for visitors to squint and marvel at.

Cost and Hours: 40 kr; late June-Aug daily 10:00-16:00, mid-April-late June and Sept-mid-Oct daily 11:00-15:00, shorter hours off-season; Smedegade 22.

Visiting the Museum: In two buildings facing each other across a cobbled courtyard, you'll see rack after rack of painstaking models in bottles and cigar boxes. Some are "right-handed" and some are "left-handed" (referring to the direction the bottle faced, and therefore which hand the model maker relied on to execute the fine details)—Bottle Peter could do it all.

In the entrance building, you'll see Peter's "American collection," which he sold to a Danish-American collector so he could have funds to retire. One of Peter's favorites was the "diver-bottle"—an extra-wide bottle with two separate ship models inside: One shipwreck on the "ocean floor" at the bottom of the bottle, and, above that, a second one floating on the "surface." A video shows the artist at work, and nearby you can see some of his tools.

The second building has some English panels about Peter's life (including his mischievous wit, which caused his friends great anxiety when he had an audience with the king) and the headstone he designed for his own grave: a cross embedded with seven ships-in-bottles, representing the seven seas he explored in his youth as a seaman.

Hammerich House (Hammerichs Hus)

These 12 funky rooms in three houses are filled with 200- to 300-year-old junk.

Cost and Hours: 30 kr, late May-mid-Aug Thu 12:00-15:00, otherwise ask for access at the Ærø Museum, closed off-season, Gyden 22.

CENTRAL DENMARK

Ærø Island Bike Ride

To Svendborg

DENMARK
Odense • Cph.
GER. Ærø

To Søby

Urehoved

To Søby

BEACH
BUNGALOWS

Drejø

Ommels-
hoved

GÆSTGIVERI
BREGNINGE

CHURCH
Bregninge

Borgnæs

CAMPING

Synneshøj

DIKE

Ærøskøbing
(start & end bike ride)

Vrå

SHORTCUTS BACK
TO ÆRØSKØBING

Lilleø

VINDEBALLE KRO

Vindeballe

Stokkeby

Lille
Rise

Kragnæs

Vodrup
Klint
(Cliffs)

Tranderup

Olde

TINGSTEDET
DOLMEN

**Store
Rise**

To Marstal
& Maritime
Museum

BREWERY

Dunkær

Baltic Sea

2 Kilometers

2 Miles

Vejnæs Nakke

ÆRØ ISLAND BIKE RIDE (OR CAR TOUR)

This 15-mile trip shows you the best of this windmill-covered island's charms. The highest point on the island is only 180 feet above sea level, but the wind can be strong and the hills seem long and surprisingly steep.

As a bike ride, it's good exercise, though it may be more exhausting than fun if you've done only light, recreational cycling at home. You'll pay more for seven gears instead of five, but it's worth it.

Rent your bike in town (see "Helpful Hints," earlier), and while my map and instructions work, a local cycle map is helpful (free loaner maps if you rent from Pilebækkens Cykler, or buy one at the TI). Bring along plenty of water, as there are few opportunities to fill up (your first good chance is at the WC at the Bregninge church; there are no real shops until downtown Bregninge).

• *Leave Ærøskøbing to the west on the road to Vrå (Vråvejen, signed Bike Route #90). From downtown, pedal up the main street (Vestergade) and turn right on Vråvejen; from the bike-rental place on Pilebækken, just turn right and pedal straight ahead—it turns into Vråvejen.*

Leaving Ærøskøbing: You'll see the first of many U-shaped farms, typical of Denmark. The three sides block the wind and store cows, hay, and people. *Gård* (farm) shows up in many local surnames.

At Øsemarksvej, bike along the coast in the protection of the dike built in 1856 to make the once-salty swampland to your left farmable. While the weak soil is good for hay and little else, they get the most out of it. Each winter, certain grazing areas flood with seawater. (Some locals claim this makes their cows produce fatter milk and meat.) As you roll along the dike, the land on your left is about eight feet below sea level. The little white pump house—alone in the field—is busy each spring and summer.

• *At the T-junction, go right (over the dike) toward...*

Borgnæs: The traditional old "straw house" (50 yards down, on left) is a café and shop selling fresh farm products. Just past that, a few roadside tables sell farm goodies on the honor system. Borgnæs is a cluster of modern summer houses. In spite of huge demand, a weak economy, and an aging population, development like this is no longer allowed.

• *Keep to the right (passing lots of wheat fields); at the next T-junction, turn right, following signs for Ø.* Bregningemark *(don't turn off for* Vindeballe*). After a secluded beach, head inland (direction: Ø. Bregninge). Pass the island's only water mill, and climb uphill over the island's 2,700-inch-high summit toward Bregninge. The tallest point on Ærø is called Synneshøj (probably means "Seems High" and it sure does—if you're even a bit out of shape, you'll feel every one of those inches).*

Gammelgård: Take a right turn marked only by a *Bike Route #90* sign. The road deteriorates (turns to gravel—and can be slushy

if there's been heavy rain, so be careful). You'll wind scenically and sometimes steeply through "Ærø's Alps," past classic thatched-roofed "old farms" (hence the name of the lane—Gammelgård).

• *At the modern road, turn left (leaving Bike Route #90) and pedal to the big village church. Before turning left to roll through Bregninge, visit the church.*

Bregninge Church: The interior of the 12th-century Bregninge church is still painted as a Gothic church would have been. Find the painter's self-portrait (behind the pulpit, right of front pew). Tradition says that if the painter wasn't happy with his pay, he'd paint a fool's head in the church (above

CENTRAL DENMARK

third pew on left). Note how the fool's mouth—the hole for a rope tied to the bell—has been worn wider and wider by centuries of ringing. (During services, the ringing bell would call those who were ill and too contagious to be allowed into the church to come for communion—distributed through the square hatches flanking the altar.)

The altarpiece—gold leaf on carved oak—is from 1528, six years before the Reformation came to Denmark. The cranium carved into the bottom indicates it's a genuine masterpiece by Claus Berg (from Lübeck, Germany). This Crucifix-ion scene is such a commotion, it seems to cause Christ's robe to billow up. The soldiers who traditionally gambled for Christ's robe have traded their dice for knives. Even the three wise men (lower right; each perhaps a Danish king) made it to this Crucifixion. Notice the escap-ing souls of the two thieves—the one who converted on the cross being carried happily to heaven, and the other, with its grim-winged escort, heading straight to hell. The scene at lower left—a dis-ciple with a bare-breasted, dark-skinned

woman feeding her child—symbolizes the Great Commission: "Go ye to all the world." Since this is a Catholic altarpiece, a roll call of saints lines the wings. During the restoration, the identity of the two women on the lower right was unknown, so the letter-ing—even in Latin—is clearly gibberish. Take a moment to study the 16th-century art on the ceiling (for example, the crucified feet ascending, leaving only footprints on earth). In the narthex, a list of pastors goes back to 1505. The current pastor (Agnes) is the first woman on the list.

• Now's the time for a bathroom break (public WC in the churchyard). If you need some food or drink, pop in to the **Gæstgiveri Bregninge** restaurant, to the right of the church as you face it (75-125-kr lunches, 135-185-kr dinners, May-mid-Sept Wed-Thu 12:00-17:00, Fri-Sun 12:00-21:00, closed Mon-Tue and in the off-season, tel. 30 23 65 55). Then roll downhill through...

Bregninge: As you bike through what is supposedly Den-mark's "second-longest village," you'll pass many more U-shaped gårds. Notice how the town is in a gully. Imagine pirates trolling along the coast, looking for church spires marking unfortified vil-lages. Ærø's 16 villages are all invisible from the sea—their church spires carefully designed not to be viewable from sea level.

• About a mile down the main road is Vindeballe. Just before the main *part of the village (soon after you pass the official* Vindeballe *sign and the* din fart *sign—which tells you "your speed"), take the* Vodrup Klint *turnoff to the right.*

Vodrup Klint: A road leads downhill (with a well-signed jog to the right) to dead-end at a rugged bluff called Vodrup Klint

(WC, picnic benches). If I were a pagan, I'd worship here for the sea, the wind, and the chilling view. Notice how the land steps in sloppy slabs down to the sea. When saturated with water, the slabs of clay that make up the land here get slick, and entire chunks can slide.

Hike down to the foamy beach (where you can pick up some flint, chalk, and wild thyme). While the wind at the top could drag a kite-flyer, the beach below can be ideal for sunbathing. Because Ærø is warmer and drier than the rest of Denmark, this island is home to plants and animals found nowhere else in the country. This southern exposure is the warmest area. Germany is dead ahead.

• *Backtrack 200 yards and follow the signs to* Tranderup. *On the way, you'll pass a lovely pond famous for its bell frogs and happy little duck houses.*

Popping out in Tranderup, you can backtrack (left) about 300 yards to get to the traditional **Vindeballe Kro**—*a handy inn for a stop if you're hungry or thirsty (35-60-kr lunches served daily July–mid-Aug 12:00–14:00, 130-225-kr dinners served daily year-round 18:00–21:00, tel. 62 52 16 13).*

If you're tired or if the weather is turning bad, you can shortcut from here back to **Ærøskøbing:** *Go down the lane across the street from the Vindeballe Kro, and you'll zip quickly downhill across the island to the dike just east of Borgnæs; turn right and retrace your steps back into town.*

But there's much more to see. To continue our pedal, head on into...

Tranderup: Still following signs for *Tranderup,* stay on Tranderupgade parallel to the big road through town. You'll pass a lovely farm and a potato stand. At the main road, turn right. At the Ærøskøbing turnoff (another chance to bail out and head home), side-trip 100 yards left to the big stone (commemorating the return of the island to Denmark from Germany in 1750) and a grand island panorama. Claus Clausen's rock (in the picnic area, next to WC) is a memorial to an extremely obscure pioneer who was born in Ærø, emigrated to America, and played a role in shaping the early history of Scandinavian Lutheranism in the US.

• *Return to the big road (continuing in direction: Marstal), pass through Olde, pedal past FAF (the local wheat farmers' co-op facility), and head toward Store Rise (STOH-reh REE-zuh), the next church spire in the distance. Think of medieval travelers using spires as navigational aids.*

Store Rise Prehistoric Tomb, Church, and Brewery: Thirty yards after the Stokkeby turnoff, follow the rough, tree-lined path on the right to the Langdysse (Long Dolmen) Tingstedet, just behind the church spire. This is a 6,000-year-old **dolmen,** an early Neolithic burial place. Though Ærø once had more than 200 of these prehistoric tombs, only 13 survive. The site is a raised mound the shape and length (about

100 feet) of a Viking ship, and archaeologists have found evidence that indicates a Viking ship may indeed have been burned and buried here.

Ting means assembly spot. Imagine a thousand years ago: Viking chiefs representing the island's various communities gathering here around their ancestors' tombs. For 6,000 years, this has been a holy spot. The stones were considered fertility stones. For centuries, locals in need of virility chipped off bits and took them home (the nicks in the rock nearest the information post are mine).

Tuck away your chip and carry on down the lane to the Store Rise **church.** Inside you'll find little ships hanging in the nave, a fine 12th-century altarpiece, a stick with offering bag and a ting-a-ling bell to wake those nodding off (right of altar), double seats (so worshippers can flip to face the pulpit during sermons), and Martin Luther in the stern keeping his Protestant hand on the rudder. The list in the church allows today's pastors to trace their pastoral lineage back to Doctor Luther himself. (The current pastor, Janet, is the first woman on the list.) The churchyard is circular—a reminder of how churchyards provided a last refuge for humble communities under attack. Can you find anyone buried in the graveyard whose name doesn't end in "-sen"?

Next follow the smell of hops (or the *Rise Bryggeri* signs) to Ærø's **brewery.** Located in a historic brewery 400 yards beyond the Store Rise church, it welcomes visitors with free samples of its various beers. The Ærø traditional brews are available in pilsner (including the popular walnut pilsner), light ale, dark ale, and a typical dark Irish-style stout. The Rise organic brews come in light ale, dark ale, and walnut (July-Aug daily 11:00-15:00; Sept Tue-Sat 11:00-15:00, closed Sun-Mon, closed Oct-June; tel. 62 52 11 32, www.risebryggeri.dk).

• *From here, climb back to the main road and continue (direction: Marstal) on your way back home to Ærøskøbing. The three 330-foot-high modern windmills on your right are communally owned and, as they are a nonpolluting source of energy, state-subsidized. At Dunkær (3 miles from Ærøskøbing), take the small road, signed* Lille Rise, *past the topless windmill. Except for the Lille Rise, it's all downhill from here, as you coast past great sea views back home to Ærøskøbing.*

Huts at the Sunset Beach: Still rolling? Bike past the campground along the Urehoved beach (*strand* in Danish) for a look at

the coziest little beach houses you'll never see back in the "big is beautiful" US. This is Europe, where small is beautiful, and the concept of sustainability is neither new nor subversive. (For more details, see "Beach Bungalow Sunset Stroll," below.)

RAINY-DAY OPTIONS

Ærø is disappointing but not unworkable in bad weather. In addition to the museums listed earlier, you could check out the evening options under "Nightlife in Ærøskøbing" (later), many of which are good in bad weather. Or hop on the free bus to Marstal to visit its maritime museum.

Marstal Maritime Museum (Marstal Søfartsmuseum)

To learn more about the island's seafaring history, visit this fine museum in the dreary town of Marstal. You'll see plenty of model ships, nautical paintings (including several scenes by acclaimed painter Carl Rasmussen), an original ship's galley, a re-created wheelhouse (with steering and navigation equipment), a collection of exotic goods brought back from faraway lands, and a children's area with a climbable mast. Designed by and for sailors, the museum presents a warts-and-all view of the hardships of the seafaring life, rather than romanticizing it.

Cost and Hours: 60 kr; June-Aug daily 9:00-17:00; May and Sept-Oct daily 10:00-16:00; shorter hours and closed Sun off-season; Prinsensgade 1, tel. 62 53 23 31, www.marmus.dk.

Getting There: Ride the free bus #790 from Ærøskøbing (see page 148) all the way to the harbor in Marstal, where you'll find the museum. It's about a 20-minute trip.

Nightlife in Ærøskøbing

These activities are best done in the evening, after a day of biking around the island.

▲▲Beach Bungalow Sunset Stroll

At sunset, stroll to Ærøskøbing's sand beach. Facing the ferry dock, go left, following the harbor. Upon leaving the town, you'll pass the Netto supermarket (convenient for picking up snacks, beer, or wine), a mini-golf course, and a children's playground. In the rosy

CENTRAL DENMARK

distance, past a wavy wheat field, is Vestre Strandvejen— a row of tiny, Monopoly-like huts facing the sunset. These beach escapes are privately owned on land rented from the town (no overnight use, WCs at each end). Each is different, but all are stained with merry memories of locals enjoying themselves Danish-style. Bring a beverage or picnic. It's perfectly acceptable—and very Danish—to borrow a porch for your sunset sit. From here, it's a fine walk out to the end of Urehoved (as this spit of land is called).

Town Walk with Night Watchman

On many summer evenings, the night watchman leads visitors through town. It's a fine time to be outside, meeting other travelers (ask at the TI for details).

Cinema

The cute little 30-seat Andelen Theater (in the Andelen Guesthouse—a former grain warehouse) plays movies in their original language (Danish subtitles, closed Mon and in July—when it hosts a jazz festival, new titles begin every Tue). It's run in a charming community-service kind of way. The management has installed heat, so tickets no longer come with a blanket (near Torvet Square at Søndergade 28A, tel. 62 52 17 11).

Bowling

Ærø-Bowl is a six-lane alley in a modern athletic club at the edge of town. In this old-fashioned town, where no modern construction is allowed in the higgledy-piggledy center, this hip facility is a magnet for young people. One local told me, "I've never seen anyone come out of there without a smile" (hot dogs, junk food, arcade games, kids on dates; Tue-Thu 16:00-22:00, later on Fri-Sat, shorter hours off-season, closed Sun-Mon, Statene 42A, tel. 62 52 23 06, www.arrebowl.dk).

Pub

Ærøskøbing's one bar, the Arrebo Pub, attracts a young crowd. It is *the* place for live music but serves no food (at the bottom of Vestergade, near ferry landing).

Sleep Code

Abbreviations   **(6 kr = about $1, country code: 45)**
S = Single, **D** = Double/Twin, **T** = Triple, **Q** = Quad, **b** = bathroom
Price Rankings
  $$$ Higher Priced—Most rooms 1,000 kr or more.
   $$ Moderately Priced—Most rooms 450-1,000 kr.
    $ Lower Priced—Most rooms 450 kr or less.
Unless otherwise noted, English is spoken, credit cards are accepted (with a 4 percent surcharge), breakfast is included, and Wi-Fi is generally free. Prices change; verify current rates online or by email. For the best prices, always book directly with the hotel.

Sleeping in Ærøskøbing

The accommodations scene here is boom or bust. Summer weekends and all of July are packed (book long in advance). It's absolutely dead in the winter. These places come with family-run personality, and each is an easy stroll from the ferry landing.

IN ÆRØSKØBING

$$$ Hotel Ærøhus is a big and sprawling last resort, with 33 uninspired rooms. It's impersonal and pretty tired, but in a small and popular town without a lot of rooms, it's worth knowing about (S-600 kr, Sb-990 kr, D-800 kr, Db-1,250 kr, Wi-Fi, bike rentals-75 kr/day, Vestergade 38, tel. 62 52 10 03, www.aeroehus.dk, mail@aeroehus.dk).

   $$ Pension Vestergade is your best home away from home in Ærøskøbing. It's lovingly run by Susanna Greve and her daughters, Henrietta and Celia. Susanna, who's fun to talk with and is always ready with a cup of tea, has a wealth of knowledge about the town's history and takes good care of her guests. Built in 1784 for a sea captain's daughter, this creaky, sagging, and venerable eight-room place—with each room named for its particular color scheme—is on the main

street in the town center. Picnic in the back garden and get to know Tillie, the live-in dog. Reserve well in advance (singles-750 kr year-round; doubles fluctuate—in spring, July, and fall: D-990 kr; winter: D-790 kr; cash only, cuddly hot-water bottles, shared bath-

rooms, Wi-Fi, Vestergade 44, tel. 62 52 22 98, www.vestergade44.
com, pensionvestergade44@post.tele.dk).

$$ På Torvet ("On the Square") is a cheery hotel/café/bou-
tique that's breathing new life into the main square. Owners Gun-
nar and Lili rent 10 modern, charming apartments, each with pri-
vate kitchen and bathroom (Db-975 kr for first night, 800 kr for
succeeding nights, 200-kr linen and cleaning fee, Wi-Fi, Torvet
7, tel. 62 52 40 50, www.paatorvet.dk, info@paatorvet.dk). The
recommended café offers seating inside and out on Torvet Square
(see "Eating in Ærøskøbing," later), plus wine and specialty foods
for purchase; the boutique sells women's clothing from Italy and
France; and the grand piano in the dining area welcomes anyone to
tickle its ivories.

$$ Andelen Guesthouse, run by Englishman Adam and his
Danish wife, Anne, is brimming with a funky nautical charm. An
old warehouse that's been converted into a hotel, it has five guest
rooms that share two bathrooms (S-600 kr, D-700 kr, T-900 kr,
breakfast-75 kr, Wi-Fi, free entry to downstairs movie theater,
guest bikes-75 kr/day, Søndergade 28A, mobile 61 26 75 11, www.
andelenguesthouse.com, info@andelenguesthouse.com).

$$ Hotel Aroma offers four bright, cheery, and modern
rooms—two standard doubles and two large quads with kitch-
ens—above the recommended Café Aroma (D-795 kr, Q-995 kr,
100 kr less in off-season, shared bathroom, laundry facilities, roof
terrace, Wi-Fi, on Vestergade, just up the street from the ferry
dock, tel. 62 52 40 02, mobile 40 40 26 84, www.cafe-aroma.dk).

$$ Det Lille Hotel is a former 19th-century captain's home
with six tidy but well-worn rooms (June-Sept: S-750 kr, D-950 kr;
Oct-May: S-650 kr, D-850 kr; extra bed-265 kr, Wi-Fi, Smedegade 33, tel. 62 52 23 00, www.det-lille-hotel.dk, mail@det-lille-
hotel.dk).

OUTSIDE OF ÆRØSKØBING

$$ Vindeballe Kro, about three miles from Ærøskøbing, is a tra-
ditional inn in Vindeballe at the island's central crossroads. Maria
and Steen rent 10 straightforward, well-kept rooms (S-500 kr,
D-700 kr; for location, see map on page 156; tel. 62 52 16 13, www.
vindeballekro.dk, mail@vindeballekro.dk). They also have a res-
taurant (see page 159).

$ Ærø Campground is set on a fine beach a few minutes' walk
out of town. This three-star campground offers a lodge with a fire-
place, campsites, cabins, and bike rental (camping-80 kr/person
plus 110-kr camping pass, 4- to 6-bed cabins-150-300 kr plus per-
person fee, 300-kr cleaning fee, open May-Sept; facing the water,
follow waterfront to the left; tel. 62 52 18 54, www.aeroecamp.dk,
info@aeroecamp.dk).

Eating in Ærøskøbing

RESTAURANTS

Ærøskøbing has a handful of charming and hardworking little eateries. Business is so light that chefs and owners come and go constantly, making it tough to predict the best value for the coming year. As each place has a distinct flavor, I'd spend 20 minutes enjoying the warm evening light and do a strolling survey before making your choice. While there are some simple burger-type joints, I've listed only the serious kitchens. Note that everything closes by 21:00—don't wait too late to eat (if you'll be taking a later ferry from Svendborg to Ærø, either eat before your boat trip or call ahead to reserve a place...otherwise you're out of luck). During the winter, some of my recommended restaurants take turns staying open, so you should be able to find a decent place to eat (ask what's open at the TI).

Restaurant Mumm is where visiting yachters go for a good and classy meal. Portions are huge, and on balmy days their garden terrace out back is a hit. Call ahead to reserve (185-kr daily specials, 80-kr starters, 150-250-kr main courses, daily 18:00-21:00, shorter hours off-season, near Torvet Square at Søndergade 12, tel. 62 52 12 12, www.restaurantmumm.com).

På Torvet Café, right on Torvet Square, offers a simple yet tasty menu of sandwiches and burgers, along with their filling signature dish, the Night Watchman's Plate, featuring smoked salmon, chicken, cheese, ham, and *panna cotta*. Dine in the cozy café or out on the square (90-100-kr lunches, 100-150-kr dinners, daily May-mid-Sept 12:00-15:30 & 17:30-20:00, shorter hours off-season, tel. 62 52 40 50).

Café Aroma, an inexpensive Danish café that feels like a rustic old diner, has a big front porch filled with tables and good, reasonably priced entrées, sandwiches, and burgers for 70-200 kr. Ask about the daily special, which will save you money and is not listed on the confusing menu. Order at the bar (daily mid-April-mid-Sept 11:00-20:00, closed mid-Sept-mid-April, on Vestergade, just up from the ferry dock, tel. 62 52 40 02). They also run a delicious ice-cream shop and a high-quality, pricey fish restaurant next door (aptly named **Fiskerestaurant;** open July only).

Ærøskøbing Røgeri serves wonderful smoked-fish meals on paper plates and picnic tables. Facing the harbor, it's great for a light meal (50-80 kr for fish with potato salad and bread). Eat there or find a pleasant picnic site at the beach or at the park behind the fish house. A smoked-fish dinner and a couple of cold Carlsbergs or Ærø brews are a well-earned reward after a long bike ride (daily mid-April-Sept 11:00-19:00, July-Aug until 21:00, Havnen 15, tel. 62 52 40 07).

Addi's Brasserie serves fresh seafood and meat dishes. Eat in the main dining room among portraits of Danish royalty, or in the larger side room (daily lunch and dinner specials, 50-85-kr lunch main courses, 180-200-kr dinner main courses, daily 11:30-15:00 & 18:00-21:00, shorter hours off-season, across street from Pension Vestergade, Vestergade 39, tel. 62 52 21 43).

Landbogården, with family-friendly indoor and outdoor dining, serves hearty fish, meat, and chicken dishes just like a Danish grandmother would make them (100-180-kr main courses, daily June-mid-Aug 17:30-21:30, closed off-season, near the top of Vestergade, tel. 30 84 49 06).

Hotel Restaurants: Two hotels in town have dining rooms with good but expensive food; I'd eat at the restaurants I've listed above, unless they're closed. But in a pinch, try these: **Det Lille Hotel** serves meals in an inviting dining room or garden (200-kr daily specials, 85-100-kr starters, 160-250-kr main courses, daily 12:00-21:00 but closed off-season, Smedegade 33, tel. 62 52 23 00, Klaus cooks with attitude). **Hotel Ærøhus** is a last resort, serving Danish fare in a sprawling complex of dining rooms, big and small (115-kr starters, 225-kr main courses, open daily but closed in off-season, on Vestergade, tel. 62 52 10 03).

SNACKS, PICNICS, AND DESSERT
Here are some places for lighter fare.

Market for Local Specialties: Run by volunteers dedicated to a healthier Ærø, **Den Gamle Købmandsgaard** ("The Old Merchants' Court") on Torvet Square sells a remarkable selection of mostly locally sourced and produced foods, including meat, sausage, salami, bread, fruit, honey, jam, chocolate, beer—even rum. Grab a seat in their café for lunch, cake, or pie (Mon-Fri 10:00-16:30, Sat 10:00-14:00, closed Sun, Torvet 5, tel. 20 24 30 07).

Grocery: The **Netto** supermarket has picnic fixings and drinks, including chilled beer and wine—handy for walks to the little huts on the beach at sunset (daily 8:00-22:00, kitty-corner from ferry dock).

Bakery: Ærøskøbing's old-school **H. E. Hansen** bakery sells homemade bread, cheese, yogurt, and tasty pastries (Tue-Fri 7:00-

17:00, Sat-Sun 7:00-14:00, closed Mon, top of Vestergade).

Ice Cream: The ice-cream shop at Café Aroma, **Ærø Ismageri**, serves good, flavorful ice cream—try gooseberry beer (made from Ærø stout—way better than it sounds), or the local favorite, the "Ærø Special"—walnut ice cream with maple syrup (daily July-mid-Aug 9:00-23:00, shorter hours off-season, closed Sept-mid-April, just up from the ferry dock).

Ærøskøbing Connections

ÆRØ-SVENDBORG FERRY

The ferry ride between **Svendborg,** with connections to Copenhagen, and **Ærøskøbing,** on the island of Ærø, is a relaxing 1.25-hour crossing. Just get on, and the crew will come to you for payment. American chip-and-PIN credit cards work (5-kr surcharge), or you can pay cash (199-kr round-trip per person, 437-kr round-trip per car—not including driver/passengers, you'll save a little money with round-trip tickets, ferry not covered by or discounted with rail pass). You can leave the island via any of the three different Ærø ferry routes.

The ferry always has room for walk-ons, but drivers should reserve a spot in advance, especially on weekends and in summer. During these busy times, reserve as far ahead as you can—ideally at least a week in advance. Car reservations by phone or email are free and easy—simply give your name and license-plate number. If you don't know your license number (i.e., you're reserving from home and haven't yet picked up your rental car), try asking nicely if they're willing to just take your name. They may want you to call them with the number when you pick up your car, but if that's not practical, you can usually just tell the attendant your name before you drive onto the boat. Ferries depart daily in summer (roughly 10/day in each direction). Call or look online for the schedule (office open Mon-Fri 8:00-15:30, Sat-Sun 9:00-15:00, tel. 62 52 40 00, www.aeroe-ferry.dk, info@aeroe-ferry.dk).

Drivers with reservations just drive on (be sure to get into the *med* reservations line). If you won't use your car in Ærø, park it in Svendborg (big, safe lot two blocks in from ferry landing, or at the far end of the harbor near the Bendix fish shop). On Ærø, parking is free.

Trains Connecting with Ærø-Svendborg Ferry

The train from **Odense** dead-ends at the Svendborg harbor (2/hour Mon-Sat, hourly on Sun, 45 minutes; don't get off at Svendborg Vest Station—wait until you get to the end of the line, called simply "Svendborg").

Arriving in Svendborg: It takes about 10 minutes to walk from the station to the dock (5 minutes if you walk briskly). Don't dawdle—the boat leaves stubbornly on time, even if trains are running late. I recommend taking a train from Odense that arrives about 30 minutes before your ferry departure to give yourself time to absorb delays and find your way. If you're cutting it close, be ready to hop off the train and walk swiftly.

To get from the Svendborg train station to the dock, turn left after exiting the train, following the sidewalk between the tracks and the station, then take a left (across the tracks) at the first street, Brogade. Head a block downhill to the harbor, make a right, and the ferry dock is ahead, across from Hotel Ærø. If you arrive early, you can head to the waiting room in the little blue building across the street from the hotel. There are several carry-out restaurants along Brogade, and a few hotels overlooking the ferry line have restaurants.

Departing from Svendborg: All Svendborg trains go to Odense (where you can connect to Copenhagen or Aarhus). A train tends to leave shortly after the ferry arrives (tight connections for hurried commuters). To reach the train from the Svendborg ferry dock, pass Hotel Ærø and continue a block along the waiting lane for the ferry, turn left and go up Brogade one block, then take a right and follow the sidewalk between the tracks and the train station. Look for a train signed *Odense* waiting on the single track.

Odense

Founded in A.D. 988 and named after Odin (the Nordic Zeus), Odense is the main city of the big island of Funen (Fyn in Danish) and the birthplace of storyteller Hans Christian Andersen (whom the Danes call simply H. C., pronounced "hoe see"). Although the author was born here in poverty and left at the tender age of 14 to pursue a career in the theater scene of Copenhagen, H. C. is Odense's favorite son—you'll find his name and image all over town. He once said, "Perhaps Odense will one day become famous because of me." Today, Odense (OH-then-za) is one of Denmark's most popular tourist destinations.

Orientation to Odense

As Denmark's third-largest city, with 170,000 people, Odense is big and industrial. But its old center, tidy and neatly urbanized, retains some pockets of the fairy-tale charm it had in the days of

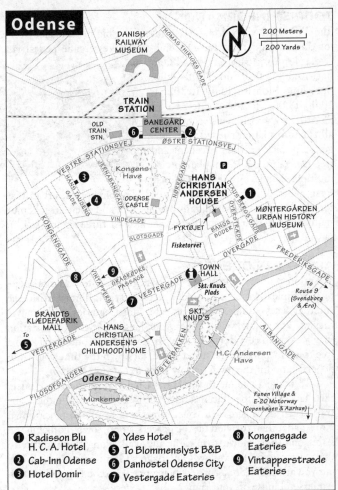

Odense

DANISH RAILWAY MUSEUM

THOMAS THIRGES GADE

200 Meters
200 Yards

TRAIN STATION

OLD TRAIN STN.
6 BANEGÅRD CENTER **2**

VESTRE STATIONSVEJ
ØSTRE STATIONSVEJ

Kongens Have

3
HANS CHRISTIAN ANDERSEN HOUSE **1**

NØRREGADE
JERNBANEGADE
HANS TAUSENS GADE

4
ODENSE CASTLE

MØNTERGÅRDEN URBAN HISTORY MUSEUM

CLAUS BERGS GADE
OVERGADE
BANGS BODER

VINDEGADE

FYRTØJET

SLOTSGADE

Fisketorvet

OVERGADE

FREDERIKSGADE

KONGENSGADE

9
GRÅBRØDRE PASSAGE

TOWN HALL

8
VINTAPPERSTR.

VESTERGADE

Skt. Knuds Plads

To Route 9 (Svendborg & Ærø)

7

SKT. KNUD'S

ALBANIGADE

BRANDTS KLÆDEFABRIK MALL

5
To VESTERGADE

HANS CHRISTIAN ANDERSEN'S CHILDHOOD HOME

KLOSTERBAKKEN

H.C. Andersen Have

FILOSOFGANGEN

Odense Å

Munkemose

To Funen Village & E-20 Motorway (Copenhagen & Aarhus)

1 Radisson Blu H. C. A. Hotel
2 Cab-Inn Odense
3 Hotel Domir
4 Ydes Hotel
5 To Blommenslyst B&B
6 Danhostel Odense City
7 Vestergade Eateries
8 Kongensgade Eateries
9 Vintapperstræde Eateries

H. C. Everything is within easy walking distance, except for the open-air folk museum.

The train station sits at the north end of the town center. A few blocks south runs the main pedestrian shopping boulevard, Vestergade. Near the eastern end of this drag, and a couple of blocks up, is a tight tangle of atmospheric old lanes, where you'll find the Hans Christian Andersen House and Møntergården, Odense's urban history museum.

TOURIST INFORMATION

The TI is in the Town Hall (Rådhuset), the big brick palace over-looking the square at the east end of the Vestergade pedestrian street (July-Aug Mon-Fri 9:30-18:00, Sat 10:00-15:00, Sun 11:00-14:00; Sept-June Mon-Fri 10:00-16:30, Sat 10:00-13:00, closed Sun; tel. 63 75 75 20, www.visitodense.com). For all the information needed for a lon-ger stop, pick up their excellent and free *Odense* guide. If you plan to visit multiple sights, consider the **Odense**

Pass, which covers the museum at H. C.'s birthplace, urban his-tory museum, art museum, railway museum, and open-air folk mu-seum. It saves you money if you visit at least three sights (169 kr, buy at TI).

ARRIVAL IN ODENSE

The train station is located in the Bånegard Center, a large shop-ping complex, which also holds the bus station, library (with free Internet access), Galaxy Internet café, shops, eateries, and a movie theater. For a quick visit, check your luggage at the train station (pay lockers in corridor next to DSB Resjebureau office), pick up a free town map inside the ticket office, jot down the time your train departs, and hit the town (follow signs to *Odense Centrum*).

To make a beeline to the **Hans Christian Andersen House,** turn left out of the station and walk to the corner (at the Cab-Inn). Turn right across the busy street and head one block down Nørregade, then turn left (at the grocery store) down Skulkenborg. After one short block, turn right and walk along the highway to the crosswalk by the yellow Oluf Bagers Gård; crossing here will put you at the start of a cute cobbled zone with the Hans Christian Andersen House on your right.

To get to the **TI,** turn right out of the station, cross the busy road, then cut through the Kongens Have (King's Garden) park and head down Jernabanegade. When you come to Vestergade, take a left and follow this fine pedestrian street 100 yards to the TI.

Sights in Odense

Note that some of Odense's museums charge higher admission (about 15-20 kr extra) during school holidays.

▲▲▲Hans Christian Andersen House

To celebrate Hans Christian Andersen's 100th birthday in 1904, the city founded this museum in the house where he was born.

Today the humble (and rebuilt) house is the corner of an expansive, high-tech museum packed with mementos from the writer's life—and hordes of children and tourists. You could spend several delightful hours here getting into his life story and work. It's fun if you like the man and his tales.

Cost and Hours: 95 kr (30 percent discount if you have a ticket for Fyrtøjet or Møntergården), free for kids under 18, daily 10:00-16:00, July-late-Aug until 17:00, Bangs Boder 29, tel. 65 51 46 01, www.museum.odense.dk.

Information: Everything is well described in English. Admission includes a nice guidebook. For more on the author, see the sidebars on pages 48 and 65.

Performances: The garden fairy-tale theater—with pleasing vignettes—thrills kids daily in July and early August in the museum garden generally at 11:00, 13:00, and 15:00, weather permitting (30-minute show in Danish, but fun regardless of language).

Eating: The café next door, with seating indoors and out, sells sandwiches, burgers, and cakes (90-120 kr).

Visiting the Museum: At the ticket desk you'll get a guidebook with a floor plan; follow the one-way route through the collection. Touchscreens invite you to delve deeper into specific topics, and headsets and benches throughout let you listen to a selection of fairy tales.

You'll kick things off with **"The Age"** exhibit, which considers the era in which Andersen lived (1805-1875), putting the author in his historical context—the time of Abraham Lincoln, Charles Darwin, and Karl Marx. **"The Man"** paints a portrait of this quirky individual, who was extremely tall and gangly, with a big nose... an ugly duckling, indeed. He spent hours in the mirror perfecting an expression of wry cleverness for photographic portraits (several of which are displayed). You'll learn how bad teeth caused H. C. a lifetime of pain, and how this deeply sensitive, introspective fellow worried about his family history of mental illness even as he astounded the world with his exuberant creativity. **"The Art"** demonstrates that H. C. was as talented with visual arts as the written word; this darkened room shows off intricate paper cutouts he created (some of which illustrated his tales) and sketches from his travels.

"**The Life**" is a circular exhibit (turn left and proceed counterclockwise, following the footprints) with a step-by-step biography of the writer, accompanied by artifacts from his life. This is arranged around a central Memorial Hall slathered with eight frescoes depicting scenes from H. C.'s past, under a dome filled with natural light. Notice that as the story of his life—starting with a tearful hug to his mother on his departure from Odense at age 14—progresses, the scenes change from daylight to sunset to evening. Under the dome are items relating to H. C.'s fervent crush on the opera singer Jenny Lind: a love letter that he wrote to her and the champagne glass she used to toast him as her

"brother" (a painful rebuff that broke H. C.'s heart—he kept the glass his entire life as a reminder).

Continuing around the biographical section, you'll pass a movie theater with a 13-minute introductory **film** about H. C. (plays every 15 minutes, alternates between Danish and English).

Down the stairs in the basement is "**Transformations**," a curious yet skippable *Little Mermaid*-inspired light installation that is supposed to respond to visitors' movements. Meh.

Near the top of the steps, you can enter H. C.'s **birth house,** with descriptions of the people his family lived with and replicas of

the type of furniture that likely filled these humble rooms. Later on, the author was highly ashamed of having been born in such a modest house in a very poor neighborhood—the theme of poverty turns up frequently in his works.

Near the end of the exhibit is a recreation of H. C.'s **study** from his apartment in Nyhavn, Copenhagen. You'll exit through "**The Works**," a library of Andersen's books from around the world (his tales have been translated into nearly 150 languages). The museum **gift shop** is full of mobiles, cut-paper models, and English versions of Andersen's fairy tales.

Another H. C. House: The writer's childhood home (with a small exhibit of its own) is a few blocks southwest of here, but it's skippable because the main museum here is so excellent and comprehensive.

Fyrtøjet ("Tinderbox")

Next door to the H. C. Andersen House is this privately run, modern, and fun hands-on center for children based on works by H. C. The centerpiece is Fairytale Land, with giant props and sets inspired by the author's tales. Kids can dress up in costumes and get their faces painted at the "magical wardrobe," act out a fairy tale, and do arts and crafts in the "atelier." Ask about performances (generally daily at 12:00 and 14:00; some are in Danish only, but others are done without dialogue).

Cost and Hours: 80 kr for ages 3-69 (free to other ages), 30 percent discount if you have a ticket for the H. C. Andersen House or Møntergården; July-mid-Aug daily 10:00-17:00; off-season Fri-Sun 10:00-16:00, closed Mon-Thu; Hans Jensens Stræde 21, tel. 66 14 44 11, www.museum.odense.dk. On school holidays, there are more activities, the museum is open later (until 17:00), and you'll pay 15 kr extra.

▲Møntergården (Urban History Museum)

This well-presented museum, three short blocks from the H. C. Andersen House, fills several medieval buildings with exhibits on the history of Odense. You'll time-travel from prehistoric times (lots of arrow, spear, and ax heads) through to 1660, when the king stripped the town of its independent status. The main exhibit, "Life of the City," fills a stately 17th-century, red house (Falk Gøyes Gård) with a high-tech, well-presented exhibit about Odense in medieval and Renaissance times, covering historical events as well as glimpses of everyday life. Wedged along the side of this building is a surviving medieval lane; at the far end are four miniscule houses that the city used to house widows and orphaned students who couldn't afford to provide for themselves. It's fascinating to squeeze into these humble interiors and imagine that people lived in these almshouses through 1955 (open only in summer, but at other times you can ask at the ticket desk to have them unlocked). A new museum building with expanded exhibits may be open by the time you visit.

Cost and Hours: 50 kr, 30 percent discount if you have a ticket for the H. C. Andersen House or Fyrtøjet; July-Aug daily 10:00-17:00; Sept-June Tue-Sun 10:00-16:00, closed Mon; Overgade 48, tel. 65 51 46 01, www.museum.odense.dk.

▲Danish Railway Museum (Danmarks Jernbanemuseum)

Conveniently (and appropriately) located directly behind the train station,

this is an ideal place to kill time while waiting for a train—and is worth a look for anyone who enjoys seeing old locomotives and train cars. Here at Denmark's biggest (and only official) rail museum, the huge roundhouse is filled with classic trains, while upstairs you'll walk past long display cases of model trains and enjoy good views down onto the trains. The information is in English, and there are lots of children's activities.

Cost and Hours: 60 kr, more during special exhibits, daily 10:00-16:00; Dannebrogsgade 24—just exit behind the station, near track 7/8, and cross the street; tel. 66 13 66 30, www. railmuseum.dk.

▲Funen Village/Den Fynske Landsby Open-Air Museum

The sleepy gathering of 26 old buildings located about two miles out of town preserves the 18th-century culture of this region. There are no explanations in the buildings because many school groups who visit play guessing games. Buy the guidebook to make your visit meaningful.

Cost and Hours: 85 kr in summer, 60 kr off-season; July-mid-Aug daily 10:00-18:00; April-June and mid-Aug-late Oct Tue-Sun 10:00-17:00, closed Mon; closed late Oct-March; bus #110 or #111 from Odense Station, or take train to Fruens Bøge Station and walk 15 minutes; tel. 65 51 46 01, www.museum.odense.dk.

Sleeping in Odense

Demand (and prices) are higher in Odense on weekdays and in winter; in summer and on weekends, you can often get a better deal.

$$$ Radisson Blu H. C. A. Hotel is big, comfortable, and impersonal, with 145 rooms a block from the Hans Christian Andersen House. It's older but nicely updated, and offers great rates every day through the summer (Sb-795-995 kr, Db-895-1,195 kr, elevator, guest computer, Wi-Fi, Claus Bergs Gade 7, tel. 66 14 78 00, www.radissonblu.com/hotel-odense, hcandersen@radissonblu. com).

$$ Cab-Inn Odense brings its no-frills minimalist economy to town, with 201 simple, comfy, and modern rooms (economy Sb-495 kr, Db-625 kr; standard Sb-545 kr, Db-675 kr; larger "Commodore" Sb-575 kr, Db-705 kr; biggest "Captains Class" Sb-675 kr, Db-805 kr; breakfast-70 kr, elevator, guest computer, Wi-Fi, parking for small cars only-80 kr/day, next to the station at Østre Stationsvej 7-9, tel. 63 14 57 00, www.cabinn.com, odense@cabinn. com). For more about this chain, see page 103.

$$ Hotel Domir has 35 tidy, basic, stylish little rooms along its tiny halls. It's located on a quiet side street just a few minutes from the train station and features extra soundproofing (Sb-575-615 kr, twin Db-650-745 kr, double bed for 100 kr more, Tb-800-995 kr, price depends on demand, elevator, guest computer, Wi-Fi, limited parking-50-100 kr/day, Hans Tausensgade 19, tel. 66 12 14 27, www.domir.dk, booking@domir.dk). They also run **Ydes Hotel,** just down the street, with industrial and metallic simplicity (about 50-70 kr cheaper).

$$ Blommenslyst B&B rents four rooms in two private guesthouses just outside Odense (Sb-350 kr, Db-480 kr, breakfast-70 kr, 10-minute drive from town center, Ravnebjerggyden 31, tel. 65 96 81 88, www.blommenslyst.dk, ingvartsen-speth@post.tele.dk, Marethe and Poul Erik Speth).

Hostel: **$ Danhostel Odense City** is a huge, efficient hostel towering above the train station, with 140 beds in 4- and 6-bed rooms with baths, plus private rooms. "Better" rooms have "better beds and a TV"; the room prices listed here reflect standard/better rooms (dorm bed-250 kr, Sb-450/500 kr, Db-620/670 kr, sheets-60 kr, breakfast-70 kr—it can add up, elevator, pay guest computer, Wi-Fi, laundry, reception open 8:00-12:00 & 16:00-20:00 but self-service check-in kiosk at other times, Østre Stationsvej 31, tel. 63 11 04 25, odensedanhostel.dk, info@cityhostel.dk).

Eating in Odense

If you're in town for just a short stopover to visit the Hans Christian Andersen House, consider the café at the museum for lunch. Otherwise, Odense's main pedestrian shopping streets, **Vestergade** and **Kongensgade,** offer the best atmosphere and most options for lunch and dinner.

Vintapperstræde is an alleyway full of restaurants just off Vestergade (look for the ornamental entryway). Choose from Danish, Mexican, Italian, and more. Study the menus posted outside each restaurant to decide, then grab a table inside or join the locals at an outdoor table.

Odense Connections

From Odense by Train to: Copenhagen (3/hour, 1.5 hours, some go direct to the airport), **Aarhus** (2/hour, 1.5 hours), **Billund/Legoland** (2/hour, 50-minute train to Vejle, then transfer to bus—see page 198; allow 2 hours total), **Svendborg/Ærø ferry** (2/hour on Mon-Sat, hourly on Sun, 45 minutes, to Svendborg dock; Ærø ferry—roughly 10/day, 1.25 hours), **Roskilde** (2/hour, 70 minutes).

ROUTE TIPS FOR DRIVERS

Aarhus or Billund to Ærø: Figure about two hours to drive from
Billund (or 2.5 hours from Aarhus) to Svendborg. The freeway
takes you over a bridge to the island of Funen (or *Fyn* in Danish);
from Odense, take the highway south to Svendborg.

Leave your car in Svendborg (at the convenient long-term
parking lot two blocks from the ferry dock or at the far end of the
harbor near the Bendix fish shop) and sail for Ærø (see page 167 for
ferry details). Cars need reservations but walk-on passengers don't.

Ærø to Copenhagen via Odense: From Svendborg, drive
north on Route 9, past Egeskov Castle, and on to Odense. To
visit the open-air folk museum just outside Odense (Den Fynske
Landsby), leave Route 9 just south of town at Højby, turning left
toward Dalum and the Odense campground (on Odensevej). Look
for *Den Fynske Landsby* signs (near the train tracks, south edge of
town). If you're going directly to the Hans Christian Andersen
House, follow the signs.

Continuing toward Copenhagen, you'll take the world's third-
longest suspension bridge (Storebælt Bridge, 235-kr toll, 12.5 miles
long). Follow signs marked *København* (Copenhagen). If you're following my three-week itinerary by car: When you get to Ringsted,
signs point you to Roskilde—aim toward the twin church spires
and follow signs for *Vikingskibene* (Viking ships). Otherwise, if
you're heading to Copenhagen or the airport, stay on the freeway,
following signs to *København C* or to *Dragør/Kastrup Airport*.

JUTLAND

Aarhus • Legoland • Jelling

Jutland (Jylland—pronounced "YEW-lan"—in Danish) is the part of Denmark that juts up from Germany. It's a land of windswept sandy beaches, inviting lakes, Lego toys, moated manor houses, and fortified old towns. In Aarhus, the lively and student-filled capital of Jutland, you can ogle the artwork in one of Denmark's best art museums, experience centuries-old Danish town life in its open-air folk museum, and meet a boggy prehistoric man. After you wander the pedestrian street, settle in for a drink along the canalside people zone. This region is particularly family-friendly. Make a pilgrimage to the most famous land in all of Jutland: the pint-sized kids' paradise, Legoland. The nearby village of Jelling is worth a quick stop to see the ancient rune stones known as "Denmark's birth certificate."

PLANNING YOUR TIME

Aarhus makes a natural stop for drivers connecting Kristiansand, Norway and Hirtshals, Denmark by ferry. Trains also link Aarhus to Hirtshals, as well as to points south, such as Odense and Copenhagen. Allow one day and an overnight to enjoy this busy port town.

Families will likely want a whole day at Legoland (near the town of Billund), while historians might consider a brief detour to Jelling, just 10 minutes off the main Billund-Vejle road. Both are best by car but doable by public transportation.

Aarhus

Aarhus (OAR-hoos, sometimes spelled Århus), Denmark's second-largest city, has a population of 310,000 and calls itself the
"World's Smallest Big City." I'd argue
it's more like the world's biggest little
town: easy to handle and easy to like.
Aarhus is Jutland's capital and cultural hub. Its Viking founders settled
here—where a river hit the sea—in
the eighth century, calling their town
Aros. Today, modern Aarhus bustles
with an important university, an in-
viting café-lined canal, a bursting-with-life pedestrian boulevard
(Strøget), a collection of top-notch museums (modern art, open-air
folk, and prehistory/ethnography), and an adorable "Latin Quarter" filled with people living very, very well. Aarhus, a pleasant
three-hour train ride from Copenhagen, is well worth a stop.

Orientation to Aarhus

Aarhus lines up along its tranquil canal—formerly a busy highway—called Åboulevarden, which runs through the middle of
town. The cathedral and lively Latin Quarter are directly north of
the canal, while the train station is about five blocks to the south
(along the main pedestrianized shopping street—the Strøget). The
main museums are scattered far and wide: The ARoS Art Museum
is at the western edge of downtown, the Den Gamle By open-air
folk museum is a bit farther to the northwest, and the Moesgård
Museum (prehistory and ethnography) is in the countryside far to
the south.

TOURIST INFORMATION

Someone on the Aarhus tourist board thinks a warm and personal
welcome is a waste of money, so the Aarhus TI is entirely virtual
outside of peak season. From June through September, however,
you will find shipping-container-type information booths parked
on the main square (Lille Torv), near the train station, and near the
bus station on Fredensgade. For the rest of the year, you can call the
TI or visit their website (tel. 87 31 50 10, www.visitaarhus.com).
Computer kiosks that access the TI website are set up in various
hotel lobbies around town. For more direct assistance, try asking
your hotelier or other helpful locals.

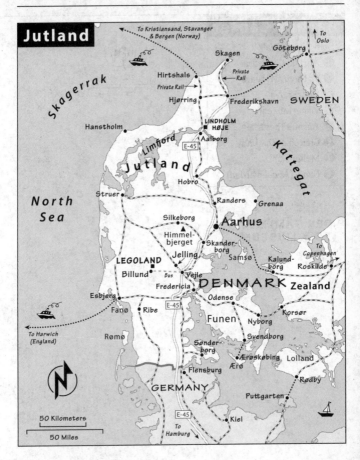

ARRIVAL IN AARHUS

At Aarhus' user-friendly **train** station, all tracks feed into a concourse, with ticket offices (*billetsalg*; open Mon-Fri 7:00-18:00, Sat-Sun 10:15-17:00) and a waiting room between tracks 2-3 and 4-5. A side entrance (marked *Bruun's Galleri*) takes you directly into a shopping mall; the other entrance (under the clock) leads into the blocky main terminal hall, with pay lockers, fast food, and ticket machines. Near the main doors, screens show departure times for upcoming city and regional buses.

To get into town, it's a pleasant 10-minute walk: Exit straight ahead, cross the street, and proceed up the wide, traffic-free shopping street known as the Strøget, which takes you directly to the canal, cathedral, and start of my "Aarhus Walk."

If arriving by **car** or **cruise ship,** see "Aarhus Connections" on page 196.

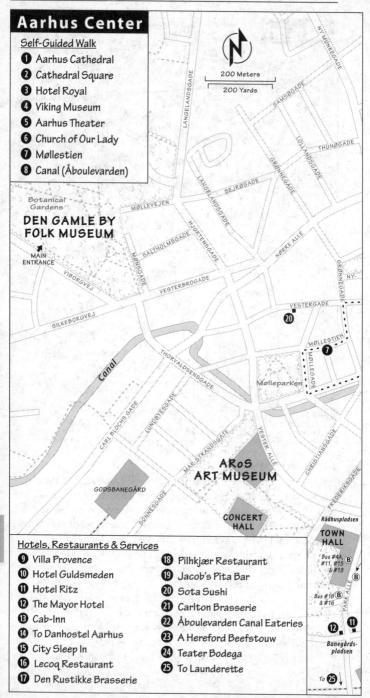

Aarhus Center

Self-Guided Walk

1. Aarhus Cathedral
2. Cathedral Square
3. Hotel Royal
4. Viking Museum
5. Aarhus Theater
6. Church of Our Lady
7. Møllestien
8. Canal (Åboulevarden)

200 Meters
200 Yards

Botanical Gardens

DEN GAMLE BY FOLK MUSEUM

MAIN ENTRANCE

AROS ART MUSEUM

Mølleparken

CONCERT HALL

GODSBANEGÅRD

Canal

TOWN HALL

Rådhuspladsen

Bus #4A, #11, #15 & #19

Bus #18 & #16

Banegårds- pladsen

To 25

Hotels, Restaurants & Services

9. Villa Provence
10. Hotel Guldsmeden
11. Hotel Ritz
12. The Mayor Hotel
13. Cab-Inn
14. To Danhostel Aarhus
15. City Sleep In
16. Lecoq Restaurant
17. Den Rustikke Brasserie
18. Pilhkjær Restaurant
19. Jacob's Pita Bar
20. Sota Sushi
21. Carlton Brasserie
22. Åboulevarden Canal Eateries
23. A Hereford Beefstouw
24. Teater Bodega
25. To Launderette

JUTLAND

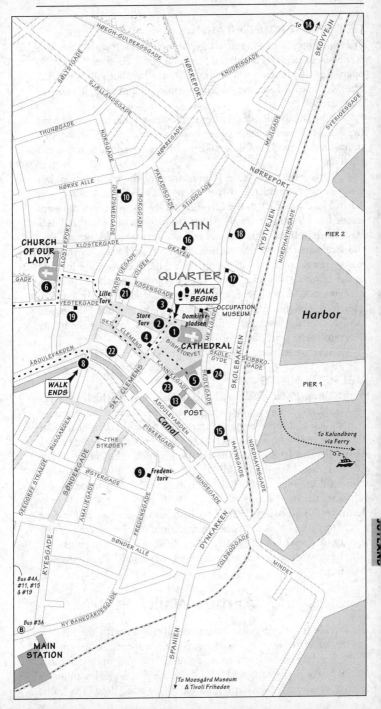

HØEGH-GULDBERGSGADE

SKOVVEJN

To ⑭

SØLYSTSGADE

SJÆLLANDSGADE

NØRREPORT

KNUDRISGADE

MEJLGADE

SVERIGESGADE

THUNØGADE

NØRGADE

NØRREGADE

PARADISGADE

STUDSGADE

NØRREPORT

KYSTVEJEN

NORDHAVNSGADE

NØRRE ALLÉ

GULDSMEDGADE

BORGGADE

⑩

PIER 2

KLOSTERPORT

KLOSTERGADE

LATIN

⑯

GRAVEN

⑱

CHURCH OF OUR LADY

GADE

✚ ⑥

Lille Torv

BADSTUEGADE

VOLDEN

ROSENSGADE

QUARTER

⑰

WALK BEGINS 👣

Occupation Museum

Harbor

VESTERGADE

⑲

⑳①

③

Store Torv

②

①

Domkirke-pladsen

SKOLE-GYDE

SKT. CLEMENS

④

BISPETORVET

CATHEDRAL

SKOLEBAKKEN

SKIBBROGADE

PIER 1

ÅBOULEVARDEN

⑧

㉒

KANNIKEGADE

SKOLEGADE

㉔

WALK ENDS

SKT. CLEMENS

㉓

⑤

To Kalundborg via Ferry

⑬

POST

ÅBOULEVARDEN

Canal

FISKERGADE

HAVNEGADE

⑮

NORDHAVNSGADE

BUSGÅRDEN

"THE STRØGET"

SØNDERGADE

ØSTERGADE

FREDENSGADE

MINDEGADE

⑨ Fredens-torv

SEEDORFF STRÆDE

AMALIEGADE

SØNDER ALLÉ

DYNKARKEN

RYESGADE

TOLDBODGADE

Bus #4A, #11, #15 & #19

MINDET

Bus #3A

NY BANEDARDESGADE

Ⓑ **MAIN STATION**

SPANIEN

JUTLAND

To Moesgård Museum & Tivoli Friheden

GETTING AROUND AARHUS

The sights mentioned in my self-guided walk, along with the ARoS Art Museum, are all within a 15-minute **walk**; the Den Gamle By open-air folk museum is a few minutes farther, but still walkable. The Moesgård Museum and Tivoli Friheden amusement park are best reached by bus.

You can buy **bus** tickets from the coin-op machines on board the bus (a 20-kr, 2-zone ticket covers any of my recommended sights, and is good for 2 hours). Bus drivers are friendly and speak English.

A few local buses leave from in front of the train station, but most depart around the corner, along Park Allé in front of the Town Hall. Bus #3A to the Den Gamle By open-air folk museum leaves from a stop across the street from the station. Other buses leave from in front of the Town Hall, about two blocks away: Cross the street in front of the station, turn left and walk to the first major corner, then turn right up Park Allé; the stops are in front of the blocky Town Hall (with the boxy tower, on the left). From here, buses #4A, #11, #15, and #19 go to Den Gamle By; bus #16 goes to the Tivoli Friheden amusement park; and bus #18 goes to the Moesgård Museum. To find your bus stop, look for the handy diagram at the start of the Strøget.

Taxis are easy to flag down but pricey (45-kr drop fee).

HELPFUL HINTS

Sightseeing Pass: Hotels sell the **Aarhus Card,** which provides small discounts on major sights and free entry to some minor sights, and includes public transportation. This can be a money-saver for busy sightseers (129 kr/24 hours, 179 kr/48 hours).

Festival: The 10-day **Aarhus Festival,** which takes place in late summer (Aug-Sept), fills the city's streets and venues with music, dance, food, kids' activities, and much more (www.aarhusfestuge.dk).

Laundry: An unstaffed, coin-op launderette *(mønt-vask)* is four short blocks south of the train station, on the square in front of St. Paul's Church (daily 7:00-21:00, bring lots of coins—30 kr to wash, about 25 kr to dry, 5 kr for soap, M.P. Bruunsgade 64).

Aarhus Walk

This quick little self-guided walk acquaints you with the historic center, covering everything of sightseeing importance except the three big museums (modern art, prehistory, and open-air folk). You'll begin at the cathedral, check out the modest sights in its vicinity, wander the cute Latin Quarter, take a stroll down the "most beautiful street" in Aarhus, and end at the canal (for walking route, see the map on page 180). After touring the impressive cathedral, the rest of the walk should take about an hour.

• *Start by touring Aarhus Cathedral.*

▲▲Aarhus Cathedral (Domkirke)

While Scandinavia's biggest church (330 feet long and tall) is typically stark-white inside, it also comes with some vivid decorations dating from before the Reformation.

Cost and Hours: Free entry; May-Sept Mon-Sat 9:30-16:00; Oct-April Mon-Sat 10:00-15:00; closed Sun except for services at 12:00 and 17:00; www.aarhus-domkirke.dk.

Visiting the Cathedral: The cathedral was finished in 1520 in all its Catholic glory. Imagine it with 55 side chapels, each dedicated to a different saint and wallpapered with colorful frescoes. Bad timing. Just 16 years later, in 1536, the Reformation hit and Protestants cleaned out the church—side altars gone, paintings whitewashed over—and added a pulpit mid-nave so parishioners could hear the sermon. The front pews were even turned away from the altar to face the pulpit (a problem for weddings today).

Ironically, that Lutheran whitewash protected the fine 16th-century Catholic art. When it was peeled back in the 1920s, the frescoes were found perfectly preserved. In 1998, the surrounding whitewash was redone, making the old original paintings, which have never been restored, pop. Noble tombs that once lined the floor (worn smooth by years of traffic) now decorate the walls. The fancy text-filled wall medallions are epitaphs, originally paired with tombs. Ships hang from the ceilings of many Danish churches (you'll find a fine example in the left transept)—in this nation of seafarers, there were invariably women praying for the safe return of their sailors.

JUTLAND

Step into the enclosed choir area at the front of the church. The main altarpiece, dating from 1479, features the 12 apostles flanking St. Clement (the patron saint of Aarhus and sailors—his symbol is the anchor), St. Anne, and John the Baptist. On top, Jesus is crowning Mary in heaven.

Head down the stairs to the apse area behind the altar. Find the model of the altarpiece, which demonstrates how the polyptych (many-paneled altarpiece) you just saw can be flipped to different scenes throughout the church year.

Also in this area, look for the fresco in the aisle (right of altar, facing windows) that shows a three-part universe: heaven, earth (at Mass), and—under the thick black line—purgatory...an ugly land with angels and devils fighting over souls. The kid on the gallows illustrates how the medieval Church threatened even little children with ugly damnation. Notice the angels trying desperately to save the damned. Just a little more money to the Church and...I...think...we...can...pull...Grandpa...OUT.

An earlier Romanesque church—just as huge—once stood on this spot. As you exit, notice the tiny, pointy-topped window in the back-right. It survives with its circa-1320 fresco from that earlier church. Even back then—when the city had a population of 1,000—the church seated 1,200. Imagine the entire community (and their dogs) assembled here to pray and worship their way through the darkness and uncertainty of medieval life.

• Then, standing at the cathedral door, survey the...

Cathedral Square

The long, triangular square is roughly the shape of the original Viking town from A.D. 770. Aarhus is the Viking word for "mouth of river." The river flows to your left to the beach, which—before modern land reclamation—was just behind the church. The green spire peeking over the buildings dead ahead is the Church of Our Lady (which we'll visit later on this walk). Fifty yards to the right, the nubile caryatids by local artist Hans Krull decorate the

entry to the **Hotel Royal** and town casino. (Krull's wildly decorated bar is just beyond, down the stairs at the corner.) Also nearby (around the corner from the cathedral) is the fine **Occupation Museum 1940-1945,** about the Danish resistance during World War II (described later, under "Sights in Aarhus").

• *Fifty yards to the left of the church (as you face the square), in the basement of the Nordea Bank, is the tiny...*

Viking Museum

When excavating the site for the bank building in 1960, remains of Viking Aarhus were uncovered. Today you can ride an escalator down to the little bank-sponsored museum showing a surviving bit of the town's original boardwalk *in situ* (where it was found), Viking artifacts, and a murder victim (missing his head)—all well-described in English.

Cost and Hours: Free, open bank hours: Mon-Fri 10:15-16:00, Thu until 17:00, closed Sat-Sun.

• *Leaving the bank, walk straight ahead along the substantial length of the cathedral (brides have plenty of time to reconsider things during their procession) to the fancy building opposite.*

Aarhus Theater

This ornate facade, with its flowery stained glass, is Danish Art Nouveau from around 1900. Under the tiny balcony is the town seal, featuring towers, the river, St. Clement with his anchor, and St. Paul with his sword. High above, on the roofline, crouches the devil. The local bishop made a stink when this "house of sin" was allowed to be built facing the cathedral. The theater builders had the

last say, finishing their structure with this smart-aleck devil triumphing (this was a hit with the secular, modern locals).

• *Return to the square in front of the cathedral.*

Latin Quarter

The higgledy-piggledy old town encompasses the six or eight square blocks in front of the cathedral and to the right. Latin was never

spoken here—the area was named in the 1960s after the cute, boutique-ish, and similarly touristy zone in Paris. Though Aarhus' canal strip is the new trendy spot, the Latin Quarter is still great for shopping, cafés, and strolling. Explore these streets: Volden (named for the rampart), Graven (moat), and Badstuegade

("Bath Street"). In the days when fires routinely decimated towns, bathhouses—with their open fires necessary to heat the water—

were located outside the walls. Back in the 15th century, finer peo-ple bathed monthly, while everyday riff-raff took their "Christmas bath" once a year.

• *Back at the far end of Cathedral Square, side-trip away from the cathedral to the green spire of the...*

Church of Our Lady (Vor Frue Kirke)

The smart brick building you see today is in the Dutch Renaissance style from the early 16th century, but this local "Notre-Dame" is the oldest church in town. After Christianity came to Viking Denmark in 965, a tiny wooden church was built here. Step down into the crypt of today's church (below the main altar). This evocative arcaded space (c. 1060) was originally an 11th-century stone rebuild of the first church (and only discovered in 1955). Four rune stones were also discovered on this site. Back upstairs, find the graphic crucifix, with its tangled thieves flanking Christ, which was carved and painted by a Lübeck artist in 1530. As at Aarhus Cathedral, the church's whitewashed walls are covered with fine epitaph medallions with family portraits.

Step through the low door behind the rear pew (on the right with your back to the altar) into the peaceful cloister. With the Reformation, this became a hospital. Today, it's a retirement home for lucky seniors.

Cost and Hours: Free; May-Sept Mon-Fri 10:00-16:00, Sat 10:00-14:00; Oct-April Mon-Fri 10:00-14:00, Sat 10:00-12:00; closed Sun year-round, www.aarhusvorfrue.dk.

• *Walk west on Vestergade to the next street, Grønnegade. Turn left, then take the next right onto...*

Møllestien

Locals call this quiet little cobbled lane the "most beautiful street in Aarhus." The small, pastel cottages—draped in climbing roses and hollyhock in summer—date from the 18th century. Notice the small mirrors on one of the windows. Known as "street spies," they allow people inside to inconspicuously watch what's going on outside.

• *At the end of the lane, head left toward the canal. The park on your*

right, **Mølleparken**, is a good spot for a picnic. The big, boxy building with the rainbow ring on top is the **ARoS Art Museum** (described below)—consider visiting it now, or backtrack here when the walk is over.

When you reach the canal, turn left and walk about four blocks toward the cathedral spire until you get to the concrete pedestrian bridge.

Canal (Åboulevarden)

You're standing on the site of the original Viking bridge. The open sea was dead ahead. A protective harbor was behind you. When the town was attacked, the bridge on this spot was raised, ships were tucked safely away, and townsmen stood here to defend their fleet. Given the choice, they'd let the town burn and save their ships.

In the 1930s, the Aarhus River was covered over to make a new road—an event marked by much celebration. In the 1980s, locals reconsidered the change, deciding that the road cut a boring, people-mean swath through the center of their town. They removed the road, artfully canalized the river, and created a trendy new people zone—the town's place to see and be seen. This strip of modern restaurants ensures the street stays as lively as possible even after the short summer.

• *Your walk is over. Retreating back up the canal takes you to **ARoS Art Museum**, then to **Den Gamle By** open-air folk museum. Following the canal ahead takes you past the best of the Aarhus canal zone. Crossing the canal bridge and going straight (with a one-block jog left) gets you to the Strøget pedestrian boulevard, which leads all the way to the train station (where you can catch a bus—either at the station or the Town Hall nearby—to Tivoli Friheden amusement park, the Den Gamle By open-air folk museum, or the Moesgård Museum). All of these sights are described in the next section.*

Sights in Aarhus

▲▲ARoS

The Aarhus Art Museum is a must-see sight, both for the building's architecture and for its knack for making cutting-edge art accessible and fun. Everything is described in English. Square and unassuming from the outside, the bright white interior—with its spiral staircase winding up the museum's eight floors—is surprising. The building has two sections, one for the exhibits and one for administration. The halves are divided by

Your rainbow panorama

JUTLAND

a vast atrium, which is free to enter if you just want to peek at the building itself (or to visit the gift shop or café). But to see any of the items described below, you'll have to buy a ticket. In addition to the permanent collections that I've described, the museum displays an impressive range of temporary exhibits—be sure to find out what's on during your visit.

Cost and Hours: 110 kr; Tue-Sun 10:00-17:00, Wed until 22:00; closed Mon, ARoS Allé 2, tel. 87 30 66 00, www.aros.dk.

Cuisine Art: The lunch café on the museum's ground floor serves 60-125-kr light meals, while the fancier restaurant on the top floor serves 190-kr lunch specials.

Visiting the Museum: After entering at the fourth-floor lobby, buy your ticket, pick up a museum floor plan, and walk two floors down the spiral staircase (to Floor 2) to find one of the museum's prized pieces: the squatting sculpture called *Boy* (by Australian artist Ron Mueck)—15 feet high, yet astonishingly realistic, from the wrinkly skin on his elbows to the stitching on his shorts.

Next, head down to the lowest level. Here, amid black walls, artists from around the world (including Tony Oursler and James Turrell) exhibit their immersive works of light and sound in each of nine spaces *(De 9 Rum)*. In this unique space, you're plunged into the imagination of the artist.

Now ride the elevator all the way to the top floor (Floor 8), then climb up the stairs (or ride a different elevator) to the rooftop.

Here you can enjoy the museum's icon: Olafur Eliasson's *Your Rainbow Panorama*, a 150-yard-long, 52-yard-diameter circular walkway enclosed in glass that gradually incorporates all the different colors of the spectrum. The piece provides 360-degree views over the city, while you're immersed in mind-bending, highly saturated hues. (It's "your" panorama because you are experiencing the colors.) It's a striking contrast to the mostly dark and claustrophobic works you've just seen in the nine spaces down below—yet, like those, it's all about playing with light. It's also practical—from a distance, it can be used by locals throughout the city as a giant compass (provided they know which color corresponds with which direction).

Back on Floor 8, stroll through the manageable permanent

collection of works from 1770 to 1930. Paintings dating from the **Danish Golden Age** (1800-1850) are evocative of the dewy-eyed Romanticism that swept Europe during that era: pastoral scenes of flat Danish countryside and seascapes, slices of peasant life, aristocratic portraits, "postcards" from travels to the Mediterranean world, and poignant scenes of departures and arrivals at Danish seaports. The **Danish Modernist** section, next, mostly feels derivative of big-name artists (you'll see the Danish answers to Picasso, Matisse, Modigliani, and others).

Continue down the spiral staircase, past various temporary exhibits. On Floor 5, take a spin through the **contemporary art gallery,** featuring temporary art and multimedia installations. Like the rest of this museum, these high-concept, navel-gazing works are well-presented and very accessible.

▲▲Den Gamle By

"The Old Town" open-air folk museum has 75 half-timbered houses and craft shops. Unlike other Scandinavian open-air museums that focus on rural folk life, Den Gamle By is designed to give you the best possible look at Danish urban life in centuries past. A fine botanical garden is next door.

Cost and Hours: Because peak-season days offer more activities, the cost depends on the time of year: July-Aug 135 kr, mid-April-June and Sept-mid-Nov 110 kr; Jan-mid-April 60 kr; mid-Nov-Dec: special Christmas-themed events and prices. Open daily mid-April-Aug 10:00-17:00, until 18:00 in July-mid-Aug; shorter hours off-season; after hours, the buildings are locked, but the peaceful park is open. Tel. 86 12 31 88, www.dengamleby.dk.

Getting There: Stroll 20 minutes up the canal from downtown, or catch a bus from near the train station: Bus #3A departs directly across the street from the station, while others (#4A, #11, #15, and #19) depart across the street from the Town Hall, on Park Allé.

Eating: This is a perfect place to enjoy a picnic lunch (bring your own, or order a lunch packet at the reception desk by the ticket booth)—outdoor and indoor tables are scattered around the grounds. The only eatery in the park open year-round is the cheery indoor/outdoor Simonsens Have, an inviting cafeteria serving affordable light meals (35-kr sandwiches, three *smørrebrød* for 65 kr). In peak season, you'll have many other options, including *pølse* and other snack stands, a café next to the ticket kiosk, and Wineke's

Cellar, an 18th-century public house serving beer, wine, and sandwiches (in the basement of the Mintmaster's Mansion).

Visiting the Museum: At the ticket desk, pick up the free map of the grounds; also pick up the flier listing what's on (and plan your time around those options). Though each building is described with a plaque, and there are maps throughout the park, the 50-kr guidebooklet is a worthwhile investment and a nice souvenir.

The grounds reward an adventurous spirit. They're designed to be explored, so don't be too shy to open doors or poke into seemingly abandoned courtyards—you may find a chatty docent inside, telling their story, answering questions, or demonstrating an old-timey handicraft. Follow sounds and smells to discover a whole world beyond the main streets.

The main part of the exhibit focuses on the 18th and 19th centuries. You'll start by heading up Navnløs, then hanging a right at Vestergade (passing a row house and a flower garden with samples for sale) to the canal. Head straight over the bridge and hike up the cute street lined with market stalls, shops, and a bakery until you pop out on the main square, Torvet. The building on the left side of Torvet, the Mayor's House (from 1597), contains a museum upstairs featuring home interiors from 1600 to 1850, including many with gorgeously painted walls. At the top of Torvet is the Mintmaster's Mansion, the residence of a Copenhagen noble (from 1683). Enter around back to tour

the boldly colorful, 18th-century Baroque rooms. Under the heavy timbers of the attic is an exhibit about the history of this restored building.

Continuing out the far end of Torvet on Søndergade, you enter the 20th century. The streets and shops here evoke the year 1927,

including a hardware store and (down Havbogade) a brewery where you can often buy samples (in the courtyard behind). At the end of Søndergade (on the left) is the Legetøj toy museum, with two floors of long hallways crammed with nostalgic playthings.

Walking into the next zone, you come to a street scene from 1974, including a hi-fi record shop and the Udstillinger building, which houses the Danish Poster Museum (a delightful collection of retro posters) and the Gallery of Decorative Arts (porcelain, clocks, and silverware).

The area under construction on the right is where they are re-creating a harborfront area from the 1970s (due to be completed by 2017). Continue down along the construction zone, cross the canal, and turn right (back toward the entrance). You'll pass idyllic pond scenery and the Simonsens Have cafeteria, before winding up at the bridge you crossed earlier.

Occupation Museum 1940-1945

Nazi occupiers used Aarhus' police station as their Gestapo head-quarters throughout World War II. It was the scene of tortures and executions. Today, it's a fine exhibit telling the story of the resistance and what it was like to live here under Nazi rule. You'll learn of heroic acts of sabotage, find out how guns were dropped out of British airplanes in the night, and see underground newspapers that kept occupied Danes connected and in the know. Sadly, much of the exhibit is without English descriptions (though free loaner English info sheets are available).

Cost and Hours: 30 kr; June-Aug Tue-Sun 11:00-16:00, closed Mon; Sept-May Sat-Sun and Tue 11:00-16:00, closed Mon and Wed-Fri; facing the cathedral, it's around to the left, just off Cathedral Square at Mathilde Fibigers Have 2; tel. 86 18 42 77, www.besaettelsesmuseet.dk.

▲▲Moesgård Museum

This museum, dedicated to prehistory and ethnography, is housed in a new, state-of-the art venue, south of Aarhus in the suburb of Højbjerg. Reopened in 2014, it juts dramatically from a hill, with grass growing on a sloping roof that visitors can walk on.

Cost and Hours: 110 kr; Tue-Sun 10:00-17:00, Wed until 21:00, closed Mon except in July-Sept, when it's open 10:00-17:00; café, tel. 87 16 10 16, www.moesmus.dk.

Getting There: The museum is located outside Aarhus at Moesgård Allé 15 in Højbjerg, in a lush, wooded park sprawling down to the sea. It's a pricey 200-kr taxi trip or easy 20-kr bus ride: Bus #18 leaves Aarhus from directly in front of the Town Hall on Park Allé (around the corner from the train station). On weekdays, the bus runs twice hourly during the museum's opening times (1-2/hour on Sat, hourly on Sun, ride 20 minutes to end of line, covered by 20-kr bus ticket that includes zone 2). Once at the museum,

JUTLAND

carefully check what time the return bus departs (posted at the bus stop, or ask at the ticket desk).

Visiting the Museum: Divided into three main periods—the Bronze Age (1800 to 500 B.C.), Iron Age (500 B.C. to A.D. 800), and Viking Age (A.D. 700 to 1050), the prehistory section features lots of real artifacts (primitive tools and pottery, plenty of spearheads and arrowheads), all well-described in English, along with an impressive collection of rune stones.

But the highlight is the well-preserved body of an Iron Age man. Believing that the gods dwelled in the bogs, prehistoric

 people threw offerings (such as spearheads) into the thick peat. The peat did a remarkable job of preserving these artifacts, many of which are now on display in the museum. The prehistoric people also sacrificed humans to the bog gods—resulting in the incredibly intact Grauballe Man, the world's best-preserved "bog-corpse." Reclining in his stately glass tomb, the more than 2,000-year-old "bog man" looks like a fellow half his age. He still has his skin, nails, hair, and even the slit in his throat he got at the sacrificial banquet (back in 300 B.C.). Spend some time with this visitor from the past. The story of his discovery (in a Jutland peat bog in 1952) and conservation is also interesting.

The Grounds: The museum sits on the pleasant grounds of the Moesgård Manor; while the manor itself is closed to the public, its grounds are fun to explore. Behind the museum, a two-mile-long circular trail stretches down to a fine beach. This "Prehistoric Trackway" runs past a few model Viking buildings, including a 12th-century stave church.

Tivoli Friheden Amusement Park

The local Tivoli, about a mile south of the Aarhus train station, offers great fun for the family.

Cost and Hours: 90-110 kr for entry only, 200-220 kr includes rides; daily early July-early Aug 11:30-20:00, longer hours in late July, May-early July and early Aug-Sept weekends only and shorter hours, closed Oct-April except for special events; bus #16 from Park Allé near Town Hall, tel. 86 14 73 00, www.friheden. dk.

Sleep Code

Abbreviations   (6 kr = about $1, country code: 45)
S = Single, **D** = Double/Twin, **T** = Triple, **Q** = Quad, **b** = bathroom
Price Rankings
   $$$ Higher Priced—Most rooms 1,000 kr or more.
    $$ Moderately Priced—Most rooms 500-1,000 kr.
     $ Lower Priced—Most rooms 500 kr or less.
Unless otherwise noted, English is spoken, credit cards are accepted, breakfast is included, and Wi-Fi is generally free. Prices change; verify current rates online or by email. For the best prices, always book directly with the hotel.

Sleeping in Aarhus

My recommendations include the following: two charming hotels with personality; two larger hotels facing the train station with rates that flex with demand; a stripped-down, functional, Motel 6-type place; and two backpacker/student-friendly hostels.

$$$ Villa Provence, named for owners Steen and Annette's favorite vacation destination, is a *petit* taste of France in the center of Aarhus, and makes a very cozy and convenient home base. Its 40 fun-yet-tasteful rooms, decorated with antique furniture and old French movie posters, surround a quiet courtyard (the pub across the street can get noisy on weekends, so ask for a room facing away from the street). Prices vary depending on the size and elegance of the room (Sb-1,195-2,300 kr, Db-1,395-3,000 kr, Wi-Fi, parking-126 kr/day, 10-minute walk from station, near Åboulevarden at the end of Fredensgade, Fredens Torv 12, tel. 86 18 24 00, www.villaprovence.dk, hotel@villaprovence.dk).

$$$ Hotel Guldsmeden ("Dragonfly") is a small, welcoming, and clean hotel with 27 rooms, fluffy comforters, a delightful stay-awhile garden, and a young, disarmingly friendly staff. A steep staircase takes you to the best rooms (Sb-1,250 kr, Db-1,395 kr), while the cheaper rooms (five rooms sharing two bathrooms) are in a ground-floor annex behind the garden (S-795 kr, D-995 kr; extra bed-300 kr, 10 percent off rooms with private bath with this book based on availability, Wi-Fi, 15-minute walk or 100-kr taxi from the station, in Aarhus' quiet Latin Quarter at Guldsmedgade 40, tel. 86 13 45 50, www.guldsmedenhotels.com, aarhus@guldsmedenhotels.com).

$$$ Hotel Ritz, across the street from the station, offers 67 clean, bright rooms done in Art Deco style (Sb-795-1,095 kr, Db-1,045-1,145 kr, bigger "superior" Db-1,095-1,245 kr, lower rates are for weekends and·July-Aug, elevator, Wi-Fi, Banegårdspladsen 12, tel. 86 13 44 44, www.hotelritz.dk, mail@hotelritz.dk).

$$$ **The Mayor Hotel** rents 160 sleek, well-furnished, business-class rooms 100 yards from the station (Sb-1,095 kr, Db-1,295 kr, lower rates on weekends and in off-season, check website for best deals, elevator, guest computer, Wi-Fi, free fitness room, parking-99 kr/day, Banegårdspladsen 14, tel. 87 32 01 00, www.themayor.dk, hotel@themayor.dk).

$$ **Cab-Inn,** overlooking the atmospheric Åboulevarden canal, is extremely practical. Rooms are minimalist yet comfy, and service is no-nonsense (Sb-495-545 kr, Db-625-805 kr, Tb-805 kr, Qb-935 kr, breakfast-70 kr, Wi-Fi, parking-80 kr/day—reserve ahead, rooms overlook boisterous canal or quieter courtyard, at Kannikegade 14 but main entrance on the canal at Åboulevarden 38, tel. 86 75 70 00, www.cabinn.dk, aarhus@cabinn.dk). For more on this chain, see page 103.

$ **Danhostel Aarhus,** an official HI hostel with six-bed dorms and plenty of two- and four-bed rooms, is near the water two miles out of town (dorm bed-250 kr, S/D-550 kr, Sb/Db-720 kr, lower prices off-season, 10 percent discount with membership card, sheets-45 kr, towels-10 kr, adult breakfast-64 kr, kids breakfast-32 kr, Wi-Fi, laundry, served by several buses from the train station—see website for details, Marienlundsvej 10, tel. 86 21 21 20, www.aarhus-danhostel.dk, info@aarhus-danhostel.dk).

$ **City Sleep In,** a creative independent hostel, has a shared kitchen, fun living and games room, laundry service, and lockers. It's on a busy road facing the harbor (with thin windows—expect some street noise), a 15-minute hike from the station. It's pretty grungy, but is the only centrally located budget option in town (180 kr/bunk in 4- to 6-bed dorms, D-450 kr, Db-500 kr, extra bed-130 kr, sheets-50 kr, towel-20 kr, organic breakfast-70 kr, elevator, guest computer, Wi-Fi, no curfew; reception open daily 8:00-11:00 & 16:00-21:00, Fri-Sat until 23:00; Havnegade 20, tel. 86 19 20 55, www.citysleep-in.dk, sleep-in@citysleep-in.dk).

Eating in Aarhus

Affluent Aarhus has plenty of great little restaurants. All of these are in the old town, within a few minutes' stroll from the cathedral.

IN AND NEAR THE LATIN QUARTER

The streets of the Latin Quarter are teeming with hardworking and popular eateries. The street called Mejlgade, along the eastern edge of downtown, has a smattering of youthful, trendy restaurants that are just far enough off the tourist trail to feel local.

Lecoq is a pricey favorite. Chef/owner Troels Thomsen and his youthful gang (proud alums from a prestigious Danish cooking school) serve up a fresh twist on traditional French cuisine in a single Paris-pleasant yet unassuming 10-table room. They pride themselves on their finely crafted presentation. Reservations are smart (245-300-kr three-course meals, 200-250-kr main courses, 85-135-kr starters, daily 11:30-15:00 & 17:30-21:30, Graven 16, tel. 86 19 50 74, www.cafe-lecoq.dk).

Den Rustikke is a French-style brasserie offering affordable, mostly French dishes, either in the rollicking interior or outside, under a cozy colonnade (45-85-kr lunches, 185-215-kr three-course dinners, daily 12:00-15:00 & 17:00-late, Mejlgade 20, tel. 86 12 00 95).

Pilhkjær is a bit more sedate, filling a cellar with elegantly casual atmosphere. The menu, which changes daily and can include fish, meat, or vegetarian offerings, is available only as a full-course meal—there's no ordering à la carte (260-275-kr two-course meal, 300-kr three-course meal; Tue-Thu 17:30-22:30, Fri-Sat 17:30-23:30, closed Sun-Mon; at the end of a long courtyard at Mejlgade 28, tel. 86 18 23 30, www.pihlkjaer-restaurant.dk).

Cheap Eats: **Jacob's Pita Bar** is a popular spot for pita sandwiches that are a cut above the average *shawarma*. Choose from grilled beef, chicken, lamb, ground beef, or turkey and melted cheese, plus your choice of a wide selection of sauces. These sandwiches are great for an inexpensive, quick meal: Sit at the counter, or get your order to go and find a spot to sit on the nearby square, along the canal, or Møllerparken (46-kr pita sandwiches, "menu" with fries and a drink-78 kr, daily 11:00-21:00, later on Fri-Sat, Vestergade 3, tel. 87 32 24 20). The pita bar is part of the adjacent, decent but overpriced steak house, Jacob's BarBQ (nightly until the wee hours).

Sushi: A few short blocks farther from the action (past the Church of Our Lady), **Sota** is a local favorite for sushi. This split-level sushi bar, in a half-timbered old house, is a sleek Tokyo-Scandinavian hybrid (80-100-kr rolls, 120-200-kr combo meals, pricier splurges available, Mon-Sat 12:00-22:00, Fri-Sat until 23:00, Sun 16:00-22:00, Vestergade 47, tel. 86 47 47 88).

Carlton Brasserie, facing a pretty square, is a solid bet for good Danish and international food in classy (verging on stuffy) surroundings. The restaurant has tables on the square, with more formal seating in back (inviting menu, 115-235-kr plates, 320-kr formal three-course dinner, Mon-Sat from 12:00, closed Sun, Rosensgade 23, tel. 86 20 21 22).

ALONG ÅBOULEVARDEN CANAL

The canal running through town is lined with trendy eateries—all overpriced unless you value making the scene with the locals (and

JUTLAND

all open daily until late). They have indoor and canalside seating with heaters and blankets, so diners can eat outdoors even when it's cold. Before settling in, cruise the entire strip, giving special consideration to **Cross Café** (with red awnings, right at main bridge) and **Ziggy,** both of which are popular for salads, sandwiches, burgers, and drinks; and **Grappa,** a classy Italian place with 135-kr pastas and pizzas, as well as pricier plates. Several places along here serve basic 40-60-kr breakfast buffets, which are popular with students for brunch.

NEAR THE CATHEDRAL

These places, while a bit past their prime and touristy, are convenient and central.

A Hereford Beefstouw, in the St. Clement's Brewery building facing the cathedral, is a bright, convivial, fun-loving, and woody land of happy eaters and drinkers. Choose from a hearty menu and eat amid shiny copper beer vats. If you're dropping by for a brew, they have enticing 15-35-kr beer snacks and little spicy *ølpølse* sausages (100-120-kr lunch and light meals; 185-385-kr hearty dinners such as steak, ribs, burgers, and fish; Mon-Sat 12:00-22:00, Sun 17:30-21:30, Kannikegade 10, tel. 86 13 53 25, www.beefstouw. com/aarhus).

Teater Bodega is the venerable best bet for traditional Danish—where local men go for "food their wives won't cook." While a bit tired and old-fashioned for Aarhus' trendy young student population, it's a sentimental favorite for old-timers. Facing the theater and cathedral, it's dressy and draped in theater memorabilia (130-270-kr main courses, 65-125-kr open-face sandwiches at lunch only, Mon-Sat 11:30-21:30, closed Sun, Skolegade 7, tel. 86 12 19 17, www.teaterbodega.dk).

Aarhus Connections

BY PUBLIC TRANSPORTATION

From Aarhus by Train to: Odense (2/hour, 1.5 hours), **Copenhagen** (2/hour, 3 hours), **Ærøskøbing** (6-7/day, transfer to ferry in Svendborg, allow 4 hours total), **Billund/Legoland** (3/hour; 45-minute train to Vejle, then transfer to bus—see page 198; allow 2 hours total), **Hamburg, Germany** (2 direct/day, more with transfers, 5 hours).

You can take the train from Aarhus to **Hirtshals,** where you can catch the **ferry to Norway** (for details on ferry options, see page 416). Trains depart Aarhus hourly and take about 2.5 hours (to meet the Color Line ferry, transfer at Hjørring and continue to Hirtshals Havn; note that rail passes don't cover the Hjørring-

Hirtshals train—www.rejseplanen.com—but do give a 50 percent discount; buy your ticket in Hjørring or on board).

BY CRUISE SHIP

Only a dozen or so ships a season (mostly Princess ships) choose to stop in Aarhus (mostly to break up the long sail from Oslo to Warnemünde in Germany). Though the pier is buried in an indus-trial-container wasteland, passengers are often greeted by a high school marching band. For security reasons, you aren't allowed to walk into town on your own—instead, a free and easy shuttle bus zips you to a welcome tent with a TI, services including currency exchange and possibly bike rental, and Danish handicrafts for sale. From there, red dots lead you on a five-minute walk into the town center (set your sights on the slender green cathedral spire). Use the big smokestacks (along with the red dots) as landmarks—when it's time to return to your ship, they'll help you find your way back to the shuttle bus, stress free.

ROUTE TIPS FOR DRIVERS

From the Ferry Dock at Hirtshals to Jutland Destinations: From the dock in Hirtshals, drive south (signs to *Hjørring*, *Ålborg*). It's about 2.5 hours to Aarhus. (To skip Aarhus, skirt the center and follow E-45 south.) To get to downtown **Aarhus,** follow signs to the center, then *Domkirke*. Park in the pay lot across from the ca-thedral. Signs all over town direct you to Den Gamle By open-air folk museum. From Aarhus, it's 60 miles to Billund/Legoland (go south on Skanderborg Road and get on E-45; follow signs to *Vejle*, *Kolding*). For **Jelling,** take the *Vejle N* exit and follow signs to *Vejle*, then veer right on the ring road (following signs to *Skovgade*), then follow Route 442 north. For **Legoland,** take the *Vejle S* exit for Bil-lund (after *Vejle N*—it's the first exit after the dramatic Vejlefjord bridge).

JUTLAND

Legoland

Legoland is Scandinavia's top kids' sight. If you have a child (or are a child at heart), it's a fun stop. This huge park is a happy combination of rides, restaurants, trees, smiles, and 33 million Lego bricks creatively arranged into such wonders as Mount Rushmore, the Parthenon, "Mad" King Ludwig's castle, and the Statue of Liberty. It's a Lego world here, as everything is cleverly related to this popular toy. If your

time in Denmark is short, or if your family has already visited a similar Legoland park in California, England, or Germany, consider skipping the trip. But if you're in the neighborhood, a visit to the mothership of all things Lego will be a hit with kids ages two through the pre-teens.

GETTING THERE

Legoland, located in the town of Billund, is easiest to visit by car (see "Route Tips for Drivers" on page 197), but doable by public transportation. The nearest train station to Billund is Vejle. Trains arrive at Vejle from **Copenhagen** (2/hour, 2-2.5 hours), **Odense** (2/hour, 50 minutes), and **Aarhus** (3/hour, 45 minutes). At Vejle, catch the bus (generally #43, #143, #166, or #179) to travel the remaining 25 miles to Billund (30-45 minutes). For train and bus details, see www.rejseplanen.dk.

ORIENTATION TO LEGOLAND

Cost: 309 kr for adults, 289 kr for kids ages 3-12 and those over 65. Legoland generally doesn't charge in the evening (free after 19:30 in July and late Aug, otherwise after 17:30).

Hours: Generally April-Oct daily 10:00-18:00, later on weekends and for much of July-Aug, closed Nov-March and Wed-Thu in Sept-mid-Oct. Activities close an hour before the park, but it's basically the same place after dinner as during the day, with fewer tour groups. Confirm exact hours before heading out (tel. 75 33 13 33, www.legoland.dk).

Crowd-Beating Tips: Legoland is crowded during the Danish summer school vacation, from early July through mid-August. To bypass the ticket line, purchase tickets in advance (simply scan them at the entry turnstile). Advance tickets, often available at a discount, are sold online at www.legoland.dk (reduced-price family tickets also available), and at many Dan-

ish locations (at stores, hotels, and TIs), including the Dagli'
Brugsen store in Vandel, just west of Billund.

Money-Saving Deals: If a one-day visit is not enough, you can pay
an extra 99 kr (once at the park) to cover the following day's
admission. If you hate waiting in lines, consider shelling out
for the Express Pass add-on, which allows holders to skip to
the front of the (often long) lines for up to 10 rides. The cost
is based on the user's height—99 kr for kids 100-119 cm tall
(3'3"-3'11"), and 179 kr for those 120 cm (3'11") and taller.

Eating: Surprisingly, the park's restaurants don't serve Lego-lamb,
but there are plenty of other food choices. Prices are high, so
consider bringing a picnic to enjoy at one of the several spots
set aside for bring-it-yourselfers.

BACKGROUND

Lego began in 1932 in the workshop of a local carpenter who named
his wooden toys after the Danish phrase *leg godt* ("play well"). In
1949, the company started making the plastic interlocking building bricks for which they are world famous. Since then, Lego has
continued to expand its lineup and now produces everything from
Ninjago ninja warriors to motorized models, Clikits jewelry, board
games, video games—many based on popular movies (*Lego Star
Wars, Lego Harry Potter,* etc.)—making kids drool in languages all
around the world. *The Lego Movie,* an animated feature, was one
of the top-grossing films of 2014. According to the company, each
person on this planet has, on average, 62 Lego blocks.

VISITING LEGOLAND

Legoland is divided into
eight different "worlds"
with fun themes such as
Adventure Land, Pirate
Land, and Knight's King-
dom. Pick up a brochure
at the entrance and make
a plan using the colorful
3-D map. You can see it
all in a day, but you'll be
exhausted. The Legoredo

JUTLAND

section (filled with Wild West clichés Europeans will enjoy more
than Americans) merits just a quick look, though your five-year-old
might enjoy roasting a biscuit-on-a-stick around the fire with a tall,
blond park employee wearing a Native American headdress.

A highlight for young and old alike is Miniland (near the
entrance), where landscaped gardens are filled with carefully constructed Lego landscapes and cityscapes. Anyone who has ever

picked up a Lego block will marvel at seeing representations of the world's famous sights, including Danish monuments, Dutch windmills, German castles, and an amazing version of the Norwegian harbor of Bergen. Children joyfully watch as tiny Lego boats ply the waters and Lego trains chug merrily along the tracks. Nearby, kids can go on mellow rides in child-size cars, trains, and boats. A highlight of Miniland is the Traffic School, where young drivers (ages 7-13) learn the rules of the road and get a souvenir license. (If interested in this popular attraction, make a reservation upon arrival.)

More rides are scattered throughout the park. While the rides aren't thrilling by Disneyland standards, most kids will find something to enjoy (parents should check the brochure for strictly enforced height restrictions). The Falck Fire Brigade ride in Lego City invites family participation as you team up to put out a (fake) fire. The Temple is an Indiana Jones-esque Egyptian-themed treasure hunt/shoot-'em-up, and the Dragon roller coaster takes you in and around a medieval castle. Note that on a few rides (including the Pirate Splash

Battle), you'll definitely get wet. Special walk-in, human-sized dryers help you warm up and dry off.

The indoor museum features company history, high-tech Lego creations, a great doll collection, and a toy exhibit full of mechanical wonders from the early 1900s, many ready to jump into action with the push of a button. A Lego playroom encourages hands-on fun, and a campground is across the street if your kids refuse to move on.

Nearby: Those looking for water fun with a tropical theme can check out the Aquadome (one of Europe's largest water parks), located outside Legoland in Billund at the family resort of Lalandia (www.lalandia.dk).

SLEEPING NEAR LEGOLAND

$$$ Legoland Hotel adjoins Legoland (Sb-1,600 kr, Db-2,500 kr, special family deals: 3,000 kr for room big enough for 2 adults and 2 kids, some room prices include 2-day admission to park, prices slightly lower Sept-May or for 2 or more nights, Wi-Fi, tel. 75 33 12 44, www.hotellegoland.dk, hotel@legoland.dk).

$$$ Hotel Svanen is close by, in Billund (standard Sb-1,095

kr, standard Db-1,195 kr, fancier rooms cost more, extra child's bed-200 kr, Wi-Fi, Nordmarksvej 8, tel. 75 33 28 33, www. hotelsvanen.dk, billund@hotelsvanen.dk).

$$ Legoland Village is a family hostel-type place offering inexpensive rooms that sleep one to five people (Db-720-1,100 kr, Tb-730-1,100 kr, Qb-1,200-1,600 kr, Quint/b-860-1,265 kr, higher prices are for mid-May-late Sept, sheets and towels extra, Ellehammers Allé 2, tel. 75 33 27 77, www.legoland-village.dk, info@legoland-village.dk).

Private Rooms: Private rooms are key to a budget visit here. In a forest just outside of Billund, Erik and Mary Sort run **$ Gregersminde,** with a great setup: six double rooms, plus a cottage that sleeps up to six people. Their guests enjoy a huge living room, a kitchen, lots of Lego toys, and a kid-friendly yard (S-210-400 kr, Sb-270-450 kr, D-330-450 kr, Db-390-550 kr, cottage-670-850 kr—towels and sheets extra, higher prices are for June-Sept, breakfast-50-60 kr, cash only, 10 percent cheaper for 2 nights or more, Wi-Fi, rental bikes-25 kr, cash only, leave Billund on Grindsted Road, turn right on Stilbjergvej, go a half-mile to Stilbjergvej 4B, tel. 61 27 33 23, www.gregersminde.dk, info@gregersminde.dk).

Jelling

On your way to or from Legoland, consider a short side-trip to the tiny village of Jelling (pronounced "YELL-ing"), a place of im-

mense importance in Danish history. Here you'll find two rune stones, set next to a 900-year-old church that's flanked by two enormous, man-made burial mounds. The two stones are often called "Denmark's birth certificate"—the first written record of Denmark's status as a nation-state. An excellent (and free) museum lies just across the street.

Two hours is ample for a visit. If pressed for time, an hour is enough to see the stones and take a quick look at the museum. Note that the museum is closed on Monday.

Jelling is too small for a TI, but the museum staff can answer most questions. If you're here around lunchtime, Jelling is a great spot for a picnic. There are several central eateries and a café and WC inside the museum, and another WC in the parking lot near the North Mound.

Getting There: Drivers can easily find Jelling, just 10 minutes off the main Vejle-Billund road (see "Route Tips for Drivers" on page 197). Train travelers coming from Copenhagen or Aarhus must change in Vejle, which is connected to Jelling by hourly trains (direction: Herning) and bus #211.

Jelling Walk

Denmark is proud of being Europe's oldest monarchy and of the fact that Queen Margrethe II, the country's current ruler, can trace her lineage back 1,300 years to Jelling. This short, self-guided walk explores this sacred place.

• *Begin your visit at the...*

Kongernes Jelling Museum: Inside this modern, light-filled building you'll find informative exhibits, historical models of the area, and replicas of the rune stones. Kids will love the room in the back on the ground level where they can write their name in the runic alphabet—and the gift shop bristling with wooden swords and Viking garb (free, June-Aug Tue-Sun 10:00-17:00, Sept-May Tue-Sun 12:00-16:00, closed between Christmas and New Year's and on Mon year-round, café, tel. 75 87 23 50, http://natmus.dk/kongernes-jelling).

• *Cross the street and walk through the graveyard to examine the actual...*

Rune Stones: The stones stand just south of the church. The modern bronze-and-glass structure is designed to protect the stones from the elements while allowing easy viewing.

The smaller stone was erected by King Gorm the Old (a.k.a. Gorm the Sleepy), who ruled Denmark for 40 years in the ninth

century. You probably don't read runic so I'll translate: *"King Gorm made this monument in memory of Thyra, his wife, Denmark's salvation."* These are the oldest recorded words of a Danish king, and the first time that the name Denmark is used to describe a country and not just the region.

The **larger stone** was erected by Gorm's son, Harald Blue-tooth, to honor his parents, commemorate the conquering of Denmark and Norway, and mark the conversion of the Danes to Christianity. (Today's Bluetooth wireless technology takes its name from Harald, who created the decidedly nonwireless connection between the Danish and Norwegian peoples.)

Harald was a shrewd politician who had practical reasons for being baptized. He knew that if he declared Denmark to be a Christian land, he could save it from possible attack by the predatory German bishops to the south. The inscription reads: *"King Harald ordered this monument made in memory of Gorm, his father, and in memory of Thyra, his mother; that Harald who won for himself all of Denmark and Norway and made the Danes Christian."*

This large stone has three sides. One side reveals an image of Jesus and a cross, while the other has a serpent wrapped around a lion. This is important imagery that speaks to the transition from Nordic paganism to Christianity. These designs carved into the rock were once brightly painted.

• *Go around the back of the church and climb the steps to the 35-foot-high, grass-covered...*

North Mound: According to tradition, Gorm was buried in a chamber inside this mound, with his queen Thyra interred in the smaller mound to the south. But excavations in the 1940s turned up no royal remains in either mound. (In the 1970s, what is believed to be Gorm's body was discovered below the church.) Scan the horizon and mentally remove the trees. Imagine the commanding view this site had in the past. Look north to stones that trace the outline of a ship. Below you lies a graveyard with typically Danish well-manicured plots.

• *Now descend the stairs to the...*

Church: Within the sparse interior, note the ship model hanging from the ceiling, a holdover from a pre-Christian tradition seeking a safe journey for ship and crew. The church, which dates from around 1100, is decorated with restored frescoes. A zigzag motif is repeated in the modern windows and the inlaid floor. The metal "Z" in the floor marks the spot where Gorm's body lies.

More Jutland Sights

JUTLAND

NORTHEAST OF BILLUND
Himmelbjerget and Silkeborg

If you're connecting the Billund and Jelling area with Aarhus, consider this slower but more scenic route north through the idyllic Danish Lake District. (With less time, return to Vejle and take the E-45 motorway.)

Himmelbjerget, best seen by car, lies in the middle of Jutland near the town of Silkeborg. Both are about an hour northeast of

Billund (22 miles west of Aarhus). Silkeborg is accessible by train from Aarhus with a change in Skanderborg.

Denmark's landscape is vertically challenged when compared to its mountainous neighbors Norway and Sweden. If you have a hankering to ascend to one of the country's highest points, consider a visit to the 482-foot-tall **Himmelbjerget,** which translates loftily as "The Heaven Mountain." That may be overstating it, but by Danish standards the view's not bad. One can literally drive to the top, where a short trail leads to an 80-foot-tall brick tower. Climb the **tower** (small admission fee, April-Oct daily 10:00-17:00, longer hours July-mid-Sept) for a commanding view. Clouds roll by above a patchwork of green and gold fields while boats ply the blue waters of the lake below. You may see the vintage paddle steamers make the hour-long trip between Himmelbjerget and Silkeborg in season (the dock is accessed by a short hike from the tower down to the lake).

Silkeborg, in the center of the Danish Lake District, has an excellent freshwater aquarium/exhibit/nature park called **AQUA** that's worth a visit, especially if you're traveling with kids (adults-140 kr, kids ages 3-11-75 kr, free for kids 2 and under; Mon-Fri 10:00-16:00, Sat-Sun 10:00-17:00, longer hours in summer, closed most of Dec; tel. 89 21 21 89, www.visitaqua.dk). Also in Silkeborg, modern-art lovers will enjoy the **Museum Jorn Silkeborg,** featuring colorful abstract works by Asger Jorn—a prominent member of the 1960s' COBRA movement—plus other Danish and foreign art (80 kr, free for kids 17 and under, April-Oct Tue-Sun 10:00-17:00, closed Mon, shorter hours off-season, tel. 86 82 53 88, www.museumjorn.dk).

SOUTHWEST OF BILLUND
▲Ribe

A Viking port 1,000 years ago, Ribe, located about 30 miles southwest of Billund, is the oldest, and possibly the loveliest, town in Denmark. It's an entertaining mix of cobbled lanes and leaning medieval houses, with a fine **cathedral** boasting modern paintings under Romanesque arches (free entry, tower-10 kr). The **TI** is on the main square (Torvet 3, tel. 75 42 15 00, www.visitribe.dk). **$ Weis Stue,** a smoky, low-ceilinged, atmospheric inn across from the church, rents primitive rooms and serves good meals (S-395 kr, D-495 kr, no breakfast, tel. 75 42 07 00, www.weis-stue.dk). Take the free **Night Watchman** tour (daily May-mid-Oct at 22:00, additional tour at 20:00 June-Aug).

NORWAY

NORWAY

Norge

Norway is stacked with superlatives—it's the most mountainous, most scenic, and most prosperous of all the Scandinavian countries. Perhaps above all, Norway is a land of intense natural beauty, its famously steep mountains and deep fjords carved out and shaped by an ancient ice age.

Norway is also a land of rich harvests—timber, oil, and fish. In fact, its wealth of resources is a major reason why Norwegians have voted *"nei"* to membership in the European Union. They don't want to be forced to share fishing rights with EU countries.

The country's relatively recent independence (in 1905, from Sweden) makes Norwegians notably patriotic and proud of their traditions and history. They have a reputation for insularity, and controversially tightened immigration laws in 2014.

Norway's Viking past (c. A.D. 800-1050) can still be seen today in the country's 28 remaining stave churches—with their decorative nods to Viking ship prows—and the artifacts housed in Oslo's Viking Ship Museum.

The Vikings, who also lived in present-day Denmark and Sweden, were great traders, shipbuilders, and explorers. However, they are probably best known for their infamous invasions, which terrorized much of Europe. The sight of their dragon-prowed ships on the horizon struck fear into the hearts of people from Ireland to the Black Sea.

Named for the Norse word *vik*, which means "fjord" or "inlet," the Vikings sailed their sleek, seaworthy ships on extensive voyages, laden with amber and furs for trading—and weapons for fighting. They traveled up the Seine and deep into Russia, through the Mediterranean east to Constantinople, and across the Atlantic to Greenland and even "Vinland" (Canada). In fact, they touched the soil of the Americas centuries before Columbus, causing proud "ya sure ya betcha" Scandinavian immigrants in the US to display bumper stickers that boast, "Columbus used a Viking map!"

Both history and Hollywood have painted a picture of the Vikings as fierce barbarians, an image reinforced by the colorful names of leaders like Sven Forkbeard, Erik Bloodaxe, and

South Norway

To Kirkenes
Trondheims-fjord
To Bodø
To Östersund & Stockholm

COASTAL STEAMER
Trondheim
Hell

Atlantic Ocean
Kristiansund
Molde
Åndalsnes
Ålesund
Dombås
Geiranger-fjord
Gudbrandsdal Valley
Nordfjord
Lom
Florø
Jostedal Glacier
Sognefjell
Kvam
Lustra-fjord
Jotunheimen Mountains
Lillehammer
Balestrand
Lærdal
Sognefjord
Aurland
Lake Mjøsa
Gudvangen
Flåm
Hamar
Voss
Myrdal
Bergen
Hardangervidda (Plateau)
Gardermoen
Eidsvoll
Hardanger-fjord
Kongsvinger
NORWAY
Charlottenberg
Bokna-fjord
Hovden
Drammen
Oslo
To Stockholm
Drøbak
Tønsberg
Stavanger
Sandefjord
Rygge
Frederikstad
Larvik
Setesdal Valley
Lake Vänern
Arendal
Flekke-fjord
Kristiansand
SWEDEN
Skagerrak Strait
North Sea
Göteborg
Hirtshals
Frederikshavn
To Cope.
To Malmö & Copenhagen
DENMARK

500 KM
250 MI
SWE
NOR.
FIN.
DEN.

50 Km
50 Miles

Harald Bluetooth. Unless you're handy with an axe, these don't sound like the kind of men you want to hoist a tankard of mead with. They kept slaves and were all-around cruel (though there is no evidence that they forced their subjects to eat lutefisk). But the Vikings also had a gentle side. Many were farmers, fishermen, and craftsmen who created delicate works with wood and metal. Faced with a growing population constrained by a lack of arable land, they traveled south not just to rape, pillage, and plunder, but in search of greener pastures. Sometimes they stayed and colonized, as in northeast England,

NORWAY

Norway Almanac

Official Name: Kongeriket Norge—"The Kingdom of Norway"—or simply Norge (Norway).

Population: Norway's 5.1 million people (about 35 per square mile) are mainly of Nordic and Germanic heritage, with a small population of indigenous Sami people in the north. The rapidly growing immigrant population is primarily from Pakistan, Sweden, Poland, Lithuania, and Somalia. Most Norwegians speak one of two official forms of Norwegian (Bokmål and Nynorsk), and the majority speak English as a second language. While church attendance is way down, the vast majority of Norwegian Christians consider themselves Lutheran.

Latitude and Longitude: 62°N and 10°E, similar latitude to Canada's Northwest Territories.

Area: 148,700 square miles, slightly larger than Montana.

Geography: Sharing the Scandinavian Peninsula with Sweden, Norway also has short northern borders with Finland and Russia. Its 51,575-mile coastline extends from the Barents Sea in the Arctic Ocean to the Norwegian Sea and North Sea in the North Atlantic. Shaped by glaciers, Norway has a rugged landscape of mountains, plateaus, and deep fjords. In the part of Norway that extends north of the Arctic Circle, the sun never sets at the height of summer, and never comes up in the deep of winter.

Biggest Cities: Norway's capital city, Oslo, has a population of 634,000; almost a million live in its metropolitan area. Bergen, Norway's second-largest city, has a population of about 240,000.

Economy: The Norwegian economy grows around 2 percent each year, contributing to a healthy $282 billion Gross Domestic Product and a per capita GDP of $55,400. Its primary export is oil—Norway ranks behind only Saudi Arabia and Russia in the amount of oil exported, making it one of the world's

---

which was called the "Danelaw," or in northwest France, which became known as Normandy ("Land of the North-men").

The Vikings worshipped many gods and had a rich tradition of mythology. Epic sagas were verbally passed down through generations or written in angular runic writing. The sagas told the heroic tales of the gods, who lived in Valhalla, the Viking heaven, presided over by Odin, the god of both wisdom and war. Like the Egyptians, the Vikings believed in life after death, and chieftains were often buried in their ships within burial mounds, along with prized possessions such as jewelry, cooking pots, food, and Hagar the Horrible cartoons.

Like the Greeks and Etruscans before them, the Vikings never

richest countries. Thanks to this oil wealth, and the country's generally prudent approach to debt, the recent economic crisis has been relatively easy on Norway.

Currency: 6 Norwegian kroner (kr, officially NOK) = about $1.

Government: As the leader of Norway's constitutional monarchy, King Harald V has largely ceremonial powers. In September of 2013, Norwegian voters elected a right-wing government, which appointed Conservative Party leader Erna Solberg as prime minister. She is Norway's second woman prime minister (after the Labor Party's Gro Harlem Brundtland) and the country's first Conservative leader since 1990. Though Solberg's party formed a coalition with the far-right anti-immigration Progress Party, the government still does not have enough votes in Parliament to enact far-reaching changes to the Norwegian welfare state. Norway's legislative body is the Stortinget (Parliament), with 169 members elected for four-year terms. The Conservative-Progress Party coalition currently holds 77 seats, followed by the Labor Party at 55 seats, and the Christian Democratic and Center parties with 10 seats each. The remaining seats are divided among smaller political parties.

Flag: The Norwegian flag is red with a blue Scandinavian cross outlined in white.

The Average Norwegian...is 39 years old, has 1.86 children, and will live to be 82. Three in four Norwegians are employed in the service sector, one in five in industry, and only 2 percent in agriculture.

organized on a large national scale and eventually faded away due to bigger, better-organized enemies and the powerful influence of Christianity. By 1150, the Vikings had become Christianized and assimilated into European society. But their memory lives on in Norway.

Beginning in the 14th century, Norway came under Danish rule for more than 400 years, until the Danes took the wrong side in the Napoleonic Wars. The Treaty of Kiel forced Denmark to cede Norway to Sweden in 1814. Sweden's rule of Norway lasted until 1905, when Norway voted to dissolve the union. Like many European countries, Norway was taken over by Germany during World War II. April 9, 1940, marked the start of five years of Nazi occupation, during which a strong resistance movement developed, hindering some of the Nazi war efforts.

Each year on May 17, Norwegians celebrate their idealistic 1814 constitution with fervor and plenty of flag-waving. Men and women wear folk costumes *(bunads)*, each specific to a region of Norway. Parades are held throughout the country. The parade in Oslo marches past the Royal Palace, where the royal family waves to the populace from their balcony. While the king holds almost zero political power (Norway has a parliament chaired by a prime minister), the royal family is still highly revered and respected.

Several holidays in spring and early summer disrupt transportation schedules: the aforementioned Constitution Day (May 17), Ascension Day (May 14 in 2015, May 6 in 2016), and Whitsunday and Whitmonday (a.k.a. Pentecost and the following day, May 24-25 in 2015, May 15-16 in 2016).

High taxes contribute to Norway's high standard of living. Norwegians receive cradle-to-grave social care: university education, health care, nearly yearlong paternity leave, and an annual six weeks of vacation. Norwegians feel there is no better place than home. Norway regularly shows up in first place on the annual UN Human Development Index.

Visitors enjoy the agreeable demeanor of the Norwegian people—friendly but not overbearing, organized but not uptight, and with a lust for adventure befitting their gorgeous landscape. Known for their ability to suffer any misfortune with an accepting (if a bit pessimistic) attitude, Norwegians are easy to get along with.

Despite being looked down upon as less sophisticated by their Scandinavian neighbors, Norwegians are proud of their rich folk

traditions—from handmade sweaters and folk costumes to the small farms that produce a sweet cheese called *geitost*. Less than 7 percent of the country's land is arable, resulting in numerous small farms. The government recognizes the value of farming, especially in the remote reaches of the country, and provides rich subsidies to keep this tradition alive. These subsidies would not be allowed if Norway joined the European Union—yet another reason the country remains an EU holdout.

Appropriate for a land with countless fjords and waterfalls, Norway is known for its pristine water. Norwegian-bottled artisanal water has an international reputation for its crisp, clean taste. Although the designer Voss water—the H2O of choice for Hollywood celebrities—comes with a high price tag, the blue-collar Olden is just as good. (The tap water is actually wonderful, too—and much cheaper.)

While the Norwegian people speak a collection of mutually understandable dialects, the Norwegian language has two official forms: *bokmål* (book language) and *nynorsk* (New Norse). During the centuries of Danish rule, people in Norway's cities and upper classes adopted a Danish-influenced style of speech and writing (called Dano-Norwegian), while rural language remained closer to Old Norse. After independence, Dano-Norwegian was renamed *bokmål*, and the rural dialects were formalized as *nynorsk*, as part of a nationalistic drive for a more purely Norwegian language. Despite later efforts to combine the two forms, *bokmål* remains the most commonly used, especially in urban areas, books, newspapers, and government agencies. Students learn both.

The majority of the population under 70 years of age also speaks English, but a few words in Norwegian will serve you well. For starters, see the Norwegian survival phrases at the end of this chapter. If you visit a Norwegian home, be sure to leave your shoes at the door; indoors is usually meant for stocking-feet only. At the end of a meal, it's polite to say "Thanks for the food"—*"Takk for maten"* (tahk for MAH-ten). Norwegians rarely feel their guests have eaten enough food, so be prepared to say *"Nei, takk"* (nay tahk; "No, thanks"). You can always try *"Jeg er mett"* (yay ehr met; "I am full"), but be careful not to say *"Jeg er full"*—"I am drunk."

STAVE CHURCHES

Norway's most distinctive architecture is the stave church. These medieval houses of worship—tall, skinny, wooden pagodas with dragon's-head gargoyles—are distinctly Norwegian and palpably historic, transporting you right back to the Viking days. On your visit, make it a point to visit at least one stave church.

Stave churches are the finest architecture to come out of medieval Norway. Wood was plentiful and cheap, and locals had an expertise with woodworking (from all that boat-building). In 1300, there were as many as 1,000

stave churches in Norway. After a 14th-century plague, Norway's population dropped, and many churches fell into disuse or burned down. By the 19th century, only a few dozen stave churches survived. Fortunately, they became recognized as part of the national heritage and were protected. Virtually all of Norway's surviving stave churches have been rebuilt or renovated, with painstaking attention to the original details.

A distinguishing feature of the "stave" design is its frame of tall, stout vertical staves (Norwegian *stav*, or "staff"). The churches typically sit on stone foundations, to keep the wooden structure away from the damp ground (otherwise it would rot). Most stave churches were made of specially grown pine, carefully prepared before being felled for construction. As the trees grew, the tips and most of the branches were cut off, leaving the trunks just barely alive to stand in the woods for about a decade. This allowed the sap to penetrate the wood and lock in the resin, strengthening the wood while keeping it elastic. Once built, a stave church was slathered with black tar to protect it from the elements.

Stave churches are notable for their resilience and flexibility. Just as old houses creak and settle over the years, wooden stave churches can flex to withstand fierce winds and the march of time. When the wind shifts with the seasons, stave churches groan and moan for a couple of weeks...until they've adjusted to the new influences, and settle in.

Even after the Vikings stopped raiding, they ornamented the exteriors of their churches with warlike, evil spirit-fighting dragons reminiscent of their ships. Inside, a stave church's structure makes you feel like you're huddled under an overturned ship. The churches are dark, with almost no windows (aside from a few small "portholes" high up). Typical decorations include carved, X-shaped crossbeams; these symbolize the cross of St. Andrew (who was crucified on such a cross). Round, Romanesque arches near the tops of the staves were made from the "knees" of a tree, where the roots bend to meet the trunk (typically the hardest wood in a tree). Overall, these churches are extremely vertical: the beams inside and the roofline outside both lead the eye up, up, up to the heavens.

Most surviving stave churches were renovated during the Reformation (16th and 17th centuries), when they acquired more horizontal elements such as pews, balconies, pulpits, altars, and other decorations to draw attention to the front of the church. In some (such as the churches in Lom and Urnes), the additions make the church feel almost cluttered. But the most authentic (including Hopperstad near Vik) feel truly medieval. These time-machine churches take visitors back to early Christian days: no pews (worshippers stood through the service), no pulpit, and a barrier between the congregation and the priest, to symbolically separate the physical world from the spiritual one. Incense filled the church, and the priest and congregation chanted the service back and forth to each other, creating an otherworldly atmosphere that likely made worshippers feel close to God. (If you've traveled in Greece, Russia, or the Balkans, Norway's stave churches might remind you of Orthodox churches, which reflect the way all Christians once worshipped.)

When traveling through Norway, you'll be encouraged to see stave church after stave church. Sure, they're interesting, but there's no point in spending time seeing more than a few of them. Of Norway's 28 remaining stave churches, seven are described in this book. The easiest to see are the ones that have been moved to open-air museums in Oslo and Lillehammer. But I prefer to appreciate a stave church in its original fjords-and-rolling-hills setting. My two favorites are both near Sognefjord: Borgund

and Hopperstad. They are each delightfully situated, uncluttered by more recent additions, and evocative as can be. Borgund is in a pristine wooded valley, while Hopperstad is situated on a fjord. Borgund comes with the only good adjacent stave church museum. (Most stave churches on the Sognefjord are operated by the same preservation society; for more details, see www.stavechurch.com.)

Other noteworthy stave churches include the one in Lom, near the Jotunheimen Mountains, which is one of Norway's biggest, and is indeed quite impressive. The Urnes church, across from Solvorn, is technically the oldest of them all—but it's been thoroughly renovated in later ages (it is still worth considering, however, if only for its exquisite carvings and the fun excursion to get to it; see the More on the Sognefjord chapter). The Fantoft church, just outside Bergen, burned down in 1992, and the replica built to replace it has none of the original's magic. The stave church in Undredal (see the Norway in a Nutshell chapter) advertises itself as the smallest. I think it's also the dullest.

Norwegian Survival Phrases

Norwegian can be pronounced quite differently from region to region.
These phrases and phonetics match the mainstream Oslo dialect, but you'll
notice variations. Vowels can be tricky: *å* sounds like "oh," *æ* sounds like
a bright "ah" (as in "apple"), and *u* sounds like the German *ü* (purse your
lips and say u). Certain vowels at the ends of words (such as *d* and *t*) are
sometimes barely pronounced (or not at all). In some dialects, the letters *sk*
are pronounced "sh." In the phonetics, ī sounds like the long i in "light,"
and bolded syllables are stressed.

English	Norwegian	Pronunciation
Hello. (formal)	God dag.	goo dahg
Hi. / Bye. (informal)	Hei. / Ha det.	hī / hah deh
Do you speak English?	Snakker du engelsk?	**snahk**-kehr dew **eng**-ehlsk
Yes. / No.	Ja. / Nei.	yah / nī
Please.	Vær så snill.	vayr soh sneel
Thank you (very much).	(Tusen) takk.	(**tew**-sehn) tahk
You're welcome.	Vær så god.	vayr soh goo
Can I help you?	Kan jeg hjelpe deg?	kahn yī **yehl**-peh dī
Excuse me.	Unnskyld.	**ewn**-shuld
(Very) good.	(Veldig) fint.	(**vehl**-dee) feent
Goodbye.	Farvel.	fahr-**vehl**
one / two	en / to	ayn / toh
three / four	tre / fire	treh / **fee**-reh
five / six	fem / seks	fehm / sehks
seven / eight	syv / åtte	seev / **oh**-teh
nine / ten	ni / ti	nee / tee
hundred	hundre	**hewn**-dreh
thousand	tusen	**tew**-sehn
How much?	Hvor mye?	voor **mee**-yeh
local currency: (Norwegian) crown	(Norske) kroner	(**norsh**-keh) **kroh**-nehr
Where is...?	Hvor er...?	voor ehr
...the toilet	...toalettet	toh-ah-**leh**-teh
men	menn / herrer	mehn / **hehr**-rehr
women	damer	**dah**-mehr
water / coffee	vann / kaffe	vahn / **kah**-feh
beer / wine	øl / vin	uhl / veen
Cheers!	Skål!	skohl
The bill, please.	Regningen, takk.	**rī**-ning-ehn tahk

OSLO

While Oslo is the smallest of the Scandinavian capitals, this brisk little city offers more sightseeing thrills than you might expect. As an added bonus, you'll be inspired by a city that simply has its act together.

Sights of the Viking spirit—past and present—tell an exciting story. Prowl through the remains of ancient Viking ships, and marvel at more peaceful but equally gutsy modern boats (the *Kon-Tiki, Ra, Fram,* and *Gjøa*). Dive into the traditional folk culture at the Norwegian open-air folk museum, and get stirred up by the country's heroic spirit at the Norwegian Resistance Museum.

For a look at modern Oslo, tour the striking City Hall, take a peek at sculptor Gustav Vigeland's people-pillars, climb the exhilarating Holmenkollen Ski Jump, walk all over the Opera House, and then celebrate the world's greatest peacemakers at the Nobel Peace Center.

Situated at the head of a 60-mile-long fjord, surrounded by forests, and populated by more than a half-million people, Oslo is Norway's cultural hub. For 300 years (1624-1924), the city was called Christiania, after Danish King Christian IV. With independence, it reverted to the Old Norse name of Oslo. As an important port facing the Continent, Oslo has been one of Norway's main cities for a thousand years and the de facto capital since around 1300. Still, Oslo has always been small by European standards; in 1800, Oslo had 10,000 people, while cities such as Paris and London had 50 times as many.

But Oslo experienced a growth spurt with the Industrial Age, and in 50 years (from 1850 to 1900) its population exploded from about 10,000 to about 250,000. Logically, most of "old Oslo" dates from this period when the city's many churches and grand buildings were made of stone in the Historicism styles (neo-Gothic and neo-Romanesque) of the late 19th century.

And Oslo's old industrial quarter, with its evocative brick factories and warehouses, is a trendy bohemian-chic zone that comes with as much of an edge as you'll find in otherwise wholesome Norway. The entire city—full of rich Norwegians—is expensive.

Today the city sprawls out from its historic core to encompass nearly a million people in its metropolitan area, about one in five Norwegians. Oslo's port hums with international shipping and a sizeable cruise industry. Its waterfront, once traffic-congested and slummy, has already undergone a huge change, and the extreme urban makeover is just starting. The vision: a five-mile people-friendly and traffic-free promenade stretching from east to west the entire length of its water-

front. Cars and trucks now travel in underground tunnels, upscale condos and restaurants are taking over, and the neighborhood has a splashy Opera House. Oslo seems to be constantly improving its infrastructure and redeveloping slummy old quarters along the waterfront into cutting-edge residential zones. The metropolis feels as if it's rushing to prepare for an Olympics-like deadline. But it isn't—it just wants to be the best city it can be.

You'll see a mix of grand Neoclassical facades, plain 1960s-style modernism, and a sprouting Nordic Manhattan-type skyline of skyscrapers nicknamed "the bar code buildings" for their sleek yet distinct boxiness.

But overall, the feel of this major capital is green and pastoral—spread out, dotted with parks and lakes, and surrounded by hills and forests. For the visitor, Oslo is an all-you-can-see *smörgåsbord* of historic sights, trees, art, and Nordic fun.

PLANNING YOUR TIME

Oslo offers an exciting slate of sightseeing thrills. Ideally, spend two days, and leave on the night boat to Copenhagen or on the scenic "Norway in a Nutshell" train to Bergen the third morning. Spend the two days like this:

Day 1: Take my self-guided "Welcome to Oslo" walk. Tour the Akershus Fortress and the Norwegian Resistance Museum. Catch the City Hall tour. Spend the afternoon at the National Gallery and at the Holmenkollen Ski Jump and museum.

Day 2: Ferry across the harbor to Bygdøy and tour the *Fram, Kon-Tiki,* and Viking Ship museums. Spend the afternoon at the

Norwegian Folk Museum. Finish the day at Vigeland Park, enjoying Gustav Vigeland's statues.

Keep in mind that the National Gallery and the Vigeland Museum (at Vigeland Park) are closed on Monday.

Orientation to Oslo

Oslo is easy to manage. Its sights cluster around the main boulevard, Karl Johans Gate (with the Royal Palace at one end and the train station at the other), and in the Bygdøy (big-doy) district, a 10-minute ferry ride across the harbor. The city's other main sight, Vigeland Park (with Gustav Vigeland's statues), is about a mile behind the palace.

The monumental, homogenous city center contains most of the sights, but head out of the core to see the more colorful neighborhoods. Choose from Majorstuen and Frogner (chic boutiques, trendy restaurants), Grünerløkka (bohemian cafés, hipsters), and Grønland (multiethnic immigrants' zone).

TOURIST INFORMATION

The city's shiny new **Oslo Visitor Center** is in the Østbanehallen, the traditional-looking building right next to the central train station. Standing in the square (Jernbanetorget) by the tiger statue and facing the train station, you'll find the TI's entrance in the red-painted section between the station and Østbanehallen. You can also enter the TI from inside the train station (May-Sept daily 9:00-18:00, Oct-April daily 9:00-16:00, tel. 81 53 05 55, www.visitoslo.com).

At the TI, pick up these freebies: an Oslo map, the helpful public-transit map, the annual *Oslo Guide* (with plenty of details on sightseeing, shopping, and eating), and the *You Are Here Oslo* map and visitors guide (a young people's guide that's full of fun and offbeat ideas). For entertainment ideas and more, the free *What's On in Oslo* monthly has the most accurate record of museum hours and an extensive listing of happenings every day, such as special events, tours, and concerts. If you like to bike, ask about the public bike-rental system (100 kr/24 hours; you can rent a card from TI to release simple one-speed bikes from racks around town).

If you're traveling on, pick up the *Bergen Guide* and information for the rest of Norway, including the useful, annual *Fjord Norway Travel Guide*. Consider buying the Oslo Pass (described next), unless you get the Oslo Package, which includes your hotel accommodation and an Oslo Pass (described under "Sleeping in Oslo," page 272).

Use It, a hardworking information center, is officially geared for those under age 26 but is generally happy to offer anyone its

OSLO

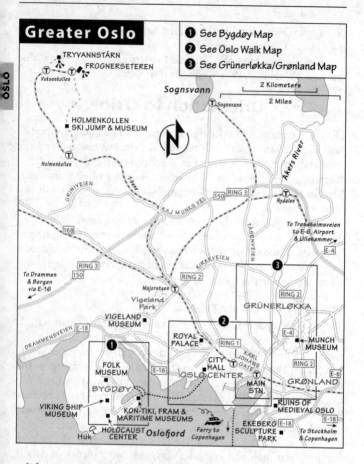

Greater Oslo

❶ See Bygdøy Map
❷ See Oslo Walk Map
❸ See Grünerløkka/Grønland Map

solid, money-saving, experience-enhancing advice (Mon-Fri 11:00-17:00, Sat 12:00-17:00, longer hours July-early Aug, closed Sun; Møllergata 3, look for *Ungdomsinformasjonen* sign, tel. 24 14 98 20, www.use-it.no). They can help find you the cheapest beds in town (no booking fee) and they offer these free services: Wi-Fi and Internet access, phone use, and luggage storage. Their free *You Are Here Oslo* guide—with practical info, maps, ideas on eating cheap, good nightspots, tips on picking up a Norwegian, the best beaches, and so on—is a must for young travelers and worthwhile for anyone curious about probing the Oslo scene.

Oslo Pass: This pass covers the city's public transit, ferry boats, and entry to nearly every major sight—all described in a useful handbook (320 kr/24 hours, 470 kr/48 hours, 590 kr/72 hours; big discounts for kids ages 4-15 and seniors age 67 and over, www. visitoslo.com). Do the math before buying; add up the individual costs of the sights you want to see to determine whether an Oslo

Pass will save you money. (Here are some sample charges: one 24-hour transit pass-90 kr, Nobel Peace Center-90 kr, three boat museums at Bygdøy-270 kr, National Gallery-50 kr. These costs, which total 500 kr, justify buying a 48-hour pass.) Students with an ISIC card may be better off without the Oslo Pass. The TI's Oslo Package (see "Sleeping in Oslo," later) includes an Oslo Pass with your discounted hotel room.

ARRIVAL IN OSLO
By Train
The central train station (Oslo Sentralstasjon, or "Oslo S" for short) is slick and helpful. You'll find free Wi-Fi, an Internet café, ATMs, and two Forex exchange desks. The station is plugged into a lively modern shopping mall called Byporten (Mon-Fri 10:00-21:00, Sat 10:00-20:00, closed Sun). You'll also find a cheap Bit sandwich shop with seating, a Joker supermarket (Mon-Fri 6:00-23:00, Sat 8:00-23:00, Sun 9:00-23:00), and a Vinmonopolet liquor store (Oslo's most central place to buy wine or liquor—which is sold only at Vinmonopolet stores, Mon-Thu 10:00-18:00, Fri 9:00-18:00, Sat 9:00-15:00, closed Sun). The new TI is in the Østbanehallen, right next to the train station.

For tickets and train info, you can go to the station's ticket office located between tracks 8 and 9 (Mon-Fri 6:30-23:00, Sat-Sun 10:00-18:00—opens at 7:45 on summer weekends) or to the helpful train office at the National Theater railway and T-bane station, which can have shorter lines (Mon-Fri 7:30-17:00, closed Sat-Sun; Ruseløkkveien, southwest of National Theater). At either ticket office, you can buy domestic and Norway in a Nutshell tickets, and pick up leaflets on the Flåm and Bergen Railway, but only the station office sells international tickets. The TI also sells domestic train tickets (same price, likely friendlier and faster).

By Plane
Oslo Airport
Oslo Lufthavn, also called Gardermoen, is about 30 miles north of the city center and has a helpful 24-hour information center (airport code: OSL, tel. 91 50 64 00, www.osl.no).

Flytoget is the speedy train that zips travelers between the airport and the central train station in 20-25 minutes (170 kr, less for students and seniors, 4/hour, runs roughly 5:00-24:00, not covered by rail passes, simply swipe your credit card through card reader at gate before boarding, then swipe it again when you get off—or buy ticket from machine or at ticket counter, where you'll pay a 30-kr surcharge; tel. 81 50 07 77, www.flytoget.no). Note that Flytoget trains alternate between those that go only to the central train station, and others that also continue on through Oslo, stopping at the National Theater station (which is closer to some recommended hotels and uses the same ticket).

Local trains are nearly half the cost of Flytoget trains and nearly as fast (90 kr, roughly 2/hour, 25 minutes, covered by rail passes, some also serve National Theater station). You'll save about 30 kr on this trip with an Oslo Pass because the pass covers transportation within Oslo; you only need to pay the fare for the stretch between the airport and the edge of town.

To reach the Flytoget and local train counters at the airport: After you leave customs, exit right and walk all the way to the far corner; you'll see two separate ticket counters (one for Flytoget, NSB for the cheaper local trains) and separate TV screens showing the timetables for Flytoget and the "lokal-InterCity-fjerntog" trains.

Flybus airport buses stop directly outside the arrival hall and make several downtown stops, including the central train station (150 kr one-way, 3/hour, 40 minutes, tel. 67 98 04 80).

Taxis run to and from the airport (895-kr fixed rate until 17:00, 1,095-kr rate after 17:00, confirm price before you commit). **Oslo Taxi** is the most reliable (tel. 02323). I prefer the slick and faster Flytoget train, but the taxi can be a good value for families and those with lots of luggage.

Other Airports near Oslo

If you arrive at the Rygge or Sandefjord airports, catch a Flybus airport bus to downtown Oslo. If you're going from Oslo *to* either airport, note that buses depart Oslo's central bus terminal (next to the train station) about three hours before all flight departures.

Rygge Airport: Ryanair and Norwegian use this airport near the city of Moss, 40 miles south of Oslo (160 kr for Flybus ticket—buy from driver, www.rygge-ekspressen.no; airport code: RYG, tel. 69 23 00 00, www.en.ryg.no).

Sandefjord Airport Torp: Ryanair, WizzAir, and other discount airlines use this airport, 70 miles south of Oslo (250 kr for Flybus ticket from driver, www.torpekspressen.no; airport code: TRF, tel. 33 42 70 00, www.torp.no).

By Boat

For details on arriving in Oslo by cruise ship, see the end of this chapter.

HELPFUL HINTS

Pickpocket Alert: They're a problem in Oslo, particularly in crowds on the street and in subways and buses. To call the police, dial 112.

Street People and Drug Addicts: Oslo's street population loiters around the train station. While a bit unnerving to some travelers, locals consider this rough-looking bunch harmless. The police have pretty much corralled them to the square called Christian Frederiks Plass, south of the station.

Money: Banks in Norway don't change money. Use ATMs or Forex exchange offices (outlets near City Hall at Fridtjof Nansens Plass 6, at train station, and at Egertorget at the crest of Karl Johans Gate; hours vary by location but generally Mon-Fri 9:00-18:00, Sat 9:00-17:00, closed Sun).

Internet Access: @rctic Internet Café is pricey but central, located in the train station's main hall and above track 13 (60 kr/hour, daily 8:00-23:00).

Post Office: It's in the train station.

Pharmacy: Jernbanetorgets Vitus Apotek is open 24 hours daily (across from train station on Jernbanetorget, tel. 23 35 81 00).

Laundry: Selva Laundry is on the corner of Wessels Gate and Ullevålsveien at Ullevålsveien 15, a half-mile north of the train station (daily self-serve 8:00-21:00, full-serve 10:00-19:00, walk or catch bus #37 from station, tel. 41 64 08 33).

Bike Rental: Viking Biking, run by Americans Curtis and Ben, rents bikes (125 kr/8 hours, 200 kr/24 hours, includes helmet, map, rain poncho, and lock, daily 9:30-18:00, Nedre Slottsgate 4, tel. 41 26 64 96, www.  vikingbikingoslo.com; see "Tours in Oslo," later, for their guided bike tours).

Or use the public bike-rental system to grab basic **city bikes** out of locked racks at various points throughout town (100 kr/24 hours; get card at TI).

Movies: The domed **Colosseum Kino** in Majorstuen, one of northern Europe's largest movie houses with 1,500 seats, is a fun place to catch a big-time spectacle. Built in 1928, this high-tech, four-screen theater shows first-run films in their original language (Fridtjof Nansens Vei 6, a short walk west from Marjorstuen T-bane station, www.oslokino.no).

Updates to This Book: For updates to this book, check www. ricksteves.com/update.

GETTING AROUND OSLO

By Public Transit: Commit yourself to taking advantage of Oslo's excellent transit system, made up of buses, trams, ferries, and a subway (*Tunnelbane,* or T-bane for short; see "Sightseeing by Public

Transit" sidebar). Use the TI's free public transit map to navigate. The system runs like clockwork, with schedules clearly posted and followed. Many stops have handy electronic reader boards showing the time remaining before the next tram arrives (usually less than 10 minutes). **Ruter,** the public-transit information center, faces the train station under the glass tower; Mon-Fri 7:00-20:00, Sat-Sun 8:00-18:00, tel. 177 or 81 50 01 76, www.ruter.no).

Individual **tickets** work on buses, trams, ferries, and the T-bane for one hour (30 kr if bought at machines, transit office, Narvesen kiosks, convenience stores such as 7-Eleven or Deli de Luca, or via smartphone app—or 50 kr if bought on board). Other options include the **24-hour ticket** (90 kr; buy at machines, transit office, or via smartphone app; good for unlimited rides in 24-hour period) and the **Oslo Pass** (gives free run of entire system; described earlier). Validate your ticket or smartcard by holding it next to the card reader when you board.

By Taxi: Taxis come with a 150-kr drop charge that covers you for three or four kilometers—about two miles (more on evenings and weekends). Taxis can be a good value if you're with a group. If you use a minibus taxi, you are welcome to negotiate an hourly rate. To get a taxi, wave one down, find a taxi stand, or call 02323.

Tours in Oslo

Oslo Fjord Tours

A fascinating world of idyllic islands sprinkled with charming vacation cabins is minutes away from the Oslo harborfront. For locals, the fjord is a handy vacation getaway. Tourists can get a glimpse of this island world by public ferry or tour boat. Cheap ferries regularly connect the nearby islands with downtown (free with Oslo Pass).

Several tour boats leave regularly from pier 3 in front of City Hall. Båtservice has a relaxing and scenic 1.5-hour hop-on, hop-off service, with recorded multilanguage commentary. It departs from the City Hall dock (185 kr, daily at 9:45, 11:15, 12:45, and 14:15; departs 30 minutes later from Opera House and one hour later from Bygdøy; tel. 23 35 68 90, www.boatsightseeing.com). They won't scream if you bring something to munch. They also offer two-hour fjord tours with lame live commentary (269 kr, 3-4/day late March-Sept) and a "Summer Evening on the Fjord" dinner cruise on a sailing ship (395 kr; joyride without narration that includes a "shrimp buffet"—just shrimp, bread, and butter; daily mid-June-Aug 19:00-22:00).

Sightseeing by Public Transit

With a transit pass or an Oslo Pass, take full advantage of the T-bane and the trams. Just spend five minutes to get a grip on the system, and you'll become amazingly empowered. Here are the only T-bane stations you're likely to use:

Jernbanetorget (central station, bus and tram hub, express train to airport)

Stortinget (top of Karl Johans Gate, near Akershus Fortress)

Nationaltheatret (National Theater, also a train station, express train to airport, near City Hall, Aker Brygge, Royal Palace)

Majorstuen (walk to Vigeland Sculpture Park, trendy shops on Bogstadveien, Colosseum cinema)

Grønland (colorful immigrant neighborhood, cheap and fun restaurant zone, bottom of Grünerløkka district; the underground mall in the station is a virtual trip to Istanbul)

Nydalen (start of my Nydalen to Grünerløkka Walk)

Holmenkollen (famous ski jump, city view)

Frognerseteren (highest point in town, jumping-off point for forest walks and bike rides)

Sognsvann (idyllic lake in forest outside of town)

Trams and buses that matter:

Trams #11 and #12 ring the city (stops at central station, fortress, harborfront, City Hall, Aker Brygge, Vigeland Park, Bogstadveien, National Gallery, and Stortorvet)

Trams #11, #12, and #13 to Olaf Ryes Plass (center of Grünerløkka district)

Trams #13 and #19, and bus #31 (south and parallel to Karl Johans Gate to central station)

Bus #30 (Nydalen, Olaf Ryes Plass in Grünerløkka, train station, near Karl Johans Gate, National Theater, and Bygdøy, with stops at each Bygdøy museum)

Bus Tours

Båtservice, which runs the harbor cruises, also offers four-hour **bus tours** of Oslo, with stops at the ski jump, Bygdøy museums, and Vigeland Park (390 kr, 2/day mid-May-mid-Sept, departs next to City Hall, longer tours also available, tel. 23 35 68 90, www.boatsightseeing.com). HMK also does daily city bus tours (220 kr/2 hours, 350 kr/4 hours, departs next to City Hall, tel. 22 78 94 00, www.hmk.no).

Open Top Sightseeing runs **hop-on, hop-off bus tours** (260 kr/all day, 19 stops, www.opentopsightseeing.no; every 30 minutes, leaves from City Hall, English headphone commentary, buy ticket from driver). While the tours help you get your bearings, most of Oslo's sightseeing is concentrated in a few discrete zones that are well-connected by the excellent public-transportation network—making pricey bus tours a lesser value. And if you hit the timing wrong, you may wait up to an hour at popular stops (such as Vigeland Park) for a chance to hop back on.

Biking Tours

Viking Biking gives several different guided tours in English, including a three-hour Oslo Highlights Tour (250 kr, May-Sept daily at 13:00, Nedre Slottsgate 4, tel. 41 26 64 96, www.vikingbikingoslo.com). They also rent bikes; see "Helpful Hints," earlier.

Guided Walking Tour

Oslo Guideservice offers 1.5-hour historic "Oslo Promenade" walks from June through August (150 kr, free with Oslo Pass; Mon, Wed, and Fri at 17:30; leaves from sea side of City Hall, confirm departures at TI, tel. 22 42 70 20, www.guideservice.no).

Local Guides

You can hire a private guide through **Oslo Guideservice** (2,000 kr/2 hours, tel. 22 42 70 20, www.guideservice.no); my guide Aksel had a passion for both history and his hometown of Oslo. Or try **Oslo Guidebureau** (prices start at 1,950 kr/3 hours, tel. 22 42 28 18, www.osloguide.no, mail@guideservice.no).

Oslo Tram Tour

Tram #12, which becomes tram #11 halfway through its loop (at Majorstuen), circles the city from the train station, lacing together many of Oslo's main sights. Apart from the practical value of being able to hop on and off as you sightsee your way around town (trams come by at least every 10 minutes), this 40-minute trip gives you a fine look at parts of the city you wouldn't otherwise see.

The route starts at the main train station, at the traffic-island tram stop located immediately in front of the transit office tower. The route makes almost a complete circle and finishes at Stortorvet (the cathedral square), dropping you off a three-minute walk from where you began the tour.

Starting out, you want tram #12 as it leaves from the second set of tracks, going toward Majorstuen. Confirm with your driver that the particular tram #12 you're boarding becomes tram #11 and finishes at Stortorvet; some of these may turn into tram #19 instead, which takes a different route. If yours becomes #19, simply hop out at Majorstuen and wait for the next #11. If #11 is canceled because of construction, leave #12 at Majorstuen and catch #19 through the center back to the train station, or hop on the T-bane (which zips every few minutes from Majorstuen to the National Theater—closest to the harbor and City Hall—and then to the station). Here's what you'll see and ideas on where you might want to hop out:

From the **station,** you'll go through the old grid streets of 16th-century Christiania, King Christian IV's planned Renaissance town. After the city's 17th fire, in 1624, the king finally got fed up. He decreed that only brick and stone buildings would be permitted in the city center, with wide streets to serve as fire breaks.

You'll turn a corner at the **fortress** (Christiana Torv stop; get off here for the fortress and Norwegian Resistance Museum), then head for **City Hall** (Rådhus stop). Next comes the harbor and upscale **Aker Brygge** waterfront neighborhood (jump off at the Aker Brygge stop for the harbor and restaurant row). Passing the harbor, you'll see on the left a few old shipyard buildings that still survive. Then the tram goes uphill, past the **House of Oslo** (a mall of 20 shops highlighting Scandinavian interior design; Vikatorvet stop) and into a district of ugly 1960s buildings (when elegance was replaced by "functionality"). The tram then heads onto the street Norwegians renamed **Henrik Ibsens Gate** in 2006 to commemorate the centenary of Ibsen's death, honoring the man they claim is the greatest playwright since Shakespeare.

After Henrik Ibsens Gate, the tram follows Frognerveien through the chic **Frogner neighborhood.** Behind the fine old facades are fancy shops and spendy condos. Here and there you'll see 19th-century mansions built by aristocratic families who wanted to live near the Royal Palace; today, many of these house foreign embassies. Turning the corner, you roll along the edge of **Frogner Park** (which includes **Vigeland Park,** featuring Gustav Vigeland's sculptures), stopping at its grand gate (hop out at the Vigelandsparken stop).

Ahead on the left, a statue of 1930s ice queen Sonja Henie marks the arena where she learned to skate. Turning onto Bogstadveien, the tram usually becomes #11 at the Majorstuen stop. **Bogstadveien** is lined with trendy shops, restaurants, and cafés—it's a fun place to stroll and window-shop. (You could get out here and walk along this street all the way to the Royal Palace park and the top of Karl Johans Gate.) The tram veers left before the palace, passing the **National Historical Museum** and stopping at the **National Gallery** (Tullinløkka stop). As you trundle along, you may notice that lots of roads are ripped up for construction. It's too cold to fix the streets in winter, so, when possible, the work is done in summer. Jump out at **Stortorvet** (a big square filled with flower stalls and fronted by the cathedral and the big GlasMagasinet department store). From here, you're a three-minute walk from the station, where this tour began.

Welcome to Oslo Walk

This self-guided stroll, worth ▲▲, covers the heart of Oslo—the zone where most tourists find themselves walking—from the train station, up the main drag, and past City Hall to the harborfront. It takes a brisk 30 minutes if done nonstop.

Train Station: Start at the plaza just outside the main entrance of Oslo's central train station (Oslo Sentralstasjon). The statue of the tiger prowling around out front alludes to the town's nickname of Tigerstaden ("Tiger Town") and commemorates the 1,000th birthday of Oslo's founding, celebrated in the year 2000. In the 1800s, Oslo was considered an urban tiger, leaving its mark on the soul of simple country folk who ventured into the wild and crazy New York City of Norway.

(These days, the presence of so many beggars, or *tigger*, has prompted the nickname "Tiggerstaden.")

With your back to the train station, look for the glass Ruter tower that marks the **public transit office;** from here, trams zip to City Hall (harbor, boat to Bygdøy), and the underground subway (T-bane, or *Tunnelbane*—look for the *T* sign to your right) goes to Vigeland Park (statues) and Holmenkollen. Tram #12—featured in the self-guided tram tour described earlier—leaves from directly across the street.

The green building behind the Ruter tower is a shopping mall called **Byporten** (literally, "City Gate," see big sign on rooftop), built to greet those arriving from the airport on the shuttle train. Oslo's 37-floor pointed-glass **skyscraper,** the Radisson Blu Plaza Hotel, looms behind that. Its 34th-floor SkyBar welcomes the public with air-conditioned views and pricey drinks (Mon-Sat 17:00-24:00, closed Sun). The tower was built with reflective glass so that, from a distance, it almost disappears. The area behind the Radisson—the lively and colorful "Little Karachi," centered along a street called Grønland—is where most of Oslo's immigrant population settled. It's become a vibrant nightspot, offering a fun contrast to the predictable homogeneity of Norwegian cuisine and culture.

Oslo allows hard-drug addicts and prostitutes to mix and mingle in the station area. (While it's illegal to buy sex in Norway, those who sell it are not breaking the law.) Troubled young people come here from small towns in the countryside for anonymity and community. The two cameras near the top of the Ruter tower monitor drug deals. Signs warn that this is a "monitored area," but victimless crimes proceed while violence is minimized. (Watch your purse and wallet here.)

• *Note that you are near the Opera House if you'd like to side-trip there now. Otherwise, turn your attention to Norway's main drag, called...*

Karl Johans Gate: This grand boulevard leads directly from the train station to the Royal Palace. The street is named for the French general Jean Baptiste Bernadotte, who was given a Swedish name, established the current Swedish dynasty, and ruled as a popular king (1818-1844) during the period after Sweden took Norway from Denmark.

Walk three blocks up Karl Johans Gate. This stretch is referred to as **"Desolation Row"** by locals because it has no soul, just shops greedily looking to devour tourists' money. If you visit in the snowy winter, you'll walk on bare concrete: Most of downtown Oslo's pedestrian streets are heated.

• *Hook right around the curved old brick structure of an old market and walk to the...*

Oslo Cathedral (Domkirke): This Lutheran church (daily 10:00-16:00) is the third cathedral Oslo has had, built in 1697 after

the second one burned down. It's where Norway commemorates its royal marriages and deaths. Seventy-seven deaths were mourned here following the tragic shootings and bombing of July 2011 (see sidebar, page 270). In the grass in front of the cathedral, you may see a semipermanent memorial to the victims, consisting of a row of stones shaped like a heart.

Look for the cathedral's cornerstone (right of entrance), a thousand-year-old carving from Oslo's first and long-gone cathedral showing how the forces of good and evil tug at each of us. Look high up on the tower. The tiny square windows midway up the copper cupola were once the lookout quarters of the fire watchman.

Step inside beneath the red, blue, and gold seal of Oslo and under an equally colorful ceiling (late Art Deco from the 1930s). The box above on the right is for the royal family. The fine Baroque pulpit and altarpiece date from 1700. The chandeliers are from the previous cathedral (which burned in the 17th century). The colorful windows in the choir (leading up to the altar) were made in 1910 by Emanuel Vigeland (Gustav's less famous brother).

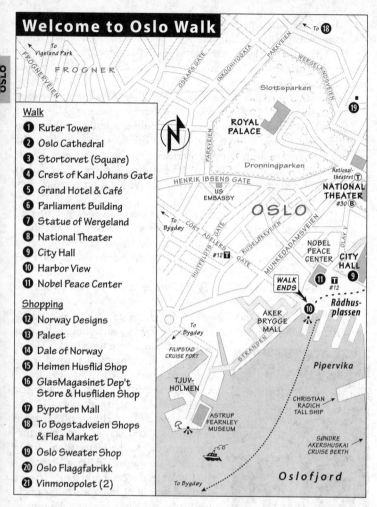

Welcome to Oslo Walk

Walk
1 Ruter Tower
2 Oslo Cathedral
3 Stortorvet (Square)
4 Crest of Karl Johans Gate
5 Grand Hotel & Café
6 Parliament Building
7 Statue of Wergeland
8 National Theater
9 City Hall
10 Harbor View
11 Nobel Peace Center

Shopping
12 Norway Designs
13 Paleet
14 Dale of Norway
15 Heimen Husflid Shop
16 GlasMagasinet Dep't Store & Husfliden Shop
17 Byporten Mall
18 To Bogstadveien Shops & Flea Market
19 Oslo Sweater Shop
20 Oslo Flaggfabrikk
21 Vinmonopolet (2)

Leaving the church, stroll around to the right, behind the church. The **courtyard** is lined by a circa-1850 circular row of stalls from an old market. Rusty meat hooks now decorate the lamps of a peaceful café, which has quaint tables around a fountain. The atmospheric **Café Bacchus,** at the far left end of the arcade, serves food outside and in a classy café downstairs (light 150-200-kr meals, Mon-Fri 11:00-22:00, Sat 12:00-22:00, closed Sun, hamburgers, salads, good cakes, coffee, tel. 22 33 34 30).

• *The big square that faces the cathedral is called…*

Stortorvet: In the 17th century, when Oslo's wall was located about here, this was the point where farmers were allowed to enter and sell their goods. Today it's still lively as a flower and produce

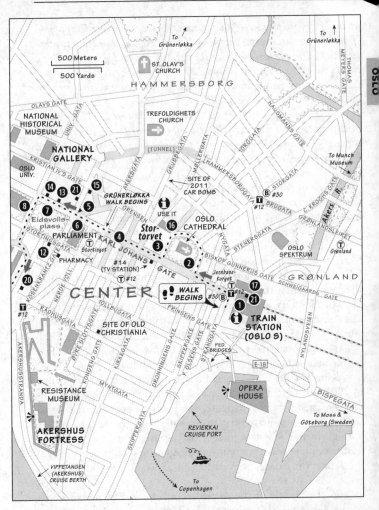

market (Mon-Fri). The statue shows Christian IV, the Danish king who ruled Norway around 1600, dramatically gesturing that-a-way. He named the city, rather immodestly, Christiania. (Oslo took back its old Norse name only in 1925.) Christian was serious about Norway. During his 60-year reign, he visited it 30 times (more than all other royal visits combined during 300 years of Danish rule). The big GlasMagasinet department store is a landmark on this square.

• *Return to Karl Johans Gate, and continue*

...e boulevard past street musicians, cafés, shops, and hordes of people. If you're here early in the morning (Mon–Fri) you may see a commotion at #14 (in the first block, on the left, look for the big 2 sign). This is the studio of a TV station (channel 2) where the Norwegian version of the Today show is shot, and as on Rockefeller Plaza, locals gather here, clamoring to get their mugs on TV.

At the next corner, Kongens Gate leads left, past the 17th-century grid-plan town to the fortress. But we'll continue hiking straight up to the crest of the hill, enjoying some of the street musicians along the way. Pause at the wide spot in the street just before Akersgata to appreciate the...

Crest of Karl Johans Gate: Look back at the train station. A thousand years ago, the original (pre-1624) Oslo was located at the foot of the wooded hill behind the station (described later). Now look ahead to the Royal Palace in the distance, which was built in the 1830s "with nature and God behind it and the people at its feet." If the flag flies atop the palace, the king is in the country. Karl Johans Gate, a parade ground laid out in about 1850 from here to the palace, is now the axis of modern Oslo. Each May 17, Norway's Constitution Day, an annual children's parade turns this street into a sea of marching student bands and costumed young flag-wavers, while the royal family watches from the palace balcony. Since 1814, Norway has preferred peace. Rather than celebrating its military on the national holiday, it celebrates its children.

King Harald V and Queen Sonja moved back into the palace in 2001, after extensive (and costly) renovations. To quell the controversy caused by this expense, the public is now allowed inside to visit each summer with a pricey one-hour guided tour (95 kr, 3 English tours/day late June–mid-Aug, fills fast—buy tickets in advance online or at many convenience stores, such as the Narvesen kiosk near the palace, or by calling 81 53 31 33, www.kongehuset. no).

In the middle of the small square, the *T* sign marks a stop of the T-bane (Oslo's subway). W. B. Samson's bakery is a good place for a quick, affordable lunch, with a handy cafeteria line (WC in back); duck inside if just to be tempted by the pastries. Two traditional favorites are *kanelboller* (cinnamon rolls) and *skolebrød* ("school bread," with an egg-and-cream filling). From here, the street called Akersgata kicks off a worthwhile stroll past the site of the July 2011 bombing, the national cemetery, and through a park-like river gorge to the trendy Grünerløkka quarter (an hour-long walk, described on page 260).

People-watching is great along Karl Johans Gate, but remember that if it's summer, half of the city's regular population is gone—vacationing in their cabins or farther away—and the city center is filled mostly with visitors.

Hike two blocks down Karl Johans Gate, past the big brick Parliament building (on the left). On your right, seated in the square, is a statue of the 19th-century painter Christian Krohg. Continue down Karl Johans Gate. If you'd like to get a city view (and perhaps some refreshment), enter the glass doors at #27 and take the elevator to the eighth-floor roof-top bar, Etoile.

A few doors farther down Karl Johans Gate, just past the Freia shop (Norway's oldest and best chocolate), the venerable **Grand Hotel** (Oslo's celebrity hotel—Nobel Peace Prize winners sleep here) overlooks the boulevard.

• *Ask the Grand Hotel staff if there is a way to view the interior of the Grand Café, which may be closed in 2016.*

Grand Café: This historic café was for many years the meeting place of Oslo's intellectual and creative elite (the playwright Henrik Ibsen was a regular here). This venerable establishment held photos and knickknacks of times gone by, as well as a mural showing Norway's literary and artistic clientele—from a century ago—enjoying this fine hangout. If you're able to view the mural at the back of the café, find Ibsen, coming in as he did every day at 13:00. Edvard Munch is on the right, leaning against the window, looking pretty drugged. Names are on the sill beneath the mural.

• *For a cheap bite with prime boulevard seating, continue past the corner to Deli de Luca, a convenience store with a super selection of takeaway food and a great people-watching perch. Across the street, a little park faces Norway's...*

Parliament Building (Stortinget): Norway's Parliament meets here (along with anyone participating in a peaceful protest outside). Built in 1866, the building seems to counter the Royal Palace at the other end of Karl Johans Gate. If the flag's flying, Parliament's in session. Today the king is a figurehead, and Norway is run by a unicameral parliament and a prime minister. Guided tours of the Stortinget are offered for those interested in Norwegian government (free, 45 minutes; mid-June-Aug Mon-Fri at 10:00 and 13:00 in English, at 11:30 in Norwegian; line up at gate in front of the main entrance off Karl Johans Gate, tel. 23 31 35 96, www.stortinget.no).

• *Cross over into the park and stroll toward the palace, past the fountain. Pause at the...*

Statue of Wergeland: The poet Henrik Wergeland helped inspire the national resurgence of Norway during the 19th century. Norway won its independence from Denmark in 1814, but within a year it lost its freedom to Sweden. For nearly a century, until Norway won independence in 1905, Norwegian culture and national spirit was stoked by artistic and literary patriots like Wergeland. In the winter, the pool here is frozen and covered with children happily ice-skating. Across the street behind Wergeland stands

Browsing

Oslo's pulse is best felt by strolling. Three good areas are along and near the central Karl Johans Gate, which runs from the train station to the palace (follow my self-guided "Welcome to Oslo" walk); in the trendy harborside Aker Brygge mall, a glass-and-chrome collection of sharp cafés, fine condos, and polished produce stalls (really lively at night, tram #12 from train station); and along Bogstadveien, a bustling shopping street with no-nonsense modern commerce, lots of locals, and no tourists (T-bane to Majorstuen and follow this street back toward the palace and tourist zone). While most tourists never get out of the harbor/Karl Johans Gate district, the real, down-to-earth Oslo is better seen elsewhere, in places such as Bogstadveien. The bohemian, artsy Grünerløkka district, described on page 260, is good for a daytime wander.

the **National Theater** and statues of Norway's favorite playwrights: Ibsen and Bjørnstjerne Bjørnson. Across Karl Johans Gate, the pale yellow building is the first university building in Norway, dating from 1854. A block behind that is the National Gallery, with Norway's best collection of paintings (self-guided tour on page 242).

Take a moment here to do a 360-degree spin to notice how quiet and orderly everything is. Many communities suffer from a "free rider" problem—which occurs when someone does something that would mess things up for all if everyone did it. (The transgressor believes his actions are OK because most people toe the line.) Norwegian society, with its heightened sense of social responsibility, doesn't experience this phenomenon.

• *Facing the theater, follow Roald Amundsens Gate left, to the towering brick...*

City Hall (Rådhuset): Built mostly in the 1930s with contributions from Norway's leading artists, City Hall is full of great art and is worth touring (see page 236). The mayor has his office here (at the base of one of the two 200-foot towers), and every December 10, this building is where the Nobel Peace Prize is presented. For the best exterior art, circle the courtyard clockwise, studying the colorful woodcuts in the arcade. Each shows a scene from Norwegian mythology, well-explained in English: Thor with his billy-goat chariot, Ask and Embla (a kind of Norse Adam and Eve), Odin on his eight-legged horse guided by ravens, the swan maidens shedding their swan disguises, and so on. Circle to the right around City Hall, until you reach the front. The statues (especially the six laborers on the other side of the building, facing the harbor, who seem to guard the facade) celebrate the nobility of the working class. Norway, a social democracy, believes in giving respect to the workers who built their society and made it what it is, and these laborers are viewed as heroes.

• *Walk to the...*

Harbor: A decade ago, you would have dodged several lanes of busy traffic to get to Oslo's harborfront. But today, most cars cross underneath the city in tunnels. In addition, the city has made its town center relatively quiet and pedestrian-friendly by levying a traffic-discouraging 35-kr toll for every car entering town. (This system, like a similar one in London, subsidizes public transit and the city's infrastructure.)

At the water's edge, find the shiny metal plaque (just left of center) listing the contents of a sealed time capsule planted in 2000 out in the harbor in the little Kavringen lighthouse straight ahead (to be opened in 1,000 years). Go to the end of the stubby pier (on the right). This is the ceremonial "enter the city" point for momentous occasions. One such instance was in 1905, when Norway gained its independence from Sweden and a Danish prince sailed in from Copenhagen to become the first modern king of Norway. Another milestone event occurred at the end of World War II, when the king returned to Norway after the country was liberated from the Nazis.

• *Stand at the harbor and give it a sweeping counterclockwise look.*

Harborfront Spin-Tour: Oslofjord is a huge playground, with 40 city-owned, park-like islands. Big white cruise ships—a large part of the local tourist economy—dock just under the Akershus Fortress on the left. Just past the fort's impressive 13th-century ramparts, a statue of FDR grabs the shade. He's here in gratitude for the safe refuge the US gave to members of the royal family (including the young prince who is now Norway's king) during World War II—while the king and his government-in-exile waged Norway's fight against the Nazis from London.

Enjoy the grand view of City Hall. The yellow building farther to the left was the old West Train Station; today it houses the **Nobel Peace Center,** which celebrates the work of Nobel Peace Prize winners (see page 238). The next pier is the launchpad for

Oslo at a Glance

▲▲▲**City Hall** Oslo's artsy 20th-century government building, lined with huge, vibrant, municipal-themed murals, best visited with included tour. **Hours:** Daily 9:00-18:00; 3 tours/day, tours run Wed only in winter. See page 236.

▲▲▲**National Gallery** Norway's cultural and natural essence, captured on canvas. **Hours:** Tue-Fri 10:00-18:00, Thu until 19:00, Sat-Sun 11:00-17:00, closed Mon. See page 242.

▲▲▲**Vigeland Park** Set in sprawling Frogner Park, with tons of statuary by Norway's greatest sculptor, Gustav Vigeland, and the studio where he worked (now a museum). **Hours:** Park—always open; Vigeland Museum—May-Aug Tue-Sun 10:00-17:00, Sept-April Tue-Sun 12:00-16:00, closed Mon year-round. See page 250.

▲▲▲**Norwegian Folk Museum** Norway condensed into 150 historic buildings in a large open-air park. **Hours:** Daily mid-May-mid-Sept 10:00-18:00, off-season park open Mon-Fri 11:00-15:00, Sat-Sun 11:00-16:00, but most historical buildings closed. See page 255.

▲▲**Norwegian Resistance Museum** Gripping look at Norway's tumultuous WWII experience. **Hours:** June-Aug Mon-Sat 10:00-17:00, Sun 11:00-17:00; Sept-May Mon-Fri 10:00-16:00, Sat-Sun 11:00-16:00. See page 241.

▲▲**Viking Ship Museum** An impressive trio of ninth-century Viking ships, with exhibits on the people who built them. **Hours:** Daily May-Sept 9:00-18:00, Oct-April 10:00-16:00. See page 256.

▲▲*Fram* **Museum** Captivating exhibit on the Arctic exploration ships *Fram* and *Gjøa*. **Hours:** June-Aug daily 9:00-18:00; May and Sept daily 10:00-17:00; Oct and March-April daily 10:00-16:00; Nov-Feb Mon-Fri 10:00-15:00, Sat-Sun 10:00-16:00. See page 258.

▲▲*Kon-Tiki* **Museum** Adventures of primitive *Kon-Tiki* and *Ra II* ships built by Thor Heyerdahl. **Hours:** Daily June-Aug 9:30-18:00, March-May and Sept-Oct 10:00-17:00, Nov-Feb 10:00-16:00. See page 258.

▲▲**Holmenkollen Ski Jump and Ski Museum** Dizzying vista and a schuss through skiing history. **Hours:** Daily June-Aug 9:00-20:00, May and Sept 10:00-17:00, Oct-April 10:00-16:00. See page 265.

▲**Nobel Peace Center** Exhibit celebrating the ideals of the Nobel Peace Prize and the lives of those who have won it. **Hours:** Mid-May-Aug daily 10:00-18:00; Sept-mid-May Tue-Sun 10:00-18:00, closed Mon. See page 238.

▲**Opera House** Stunning performance center that's helping revitalize the harborfront. **Hours:** Foyer and café/restaurant open Mon-Fri 10:00-23:00, Sat 11:00-23:00, Sun 12:00-22:00; usually 3 tours/day of Opera House in summer. See page 238.

▲**Akershus Fortress Complex and Tours** Historic military base and fortified old center, with guided tours, a ho-hum castle interior, and a couple of museums (including the excellent Norwegian Resistance Museum, listed earlier). **Hours:** Park generally open daily 6:00-21:00; generally 3 one-hour tours/day, fewer off-season. See page 240.

▲**Norwegian Maritime Museum** Dusty cruise through Norway's rich seafaring heritage. **Hours:** Mid-May-Aug daily 10:00-17:00; Sept-mid-May Tue-Fri 10:00-15:00, Sat-Sun 10:00-16:00, closed Mon. See page 259.

▲**Norwegian Holocaust Center** High-tech walk through rise of anti-Semitism, the Holocaust in Norway, and racism today. **Hours:** June-Aug daily 10:00-18:00, Sept-May Mon-Fri 10:00-16:00, Sat-Sun 11:00-16:00. See page 259.

▲**Ekeberg Sculpture Park** Hilly, hikeable 63-acre forest park dotted with striking contemporary art. **Hours:** Always open. See page 266.

▲**Edvard Munch Museum** Works of Norway's famous Expressionistic painter. **Hours:** Mid-June-Sept daily 10:00-17:00; Oct-mid-June Wed-Mon 11:00-17:00, closed Tue. See page 267.

▲**Grünerløkka** Oslo's bohemian district, with bustling cafés and pubs. **Hours:** Always open. See page 260.

▲**Aker Brygge and Tjuvholmen** Oslo's harborfront promenade, and nearby trendy Tjuvholmen neighborhood with Astrup Fearnley Museum, upscale galleries, shops, and cafés. **Hours:** Always strollable. See page 239.

OSLO

harbor boat tours and the shuttle boat to the Bygdøy museums. A fisherman often moors his boat here, selling shrimp from the back.

At the other end of the harbor, shipyard buildings (this was the former heart of Norway's once-important shipbuilding industry) have been transformed into **Aker Brygge**—Oslo's thriving restaurant/shopping/nightclub zone (see "Eating in Oslo").

Just past the end of Aker Brygge is a new housing development—dubbed Norway's most expensive real estate—called **Tjuvholmen.** It's anchored by the Astrup Fearnley Museum, an international modern art museum complex designed by renowned architect Renzo Piano (most famous for Paris' Pompidou Center; www.afmuseet.no). This zone is just one more reminder of Oslo's bold march toward becoming a city that is at once futuristic and people-friendly.

An ambitious urban renewal project called Fjord City (Fjordbyen)—which kicked off years ago with Aker Brygge, and led to the construction of Oslo's dramatic Opera House (see page 238)—is making remarkable progress in turning the formerly industrial waterfront into a flourishing people zone.

• *From here, you can stroll out Aker Brygge and through Tjuvholmen to a tiny public beach at the far end, tour City Hall, visit the Nobel Peace Center, hike up to Akershus Fortress, take a harbor cruise (see "Tours in Oslo," earlier), or catch a boat across the harbor to the museums at Bygdøy (from pier 3). The sights just mentioned are described in detail in the following section.*

Sights in Oslo

NEAR THE HARBORFRONT
▲▲▲City Hall (Rådhuset)

In 1931, Oslo tore down a slum and began constructing its richly decorated City Hall. It was finally finished—after a WWII delay—in 1950 to celebrate the city's 900th birthday. Norway's leading artists all contributed to the building, which was an avant-garde thrill in its day. City halls, rather than churches, are the dominant buildings in Scandinavian capitals. The prominence of this building on the harborfront makes sense in this most humanistic, yet least churchgoing, northern end of the Continent. Up here, people pay high taxes, have high expectations, and are generally satisfied with what their governments do with their money.

Cost and Hours: Free, daily 9:00-18:00, free 50-minute guided tours daily at 10:00, 12:00, and 14:00 in summer, tours run Wed only in winter, free and fine WC, enter on Karl Johans Gate side, tel. 23 46 12 00.

Visiting City Hall: At Oslo's City Hall, the six statues facing the waterfront—dating from a period of Labor Party rule in Norway—celebrate the nobility of the working class. The art implies a classless society, showing everyone working together. The theme continues inside, with 20,000 square feet of bold and colorful Socialist Realist murals showing town folk, country folk, and people from all walks of life working harmoniously for a better society. The huge murals take you on a voyage through the collective psyche of Norway, from its simple rural beginnings through the scar tissue of the Nazi occupation and beyond. Filled with significance and symbolism—and well-described in English—the murals become even more meaningful with the excellent guided tours.

The main hall feels like a temple to good government, with its altar-like mural celebrating "work, play, and civic administration." The mural emphasizes Oslo's youth participating in community life—and rebuilding the country after Nazi occupation. Across the bottom, the slum that once cluttered up Oslo's harborfront is being cleared out to make way for this building. Above that, scenes show Norway's pride in its innovative health care and education systems. Left of center, near the top, Mother Norway rests on a church—reminding viewers that the Lutheran Church of Norway (the official state religion) provides a foundation for this society. On the right, four forms represent the arts; they illustrate how creativity springs from children. And in the center, the figure of Charity is

surrounded by Culture, Philosophy, and Family.

The "Mural of the Occupation" lines the left side of the hall. It tells the story of Norway's WWII experience. Looking left to right, you'll see the following: The German blitzkrieg overwhelms the country. Men head for the mountains to organize a

resistance movement. Women huddle around the water well, traditionally where news is passed, while Quislings (traitors named after the Norwegian fascist who ruled the country as a Nazi puppet) listen in. While Germans bomb and occupy Norway, a family gathers in their living room. As a boy clenches his fist (showing determination) and a child holds the beloved Norwegian flag, the

Gestapo steps in. Columns lie on the ground, symbolizing how Germans shut down the culture by closing newspapers and the university. Two resistance soldiers are executed. A cell of resistance fighters (wearing masks and using nicknames, so if tortured they can't reveal their compatriots' identities) plan a sabotage mission. Finally, prisoners are freed, the war is over, and Norway celebrates its happiest day: May 17, 1945—the first Constitution Day after five years under Nazi control.

While gazing at these murals, keep in mind that the Nobel Peace Prize is awarded in this central hall each December (though the general Nobel Prize ceremony occurs in Stockholm's City Hall). You can see videos of the ceremony and acceptance speeches in the adjacent Nobel Peace Center (see next).

Eating: Fans of the explorer Fridtjof Nansen might enjoy a coffee or beer across the street at Fridtjof, an atmospheric bar filled with memorabilia from Nansen's Arctic explorations. A model of his ship, the *Fram*, hangs from the ceiling, and 1894 photos and his own drawings are upstairs (Mon-Sat 12:00 until late, Sun 14:00-22:00, Nansens Plass 7, near Forex, tel. 93 25 22 30).

▲Nobel Peace Center (Nobels Fredssenter)

This thoughtful and thought-provoking museum, housed in the former West Train Station (Vestbanen), poses the question, "What is the opposite of conflict?" It celebrates the 800-some past and present Nobel Peace Prize winners with engaging audio and video exhibits and high-tech gadgetry (all with good English explanations). Allow time for reading about past prizewinners and listening to acceptance speeches by recipients from President Carter to Mother Theresa. Check out the astonishing interactive book detailing the life and work of Alfred Nobel, the Swedish inventor of dynamite, who initiated the prizes—perhaps to assuage his conscience.

Cost and Hours: 90 kr; mid-May-Aug daily 10:00-18:00; Sept-mid-May Tue-Sun 10:00-18:00, closed Mon; included English guided tours at 12:00 and 15:00, fewer in winter; Brynjulfs Bulls Plass 1, tel. 48 30 10 00, www.nobelpeacecenter.org.

▲Opera House

Opened in 2008, Oslo's striking Opera House is still the talk of the town and a huge hit. The building rises from the water on the city's eastern harbor, across the highway from the train station (use the sky-bridge). Its boxy, low-slung, glass center holds a state-of-the-art 1,400-seat main theater with a 99-piece orchestra "in

the pit," which can rise to put the orchestra "on the pedestal." The season is split between opera and ballet.

Information-packed, 50-minute tours explain what makes this one of the greenest buildings in Europe and why Norwegian taxpayers helped foot the half-billion dollar cost for this project—to make high culture (ballet and opera) accessible to the younger generation and a strata of society who normally wouldn't care. You'll see a workshop employing 50 people who hand-make costumes, and learn how the foundation of 700 pylons set 40 or 50 meters deep support the jigsaw puzzle of wood, glass, and 36,000 individual pieces of marble. The construction masterfully integrates land and water, inside and outside, nature and culture.

The jutting white marble planes of the Opera House's roof double as a public plaza. When visiting, you feel a need to walk all over it. The Opera House is part of a larger harbor-redevelopment plan that includes rerouting traffic into tunnels and turning a once-derelict industrial zone into an urban park.

Cost and Hours: Foyer and café/restaurant open Mon-Fri 10:00-23:00, Sat 11:00-23:00, Sun 12:00-22:00.

Tours: In summer, the Opera House offers sporadic foyer concerts (50 kr, generally at 13:00) and fascinating 50-minute guided tours of the stage, backstage area, and architecture (100 kr, usually 3 tours/day in English—generally at 11:00, 12:00, and 14:00, reserve by email at omvisninger@operaen.no or online at www. operaen.no, tel. 21 42 21 00).

Getting There: The easiest way to get to the Opera House is from the train station. Just follow signs for *Exit South/Utgang Syd* (standing in the main hall with the tracks to your back, it's to the left). Exiting the station, proceed straight ahead onto the pedestrian bridge (marked *Velkommen til Operaen*), which takes you effortlessly above traffic congestion to your goal.

▲Aker Brygge and Tjuvholmen

Oslo's harborfront was dominated by the Aker Brygge shipyard until it closed in 1986. Today this is the first finished part of a project (called Fjordbyen, or Fjord City) that will turn the central stretch of Oslo's harborfront into a people-friendly park and culture zone. Aker Brygge is a stretch of trendy yacht-club style restaurants facing a fine promenade—just the place to join in on a Nordic paseo on a balmy summer's eve.

The far end of Aker Brygge is marked by a big black anchor (from the German warship *Blücher*, sunk by Norwegian forces near Drøbak during the Nazi invasion on April 9, 1940). From there a bridge crosses over into Tjuvholmen (named for the place they hung thieves back in the 17th century). This is a planned and future-esque community, with the trendiest and costliest apartments in town, lots of galleries, elegant shops and cafés, and the strik-ing Astrup Fearnley Museum of Modern Art nearby. As you stroll through Tjuvholmen, admire how each building has its own per-sonality.

Eating: Dining here is a great idea in the evening. Choose from many restaurants, or take advantage of the generous public benches, lounge chairs, and picnic tables that allow people who can't afford a fancy restaurant meal to enjoy the best seats of all (grocery stores are a block away from the harborfront views).

▲AKERSHUS FORTRESS COMPLEX

This park-like complex of sights scattered over Oslo's fortified old center is still a military base. (The Royal Guard is present because the castle is a royal mausoleum.) But the public is welcome, and as you dodge patrol guards and vans filled with soldiers, you'll see the castle, a prison, war memorials, the Norwegian Resistance Mu-seum, the Armed Forces Museum, and cannon-strewn ramparts affording fine harbor views and picnic perches. There's an unim-pressive changing of the guard daily at 13:30 (at the parade ground, deep in the castle complex). The park is generally open daily 6:00-21:00, but because the military is in charge here, times can change without warning. Expect bumpy cobblestone lanes and steep hills. To get here from the harbor, follow the stairs (which lead past the FDR statue) to the park.

Fortress Visitors Center: Located immediately inside the gate, the information center has an exhibit tracing the story of Os-lo's fortifications from medieval times through the environmental struggles of today. Stop here to pick up the fortress trail and site map, quickly browse through the museum, and consider catching a tour (see next; museum entry free, mid-June-mid-Aug Mon-Fri 10:00-17:00, Sat-Sun 11:00-17:00, shorter hours off-season, tel. 23 09 39 17, www.mil.no/felles/ak).

▲Fortress Tours

The 50-kr hour-long English walking tours of the grounds help you make sense of the most historic piece of real estate in Oslo (mid-June-mid-Aug 3/day, fewer off-season; depart from Fortress Visitors Center, call center at tel. 23 09 39 17 in advance to confirm times).

Akershus Castle

The first fortress here was built by Norwegians in 1299. It was rebuilt much stronger by the Danes in 1640 so the Danish king (Christian IV) would have a suitable and safe place to stay during his many visits. When

Oslo was rebuilt in the 17th century, many of the stones from the first Oslo cathedral were reused here, in the fortress walls.

Although it's one of Oslo's oldest buildings, the castle overlooking the harbor is mediocre by European standards; the big, empty rooms recall Norway's medieval poverty. From the old kitchen, where the ticket desk and gift shop are located, you'll follow a one-way circuit of rooms open to the public. Descend through a secret passage to the dungeon, crypt, and royal tomb. Emerge behind the altar in the chapel, then walk through echoing rooms including the Daredevil's Tower, Hall of Christian IV (with portraits of Danish kings of Norway on the walls), and Hall of Olav I. There are terrific harbor views (often filled with a giant cruise ship) from the rampart just outside.

Cost and Hours: 70 kr, includes audioguide with 45-minute tour and ghost story options; May-Aug Mon-Sat 10:00-16:00, Sun 12:30-16:00; Sept-April Sat-Sun 12:00-17:00 only, closed Mon-Fri; tel. 22 41 25 21.

▲▲Norwegian Resistance Museum (Norges Hjemmefrontmuseum)

This fascinating museum tells the story of Norway's WWII experience: appeasement, Nazi invasion (they made Akershus their headquarters), resistance, liberation, and, finally, the return of the king.

Cost and Hours: 50 kr; June-Aug Mon-Sat 10:00-17:00, Sun 11:00-17:00; Sept-May Mon-Fri 10:00-16:00, Sat-Sun 11:00-16:00; next to castle, overlooking harbor, tel. 23 09 31 38, www.forsvaretsmuseer.no.

Visiting the Museum: It's a one-way, chronological, can't-get-lost route. As you enter the museum, you're transported back to 1940, greeted by an angry commotion of rifles aimed at you. A German notice proclaiming "You will submit or die" is bayonetted onto a gun in the middle.

You'll see propaganda posters attempting to get Norwegians to join the Nazi party, and the German ultimatum to which the king gave an emphatic "No." Various displays show secret radios, transmitters, underground newspapers, crude but effective homemade weapons, and the German machine that located clandestine radio stations. Exhibits explain how the country coped with 350,000 occupying troops; how airdrops equipped a home force of 40,000 so they were ready to coordinate with the Allies when liberation was imminent; and the happy day when the resistance army came out of the forest, and peace and freedom returned to Norway.

The museum is particularly poignant because many of the patriots featured inside were executed by the Germans right outside the museum's front door; a stone memorial marks the spot. (At war's end, the traitor Vidkun Quisling was also executed at the

fortress, but at a different location.)
With good English descriptions, this
is an inspirational look at how the
national spirit can endure total occupation by a malevolent force. (Note:
Copenhagen's Resistance Museum
burned down and neutral Sweden
didn't have a resistance.)

Armed Forces Museum (Forsvarsmuseet)

Across the fortress parade ground, a too-spacious museum traces
Norwegian military history from Viking days to post-World War
II. The early stuff is sketchy, but the WWII story is compelling.

Cost and Hours: Free, May-Aug Mon-Fri 10:00-16:00, Sat-
Sun 11:00-17:00, shorter hours off-season, tel. 23 09 35 82.

Old Christiania

In the mid-1600s, the ruling Danes had the original Oslo leveled
and built a more modern grid-planned city. They built with stone
so it wouldn't burn, and located it just below the castle so it was
easier to control and defend. They named it Christiania, after their
king. The checkerboard zone between the castle and the cathedral
today marks that original Christiania town. While Oslo didn't
do a good job of protecting it through the 20th century, bits of
Christiania's original Dutch Renaissance-style buildings survive.
(Norwegian builders, accustomed to working with wood, lacked
skill with stone, so the Danes imported Dutch builders.) The main
square, Christiania Torv, is marked by a modern fountain called
"The Glove." The sculpture of Christian IV's glove points as if to
indicate, "This is where we'll build my city." The old City Hall, now
the Gamle Raadhus restaurant, survives. If you explore this district
you'll see several 17th-century buildings.

DOWNTOWN MUSEUMS

▲▲▲National Gallery (Nasjonalgalleriet)

While there are many schools of painting and sculpture displayed
in Norway's National Gallery, focus on what's uniquely Norwegian. Paintings come and go in this museum (pesky curators may
have even removed some of the ones listed in the self-guided tour
on the next page), but you're sure to see plenty that showcase the
harsh beauty of Norway's landscape and people. A thoughtful visit
here gives those heading into the mountains and fjord country a
chance to pack along a little of Norway's cultural soul. Tuck these
images carefully away with your goat cheese—they'll sweeten your
explorations.

The gallery also has several Picassos, a noteworthy Impressionist collection, a Van Gogh self-portrait, and some Vigeland statues. Its many raving examples of Edvard Munch's work, including one of his famous *Scream* paintings, make a trip to the Munch Museum unnecessary for most (see page 267). It has about 50 Munch paintings in its collection, but only about a third are on display. Be prepared for changes, but don't worry—no matter what the curators decide to show, you won't have to scream for Munch's masterpieces.

Cost and Hours: 50 kr, free on Sun, Tue-Fri 10:00-18:00, Thu until 19:00, Sat-Sun 11:00-17:00, closed Mon, chewing gum prohibited, Universitets Gata 13, tel. 22 20 04 04, www.nasjonalmuseet.no. Pick up the guidebooklet to help navigate the collection.

Eating: The richly ornamented French Salon café offers an elegant break.

➲ **Self-Guided Tour:** This easy-to-handle museum gives an effortless tour back in time and through Norway's most beautiful valleys, mountains, and fjords, with the help of its Romantic painters (especially Johan Christian Dahl).

• *Go up the stairs into Room 24 and turn left into Room 13.*

Landscape Paintings and Romanticism

Landscape painting has always played an important role in Norwegian art, perhaps because Norway provides such an awesome and varied landscape to inspire artists. The style reached its peak during the Romantic period in the mid-1800s, which stressed the beauty of unspoiled nature. (This passion for landscapes sets Norway apart from Denmark and Sweden.) After 400 years of Danish rule, the soul of the country was almost snuffed out. But with semi-independence and a constitution in the early 1800s, there was a national resurgence. Romantic paintings featuring the power of Norway's natural wonders and the toughness of its salt-of-the-earth folk came into vogue.

❶ **Johan Christian Dahl—*View from Stalheim* (1842):** This painting epitomizes the Norwegian closeness to nature. It shows a view very similar to the one that 21st-century travelers enjoy on their Norway in a Nutshell excursion (see page 289): mountains, rivers, and farms clinging to hillsides. Painted in 1842, it's quintessential Romantic style. Nature rules—the background is as detailed as the foreground, and you are sucked in.

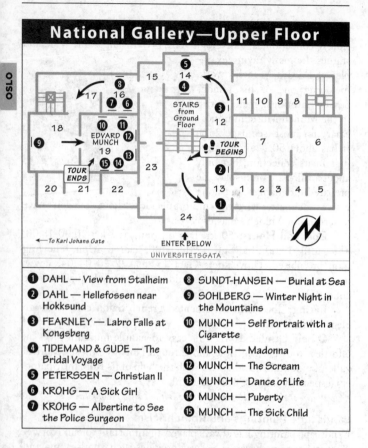

National Gallery—Upper Floor

1 DAHL — View from Stalheim

2 DAHL — Hellefossen near Hokksund

3 FEARNLEY — Labro Falls at Kongsberg

4 TIDEMAND & GUDE — The Bridal Voyage

5 PETERSSEN — Christian II

6 KROHG — A Sick Girl

7 KROHG — Albertine to See the Police Surgeon

8 SUNDT-HANSEN — Burial at Sea

9 SOHLBERG — Winter Night in the Mountains

10 MUNCH — Self Portrait with a Cigarette

11 MUNCH — Madonna

12 MUNCH — The Scream

13 MUNCH — Dance of Life

14 MUNCH — Puberty

15 MUNCH — The Sick Child

Johan Christian Dahl (1788-1857) is considered the father of Norwegian Romanticism. Romantics such as Dahl (and Turner, Beethoven, and Lord Byron) put emotion over rationality. They reveled in the power of nature—death and pessimism ripple through their work, though in this scene a double rainbow and a splash of sunlight give hope of a better day. The birch tree—standing boldly front and center—is a standard symbol for the politically downtrodden Norwegian people: hardy, weathered, but defiantly sprouting new branches. In the mid-19th century, Norwegians were awakening to their national identity. Throughout Europe, nationalism and Romanticism went hand in hand.

Find the farm buildings huddled near the cliff's edge, smoke rising from chimneys, and the woman in traditional dress tending her herd of goats, pausing for a moment to revel in the glory of nature. It reminds us that these farmers are hardworking, independent, small landowners. There was no feudalism in medieval

Norway. People were poor...but they owned their own land. You can almost taste goat cheese.

• *Look at the other works in Rooms 13 and 12. Dahl's paintings and those by his Norwegian contemporaries, showing heavy clouds and glaciers, repeat these same themes—drama over rationalism, nature pounding humanity. Human figures are melancholy. Norwegians, so close to nature, are fascinated by those plush, magic hours of dawn and twilight. The dusk makes us wonder: What will the future bring?*

In particular, focus on the painting to the left of the door in Room 13.

❷ **Dahl**—*Hellefossen near Hokksund* **(1838):** Another typical Dahl setting: romantic nature and an idealized scene. A fisherman checks on wooden baskets designed to catch salmon migrating up the river. In the background, a water-powered sawmill slices trees into lumber. Note another Dahl birch tree at the left, a subtle celebration of the Norwegian people and their labor.

• *Now continue into Room 12. On the right is...*

❸ **Thomas Fearnley**—*Labro Falls at Kongsberg* **(1837):** Man cannot control nature or his destiny. The landscape in this painting is devoid of people—the only sign of humanity is the jumble of sawn logs in the foreground. A wary eagle perched on one log seems to be saying, "While you can cut these trees, they'll always be mine."

• *Continue to the end of Room 12, and turn left into Room 14.*

❹ **Adolph Tidemand and Hans Gude**—*The Bridal Voyage* **(1848):** This famous painting shows the ultimate Norwegian

scene: a wedding party with everyone decked out in traditional garb, heading for the stave church on the quintessential fjord (Hardanger). It's a studio work (not real) and a collaboration: Hans Gude painted the landscape, and Adolph Tidemand painted the people. Study their wedding finery. This work trumpets the greatness of both the landscape and Norwegian culture.

• *Also in Room 14, on the opposite wall, is an example of...*

The Photographic Eye

At the end of the 19th century, Norwegian painters traded the emotions of Romanticism for more slice-of-life detail. This was the end of the Romantic period and the beginning of Realism. With the advent of photography, painters went beyond simple realism and into extreme realism.

❺ **Eilif Peterssen**—*Christian II* **(1875):** The Danish king signs the execution order for the man who'd killed the king's beloved mistress. With camera-like precision, the painter captures the whole story of murder, anguish, anger, and bitter revenge in the king's set jaw and steely eyes.

• *Go through Room 15 and into Room 16. Take time to browse the paintings.*

Vulnerability

Death, disease, and suffering were themes seen again and again in art from the late 1800s. The most serious disease during this period was tuberculosis (which killed Munch's mother and sister).

❻ Christian Krohg—A Sick Girl (1880): Christian Krohg (1852-1925) is known as Edvard Munch's inspiration, but to Nor-

wegians, he's famous in his own right for his artistry and giant personality. This extremely realistic painting shows a child dying of tuberculosis, as so many did in Norway in the 19th century. The girl looks directly at you. You can almost feel the cloth, with its many shades of white.

• *And just to the right of this painting, find...*

❼ Krohg—*Albertine to See the Police Surgeon* (c. 1885-1887): Krohg had a sharp interest in social justice. In this painting, Albertine, a sweet girl from the countryside, has fallen into the world of prostitu-

tion in the big city. She's the new kid on the Red Light block in the 1880s, as Oslo's prostitutes are pulled into the police clinic for their regular checkup. Note her traditional dress and the disdain she gets from the more experienced girls. Krohg has buried his subject in this scene. His technique requires the viewer to find her, and that search helps humanize the prostitute.

• *In Room 16 you may also find...*

❽ Carl Sundt-Hansen—*Burial at Sea* (1890): While Monet and the Impressionists were busy abandoning the realistic style, Norwegian artists continued to embrace it. In this painting, you're invited to participate. A dead man's funeral is attended by an ethnically diverse group of sailors and passengers, but only one is a woman—the widow. Your presence completes the half-circle at the on-deck ceremony. Notice how each person in the painting has his or her own way of confronting death. Their faces speak volumes about the life of toil here. A common thread in Norwegian art is the cycle—the tough cycle—of life. There's also an interest in

everyday experiences. *Burial at Sea* may not always be on display. If it's not here, you may instead see a similar canvas, **Erik Werenskiold's** *A Peasant Burial* (1885).
• *Continue through Room 17 and into Room 18.*

Atmosphere

Landscape painters were often fascinated by the phenomena of nature, and the artwork in this room takes us back to this ideal from the Romantic Age. Painters were challenged by capturing atmospheric conditions at a specific moment, since it meant making quick sketches outdoors, before the weather changed yet again.

❾ **Harald Sohlberg**—*Winter Night in the Mountains* (1914): Harald Sohlberg was inspired by this image while skiing in the

mountains in the winter of 1899. Over the years, he attempted to re-create the scene that inspired this remark: "The mountains in winter reduce one to silence. One is overwhelmed, as in a mighty, vaulted church, only a thousand times more so."
• *Follow the crowds into Room 19, the Munch room.*

Turmoil

Room 19 is filled with works by Norway's single most famous painter, Edvard Munch (see sidebar). Norway's long, dark winters and social isolation have produced many gloomy artists, but none gloomier than Munch. He infused his work with emotion and expression at the expense of realism. After viewing the paintings in general, take a look at these in particular (listed in clockwise order).

❿ **Edvard Munch**—*Self Portrait with a Cigarette* (1895): In this self-portrait, Munch is spooked, haunted—an artist working, immersed in an oppressive world. Indefinable shadows inhabit the background. His hand shakes as he considers his uncertain future. (Ironic, considering he created his masterpieces during this depressed period.) After eight months in a Danish clinic, he found peace—and lost his painting power. Afterward, Munch never again painted another strong example of what we love most about his art.

⓫ **Munch**—*Madonna* (1894-1895): Munch had a tortured relationship with women. He never married. He dreaded and struggled with love, writing that he feared if he loved too much, he'd lose his painting talent. This painting is a mystery: Is she standing or lying? Is that a red halo or some devilish accessory? Munch

OSLO

Edvard Munch (1863-1944)

Edvard Munch (pronounced "moonk") is Norway's most famous and influential painter. His life was rich, complex, and sad. His father was a doctor who had a nervous breakdown. His mother and sister both died of tuberculosis. He knew suffering. And he gave us the enduring symbol of 20th-century pain, *The Scream*.

He was also Norway's most forward-thinking painter, a man who traveled extensively through Europe, soaking up the colors of the Post-Impressionists and the curves of Art Nouveau. He helped pioneer a new style—Expressionism—using lurid colors and wavy lines to "express" inner turmoil and the angst of the modern world.

After a nervous breakdown in late 1908, followed by eight months of rehab in a clinic, Munch emerged less troubled—but a less powerful painter. His late works were as a colorist: big, bright, less tormented...and less noticed.

---

wrote that he would strive to capture his subjects at their holiest moment. His alternative name for this work: *Woman Making Love*. What's more holy than a woman at the moment of conception?

⓱ Munch—*The Scream* (1893): Munch's most famous work shows a man screaming, capturing the fright many feel as the human "race" does just that. The figure seems isolated from the people on the bridge—locked up in himself, unable to stifle his scream. Munch made four versions of this scene, which has become *the* textbook example of Expressionism. On one, he graffitied: "This painting is the work of a madman." He explained that the painting "shows today's society, reverberating within me...making me want to scream." He's sharing his internal angst. In fact, this Expressionist masterpiece is a breakthrough painting; it's angst personified.

⓲ Munch—*Dance of Life* (1899-1900): In this scene of five dancing couples, we glimpse Munch's notion of femininity. To him, women were a complex mix of Madonna and whore. We see

Munch's take on the cycle of women's lives: She's a virgin (discarding the sweet flower of youth), a whore (a jaded temptress in red), and a widow (having destroyed the man, she is finally alone, aging, in black). With the phallic moon rising on the lake, Munch demonizes women as they turn men into green-faced, lusty monsters.

OSLO

❹ **Munch—*Puberty* (1894-1895):** One of the artist's most important non-*Scream* canvases reveals his ambivalence about women (see also his *Madonna*, earlier). This adolescent girl, grappling with her emerging sexuality, covers her nudity self-consciously. The looming shadow behind her—frighteningly too big and amorphous—threatens to take over the scene. The shadow's significance is open to interpretation—is it phallic, female genitalia, death, an embodiment of sexual anxiety...or Munch himself?

❺ **Munch—*The Sick Child* (1896):** The death of Munch's sister in 1877 due to tuberculosis likely inspired this painting. The girl's face melts into the pillow. She's becoming two-dimensional, halfway between life and death. Everything else is peripheral, even her despairing mother saying good-bye. You can see how Munch scraped and repainted the face until he got it right.

• *Our tour is over, but there's more to see in this fine collection. Take a break from Nordic gloom and doom by visiting Rooms 15 and 23, with works by Impressionist and Post-Impressionist artists...even Munch got into the spirit with his Parisian painting, titled* Rue Lafayette. *You'll see lesser-known, but still beautiful, paintings by non-Norwegian big names such as Picasso, Modigliani, Monet, Manet, Van Gogh, Gauguin, and Cézanne.*

National Historical Museum (Historisk Museum)

Directly behind the National Gallery and just below the palace is a fine Art Nouveau building offering an easy (if underwhelming) peek at Norway's history.

Cost and Hours: 50 kr, mid-May-mid-Sept Tue-Sun 10:00-17:00, mid-Sept-mid-May Tue-Sun 11:00-16:00, closed Mon year-round; Frederiks Gate 2, tel. 22 85 99 12, www.khm.uio.no.

Visiting the Museum: The ground floor offers a walk through the local history from prehistoric times. It includes the country's top collection of Viking artifacts, displayed in low-tech, old-school exhibits with barely a word of English to give it meaning. There's also some medieval church art. The museum's highlight is upstairs: an exhibit (well-described in English) about life in the Arctic for the Sami people (previously known to outsiders as Laplanders). In this overview of the past, a few Egyptian mummies and Norwegian coins through the ages are tossed in for good measure.

Gustav Vigeland (1869-1943)

As a young man, Vigeland studied sculpture in Oslo, then supplemented his education with trips abroad to Europe's art capitals. Back home, he carved out a successful, critically acclaimed career feeding newly independent Norway's hunger for homegrown art.

During his youthful trips abroad, Vigeland had frequented the studio of Auguste Rodin, admiring Rodin's naked, restless, intertwined statues. Like Rodin, Vigeland explored the yin/yang relationship of men and women. Also like Rodin, Vigeland did not personally carve or cast his statues. Rather, he formed them in clay or plaster, to be executed by a workshop of assistants. Vigeland's sturdy humans capture universal themes of the cycle of life—birth, childhood, romance, struggle, child-rearing, growing old, and death.

A PARK AND TWO MUSEUMS
▲▲▲Vigeland Park

Within Oslo's vast Frogner Park is Vigeland Park, containing a lifetime of work by Norway's greatest sculptor, Gustav Vigeland (see sidebar). In 1921, he made a deal with the city. In return for a great studio and state support, he'd spend his creative life beautifying Oslo with this sculpture garden. From 1924 to 1943 he worked on-site, designing 192 bronze and granite statue groupings—600 figures in all, each nude and unique. Vigeland even planned the landscaping. Today the park is loved and respected by the people of Oslo (no police, no fences—and no graffiti). The Frognerbadet swimming pool is nearby in Frogner Park.

Cost and Hours: The garden is always open and free. The park is safe (cameras monitor for safety) and lit in the evening.

Getting There: Tram #12—which leaves from the central train station, Rådhusplassen in front of City Hall, Aker Brygge, and other points in town—drops you off right at the park gate (Vigelandsparken stop). Tram #19 (with stops along Karl Johans Gate) takes you to Majorstuen, a 10-minute walk to the gate (or you can change at Majorstuen to tram #12 and ride it one stop to Vigelandsparken).

Visiting the Park: Vigeland Park is more than great art: It's a city at play. Appreciate its urban Norwegian ambience.

The park is huge, but this visit is a snap. Here's a quick, four-stop, straight-line, gate-to-monolith tour:

Enter the Park from Kirkeveien: For an illustrated guide and fine souvenir, pick up the 75-kr book in the Visitors Center (Besøkssenter) on your right

as you enter. The modern cafeteria has sandwiches (indoor/outdoor seating, daily 9:00-20:30, shorter hours Sun and off-season), plus books, gifts, and WCs. Look at the statue of Gustav Vigeland (hammer and chisel in hand, drenched in pigeon poop) and consider his messed-up life. He lived with his many models. His marriages failed. His children entangled his artistic agenda. He didn't age gracefully. He didn't name his statues, and refused to explain their meanings. While those who know his life story can read it clearly in the granite and bronze, I'd forget Gustav's troubles and see his art as observations on the bittersweet cycle of life in general—from a man who must have had a passion for living.

Bridge: The 300-foot-long bridge is bounded by four granite columns: Three show a man fighting a lizard, the fourth shows a woman submitting to the lizard's embrace. Hmmm. (Vigeland was familiar with medieval mythology, where dragons represent man's primal—and sinful—nature.) But enough lizard love; the 58 bronze statues along the bridge are a general study of the human body. Many deal with relationships between people. In the middle, on the right, find the circular statue of a man and woman going round and round—perhaps the eternal attraction and love between the sexes. But directly opposite, another circle feels like a prison—

man against the world, with no refuge. From the man escaping, look down at the children's playground: eight bronze infants circling a head-down fetus.

On your left, see the famous *Sinnataggen,* the hot-headed little boy. It's said Vigeland gave him chocolate and then took it away to get this reaction. The statues capture the joys of life (and, on a sunny day, so do the Norwegians filling the park around you).

Fountain: Continue through a rose garden to the earliest sculpture unit in the park. Six giants hold a fountain, symbolically toiling with the burden of life, as water—the source of life—cascades steadily around them. Twenty tree-of-life groups surround the fountain. Four clumps of trees (on each corner) show humanity's relationship to nature and the seasons of life: childhood, young love, adulthood, and winter.

Take a quick swing through life, starting on the right with youth. In the branches you'll see a swarm of children (Vigeland

called them "geniuses"): A boy sits in a tree, boys actively climb while most girls stand by quietly, and a girl glides through the branches wide-eyed and ready for life...and love. Circle clockwise to the next stage: love scenes. In the third corner, life becomes more complicated: a sad woman in an animal-like tree, a lonely child, a couple plummeting downward (perhaps falling out of love), and finally an angry man driving away babies. The fourth corner completes the cycle, as death melts into the branches of the tree of life and you realize new geniuses will bloom.

The 60 bronze reliefs circling the basin develop the theme further, showing man mixing with nature and geniuses giving the carousel of life yet another spin. Speaking of another spin, circle again and follow these reliefs.

The sidewalk surrounding the basin is a maze—life's long and winding road with twists, dead ends, frustrations, and, ultimately, a way out. If you have about an hour to spare, enter the labyrinth (on the side nearest the park's entrance gate, there's a single break in the black border) and follow the white granite path until (on the monolith side) you finally get out. (Tracing this path occupies older kids, affording parents a peaceful break in the park.) Or you can go straight up the steps to the monolith.

Monolith: The centerpiece of the park—a teeming monolith of life surrounded by 36 granite groups—continues Vigeland's cycle-of-life motif. The figures are hunched and clearly earthbound, while Vigeland explores a lifetime of human relationships. At the center, 121 figures carved out of a single block of stone rocket skyward. Three stone carvers worked daily for 14 years, cutting Vigeland's full-size plaster model into the final 180-ton, 50-foot-tall erection.

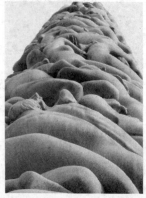

Circle the plaza, once to trace the

stages of life in the 36 statue groups, and a second time to enjoy how Norwegian kids relate to the art. The statues—both young and old—seem to speak to children.

Vigeland lived barely long enough to see his monolith raised. Covered with bodies, it seems to pick up speed as it spirals skyward. Some people seem to naturally rise. Others struggle not to fall. Some help others. Although the granite groups around the monolith are easy to understand, Vigeland left the meaning of the monolith itself open. Like life, it can be interpreted many different ways.

From this summit of the park, look a hundred yards farther, where four children and three adults are intertwined and spinning in the Wheel of Life. Now, look back at the entrance. If the main gate is at 12 o'clock, the studio where Vigeland lived and worked—now the Vigeland Museum—is at 2 o'clock (see the green copper tower poking above the trees). His ashes sit in the top of the tower in clear view of the monolith. If you liked the park, visit the Vigeland Museum (described next), a delightful five-minute walk away, for an intimate look at the art and how it was made.

▲▲Vigeland Museum

Filled with original plaster casts and well-described exhibits on his work, this palatial city-provided studio was Gustav Vigeland's home and workplace. The high south-facing windows provided just the right light.

Vigeland, who had a deeply religious upbringing, saw his art as an expression of his soul. He once said, "The road between feeling and execution should be as short as possible."

Here, immersed in his work, Vigeland supervised his craftsmen like a father, from 1924 until his death in 1943.

Cost and Hours: 60 kr; May-Aug Tue-Sun 10:00-17:00, Sept-April Tue-Sun 12:00-16:00, closed Mon year-round; bus #20 or tram #12 to Frogner Plass, Nobels Gate 32, tel. 23 49 37 00, www.vigeland.museum.no.

Oslo City Museum (Oslo Bymuseum)

This hard-to-be-thrilled-about little museum tells the story of Oslo. For a quick overview of the city, watch the 15-minute English video.

Cost and Hours: Free, Tue-Sun 11:00-16:00, closed Mon, borrow English description sheet, located in Frogner Park at Frogner Manor Farm across street from Vigeland Museum, tel. 23 28 41 70, www.oslomuseum.no.

▲▲OSLO'S BYGDØY NEIGHBORHOOD

This thought-provoking and exciting cluster of sights is on a park-like peninsula just across the harbor from downtown. It provides a busy and rewarding half-day (at a minimum) of sightseeing. Here, within a short walk, are six major sights (listed in order of importance):

• **Norwegian Folk Museum,** an open-air park with traditional log buildings from all corners of the country.

• **Viking Ship Museum,** showing off the best-preserved Viking longboats in existence.

• **Fram Museum,** showcasing the modern Viking spirit with the *Fram,* the ship of Arctic-exploration fame, and the *Gjøa,* the first ship to sail through the Northwest Passage.

• **Kon-Tiki Museum,** starring the *Kon-Tiki* and the *Ra II,* in which Norwegian explorer Thor Heyerdahl proved that early civilizations—with their existing technologies—could have crossed the oceans.

• **Norwegian Maritime Museum,** interesting mostly to old salts, has a wonderfully scenic movie of Norway.

• **Norwegian Holocaust Center,** a high-tech look at the Holocaust in Norway and contemporary racism.

Getting There: Sailing from downtown to Bygdøy is fun, and it gets you in a seafaring mood. Ride the Bygdøy ferry—marked *Public Ferry Bygdøy Museums*—from pier 3 in front of City Hall (50 kr one-way; covered by Oslo Pass; mid-May-Aug daily 8:55-20:55, usually 3/hour; fewer sailings April and Sept; doesn't run Oct-March). Boats generally leave from downtown and from the museum dock at :05, :25, and :45 past each hour. In summer, avoid the nearby (much more expensive) tour boats. For a less memorable approach, you can take bus #30 (from train station or National Theater, direction: Bygdøy).

Getting Around Bygdøy: The Norwegian Folk and Viking Ship museums are a 10-minute walk from the ferry's first stop (Dronningen). The other boating museums (Fram, Kon-Tiki, and Maritime) are at the second ferry stop (Bygdøynes). The Holocaust Center is off Fredriksborgveien, about halfway between these two museum clusters. All Bygdøy sights are within a pleasant (when sunny) 15-minute walk of each other. The walk gives you a picturesque taste of small-town Norway.

City bus #30 connects the sights four times hourly in this order: Norwegian Folk Museum, Viking Ship Museum, Kon-Tiki Museum, Norwegian Holocaust Center. (For the Holocaust Center, you'll use the Bygdøyhus stop a long block away; tell the bus

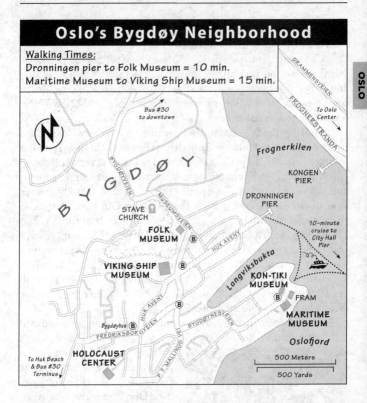

Oslo's Bygdøy Neighborhood

Walking Times:
Dronningen pier to Folk Museum = 10 min.
Maritime Museum to Viking Ship Museum = 15 min.

OSLO

driver you want the stop for the "HL-Senteret.") The bus turns around at its final stop (Huk), then passes the sights in reverse order on its way back to the city center. Note that after 17:00, bus and boat departures are sparse. If returning to Oslo by ferry, get to the dock a little early—otherwise the boat is likely to be full, and you'll have to wait for the next sailing.

Eating at Bygdøy: Lunch options near the Kon-Tiki are a sandwich bar (relaxing picnic spots along the grassy shoreline) and a cafeteria (with tables overlooking the harbor). The Norwegian Folk Museum has a decent cafeteria inside and a fun little farmers' market stall across the street from the entrance. The Holocaust Center has a small café on its second floor.

Beach at Bygdøy: A popular beach is located at Huk, on the southwest tip of the peninsula.

▲▲▲Norwegian Folk Museum (Norsk Folkemuseum)

Brought from all corners of Norway, 150 buildings have been reassembled here on 35 acres. While Stockholm's Skansen was the first museum of this kind to open to the public (see page 468), this museum is a bit older, started in 1882 as the king's private collection (and the inspiration for Skansen).

Cost and Hours: 110 kr, daily mid-May-mid-Sept 10:00-18:00, off-season park open Mon-Fri 11:00-15:00, Sat-Sun 11:00-16:00 but most historical buildings closed, free lockers, Museumsveien 10, bus #30 stops immediately in front, tel. 22 12 37 00, www.norskfolkemuseum.no.

Visiting the Museum: Think of the visit in three parts: the park sprinkled with old buildings, the re-created old town, and the folk-art museum. In peak season, the park is lively, with craftspeople doing their traditional things, barnyard animals roaming about, and costumed guides all around. (They're paid to happily answer your questions—so ask many.) The evocative Gol stave church, at the top of a hill at the park's edge, is a must-see (built in 1212 in Hallingdal and painstakingly reconstructed here; for more on stave churches, see page 211). Across the park, the old town comes complete with apartments from various generations (including some reconstructions of people's actual homes) and offers an intimate look at lifestyles here in 1905, 1930, 1950, 1979, and even a modern-day Norwegian-Pakistani apartment.

The museum beautifully presents woody, colorfully painted folk art (ground floor), exquisite-in-a-peasant-kind-of-way folk

costumes (upstairs), and temporary exhibits. Everything is thoughtfully explained in English. Don't miss the best Sami culture exhibit I've seen in Scandinavia (across the courtyard in the green building, behind the toy exhibit).

Upon arrival, pick up the site map and review the list of the day's activities, concerts, and guided tours. In summer, there are two guided tours in English per day; the Telemark Farm hosts a small daily fiddle-and-dance show; and a folk music-and-dance show is held each Sunday. The folk museum is most lively June through mid-August, when buildings are open and staffed. Otherwise, the indoor museum is fine, but the park is just a walk past lots of locked-up log cabins. If you don't take a tour, pick up a guidebook and ask questions of the informative attendants stationed in buildings throughout the park.

▲▲Viking Ship Museum (Vikingskiphuset)

In this impressive museum, you'll gaze with admiration at two finely crafted, majestic oak Viking ships dating from the 9th and 10th centuries, and the scant remains of a third vessel. Along with

the two well-preserved ships, you'll see the bones of Vikings buried with these vessels and remarkable artifacts that may cause you to consider these notorious raiders in a different light. Over a thousand years ago, three things drove Vikings on their far-flung raids: hard economic times in their bleak homeland, the lure of prosperous and vulnerable communities to the south, and a mastery of the sea. There was a time when most frightened Europeans closed every prayer with, "And deliver us from the Vikings, Amen." Gazing up at the prow of one of these sleek, time-stained vessels, you can almost hear the screams and smell the armpits of those redheads on the rampage.

Cost and Hours: 80 kr, daily May-Sept 9:00-18:00, Oct-April 10:00-16:00, Huk Aveny 35, tel. 22 13 52 80, www.khm.uio.no.

Visiting the Museum: Focus on the two well-preserved ships, starting with the *Oseberg*, from A.D. 834. With its ornate carving and impressive rudder, it was likely a royal pleasure craft. It seems designed for sailing on calm inland waters during festivals, but not in the open ocean.

The *Gokstad*, from A.D. 950, is a practical working boat, capable of sailing the high seas. A ship like this brought settlers to the west of France (Normandy was named for the Norsemen). And in such a vessel, explorers such as Eric the Red hopscotched from Norway to Iceland to Greenland and on to what they called Vinland—today's Newfoundland in Canada. Imagine 30 men hauling on long oars out at sea for weeks and months at a time. In 1892, a replica of this ship sailed from Norway to America in 44 days to celebrate the 400th anniversary of Columbus *not* discovering America.

The ships tend to steal the show, but don't miss the hall displaying **jewelry and personal items** excavated along with the ships. The ships and related artifacts survived so well because they were buried in clay as part of a gravesite. Many of the finest items were not actually Viking art, but goodies they brought home after raiding more advanced (but less tough) people. Still, there are lots of actual Viking items, such as metal and leather goods, that give insight into their culture. Highlights are the cart and sleighs, ornately carved with scenes from Viking sagas.

The museum doesn't offer tours, but it's easy to eavesdrop on the many guides leading big groups through the museum. Everything is well-described in English. You probably don't need the little museum guidebook—it repeats exactly what's already posted on the exhibits.

▲▲Fram Museum (Frammuseet)

This museum holds the 125-foot, steam- and sail-powered ship that took modern-day Vikings Roald Amundsen and Fridtjof Nansen deep into the Arctic and Antarctic, farther north and south than any vessel had gone before. For three years, the *Fram*—specially designed to survive the crushing pressures of a frozen-over sea—drifted, trapped in the Arctic ice. The museum was recently enlarged to include Amundsen's *Gjøa*, the first ship to sail through the Northwest Passage.

Cost and Hours: 100 kr; June-Aug daily 9:00-18:00; May and Sept daily 10:00-17:00; Oct and March-April daily 10:00-16:00; Nov-Feb Mon-Fri 10:00-15:00, Sat-Sun 10:00-16:00; Bygdøynesveien 36, tel. 23 28 29 50, www.frammuseum.no.

Visiting the Museum: Read the ground-floor displays, check out the videos below the bow of the ship, then climb the steps to the third-floor gangway to explore the *Fram*'s claustrophobic but fascinating interior. Also featured are a tent like the one Amundsen used, reconstructed shelves from his Arctic kitchen, models of the *Fram* and the motorized sled they used to traverse the ice and snow, and a "polar simulator" plunging visitors to a 15° Fahrenheit environment. A "Northern Lights Show," best viewed from the *Fram*'s main deck, is presented every 20 minutes.

Next, take the underground passageway to the adjacent A-frame building that displays the *Gjøa*, the motor- and sail-powered ship that Amundsen and a crew of six used from 1903 to 1906 to successfully navigate the Northwest Passage. Exhibits describe their ordeal as well as other Arctic adventures, such as Amundsen's 1926 airship (zeppelin) expedition from Oslo over the North Pole to Alaska. And pop into the 100-seat cinema for a film about the polar regions (every 15 minutes).

▲▲Kon-Tiki Museum (Kon-Tiki Museet)

Next to the *Fram* is a museum housing the *Kon-Tiki* and the *Ra II*, the ships built by Thor Heyerdahl (1914-2002). In 1947, Heyerdahl and five crewmates constructed the *Kon-Tiki* raft out of balsa wood, using only pre-modern tools and techniques. They set sail from Peru on the tiny craft, surviving for 101 days on fish, coconuts, and sweet potatoes (which were native to Peru). About 4,300 miles later, they arrived in Polynesia. The point was to show that early South Americans could have settled Polynesia. (While Heyerdahl proved they could have, anthropologists doubt they did.) The *Kon-Tiki* story became a bestselling book and award-winning documentary (and helped spawn the "Tiki" culture craze in the US). In 1970, Heyerdahl's *Ra II* made a similar 3,000-mile journey from Morocco to Barbados to prove that Africans could have populated America. Both ships are well-displayed and described in English. Short clips from *Kon-Tiki*, the Oscar-winning 1950 documentary film, play in a small theater at the end of the exhibit.

Cost and Hours: 90 kr, daily June-Aug 9:30-18:00, March-May and Sept-Oct 10:00-17:00, Nov-Feb 10:00-16:00, Bygdøynesveien 36, tel. 23 08 67 67, www.kon-tiki.no.

▲Norwegian Maritime Museum (Norsk Sjøfartsmuseum)

If you like the sea, this museum is a salt lick, providing a wide-ranging look at Norway's maritime heritage. The collection was recently updated, with new exhibits such as "The Ship" ("Skipet"), tracing 2,000 years of maritime development, and "At Sea" ("Til Sjøs"), exploring what life is like on the ocean, from Viking days to the present. Don't miss the movie *The Ocean: A Way of Life*, included with your admission. It's a breathtaking widescreen film swooping you scenically over Norway's dramatic sea and fishing townscapes from here all the way to North Cape in a comfy theater (20 minutes, shown at the top and bottom of the hour, follow *Supervideografen* signs). And if you appreciate maritime art, the collection in the gallery should float your boat.

Cost and Hours: 80 kr, kids under 6 free; mid-May-Aug daily 10:00-17:00; Sept-mid-May Tue-Fri 10:00-15:00, Sat-Sun 10:00-16:00, closed Mon; Bygdøynesveien 37, tel. 24 11 41 50, www.marmuseum.no.

▲Norwegian Holocaust Center (HL-Senteret)

Located in the stately former home of Nazi collaborator Vidkun Quisling, this museum and study center offers a high-tech look at the racist ideologies that fueled the Holocaust. To show the Holocaust in a Norwegian context, the first floor displays historical documents about the rise of anti-Semitism and personal effects from Holocaust victims. Downstairs, the names of 760 Norwegian Jews killed by the Nazis are listed in a bright, white room. The *Innocent Questions* glass-and-neon sculpture outside shows an old-fashioned punch card, reminding viewers of how the Norwegian puppet government collected seemingly innocuous information before deporting its Jews. The *Contemporary Reflections* video is a reminder that racism and genocide continue today.

Cost and Hours: 50 kr, ask for free English audioguide or tablet, June-Aug daily 10:00-18:00, Sept-May Mon-Fri 10:00-16:00, Sat-Sun 11:00-16:00, Huk Aveny 56—take bus #30 to the Byg-

døyhus stop, follow signs to *HL-Senteret*, tel. 22 84 21 00, www.
hlsenteret.no.

GRÜNERLØKKA AND GRØNLAND DISTRICTS

The Grünerløkka district is trendy, and workaday Grønland is
emerging as a fun spot. The Akers Rivers bisects Grünerløkka. You
can connect the dots by taking the self-guided "Up Akers River
and Down Grünerløkka Walk." For a longer hike, start with my
"Nydalen to Grünerløkka Walk," which intersects the Akers/
Grünerløkka Walk. Everything is described in this section.

Akers River

This river, though only about five miles long, powered Oslo's early
industry: flour mills in the 1300s, sawmills in the 1500s, and Norway's Industrial Revolution in the 1800s. A walk along the river
not only spans Oslo's history, but also shows the contrast the city
offers. The bottom of the river (where this walk doesn't go)—bordered by the high-rise Oslo Radisson Blu Plaza Hotel and the "Little Pakistan" neighborhood of Grønland—has its share of drunks
and drugs, reflecting a new urban reality in Oslo. Farther up, the
river valley becomes a park as it winds past decent-size waterfalls
and red-brick factories. The source of the river (and Oslo's drinking water) is the pristine Lake Maridal, situated at the edge of the
Nordmarka wilderness. The idyllic recreation scenes along Lake
Maridal are a favorite for nature-loving Norwegians.

▲Grünerløkka

The Grünerløkka district is the largest planned urban area in Oslo.
It was built in the latter half of the 1800s to house the legions
of workers employed at the factories powered by the Akers River.
The first buildings were modeled on similar places built in Berlin.
(German visitors observe that there's now more turn-of-the-20th-
century Berlin here than in present-day Berlin.) While slummy in
the 1980s, today it's trendy. Locals sometimes refer to it as "Oslo's
Greenwich Village." Although that's a stretch, it is a bustling area
with lots of cafés, good spots for a fun meal, and few tourists.

Getting There: Grünerløkka can be reached from the center
of town by a short ride on tram #11, #12, or #13, or by taking the
short but interesting walk described next.

▲Up Akers River and Down Grünerløkka Walk

While every tourist explores the harborfront and main drag of
Oslo, few venture into this neighborhood that evokes the Industrial Revolution. Once housing poor workers, it now attracts hip
professionals. A hike up the Akers River, finishing in the stylish
Grünerløkka district, shines a truly different light on Oslo. Allow
about an hour at a brisk pace, including a fair bit of up and down.

OSLO

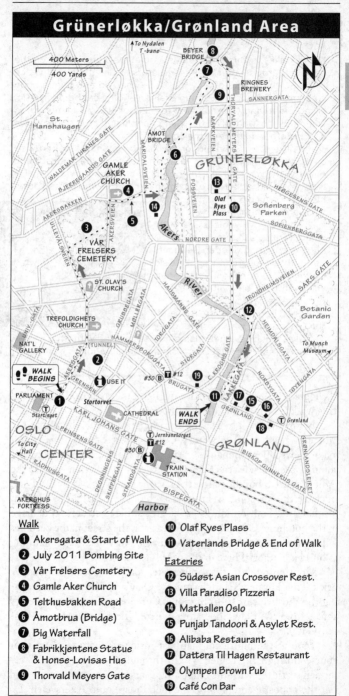

Grünerløkka/Grønland Area

Walk
1. Akersgata & Start of Walk
2. July 2011 Bombing Site
3. Vår Frelsers Cemetery
4. Gamle Aker Church
5. Telthusbakken Road
6. Åmotbrua (Bridge)
7. Big Waterfall
8. Fabrikkjentene Statue & Honse-Lovisas Hus
9. Thorvald Meyers Gate
10. Olaf Ryes Plass
11. Vaterlands Bridge & End of Walk

Eateries
12. Südøst Asian Crossover Rest.
13. Villa Paradiso Pizzeria
14. Mathallen Oslo
15. Punjab Tandoori & Asylet Rest.
16. Alibaba Restaurant
17. Dattera Til Hagen Restaurant
18. Olympen Brown Pub
19. Café Con Bar

In Cold Blood

Norway likes to think of itself as a quiet, peaceful nation on the edge of Europe—after all, its legislators award the Nobel Peace Prize. So the events of July 22, 2011—when an anti-immigration fanatic named Anders Behring Breivik set off a car bomb in Oslo, killing eight, and then traveled to a Labor Party summer camp where he shot and killed 69 young people and counselors—have had a profound effect on the country's psyche.

Unlike the US, Britain, or Spain, Norway had escaped 21st-century terrorism until Breivik's attack. When the public found out that the man behind the bombing and gunfire was a native Norwegian—dressed in a policeman's uniform—who hunted down his victims in cold blood, it became a national nightmare.

Though Norwegians are often characterized as stoic, there was a huge outpouring of grief. Bouquets flooded the square in front of Oslo Cathedral. Permanent memorials will eventually be built at the sites of the tragedies.

Breivik, who was arrested after the shootings, was described by police as a gun-loving fundamentalist obsessed with what he saw as the "threat" of multiculturalism and immigration to Norwegian

Navigate with the TI's free city map and the map in this chapter. This walk is best during daylight hours.

Begin the walk by leaving Karl Johans Gate at the top of the hill, and head up **Akersgata**—Oslo's "Fleet Street" (lined with major newspaper companies). After two blocks, at Apotekergata, you may see the side street blocked off and construction work to the right. They're rebuilding after the horrific bombing of July 2011 (see sidebar); the car bomb went off just a block to the right of here, on Grubbegata. Four buildings in the area suffered structural damage in the bombing. Continuing up Akersgata, the street name becomes Ullevålsveien as it passes those buildings. Norwegians are planning to build a memorial here in the near future.

Continuing past this somber site, you'll approach the massive brick Trefoldighets Church and St. Olav's Church before reaching the **Vår Frelsers (Our Savior's) Cemetery.** Enter the cemetery across from the Baby Shop store (where Ullevålsveien meets Wessels Gate).

Stop at the big metal map just inside the gate to chart your course through the cemetery: Go through the light-green Æreslunden section—with the biggest plots and highest elevation—and out the opposite end (#13 on the metal map) onto Akersveien. En

values. His targets were the Norwegian government and politically active youths—some only 14 years old—and their counselors at an island summer camp sponsored by Norway's center-left party.

It's true that Norway has a big and growing immigrant community. More than 11 percent of today's Norwegians are not ethnic Norwegians, and a quarter of Oslo's residents are immigrants. These "new Norwegians" have provided a much-needed and generally appreciated labor force, filling jobs that wealthy Norwegians would rather not do.

Horrified by Breivik's actions, many Norwegians went out of their way to make immigrants feel welcome after the attack. But there is some resentment in a country that is disinclined to be a melting pot. There have been scuffles between Norwegian gangs and immigrant groups. Another source of friction is the tough love Norwegians feel they get from their government compared to the easy ride offered to needy immigrants: "They even get pocket money in jail!" The country recently strengthened its immigration laws in 2014.

Norway seems determined not to let the July 22 massacre poison its peaceful soul. Calls for police to start carrying weapons or to reinstate the death penalty were quickly rejected. "Breivik wanted to change Norway," an Oslo resident told me. "We're determined to keep Norway the way it was."

route, check out some of the tombstones of the illuminati and literati buried in the honorary Æreslunden section. They include Munch, Ibsen, Bjørnson, and many of the painters whose works you can see in the National Gallery (all marked on a map posted at the entrance). Exiting on the far side of the cemetery, walk left 100 yards up Akersveien to the church.

The Romanesque **Gamle Aker Church** (from the 1100s), the oldest building in Oslo, is worth a look inside (free, generally Mon-Thu 14:00-16:00, Fri 12:00-14:00). The church, which fell into ruins and has been impressively rebuilt, is pretty bare except for a pulpit and baptismal font from the 1700s.

From the church, backtrack 20 yards, head left at the playground, and go downhill on the steep **Telthusbakken Road** toward the huge, gray former grain silos (now student housing). The cute lane is lined with colorful old wooden houses: The people who constructed these homes were too poor to meet the no-wood fire-safety building codes within the city limits, so they built in what used to be suburbs. At the bottom of Telthusbakken, cross the busy Maridalsveien and walk directly through the park to the Akers River. The lively Grünerløkka district is straight across the river from here, but if you have 20 minutes and a little energy, detour upstream first and hook back down. Don't cross the river yet.

Walk along the riverside bike lane upstream through the river gorge park. Just above the first waterfall, cross **Åmotbrua,** the big white springy suspension footbridge from 1852 (moved here in 1958). Keep hiking uphill along the river. At the base of the next big waterfall, cross over again to the large brick buildings, hiking up the stairs to the **Beyer Bridge** (above the falls) and *Fabrikkjentene,* a statue of four women laborers. They're pondering the textile factory where they and 700 others toiled long and hard. This gorge

was once lined with the water mills that powered Oslo through its 19th-century Industrial Age boom.

Look back (on the side you just left) at the city's two biggest former textile factories. Once you could tell what color the fabric was being dyed each day by the color of the river. Just beyond them, between the two old factories, is a small white building housing the **Labor Museum** (Arbeidermuseet, free; late June-mid-Aug Tue-Sun 11:00-16:00, closed Mon; off-season Sat-Sun 11:00-16:00, closed Mon-Fri; borrow English handout). Inside you'll see old photos that humanize the life of laborers there, and an 1899 photo exhibit by Edvard Munch's sister, Inger Munch.

The tiny red house just over and below the bridge—the **Honse-Lovisas Hus** cultural center—makes a good rest-stop (Tue-Sun 11:00-18:00, closed Mon, coffee and wafels). Cross over to the red-brick Ringnes Brewery and follow **Thorvald Meyers Gate** downhill directly into the heart of Grünerløkka. The main square, called **Olaf Ryes Plass,** is a happening place to grab a meal or drink (see "Eating," later). Trams take you from here back to the center.

• *To continue exploring, you could keep going straight and continue walking until you reach a T-intersection with a busy road (Trondheimsveien). From there (passing the recommended Südøst Asian Crossover Restaurant) you can catch a tram back to the center, or drop down to the riverside path and follow it downstream to Vaterlands bridge in the* **Grønland** *district. From here the train station is a five-minute walk down Stenersgata.*

▲Nydalen to Grünerløkka Walk

For a longer hike than the "Up Akers River and Down Grüner-løkka Walk" described previously, consider this 30-minute walk, downhill and through peaceful riverside parks all the way (see map on page 218). This walk intersects the Akers River/Grünerløkka Walk at its halfway (and highest altitude) point, Beyer Bridge, where you can choose to finish the downhill ramble following its route—either doing the first half in reverse order (visiting the Gamle Aker Church and the Vår Frelsers Cemetery on your way into the city center), or picking up the last half of the walk (through the heart of Grünerløkka and on to Grønland). Walking at a brisk pace, it'll take you 30 minutes to get from the Nydalen T-bane stop to the top of the Akers River/Grünerløkka Walk. Allow an hour from the top all the way back into town. If you follow these easy directions, I promise you won't get lost.

Ride the T-bane to **Nydalen,** where you'll be high above the city, surrounded by modern apartments and university buildings. From the T-bane stop, walk to the Akers River and head down-hill...like the water that powered the Industrial Revolution in Oslo. From here it's all downhill and along the river. Stay on the right side of the river until the second street with cars, where you'll cross the bridge to the left side of the river.

From the top, after about 15 minutes, you'll hit the first street with cars. Don't cross it: Stay right and follow the lane under an overpass and you'll once again hear the babbling sounds of the brook. Continue along the Akers River. Across the river you'll see the fine brickwork of **Lilleborg,** a huge former soap factory. Started in 1712, it was the last factory in use here (until 1997) and, ironically, infamous as a source of pollution.

Notice the lights along the path, a reminder that in the winter it gets dark early, before 16:00.

At the next big road with cars (Griffenfeldts Gate), cross the river. Pause on the bridge and consider that from 1624, wooden pipes laid from here (just upstream from the river-based industry) ran all the way to the center, providing drinking water to Oslo. This remained Oslo's water source until 1879, when encroaching industry forced its relocation upstream to higher ground.

Soon you'll arrive at **Beyer Bridge,** with the statue of four female factory workers on it. Across the bridge, between what used to be the city's two biggest textile factories, stands the little Labor Museum.

At Beyer Bridge, you hit the Akers River/Grünerløkka Walk" (described previously) and need to decide which leg of the walk you'd like to take (or you could head left a block or so and hop on any tram heading downhill). And, as mentioned earlier, you could walk through the core of Grünerløkka to the suburb of...

Grønland

With the Industrial Revolution, Oslo's population exploded. The city grew from an estimated 10,000 in 1850 to 250,000 in 1900. The T-bane's Grønland stop deposits you in the center of what was the first suburb to accommodate workers of Industrial Age Oslo. If you look down side streets, you'll see fine 19th-century facades from this period. While the suburb is down-and-dirty like working-class and immigrant neighborhoods in other cities, Grønland is starting to emerge as a trendy place for eating out and after-dark fun. Locals know you'll get double the food and lots more beer for the kroner here (see "Eating in Oslo," later). If you'd enjoy a whiff of Istanbul, make a point to wander through the underground commercial zone at the Grønland station (easy to visit even if you're not riding the T-bane).

OUTER OSLO

▲▲Holmenkollen Ski Jump and Ski Museum

The site of one of the world's oldest ski jumps (from 1892), Holmenkollen has hosted many championships, including the 1952 Winter Olympics. To win the privilege of hosting the 2011 World Ski Jump Championship, Oslo built a bigger jump to match modern ones built elsewhere. This futuristic, cantilevered, Olympic-standard **ski jump** has a tilted elevator that you can ride to the top (on a sunny day, you may have to wait your turn for

the elevator). Stand right at the starting gate, just like an athlete, and get a feel for this daredevil sport. The jump empties into a 30,000-seat amphitheater, and if you go when it's clear, you'll see one of the best possible views of Oslo. While the view is exciting from the top, even more exciting is watching thrill-seekers rocket down the course on a zip-line from the same lofty perch (600 kr per trip).

As you ponder the jump, consider how modern athletes continually push the boundaries of their sport. The first champion here in 1892 jumped 21 meters (nearly 69 feet). In 1930 it took a 50-meter jump to win. In 1962 it was 80 meters, and in 1980 the champ cracked 100 meters. And, most recently, a jump of 140 meters (459 feet) took first place.

The **ski museum,** a must for skiers, traces the evolution of the sport, from 4,000-year-old rock paintings to crude 1,500-year-old wooden sticks to the slick and quickly evolving skis of modern times, including a fun exhibit showing the royal family on skis. You'll see gear from Roald Amundsen's famous trek to the South

Pole, including the stuffed remains of Obersten (the Colonel), one of his sled dogs.

Cost and Hours: 120-kr ticket includes museum and viewing platform at top of jump; daily June-Aug 9:00-20:00, May and Sept 10:00-17:00, Oct-April 10:00-16:00; tel. 22 92 32 64, www.holmenkollen.com or www.skiforeningen.no.

Simulator: To cap your Holmenkollen experience, step into the simulator and fly down the ski jump and ski in a virtual downhill race. My legs were exhausted after the five-minute terror. This simulator (or should I say stimulator?) costs 60 kr. It's located at the lower level of the complex, near the entry of the ski museum. Outside, have fun watching a candid video of those shrieking inside.

Getting There: T-bane line #1 gets you out of the city, through the hills, forests, and mansions that surround Oslo, and to the jump (direction: Frognerseteren). From the Holmenkollen station, you'll hike steeply up the road 15 minutes to the ski jump. (Getting back is just 5 minutes. Note T-bane departure times before you leave.)

Nearby: For an easy downhill jaunt through the Norwegian forest, with a woodsy coffee or meal break in the middle, stay on the T-bane past Holmenkollen to the end of the line (Frognerseteren) and walk 10 minutes downhill to the recommended **Frognerseteren Hovedrestaurant,** a fine traditional eatery with a sod roof, reindeer meat on the griddle, and a city view (see page 285). Continue on the same road another 20 minutes downhill to the ski jump, and then to the Holmenkollen T-bane stop. The **Holmenkollen Restaurant,** described on page 285, is just a few steps above the T-bane stop and offers a similar view and better food and prices, but without the pewter-and-antlers folk theme.

▲Ekeberg Sculpture Park and Ruins of Medieval Oslo

The buzz in Oslo is its modern sculpture park (opened in 2013), with striking art sprinkled through a forest with grand city views. There's lots of climbing. The park has a long story, from evidence of the Stone Age people who chose to live here 7,000 years ago to the memory of its days as a Nazi military cemetery in World War II.

Getting There: The park, always open and free, is a 10-minute tram ride southeast of the center (catch tram #18 or #19 from station, platform E). From the Ekebergparken tram stop, climb uphill to the visitors center with its small museum (30 kr), where you can join a guided walk in English (150 kr, 90 minutes, Mon-Sat at 13:00, Sun at 14:00), or just pick up a map and start your hike.

Background: Ekeberg Park is the big project and gift to the city from real estate tycoon Christian Ringnes (grandson of Norwegian brewery tycoons, who—like Coors in Denver and Carlsberg in Copenhagen—have lots of money for grand city projects). Norwegians tend to be skeptical of any fat cat giving something to the city. What's the real motive? They note that the park's popularity will bring lots more business to the fancy Ringnes-owned restaurant within the park. But critics are getting over that, and today the people of Oslo are embracing this lovely 63-acre mix of forest and contemporary art. Art collector Ringnes loves women and wanted to the park to be a celebration of femininity. While that vision was considered a bit ill-advised and scaled back, the park is plenty feminine and organic.

Nearby: The faint **medieval remains of Oslo** (free, always open) are immediately below Ekeberg Park. While a bit obscure for most, history buffs can spend a few minutes wandering a park with the ruins of the 11th-century town—back when it was 3,000 people huddled around a big stone cathedral, seat of the Norwegian bishop. The arcade of a 13th-century Dominican monastery still stands (office of today's Lutheran bishop). To get there, hop off at the St. Halvards Plass stop on your way to the Ekebergparken tram stop (note when the next tram is due). The ruins are across the street from the bus stop.

▲Edvard Munch Museum (Munch Museet)

The only Norwegian painter to have had a serious impact on European art, Munch (pronounced "moonk") is a surprise to many who visit this fine museum, located one mile east of Oslo's center. The emotional, disturbing, and powerfully Expressionistic work of this strange and perplexing man is arranged chronologically. You'll see an extensive collection of paintings, drawings, lithographs, and photographs. (Note that Oslo's centrally located National Gallery, which also displays many of Munch's most popular works, is a better alternative for those who just want to see a dozen great Munch paintings, including "The Scream," without leaving the city center.)

The Munch Museum was in the news in August of 2004, when two Munch paintings, *Madonna* and a version of his famous *Scream,* were brazenly stolen right off the walls in broad daylight. Two men in black hoods simply entered through the museum café, waved guns at the stunned guards and tourists, ripped the paintings off the wall, and sped off in a black Audi station wagon. Happily, in 2006, the thieves were caught and the stolen paintings recovered. Today they are on display again, behind glass and with heightened security.

Cost and Hours: 95 kr; mid-June-Sept daily 10:00-17:00; Oct-mid-June Wed-Mon 11:00-17:00, closed Tue; 25-kr audioguide, guided tours in English daily July-Aug at 13:00, T-bane or bus #60 to Tøyen, Tøyengata 53, tel. 23 49 35 00, www.munch.museum.no. For more on Munch, see page 248.

OSLO

ESCAPES FROM THE CITY

Oslo is surrounded by a vast forest dotted with idyllic little lakes, huts, joggers, bikers, and sun-worshippers. Mountain-biking possibilities are endless (as you'll discover if you go exploring without a good map). Consider taking your bike on the T-bane (free outside of rush hour, otherwise half the normal adult fare) to the end of line #1 (Frognerseteren, 30 minutes from National Theater) to gain the most altitude possible. Then follow the gravelly roads (mostly downhill but with some climbing) past several dreamy lakes to Sognsvann at the end of T-bane line #6. Farther east, from Maridalsvannet, a bike path follows the Akers River all the way back into town. (The TI has details.) While Oslo isn't much on bike rentals, you can rent quality bikes at Viking Biking (see page 220).

For plenty of trees and none of the exercise, ride T-bane line #6 to its last stop, Sognsvann (with a beach towel rather than a bike), and join the lakeside scene. A pleasant trail leads around the lake.

Oslofjord Island Beaches

On a hot day it seems the busy ferry scene at Oslo's harborfront is primarily designed to get locals out of their offices and onto the cool, green islands across the harbor so they can take a dip in the fjord, enjoy a little beach time, or simply stroll and enjoy views of the city. The larger Hovedøya offers good beaches, the ruins of a Cistercian monastery from 1147, some old cannons from the early 1800s, a marina, and a café. Little Gressholmen has good swimming, easy wandering to a pair of connected islands, and Gressholmen Kro, a rustic café dating to the 1930s.

Getting to the Islands: Take bus #60 to Vippetangen and catch ferry #92 or #93 to Hovedøya or ferry #93 to Gressholmen (both covered by city transit passes). Ferry #92 takes you directly to Hovedøya in five minutes, while ferry #93 takes a slightly longer, scenic route past several islands (including Gressholmen) on its way to Hovedøya. For schedules and fare info, check www.ruter.no.

Beach at Bygdøy: Remember there's also a beach at Huk on the Bygdøy peninsula; take the direct boat from pier 3 in front of City Hall or bus #30.

Tusenfryd

This giant amusement complex just out of town offers a world of family fun. It's sort of a combination Norwegian Disneyland/Viking Knott's Berry Farm, with more than 50 rides, plenty of entertainment, and restaurants.

Cost and Hours: Admission is based on your height: under 95 centimeters (3 feet)—free, under 1.2 meters (4 feet)—315 kr, over 1.2 meters (4 feet)—389 kr. Daily July-mid-Aug 10:30-19:00, shorter hours April-June and mid-Aug-Sept, closed in winter, tel. 64 97 66 99, www.tusenfryd.no.

Getting There: Bus #541 takes fun-seekers to the park from behind Oslo's train station (50 kr, 2/hour, 20-minute ride).

Wet Fun

Oslo offers a variety of water play. Located near Vigeland Park, the **Frognerbadet** has three outdoor pools, a waterslide, high dives, a cafeteria, and lots of young families (100 kr, students-70 kr, mid-May-late Aug Mon-Fri 7:00-19:30, Sat-Sun 10:00-18:00, last entry 30 minutes before closing, closed late Aug-mid-May, Middelthunsgate 28, tel. 23 27 54 50).

Tøyenbadet, a modern indoor/outdoor pool complex with a 330-foot-long waterslide, also has a gym and sauna (100 kr, children-50 kr, Mon-Fri 7:00-19:00, Sat-Sun 9:00-19:00, sometimes closed mornings for school events, 10-minute walk from Edvard Munch Museum, Helgengate 90, tel. 23 30 44 70). Oslo's free botanical gardens are nearby.

NEAR OSLO

▲Eidsvoll Manor

During the Napoleonic period, control of Norway changed from Denmark to Sweden. This ruffled the patriotic feathers of Norway's Thomas Jeffersons and Ben Franklins, and on May 17, 1814, Norway's constitution was written and signed in this stately mansion (in the town of Eidsvoll Verk, north of Oslo). While Sweden still ruled, Norway had more autonomy than ever.

To get ready for the bicentennial of Norway's constitution, the manor itself was restored to how it looked in 1814. A visitors center in the nearby Wergeland House tells the history of Norway's march to independence with 21st-century high-tech touches.

Cost and Hours: 100 kr, includes Eidsvoll Manor, Wergeland House, and guided tour; May-Aug daily 10:00-17:00; Sept Mon-Fri 10:00-16:00, Sat-Sun 11:00-16:00; Oct-April Tue-Fri 10:00-16:00, Sat-Sun 11:00-16:00, closed Mon; tel. 63 92 22 10, www.eidsvoll1814.no.

Getting There: Eidsvoll is 45 minutes from Oslo by car (take road E-6 toward Trondheim, turn right at *Eidsvolls Bygningen* sign, free parking) or bus (direct bus #854 runs hourly from Oslo Airport). You can also take the train to Eidsvoll (hourly, 45 minutes plus 15-minute walk). If you're driving from Oslo to Lillehammer and the Gudbrandsdal Valley, it's right on the way and worth a stop.

Drøbak

This delightful fjord town is just an hour from Oslo by bus (70 kr one-way if bought in advance, 90 kr on board, 2/hour, bus #541 or

#542 from behind the train station) or ferry (70 kr one-way, sporadic departures usually Wed and Fri-Sun, check at pier 1 or ask at Oslo TI). Consider taking the 1.25-hour boat trip down, exploring the town, having dinner, and taking the bus back.

For holiday cheer year-round, stop into **Tregaarden's Julehuset** Christmas shop, right off Drøbak's main square (generally Mon-Fri 10:00-17:00, Sat 10:00-15:00, Sun 12:00-16:00, longer hours in Dec, closed Jan-Feb, tel. 64 93 41 78, www.julehus.no). Then wander out past the church and cemetery on the north side of town to a pleasant park. Looking out into the fjord, you can see the old **Oscarsborg Fortress,** where Norwegian troops fired cannons and torpedoes to sink Hitler's warship, *Blücher.* The attack bought enough time for Norway's king and parliament to escape capture and eventually set up a government-in-exile in London during the Nazi occupation of Norway (1940-1945). Nearby, a monument is dedicated to the commander of the fortress, and one of *Blücher's* anchors rests aground (the other is at Aker Brygge in Oslo). A 100-kr round-trip summer ferry shuttles visitors from the town harbor.

If you want to spend the night, the **TI** can recommend accommodations (June-Aug Mon-Fri 8:30-16:00, Sat-Sun 10:00-14:00; Sept-May Mon-Fri 8:30-16:00, closed Sat-Sun; tel. 64 93 50 87, www.visitdrobak.no). **Restaurant Skipperstuen** is a good option for dinner, with outdoor seating that overlooks the fjord and all the Oslo-bound boat traffic (entrées from 300 kr, Mon-Sat 12:00-22:00, Sun 12:00-20:00, tel. 64 93 07 03).

Shopping in Oslo

Shops in Oslo are generally open 10:00-18:00 or 19:00. Many close early on Saturday and all day Sunday. Shopping centers are open Monday through Friday 10:00-21:00, Saturday 9:00-18:00, and are closed Sunday. Remember, when you make a purchase of 315 kr or more, you can get the 25 percent tax refunded when you leave the country if you hang on to the paperwork (see page 719). Here are a few favorite shopping opportunities many travelers enjoy, but not on Sunday, when they're all closed.

Norway Designs, just outside the National Theater, shows off the country's sleek, contemporary designs in clothing, kitchenware, glass, textiles, jewelry—and high prices (Stortingsgata 12, T-bane: Nationaltheatret, tel. 23 11 45 10).

Paleet is a mall in the heart of Oslo, with 30 shops on three levels and a food court in the basement (Karl Johans Gate 37, tel. 23 08 08 11).

Dale of Norway, considered Norway's biggest and best maker of traditional and contemporary sweaters, offers its complete collection at this "concept store" (Karl Johans Gate 45, tel. 97 48 12 07).

Heimen Husflid has a superb selection of authentic Norwegian sweaters, *bunads* (national costumes), traditional jewelry, and other Norwegian crafts (top quality at high prices, Rosenkrantz Gate 8, tel. 23 21 42 00).

GlasMagasinet is one of Oslo's oldest and fanciest department stores (top end, good souvenir shop, near the cathedral at Stortorvet 9, tel. 22 82 23 00).

The Husfliden Shop, in the basement of the GlasMagasinet department store (listed previously), is popular for its Norwegian-made sweaters, yarn, and colorful Norwegian folk crafts (tel. 22 42 10 75).

The Oslo Sweater Shop has competitive prices for Norwegian-made sweaters (in Radisson Blu Scandinavia Hotel at Tullinsgate 5, tel. 22 11 29 22).

Byporten, the big, splashy mall adjoining the central train station, is filled with youthful and hip shops, specialty stores, and eateries (Jernbanetorget 6, tel. 23 36 21 60).

The street named **Bogstadveien** is considered to have the city's trendiest boutiques and chic, high-quality shops (stretches from behind the Royal Palace to Majorstuen near Vigeland Park).

Oslo's Flea Market makes Saturday morning a happy day for those who brake for garage sales (at Vestkanttorvet, March-Nov only, two blocks east of Frogner Park at the corner of Professor Dahl's Gate and Neubergsgate).

Oslo Flaggfabrikk sells quality flags of all shapes and sizes, including the long, pennant-shaped *vimpel*, seen fluttering from flagpoles all over Norway (875 kr for 11.5-foot *vimpel*—dresses up a boat or cabin wonderfully, near City Hall at Hieronymus Heyerdahlsgate 1, entrance on Tordenskioldsgate—on the other side of the block, tel. 22 40 50 60).

Vinmonopolet stores are the only places where you can buy wine and spirits in Norway. The most convenient location is at the central train station. Another location, not far from Stortinget, is at Rosenkrantzgate 11. The bottles used to be kept behind the counter, but now you can actually touch the merchandise. Locals say it went from being a "jewelry store" to a "grocery store." (Light beer is sold in grocery stores, but strong beer is still limited to Vinmonopolet shops.)

Sleeping in Oslo

In Oslo, like in many other big cities, supply and demand dictate hotel room prices. And yet, some hotels may still offer lower rates on weekends and during some parts of the summer. The only way to

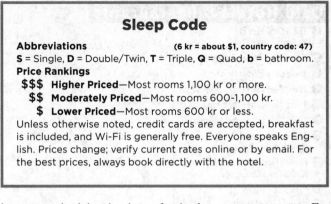

Sleep Code

Abbreviations   **(6 kr = about $1, country code: 47)**
S = Single, **D** = Double/Twin, **T** = Triple, **Q** = Quad, **b** = bathroom.
Price Rankings
$$$ **Higher Priced**—Most rooms 1,100 kr or more.
  $$ **Moderately Priced**—Most rooms 600-1,100 kr.
   $ **Lower Priced**—Most rooms 600 kr or less.
Unless otherwise noted, credit cards are accepted, breakfast is included, and Wi-Fi is generally free. Everyone speaks English. Prices change; verify current rates online or by email. For the best prices, always book directly with the hotel.

know is to check hotel websites for the dates you want to visit. For convenience and modern comfort, I like the Thon Budget Hotels. For lower prices, consider a cheap hotel or a hostel.

If you arrive without a reservation, the TI can try to sort through all of the confusing hotel specials and get you the best deal going on fancy hotel rooms on the push list. With "dynamic pricing," it's tough to get a hotel to give a firm rate. If booking on your own and on a budget, check hotel websites far in advance to see who's willing to offer the most aggressive discount.

The TI's **Oslo Package** offers business-class rooms plus an Oslo Pass for around 800 kr per person (based on double occupancy); prices vary depending on the hotel—though note that the Oslo Package may be discontinued in 2016. If it's still available, it's a good deal for couples and ideal for families with young children. Two kids under 16 sleep free, breakfast is included, and up to four family members get free Oslo Passes, covering admission to sights and all public transportation (see page 217). These passes are valid for four days, even if you only stay one night at the hotel (allowing you to squeeze two days of sightseeing out of a one-night stay—for example, if you take an overnight train or boat out of town on your second evening). Buy the Oslo Package through your travel agent at home or, simpler and quicker, upon arrival in Oslo at the TI. Even if you show up late in the day when prices may be deeply discounted, you still get the Oslo Pass along with your room. For details on the Oslo Package, see www.visitoslo.com.

NEAR THE TRAIN STATION AND KARL JOHANS GATE

These accommodations are within a 15-minute walk of the station. While evidence of an earlier, shadier time survives nearest the station, the hotels feel secure and comfortable. Parking in a central garage will run you about 250-300 kr per day.

OSLO

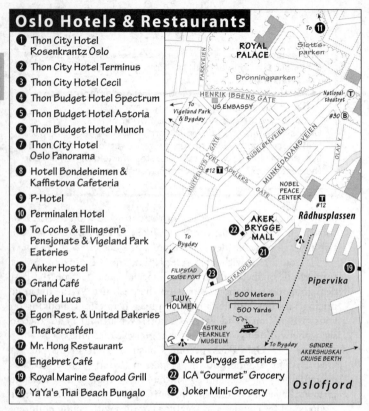

Oslo Hotels & Restaurants

1. Thon City Hotel Rosenkrantz Oslo
2. Thon City Hotel Terminus
3. Thon City Hotel Cecil
4. Thon Budget Hotel Spectrum
5. Thon Budget Hotel Astoria
6. Thon Budget Hotel Munch
7. Thon City Hotel Oslo Panorama
8. Hotell Bondeheimen & Kaffistova Cafeteria
9. P-Hotel
10. Perminalen Hotel
11. To Cochs & Ellingsen's Pensjonats & Vigeland Park Eateries
12. Anker Hostel
13. Grand Café
14. Deli de Luca
15. Egon Rest. & United Bakeries
16. Theatercaféen
17. Mr. Hong Restaurant
18. Engebret Café
19. Royal Marine Seafood Grill
20. YaYa's Thai Beach Bungalo
21. Aker Brygge Eateries
22. ICA "Gourmet" Grocery
23. Joker Mini-Grocery

Thon Hotels

This chain of business-class hotels (found in big cities throughout Norway) knows which comforts are worth paying for and which are not. They offer little character, but provide maximum comfort per krone in big, modern, conveniently located buildings. Each hotel has a cheery staff and lobby, tight but well-designed rooms, free Wi-Fi, and a big buffet breakfast. All are non-smoking.

Thon Hotels come in categories: Their "City Hotels" are a cut above their "Budget Hotels" and are generally more expensive. But depending on demand, you may be able to find a City Hotel that's discounted below the cost of the Budget Hotels. Both Budget and City Hotels are usually cheaper during the summer. Most City Hotels offer free juice and coffee all day. In Budget Hotels, all rooms lack phones and mini-fridges; also, rooms with double beds are a bit bigger than twin-bedded rooms for the same price.

Because Thon Hotels base their prices on demand, their rates vary wildly, so the following prices are roughly the midpoint of a huge range: **Thon City Hotels**—Sb-1,525, Db-1,825 kr; **Thon**

OSLO

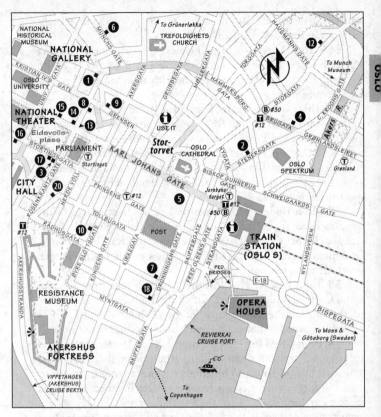

Budget Hotels—Sb-795 kr, Db-1,100 kr. Extra beds are 200 kr for an adult and 100 kr for a child under 13. Book by phone or online (central booking tel. 81 55 24 00, www.thonhotels.no).

For the best prices, check the "price calendar" on the Thon Hotels website. Booking via the Thon website gets you a 12 percent "Thon WebDeal" discount (with some exceptions) if you prepay, with no option to change or cancel your reservation 24 hours after booking. My price ratings for Thon Hotels are based on their average summer rates. Of the 14 Thon Hotels in Oslo, I find the following most convenient:

$$$ Thon City Hotel Rosenkrantz Oslo offers 151 modern, comfortable rooms in a classy and central location two blocks off Karl Johans Gate. Its eighth-floor lounge offers views of the Royal Palace park. If you want to splurge, this is the place to do it (Rosenkrantz Gate 1, tel. 23 31 55 00, www.thonhotels.no/rosenkrantzoslo, rosenkrantzoslo@thonhotels.no).

$$$ Thon City Hotel Terminus is similar but closer to the station (Steners Gate 10, tel. 22 05 60 00, www.thonhotels.no/terminus, terminus@thonhotels.no).

$$$ Thon City Hotel Cecil is near the Parliament building a block below Karl Johans Gate (Stortingsgata 8, tel. 23 31 48 00, www.thonhotels.no/cecil, cecil@thonhotels.no, manager Livanne loves my readers).

$$ Thon Budget Hotel Spectrum is four blocks from the station near the Grønland Torg shopping street. A quarter of its rooms are plagued by disco noise on weekends (leave station out north entrance toward bus terminal, go across footbridge toward tall glass Radisson Blu Plaza Hotel, and pass through Grønland Torg, Brugata 7; tel. 23 36 27 00, www.thonhotels.no/spectrum, spectrum@thonhotels.no).

$$ Thon Budget Hotel Astoria has the least charm of my recommended Thon Hotels, but it's well-located and perfectly serviceable (3 blocks in front of station, 50 yards off Karl Johans Gate, Dronningens Gate 21, tel. 24 14 55 50, www.thonhotels.no/astoria, astoria@thonhotels.no).

$$ Thon Budget Hotel Munch, a few blocks from the National Gallery, is like its sisters. Of all the Thon Budget hotels listed, this one has the most upscale location (Munchs Gate 5, tel. 23 21 96 00, www.thonhotels.no/munch, munch@thonhotels.no).

$$ Thon City Hotel Oslo Panorama is a 15-story attempt at a downtown condominium building (the condos didn't work, so now it's a budget hotel). While higher rooms are more expensive, even those reserving a cheap room often get bumped up. If you request anything higher than the fourth floor, you'll likely enjoy a bigger room, perhaps with a balcony (just off Dronningens Gate at Rådhusgata 7, about 6 blocks from station, tel. 23 31 08 00, www.thonhotels.no/oslopanorama, oslopanorama@thonhotels.no).

More Hotels near the Train Station

$$$ Hotell Bondeheimen ("Farmer's Home") is a historic hotel run by the farmers' youth league, *Bondeungdomslaget*. It once housed the children of rural farmers attending school in Oslo. Now a Best Western, its 127 rooms have all the comforts of a modern hotel (Db-1,195-1,990 kr, prices can vary wildly—check website for best deals, lower prices in July; non-smoking, elevator, Rosenkrantz Gate 8, tel. 23 21 41 00, www.bondeheimen.com, bookingoffice@bondeheimen.com). This almost-100-year-old building is also home to the Kaffistova cafeteria (see "Eating in Oslo") and the Heimen Husflid shop (see "Shopping in Oslo").

$$$ P-Hotel rents 93 comfortable rooms—some with hardwood-slick floors—for the same price every day of the year. You get a boxed breakfast delivered each morning, as well as a guest computer and Wi-Fi. Avoid late-night street noise by requesting a room high up or in the back (Db-895-1,250 kr, bigger rooms add 200 kr per person up to five, some sixth-floor rooms have balconies, pay by credit card—no cash accepted, Grensen 19, T-bane: Stortinget, tel. 23 31 80 00, www.p-hotels.com, oslo@p-hotels.no).

$$ Perminalen Hotel, a place for military personnel on leave, is perfectly central, spartan, inexpensive, and welcoming to civvies. They have the same fair prices all year. Spliced invisibly into a giant office block on a quiet street, it has sleek woody furniture and a no-nonsense reception desk (Sb-620 kr, twin Db-860 kr, some seventh-floor rooms have balconies, entirely non-smoking, elevator, pay guest computer, Wi-Fi in lobby, tram #12 from station to Øvre Slottsgate 2, tel. 23 09 30 81, www.perminalen.com, post.perminalen@iss.no). Single beds in shared quads segregated by sexes (with lockers and breakfast) rent for 380 kr each. Its cheap mess hall is open all day.

THE WEST END

$$ Cochs Pensjonat has 89 characteristic rooms (20 remodeled doubles), many with kitchenettes. It's on the far side of the Royal Palace (S-510 kr, Sb-610-660 kr, D-720 kr, Db-840-900 kr, Q-1,180 kr, Qb-1,340 kr, July usually cheaper, discounts for breakfast at nearby cafés, non-smoking rooms, elevator; T-bane: Nationaltheatret, exit to Parkveien, and 10-minute walk through park; or more-convenient trams #11, #17, or #18 to Welhavens Gate; Parkveien 25; tel. 23 33 24 00, www.cochspensjonat.no, booking@cochs.no, three generations of the Skram family).

$$ Ellingsen's Pensjonat rents 18 clean, bright rooms with fluffy down comforters. It's in a residential neighborhood four blocks behind the Royal Palace (S-500 kr, Sb-600 kr, D-800 kr, Db-990 kr, extra bed-350 kr, breakfast-85 kr, lower prices Sept-Feb, non-smoking, back rooms have less street noise, tram #19 from central station to Rosenborg stop, near Uranienborg church at Holtegata 25, tel. 22 60 03 59, www.ellingsenspensjonat.no, post@ellingsenspensjonat.no).

PRIVATE HOMES

To find a room in a private home, which can save you money but at the cost of being farther from the center, try Airbnb or www.bbnorway.com. The TI does not offer a booking service for private homes, but they do list B&Bs and pensions on their website, www.visitoslo.com.

HOSTELS

$ Anker Hostel, a huge student dorm open to travelers of any age, offers 250 of Oslo's best cheap doubles. Though it comes with the ambience of a bomb shelter, each of its rooms is spacious, simple, and clean. There are kitchens and elevators (bed in 6-bed room-240-260 kr, bed in quad-270-290 kr, Db-620-640 kr, Tb-810-870 kr, higher prices are weekend rates, sheets-50 kr, towel-20 kr, no breakfast, self-serve laundry, parking-230 kr/day; tram #12 or #13, or bus #30 or #31 from central station, bus and tram stop: Hausmannsgate; or 10-minute walk from station; Storgata 55, tel. 22 99 72 00, www.ankerhostel.no, hostel@anker.oslo.no).

$ Haraldsheim Youth Hostel (IYHF), a huge, modern hostel open all year, comes with a grand view, laundry, self-service kitchen, 315 beds—most of them in four-bed rooms...and a long commute (2.5 miles out of town). Beds in the fancy quads with private showers and toilets are 280 kr per person (bed in simple quad with bathroom down the hall-255 kr). They also offer private rooms (S-455 kr, Sb-510 kr, D-610 kr, Db-690 kr, bunk-bed D-540 kr, Db-625 kr; all include breakfast, members get 10 percent off, sheets-50 kr, catch bus #31 or tram #17 or T-bane lines #4 or #6 from Oslo's central train station to Sinsenkrysset, then 5-minute uphill hike to Haraldsheimveien 4, tel. 22 22 29 65, www.haraldsheim.no, oslo.haraldsheim@hihostels.no). Eurailers can train to the hostel with their rail pass (2/hour, to Grefsen and walk 10 minutes).

SLEEPING ON THE TRAIN OR BOAT
Norway's trains and ferries offer ways to travel while sleeping. The eight-hour night train between Bergen and Oslo leaves at about 23:00 in each direction (nightly except Sat). The overnight cruise between these Nordic capitals is a clever way to avoid a night in a hotel and to travel while you sleep, saving a day in your itinerary (see "Oslo Connections," later).

Eating in Oslo

EATING CHEAPLY
How do the Norwegians afford their high-priced restaurants? They don't eat out much. This is one city in which you might just settle for simple or ethnic meals—you'll save a lot and miss little. Many menus list small and large plates. Because portions tend to be large, choosing a small plate or splitting a large one makes some otherwise pricey options reasonable. You'll notice many locals just drink free tap water, even in fine restaurants. For a description of Oslo's classic (and expensive) restaurants, see the TI's *Oslo Guide* booklet.

Splurge for a hotel that includes breakfast, or pay for it if it's

Oslo's One-Time Grills

Norwegians are experts at completely avoiding costly restaurants. "One-time grills," or *engangsgrill*, are the rage for locals on a budget. For about 25 kr, you get a disposable outdoor cooker consisting of an aluminum tray, easy-to-light charcoal, and a flimsy metal grill. All that's required is a sunny evening, a grassy park, and a group of friends. During balmy summer evenings, the air in Oslo's city parks is thick with the smell of disposable (and not terribly eco-friendly) grills. It's fun to see how prices for this kind of "dining" aren't that bad in the supermarket: Norwegian beer-28 kr/half-liter, potato salad-30 kr/tub, cooked shrimp-50

kr/half kilo, "ready for grill" steak-two for 120 kr, *grill polse* hot dogs-75 kr per dozen, *lomper* (Norwegian tortillas for wrapping hot dogs)-20 kr per stack, and the actual grill itself.

Bars are also too expensive for the average Norwegian. Young night owls drink at home before *(forspiel)* and after *(nachspiel)* an evening on the town, with a couple of hours, generally around midnight, when they go out for a single drink in a public setting. A beer in a bar costs about $12 for a half-liter (compared to $6 in Ireland and $2 in the Czech Republic), while they can get a six-pack for about twice that price in a grocery store.

optional. At around 80 kr, a Norwegian breakfast fit for a Viking is a good deal. Picnic for lunch or dinner. Basements of big department stores have huge, first-class supermarkets with lots of alternatives to sandwiches for picnic dinners. The little yogurt tubs with cereal come with collapsible spoons. Wasa crackers and meat, shrimp, or cheese spread in a tube are cheap and pack well. The central station has a Joker supermarket with long hours (Mon-Fri 6:00-23:00, Sat 8:00-23:00, Sun 9:00-23:00). Some supermarkets have takeout food that is discounted just before closing—showing up just before 20:00 or so to buy some roast chicken could be your cheapest meal in Oslo. My favorite meals in Oslo are picnic dinners harborside.

You'll save 12 percent by getting takeaway food from a restaurant rather than eating inside. (The VAT on takeaway food is 12 percent; restaurant food is 24 percent.) Fast-food restaurants ask if you want to take away or not before they ring up your order on the cash register. Even McDonald's has a two-tiered price list.

Oslo is awash with little budget eateries (modern, ethnic, fast food, pizza, department-store cafeterias, and so on). **Deli de Luca,** a cheery convenience store chain, notorious for having a store on every key corner in Oslo, is a step up from the similarly ubiquitous 7-Elevens. Most are open 24/7, selling sandwiches, pastries, sushi, and to-go boxes of warm pasta or Asian noodle dishes. You can fill your belly here for about 80 kr. Some outlets (such as the one at the corner of Karl Johans Gate and Rosenkrantz Gate) have seating on the street or upstairs. Beware: Because this is still a *convenience* store, not everything is well-priced. Convenience stores—while convenient—charge double what supermarkets do.

KARL JOHANS GATE STRIP

Strangely, **Karl Johans Gate** itself—the most Norwegian of boulevards—is lined with a strip of good-time American chain eateries and sports bars where you can get ribs, burgers, and pizza, including T.G.I. Fridays and the Hard Rock Cafe. **Egon Restaurant** offers a daily 110-kr all-you-can-eat pizza deal (available Tue-Sat 11:00-18:00, Sun-Mon all day). Each place comes with great sidewalk seating and essentially the same prices.

Grand Café is perhaps the most venerable place in town—though it may be closed in 2016. At lunchtime, try the sandwich buffet (315-kr all-you-like). Lunch plates are 150-200 kr, and dinner plates run about 250-300 kr. Reserve a window, and if you hit a time when there's no tour group, you're suddenly a posh Norwegian (daily 11:00-23:00, Karl Johans Gate 31, tel. 23 21 20 18).

Deli de Luca, just across from the Grand Café, offers good-value food and handy seats on Karl Johans Gate. For a fast meal with the best people-watching view in town, you may find yourself dropping by here repeatedly (for 60 kr you can get a calzone, or a portion of chicken noodles, beef noodles, or chicken vindaloo with rice—ask to have it heated up, open 24/7, Karl Johans Gate 33, tel. 22 33 35 22).

United Bakeries, next to the Paleet mall, is a quiet bit of Norwegian quality among sports bars, appreciated for its salads, light lunches, and fresh pastries (seating inside and out, Mon-Fri 7:00-20:00, Sat 9:00-20:00, Sun 9:00-16:00).

Kaffistova, a block off the main drag, is where my thrifty Norwegian grandparents always took me. And it remains almost unchanged since the 1970s. This alcohol-free cafeteria still serves simple, hearty, and typically Norwegian (read: bland) meals for a good price (140-kr daily specials, Mon-Fri 10:00-21:00, Sat-Sun 11:00-19:00, Rosenkrantz Gate 8, tel. 23 21 42 10).

Theatercaféen, since 1900 the place for Norway's illuminati to see and be seen (note the celebrity portraits adorning the walls), is a swanky splurge steeped in Art Nouveau elegance (175-195-kr starters, 200-375-kr main dishes, 655-kr three-course meal,

Norwegian Cuisine

Traditionally Norwegian cuisine doesn't rank very high in terms of excitement value. But the typical diet of meat, fish, and potatoes is definitely evolving to incorporate more diverse products, and the food here is steadily improving. Fresh produce, colorful markets, and efficient supermarkets abound in Europe's most expensive corner.

In this land of farmers and fishermen, you'll find raw ingredients like potatoes, salmon, or beef in traditional recipes. Norway's national dish is *Fårikål*, a lamb or mutton stew with cabbage, peppercorns, and potatoes. It's served with lingonberry jam and lefse—a soft flatbread made from potatoes, milk, and flour. This dish is so popular that the last Thursday in September is *Fårikål* day in Norway. Norwegian grandmothers prepare this hearty stew by throwing together the basic ingredients with whatever leftovers are lying around the kitchen. There's really no need for a recipe, so every stew turns out differently—and every grandma claims hers is the best.

Because of its long, cold winters, Norway relies heavily on the harvesting and preservation of fish. Smoked salmon, called *røkt laks*, is prepared by salt-curing the fish and cold-smoking it, ensuring the temperature never rises above 85°F. This makes the texture smooth and almost raw. *Bacalao* is another favorite: salted and dried cod that is soaked in water before cooking. You'll often find *bacalao* served with tomatoes and olives.

Some Norwegians serve lutefisk around Christmas time, but you'll rarely see this salty, pungent dish on the menu. Instead, try the more pleasant *fiskekake*, a small white fish cake made with cream, eggs, milk, and flour. You can find these patties year-round. For a break from the abundance of seafood, try local specialties such as reindeer meatballs, or pork-and-ground beef meat cakes called *kjøttkaker*. True to Scandinavian cuisine, *kjøttkaker* are usually slathered in a heavy cream sauce.

Dessert and coffee after a meal are essential. *Bløtkake*, a popular delight on Norway's Constitution Day (May 17), is a layered cake drizzled with strawberry juice, covered in whipped cream, and decorated with fresh strawberries. The cloudberry (*multe*), which grows in the Scandinavian tundra, makes a unique jelly that tastes delicious on vanilla ice cream, or even whipped into a rich cream topping for heart-shaped waffles. Norwegians are proud of their breads and pastries, and you'll never be too far from a bakery that sells an almond-flavored *kringle* or a cone-shaped *krumkake* cookie filled with whipped cream.

Mon-Sat 11:00-23:00, Sun 15:00-22:00, in Hotel Continental at Stortingsgata 24, across from National Theater, tel. 22 82 40 50).

Mr. Hong Restaurant is a busy Asian eatery serving fish, duck, chicken, pork, and beef dishes and an all-day, all-you-can-eat grill buffet (165-240-kr main dishes, 200-kr buffet, Mon-Fri 14:00-23:00, Sat 13:00-23:30, Sun 14:00-22:00, Stortingsgata 8, entrance on Rosenkrantz Gate, right next to recommended Hotel Cecil, tel. 22 42 20 08).

EATING IN THE SHADOW OF THE FORTRESS

Engebret Café is a fine old restaurant in a 17th-century building in the Christiania section of town below the fortress. Since 1857 it's been serving old-fashioned Norse food (reindeer is always on the menu) in a classic old Norwegian setting, with outdoor dining in spring and summer (250-350-kr main dishes, Mon-Fri 11:30-23:00, Sat in summer 13:00-23:00, closed Sun and July, Bankplassen 1, tel. 22 82 25 25).

Royal Marine Seafood Grill is a good bet for affordable dining on the harborfront on a balmy evening. All seats are outside, where you'll enjoy nice views and sunsets on the Oslofjord. In contrast to the Aker Brygge scene, this is a casual place under the castle with nothing trendy about it (150-180-kr salads, burgers, fish-and-chips, 200-kr seafood dishes, daily May-Aug 14:00-22:00, closed Sept-April, Akershusstranda 5, tel. 22 08 03 00).

YaYa's Thai Beach Bungalow is a welcome change from Norwegian bland. The tiki-bar decor is infectious, the menu is fun and accessible, and the food is surprisingly authentic—I slurped up every morsel of my green curry pork. Don't be surprised if your dinner is accompanied by the sounds and lights of an hourly tropical thunderstorm (100-kr starters, 170-kr main dishes, vegetarian options, daily 16:00-22:00, Fri-Sat until 23:00, between the Parliament building and City Hall at Øvre Vollgate 13, tel. 22 83 71 10).

HARBORSIDE DINING IN AKER BRYGGE

Aker Brygge, the harborfront mall, is popular with businesspeople and tourists. While it isn't cheap, its inviting cafés and restaurants with outdoor, harborview tables make for a memorable waterfront meal. Before deciding where to eat, you might want to walk the entire lane (including the back side), considering both the regular places (some with second-floor view seating) and the various floating options. Nearly all are open for lunch and dinner.

Lekter'n Lounge, right on the water, offers the best harbor view (rather than views of strolling people). This trendy bar has a floating dining area open only when the weather is warm. It serves hamburgers, fish-and-chips, 150-180-kr salads, mussels, and shrimp buckets. Budget eaters can split a 160-kr pizza (all out-doors, Stranden 3, tel. 22 83 76 46). If you go just for drinks, the sofas make you feel right at home and a DJ adds to the ambience.

Rorbua, the "Fisherman's Cabin," is a lively yet cozy eatery tucked into this mostly modern stretch of restaurants. The specialty is food from Norway's north, such as whale and reindeer. Inside, it's extremely woody with a rustic charm and candlelit picnic tables surrounded by harpoons and old B&W photos. Grab a stool at one of the wooden tables, and choose from a menu of meat-and-potato dishes (200-300 kr). A hearty daily special with coffee for 165 kr is one of the best restaurant deals in the city (daily 12:30-23:00, Stranden 71, tel. 22 83 64 84).

Lofoten Fiskerestaurant serves fish amid a dressy yacht-club atmosphere at the end of the strip. While it's beyond the people-watching action, it's comfortable even in cold and blustery weather because of its heated atrium, which makes a meal here practically outdoor dining. Reservations are a must, especially if you want a harborside window table (lunch-200 kr, dinner from 300 kr, open daily, Stranden 75, tel. 22 83 08 08, www.lofoten-fiskerestaurant. no).

Budget Tips: If you're on a budget, try a hotdog from a *pølse* stand or get a picnic from a nearby grocery store and grab a bench along the boardwalk. The **ICA "Gourmet"** grocery store—in the middle of the mall a few steps behind all the fancy restaurants—has salads, warm takeaway dishes (sold by the weight), and more (turn in about midway down the boardwalk, Mon-Fri 8:00-22:00, Sat 9:00-20:00, closed Sun). Farther down, the **Joker mini-grocery** (just over the bridge and to the right on Lille Stranden in Tjuvhol-men) is open until 22:00.

DINING NEAR VIGELAND PARK

Lofotstua Restaurant feels transplanted from the far northern is-lands it's named for. Kjell Jenssen and his son, Jan Hugo, proudly serve up fish Lofoten-style. Evangelical about fish, they will pa-tiently explain to you the fine differences between all the local va-rieties, with the help of a photo-filled chart. They serve only the freshest catch, perfectly—if simply—prepared. If you want meat, they've got it—whale or seal (170-290-kr plates, Mon-Fri 15:00-22:00, generally closed in July, 5-minute walk from gate of Vige-land statue garden, tram #12, in Majorstuen at Kirkeveien 40, tel. 22 46 93 96). This place is packed daily in winter for their famous lutefisk.

Curry and Ketchup Indian Restaurant is filled with in-the-know locals enjoying tasty and hearty meals for about 100 kr. This happening place requires no reservations and feels like an Indian market. If you want a reasonable Indian meal in Oslo, this is hard to beat (daily 14:00-23:00, cash only, a 5-minute walk from gate of Vigeland statue garden, tram #12, in Majorstuen at Kirkeveien 51, tel. 22 69 05 22).

TRENDY DINING AT THE BOTTOM OF GRÜNERLØKKA

These spots are located on the map on page 261.

Südøst Asian Crossover Restaurant, once a big bank, now fills its vault with wine (which makes sense, given Norwegian alcohol prices). Today it's popular with young Norwegian professionals as a place to see and be seen. It's a fine mix of Norwegian-chic woody ambience inside with a trendy menu, and a big riverside terrace outdoors with a more casual menu. Diners enjoy its chic setting, smart service, and modern creative Asian-fusion cuisine (200-kr dinner plate, 300-kr dinner menu, daily 16:00-24:00, at bottom of Grünerløkka, tram #11, #12, or #17 to Trondheimsveien 5, tel. 23 35 30 70).

Olaf Ryes Plass, Grünerløkka's main square (and the streets nearby), is lined with inviting eateries and has a relaxed, bohemian-chic vibe. The top side of the square (near Villa Paradiso Pizzeria) has several pubs selling beer-centric food to a beer-centric crowd. To get here, hop on tram #11, #12, or #13 to Olaf Ryes Plass.

Villa Paradiso Pizzeria serves Oslo's favorite pizza. Youthful and family-friendly, it has a rustic interior and a popular terrace overlooking the square and people scene (120-180-kr pizza, Olaf Ryes Plass 8, tel. 22 35 40 60).

Mathallen Oslo is a former 19th-century factory, spiffed up and morphed into a neighborhood market with a mix of produce stalls and enticing eateries all sharing food-circus-type seating in the middle (Tue-Sun until late, closed Mon, on the river, 5-minute walk from Olaf Ryes Plass).

EATING CHEAP AND SPICY IN GRØNLAND

The street called Grønland leads through this colorful immigrant neighborhood (a short walk behind the train station or T-bane: Grønland; see the map on page 266). After the cleanliness and orderliness of the rest of the city, the rough edges and diversity of people here can feel like a breath of fresh air. Whether you eat here or not, the street is fun to explore. In Grønland, backpackers and immigrants munch street food for dinner. Cheap and tasty *börek* (feta, spinach, mushroom) is sold hot and greasy to go for 25 kr.

Punjab Tandoori is friendly and serves hearty meals (70-100-kr, lamb and chicken curry, tandoori specials). I like eating outside here with a view of the street scene (daily 11:00-23:00, Grønland 24).

Alibaba Restaurant is clean, simple, and cheap for Turkish food. They have good indoor or outdoor seating (139-kr fixed-price meal Mon-Thu only, open daily 12:30-22:30, corner of Grønland-sleiret and Tøyengata at Tøyengata 2, tel. 22 17 22 22).

Asylet is more expensive and feels like it was here long before Norway ever saw a Pakistani. This big, traditional eatery—like a Norwegian beer garden—has a rustic, cozy interior and a cobbled backyard filled with picnic tables (150-240-kr plates and hearty dinner salads, daily 11:00-24:00, Grønland 28, tel. 22 17 09 39).

Dattera Til Hagen feels like a college party. It's a lively scene filling a courtyard with picnic tables and benches under strings of colored lights. If it's too cold, hang out inside. Locals like it for the tapas, burgers, salads, and Norwegian microbrews on tap (180-kr plates, Grønland 10, tel. 22 17 18 61). On weekends after 22:00, it becomes a disco.

Olympen Brown Pub is a dressy dining hall that's a blast from the past. You'll eat in a spacious, woody saloon with big dark furniture, faded paintings of circa-1920 Oslo lining the walls, and huge chandeliers. It's good for solo travelers, because sharing the long dinner tables is standard practice. They serve hearty 200-kr plates and offer a huge selection of beers. Traditional Norwegian cuisine is served downstairs, while upstairs on the rooftop, the food is grilled (daily 11:00-2:00 in the morning, Grønlandsleiret 15, tel. 22 17 28 08).

Café Con Bar is a trendy yuppie eatery on the downtown edge of Grønland. Locals consider it to have the best burgers in town (150 kr). While the tight interior seating is very noisy, the sidewalk tables are great for people-watching (160-kr daily specials, 150-190-kr main dishes, Mon-Sat 10:00-late, Sun 12:00-late, kitchen closes at 23:00, where Grønland hits Brugata).

NEAR THE SKI JUMP, HIGH ON THE MOUNTAIN

Frognerseteren Hovedrestaurant, nestled high above Oslo (and 1,400 feet above sea level), is a classy, sod-roofed old restaurant. Its terrace, offering a commanding view of the city, is a popular stop for famous apple cake and coffee. The café is casual and less expensive, with indoor and outdoor seating (90-kr sandwiches and cold dishes, 140-190-kr entrées, Mon-Sat 11:00-22:00, Sun 11:00-21:00, reservations unnecessary). The elegant view restaurant is pricier (375-395-kr plates, Mon-Fri 12:00-22:00, Sat 13:00-22:00, Sun 13:00-21:00, reindeer specials, reserve for evening dining, tel. 22 92 40 40).

The **Holmenkollen** restaurant, just below the ski jump and a few steps above the Holmenkollen T-bane stop, is a practical al-ternative to the Frognerseteren restaurant. It serves better food at better prices with a similarly grand Oslo fjord view, but without the folk charm.

You can combine a trip into the forested hills surrounding the city with lunch or dinner and get a chance to see the famous Holmenkollen Ski Jump up close (see page 265).

Oslo Connections

BY TRAIN, BUS, OR CAR

For train information, call 81 50 08 88 and press 9 for English. For international trains, press 3. Even if you have a rail pass, reservations are required for long rides (free with first-class pass, 50 kr for second-class; SJ InterCity reservation fee for tickets to Stockholm in costs about 35 kr regardless of class). First class often comes with a hot meal, fruit bowl, and unlimited juice and coffee.

Be warned that international connections from Oslo are often in flux. Schedules can vary depending on the day of the week, so carefully confirm the specific train you need and purchase any required reservations in advance. Aside from the occasional direct train to Stockholm, most trips from Oslo to Copenhagen or Stockholm require a change in Sweden.

From Oslo by Train to Bergen: Oslo and Bergen are linked by a spectacularly scenic train ride (3-5/day, 7 hours, overnight possible daily except Sat). Many travelers take it as part of the **Norway in a Nutshell** route, which combines train, ferry, and bus travel in an unforgettably beautiful trip. For information on times and prices, see the next chapter.

By Train to: Lillehammer (almost hourly, 2.25 hours), **Kristiansand** (5/day, 4.5 hours, overnight possible), **Stavanger** (4/day, 8-8.5 hours, overnight possible), **Copenhagen** (2/day, 8.5 hours, transfer at Göteborg, more with multiple changes), **Stockholm** (2/day direct InterCity trains, 5.75 hours; 2/day with change in Göteborg, 6-7.5 hours).

By Bus to Stockholm: Taking the bus to Stockholm is cheaper but slower than the train (3/day, 8 hours, www.swebus.se).

By Car to the Jotunheimen Mountains: See "Route Tips for Drivers" on page 359.

BY CRUISE SHIP

Oslo has three cruise ports, described next. For more in-depth cruising information, pick up my *Rick Steves Northern European Cruise Ports* guidebook.

Getting Downtown: To varying degrees, all of Oslo's cruise ports are within walking distance of the city center—but from the farthest-

flung port, Filipstad, your best option is probably to take advantage of your cruise line's shuttle bus, even if you have to pay for it (most drop off by the Nobel Peace Center, near City Hall on the harborfront). No public transit serves the ports, but Open Top Sightseeing's hop-on, hop-off bus tours meet arriving cruise ships at or near all ports (pricey but convenient; see page 223). A taxi into town from any of the ports costs a hefty 150 kr.

Once you arrive at the City Hall/harbor area, you can simply walk up the street behind City Hall to find Karl Johans Gate, and the National Gallery; hop on tram #12 (ride it toward Majorstuen to reach Vigeland Park—use the Vigelandsparken stop; or ride it toward Disen to reach the train station—use the Jernbanetorget stop); or take the shuttle boat across the harbor to the museums at Bygdøy.

Port Details: Akershus, right on the harbor below Akershus Fortress, has two berths: **Søndre Akershuskai,** a bit closer to town, and **Vippetangen,** a bit farther out (at the tip of the peninsula). Both are within an easy 10-minute walk of City Hall (just stroll with the harbor on your left).

Revierkai, around the east side of the Akershus Fortress peninsula, faces Oslo's can't-miss-it, cutting-edge Opera House. From the Opera House, a pedestrian overpass takes you directly to the train station and the start of my self-guided "Welcome to Oslo" walk, or you can head up the street called Rådhusgata to City Hall.

Filipstad is just west of downtown, next to the brand-new Tjuvholmen development (around the far side of Aker Brygge from City Hall). From here, it's a dull 20-minute walk into town: Walk out of the port, turn right at the roundabout, then head to the busy highway and follow the path to the right and signs to *sentrum*. When construction around Filipstad and Tjuvholmen is finally finished (years from now), it will be possible to cross directly from the port to Tjuvholmen and then it will be a quick walk along Aker Brygge to the city center. Your ship's upper deck provides the perfect high-altitude vantage point for scouting your options before disembarking.

BY OVERNIGHT BOAT TO COPENHAGEN

Consider connecting Oslo and Copenhagen by cruise ship. The boat leaves daily from Oslo at 16:30 (arrives in Copenhagen at 9:45 the following morning; going the other way, it departs Copenhagen at 16:30 and arrives in Oslo at 9:45; about 17 hours sailing each way). The boat leaves Oslo from the far (non-City Hall) side of the Akershus Fortress peninsula (get there via bus #60 from the train station, 2-3/hour, get off at Vippetangen stop and follow signs to DFDS ticket office). Boarding is from 15:00 to 16:15. From Oslo, you'll sail through the Oslofjord—not as dramatic as Norway's western fjords, but impressive if you're not going to Bergen. On board are gourmet restaurants, dinner and breakfast buffets, cafés, nightclubs, shops, a sauna, hot tub, and swimming pool. This is fun and convenient, but more expensive and not as swanky as the Stockholm-Helsinki cruise (see the Helsinki chapter).

You can take this cruise one-way or do a round-trip from either city. Book online or by phone (from Norway, call DFDS Seaways' Denmark office: Mon-Fri 9:00-16:30, closed Sat-Sun, tel. 00 45 33 42 30 10, www.dfdsseaways.us). Book in advance for the best prices. For more specifics and sample prices, see "By Overnight Boat to Oslo" on page 120.

NORWAY IN A NUTSHELL

A Scenic Journey to the Sognefjord

While Oslo and Bergen are the big draws for tourists, Norway is first and foremost a place of unforgettable natural beauty. There's a certain mystique about the "land of the midnight sun," but you'll get the most scenic travel thrills per mile, minute, and dollar by going west from Oslo rather than north.

Norway's greatest claims to scenic fame are her deep, lush fjords. Three million years ago, an ice age made this land as inhabitable as the center of Greenland. As the glaciers advanced and cut their way to the sea, they gouged out long grooves—today's fjords.

The entire west coast is slashed by stunning fjords, and the Sognefjord—Norway's longest (120 miles) and deepest (1 mile)—is tops. The seductive Sognefjord has tiny but tough ferries, towering canyons, and isolated farms and villages marinated in the mist of countless waterfalls.

A series of well-organized and spectacular bus, train, and ferry connections—appropriately nicknamed "Norway in a Nutshell"—lays Norway's beautiful fjord country before you on a scenic platter. With the Nutshell, you'll delve into two offshoots of the Sognefjord, which make an upside-down "U" route: the Aurlandsfjord and the Nærøyfjord. You'll link the ferry ride to the rest of Norway with two trains and a bus: The main train is an express route that takes you through stark and icy scenery above the tree line. To get from the express train down to the ferry, you'll catch an old-fashioned slow train one way (passing waterfalls and forests) and a bus the other way (offering fjord views and more waterfalls). All connections are designed for tourists, explained in English, convenient, and easy. At the start of the fjord, you'll go through the town of Flåm (a transit hub), then pass briefly by the workaday town of

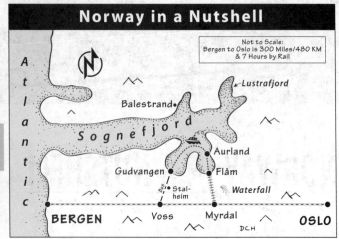

Aurland and the hamlet of Undredal (by taking the Nutshell trip segments at your own pace, you can visit the latter two fjord towns on your own; all are described in this chapter).

This region enjoys mild weather for its latitude, thanks to the warm Gulf Stream. (When it rains in Bergen, it just drizzles here.) But if the weather is bad—don't fret. I've often arrived to gloomy weather, only to enjoy sporadic splashes of brilliant sunshine all day long.

Recently the popularity of the Nutshell route has skyrocketed. And the 2005 completion of the longest car tunnel in the world (15 miles between Flåm and Lærdal) rerouted the main E-16 road between Bergen and Oslo through this idyllic fjord corner. All of this means that July and August come with a crush of crowds, dampening some of the area's magic. Unfortunately, many tourists are overcome by Nutshell tunnel-vision, and spend so much energy scurrying between boats, trains, and buses that they forget to simply enjoy the fjords. Relax—you're on vacation.

PLANNING YOUR TIME

Even the blitz tourist needs a day for the Norway in a Nutshell trip. With more time, sleep in a town along the fjord, and customize your fjord experience to include sights outside the Nutshell.

Day 1: The Nutshell works well as a single day (one-way between Oslo and Bergen in either direction, or as a long day trip from either city). Those with a car and only one day can leave the car in Oslo and do the Nutshell by train, bus, and boat. If you're using public transportation and want to make efficient use of your time, organize your trip so that it ends in Bergen, or return to Oslo on a night train (sleeping through all the scenery you saw west-bound).

Day 2: If you have enough time, spend the night somewhere on the Sognefjord—either along the Nutshell route itself (in Flåm

or Aurland; accommodations listed later), or in another, even more appealing fjordside town (such as Balestrand or Solvorn, both described in the next chapter).

With More Time: The Sognefjord deserves more than a day. If you can spare the time, venture off

the Nutshell route. You can easily connect to some non-Nutshell towns (such as Balestrand) via ferry or express boat. Drivers can improve on the Nutshell by taking a northern route: From Oslo, drive through the Gudbrandsdal Valley, go over the Jotunheimen Mountains, then along Lustrafjord to Balestrand; from there, you can cross the Sognefjord on a car ferry (such as Kaupanger-Gudvangen) and drive the Nutshell route on to Bergen. (Most of these sights, and the car ferry connection, are covered in the next two chapters.) For more tips, see the "Beyond the Nutshell" sidebar.

Orientation to the Nutshell

The most exciting single-day trip you could make from Oslo or Bergen is this circular train/boat/bus/train jaunt through fjord country.

Local TIs (listed throughout this chapter) are well-informed about your options, and they sell tickets for various segments of the trip. At TIs, train stations, and hotels, look for souvenir-worthy brochures with photos, descriptions, and exact times (see sample schedules later in this chapter).

Route Overview: The basic idea is this: Take a train halfway across the mountainous spine of Norway, make your way down to the Sognefjord for a boat cruise, then climb back up out of the fjord to rejoin the main train line. Each of these steps is explained in the self-guided "Nutshell Tour" in this chapter. Transportation along the Nutshell route is carefully coordinated. If any segment of your journey is delayed, the transportation for the next segment

---

"Norway in a Nutshell" in a Nutshell

The essential five Nutshell segments (all described in detail in this chapter) are:

Norwegian State Railways (NSB) Oslo to Myrdal Train: Five hours, two departures each morning—6:43 (recommended) and 8:05 (for sleepyheads), www.nsb.no. Confirm times online or locally.

Private Train from Myrdal to Flåm (Flåmsbana): One hour, hourly departures, generally timed for arrival of Oslo train.

Boat Through the Fjords: Flåm to Gudvangen, 2 hours, about hourly departures, two boat companies, same route and cost.

Bus from Gudvangen to Voss: 25 miles, one hour, departures timed with boat arrivals.

Train from Voss to Bergen: One hour, hourly departures.

Nutshell travelers originating in Bergen can use this route in reverse. Check schedules at www.scandinavianrail.com and ruteinfo.net.

---

will wait for you (because everyone on board is catching the same connection).

The route works round-trip from Oslo or Bergen, or one-way between those two cities (going in either direction). Doing the Nutshell one-way between Oslo and Bergen (or vice versa) is most satisfying—you'll see the whole shebang, and it's extremely efficient if you're connecting the two cities anyway. Doing the Nutshell as a round-trip from Bergen is cheaper, but it doesn't include the majestic train ride between Myrdal and Oslo. Conversely, even though the round-trip from Oslo doesn't go all the way to Bergen, it still includes all the must-sees (the Voss-Bergen leg is the least thrilling, anyway).

When to Go: The Nutshell trip is possible all year. In the summer (late June-late Aug), the connections are most convenient, the weather is most likely to be good...and the route is at its most crowded. Outside of this time, sights close and schedules become more challenging. Some say the Nutshell is most beautiful in winter, though schedules are severely reduced (and you can't do it as a day trip from Oslo). It's easy to confirm schedules, connections, and prices locally or online (www.ruteinfo.net).

Sample Oslo-Bergen Schedule: You must take one of two morning departures (6:43 or 8:05) to do the entire trip from Oslo to Bergen in a day. I recommend the earlier departure to enjoy an hour more free time in Flåm and generally fewer crowds. This itinerary shows typical sample times for summer travel; confirm exact times before your trip (www.nsb.no for trains and www.ruteinfo. net for boats and buses):

- Oslo to Myrdal—6:43-12:05
- Myrdal to Flåm—12:13-13:10
- Free time in Flåm—13:10-15:10
- Boat from Flåm to Gudvangen—15:10-17:30
- Bus from Gudvangen to Voss—17:45-19:00
- Train from Voss to Bergen—19:41-21:08
- Free time in Bergen—21:08-22:59
- Overnight train from Bergen to Oslo—22:59-6:27

If you leave Oslo on the 8:05 train, you'll have only one hour of free time on the fjord in Flåm and arrive in Bergen at the same time (21:08). If overnighting in Flåm, you have nearly hourly boats, buses, and trains the next day to continue on into Bergen. Doing the Nutshell route round-trip from Bergen, or from Bergen to Oslo, requires leaving Bergen at 8:40.

Reservations: While reservations are possible for most of the legs, they're only really worth considering for two: The Oslo-Myrdal train (essential), and the Flåmsbana train between Myrdal and Flåm (less critical, but worth having—especially at times when cruise passengers docked in Flåm can jam up the train). Fortunately, both of these legs can be reserved at www.nsb.no or at the Oslo train station; to avoid disappointment, you may as well book both trains at once. The other legs—the boat trip, the bus ride, and the Voss-Bergen train—are less crowded and it's easy to just wing it (though it's wise to book your specific boat departure in Flåm once you know which one you'd like to take).

Buying Tickets: Without a rail pass, you'll save about 100 kr by purchasing Norwegian State Railways tickets in advance. If you have a Eurail pass, the train connections from Oslo-Myrdal and Voss-Bergen are free, and you get a 30 percent discount on the Myrdal-Flåm ride (no rail pass discounts on boat or bus). Standard ticket prices for the Nutshell legs are 320 kr for Myrdal-Flåm (220 kr with rail pass, same price in advance, at station, or on train from conductor); 300 kr on either line for the Flåm-Gudvangen boat; and 100 kr for the Gudvangen-Voss bus (buy from driver).

Dealing with Your Luggage: Many travelers connect Oslo and Bergen with the Nutshell trip and are therefore carrying their luggage. Luckily, the connections require almost no walking: At Myrdal, you just cross the platform; in Flåm, you walk 50 yards from the train to the dock; in Gudvangen, the bus meets the ferry at the dock (look for buses marked *Norway in a Nutshell*); in Voss, the bus drops you at the train station. On the three train segments, simply put your bag in the overhead rack. If you want to check your bag during your free time in Flåm, use the baggage-check cabin at the head of the train track, across the lane from the boat dock.

On the ferry, leave your bag with the stack of bags on the car deck. And on the bus (which meets the boat), the driver will help you stow your bag underneath, or you can take it on board. The biggest chore is getting your bags to and from the train stations in Oslo and Bergen.

MORE SAMPLE NUTSHELL ITINERARIES

Here are non-Oslo-Bergen one-day options for doing the Nutshell in the summer. Confirm specific times before your trip (www.ruteinfo.net).

Bergen-Oslo: Train departs Bergen-8:40, arrives Voss-9:56; bus departs Voss-10:10, arrives Gudvangen-11:20; boat departs Gudvangen-11:45, arrives Flåm-14:10; Flåmsbana train departs Flåm-16:05, arrives Myrdal-17:03; train departs Myrdal-17:53, arrives Oslo-22:45.

Day Trip from Oslo: Train departs Oslo-6:43, arrives Myrdal-12:01; Flåmsbana train departs Myrdal-12:13; arrives Flåm-13:10; boat departs Flåm-13:20, arrives Gudvangen-15:30; bus departs Gudvangen-15:40, arrives Voss-16:55; train departs Voss-17:08, arrives Oslo-22:45.

Day Trip from Bergen: Train departs Bergen-8:40, arrives Voss-9:56; bus departs Voss-10:10, arrives Gudvangen-11:20; boat departs Gudvangen-11:45, arrives Flåm-14:10; Flåmsbana train departs Flåm-14:40, arrives Myrdal-15:40; train departs Myrdal-17:01, arrives Bergen-19:05.

Express Boat to Balestrand and Bergen: If you don't want to do the entire Nutshell route, take note of the very handy and speedy express boat connecting this area (Aurland and Flåm) with two other worthwhile destinations: Balestrand (on the Sognefjord's northern bank) and Bergen. While this boat misses the best fjord (Nærøyfjord), many travelers use it to craft their own itinerary that escapes the Nutshell rut. For more on this boat, see page 332.

Eating: Options along the route aren't great—on the Nutshell I'd consider food just as a source of nutrition and forget about fine dining. You can buy some food on the fjord cruises (50-75-kr hot dogs, burgers, and pizza) and the Oslo-Bergen train (50-100-kr hot meals, 150-kr daily specials). Depending on the timing of your layovers, Myrdal, Voss, or Flåm are your best lunch-stop options (the Myrdal and Flåm train stations have decent cafeterias, and other eateries surround the Flåm and Voss stations)—although you won't have a lot of time there if you're making the journey all in one day. Your best bet is to pack picnic meals and munch en route. If catching an early train in Oslo, the station has several handy grocery stores open at 6:00.

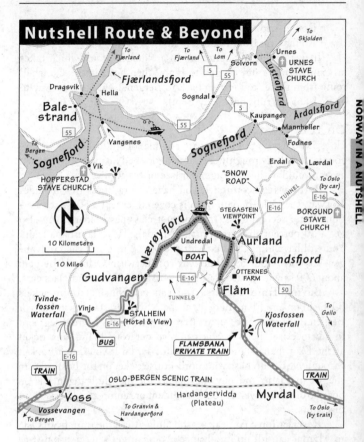

Nutshell Route & Beyond

WITH A PACKAGE DEAL OR ON YOUR OWN?

The Fjord Tours package deals are easy to book—they'll save you time as well as a little money. If you have a rail pass, or if you're a student or a senior (and therefore eligible for discounts), you'll save money doing the Nutshell on your own. Just buy tickets as you go (described on the next page).

Package Deals

Fjord Tours sells the Nutshell package and other package trips at all Norwegian State Railways stations, including Oslo and Bergen, or through their customer-service line in Norway (tel. 81 56 82 22, www.fjordtours.no). With these packages, your train departures are fixed and you can catch whichever boat and bus you like.

The costs of the Nutshell packages are as follows:
- One-way from Bergen or Oslo-1,630 kr
- Round-trip from Oslo via Voss (but not Bergen)-2,205 kr
- Round-trip from Oslo via Bergen-2,490 kr

- Round-trip from Bergen via Myrdal (but not Oslo)-1,220 kr
- Round-trip from Flåm-840 kr

They also sell a "Sognefjord in a Nutshell" tour, which takes an express boat from Bergen to Flåm, then picks up the Nutshell route from there (round-trip back to Bergen-1,465 kr; one-way to Oslo-1,865 kr; runs only May-Sept).

On Your Own

Unless you have a rail pass or are eligible for student or senior discounts, you'll pay roughly the same to do the Nutshell on your own as you would with a package tour (see prices above).

Rail Pass Discounts: If you have any rail pass that includes Norway, the Oslo-Bergen train is covered (except a 50-kr reservation fee for second class; free for first-class passholders); you also get a 30 percent discount on the Myrdal-Flåm Flåmsbana train. You still have to pay full fare for the boat cruise and the Gudvangen-Voss bus. Your total one-way cost between Oslo and Bergen: about 600 kr with a first-class pass, 650 kr with a second-class pass.

Buying Train Tickets: You can get Nutshell train tickets (Oslo-Flåm and Flåm-Bergen) at the NSB train stations in Oslo or Bergen. In summer, it's smart to reserve the Oslo-Myrdal segment in advance (see below). You can also get your Flåmsbana ticket at the Flåmsbana station in Flåm or Myrdal if you didn't book it through NSB; purchase your fjord-cruise ticket on the boat or from the TI in Flåm; and buy the tickets for the Gudvangen bus on board from the driver. If you're a student or senior, always ask about discounts.

Reservations: At peak season (July-Aug), the train from Oslo to Myrdal can fill up in advance. You can get a reservation (free with first-class rail pass) at any Norwegian train station (including at the Oslo airport) or at the Oslo TI. To reserve further in advance, book your seat online at www.nsb.no. You'll be given a choice of picking up your ticket at the train station, sending it to your smartphone, or printing it out. If you have any difficulty paying for your ticket with a US credit card online, call 81 50 08 88 or 23 62 00 00; press 9 for English, and you'll be given a Web link where you can finish processing your credit-card payment.

The **Flåmsbana train** is usually no problem to just hop on, but certain departures are greatly affected by cruise ships docked in Flåm. Morning departures from Flåm to Myrdal can sell out, and late-morning or early-afternoon trains from Myrdal back to Flåm can be jammed. If you're booking ahead for your Oslo-Myrdal leg, you may as well book a Flåmsbana seat at the same time. At other times, you can just buy your ticket on the spot at either the Myrdal or Flåm stations, or from the conductor on the train (same price). While you may be told in Oslo that the Flåmsbana train is sold out,

Beyond the Nutshell

The Sognefjord is the ultimate natural thrill Norway has to offer, and there's no doubt that the Nutshell route outlined in this chapter is the most efficient way to see it quickly. Unfortunately, its trains, buses, and boats are thronged with other visitors who have the same idea.

Travelers with a bit more time, and the willingness to chart their own course, often have a more rewarding Sognefjord experience. It's surprisingly easy to break out of the Nutshell and hit the northern part of the Sognefjord (for example, using the Bergen-Vik-Balestrand-Aurland-Flåm express boat, described on page 332).

In the next chapter, you'll find some tempting stopovers on the north bank of the Sognefjord, including adorable fjordside villages (such as Balestrand and Solvorn), evocative stave churches (including Hopperstad and Urnes), and a chance to get up close to a glacier (at the Nigard Glacier).

Read up on your options, then be adventurous about mixing and matching the fjordside attractions that appeal to you most. Ideally, use the Nutshell as a springboard for diving into the Back Door fjords of your travel dreams.

you most likely can still catch it at the time you wanted (or an hour later, since it runs about hourly).

You don't need to reserve the **Flåm-Gudvangen fjord** boat trip, but it's smart to buy your boat ticket upon arrival in Flåm (see page 300). You don't need a reservation for the **Gudvangen-Voss bus.**

Tips for Cruise-Ship Passengers Arriving in Flåm

Tiny Flåm—in the heart of Nutshell country—is an increasingly popular destination for huge cruise ships. If your cruise is stopping in Flåm, you can do the middle part of the Nutshell loop in a day, but it helps to know a few pointers:

• Plan your day in advance (using this chapter), disembark as early as possible, and head straight for the train station (a short walk from the dock). Many ships arrive around 8:00; Flåm's TI and train-station ticket office both open at 8:15; and the first Nutshell fjord boat sets sail at 9:00—leaving you a narrow window of time to confirm schedules and book tickets. Stragglers may get stuck in long lines and (literally) miss the boat.

• The Nutshell loop is practical for cruisers only if done counterclockwise: Flåm-Gudvangen boat, 9:00-11:25; Gudvangen-Voss bus, 11:40-12:55; Voss-Myrdal train, 13:10-14:00; Flåmsbana train from Myrdal to Flåm, 14:40-15:40 (these are 2014 times; confirm locally). The opposite direction (Flåm-Myrdal-Voss-Gudvangen-Flåm) returns to Flåm too late for most cruise ships.

• The same "package vs. on your own" considerations, explained earlier, apply to cruisers. Unless you're eligible for student, senior, or rail pass discounts, book the Flåm round-trip package (at the Flåm TI).

• If you'd rather not do the Nutshell loop on your day in port, you could do one or two legs: For example, cruise to Gudvangen, then take a bus straight back to Flåm (skipping the train rides); or simply go for a round-trip ride on the Flåmsbana train to Myrdal and back (this popular-with-cruisers option often sells out—get your tickets as quickly as possible on arrival in Flåm). For other ideas of what to do in Flåm, see page 306.

Nutshell Tour

If you only have one day for this region, it'll be a thrilling day—worth ▲▲▲. The following self-guided segments of the Nutshell route are narrated from Oslo to Bergen. If you're going the other way, hold the book upside down.

▲▲Oslo-Bergen Train

This is simply the most spectacular train ride in northern Europe. The scenery crescendos as you climb over Norway's mountainous spine. After a mild three hours of deep woods and lakes, you're into the barren, windswept heaths and glaciers. These tracks were begun in 1894 to link Stockholm and Bergen, but Norway won its independence from Sweden in 1905, so the line served to link the two main cities in the new country—Oslo and Bergen. The entire railway, an amazing engineering feat completed in 1909, is 300 miles long; peaks at 4,266 feet, which, at this Alaskan latitude, is far above the tree line; goes under 18 miles of snow sheds; trundles over 300 bridges; and passes through 200 tunnels in just under seven hours.

Here's what you'll see traveling westward from Oslo: Leaving Oslo, you pass through a six-mile-long tunnel and stop in Drammen, Norway's fifth-largest town. The scenery stays low-key and woodsy up Hallingdal Valley until you reach Geilo, a popular ski resort. Then you enter a land of big views and tough little cabins. Finse, at about 4,000 feet, is the highest stop on the line. At several towns, the conductor may announce how many minutes the train will be stopped there. This gives you a few fun moments to get out, stretch, take a photograph, and look around.

Before Myrdal, you enter the longest high-mountain stretch of railway in Europe. Much of the line is protected by snow tunnels. The scenery gets more dramatic as you approach Myrdal (MEER-

NORWAY IN A NUTSHELL

doll). Just before Myrdal, look to the right and down into the Flåm Valley, where the Flåmsbana branch line winds its way down to the fjord. Nutshell travelers get off at Myrdal.

Cost: Note that the Nutshell route includes only part of this train ride (as a day trip from Oslo, for instance, you take the Oslo-Myrdal and Voss-Oslo segments). Here are the one-way fares for various segments: Oslo-Bergen-815 kr, Oslo-Myrdal-660 kr, Myrdal-Voss-117 kr, Myrdal-Bergen-286 kr, Voss-Bergen-200 kr. You can save money on these fares if you book in advance at www.nsb.no.

Remember, second-class rail-pass holders pay just 50 kr to reserve, and first-class passholders pay nothing. If you have a second-class rail pass or ticket, you can pay 90 kr to upgrade to "Komfort" class, with more legroom, reclining seats, free coffee and tea, and an electrical socket for your laptop (just ask the conductor when you board).

Schedule: This train runs three to five times per day (overnight possible daily except Sat). The segment from Oslo to Myrdal takes about 5 hours; going all the way to Bergen takes about 7 hours.

Reservations: In peak season, get reservations for this train at least a week in advance (see page 296).

▲▲Myrdal-Flåm Train (Flåmsbana)

The little 12-mile spur line leaves the Oslo-Bergen line at Myrdal (2,800 feet), which is nothing but a scenic high-altitude train junction with a decent cafeteria.
From Myrdal, the Flåmsbana train winds down to Flåm (sea level) through 20 tunnels (more than three miles' worth) in 55 thrilling minutes. It's party time on board, and the engineer even stops the train for photos at the best waterfall,

Kjosfossen. According to a Norwegian legend, a temptress lives behind these falls and tries to lure men to the rocks with her singing...look out for her...and keep a wary eye on your partner.

The train line is an even more impressive feat of engineering when you realize it's not a cogwheel train—it's held to the tracks only by steel wheels, though it does have five separate braking systems. Before boarding, pick up the free, multilingual souvenir pamphlet with lots of info on the trip (or see www.flaamsbana.

no). Video screens onboard and sporadic English commentary on the loudspeakers explain points of interest, but there's not much to say—it's all about the scenery.

If you're choosing seats, you'll enjoy slightly more scenery if you sit on the left going down.

Cost: 320 kr one-way (rail-pass holders pay 220 kr), 420 kr round-trip. You can buy tickets at the Flåmsbana stations in Myrdal or Flåm or on the train (same price). Train-information staff in Oslo may tell you that the Mrydal-Flåm train is booked—don't worry, it very rarely fills up. Simply get to Myrdal and hop on that train.

Schedule: The train departs in each direction nearly hourly.

Reservations: On trains going from Myrdal down to Flåm, you can always squeeze in, even if it's standing-room only. However, morning trains ascending from Flåm to Myrdal (when there are several cruise ships in port) can sell out. This is a concern only for those wanting to leave Flåm to Myrdal in the morning. If that's you, try to buy your ticket the night before or right when the Flåm ticket office opens (at 8:15).

▲▲▲Flåm-Gudvangen Fjord Cruise

The Flåmsbana train deposits you at **Flåm,** a scenic, functional transit hub at the far end of the Aurlandsfjord. If you're doing the Nutshell route nonstop, follow the crowds and hop on the sightseeing boat that'll take you to **Gudvangen.** With minimal English narration, the boat takes you close to the goats, sheep, waterfalls, and awesome cliffs.

There are two boat companies to choose from: Fjord 1 and Sognefjorden. Between them, there are departures about hourly from Flåm to Gudvangen. Beware: The first ticket desk you hit in Flåm's visitors center is the Sognefjorden boat desk, and they'll sell you a boat ticket implying it's your only option.

Fjord 1 is the public ferry with cars and lots of open space. It stops at Aurland and Undredal, which is handy if you want to hop off and on along the way—though you'll need to buy separate tickets for each leg of your trip, and it'll end up costing you at least

The Facts on Fjords

The process that created the majestic Sognefjord began during an ice age about three million years ago. A glacier up to 6,500 feet thick slid downhill at an inch an hour, following a former river valley on its way to the sea. Rocks embedded in the glacier gouged out a steep, U-shaped valley, displacing enough rock material to form a mountain 13 miles high. When the climate warmed up, the ice age came to an end. The melting glaciers retreated and the sea level rose nearly 300 feet, flooding the valley now known as the Sognefjord. The fjord is more than a mile deep, flanked by 3,000-foot mountains—for a total relief of 9,300 feet. Waterfalls spill down the cliffs, fed by runoff from today's glaciers. Powdery sediment tinges the fjords a cloudy green, the distinct color of glacier melt.

Why are there fjords on the west coast of Norway, but not, for instance, on the east coast of Sweden? The creation of a fjord requires a setting of coastal mountains, a good source of moisture, and a climate cold enough for glaciers to form and advance. Due to the earth's rotation, the prevailing winds in higher latitudes blow from west to east, so chances of glaciation are ideal where there is an ocean to the west of land with coastal mountains. When the winds blow east over the water, they pick up a lot of moisture, then bump up against the coastal mountain range, and dump their moisture in the form of snow—which feeds the glaciers that carve valleys down to the sea.

You can find fjords along the northwest coast of Europe—including western Norway and Sweden, Denmark's Faroe Islands, Scotland's Shetland Islands, Iceland, and Greenland; the northwest coast of North America (from Puget Sound in Washington state north to Alaska); the southwest coast of South America (Chile); the west coast of New Zealand's South Island; and on the continent of Antarctica.

As you travel through Scandinavia, bear in mind that, while we English-speakers use the word "fjord" to mean only glacier-cut inlets, Scandinavians often use it in a more general sense to include bays, lakes, and lagoons that weren't formed by glacial action.

85 kr more (be sure to notify the ticket-seller where you want to get off, to make certain they'll stop).

The Sognefjorden boat (same price, route, and journey time) is more of a sightseeing boat rather than a public car and post boat—but it's mostly closed in.

I much prefer the Fjord 1 boat because I like to be in the open air, I enjoy hanging out on the car deck, and the Gudvangen-Voss Nutshell bus connection in Gudvangen is immediate and reliable.

You'll cruise up the lovely **Aurlandsfjord,** motoring by the town of **Aurland** (a good home base, but your boat may not stop

here unless you ask), pass the town of **Undredal** (or stop here if you request it), and hang a left at the stunning **Nærøy-fjord.** The cruise ends at the apex of the Nærøyfjord, in **Gudvangen.**

The trip is breathtaking in any weather. For the last hour, as you sail down the Nærøyfjord, camera-clicking tourists scurry around struggling to get a photo that will catch the magic. Waterfalls turn the black cliffs into bridal veils, and you can nearly reach out and touch the cliffs of the Nærøyfjord. It's the world's narrowest fjord: six miles long and as little as 820 feet wide and 40 feet deep. On a sunny day, the ride is one of those fine times—like when you're high on the tip of an Alp—when a warm camaraderie spontaneously combusts between the strangers who've come together for the experience.

Cost: For the whole route (Flåm-Gudvangen), you'll pay 300 kr one-way (150 kr for students with ISIC cards; 450 kr round-trip).

Schedule: In summer (May-Sept), boats run four to five times each day in both directions. Specific departure times can vary, but generally boats leave Flåm at 9:00, 13:20, 15:10, and 18:00 (with an additional 11:00 departure from late June to late August) and leave Gudvangen at 10:30, 11:45, 15:45, and 17:40 (with an additional 13:30 departure from late June to late August). Frequency drops off-season. The trip takes about two hours and 15 minutes. Your only concern is that the Nutshell bus may not meet the last departure of day (check locally); the worst-case scenario is that you'd need to catch the regular commuter bus to Voss, which makes more stops and doesn't take the razzle-dazzle Stalheimskleiva corkscrew road.

Reservations: Don't bother. Just buy your ticket in Flåm as soon as you know which boat you want.

Other Ways to Cruise Nærøyfjord: If staying in Flåm, you could take a thrilling ride on a little inflatable FjordSafari speedboat (described later, under "Sights in and near Flåm"; see page 307).

▲Gudvangen-Voss Bus

Nutshellers get off the boat at Gudvangen and take the 25-mile bus ride to Voss. Gudvangen is little more than a boat dock and giant tourist kiosk. If you want, you can browse through the grass-roofed souvenir stores and walk onto a wooden footbridge—then catch your bus. Buses meet each ferry, or will show up soon. (Confirm this in advance if you plan to take the last boat of the day—the ferry crew can call ahead to be sure the bus waits for you.) While some buses—designed for commuters rather than sightseers—take the direct route to Voss, buses tied to the Nutshell schedule take a super-scenic detour via Stalheim (described below). If you're a waterfall junkie, sit on the left.

First the bus takes you up the **Nærøydal** and through a couple of long tunnels. Then you'll take a turnoff to drive past the land-

mark **Stalheim Hotel** for the first of many spectacular views back into fjord country. Though the hotel dates from 1885, there's been an inn here since about 1700, where the royal mailmen would change horses. The hotel is geared for tour groups (genuine trolls sew the pewter buttons on the sweaters), but the priceless view from the backyard is free. Drivers should be sure to stop here for the view and peruse the hotel's living room to survey the art showing this perch in the 19th century.

Leaving the hotel, the bus wends its way down a road called **Stalheimskleiva,** with a corkscrew series of switchbacks flanked by a pair of dramatic waterfalls. With its 18 percent grade, it's the steepest road in Norway.

After winding your way down into the valley, you're back on the same highway. The bus goes through those same tunnels again, then continues straight on the main road through pastoral countryside to Voss. You'll pass a huge lake, then follow a crystal-clear, surging river. Just before Voss, look to the right for the wide **Tvindefossen waterfall,** tumbling down its terraced cliff. Drivers will find the grassy meadow and flat rocks at its base ideal for letting the mist fog their glasses and enjoying a drink or snack (be discreet, as "picnics are forbidden").

Cost: 100 kr, pay on board, no rail pass discounts.

Reservations: Not necessary.

Voss

The Nutshell bus from Gudvangen drops you at the Voss train station, which is on the Oslo-Bergen train line. This connection is generally not well-coordinated; you'll likely have 40 minutes or so to kill before the next train to Bergen.

A plain town in a lovely lake-and-mountain setting, Voss lacks the striking fjordside scenery of Flåm, Aurland, or Undredal, and is basically a home base for summer or winter sports (Norway's Winter Olympics teams often practice here). Voss surrounds its fine, 13th-century church with workaday streets—busy with both local shops and souvenir stores—stretching in several directions. Fans of American football may want to see the humble monument to player and coach Knute Rockne, who was born in Voss in 1888; look for the metal memorial plaque on a rock near the train station.

Voss' helpful **TI** is a five-minute walk from the train station—just head toward the church (June-Aug daily 8:00-19:00; Sept-May Mon-Sat 8:30-17:00, closed Sun; facing the church in the center of town at Vangsgatan 20, mobile 40 61 77 00, www.visitvoss.no).

Drivers should zip right through Voss, but two miles outside town, you can stop at the **Mølstertunet Folk Museum,** which has 16 buildings showing off farm life in the 17th and 18th centuries (70 kr; mid-May-Aug daily 10:00-17:00; Sept-mid-May Mon-Fri 10:00-15:00, Sun 12:00-15:00, closed Sat; Mølstervegen 143, tel. 47 47 97 94, www.vossfolkemuseum.no).

▲Voss-Bergen Train

The least exciting segment of the trip—but still pleasantly scenic—this train chugs 60 miles along the valley between the midsize town of Voss (described above) and Bergen. For the best scenery, sit on the right side of the train if coming from Oslo/Voss, or the left side if coming from Bergen. Between Voss and Dale, you'll pass several scenic lakes; near Bergen, you'll go along the Veafjord.

Cost: The train costs 200 kr between Voss and Bergen and is fully covered by rail passes that include Norway.

Schedule and Reservations: Unlike the long-distance Oslo-Bergen journey, this line is also served by more frequent commuter trains (about hourly, 75 minutes), and reservations aren't necessary.

Voss-Oslo Train: Note that if you're doing the Nutshell round-trip from Oslo, you should catch the train from Voss (rather than Bergen) back to Oslo. The return trip takes 6 hours and costs 747 kr; reservations are strongly recommended in peak season.

Flåm

Flåm (pronounced "flome")—
where the boat and Flåmsbana
train meet, at the head of the
Aurlandsfjord—feels more like
a transit junction than a village. But its striking setting,
easy transportation connections, and touristy bustle make
it appealing as a home base for
exploring the nearby area.

Orientation to Flåm

Most of Flåm's services are in a modern cluster of buildings in and
around the train station, including the TI (see below), train ticket
desk, public WC, cafeteria, and souvenir shops. Just outside the
station, the little red shed at the head of the tracks serves as a left-
luggage desk (40 kr, daily 8:00-19:45, on your right as you depart
the train, ring bell if nobody's there), and displays a chart of the
services you'll find in the station. The boat dock for fjord cruises
is just beyond the end of the tracks. Surrounding the station are a
Co-op Marked grocery store (with a basic pharmacy and post office inside, Mon-Sat 9:00-20:00, shorter hours off-season, closed
Sun year-round) and a smattering of hotels, travel agencies, and
touristy restaurants. Aside from a few scattered farmhouses and
some homes lining the road, there's not much of a town here. (The
extremely sleepy old town center—where tourists rarely venture,
and which you'll pass on the Flåmsbana train—is a few miles up
the river, in the valley.)

TOURIST INFORMATION

At the TI inside the train station, you can purchase your boat tickets (for Fjord 1 but not Sognefjorden) and load up on handy brochures (daily May and late Sept 8:15-16:00, June-mid-Sept 8:15-
20:00, closed Oct-April, tel. 57 63 21 06, www.visitflam.com or
www.alr.no). The TI hands out a variety of useful items: an excellent flier with a good map and up-to-date schedules for public transit options; a diagram of the train-station area, identifying services
available in each building; and a map of Flåm and the surrounding
area, marked with suggested walks and hikes. Answers to most of
your questions can be found posted on the walls and from staff at
the counter. Bus schedules, boat and train timetables, maps, and

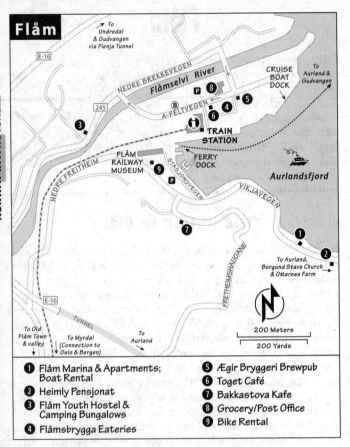

Flåm

1. Flåm Marina & Apartments; Boat Rental
2. Heimly Pensjonat
3. Flåm Youth Hostel & Camping Bungalows
4. Flåmsbrygga Eateries
5. Ægir Bryggeri Brewpub
6. Toget Café
7. Bakkastova Kafe
8. Grocery/Post Office
9. Bike Rental

more are photocopied and available for your convenience. You can pick up Bergen or Oslo information as well.

Sights in and near Flåm

ALONG THE WATERFRONT

Flåm's village activities are all along or near the pier.

The **Flåm Railway Museum** (Flåmsbana Museet), sprawling through the long old train station building alongside the tracks, has surprisingly good exhibits about the history of the train that connects Flåm to the main line up above. You'll find good English explanations, artifacts, re-creations of historic interiors (such as a humble schoolhouse), and an old train car. It's the only real museum in town and a good place to kill time while waiting for your boat or train (free, daily 9:00-17:00, until 20:00 in summer).

A pointless and overpriced **tourist train** does a 45-minute loop around Flåm (95 kr).

The pleasantly woody **Ægir Bryggeri,** a microbrewery designed to resemble an old Viking longhouse, offers tastes of its five beers (135 kr; also restaurant meals in evening with a matching beer menu).

The TI hands out a map suggesting several **walks and hikes** in the area, starting from right in town.

Consider renting a **boat** to go out on the peaceful waters of the fjord. You can paddle near the walls of the fjord and really get a sense of the immensity of these mountains. You can rent rowboats, motorboats, and paddleboats at the little marina across the harbor. If you'd rather have a kayak, Njord does kayak tours, but won't rent you one unless you're certified (tel. 91 32 66 28, www.njord.as).

But the main reason people come to Flåm is to leave it—see some options below. Because Aurland and Flåm are close together (10 minutes away by car or bus, or 20 minutes by boat), I've also listed attractions near Aurland, below.

▲▲▲Cruising Nærøyfjord

The most scenic fjord I've seen anywhere in Norway is about an hour from Flåm (basically the last half of the 2-hour Flåm-Gudvangen trip). There are several ways to cruise it: You can take the Fjord 1 ferry, described earlier as part of the Norway in a Nutshell trip (4.5-hour round-trips departing Flåm in peak season at 9:00, 11:00, and 13:20, 400 kr; these should also stop in Aurland and Undredal—make sure the crew knows that you want to get off, and that the cruise ends in Gudvangen). Or you can consider two other Flåm-based options:

Sognefjorden Sightseeing & Tours: This private company runs trips from Flåm to Gudvangen and back to Flåm, using their own boats and buses (rather than the public ones on the "official" Nutshell route). If the Nutshell departures don't work for you, consider these trips as an alternative. Their main offering, the World Heritage Cruise, is a boat trip up the Nærøyfjord with a return by bus (365 kr, 3 hours, multiple departures daily mid-May-mid-Sept). They also do a variation on this trip with a 45-minute stop in the village of Undredal for lunch and a goat-cheese tasting (495 kr, June-Aug only); a bus trip up to the Stalheim Hotel for the view (290 kr, or combined with return from Gudvangen by boat for 510 kr); a bus ride up to the thrilling Stegastein viewpoint (a concrete-and-wood viewing pier sticking out from a mountainside high above Aurland, 190 kr, mid-May-mid-Sept); and more. For details, drop by their office inside the Flåm train station, call 57 66 00 55, or visit www.visitflam.com/sognefjorden.

▲▲FjordSafari to Nærøyfjord: FjordSafari takes little

NORWAY IN A NUTSHELL

groups out onto the fjord in small, open Zodiac-type boats with an English-speaking guide. Participants wear full-body weather suits, furry hats, and spacey goggles (making everyone on the boat look like crash-test dummies). As the boat rockets across the water, you'll be thankful for the gear, no matter what the weather. Their two-hour Flåm-Gudvangen-Flåm tour focuses on the Nærøyfjord, and gets you all the fjord magnificence you can imagine (610 kr). Their three-hour tour is the same as the two-hour tour, except that it includes a stop in Undredal, where you can see goat cheese being made, taste the finished product, and wander that sleepy village (720 kr, several departures daily June-Aug, fewer off-season, kids get discounts, tel. 99 09 08 60, www.fjordsafari.no, Maylene). Their 1.5-hour "mini" tour costs 510 kr and just barely touches on the Nærøyfjord...so what's the point?

▲Flåm Valley Bike Ride or Hike

For the best single-day, non-fjord activity from Flåm, take the Flåmsbana train to Myrdal, then hike or mountain-bike along the

road (half gravel, half paved) back down to Flåm (2-3 hours by bike, gorgeous waterfalls, great mountain scenery, and a cute church with an evocative graveyard, but no fjord views).

Walkers can just hike the best two hours from Myrdal to Blomheller, and catch the train from there into the valley. Or, without riding the train, you can simply walk up the valley 2.5 miles to the church and a little farther to a waterfall. Whenever you get tired hiking up or down the valley, you can hop on the next train. Pick up the helpful map with this and other hiking options (ranging from easy to strenuous) at the Flåm TI.

Bikers can rent good mountain bikes from the bike-rental cabin next to the Flåm train station (daily June-Sept 8:00-20:00, 50 kr/hour, 250 kr/day, includes helmet). It costs 100 kr to take a bike to Myrdal on the train.

▲▲Otternes Farms

This humble but magical cluster of four centuries-old farms is about three miles from Flåm (easy for drivers; a decent walk or bike ride otherwise). It's perched high on a ridge, up a twisty gravel road midway

between Flåm and Aurland. Laila Kvellestad runs this low-key sight, valiantly working to save and share traditional life as it was back when butter was the farmers' gold. (That was before emigration decimated the workforce, coinage replaced barter, and industrialized margarine became more popular than butter—all of which left farmers to eke out a living relying only on their goats and the cheese they produced.) Until 1919 the only road between Aurland and Flåm passed between this huddle of 27 buildings, high above the fjord. First settled in 1522, farmers lived here until the 1990s. Laila gives 45-minute English tours through several time-warp houses and barns at 10:00, 12:00, 14:00, and 16:00 (50-kr entry plus 30 kr for guided tour, June-mid-Sept daily 10:00-17:00, tel. 48 12 51 38, www.otternes.no). It's wise to call first to confirm tour times and that it's open. For an additional 70 kr, Laila serves a traditional snack of pancakes and coffee or tea with your tour. Or book in advance for a 175-kr full lunch featuring locally sourced specialties such as *rømmegrøt* (porridge) and meatballs.

OVER (OR UNDER) THE MOUNTAINS, TO LÆRDAL AND BORGUND

To reach these sights, you'll first head along the fjord to Aurland (described on page 312). Of the sights below, the Lærdal Tunnel, Stegastein viewpoint, and Aurlandsvegen "Snow Road" are best for drivers. The Borgund Stave Church can be reached by car, or by bus from Flåm or Aurland.

For more specifics on driving through the Lærdal Tunnel or on the Aurlandsvegen "Snow Road," see below.

Lærdal Tunnel

Drivers find that this tunnel makes connecting Flåm and Lærdal a snap. It's the world's longest road-vehicle tunnel, stretching 15 miles between Aurland and Lærdal as part of the E-16 highway. It also makes the wonderful Borgund Stave Church (described on the next page) less than an hour's drive from Aurland. The downside to the tunnel is that it goes beneath my favorite scenic drive in Norway (the Aurlandsvegen "Snow Road," described next). But with about two hours, you can drive through the tunnel to Lærdal and then return via the "Snow Road," with the Stegastein viewpoint as a finale, before dropping back into Aurland.

▲▲Stegastein Viewpoint and Aurlandsvegen "Snow Road"

With a car, clear weather, and a little nerve, consider twisting up the mountain behind Aur-

land on route 243 for about 20 minutes to a magnificent view over the Aurlandsfjord. A viewpoint called Stegastein—which looks like a giant, wooden, sideways number "7"—provides a platform from which you can enjoy stunning views across the fjord and straight down to Aurland. Immediately beyond the viewpoint, you leave the fjord views and enter the beautifully desolate mountain-top world of the Aurlandsvegen "Snow Road." When this narrow ribbon of a road finally hits civilization on the other side, you're a mile from the Lærdal tunnel entrance and about 30 minutes from the fine Borgund Stave Church.

▲▲Borgund Stave Church

About 16 miles east of Lærdal, in the village of Borgund, is Norway's most-visited and one of its best-preserved stave churches.

Borgund's church comes with one of this country's best stave-church history museums, which beautifully explains these icons of medieval Norway. Dating from around 1180, the interior features only a few later additions, including a 16th-century pulpit, 17th-century stone altar, painted decorations, and crossbeam reinforcements.

The oldest and most authentic item in the church is the stone baptismal font. In medieval times, priests conducting baptisms would go outside to shoo away the evil spirits from an infant before bringing it inside the church for the ritual. (If infants died before being baptized, they couldn't be buried in the churchyard, so parents would put their bodies in little coffins and hide them under the church's floorboards to get them as close as possible to God.)

Explore the dimly lit interior, illuminated only by the original, small, circular windows up high. Notice the X-shaped crosses of St. Andrew (the church's patron), carvings of dragons, and medieval runes.

Cost and Hours: 75 kr, buy tickets in museum across street, daily June-Aug 8:00-20:00, May and Sept 10:00-17:00, closed Oct-April. The museum has a shop and a fine little cafeteria serving filling and tasty lunches (70-kr soup with bread, tel. 57 66 81 09, www.stavechurch.com).

Getting There: It's about a 30-minute **drive** east of Lærdal, on E-16 (the road to Oslo—if coming from Aurland or Flåm, consider taking the scenic route via the Stegastein viewpoint, described above). There's also a convenient **bus** connection: The bus departs Flåm and Aurland around midday (direction: Lillehammer) and heads for the church, with a return bus departing Borgund in mid-

> ## Sleep Code
>
> **Abbreviations**   **(6 kr = about $1, country code: 47)**
> **S** = Single, **D** = Double/Twin, **T** = Triple, **Q** = Quad, **b** = bathroom
> **Price Rankings**
> **$$$** **Higher Priced**—Most rooms 1,100 kr or more.
>   **$$** **Moderately Priced**—Most rooms 600-1,100 kr.
>   **$** **Lower Priced**—Most rooms 600 kr or less.
> You can assume that staff speak English, breakfast is included,
> Wi-Fi is free, and credit cards are accepted unless otherwise
> noted. Note that the season is boom or bust here. It can be
> dead in June and packed in July and August. Prices change;
> verify current rates online or by email. For the best prices, al-
> ways book directly with the hotel.

afternoon (170-kr round-trip, get ticket from driver, about 1 hour each way with about 1 hour at the church, bus runs daily May-Sept, tell driver you want to get off at the church).

Sleeping in Flåm

My recommended accommodations are away from the tacky train-station bustle, but a close enough walk to be convenient. The first two places are located along the waterfront a quarter-mile from the station: Walk around the little harbor (with the water on your left) for about 10 minutes. It's more enjoyable to follow the level, waterfront dock than to hike up the main road.

$$$ Flåm Marina and Apartments, perched right on the fjord, is ideal for families and longer stays. They offer 10 new-feeling, self-catering apartments that each sleep 2-5 people. All units offer views of the fjord with a balcony, kitchenette, and small dining area (Db-1,198 kr May-mid-Sept, less off-season, 450 kr more for each additional adult, check online or ask about specials for longer stays, no breakfast, café open during high season, boat rental, laundry facilities, next to the guest harbor just below Heimly Pensjonat—see next listing, tel. 57 63 35 55, www.flammarina.no, booking@flammarina.no).

$$ Heimly Pensjonat, with 22 straightforward rooms, is clean, efficient, and the best small hotel in town. Sit on the porch with new friends and watch the clouds roll down the fjord (Sb-895 kr, Db-1,095 kr, view Db costs 100 kr more in summer, extra bed-395 kr for adult or 295 kr for child, cheaper Oct-May, Db rooms are mostly twins, try to reserve a room with a view at the standard price, car rental, tel. 57 63 23 00, www.heimly.no, post@heimly.no).

$-$$ Flåm Youth Hostel and Camping Bungalows, voted

Scandinavia's most beautiful campground, is run by the friendly Håland family, who rent the cheapest beds in the area (hostel: bunk in 4-bed room-240 kr, S-390 kr, D-620-650 kr; newer, fancier building: bunk in 4-bed room-260-315 kr, Db-800-865 kr; hostel prices include sheets and towels; cabins-700-1,300 kr; sheets and towels-50 kr, showers-10 kr, 10 percent discount for members, no meals but kitchen access, laundry, apple grove, tel. 57 63 21 21, www.flaam-camping.no, camping@flaam-camping.no). It's a five-minute walk toward the valley from the train station: Cross the bridge and turn left up the main road; then look for the hostel on the right.

Eating in Flåm

Dining options beyond your hotel's dining room or kitchenette are expensive and touristy. Don't aim for high cuisine here—go practical. Almost all eateries are clustered near the train station complex. Hours can be unpredictable, flexing with the season, but you can expect these to be open daily in high season. Places here tend to close pretty early (especially in shoulder season)—don't wait too long for dinner.

The **Flåmsbrygga** complex, sprawling through a long building toward the fjord from the station, includes a hotel, the affordable **Furukroa Caféteria** (daily 8:00-20:00 in season, cafeteria with 50-65-kr cold sandwiches, 100-150-kr fast-food meals, and 200-225-kr pizzas), and the pricey **Flåmstova Restaurant** (235-kr lunch buffet, 325-kr dinner buffet, plus other menu options at dinner). Next door is their fun, Viking-longhouse-shaped brewpub, **Ægir Bryggeri** (daily 17:00-22:00, local microbrews, 200-300-kr Viking-inspired meals). **Toget Café,** with seating in old train cars, prides itself on using as many locally sourced and organic ingredients as possible (65-75-kr sandwiches, 160-195-kr main dishes). **Bakkastova Kafe,** at the other end of town, feels cozier; it's in a traditional Norwegian red cabin just above the Fretheim Hotel, with a view terrace, and serves sandwiches, salads, and authentic Norwegian fare (daily 10:00-18:00).

Aurland

A few miles north of Flåm, Aurland is more of a real town and less of a tourist depot. While it's nothing exciting (Balestrand is more lively and appealing, and Solvorn is cuter—see next chapter), it's a good, easygoing fjordside home base. And thanks to its lo-

cation—on the main road and boat lines, near Flåm—it's relatively handy for those taking public transportation.

Getting There: Aurland is an easy 10-minute drive or bus trip from Flåm. If you want to stay overnight in Aurland, note that every train (except the late-night one) arriving in Flåm connects with a bus or boat to Aurland. Eleven buses and at least four ferries link the towns daily in summer (bus-40 kr, 10 minutes; boat-100 kr, 20 minutes). The Flåm-Gudvangen boat doesn't always have a scheduled stop at Aurland, but they're willing to stop there if you ask—so it's possible to continue the Nutshell route from Aurland without backtracking to Flåm. Boat tickets bought at the Aurland TI come with a reservation (helpful on the busiest days in July and August, when the boats can fill up in Flåm). The Bergen-Balestrand-Flåm express boat stops in Aurland (for details, see page 332).

Orientation to Aurland

From Aurland's dingy boat dock area, walk one block up the paved street into the heart of town. On your right are the Matkroken and Spar supermarkets (handy for picnic supplies) and Marianne Bakeri and Café (at the bridge). To your left is the Vangsgården Guest House and, behind it, Aurland Fjordhotel. To reach the TI, go straight ahead and bear right, then look behind the white church (800 years old and worth a peek). The bus stop, with buses to Flåm, is in front of the TI. For attractions near Aurland, see page 306.

TOURIST INFORMATION

The TI stocks English-language brochures about hikes and day trips from the area, offers free Internet terminals, and hosts a small history exhibit (June-Aug Mon-Fri 9:00-17:00, Sat-Sun 10:30-17:00, Sept-May Mon-Fri 9:00-16:00, closed Sat-Sun; behind the white church—look for green-and-white *i* sign; tel. 57 63 33 13, www.alr.no).

Sleeping in Aurland

$$$ Aurland Fjordhotel is big, modern, and centrally located. While it has a business-hotel vibe, most of its 30 rooms come with gorgeous fjord-view balconies (Sb-995 kr, Db-1,490 kr, Tb-1,580, prices lower off-season, check website for deals, Wi-Fi, tel. 57 63

35 05, www.aurland-fjordhotel.com, post@aurland-fjordhotel. com, Steinar Kjerstein).

$$$ Vangsgården Guest House, closest to the boat landing, is a complex of old buildings dominating the old center of Aurland and run from one reception desk (Wi-Fi in main building, tel. 57 63 35 80, www.vangsgaarden.no, vangsgaarden@alb.no, open all year, Astrid). The main building is a simple, old guesthouse offering basic rooms and a fine old-timey living room (Sb-830 kr, Db-1,250 kr). Their old-fashioned **Aabelheim Pension** is Aurland's best *koselig* (cozy)-like-a-farmhouse place (same prices). And lining the waterfront are their six adorable wood cabins, each with a kitchen, bathroom, and two bedrooms (1,250 kr for 2-6 people, sheets-65 kr/person, book 2 months in advance). The owners also run the Duehuset Pub (see "Eating in Aurland," below) and rent bikes for 200 kr/day.

NEAR AURLAND

$$ Skahjem Gard is an active farm run by Aurland's former deputy mayor, Nils Tore. He's converted his old sheep barn into seven spic-and-span family apartments with private bathrooms and kitchenettes, each sleeping up to four people (750-800 kr for studio, 900 kr with separate bedroom; sheets and towels-60 kr/person, Wi-Fi, two miles up the valley—road #50, follow *Hol* signs, tel. 57 63 33 29, mobile 95 17 25 67, www.skahjemgard.com, nskahjem@online. no). It's a 25-minute walk from town, but Nils will pick up and drop off travelers at the ferry. This is best for families and foursomes with cars.

$ Winjum Huts, about a half-mile from Aurland's dock, rents 14 basic cabins on a peaceful perch overlooking the majestic fjord. The washhouse/kitchen is where you'll find the toilets and showers. Follow the road uphill past the Aurland Fjordhotel; the huts are after the first hairpin curve (450-500 kr for up to 4 people, 2-bed apartment-900-1,200 kr, sheets-50 kr/person, showers-10 kr/5 minutes, no food available—just beer, tel. 57 63 34 61, mobile 41 47 47 51).

Eating in Aurland

Marianne Bakeri and Café is a basic little bakery/café serving the best-value food in town. It's a block from the main square, at the bridge over the river. Sit inside or on its riverside terrace (55-95-kr sandwiches, 155-kr pizza, 165-kr quiche, daily 10:00-17:00, tel. 57 63 36 66).

Duehuset Pub ("The Dove's House"), run by Vangsgården Guest House, serves up decent food in the center of town (190-240-kr pizzas big enough for four, 160-240-kr main dishes; June-

Sept daily 15:00-23:00; Oct-May Fri-Sun 18:00-23:00, closed Mon-Thu).

The **Aurland Fjordhotel** is your only alternative for splurges (200-kr main dishes, 70-kr starters, 250-300-kr dinner buffet, daily 19:00-22:00, shorter hours off-season, bar open later, tel. 57 63 35 05).

For cheap eats on dockside benches, gather a picnic at the **Spar** or **Matkroken** supermarkets (both open Mon-Fri 9:00-20:00, Sat 9:00-18:00, closed Sun).

Undredal

This almost impossibly remote community is home to about 80 people and 400 goats. A huge percentage of the town's former pop-ulation (300 people) emigrated to the US between 1850 and 1925. Undredal was accessible only by boat until 1988, when the road from Flåm opened. There's not much in the town, which is famous for its church and its goat cheese, but I'll never forget the picnic I had on the ferry wharf. While appeal-ing, Undredal is quiet (some say better from the boat) and difficult to reach—you'll have to be patient to connect to other towns. For more information on the town, see www.undredal.no.

Undredal has Norway's smallest still-used **church,** seating 40 people for services every fourth Sunday. The original church was built in 1147 (look for the four original stave pillars inside). It was later expanded, pews added, and the interior painted in the 16th century in a way that resembles the traditional Norwegian *rosemal-ing* style (which came later). You can get in only with a 30-minute tour (60 kr, June-mid-Aug daily 10:00-17:00, less in shoulder sea-son, closed Oct-April, tel. 95 29 76 68).

Undredal's farms exist to produce cheese. The beloved local cheese comes in two versions: brown and white. The brown ver-sion is unaged and slightly sweet, while the white cheese has been aged and is mild and a bit salty. For samples, visit the Undredalsbui grocery store at the harbor (Mon-Sat 9:00-17:00, Sun 12:00-16:00, shorter hours and closed Sun off-season).

The 15-minute drive from Flåm is mostly through a tunnel. By sea, you'll sail past Undredal on the Flåm-Gudvangen boat (you can request a stop). To get the ferry to pick you up in Undredal, turn on the blinking light (though some express boats will not stop).

This sleepy town can accommodate maybe a dozen visitors a night. **$$ Undredal Overnatting** rents four modern, woody, comfortable rooms and two apartments. The reception is at the café on the harbor, while the accommodations are at the top of town (Db-795 kr, D-645-695 kr in guesthouse with shared kitchen, apartments start at 1,290 kr, includes sheets, breakfast-110 kr, tel. 57 63 30 80 or 57 63 31 00, www.visitundredal.no, visit@undredal.no).

MORE ON THE SOGNEFJORD

Balestrand • The Lustrafjord • Scenic Drives

Norway's world of fjords is decorated with medieval stave churches, fishing boats, cascading waterfalls, dramatic glaciers, and brightly painted shiplap villages. Travelers in a hurry zip through the fjords on the Norway in a Nutshell route (see previous chapter). Their heads spin from all the scenery, and most wish they had more time on the Sognefjord. If you can linger in fjord country, this chapter is for you.

Snuggle into the fjordside village of Balestrand, which has a variety of walking and biking options and a fun local arts scene. Balestrand is also a handy jumping-off spot for adventures great and small, including a day trip up the Fjærlandsfjord to gaze at a receding tongue of the Jostedal Glacier, or across the Sognefjord to the truly medieval-feeling Hopperstad Stave Church. Farther east is the Lustrafjord, a tranquil branch of the Sognefjord offering drivers an appealing concentration of visit-worthy sights. On the Lustrafjord, you'll enjoy enchanting hamlets with pristine fjord views (such as Solvorn), historic churches (including Norway's oldest stave church at Urnes and the humble village Dale Church in Luster), an opportunity to touch and even hike on a glacier (the Nigard), and more stunning fjord views.

This region is important to the people of Norway. After four centuries under Danish rule, the soul of the country was nearly lost. With semi-independence and its own constitution in the early 1800s, the country experienced a resurgence of national pride. Urban Norwegians headed for the fjord country here in the west. Norway's first Romantic painters and writers were drawn to Balestrand, inspired by the unusual light and dramatic views of mountains plunging into the fjords. The Sognefjord, with its many

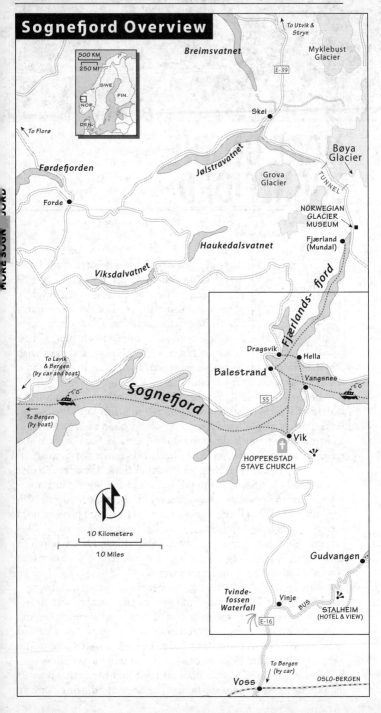

Sognefjord Overview

To Utvik & Stryn

Breimsvatnet

Myklebust Glacier

500 KM
250 MI
SWE.
FIN.
NOR.
DEN.

E-39

Skei

Bøya Glacier

TUNNEL

To Florø

Førdefjorden

Jølstravatnet

Grova Glacier

Forde

NORWEGIAN GLACIER MUSEUM

Haukedalsvatnet

Fjærland (Mundal)

Viksdalvatnet

Fjærlands-fjord

Dragsvik

Hella

To Lavik & Bergen (by car and boat)

Balestrand

Sognefjord

55

Vangsnes

To Bergen (by boat)

Vik

HOPPERSTAD STAVE CHURCH

10 Kilometers

10 Miles

Gudvangen

Tvinde-fossen Waterfall

Vinje

BUS

STALHEIM (HOTEL & VIEW)

E-16

To Bergen (by car)

Voss

OSLO-BERGEN

MORE SOGN JORD

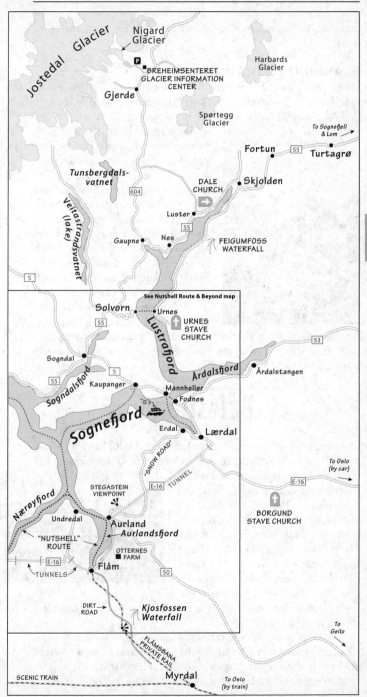

branches, is featured in more Romantic paintings than any other fjord.

PLANNING YOUR TIME

If you can spare a day or two off the Norway in a Nutshell route, spend it here. Balestrand is the best home base, especially if you're

relying on public transportation (it's well-connected by express boat both to the Nutshell scene and to Bergen). If you have a car, consider staying in the heart of the Lustrafjord region in sweet little Solvorn (easy ferry connection to the Urnes Stave Church and a short drive to the Nigard Glacier). As fjord home bases go, Balestrand and Solvorn are both better—but less convenient—than Flåm or Aurland on the Nutshell route (see previous chapter).

With one night in this area, you'll have to blitz the sights on the way between destinations; with two nights, you can slow your pace (and your pulse) to enjoy the fjord scenery and plenty of day-trip possibilities.

Balestrand

The pleasant fjord town of Balestrand (pop. 2,000) has a long history of hosting tourists, thanks to its landmark Kviknes Hotel. But

it also feels real and lived-in, making Balestrand a nice mix of cuteness and convenience. The town is near, but not *too* near, the Nutshell bustle is across the fjord—and yet it's an easy express-boat trip away if you'd like to dive into the Nuttiness. In short, consider Balestrand a worthwhile de-

tour from the typical fjord visit—allowing you to dig deeper into the Sognefjord, just like the glaciers did during the last ice age.

With two nights, you can relax and consider some day trips: Cruise up the nearby Fjærlandsfjord for a peek at a distant tongue of the ever-less-mighty Jostedal Glacier, or head across the Sognefjord to the beautiful Hopperstad Stave Church in Vik. Balestrand also has outdoor activities for everyone, from dreamy fjordside strolls and strenuous mountain hikes to wildly scenic bike rides. For dinner, splurge on the memorable *smörgåsbord*-style *store koldt bord* dinner in the Kviknes Hotel dining room, then sip coffee from its balcony as you watch the sun set (or not) over the fjord.

PLANNING YOUR TIME

Balestrand's key advantage is its easy express-boat connection to Bergen, offering an alternative route to the fjord from the typical Nutshell train-bus combo. Consider zipping here on the Bergen boat, then continuing on via the Nutshell route.

One night is enough to get a taste of Balestrand. But two nights buy you some time for day trips. Note that the first flurry of day trips departs early, around 7:30-8:05 (includes the boat to Vik/Hopperstad Stave Church or the full-day Fjærlandsfjord glacier excursion), and the next batch departs around noon (the half-day Fjærlandsfjord glacier excursion and the boat to Flåm). If you wait until after 12:00 to make your choice, you'll miss the boat...literally.

Balestrand pretty much shuts down from mid-September through mid-May—when most of the activities, sights, hotels, and restaurants listed here likely are closed.

Orientation to Balestrand

Most travelers arrive in Balestrand on the express boat from Bergen or Flåm. The tidy harbor area has a TI, two grocery stores, a couple of galleries, a town history museum, and a small aquarium devoted to marine life found in the fjord. The historic wooden Kviknes Hotel and its ugly modern annex dominate Balestrand's waterfront.

Even during tourist season, Balestrand is quiet. How quiet? The police station closes on weekends. And it's tiny—from the harbor to the Balestrand Hotel is a five-minute stroll, and you can walk from the aquarium to Kviknes Hotel in less time than that.

Balestrand became accessible to the wider world in 1858 when an activist minister (from the church you see across the fjord from town) brought in the first steamer service. That put Balestrand on the Grand Tour map of the Romantic Age. Even the German *Kaiser* chose to summer here. Today, people from around the world come here to feel the grandeur of the fjord country and connect with the essence of Norway.

TOURIST INFORMATION

At the TI, located next to the Joker supermarket at the harbor, pick up the free, helpful *Outdoor Activities in Balestrand* brochure.

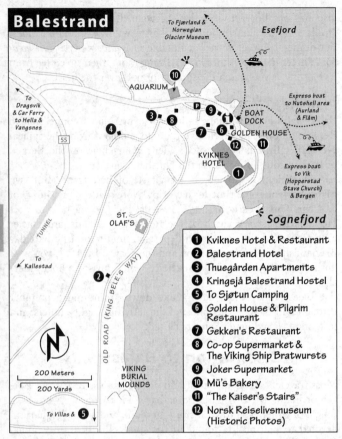

Balestrand

To Fjærland &
Norwegian
Glacier Museum

Esefjord

AQUARIUM

To
Dragsvik
& Car Ferry
to Hella &
Vangsnes

55

Express boat
to Nutshell area
(Aurland
& Flåm)

BOAT
DOCK

GOLDEN HOUSE

KVIKNES
HOTEL

Express boat
to Vik
(Hopperstad
Stave Church)
& Bergen

TUNNEL

To
Kallestad

ST.
OLAF'S

Sognefjord

OLD ROAD (KING BELE'S WAY)

N

200 Meters

200 Yards

VIKING
BURIAL
MOUNDS

To Villas & ⑤

MORE SOGNEFJORD

❶ Kviknes Hotel & Restaurant
❷ Balestrand Hotel
❸ Thuegården Apartments
❹ Kringsjå Balestrand Hostel
❺ To Sjøtun Camping
❻ Golden House & Pilgrim
   Restaurant
❼ Gekken's Restaurant
❽ Co-op Supermarket &
   The Viking Ship Bratwursts
❾ Joker Supermarket
❿ Mü's Bakery
⓫ "The Kaiser's Stairs"
⓬ Norsk Reiselivsmuseum
   (Historic Photos)

If you're planning on a longer hike, consider buying the good 70-kr hiking map. The TI has numerous brochures about the Sognefjord area and detailed information on the more challenging hikes. It offers terminals with Internet access (1 kr/minute) and pay Wi-Fi, rents bikes (70 kr/hour, 270 kr/day), sells day-trip excursions to the glacier, and more (late June-late Aug Mon-Fri 9:00-17:30, Sat-Sun 10:00-17:30, shorter hours in spring and fall, closed Oct-April, tel. 57 69 12 55—answered all year).

Local Guide: Bjørg Bjøberg, who runs the Golden House (Det Gylne Hus) art gallery, knows the town well and is happy to show visitors around (1,000-1,500 kr/2 hours per group—gather several people and divvy up the cost, mobile 91 56 28 42).

Car Rental: The **Balholm Car Rental** agency will deliver a car to your Balestrand hotel, and they'll pick it up, too (daily 8:00-20:00, tel. 41 24 82 53, www.rentacarbalholm.com, post@

rentacarbalholm.com). Also, the Kviknes Hotel can arrange a one-day car rental for you (tel. 57 69 42 00).

Sights in Balestrand

Balestrand Harborfront Stroll

The tiny harbor stretches from the aquarium to the big, old Kviknes Hotel. Stroll its length, starting at the aquarium (described later) and little marina. Across the street, at The Viking Ship shack, a German woman named Carola sells German sausages with an evangelical zeal (see "Eating in Balestrand," later). A couple of doors down, the Spindelvev ("Spider's Web") shop sells handicrafts made by people with physical and mental disabilities. A local home for the disabled was closed in the 1980s, but many of its former residents stayed in Balestrand because the government gave them pensions and houses in town.

Then, in the ugly modern strip mall, you'll find the TI, supermarket, and a community bulletin board with the schedule for the summer cinema (the little theater, 800 yards away, runs films nightly in their original language). On the corner is the Golden House art gallery and museum (described later). Behind it—and built into solid rock—is the boxy new moss-covered home of the Norwegian Travel Museum (Norsk Reiselivsmuseum), featuring photos showing this part of Norway over the past 150 years, interactive exhibits, and souvenirs. And just beyond that is the dock where the big Bergen-Sognefjord express catamaran ties up.

Across the street is a cute white house (at #8), which used to stand at the harborfront until the big Joker supermarket and Kviknes Hotel, with its modern annex, partnered to ruin the town center. This little house was considered historic enough to be air-lifted 100 yards to this new spot. It's flanked by two other historic buildings, which house a gallery and an artisans' workshop.

Farther along, find the rust-red building that was the waiting room for the 19th-century steamer that first brought tourism to town. Walk a few steps farther, and stop at the tall stone monument erected to celebrate the North Bergen Steamship Company. Its boats first connected Balestrand to the rest of the world in 1858. In front of the monument, some nondescript concrete steps lead into the water. These are "The Kaiser's Stairs," built for the German emperor, Kaiser Wilhelm II, who made his first summer visit (complete with navy convoy) in 1899 and kept returning until the outbreak of World War I.

Behind the monument stands one of the largest old wooden buildings in Norway, Kviknes Hotel. It was built in the 1870s and faces the rare little island in the fjord, which helped give the town its name: "Balestrand" means the strand or promenade in front of an island. (The island is now connected to the hotel's front yard and is part of a playground for its guests.) Hike up the black driveway that leads from the monument to the hotel's modern lobby. Go inside and find (to your left) the plush old lounge, a virtual painting gallery. All the pieces are by artists from this area, celebrating the natural wonder of the fjord country—part of the trend that helped 19th-century Norway reconnect with its heritage. (While you're here, consider making a reservation and choosing a table for a *smörgåsbord* dinner tonight.) Leave the hotel lobby (from the door opposite to the one you entered), and head up to St. Olaf's Church (300 yards, described next). To continue this stroll, take King Bele's Way (described later) up the fjord.

St. Olaf's Church

This distinctive wooden church was built in 1897. Construction was started by Margaret Sophia Kvikne, the wife of Knut Kvikne

(of the Kviknes Hotel family; her portrait is in the rear of the nave), but she died in 1894, before the church was finished. This devout Englishwoman wanted a church in Balestrand where English services were held...and to this day, bells ring to announce services by British clergy. St. Olaf, who brought Christianity to Norway in the 11th century, was the country's patron saint in Catholic times. The church was built in a "Neo-stave" style, with lots of light from its windows and an altar painting inspired by the famous *Risen Christ* statue in Copenhagen's Cathedral of Our Lady. Here, Christ is flanked by fields of daisies (called "priests' collars" in Norwegian) and peace lilies. From the door of the church, enjoy a good view of the island in the fjord.

Cost and Hours: Free, open daily, services in English every Sun from late May through August.

Golden House (Det Gylne Hus)

This golden-colored house facing the ferry landing was built as a general store in 1928. Today it houses an art installation called "Golden Memories" and a quirky museum created by local watercolorist and historian Bjørg Bjøberg, and her husband, Arthur Adamson.

On the ground floor, you'll find Bjørg's gallery, with her watercolors celebrating the beauty of Norway, and Arthur's paintings, celebrating the beauty of women. Upstairs is the Pilgrimage Balestrand room, focusing on their local nature pilgrimage program, along with a free exhibit of historical knickknacks, contributed by locals wanting to preserve treasures from their families' past. You'll see a medicine cabinet stocked with old-fashioned pills, an antiquated tourist map, lots of skis, and WWII-era mementos. A wheel in the wall once powered a crane that could winch up goods from the fjord below (back when this store was actually on the waterfront). While there are no written English explanations, Bjørg is happy to explain things.

Unable to contain her creative spirit, Bjørg has paired an eccentric wonderland experience with her private tour of the Golden House's hidden rooms. The tour includes a 30-minute movie (at 17:00 and 18:00), either about her art and local nature, or about Balestrand in winter. Bjørg and Arthur also run the recommended on-site restaurant, Pilgrim. Diners have free access to the glass dome on top of the building, with a telescope and lovely views.

Cost and Hours: Free entry; optional private one-hour tour-50/kr person, 100-kr minimum, 200-kr maximum; May-Aug daily 10:00-22:00, shorter hours late April and Sept, mobile 91 56 28 42, www.detgylnehus.no.

Strolling King Bele's Way up the Fjord

For a delightful walk (or bike ride), head west out of town up the "old road"—once the main road from the harbor—for about a mile. It follows the fjord's edge, passing numerous "villas" from the late 1800s. At the time, this Swiss style was popular with some locals, who hoped to introduce a dose of Romanticism into Norwegian architecture. Look for the dragons' heads (copied from Viking-age stave churches) decorating the gables. Along the walk, you'll pass a swimming area, a campground, and two burial mounds from the Viking age, marked by a ponderous statue of the Viking King Bele. Check out the wooden shelters for the mailboxes; some give the elevation (*m.o.h.* stands for "meters over *havet*"—the sea)—not too high, are they? The walk is described in the *Outdoor Activities in Balestrand* brochure (free at the TI or your hotel).

Aquarium

The tiny aquarium gives you a good look at marine life in the Sognefjord. For descriptions, borrow the English booklet at the front desk. While not thrilling, the well-explained place is a decent rainy-day option. A 15-minute slide show starts at the top and bottom of each hour. The last room is filled with wood carvings depicting traditional everyday life in the fjordside village of Munken. The fish-filled tanks on the dock outside are also worth a look.

Cost and Hours: 70 kr, May-Aug daily 9:00-19:00, closed Sept-April, tel. 57 69 13 03.

Biking

You can cycle around town, or go farther by circling the scenic Esefjord (north of town, en route to the ferry landing at Drags-vik—about 6 miles each way). Or pedal west up Sognefjord along the scenic King Bele's Way (described above). The roads here are relatively flat. Rental bikes are available at the TI and through Kviknes Hotel.

NEAR BALESTRAND

These two side-trips are possible only if you've got the better part of a day in Balestrand. With a car, you can see Hopperstad Stave Church on the drive to Bergen.

▲▲Hopperstad Stave Church (Hopperstad Stavkyrkje) in Vik

The most accessible stave church in the area—and perhaps the most scenically situated in all Norway—is located just a 15-minute express-boat ride across the Sognefjord, in the town of Vik. Hopperstad Stave Church boasts a breathtaking exterior, with several tiers of dragon heads over-looking rolling fields between fjord cliffs. The interior is notable for its emptiness. Instead of being crammed full of later additions, the church is blissfully unclut-tered, as it was when it was built in the mid-12th century. (For more on stave churches, see page 211.)

Cost and Hours: 60 kr, good 30-kr color booklet in English, daily mid-May-mid-Sept 10:00-17:00, mid-June-mid-Aug opens at 9:00, closed mid-Sept-mid-May, tel. 57 69 52 70, www.stavechurch.com.

Tours: The attendant will give you a free tour at your request, provided she's not too busy. (Ask where the medieval graffiti is, and she'll grab her flashlight and show you.)

Location: The church is a 20-minute walk up the valley from Vik's harbor. From the boat landing, walk up the main street from the harbor about 200 yards (past the TI, a grocery store, and hotel). Take a right at the sign for *Hopperstad Stavkyrkje*, walk 10 minutes, and you'll see the church perched on a small hill in the distance.

Getting There: Pedestrians can ride the express passenger boat between Balestrand and Vik (78 kr each way, 15 minutes). The only way to get to the church and back in one day (only possible Mon-Sat) is to take the 7:50 departure from Balestrand, then re-turn on the 11:30 departure from Vik, arriving back in Balestrand at 11:50—just in time to join a 12:00 glacier excursion (described next). Because schedules can change, be sure to double-check these times at the TI or www.norled.no. Since cars can't go on this express boat, **drivers** must go around the small Esefjord to the town of Dragsvik, then catch the ferry across the Sognefjord to Vangsnes (a 20-minute drive from Vik and the church).

Visiting the Church: Originally built around 1140 and retaining most of its original wood, Hopperstad was thoroughly re-

stored and taken back to basics in the 1880s by renowned architect Peter Blix. Unlike the famous stave church at Urnes (described later), whose interior has been rejiggered by centuries of engineers and filled with altars and pews, the Hopperstad church looks close to the way it did when it was built. You'll see only a few non-

original features, including the beautifully painted canopy that once covered a side altar (probably dating from around 1300), and a tombstone from 1738. There are only a few colorful illustrations and some very scant medieval "graffiti" carvings and runic inscriptions. Notice the intact chancel screen (the only one surviving in Norway), which separates the altar area from the congregation. As with the iconostasis (panel of icons) in today's Orthodox faith, this screen gave priests privacy to do the spiritual heavy lifting. Because Hopperstad's interior lacks the typical adornments, you can really grasp the fundamentally vertical nature of stave church architecture, leading your gaze to the heavens. Follow that impulse and look up to appreciate the Viking-ship rafters. Imagine the comfort this ceiling brought the church's original parishioners, whose seafaring ancestors had once sought refuge under overturned boats. For a unique angle on this graceful structure, lay your camera on the floor and shoot the ceiling.

▲Excursion to Fjærland and the Jostedal Glacier

From Balestrand, cruise up the Fjærlandsfjord to visit the Norwegian Glacier Museum in Fjærland and to see a receding tongue of the Jostedal Glacier (Jostedalbreen). Half-day and full-day (685 kr for either tour) excursions are sold by Balestrand's TI or onboard the boat. Reservations are smart (tours offered daily June-Aug only, tel. 57 63 32 00, www.visitflam.com/sognefjorden and follow links for "Fjærlandsfjord").

While the museum and the glacier's tongue are underwhelming, it's a pleasant excursion with a dreamy fjord cruise (80 minutes each way). To take the all-day trip, catch the 8:05 ferry; for the shorter trip, hop on the 11:55 boat. They both return on the same boat, getting you back in Balestrand at 16:50 (in time to catch the fast boat back to Bergen). Both tours offer the same fjord ride, museum visit, and trip to the glacier. The all-day version, however, gives you a second glacier viewing point and 2.5 hours to hang out in the town of Fjærland. (This sleepy village, famous for its second-hand book shops, is about as exciting as Walter Mondale, the US vice president whose ancestors came from here.)

The ferry ride (no stops, no narration) is just a scenic glide with the gulls. Bring a picnic, as there's almost no food sold onboard, and some bread to toss to the gulls (they do acrobatics to catch whatever you loft into the air). You'll be met at the ferry dock (labeled *Mundal*) by a bus—and your guide, who reads a script about the glacier as you drive up the valley for about 15 minutes. You'll stop for an hour at the **Norwegian Glacier Museum** (Norsk Bremuseum). After watching an 18-minute aerial tour of the dramatic Jostedal Glacier in the theater, you'll learn how glaciers were formed, experiment with your own hunk of glacier, weigh evidence of the woolly mammoth's existence in Norway, and learn about the effect of global climate change on the fjords (way overpriced at 120 kr, included in excursion price, daily June-Aug 9:00-19:00, April-May and Sept-Oct 10:00-16:00, closed Nov-March, tel. 57 69 32 88, www.bre.museum.no). From the museum, the bus runs you up to a café near a lake, at a spot that gives you a good look at the Bøyabreen, a tongue of the Jostedal Glacier. Marvel at how far the glacier has retreated—10 years ago, the visit was more dramatic. With global warming, glacier excursions like this become more sad than majestic. I wonder how long they'll even be able to bill this as a "glacier visit."

Considering that the fjord trip is the highlight of this journey, you could save time and money by just riding the ferry up and back (8:05-11:30). At 390 kr for the round-trip boat ride, it's much cheaper than the 685-kr tour.

Note that if you're into glaciers, a nearby arm of the Jostedal, called the **Nigard Glacier,** is a more dramatic and boots-on experience (see page 335). It's easy for drivers to reach; see page 321 for car-rental info.

Sleeping in Balestrand

$$$ Kviknes Hotel is the classy grande dame of Balestrand, dominating the town and packed with tour groups. The picturesque wooden hotel—and five generations of the Kvikne family—have welcomed tourists to Balestrand since the late 19th century. The hotel has two parts: a new wing, and the historic wooden section, with 25 older, classic rooms, and no elevator. All rooms come with balconies. The elegant Old World public spaces in the old section make you want to just sit there and sip tea all afternoon (Db-1,720

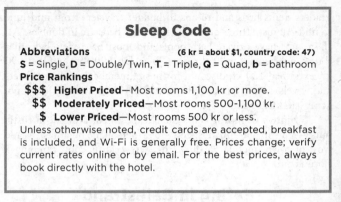

Sleep Code

Abbreviations   **(6 kr = about $1, country code: 47)**
S = Single, **D** = Double/Twin, **T** = Triple, **Q** = Quad, **b** = bathroom
Price Rankings
  $$$ Higher Priced—Most rooms 1,100 kr or more.
   $$ Moderately Priced—Most rooms 500-1,100 kr.
    $ Lower Priced—Most rooms 500 kr or less.
Unless otherwise noted, credit cards are accepted, breakfast
is included, and Wi-Fi is generally free. Prices change; verify
current rates online or by email. For the best prices, always
book directly with the hotel.

kr in new building, about 350 kr more with view, Db-2,270 kr in old building, non-smoking, Wi-Fi, family rooms available, closed Oct-April, tel. 57 69 42 00, www. kviknes.no, booking@kviknes.no). Part of the Kviknes ritual is gorging on the *store koldt bord* buffet dinner— open to non-guests, and a nice way to soak in the hotel's old-time elegance without splurging on an overnight (see "Eating in Balestrand," later; cheaper if you stay at the hotel for 2 or more nights).

$$ Balestrand Hotel, family-run by Unni-Marie Kvikne, her California-born husband Eric Palmer, and their three children, is your best fjordside home. Open mid-May through early September, this cozy, welcoming place has 30 well-appointed, comfortable, quiet rooms; a large, modern common area with lots of English paperbacks; laundry service, Wi-Fi, balconies (in some rooms), and outdoor benches for soaking in the scenery. The waterfront yard has inviting lounge chairs and a mesmerizing view. When reserving, let them know your arrival time, and they'll pick you up at the harborfront (non-view Sb-750 kr, view Sb-890 kr, non-view Db-1,090 kr, view Db-1,390 kr, 5-minute walk from dock, past St. Olaf's Church—or free pick-up, tel. 57 69 11 38, www.balestrand. com, info@balestrand.com).

$$ Thuegården offers five clean, bright, modern doubles with mini-kitchens, conveniently located near the ferry dock and just up the street from the Co-op grocery store. Some rooms have balconies and some come with a fjord view (Db-850-950 kr, discount if staying more than 3 nights, no breakfast, Wi-Fi, office inside ground-floor hair salon, tel. 57 69 15 95, mobile 97 19 92 63, www. thuegaarden.com, thuegaarden@gmail.com).

$-$$ Kringsjå Balestrand Hostel, a camp school for sixth-graders, rents beds and rooms to budget travelers from mid-June to mid-August. Three-quarters of their 58 beds are in doubles. All the rooms have private bathrooms and most have view balconies (bunk in 4-bed dorm-295 kr, Sb-690 kr, Db-890-990 kr, Qb-1,090 kr, extra bed-120 kr, discount for hostel members, includes sheets and towels, game room, Wi-Fi, tel. 57 69 13 03, www.kringsja.no, kringsja@kringsja.no).

$ Sjøtun Camping rents the cheapest beds around, in rustic huts (4-person hut-300 kr, sheets-60 kr/person, no breakfast, a mile west of town, mobile 95 06 72 61, www.sjotun.com, camping@sjotun.com).

Eating in Balestrand

Balestrand's dining options are limited, but good.

Kviknes Hotel offers a splendid, spendy *store koldt bord* buffet dinner in a massive yet stately old dining room. For a memorable fjordside *smörgåsbord* experience, it doesn't get any better than this. Don't rush. Consider taking a pre-view tour—surveying the reindeer meat, lingonberries, and fjord-caught seafood—before you dive in, so you can budget your stomach space. Get a new plate with each course and save room for dessert. Each dish is labeled in English (545 kr/person, May-Sept daily 19:00-21:00, closed Oct-April). They also offer a four-course, locally

sourced dinner for 645 kr. After dinner, head into the rich lounge to pick up your cup of coffee or tea (included), which you'll sip sitting on classy old-fashioned furniture and basking in fjord views. For tips on enjoying this feast, see page 732.

Pilgrim, inside the Golden House at the harbor, dishes up Norwegian home cooking and a variety of salads. Sit outside or inside, in a dining area built to resemble a traditional Norwegian kitchen. The restaurant upstairs shows off part of owner Bjørg's antique collection. They serve 100-130-kr lunches and pricier meals for dinner, such as 150-220-kr meat and fish dishes (May-Sept Mon-Sat 13:00-21:00, Sun 16:00-21:00, closed Oct-April, mobile 91 56 28 42).

Gekken's is an informal summer restaurant serving good-value meat, fish, and vegetarian dishes, along with burgers, fish-and-chips, and other fried fare. Sit in the simply decorated interior, or out on the shaded little terrace. Geir Arne "Gekken" Bale can trace his family's roots back 400 years in Balestrand. He has filled his walls with fascinating historic photos and paintings, making his dining hall an art gallery of sorts (light dishes-60-100 kr, daily dinner plates-100-200 kr, May-Aug daily 12:00-22:00, closed Sept-April, above and behind the TI from the harbor, tel. 57 69 14 14).

The Viking Ship, the hot-dog stand facing the harbor, is proudly run by Carola. A bratwurst missionary from Germany, she claims it took her years to get Norwegians to accept the tastier bratwurst over their beloved *pølser* weenies. Eat at her picnic tables or across the street on the harbor park (fine sausages, fish-and-chips, May-Sept daily 11:00-20:00, closed Oct-April).

Picnic: The delightful waterfront park next to the aquarium has benches and million-dollar fjord views. The Co-op and Joker **supermarkets** at the harbor have basic grocery supplies, including bread, meats, cheeses, and drinks; the Co-op is bigger and has a wider selection (Co-op open Mon-Fri 8:00-20:00, Sat 8:00-18:00; Joker open Mon-Fri 9:00-18:00—until 20:00 in summer, Sat 9:00-15:00; both closed Sun). **Mü's Bakery** offers a healthy assortment of sandwiches and fresh-baked goodies (Mon-Sat 9:30-18:00, Sun 9:30-15:00, closed mid-Sept-early May, just inside the aquarium entrance).

Balestrand Connections

Because Balestrand is separated from the Lustrafjord by the long Fjærlandsfjord, most Balestrand connections involve a boat trip.

BY EXPRESS PASSENGER BOAT

The easiest way to reach Balestrand is on the handy express boat, which connects to **Bergen, Vik** (near Hopperstad Stave Church), **Aurland,** and **Flåm** (see sidebar on next page for schedules). Note that you can also use this boat to join the Nutshell trip in Flåm. From here, continue on the Nutshell boat down the Nærøyfjord to Gudvangen, where you'll join the crowd onward to Voss, then Bergen or Oslo. As you're making schedule and sightseeing decisions, consider that the Balestrand-Flåm boat skips the Nærøyfjord, the most dramatic arm of the Sognefjord.

BY CAR FERRY

Balestrand's main car-ferry dock is at the village of **Dragsvik,** a six-mile, 15-minute drive around the adorable little Eselfjord. From Dragsvik, a car ferry makes the short crossing east to **Hella** (a 30-minute drive from Sogndal and the Lustrafjord), then crosses the Sognefjord south to **Vangsnes** (a 20-minute drive to Hopperstad Stave Church and onward to Bergen). The ferry goes at least once per hour (2/hour in peak times, fewer boats Sun, 87 kr for car and driver).

MORE SOGNEFJORD

Express Boat Between Bergen and the Sognefjord

The made-for-tourists express boat makes it a snap to connect Bergen with Balestrand and other Sognefjord towns (for foot passengers only—no cars). In summer, the boat links Bergen, Vik, Balestrand, Aurland, and Flåm. You can also use this boat to connect towns on the Sognefjord, such as zipping from quiet Balestrand to busy Flåm, in the heart of the Nutshell action (reservations are smart—call 51 86 87 00 or visit www.norled.no; discounts for students and seniors, tickets also sold on boat and at TI). The following times were good for 2014—confirm them locally.

Between Bergen and the Sognefjord: The boat trip between Bergen and **Balestrand** takes four hours (545 kr, departs Bergen May-Sept daily at 8:00, also Mon-Fri at 16:30, Sat at 14:15, some Sun at 16:30—but not mid-June-mid-Aug; Oct-April Sun-Fri at 16:30, Sat at 14:15; departs Balestrand May-Sept daily at 16:55, Mon-Sat also at 7:50, some Sun at 11:30—but not mid-June-mid Aug; Oct-April Mon-Sat at 7:50, Sun at 16:25). In summer, the 8:00 boat from Bergen continues to Flåm.

Between Flåm and Balestrand: Going by boat between Flåm and Balestrand takes about 1.5 hours (250 kr, departs Flåm May-Sept daily at 15:30, stops at Aurland, arrives in Balestrand at 16:55; departs Balestrand daily at 11:50 arriving Flåm at 13:25; no express boats between Flåm and Balestrand Oct-April).

From Oslo to Balestrand via the Nutshell: This variation on the standard Norway in a Nutshell route is called "Sognefjord in a Nutshell" (Oslo-Myrdal-Flåm-Balestrand-Bergen). From Oslo, you can take an early train to Flåm (no later than the 8:05 train as part of the Norway in a Nutshell route—see previous chapter), then catch the 15:30 express boat to Balestrand. After your visit, you can continue on the express boat to Bergen, or return to the Nutshell route by taking the express boat to Flåm, and transferring to the next boat to Gudvangen.

Note that you can also drive through Sogndal to catch the **Kaupanger-Gudvangen** or **Mannheller-Fodnes** ferries (described under "Lustrafjord Connections," near the end of this chapter).

BY BUS

A local bus links Balestrand to **Sogndal** (Mon-Fri only, 1/day, maybe more in summer, 1.25 hours, includes ride on Dragsvik-Hella ferry, get details at TI).

The Lustrafjord

This arm of the Sognefjord is rugged country—only 2 percent of the land is fit to build on or farm. The Lustrafjord is ringed with

tiny villages where farmers sell cherries and giant raspberries. A few interesting attractions lie along the Lustrafjord: the village Dale Church at Luster; the impressive Nigard Glacier (a 45-minute drive up a valley); the postcard-pretty village of Solvorn; and, across the fjord, Norway's oldest stave church at Urnes. While a bit trickier to explore by public transportation, this beautiful region is easy by car, but still feels remote. There are no ATMs between Lom and Gaupne—that's how remote this region is.

MORE SOGNEFJORD

SUGGESTED ROUTE FOR DRIVERS

The Lustrafjord can be seen either coming from the north (over the Sognefjell pass from the Jotunheimen region—see next chapter) or from the south (from Balestrand or the Norway in a Nutshell route—see previous chapter). Note that public buses between Lom and Sogndal follow this same route (see "Lustrafjord Connections," later).

Here's what you'll see if you're driving from the north (if you're coming from the south, read this section backward): Descending from Sognefjell, you'll hit the fjord at the village of Skjolden (decent TI in big community center, mobile 99 23 15 00). Follow Route 55 along the west bank of the fjord. In the town of Luster, consider visiting the beautifully decorated Dale Church (described next). Farther along, near the hamlet of Nes, you'll have views across the fjord of the towering Feigumfoss waterfall. Drops and dribbles come from miles around for this 650-foot tumble. Soon Route 55 veers along an inlet to the town of Gaupne, where you can choose to detour about an hour to the Nigard Glacier (up Route 604; described under "Sights on the Lustrafjord," next). After Gaupne, Route 55 enters a tunnel and cuts inland, emerging at a long, fjord-like lake at the town of Hafslo. Just beyond is the turnoff for Solvorn, a fine home-base town with the ferry across to Urnes and its stave church (Solvorn and Urnes Stave Church both described under "Sights on the Lustrafjord," next). Route 55 continues to Sogndal, where you can choose to turn off for the Kaupanger and Mannheller ferries across the Sognefjord, or continue on Route 55 to Hella and the boat across to either Dragsvik (near Balestrand) or Vangsnes (across the Sognefjord, near Vik and Hopperstad Stave Church).

Route Timings: If you're approaching from Lom in the Gudbrandsdal Valley, figure about 1.5 hours over Sognefjell to the start of the Lustrafjord at Skjolden, then another 30 minutes to Gaupne (with the optional glacier detour: 2 hours to see it, 4 hours to hike on it). From Gaupne, figure 30 minutes to Solvorn or 40 minutes to Sogndal. Solvorn to Sogndal is about 30 minutes. Sogndal to Hella, and its boat to Balestrand, takes about 40 minutes. These estimated times are conservative, but they don't include photo stops.

Sights on the Lustrafjord

These attractions are listed as you'll reach them driving from north to south along the fjordside Route 55. If you're sleeping in this area, you could visit all four sights in a single day (but it'd be a busy, somewhat rushed day). If you're just passing through, Dale Church and Solvorn are easy, but the other two involve major detours—choose one or skip them both.

▲Dale Church (Dale Kyrkje) in Luster

The namesake town of Luster, on the west bank of the Lustrafjord, boasts a unique 13th-century Gothic church. In a land of wooden stave churches, this stone church, with its richly decorated interior, is worth a quick stop as you pass through town.

Cost and Hours: Free entry but donation requested, daily 10:00-20:00 but often closed for services and off-season, good posted English info inside, 5-kr English brochure, just off the main road—look for red steeple, WC in graveyard, fresh goodies at bakery across the street.

Visiting the Church: The soapstone core of the church dates from about 1250, but the wooden bell tower and entry porch were likely built around 1600. As you enter, on the left you'll see a tall, elevated platform with seating, surrounded by a wooden grill. Nicknamed a "birdcage" for the feathery fashions worn by the ladies of the time, this high-profile pew—three steps higher than the pulpit—was built in the late-17th century by a wealthy parishioner.

The beautifully painted pulpit, decorated with faded images of the four evangelists, dates from the 13th century. In the chancel (altar area), restorers have uncovered frescoes from three different time periods: the 14th, 16th, and 17th centuries. Most of the ones you see here were likely created around the year 1500. The crucifix high over the pews, carved around 1200, predates the church, as does the old bench (with lots of runic carvings)—making them more than eight centuries old.

▲▲Jostedal's Nigard Glacier

The Nigard Glacier (Nigardsbreen) is the most accessible branch of mainland Europe's largest glacier (the Jostedalsbreen, 185 square

miles). Hiking to or on the Nigard offers Norway's best easy opportunity for a hands-on glacier experience. It's a 45-minute detour from the Lustrafjord up Jostedal Valley. Visiting a glacier is a quintessential Norwegian experience, bringing you face-to-face with the majesty of nature. If you can spare the time, it's worth the detour (even if you don't do a guided hike). But if glaciers don't give you tingles and you're feeling pressed, skip it.

Getting There: It's straightforward for **drivers.** When the main Route 55 along the Lustrafjord reaches Gaupne, turn onto Route 604, which you'll follow for 25 miles up the Jostedal Valley to the Breheimsenteret Glacier Information Center. Access to the glacier itself is down the toll road past the information center (all described next).

From late June through August, a **Glacier Bus** connects the Nigard Glacier to various home-base towns around the region (leaves Sogndal at 8:45, passes through Solvorn en route, arrives at the glacier around 10:00; departs glacier at 17:00, arrives back in Sogndal around 18:35; buses or boats from other towns—including Flåm and Aurland—coordinate to meet this bus in Sogndal; combo-tickets include various glacier visits and hikes; no bus Sept-June; for complete timetable, see www.jostedal.com). While handy, the bus is designed for those spending the entire day at the glacier.

Visiting the Glacier: The architecturally striking Breheimsenteret Glacier Information Center services both Breheimen and

Jostedalsbreen national parks. Drop by to confirm your glacier plans; you can also book excursions here. The center's highlights include a relaxing 15-minute film with highlights of the region, along with interactive glacier-related exhibits that explain these giant, slow-moving rivers of ice. The center also has a restaurant and gift shop (daily mid-June-mid-Aug 9:00-18:00, May-mid-June and mid-Aug-Sept 10:00-17:00, closed Oct-April, tel. 57 68 32 50, www.jostedal.com).

The best quick visit is to walk to, but not on, the glacier. (If you want to walk *on* it, see "Hikes on the Glacier," next.) From the information center, a 40-kr toll road continues two miles to a lake facing the actual tongue of the glacier. About 75 years ago, the glacier reached all the way to today's parking lot. (It's named for the ninth farm—*ni gard*—where it finally stopped, after crushing eight farms higher up the valley.) From the lot, you can hike all the way to the edge of today's glacier (about 45 minutes each way); or, to save about 20 minutes of walking, take a special boat to a spot that's a 20-minute hike from the glacier (30 kr one-way, 40 kr round-trip, 10-minute boat trip, 4/hour, mid-June-mid-Sept 10:00-17:00).

The walk is uneven but well-marked—follow the red *T*'s and take your time. You'll hike on stone polished smooth by the glacier, and scramble over and around boulders big and small that were deposited by it. The path takes you right up to the face of the Nigardsbreen. Respect the glacier. It's a powerful river of ice, and fatal accidents do happen. If you want to walk on the glacier, read the next listing first.

Hikes on the Glacier: Don't attempt to walk on top of the glacier by yourself. The Breheimsenteret Glacier Information Center offers guided family-friendly walks that include about one hour on the ice (260 kr, 130 kr for kids, cash only, minimum age 6, I'd rate the walks PG-13 myself, about 4/day, generally between 11:30-15:00, no need to reserve—just call glacier center to find out time and show up). Leave the information center one hour before your tour, then meet the group on the ice, where you'll pay and receive your clamp-on crampons. One hour roped up with your group gives you the essential experience. You'll find yourself marveling at how well your crampons work on the 5,000-year-old-ice. Even if it's hot, wear long pants, a jacket, and your sturdiest shoes. (Think ahead. It's awkward to empty your bladder after you're roped up.)

Longer, more challenging, and much more expensive hikes get you higher views, more exercise, and real crampons (starting at 460

kr, includes boots, mid-May-mid-Sept daily at 11:45, also July-Aug daily at 13:00, 4 hours including 2 hours on the ice, book by phone the day before—tel. 57 68 32 50, arrive at the information center 45 minutes early to pay for tickets and pick up your gear). If you're adventurous, ask about even longer hikes and glacier kayaking. While it's legal to go on the glacier on your own, it's dangerous and crazy to do so without crampons.

▲▲Solvorn

On the west bank of the Lustrafjord, 10 miles northeast of Sogndal, idyllic Solvorn is a sleepy little Victorian town with colorful wood-

en sheds lining its waterfront. My favorite town on the Lustrafjord is tidy and quaint, well away from the bustle of the Nutshell action. Its tiny ferry crosses the fjord regularly to Urnes and its famous stave church (next). While not worth going far out of your way for, Solvorn is a mellow and surprisingly appealing place to kill some time waiting for the ferry...or just munching a picnic while looking across the fjord. A pensive stroll or photo shoot through the village's back lanes is a joy (look for plaques that explain historic buildings in English). Best of all, Solvorn also has a pair of excellent accommodations: a splurge (Walaker Hotel) and a budget place (Eplet Bed & Apple), described later under "Sleeping on the Lustrafjord."

Getting There: Solvorn is a steep five-minute **drive** down a switchback road from the main Route 55. The main road into town leads right to the Urnes ferry (see next) and dead-ends into a handy parking lot (free, 2-hour posted—but unmonitored—limit). It's a 30-minute drive or bus trip into Sogndal, where you can transfer to other **buses** (2-4 buses/day between Solvorn and Sogndal, including the Glacier Bus to the Nigard Glacier—described earlier).

▲▲Urnes Stave Church

The hamlet of Urnes (sometimes spelled "Ornes") has Norway's oldest surviving stave church, dating from 1129. While not easy to reach (it's across the Lustrafjord from other attractions), it's worth the scenic ferry ride. The exterior is smaller and simpler than most stave churches, but its interior—modified in fits and starts over the centuries—is uniquely eclectic. For more on stave

churches, see page 211. If you want to pack along a bike (rentable in Solvorn), see "Bring a Bike?" at the end of this listing.

Cost and Hours: 80 kr, includes 20-minute English tour (departs at :40 past most hours, to coincide with ferry arrival—described below); May-Sept daily 10:30-17:45, closed off-season, tel. 57 68 39 45, www.stavechurch.com.

Services: A little café/restaurant is at the farm called Urnes Gard, across from the church (same hours as church, homemade apple cakes, tel. 57 68 39 44).

Getting There: Urnes is perched on the east bank of the Lustrafjord (across the fjord from Route 55 and Solvorn). Ferries running between Solvorn and Urnes depart Solvorn at the top of most hours and Urnes at the bottom of most hours (34 kr one-way passenger fare, 93 kr one-way for car and driver, no round-trip discount, 15-minute ride, mobile 91 79 42 11, www.lustrabaatane.no). You can either drive or walk onto the boat—but, since you can't drive all the way up to the church, you might as well leave your car in Solvorn. Once across, it's about a five-minute uphill walk to the main road and parking lot (where drivers must leave their cars; parking lot at the church only for disabled visitors). From here, it's a steep 15-minute walk up a switchback road to the church (follow signs for *Urnes*).

Planning Your Time: Don't dawdle on your way up to the church, as the tour is scheduled to depart at :40 past most hours, about 25 minutes after the ferry arrives (giving most visitors just enough time to make it up the hill to the church). The first boat of the day departs Solvorn at 10:00; the last boat departs Solvorn at 16:00 (last tour at 16:40); and the last boat back to Solvorn departs Urnes at 18:00. Confirm the "last boat" time, and keep an eye on your watch to avoid getting stranded in Urnes.

Visiting the Church: Most visitors to the church take the included 20-minute tour (scheduled to begin soon after the ferry arrives—described earlier). Here are some highlights:

Buy your ticket in the white house across from the church. Visit the little museum here after you see the church, so you don't miss the tour.

Many changes were made to the exterior to modernize the church after the Reformation (the colonnaded gallery was replaced, the bell tower was added, and mod-

designmuseo

DESIGNMUSEO

#UUSIMUSEO

ADULT	1	12,00	12,00
STUDENT	1	6,00	6,00

==

YHTEENSÄ EUR			**18.00**
KORTTI			18,00
TAKAISIN			0,00

# ALV %	ALV	NETTO	YHTEENSÄ
4 0 %	0,00	18,00	18,00

Veloitus 18,00 EUR
Kortti: CHASE VISA
Numero: ************8039 01 C
AID: A0000000031010
Varm: 02260D
Aviite: 190825142443 00025884
Yritys: 0781251-1 Ala: 7991
TVR: 0080008000 TSI: E800 CVM: 5E0000
TC: 95CCD21EDD8063EE
RC: 00
T: 190825171403

KORKEAVUORENKATU 23, 00130 HELSINKI
09-6220 540
WWW.DESIGNMUSEUM.FI
DESIGNMUSEO Y-TUNNUS 0781251-1
DESIGN MUSEUM SHOP OY Y-TUNNUS 1052841-5

TEITÄ PALVELI: MYYJÄ 1

352153 17:14:17 25.8.2019 183255 3 1

designmuseo

DESIGNMUSEO
DESIGNMUSEO

| AIKUA | 1 × 12,00 | 12,00 |
| STUDENT | 1 × 6,00 | 6,00 |

YHTEENSÄ EUR		**18,00**
KORTTI		18,00
TAKAISIN		0,00

| # ALV % | ALV | NETTO | YHTEENSÄ |
| 4 0 % | 0,00 | 18,00 | 18,00 |

Veloitus 18,00 EUR
Kortti: CHASE VISA
Numero: ************6093 01 C
AID: A0000000003101 0
Varm: 02280D
Avite: 190825124443 0002388A
Yritys: 07812521-1 Alat 2991
TVR: 00800000000 TSI: E800 CVM: 3E0000
TC: 85CC02IE0080858E
RC: 00
T: 1908251714O3

KORKEAVUORENKATU 23, 00130 HELSINKI
09-6220 540
WWW.DESIGNMUSEUM.FI
DESIGNMUSEO Y-TUNNUS 0781252-1
DESIGN MUSEUM SHOP OY Y-TUNNUS 1052841-5

TEITÄ PALVELI: MYYJÄ 1

352153 17-14:17 28.8.2019 18:29:59 3 3

ern square windows were cut into the walls). Go around the left side of the church, toward the cemetery. This is the third church on this spot, but the carved doorway embedded in the wall here was inherited from the second church. Notice the two mysterious beasts—a warm-blooded predator (standing) and a cold-blooded dragon—weaving and twisting around each other, one entwining the other. Yet, as they bite each other on the neck, it's impossible to tell which one is "winning"...perhaps symbolizing the everlasting struggle of human existence. The door you see in the middle, however, has a very different message: the harmony of symmetrical figure-eights, an appropriately calming theme for those entering the church.

Now go around to the real entry door (with a wrought-iron lock and handle probably dating from the first church) and head inside. While it feels ancient and creaky, a lot of what you see in here is actually "new" compared to the 12th-century core of the church. The exquisitely carved, voluptuous, column-topping capitals are remarkably well-preserved originals. The interior was initially stark (no pews) and dark—lit not by windows (which were added much later), but by candles laid on the floor in the shape of a cross. Looking straight ahead, you see a cross with Mary on the left (where the women stood) and John the Baptist on the right (with the men). When they finally added seating, they kept things segregated: Notice the pews carved with hearts for women, crowns for men.

When a 17th-century wealthy family wanted to build a special pew for themselves, they simply sawed off some of the pinecone-topped columns to make way for it. When the church began to lean, it was reinforced with the clumsy, off-center X-shaped supports. Churchgoers learned their lesson, and never cut anything again.

The ceiling, added in the late 17th century, prevents visitors from enjoying the Viking-ship roof beams. But all of these additions have stories to tell. Experts can read various cultural influences into the church decorations, including Irish (some of the carvings) and Romanesque (the rounded arches).

Bring a Bike? To give your Lustrafjord excursion an added dimension, take a bike on the ferry to Urnes (free passage, rentable for 200 kr/day with helmets from Eplet Bed & Apple hostel in Solvorn, where you can park your car for free). From the stave church, bike the super-scenic fjordside road (4.5 miles—with almost no traffic—to big Feigumfossen waterfall and back).

Sleeping on the Lustrafjord

These accommodations are along the Lustrafjord, listed from north to south.

MORE SOGNEFJORD

IN NES

$$ Nes Gard Farmhouse B&B rents 15 homey rooms, offering lots of comfort in a grand 19th-century farmhouse (S-760-820 kr, Db-980-1,080 kr, higher prices for July-Aug, rooms in main building more traditional, family apartment, bike rental-150 kr/day, tel. 57 68 39 43, mobile 95 23 26 94, www.nesgard.no, post@nesgard.no, Månum family). Mari and Asbjørn serve a three-course breakfast and dinner for 350 kr.

$ Viki Fjord Camping has great fjordside huts—many directly on the water, with fjord views and balconies—located directly across from the Feigumfossen waterfall (300-350 kr without a private bathroom, 400-900 kr with bathroom, price depends on size and season, no breakfast, sheets-70 kr, tel. 57 68 64 20, mobile 99 53 97 30, www.vikicamping.no, post@vikicamping.no, Berit and Svein).

IN SOLVORN

For more on this delightful little fjordside town—my favorite home base on the Lustrafjord—see the description earlier in this chapter. While it lacks the handy boat connections of Flåm, Aurland, or Balestrand, that's part of Solvorn's charm.

$$$ Walaker Hotel, a former inn and coach station, has been run by the Walaker family since 1690 (that's a lot of pressure on ninth-generation owner Ole Henrik). The hotel, set right on the Lustrafjord (with a garden perfect for relaxing and, if necessary, even convalescing), is open May through September. In the main house, the halls and living rooms are filled with tradition. Notice the patriotic hymns on the piano. The 22 rooms are divided into two types: nicely appointed standard rooms in the modern annex (big Sb-1,500 kr, Db-1,750 kr); or recently renovated "historic" rooms with all the modern conveniences in two different old buildings: rooms with Old World elegance in the main house, and brightly painted rooms with countryside charm in the Tingstova house next door (Sb-1,950 kr, Db-2,250 kr, 500 kr more for larger room #20 or room #23; non-smoking, Wi-Fi, sea kayak rental-350 kr/day, tel. 57 68 20 80, www.walaker.com, hotel@walaker.com). They serve excellent four-course dinners (575 kr plus drinks, nightly at 19:30, savor your dessert with fjordside setting on the balcony). Their impressive gallery of Norwegian art is in a restored, historic farmhouse out back (free for guests; Ole Henrik leads one-hour tours of the collection, peppered with some family history, nightly after dinner).

$-$$ Eplet Bed & Apple is my kind of hostel: innovative and friendly. It's creatively run by Trond and Agnethe, whose entrepreneurial spirit and positive attitude attract enjoyable guests. With welcoming public spaces and 22 beds in seven rooms (all with views, some with decks), this place is worth considering even if you don't normally sleep at hostels (open April-Sept only; camping space-100 kr, bunk in 7-bed dorm-200 kr, S-500 kr, D-600 kr, T-800 kr, S/D/T cost 50 kr less for 2 nights or more, no breakfast, no elevator, laundry-50 kr, kitchen, guest computer and Wi-Fi, free loaner bikes for guests, tel. 41 64 94 69, www.eplet.net, trondhenrik@eplet.net). It's about 300 yards uphill from the boat dock—look for the white house with a giant red apple painted on it. It's surrounded by a raspberry and apple farm (they make and sell tasty juices from both). The hostel rents bikes and helmets to non-guests for 200 kr/day. If you plan to bike along the fjord from Urnes, consider that if you stay at the hostel, the free bikes will save you 400 kr (for two people).

Eating in Solvorn: The **Linahagen Kafé,** next door to Walaker Hotel, serves good meals (150-kr salads and main dishes, June-Aug Mon-Fri 12:00-18:00, Sat 12:00-16:00, Sun 13:00-18:00, closed Sept-May, run by Tordis and her family).

IN SOGNDAL

Sogndal is the only sizeable town in this region. While it lacks the charm of Solvorn and Balestrand, it's big enough to have a busy shopping street and a helpful **TI** (daily 10:00-22:00, inside the MIX mini-mart at Parkvegen 5, mobile 99 23 15 00).

$$ Loftesnes Pensjonat, with 13 rooms, houses travelers mid-June through mid-August, and mostly students—reserving four rooms for travelers—during the school year (S-400 kr, Sb-420 kr, D-600 kr, Db-650 kr, no breakfast, kitchen, above a Chinese restaurant near the water, tel. 57 67 15 77, mobile 90 93 51 71, loftesnes.pensjonat@gmail.com).

$$ Sogndal Youth Hostel rents good, cheap beds (bunk in 4-bed room-310 kr, S-410 kr, D-620 kr, Db-755 kr, 10 percent less for members, sheets-70 kr, towel-40 kr, fully equipped members' kitchen, mid-June–mid-Aug only, closed 10:00-17:00, at fork in the road as you enter town, tel. 57 62 75 75, www.vandrerhjem.no, sogndal@hihostels.no).

Lustrafjord Connections

Sogndal is the transit hub for the Lustrafjord region.

FROM SOGNDAL BY BUS

Buses go to **Lom** over the Sognefjell pass (2/day late June-Aug only, road closed off-season, 3.5 hours, 1/day off-season, goes around the pass, 4.75 hours, change in Skei), **Solvorn** (5/day, fewer Sat-Sun, 30 minutes), **Balestrand** (3/Mon-Fri, none Sat-Sun, 1.25 hours, includes ride on Hella-Dragsvik ferry), **Nigard Glacier** via the Glacier Bus (1/day, 3 hours, departs Sogndal daily at 8:45, returns to Sogndal in the afternoon, also stops at Solvorn in each direction, late June-Aug only). Most buses run less (or not at all) on weekends—check the latest at www.ruteinfo.net.

BY BOAT

Car ferries cost roughly $5 per hour for walk-ons and $20 per hour for a car and driver. Reservations are generally not necessary, and on many short rides, aren't even possible (for info and free and easy reservations for longer rides, call 55 90 70 70). Confirm schedules at www.ruteinfo.net. From near Sogndal, various boats fan out to towns around the Sognefjord. Most leave from two towns at the southern end of the Lustrafjord: **Kaupanger** (a 15-minute drive from Sogndal) and **Mannheller** (a 5-minute drive beyond Kaupanger, 20 minutes from Sogndal).

From Kaupanger: While Kaupanger is little more than a ferry landing, the small stave-type church at the edge of town merits a look. Boats go from Kaupanger all the way down the gorgeous Nærøyfjord to **Gudvangen,** which is on the Norway in a Nutshell route (where you catch the bus to Voss). Taking this boat allows you to see the best part of the Nutshell fjord scenery (the Nærøyfjord), but misses the other half of that cruise (Aurlandsfjord). From June through September, boats leave Kaupanger daily at 9:00 and 15:00 for the 2.75-hour trip (check in 15 minutes before departure); car and driver-700 kr, adult passenger-300 kr; reserve at least one day in advance—or longer in July-Aug; www.fjord2.no, post@fjord2.no). Prices are high because this route is mainly taken by tourists, not locals. The service was taken over by new owners in 2015 and may change; verify schedules and prices online. Boats also connect Kaupanger to **Lærdal,** but the crossing from Mannheller to Fodnes is easier (described next).

From Mannheller: Ferries frequently make the speedy 15-minute crossing to **Fodnes** (74 kr for a car and driver, 3/hour, no reservations possible). From Fodnes, drive through the five-mile-long tunnel to Lærdal and the main E-16 highway (near Borgund Stave Church, the long tunnel to Aurland, and the scenic overland road to the Stegastein fjord viewpoint—all described in the previous chapter).

To Balestrand: To reach Balestrand from the Lustrafjord, you'll take a short ferry trip (Hella-Dragsvik). For information on the car ferries to and from Balestrand, see "Balestrand Connections," earlier.

Scenic Drives from the Sognefjord

If you'll be doing a lot of driving, pick up a good local map. The 1:335,000-scale *Sør-Norge nord* map by Cappelens Kart is excellent (about 150 kr, available at local TIs and bookstores).

▲▲From the Lustrafjord to Aurland

The drive to the pleasant fjordside town of Aurland (see previous chapter) takes you either through the world's longest car tunnel, or

over an incredible mountain pass. If you aren't going as far as Lom and Jotunheimen, consider taking the pass, as the scenery here rivals the famous Sognefjell pass drive.

From Sogndal, drive 20 minutes to the Mannheller-Fodnes ferry (described under "Lustrafjord Connections," earlier), float across the Sognefjord, then drive from Fodnes to Lærdal. From Lærdal, you have two options to Aurland: The speedy route is on E-16 through the 15-mile-long **tunnel** from Lærdal, or the Aurlandsvegen **"Snow Road"** over the pass.

The tunnel (described on page 309) is free, and impressively nonchalant—it's signed as if it were just another of Norway's countless tunnels. But driving it is a bizarre experience: A few miles in, as you find yourself trying not to be hypnotized by the monotony, it suddenly dawns on you what it means to be driving under a mountain for 15 miles. To keep people awake, three rest chambers, each illuminated by a differently colored light, break up the drive visually. Stop and get out—if no cars are coming, test the acoustics from the center.

The second, immeasurably more scenic, route is a breathtaking one-hour, 30-mile drive that winds over a pass into Aurland, cresting at over 4,000 feet and offering classic aerial fjord views (it's worth the messy pants). From the Mannheller-Fodnes ferry, take the first road to the right (to Erdal), then leave E-68 at Erdal

THE SOGNEFJORD

(just west of Lærdal) for the Aurlandsvegen. This road, while well-maintained, is open only in summer, and narrow and dangerous during snowstorms (which can hit with a moment's notice, even in warm weather). Even in good weather, parts of the road can be a white-knuckle adventure, especially when meeting oncoming vehicles on the tiny, exposed hairpin turns. You'll enjoy vast and terrifying views of lakes, snowfields, and remote mountain huts and farmsteads on what feels like the top of Norway. As you begin the 12-hairpin zigzag descent to Aurland, you'll reach the "7"-shaped **Stegastein viewpoint**—well worth a stop. The "Snow Road" and viewpoint are both described on page 309.

▲From the Lustrafjord to Bergen, via Nærøyfjord and Gudvangen

Car ferries take tourists between Kaupanger and the Nutshell town of Gudvangen through an arm and elbow of the Sognefjord, including the staggering Nærøyfjord (for details on the ferry, see "Lustrafjord Connections," earlier). From Gudvangen, it's a 90-mile drive to Bergen via Voss (figure about one hour to Voss, then another two hours into Bergen). This follows essentially the same route as the Norway in a Nutshell (Gudvangen-Voss bus, Voss-Bergen train). For additional commentary on the journey, see page 302.

Get off the ferry in Gudvangen and drive up the Nærøy valley past a river. You'll see the two giant falls and then go uphill through a tunnel. After the tunnel, look for a sign marked *Stalheim* and turn right. Stop for a break at the touristy Stalheim Hotel (described on page 302). Then follow signs marked *Stalheimskleiva*. This incredible road doggedly worms its way downhill back into the depths of the valley. My brakes started overheating in a few minutes. Take it easy. As you wind down, you can view the falls from several turnouts.

The road rejoins E-16. You retrace your route through the tunnel and then continue into a mellower beauty, past lakes and farms, toward Voss. Just before you reach Voss itself, watch the right side of the road for Tvindefossen, a waterfall with a handy campground/WC/kiosk picnic area that's worth a stop. Highway E-16 takes you through Voss and into Bergen. If you plan to visit Edvard Grieg's Home and the nearby Fantoft Stave Church, now is the ideal time, since you'll be driving near them—and they're a headache to reach from downtown. Both are worth a detour if you're not rushed, and are open until 18:00 in summer (see pages 389 and 390 of the Bergen chapter).

▲▲From Balestrand to Bergen, via Vik

If you're based in Balestrand and driving to Bergen, you have two options: Take the Dragsvik-Hella ferry, drive an hour to Kaupanger (via Sogndal), and drive the route just described; or, take the following slower, twistier, more remote, and more scenic route, with a stop at the beautiful Hopperstad Stave Church. This route is slightly longer, with more time on mountain roads and less time on the boat. Figure 20 minutes from Vangsnes to Vik, then about 1.5 hours to Voss, then another 2 hours into Bergen.

From Vagsnes, head into Vik on the main Route 13. In Vik, follow signs from the main road to Hopperstad Stave Church (de-

scribed earlier in this chapter). Then backtrack to Route 13 and follow it south, to Voss. You'll soon begin a series of switchbacks that wind you up and out of the valley. The best views are from the Storesvingen Fjellstove restaurant (on the left). Soon after, you'll crest the ridge, go through a tunnel, and find yourself on top of the world, in a desolate and harshly scenic landscape of scrubby mountaintops, snow banks, lakes, and no trees, scattered with vacation cabins. After cruising atop the plateau for a while, the road twists its way down (next to a waterfall) into a very steep valley, which it meanders through the rest of the way to Voss. This is an hour-long, middle-of-nowhere journey, with few road signs—you might feel lost, but keep driving toward Voss. When Route 13 dead-ends into E-16, turn right (toward Voss and Bergen) and re-enter civilization. From here, the route follows the same roads as in the Lustrafjord-Bergen drive described earlier (including the Tvindefossen waterfall).

GUDBRANDSDAL VALLEY AND JOTUNHEIMEN MOUNTAINS

Norway in a Nutshell is a great day trip, but with more time and a car, consider a scenic meander from Oslo to Bergen. You'll arc up the Gudbrandsdal Valley and over the Jotunheimen Mountains, then travel along the Lustrafjord (see previous chapter).

After an introductory stop in Lillehammer, with its fine folk museum, you might spend the night in a log-and-sod farmstead-turned-hotel, tucked in a quiet valley under Norway's highest peaks. Next, Norway's highest pass takes you on an exhilarating roller-coaster ride through the heart of the myth-inspiring Jotunheimen, bristling with Norway's biggest mountains. Then the road hairpins down into fjord country (see previous chapter).

PLANNING YOUR TIME

While you could spend five or six days in this area on a three-week Scandinavian rampage, this slice of the region is worth three days. By car, I'd spend them like this:

Day 1: Leave Oslo early, and spend midday at Lillehammer's Maihaugen Open-Air Folk Museum for a tour and picnic. Drive up the Gudbrandsdal Valley, stopping at the stave church in Lom. Stay overnight in the Jotunheimen countryside.

Day 2: Drive the Sognefjell road over the mountains, then down along the Lustrafjord, stopping to visit the Dale Church and the Nigard Glacier (see previous chapter). Sleep in your choice of fjord towns,

Gudbrandsdal Valley &
Jotunheimen Mountains

To Åndalsnes
To Trondheim
27
E-6
To Geiranger-fjord
15
Dombås
STAVE CHURCH
Lom
55
PEER GYNT SETERVEIEN
(TOLL ROAD)
Røisheim
TOLL ROADS
Gudbrandsdal
Bøverdal
Leirdalen
Otta
51
Glitter-tinden
Kvam
Turtagrø
Galdhøpiggen
Fortun
Jotunheimen Mtns.
To Sogndal
55
Vinstra
Skjolden
Kyrkja
Hurrungane Range
Bessvatnet
Besseggen Ridge
Gaupne
Memurubu
Maurvangen
Lustrafjord
Gjende
PEER GYNT VEIEN
(TOLL ROAD)
Tretten
Gjendesheim
51
To Hamar & Oslo
Sognefjord
E-16
Lillehammer
Lake Mjøsa
To Myrdal, Voss & Bergen
51
To Gjøvik & Oslo
E-16
To Oslo
30 Kilometers
30 Miles

1 Røisheim Hotel
2 Elvesæter Hotel
3 Bøverdalen Youth Hostel
4 Strind Gard
5 Spiterstulen Lodge
6 Juvasshytta Lodge
7 Leirvassbu Lodge

GUDBRANDSDAL

described in previous chapters (such as Solvorn—see page 340, Balestrand—see page 328, or Aurland—see page 313).

Day 3: Cruise the Aurland and/or Nærøy fjords and try to visit another stave church or two (such as Urnes—see page 337, Hopperstad—see page 326, or Borgund—see page 310) before carrying on to Bergen.

This plan can be condensed into two days if you skip the Nigard Glacier side-trip.

Lillehammer and the Gudbrandsdal Valley

The Gudbrandsdal Valley is the tradition-steeped country of Peer Gynt, the Norwegian Huck Finn. This romantic valley of time-worn hills, log cabins, and velvet farms has connected northern and southern Norway since ancient times. While not as striking as other parts of the Norwegian countryside, Gudbrandsdal offers a suitable first taste of the natural wonders that crescendo farther north and west (in Jotunheimen and the Sognefjord). Throughout this region, the government subsidizes small farms to keep the countryside populated and healthy. (These subsidies would not be permitted if Norway were a member of the European Union.)

Orientation to Lillehammer

The de facto capital of Gudbrandsdal, Lillehammer is a pleasant winter and summer resort town of 27,000. While famous for its brush with Olympic greatness (as host of the 1994 Winter Olympiad), Lillehammer is a bit disappointing—worthwhile only for its excellent Maihaugen Open-Air Folk Museum, or to break up the long drive between Oslo and the Jotunheimen region. If you do wind up here, Lillehammer has happy, old, woody pedestrian zones (Gågata and Storgata).

Tourist Information: Lillehammer's TI is inside the train station (mid-June-mid-Aug Mon-Fri 8:00-18:00, Sat-Sun 10:00-16:00; mid-Aug-mid-June Mon-Fri 8:00-16:00, Sat 10:00-14:00, closed Sun; Jernbanetorget 2, tel. 61 28 98 00, www.lillehammer.com).

Sights in Lillehammer

Lillehammer's two most worthwhile sights are up the hill behind the center of town. It's a fairly steep 15-minute walk from the train station to either sight and a 10-minute, mostly level walk between the two (follow the busy main road that connects them). Because the walk from the station is uphill (and not very well-signed), consider catching the bus from in front of the train station (bus #003 or #002 to Olympics Museum, 2/hour; bus #006 to Maihaugen, 1/hour; 35 kr one-way for either bus).

▲▲Maihaugen Open-Air Folk Museum (Maihaugen Friluftsmuseet)

This idyllic park, full of old farmhouses and pickled slices of folk culture, provides a good introduction to what you'll see as you drive

through the Gudbrandsdal Valley. Anders Sandvig, a "visionary dentist," started the collection in 1887. You'll divide your time between the fine indoor museum at the entrance and the sprawling exterior exhibits.

Upon arrival, ask about special events, crafts, or musical performances. A TV monitor shows what's going on in the park. Summer is busy

with crafts in action and people re-enacting life in the past, à la Colonial Williamsburg. There are no tours, so it's up to you to initiate conversations with the "residents." Off-season it's pretty dead, with no live crafts and most buildings locked up.

Cost and Hours: 150 kr in summer, 110 kr off-season; 25 percent off when combined with Olympics Museum; June-Aug daily 10:00-17:00; Sept-May Tue-Sun 11:00-16:00, closed Mon; paid parking.

Information: Because English descriptions are scant, consider purchasing the English guidebook. Tel. 61 28 89 00, www. maihaugen.no.

Visiting the Museum: The outdoor section, with 200 buildings from the Gudbrandsdal region, is divided into three areas: the

"Rural Collection," with old sod-roof log houses and a stave church; the "Town Collection," with reconstructed bits of old-time Lillehammer; and the "Residential Area," with 20th-century houses that look like most homes in today's Norway. The time trip can be jarring: In the 1980s house, a bubble-gum-chewing girl enthuses about her new, "wireless" TV remote and plays ABBA tunes from a cassette-tape player.

The museum's excellent "We Won the Land" exhibit (at the entry) sweeps you through Norwegian history from the Ice Age to the Space Age. The Gudbrandsdal art section shows village life at its best. And you can walk through Dr. Sandvig's old dental office and the original shops of various crafts- and tradespeople.

Though the museum welcomes picnickers and has a simple

cafeteria, Lillehammer's town center (a 15-minute walk below the museum), with lots of fun eateries, is better for lunch (see "Eating in the Gudbrandsdal Valley," later).

Norwegian Olympics Museum (Norges Olympiske Museum)

This cute museum is housed in the huge Olympic ice-hockey arena, Håkon Hall. With brief English explanations, an emphasis on Norwegians and Swedes, and an endearingly gung-ho Olympic spirit, it's worth a visit on a rainy day or for sports fans. The ground-floor exhibit traces the ancient history of the Olympics, then devotes one wall panel to each of the summer and winter Olympiads of the modern era (with special treatment for the 1952 Oslo games). Upstairs, walk the entire concourse, circling the arena seating while reviewing the highlights (and lowlights) of the 1994 games (remember Tonya Harding?). While you're up there, check out the gallery of great Norwegian athletes and the giant egg used in the Lillehammer opening ceremony.

Cost and Hours: 110 kr, 25 percent off when combined with Maihaugen Museum; June-Aug daily 10:00-17:00; Sept-May Tue-Sun 11:00-16:00, closed Mon; tel. 61 25 21 00, www.maihaugen. no.

Nearby: On the hillside above Håkon Hall (a 30-minute hike or quick drive) are two ski jumps that host more Olympics sights, including a ski lift, the ski jump tower, and a bobsled ride (www. olympiaparken.no). In the summer, ski jumpers practice on the jumps, which are sprayed with water.

IN THE GUDBRANDSDAL VALLEY

If you're driving from Oslo to the Gudbrandsdal Valley, you'll go right past the historic Eidsvoll Manor (described on page 269).

Scenic Drives

The main E-6 road north of Lillehammer (en route to Otta and Lom) passes through a bucolic valley with fine but unremarkable scenery. Along this road, a pair of toll-road side-trips (Gynt Veien and Peer Gynt Seterveien) loop off the E-6 road. While they sound romantic, they're basically windy, curvy dirt roads over high, desolate heath and scrub-brush plateaus with fine mountain views. They're scenic, but pale in comparison with the Sognefjell road between Lom and the Lustrafjord (described later in this chapter).

Sleep Code

Abbreviations   **(6 kr = about $1, country code: 47)**
S = Single, **D** = Double/Twin, **T** = Triple, **Q** = Quad, **b** = bathroom
Price Rankings
  $$$ **Higher Priced**—Most rooms 1,000 kr or more.
    $$ **Moderately Priced**—Most rooms 600-1,000 kr.
      $ **Lower Priced**—Most rooms 600 kr or less.
Unless otherwise noted, credit cards are accepted, breakfast is included, and Wi-Fi is generally free. Everyone speaks English. Prices change; verify current rates online or by email. For the best prices, always book directly with the hotel.

Sleeping in the Gudbrandsdal Valley

I prefer sleeping in the more scenic and Norwegian-feeling Jotunheimen area (described later). But if you're sleeping here, Lillehammer and the surrounding valley offer several good options. My choices for Lillehammer are near the train station; the accommodations in Kvam provide a convenient stopping point in the valley.

IN LILLEHAMMER

$$$ Mølla Hotell, true to its name, is situated in an old mill along the little stream running through Lillehammer. The 58 rooms blend Old World charm with modern touches. It's more cutesy-cozy and less businesslike than other Lillehammer hotels in this price range (Db-1,000-1,450 kr depending on demand, elevator, guest computer and Wi-Fi, a block below Gågata at Elvegata 12, tel. 61 05 70 80, www.mollahotell.no, post@mollahotell.no).

    $$$ First Hotel Breiseth is a business-class hotel with 89 rooms in a handy location directly across from the train station (Sb-820-1,200 kr, Db-1,000-1,320 kr, Wi-Fi, free parking, Jernbanegaten 1-5, tel. 61 24 77 77, www.firsthotels.no/breiseth, breiseth@firsthotels.no).

    $ Vandrerhjem Stasjonen, Lillehammer's youth hostel, is actually upstairs inside the train station. With 100 beds in 33 institutional but new-feeling rooms—including 21 almost hotel-like doubles—it's a winner (340-kr bunk in a 3- to 4-bed dorm, Sb-745 kr, Db-990 kr, 15 percent cheaper for members, includes sheets and breakfast, elevator, Wi-Fi, Jernbanetorget 2, tel. 61 26 00 24, www.stasjonen.no, lillehammer@hihostels.no).

IN KVAM

This is a popular vacation valley for Norwegians, and you'll find loads of reasonable small hotels and campgrounds with huts for those who aren't quite campers (*hytter* means "cottages" or "cabins," *rom* is "private room," and *ledig* means "vacancy"). These huts normally cost about 400-600 kr, depending on size and amenities, and can hold from four to six people. Although they are simple, you'll have a kitchenette and access to a good WC and shower. When available, sheets rent for around 60 kr per person. Here are a couple of listings in the town of Kvam, located midway between Lillehammer and Lom.

$$$ Vertshuset Sinclair has a quirky Scottish-Norwegian ambience. The 15 fine rooms are in old-fashioned motel wings, while the main building houses an inexpensive cafeteria, described later (Sb-890 kr, Db-1,090 kr, family deals, free guest computer and Wi-Fi, tel. 61 29 54 50, www.vertshuset-sinclair.no, post@ vertshuset-sinclair.no). The motel was named after a Scotsman who led a band of adventurers into this valley, attempting to set up their own Scottish kingdom. They failed. All were kilt.

$-$$ Kirketeigen Ungdomssenter ("Church Youth Center"), behind the town church, welcomes travelers year-round (camping spots-120 kr/tent; small cabins without water-400 kr; cabins with kitchen and bath-800 kr, sleeps up to 5 people; simple 4-bed rooms in the main building-450 kr for 2-4 people with sheets; sheets and blankets-100 kr, Wi-Fi, tel. 61 21 60 90, www.kirketeigen.no, post@kirketeigen.no).

Eating in the Gudbrandsdal Valley

In Lillehammer: Good restaurants are scattered around the city center, but for the widest selection, head to where the main pedestrian drag (Gågata) crosses the little stream running downhill through town. Poke a block or two up and down **Elvegata,** which stretches along the river and hosts a wide range of tempting eateries—from pubs (both rowdy and upscale) to pizza and cheap sandwich stands.

In the Valley: **Vertshuset Sinclair,** described earlier, has a cafeteria handy for a quick and filling bite on the road between Lillehammer and Lom (50-70-kr small dishes, 100-200-kr meals, daily 7:00-late).

Jotunheimen Mountains

Norway's Jotunheimen ("Giants' Home") Mountains feature the country's highest peaks and some of its best hikes and drives. This national park stretches from the fjords to the glaciers. You can play roller-coaster with mountain passes, take rugged hikes, wind up scenic toll roads, get up close to a giant stave church...and sleep in a time-passed rural valley. The gateway to the mountains is the unassuming town of Lom.

Lom

Pleasant Lom—the main town between Lillehammer and Sogndal—feels like a modern ski resort village. It's home to one of Norway's most impressive stave churches. While Lom has little else to offer, the church causes the closest thing to a tour-bus traffic jam this neck of the Norwegian woods will ever see.

Orientation to Lom

Park by the stave church—you'll see its dark spire just over the bridge. The church shares a parking lot with a gift shop/church museum and some public WCs. Across the street is the TI, in the sod-roofed building that also houses the Norwegian Mountain Museum. If you're heading over the mountains, Lom's bank (at the Kommune building) has the last ATM until Gaupne.

TOURIST INFORMATION

Lom's TI, a good source of information for hikes and drives in the Jotunheimen Mountains, may close for a couple of years starting in 2015; if it does, an alternate TI may open just across the river in Lom's Co-op Mega grocery store—ask around (if open, TI's hours likely July-mid-Aug Mon-Fri 9:00-17:00, Sat-Sun 9:00-15:00; shorter hours off-season and closed Sat-Sun Oct-April; tel. 61 21 29 90, www.visitjotunheimen.com).

Sights in Lom

▲▲Lom Stave Church (Lom Stavkyrkje)

Despite extensive renovations, Lom's church (from 1158) remains a striking example of a Nordic stave church. For more on these distinctive medieval churches, see page 211.

Cost and Hours: Church—60 kr, daily mid-June-mid-Aug 9:00-19:00 (until 17:00 last half of Aug), mid-May-mid-June and Sept 10:00-16:00, closed in winter and during funerals; museum—10 kr, same hours as church, progressively shorter hours in shoulder season, in winter Mon-Sat 10:00-15:00, closed Sun; tel. 40 43 84 86.

Tours: Try to tag along with a guided tour of the church—or, if it's not too busy, a docent can give you a quick private tour (included in ticket). Even outside of opening times—including winter—small groups can arrange a tour (60 kr/person, 600-kr mini-

GUDBRANDSDAL

mum, call 97 07 53 97 in summer or 61 21 73 00 in winter).

Visiting the Church: Buy your ticket and go inside to take in the humble **interior** (still used by locals for services—notice the posted hymnal numbers). Men sat on the right, women on the left, and prisoners sat with the sheriff in the caged area in the rear. Standing in the middle of the nave, look overhead to see the earliest surviving parts of the church, such as the circle of X-shaped St. Andrew crosses and the Romanesque arches above them. High above the door (impossible to see without a flashlight—ask a docent to show you) is an old painting of a dragon- or lion-like creature—likely an old Viking symbol, possibly drawn here to smooth the forced conversion local pagans made to Christianity. When King Olav II (later to become St. Olav) swept through this valley in 1021, he gave locals an option: convert or be burned out of house and home.

On the white town flag, notice the spoon—a symbol of Lom. Because of its position nestled in the mountains, Lom gets less rainfall than other towns, so large spoons were traditionally used to spread water over the fields. The apse (behind the altar) was added in 1240, when trendy new Gothic cathedrals made an apse a must-have accessory for churches across Europe. Lepers came to the grilled window in the apse for a blessing. When the Reformation hit in 1536, the old paintings were whitewashed over. The church has changed over the years: Transepts, pews, and windows were added in the 17th century. And the circa-1720 paintings were done by a local priest's son.

Drop into the **gift shop/church museum** in the big black building in the parking lot. Its one-room exhibit celebrates 1,000 years of the stave church—interesting if you follow the loaner English descriptions. Inside you'll find a pair of beautiful model churches, headstones and other artifacts, and the only surviving stave-church dragon-head "steeple." In the display case near the early-1900s organ, find the little pencil-size stick carved with runes, dating from around 1350. It's actually a love letter from a would-be suitor. The woman rejected him, but she saved them both from embarrassment by hiding the stick under the church floorboards beneath a pew...where it was found in 1973. (Docents inside the church like to show off a replica of this stick.)

Before or after your church visit, explore the tidy, thought-provoking **graveyard** surrounding the church. Also, check out the precarious-looking little footbridge over the waterfall (the best view is from the modern road bridge into town).

Norwegian Mountain Museum (Norsk Fjellmuseum)

This worthwhile museum traces the history of the people who have lived off the land in the Jotunheimen Mountains from the Stone Age to today (and also serves as a national park office). It is one of the better museums in fjord country, with well-presented displays and plenty of actual artifacts. Beginning in 2015, a new exhibit, "Over the Ice: Discoveries from the Ice Show the Way," will explore prehistoric human and animal migrations in the surrounding mountains based on recent archaeological finds, including a 1,300-year-old ski.

Cost and Hours: 70 kr, mid-May-early-Oct daily 9:00-16:00, except until 19:00 daily July-mid-Aug, generally closed off-season, in the sod-roofed building across the road from the Lom Stave Church parking lot, tel. 61 21 16 00, http://fjell.museum.no.

Sleeping near Lom

Lom itself has a handful of hotels, but the most appealing way to overnight in this area is at a rural rest stop in the countryside. All of these are on Route 55 south of Lom, toward Sognefjord—first is Strind Gard, then Bøverdalen, Røisheim, and finally Elvesæter (all within 20 minutes of Lom).

$$$ Røisheim, in a marvelously remote mountain setting, is an extremely expensive storybook hotel composed of a cluster of centuries-old, sod-roofed log farmhouses. Its posh and generous living rooms are filled with antiques. Each of the 20 rooms (in 14 different buildings) is rustic but elegant, with fun "barrel bathtubs" and four-poster or canopy beds. Some rooms are in old, wooden farm buildings—*stabburs*—with low ceilings and heavy beams. The deluxe rooms are larger, with king beds and fireplaces. Call ahead so they'll be prepared for your arrival (open May-Sept; standard Db-3,000 kr, deluxe Db-3,600 kr; includes breakfast, packed lunch, and an over-the-top four-course traditional dinner served at 19:30; non-smoking, Wi-Fi, 10 miles south of Lom on Route 55, tel. 61 21 20 31, www.roisheim.no, booking@roisheim.no).

$$$ Elvesæter Hotel has its own share of Old World romance, but is bigger, cheaper, and more modest. Delightful public spaces bunny-hop through its traditional shell, while its 200 beds sprawl through nine buildings. The Elvesæter family has done a great job of retaining the historic character of their medieval farm, even though the place is big enough to handle large tour groups. The renovated "superior" rooms are new-feeling, but have sterile modern furniture; the older, cheaper "standard" rooms are well-worn but more characteristic (open May-Sept, standard Db-1,150 kr, superior Db-1,550 kr, extra bed-450 kr, family deals, includes breakfast, good 325-kr three-course dinners, Wi-Fi, swimming pool, farther up Route 55, just past Bøverdal, tel. 61 21 12 10, www.topofnorway.no, elveseter@topofnorway.no). Even if you're not staying here, stop by to wander through the public spaces and pick up a flier explaining the towering Sagasøyla (Saga Column). It was started in 1926 to celebrate the Norwegian constitution, and was to stand in front of Oslo's Parliament Building—but the project stalled after World War II (thanks to the artist's affinity for things German and membership in Norway's fascist party). It was eventually finished and erected here in 1992.

$ **Bøverdalen Youth Hostel** offers 32 cheap-but-comfortable beds and a far more rugged clientele—real hikers rather than car hikers. While a bit institutional, it's well-priced and well-run (open late May-Sept, bunk in 4- to 6-bed room-180 kr, D-550 kr, 4-person cabins-980 kr, sheets-65 kr, breakfast-85 kr, Wi-Fi, kitchen, hot meals, self-serve café, tel. 61 21 20 64, www.hihostels.no, boverdalen@hihostels.no, Anna Berit). It's in the center of the little community of Bøverdal (store, campground, and toll road up to Galdhøpiggen area).

$ **Strind Gard** is your very rustic option if you can't spring for Røisheim or Elvesæter, but still want the countryside-farm experience. This 150-year-old farmhouse, situated by a soothing waterfall, rents two rooms and one apartment, plus four sod-roofed log huts. The catch: Many of the buildings have no running water, so you'll use the shared facilities at the main building. While not everyone's cup of tea, this place will appeal to romantics who always wanted to sleep in a humble log cabin in the Norwegian mountains—it's downright idyllic for those who like to rough it (2-person huts: without bathroom-300-500 kr depending on size, beautiful private hut with bathroom-700 kr; rooms in main house: D-400-500 kr depending on size, apartment for 4-6 with private bath-700 kr; sheets and towels-70 kr, no breakfast, Wi-Fi, low ceilings, farm smells, valley views, 2 miles south of Lom on Route 55, tel. 61 21 12 37, www.strind-gard.no, post@strind-gard.no, Anne Jorunn and Trond Dalsegg).

Drives and Hikes in the Jotunheimen Mountains

Route 55, which runs between Lom and the Sognefjord to the south, is the sightseeing spine of this region. From this main (and already scenic) drag, other roads spin upward into the mountains—

offering even better views and exciting drives and hikes. Many of these get you up close to Norway's highest mountain, Galdhøpiggen (8,100 feet). I've listed these attractions from north to south, as you'll reach them driving from Lom to the Sognefjord; except for the first, they all branch off from Route 55. Another great high-mountain experience nearby—the hike to the Nigard Glacier near Lustrafjord—is covered on page 336.

Remember that the Norwegian Mountain Museum in Lom acts as a national park office, offering excellent maps and advice for drivers and hikers—a stop here is obligatory if you're planning a jaunt into the mountains (see "Orientation to Lom," earlier). For locations, see the map on page 347.

Besseggen

This trail offers an incredible opportunity to walk between two lakes separated by a narrow ridge and a 1,000-foot cliff. It's one of Norway's most beloved hikes, which can make it crowded in the summer. To get to the trailhead, drivers detour down Route 51 after Otta south to Maurvangen. Turn right to Gjendesheim to park your car. From Gjendesheim, catch the boat to Memurubu, where the path starts at the boat dock. Hike along the ridge—with a blue lake (Bessvatnet) on one side and a green lake (Gjende) on the other—and keep your balance. The six-hour trail loops back to Gjendesheim. Because the boat runs sporadically, time your visit to catch one (120 kr for 20-minute ride, 3 morning departures daily, latest schedules at www.gjende.no, mobile 91 30 67 44). This is a thrilling but potentially hazardous hike, and it's a major detour: Gjendesheim is about 1.5 hours and 50 miles from Lom.

Spiterstulen

From Røisheim, this 11-mile toll road (80 kr) takes you from Route 55 to the Spiterstulen mountain hotel/lodge in about 30 minutes (3,600 feet). This is the best destination for serious all-day hikes to Norway's two mightiest mountains, Glittertinden and Galdhøpiggen (a 5-hour hike up and a 3-hour hike down, doable without a guide). Or consider a guided, two-hour glacier walk (tel. 61 21 94 00, www.spiterstulen.no).

Juvasshytta

This toll road takes you (in about 40 minutes) to the highest you can drive and the closest you can get to Galdhøpiggen (6,050 feet) by car. The road starts in Bøverdal, and costs 85 kr; at the end of it, daily, guided, six-hour hikes go across the glacier to the summit and back (200 kr, late June-late Sept daily at 10:00, July-mid-Aug also daily at 11:30, check in 30 minutes before, strict age limit—no kids under age 7, 4 miles each way, easy ascent but can be dangerous without a guide, hiking boots required—possible to rent from nearby ski resort). You can sleep in the newly updated **$$$ Ju-vasshytta lodge** (Db-1,140 kr with sheets, D without sheets-860 kr, sheets-100 kr, includes breakfast, dinner-330 kr, open June-Sept, tel. 61 21 15 50, www.juvasshytta.no).

Leirvassbu

This 11-mile, 50-kr toll road (about 30 minutes one-way from Bøverkinnhalsen, south of Elvesæter) is most scenic for car hikers. It takes you to a lodge at 4,600 feet with great views and easy walks. A serious (5-hour round-trip) hike goes to the lone peak, Kyrkja—"The Cathedral," which looms like a sanded-down mini-Matterhorn on the horizon (6,660 feet).

▲▲Sognefjell Drive to the Sognefjord

Norway's highest pass (at 4,600 feet, the highest road in northern Europe) is a thrilling drive through a cancan line of mountains, from Jotunheimen's Bøverdal Valley to the Lustrafjord (an arm of the Sognefjord—see previous chapter). Centuries ago, the farmers of Gudbrandsdal took their horse caravans over this difficult mountain pass on treks to Bergen. Today, the road (Route 55) is still narrow, windy, and otherworldly (and usually closed mid-Oct-May).

As you begin to ascend just beyond Elvesæter, notice the viewpoint on the left for the Leirdalen Valley—capped at the end with the Kyrkja peak (described earlier). Next you'll twist up into a lake-filled valley, then through a mild canyon with grand waterfalls. Before long, as you corkscrew up more switchbacks, you're above the tree line, enjoying a "top of the world" feeling. The best views (to the south) are of the cut-glass range called Hurrungane ("Noisy Children"). The 10 hairpin turns between Turtagrø and

Fortun are exciting. Be sure to stop, get out, look around, and enjoy the lavish views. Treat each turn as if it were your last.

Just before you descend to the fjord, the terrain changes, and you reach a pullout on the right, next to a hilltop viewpoint—offering your first glimpse of the fjord. The Lustrafjord village of Skjolden is just around the bend (and down several more switchbacks). Entering Skjolden, continue following Route 55, which now traces the west bank of the Lustrafjord. For more on the sights from here on out, turn to page 334.

Gudbrandsdal and Jotunheimen Connections

Cars are better, but if you're without wheels: **Oslo to Lillehammer** (trains almost hourly, 2.5 hours, just 2 hours from Oslo airport), **Lillehammer to Otta** (6 trains/day, 1.5 hours); a bus meets some trains (confirm schedule at the train station in Oslo) for travelers heading on to **Lom** (2 buses/day, 1 hour) and onward from **Lom to Sogndal** (2 buses/day late June-Aug only, road closed off-season, 3.5 hours).

ROUTE TIPS FOR DRIVERS

Use low gears and lots of patience both up (to keep the engine cool) and down (to save your brakes). Uphill traffic gets the right-of-way, but drivers, up or down, dive for the nearest fat part of the road whenever they meet. Ask backseat drivers not to scream until you've actually been hit or have left the road.

From Oslo to Jotunheimen: It's 2.5 hours from Oslo to Lillehammer and 3 hours after that to Lom. Wind out of Oslo following signs for *E-6* (not to *Drammen*, but for *Stockholm* and then to *Trondheim*). In a few minutes, you're in the wide-open pastoral countryside of eastern Norway. Norway's Constitution Hall— Eidsvoll Manor—is a five-minute detour off E-6, several miles south of Eidsvoll in Eidsvoll Verk (described on page 269; follow the signs to *Eidsvoll Bygningen*). Then E-6 takes you along Norway's largest lake (Mjøsa), through the town of Hamar, and past more lake scenery into Lillehammer. Signs direct you uphill from downtown Lillehammer to the Maihaugen Open-Air Folk Museum. From Lillehammer, signs to *E-6/Trondheim* take you up the valley of Gudbrandsdal. At Otta, exit for Lom. Halfway to Lom, on the left, look for the long suspension bridge spanning the milky-blue river—a good opportunity to stretch your legs, and a scenic spot to enjoy a picnic.

BERGEN

Bergen is permanently salted with robust cobbles and a rich sea-trading heritage. Norway's capital in the 13th century, Bergen's wealth and importance came thanks to its membership in the heavyweight medieval trading club of merchant cities called the Hanseatic League. Bergen still wears her rich maritime heritage proudly—nowhere more scenically than the colorful wooden warehouses that make up the picture-perfect Bryggen district along the harbor.

Protected from the open sea by a lone sheltering island, Bergen is a place of refuge from heavy winds for the giant working boats that serve the North Sea oil rigs. (Much of Norway's current affluence is funded by the oil it drills just offshore.) Bergen is also one of the most popular cruise-ship ports in northern Europe, hosting about 300 ships a year and up to five ships a day in peak season. Each morning is rush hour, as cruisers hike past the fortress and into town.

Bergen gets an average of 80 inches of rain annually (compared to 30 inches in Oslo). A good year has 60 days of sunshine. The natives aren't apologetic about their famously lousy weather. In fact, they seem to wear it as a badge of pride. "Well, that's Bergen," they'll say matter-of-factly as they wring out their raincoats. When I complained about an all-day downpour, one resident cheerfully informed me, "There's no such thing as bad weather—just inappropriate clothing"...a local mantra that rhymes in Norwegian.

With about 240,000 people, Bergen has big-city parking problems and high prices, but visitors sticking to the old center find it charming. Enjoy Bergen's salty market, then stroll the easy-on-foot old quarter, with cute lanes of delicate old wooden houses.

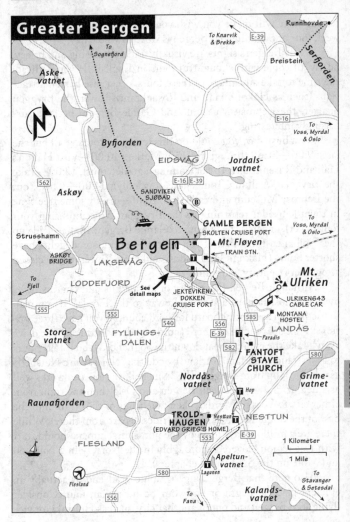

From downtown Bergen, a funicular zips you up a little mountain for a bird's-eye view of this sailors' town. A short foray into the countryside takes you to a variety of nearby experiences: a dramatic cable-car ride to a mountaintop perch (Ulriken643); a scenic stave church (Fantoft); and the home of Norway's most beloved composer, Edvard Grieg, at Troldhaugen.

PLANNING YOUR TIME

Bergen can be enjoyed even on the tail end of a day's scenic train ride from Oslo before returning on the overnight train. But that teasing taste will make you wish you had more time. On a three-week tour of Scandinavia, Bergen is worth a whole day.

While Bergen's sights are visually underwhelming and pricey, nearly all come with thoughtful tours in English. If you dedicate the time to take advantage of these tours, otherwise barren attractions (such as Håkon's Hall and Rosenkrantz Tower, the Bryggen quarter, the Leprosy Museum, and Gamle Bergen) become surprisingly interesting.

For a busy day, you could do this (enjoying tours at all but the last): 9:00—Stroll through the Fish Market; 10:00—Visit Håkon's Hall and Rosenkrantz Tower (joining a guided tour); 12:00—Take the Bryggen Walking Tour (June-Aug only); 14:00—Check out the Leprosy Museum and cathedral; 16:00—Enjoy some free time in town (consider returning to the Bryggens Museum using your tour ticket), or catch the bus out to Gamle Bergen; 18:00—Ride up the Fløibanen funicular. If you visit off-season, some sights have shorter hours (Håkon's Hall and Rosenkrantz Tower) or are closed altogether (Leprosy Museum).

Although Bergen has plenty of attractions and charms of its own, it's most famous as the "Gateway to the Fjords." If you plan to use Bergen as a springboard for fjord country, you have three options: Pick up a rental car here (fjord wonder is a three-hour drive away); take the express boat down the Sognefjord (about four hours to Balestrand and Flåm/Aurland); or do the "Norway in a Nutshell" as a scenic loop from Bergen. The "Nutshell" option also works well as a detour midway between Bergen and Oslo (hop the train from either city to Voss or Myrdal, then take a bus or spur train into the best of the Sognefjord; scenic ferry rides depart from there). While there are a million ways to enjoy the fjords, first-timers should start with this region (covered thoroughly in the Norway in a Nutshell and More on the Sognefjord chapters).

Also note that Bergen, a geographic dead-end, is actually an efficient place to begin or end your Scandinavian tour. Consider flying into Bergen and out of another city, such as Helsinki (or vice versa).

Orientation to Bergen

Bergen clusters around its harbor—nearly everything listed in this chapter is within a few minutes' walk. The busy Torget (the square with the Fish Market) is at the head of the harbor. As you face the sea from here, Bergen's TI is at the left end of the Fish Market. The town's historic Hanse-

atic Quarter, Bryggen (BREW-gun), lines the harbor on the right. Express boats to the Sognefjord (Balestrand and Flåm) dock at the harbor on the left.

Charming cobbled streets surround the harbor and climb the encircling hills. Bergen's popular Fløibanen funicular climbs high above the city to the top of Mount Fløyen for the best view of the town. Surveying the surrounding islands and inlets, it's clear why this city is known as the "Gateway to the Fjords."

TOURIST INFORMATION

The centrally located TI is upstairs in the long, skinny, modern, Torghallen market building, next to the Fish Market (June-Aug daily 8:30-22:00; May and Sept daily 9:00-20:00; Oct-April Mon-Sat 9:00-16:00, closed Sun; handy budget eateries downstairs and in Fish Market; tel. 55 55 20 00, www.visitbergen.com).

The TI covers Bergen and western Norway, provides information and tickets for tours, has a fjord information desk, books rooms, and maintains a very handy events board listing today's and tomorrow's slate of tours, concerts, and other events. Pick up this year's edition of the free *Bergen Guide* (also likely at your hotel), which has a fine map and lists all sights, hours, and special events. This booklet can answer most of your questions. If you need assistance and there's a line, take a number. They also have free Wi-Fi (password posted on wall).

Bergen Card: You have to work hard to make this greedy little card pay off (200 kr/24 hours, 260 kr/48 hours, sold at TI and Montana Family & Youth Hostel). It gives you free use of the city's tram and buses, half off the Mount Fløyen funicular, free admission to most museums (but not the Hanseatic Museum; aquarium included only in winter), and discounts on some events and sights such as Edvard Grieg's Home.

ARRIVAL IN BERGEN

By Train or Bus: Bergen's train and bus stations are on Strømgaten, facing a park-rimmed lake. The small, manageable train station has an office open long hours for booking all your travel in Norway—you can get your Nutshell reservations here (Mon-Fri 6:35-19:00, Sat 7:30-16:00, Sun 7:30-16:00). There are luggage lockers (50 kr/day, daily 6:00-23:30), pay toilets, a newsstand, sandwich shop, and coffee shop. (To get to the bus station, follow the covered walkway behind the Narvesen newsstand via the Storcenter shopping mall.) Taxis wait to the right (with the tracks at your back); a tram stop is to your left, just around the corner. From the train station, it's a 10-minute walk to the TI: Cross the street (Strømgaten) in front of the station and take Marken, a cobbled street that eventually turns

BERGEN

into a modern retail street. Continue walking in the same direction until you reach the water.

By Plane: Bergen's cute little Flesland Airport is 12 miles south of the city center (airport code: BGO, tel. 67 03 15 55, www. avinor.no/bergen). The airport bus runs between the airport and downtown Bergen, stopping at the Radisson Blu Royal Hotel in Bryggen, the harborfront area near the TI (if you ask), the Radisson Blu Hotel Norge (in the modern part of town at Ole Bulls Plass), and the bus station (about 95 kr, pay driver, 4/hour at peak times, less in slow times, 30-minute ride). Two different companies run this bus, but the cost and frequency is about the same—just take the first one that shows up. Taxis take up to four people and cost about 400 kr for the 20-minute ride (depending on the time of day).

By Car: Driving is a headache in Bergen; avoid it if you can. Approaching town on E-16 (from Voss and the Sognefjord area), follow signs for *Sentrum*, which spits you out near the big, modern bus station and parking garage. Parking is difficult and costly—ask your hotelier for tips. Note that all drivers entering Bergen must pay a 25-kr toll, but there are no toll-collection gates (since the system is automated). Assuming they bill you, it'll just show up on your credit card (which they access through your rental-car company). For details, ask your rental company or see www.autopass. no.

By Cruise Ship: Bergen is easy for cruise passengers, regardless of which of the city's two ports your ship uses.

The **Skolten** cruise port is just past the fortress on the main harborfront road. Arriving here, simply walk into town (stroll with the harbor on your right, figure about 10 minutes to Bryggen, plus five more minutes to the Fish Market and TI). After about five minutes, you'll pass the fortress—the starting point for my self-guided walk. A taxi into downtown costs about 70-80 kr, and hop-on, hop-off buses pick up passengers at the port (though in this compact town, I'd just walk).

The **Jekteviken/Dokken** cruise port is in an industrial zone to the south, a bit farther out (about a 20-minute walk). To discourage passengers from walking through all the containers, the port operates a convenient and free **shuttle bus** that zips you into town. It drops you off along Rasmus Meyers Allé right in front of the Kode Art Museums, facing the cute manmade lake called Lille Lungegårdsvann. From here, it's an easy 10-minute walk to the TI and Fish Market: Walk with the lake on your right, pass through the park (with the pavilion) and head up the pedestrian mall called Ole Bulls Plass, and turn right (at the bluish slab) up the broad square called Torgallmenningen. Note that my self-guided Bergen walk conveniently ends near the shuttle-bus stop. A taxi from the cruise port into downtown runs about 110 kr.

For more in-depth cruising information, pick up my *Rick Steves Northern European Cruise Ports* guidebook.

HELPFUL HINTS

Museum Tours: Many of Bergen's sights are hard to appreciate without a guide. Fortunately, several include a wonderful and intimate guided tour with admission. Make the most of the following sights by taking advantage of their included tours: Håkon's Hall and Rosenkrantz Tower, Bryggens Museum, Hanseatic Museum, Leprosy Museum, Gamle Bergen, and Edvard Grieg's Home.

Crowd Control: In high season, cruise-ship passengers mob the waterfront between 10:00 and 15:00; to avoid the crush, consider visiting an outlying sight during this time, such as Gamle Bergen or Edvard Grieg's Home.

Internet Access: The **TI** offers free, fast Wi-Fi (look for the password posted on the wall), but no terminals. The **Bergen Public Library,** next door to the train station, has free terminals in their downstairs café (30-minute limit, Mon-Thu 10:00-18:00, Fri 10:00-16:00, Sat 10:00-15:00, closed Sun, Strømgaten 6, tel. 55 56 85 60). The church-run **Kafe Magdalena,** just off the harbor at Kong Oscars Gate 5, has two free terminals.

Laundry: If you drop your laundry off at **Hygienisk Vask & Rens,** you can pick it up clean the next day (70 kr/kilo, no self-service, Sun-Fri 8:30-16:30, closed Sat, Halfdan Kjerulfsgate 8, tel. 55 31 77 41).

Updates to This Book: For updates to this book, check www.ricksteves.com/update.

GETTING AROUND BERGEN

Most in-town sights can easily be reached by foot; only the aquarium and Gamle Bergen (and farther-flung sights such as the Fantoft Stave Church, Edvard Grieg's Home at Troldhaugen, and the Ulriken643 cable car) are more than a 10-minute walk from the TI.

By Bus: City buses cost 41 kr per ride (pay driver in cash), or 31 kr per ride if you buy a single-ride ticket from a machine or convenience stores such as Narvesen, 7-Eleven, Rimi, and Deli de Luca. The best buses for a Bergen joyride are #6 (north along the coast) and #11 (into the hills).

By Tram: Bergen's recently built light-rail line (Bybanen) is a convenient way to visit Edvard Grieg's Home or the Fantoft Stave Church. The tram begins next to Byparken (on Kaigaten, between Bergen's little lake and Ole Bulls Plass), then heads to the train station and continues south. Buy your 31-kr ticket from the machine prior to boarding (to use a US credit card, you'll need to know your PIN code). You can also buy single-ride tickets at Narvesen, 7-Eleven, Rimi, and Deli de Luca stores. You'll get a gray *minikort* pass. Validate the pass when you board by holding it next to the card reader (watch how other passengers do it). Ride it about 20 minutes to the Paradis stop for Fantoft Stave Church (don't get off at the "Fantoft" stop, which is farther from the church); or continue to the next stop, Hop, to hike to Troldhaugen.

By Ferry: The *Beffen*, a little orange ferry, chugs across the harbor every half-hour, from the dock a block south of the Bryggens Museum to the dock—directly opposite the fortress—a block from the Nykirken church (20 kr, Mon-Fri 7:30-16:00, plus Sat May-Aug 11:00-16:00, never on Sun, 3-minute ride). The *Vågen* ferry runs from the Fish Market every half-hour to a dock near the aquarium (50 kr one-way, daily June-Aug 10:00-17:30, off-season 10:00-16:00, 10-minute ride). These short "poor man's cruises" have good harbor views.

By Taxi: For a taxi, call 07000 or 08000 (they're not as expensive as you might expect).

Tours in Bergen

▲▲▲Bryggen Walking Tour

This tour of the historic Hanseatic district is one of Bergen's best activities. Local guides take visitors on an excellent 1.5-hour walk

in English through 900 years of Bergen history via the old Hanseatic town (20 minutes in Bryggens Museum, 20-minute visit to the medieval Hanseatic Assembly Rooms, 20-minute walk through Bryggen, and 20 minutes in Hanseatic Museum). Tours leave from the Bryggens Museum (next to the Radisson Blu Royal Hotel). When you consider that the price includes entry tickets to all three sights, the tour more than pays for itself (120 kr, June-Aug daily at 11:00 and 12:00, maximum 30 in group, no tours Sept-May, tel. 55 58 80 10, bryggens. museum@bymuseet.no). While the museum visits are a bit rushed, your tour ticket allows you to re-enter the museums for the rest of the day. The 11:00 tour can sell out, especially in July; to be safe, you can call, email, or drop by ahead of time to reserve a spot.

Local Guide

Sue Lindelid is a British expat who has spent more than 25 years showing visitors around Bergen (800 kr/2-hour tour, 900 kr/3 or more people; 1,000 kr/3-hour tour, 1,200 kr/3 or more people; mobile 90 78 59 52, suelin@hotmail.no).

▲Bus Tours

The TI sells tickets for various bus tours, including a 2.5-hour Grieg Lunch Concert tour that goes to Edvard Grieg's Home at Troldhaugen—a handy way to reach that distant sight (250 kr, discount with Bergen Card, includes 30-minute concert but not lunch, June-mid-Sept daily at 11:30, departs from TI). Buses are comfy, with big views and a fine recorded commentary. There are also several full-day tour options from Bergen, including bus/boat tours to nearby Hardanger and Sogne fjords. The TI is packed with brochures describing all the excursions.

Hop-On, Hop-Off Buses

City Sightseeing links most of Bergen's major sights and also stops at the Skolten cruise port, but doesn't go to the Fantoft Stave Church, Troldhaugen, or Ulriken643 cable car. If your sightseeing plans don't extend beyond the walkable core of Bergen, skip the bus and save some kroner (150 kr/24 hours, late May-Aug 9:00-16:30, 2/hour, also stops right in front of Fish Market, mobile 97 78 18 88, www.citysightseeing-bergen.net).

▲Harbor Tour

The *White Lady* leaves once daily at 11:00 (summer only) from the Fish Market for a 1.5-hour cruise. The ride is both scenic and informative, with a relaxing sun deck and good—if scant—recorded narration (150 kr, June-Aug). A daily four-hour afternoon fjord trip is also available (500 kr, June-Aug, tel. 55 25 90 00, www.whitelady.no).

Tourist Train

The tacky little "Bergen Express" train departs from in front of the Hanseatic Museum for a 55-minute loop around town (150 kr, 2/hour in peak season, otherwise hourly; runs daily May 10:00-16:00, June-Aug 10:00-19:00, Sept 10:00-15:00; headphone English commentary).

Bergen Walk

For a quick self-guided orientation stroll through Bergen, follow this walk from the city's fortress, through its old wooden Hanseatic Quarter and Fish Market, to the modern center of town. This walk is also a handy sightseeing spine, passing most of Bergen's best museums; ideally, you'll get sidetracked and take advantage

Bergen

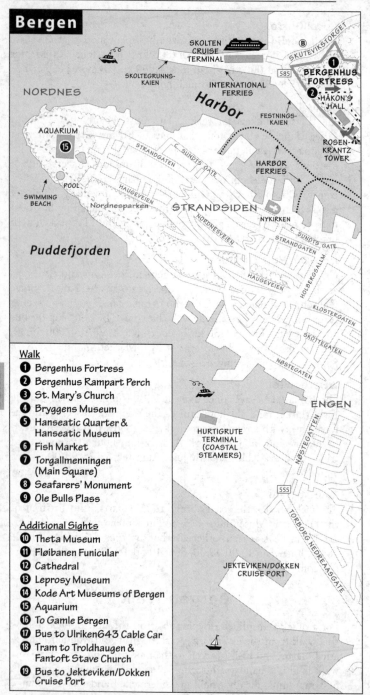

Walk

1. Bergenhus Fortress
2. Bergenhus Rampart Perch
3. St. Mary's Church
4. Bryggens Museum
5. Hanseatic Quarter & Hanseatic Museum
6. Fish Market
7. Torgallmenningen (Main Square)
8. Seafarers' Monument
9. Ole Bulls Plass

Additional Sights

10. Theta Museum
11. Fløibanen Funicular
12. Cathedral
13. Leprosy Museum
14. Kode Art Museums of Bergen
15. Aquarium
16. To Gamle Bergen
17. Bus to Ulriken643 Cable Car
18. Tram to Troldhaugen & Fantoft Stave Church
19. Bus to Jekteviken/Dokken Cruise Port

BERGEN

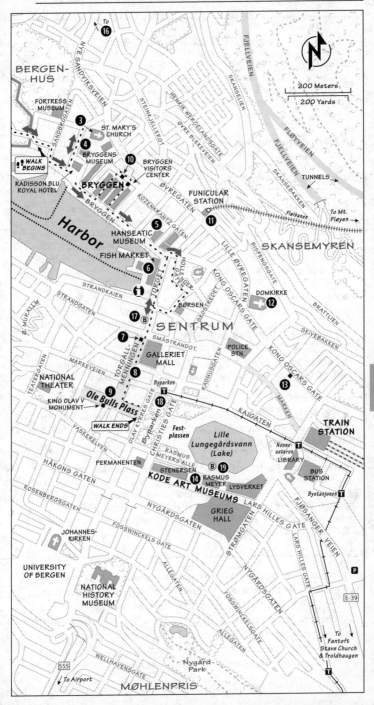

Bergen at a Glance

▲▲▲**Bryggen Walking Tour** Wonderful 1.5-hour tour of the historic Hanseatic district that covers 900 years of history and includes short visits to the Bryggens Museum, Hanseatic Assembly Rooms, and Hanseatic Museum, plus a walk through Bryggen. **Hours:** June-Aug daily at 11:00 and 12:00. See page 366.

▲▲**Bryggens Museum** Featuring early bits of Bergen (1050-1500), found in a 1950s archaeological dig. **Hours:** Mid-May-Aug daily 10:00-16:00; Sept-mid-May Mon-Fri 11:00-15:00, Sat 12:00-15:00, Sun 12:00-16:00. See page 383.

▲▲**Hanseatic Museum** Small museum highlighting Bryggen's glory days, located in an old merchant house furnished with artifacts from the time German merchants were tops in trading—most interesting with included tour. **Hours:** Daily May-Sept 9:00-17:00; Oct-April Tue-Sat 11:00-14:00, Sun 11:00-16:00, closed Mon. See page 383.

▲▲**Fløibanen Funicular** Zippy lift to top of Mount Fløyen for super views of Bergen, islands, and fjords, with picnic ops, an eatery, playground, and hiking trails. **Hours:** Mon-Fri 7:30-23:00, Sat-Sun 8:00-23:00. See page 384.

▲**Harbor Tour** Scenic 1.5-hour cruise, with recorded narration, leaving from the Fish Market. **Hours:** June-Aug at 11:00. See page 367.

▲**Fish Market** Lively market with cheap seafood eateries and free samples. **Hours:** Daily 7:00-19:00; Sept-May Mon-Sat 7:00-16:00, closed Sun. See page 378.

▲**Bergenhus Fortress: Håkon's Hall and Rosenkrantz Tower** Fortress with a 13th-century medieval banquet hall, a climbable tower offering a history exhibit and views, and a worthwhile, included tour. **Hours:** Mid-May-Aug—hall open daily 10:00-16:00, tower open daily 9:00-16:00; Sept-mid-May—hall open daily 12:00-15:00, tower open Sun only 12:00-15:00. See page 382

of their excellent tours (included with admission) along the way. I've pointed out the museums you'll pass en route—all of them are described in greater detail later, under "Sights in Bergen."

• *Begin where Bergen did, at its historic fortress. From the harborfront road, 50 yards before the stone tower with the water on your left, veer up the ramp behind the low stone wall on the right, through a gate, and into the fortress complex. Stand before the stony skyscraper.*

▲**Kode Art Museums of Bergen** Collection spread among four neighboring lakeside buildings: Lysverket (international and Norwegian artists), Rasmus Meyer (Norwegian artists, including Munch), Stenersen (contemporary art), and Permanenten (decorative arts). **Hours:** Daily 11:00-17:00, closed Mon mid-Sept-mid-May. See page 386.

▲**Aquarium** Well-presented sea life, with a walk-through "shark tunnel" and feeding times at the top of most hours in summer. **Hours:** Daily May-Aug 10:00-18:00, Sept-mid-Oct daily 10:00-16:00, mid-Oct-April Tue-Sun 10:00-16:00, closed Mon. See page 386.

▲**Gamle Bergen (Old Bergen)** Quaint gathering of 50 homes and shops dating from 18th-20th century, with guided tours of museum interiors at the top of the hour. **Hours:** Mid-May-Aug daily 9:00-16:00, closed Sept-mid-May. See page 387.

Leprosy Museum Former hospital for lepers, with small exhibit and worthwhile free tour offered on the top of every hour. **Hours:** Mid-May-Aug daily 11:00-15:00, closed Sept-mid-May. See page 385.

Near Bergen
▲▲**Edvard Grieg's Home, Troldhaugen** Home of Norway's greatest composer, with artifacts, tours, and concerts. **Hours:** Daily May-Sept 9:00-18:00, Oct-April 10:00-16:00. See page 389.

▲**Ulriken643 Cable Car** A quick ride up to the summit of Ulriken, Bergen's tallest mountain, with nonstop views, a restaurant, and hiking trails. **Hours:** Daily 9:00-21:00, off-season 9:00-17:00. See page 388.

Fantoft Stave Church Replica of a 12th-century wooden church in atmospheric wooded setting. **Hours:** Mid-May-mid-Sept daily 10:30-18:00, interior closed off-season. See page 390.

BERGEN

❶ Bergenhus Fortress
In the 13th century, Bergen became the Kingdom of Norway's first real capital. (Until then, kings would circulate, staying on royal farms.) This fortress—built in the 1240s, and worth ▲—was a garrison, with a tower for the king's residence (Rosenkrantz Tower) and a large hall for his banquets (Håkon's Hall).

Rosenkrantz Tower, the keep of the 13th-century castle, was expanded in the 16th century by the Danish-Norwegian king, who wanted to exercise a little control over the German merchants who dominated his town. He was tired of the Germans making all the money without paying taxes. This tower—with its cannon trained not on external threats but toward Bryggen—while expensive, paid for itself many times over as Germans got the message and paid their taxes.

• *Step through the gate (20 yards to the right of the tower) marked 1728 and into the courtyard of the Bergenhus Fortress. In front of you stands Håkon's Hall with its stepped gable. Tours for both the hall and the tower leave from the building to the right of Håkon's Hall (for details, see page 382).*

Pop into the museum lobby to enjoy a free exhibit about the massive 1944 explosion of the German ammunition ship in the harbor. For the best view of Håkon's Hall, walk through the gate and around the building to the left. Stand on the rampart between the hall and the harbor.

Håkon's Hall is the largest secular medieval building in Norway. When the pope sent a cardinal to perform Håkon's coronation there was no suitable building in Norway for such a VIP. King Håkon fixed that by having this impressive banqueting hall built in the mid-1200s. When Norway's capital moved to Oslo in 1299, the hall was abandoned and eventually used for grain storage. For a century it had no roof. In the Romantic 19th century, it was appreciated and restored. It's essentially a giant, grand reception hall used today as it was eight centuries ago, for banquets.

• *Continue walking along the rampart (climbing some steps and going about 100 yards past Håkon's Hall) to the far end of Bergenhus Fortress where you find a statue of a king and a fine harbor view.*

❼ Bergenhus Rampart Perch and Statue of King Håkon VII

The cannon on the ramparts here illustrates how the fort protected this strategic harbor. The port is busy with both cruise ships and support ships for the nearby North Sea oil rigs. Long before this modern commerce, this is where the cod fishermen of the north met the traders of Europe. Travelers in the 12th century described how there were so many trading vessels here "you could cross the harbor without getting your feet wet." Beyond the ships is an island protecting Bergen from the open sea.

Look left and right at the dangerous edge with no railing. If someone were to fall and get hurt here and then try to sue, the Norwegian judge's verdict would be: stupidity—case dismissed. Around you are Bergen's "seven mountains." One day each summer locals race to climb each of these in rapid succession, accomplishing the feat in less than 12 hours.

The statue is of the beloved King Håkon VII (1872-1957),

grandfather of today's king. While exiled in London during World War II, King Håkon kept up Norwegian spirits through radio broadcasts. The first king of modern Norway (after the country won its independence from Sweden in 1905), he was a Danish prince married to Queen Victoria's granddaughter—a savvy monarch who knew how to play the royalty game.

A few steps behind the statue (just right of tree-lined lane) is the site of Bergen's first cathedral, built in 1070. A hedge grows where its walls once stood. The statue of Mary marks the place of the altar, its pedestal etched with a list of 13th-century kings of Norway crowned and buried here.

These castle grounds (notice the natural amphitheater on the left) host cultural events and music festivals; Bruce Springsteen, the Stones, and Rihanna have all packed this outdoor venue in recent years.

Continuing around Håkon's Hall, follow the linden tree-lined lane. On the left, a massive concrete structure disguised by ivy looms as if evil. It was a German bunker built during the Nazi occupation—easier now to ignore than dismantle.

Twenty yards ahead on the right is a rare set of free public toilets. Notice they come with blue lights to discourage heroin junkies from using these WCs as a place to shoot up. The blue lights make it hard to see veins.

• *You've now returned to the tower and circled the castle grounds. Before leaving, consider taking one of the guided tours of the hall and tower that leave at the top of each hour (described in "Sights in Bergen," later). Head back down the ramp, out to the main road, and continue with the harbor on your right. (After a block, history buffs could follow Bergen-hus signs, up the street to the left, to the free and fascinating **Fortress Museum**—with its collection of Norwegian military history and Nazi occupation exhibits.) Proceed one more block along the harbor until you reach the open, park-like space on your left. Walk 100 yards (just past the handy Rema 1000 supermarket) to the top of this park where you'll see...*

❸ St. Mary's Church (Mariakirken)

Dating from the 12th century, this is Bergen's oldest building in continuous use. It's closed for a couple of years while a 100-million-kroner renovation is under way. This stately church of the Hanseatic merchants has a dour stone interior, enlivened by a colorful, highly decorated pulpit.

In the park below the church, find the statue of Snorri Sturluson. In the 1200s, this Icelandic scribe and scholar wrote down the Viking sagas. Thanks to him, we have a better understanding of this Nordic era. A few steps to the right, look through the window of the big modern building at an archaeological site showing the oldest remains of Bergen—stubs of the 12th-century trading town's streets tumbling to the harbor before land reclamation pushed the harbor farther out.

*• The window is just a sneak peek at the excellent ❹ Bryggens Museum, which provides helpful historical context for the Hanseatic Quarter we're about to visit (see listing later, under "Sights in Bergen.") The museum's outstanding **Bryggen Walking Tour** is your best bet for seeing this area (June-Aug daily at 11:00 and 12:00, see "Tours in Bergen," earlier). Continue down to the busy harborfront. On the left is the most photographed sight in town, the Bryggen quarter. To get your bearings, first read the "Bryggen's History" sidebar; if it's nice out, cross the street to the wharf and look back for a fine overview of this area. (Or, in the rain, huddle under an awning.)*

❺ Bergen's Hanseatic Quarter (Bryggen)

Bergen's fragile wooden old town is its iconic front door. The long "tenements" (rows of warehouses) hide atmospheric lanes that creak and groan with history.

Remember that while we think of Bergen as "Norwegian," Bryggen was German—the territory of *Deutsch*-speaking merchants and traders. (The most popular surname in Bergen is the German name Hanson—"son of Hans.") From the front of Bryggen, look back at the Rosenkrantz Tower. The little red holes at its top mark where cannons once pointed at the German quarter, installed by Norwegian royalty who wanted a slice of all that taxable trade revenue. Their threat was countered by German grain—without which the Norwegians would've starved.

Notice that the first six houses are perfectly straight; they were built in the 1980s to block the view of a modern hotel behind. The more ramshackle stretch of 11 houses beyond date from the early 1700s. Each front hides a long line of five to ten businesses.

• To wander into the heart of this woody medieval quarter, head down Bredsgården, the lane a couple of doors before the shop sign featuring the anatomically correct unicorn. We'll make a loop to the right: down this lane nearly all the way, under a passage into a square (with a well, a

vibrant outdoor restaurant, and a big wooden cod), and then back to the harbor down a parallel lane. Read the information below, then explore, stopping at the big wooden cod.

Bit by bit, Bryggen is being restored using medieval techniques and materials. As you explore, you may stumble upon a rebuilding project in action.

Strolling through Bryggen, you feel swallowed up by history. Long rows of planky buildings (medieval-style double tenements) lean haphazardly across narrow alleys. The last Hanseatic merchant moved out centuries ago, but this is still a place of (touristy) commerce. You'll find artists' galleries, T-shirt boutiques, leather workshops, atmospheric restaurants, fishing tackle shops, sweaters, sweaters, sweaters...and trolls.

Look up at the winch and pulley systems on the buildings. These connected ground-floor workrooms with top-floor storerooms. Notice that the overhanging storerooms upstairs were supported by timbers with an elbow created by a tree trunk and its root—considered the strongest way to make a right angle in construction back then. Turning right at the top of the lane, you enter a lively cobbled square. On the far side is that big wooden fish.

The wooden cod (next to a well) is a reminder that the economic foundation of Bergen—the biggest city in Scandinavia until 1650 and the biggest city in Norway until 1830—was this fish. The stone building behind the carved cod was one of the fireproof cookhouses serving a line of buildings that stretched to the harbor. Today it's the Hetland Gallery, filled with the entertaining work of a popular local artist famous for fun caricatures of the city. Facing the same square is the Bryggen visitors center, worth peeking into.

• *Enjoy the center and the shops. Then return downhill to the harborfront, turn left, and continue the walk.*

Half of Bryggen (the brick-and-stone stretch to your left between the old wooden facades and the head of the bay) was torn down around 1900. Today the stately buildings that replaced it—far less atmospheric than Bryggen's original wooden core—are filled with tacky trinket shops and touristy splurge restaurants. They do make a nice architectural cancan of pointy gables, each with its date of construction indicated near the top.

Head to the lone wooden red house at the end of the row,

Bryggen's History

Pretty as Bryggen is today, it has a rough-and-tumble history. A horrific plague decimated the population and economy of Norway in 1350, killing about half of its people. A decade later, German merchants arrived and established a Hanseatic trading post, bringing order to that rustic society. For the next four centuries, the port of Bergen was essentially German territory.

Bergen's old German trading center was called "the German wharf" until World War II (and is now just called "the wharf," or "Bryggen"). From 1370 to 1754, German merchants controlled Bergen's trade. In 1550, it was a Germanic city of 1,000 workaholic merchants—surrounded and supported by some 5,000 Norwegians.

The German merchants were very strict and lived in a harsh, all-male world (except for Norwegian prostitutes). This wasn't a military occupation, but a mutually beneficial economic partnership. The Norwegian cod fishermen of the far north shipped their dried cod to Bergen, where the Hanseatic merchants marketed it to Europe. Norwegian cod provided much of Europe with food (a source of easy-to-preserve protein) and cod oil (which lit the lamps until about 1850).

While the city dates from 1070, little survives from before the last big fire in 1702. In its earlier hey-  day, Bergen was one of the largest wooden cities in Europe. Congested wooden buildings, combined with lots of small fires (to provide heat and light in this cold and dark corner of Europe), spelled disaster for Bergen. Over the centuries, the city suffered countless fires, including 10 devastating ones. Back then, it wasn't a question of *if* there would be a fire, but *when* there would be a fire—with major blazes every 20 or so years. Each time the warehouses burned, the merchants would toss the refuse into

which houses the **Hanseatic Museum.** The man who owned this building recognized the value of the city's heritage and kept its 18th-century interior intact. Once considered a nutcase, today he's celebrated as a visionary, as his decision has left visitors with a fine example of an old merchant house that they can tour. This highly recommended museum is your best chance to get a peek inside one of those old wooden tenements.

• *The Fish Market is just across the street. Before enjoying that, we'll circle a few blocks inland and around to the right.*

The red-brick building (with frilly white trim, stepped gable, and a Starbucks) is the old meat market. It was built in 1877, after the importance of hygiene was recognized and the meat was moved

the bay and rebuild. Gradually, the land crept out, and so did the buildings. (Looking at the Hanseatic Quarter from the harborfront, you can see how the buildings have settled. The foundations, composed of debris from the many fires, settle as they rot.)

After 1702, the city rebuilt using more stone and brick, and suffered fewer fires. But this one small wooden quarter was built after the fire, in the early 1700s. To prevent future blazes, the Germans forbade all fires and candles for light or warmth except in isolated and carefully guarded communal houses behind each tenement. It was in these communal houses that apprentices studied, people dried out their soggy clothes, hot food was cooked, and the men drank and partied. When there was a big banquet, one man always stayed sober—a kind of designated fire watchman.

Flash forward to the 20th century. One of the biggest explosions of World War II occurred in Bergen's harbor on April 20, 1944. An ammunition ship loaded with 120 tons of dynamite blew up just in front of the fortress. The blast leveled entire neighborhoods on either side of the harbor (notice the ugly 1950s construction opposite the fortress) and did serious damage to Håkon's Hall and Rosenkrantz Tower. How big was the blast? There's a hut called "the anchor cabin" a couple of miles away in the mountains. That's where the ship's anchor landed. The blast is considered to be accidental, despite the fact that April 20 happened to be Hitler's 55th birthday and the ship blew up about 100 yards away from the Nazi commander's headquarters (in the fortress).

After World War II, Bryggen was again slated for destruction. Most of the locals wanted it gone—it reminded them of the Germans who had occupied Norway for the miserable war years. Then excavators discovered rune stones indicating that the area predated the Germans. This boosted Bryggen's approval rating, and the quarter was saved. Today this picturesque and historic zone is the undisputed tourist highlight of Bergen.

BERGEN

inside from today's Fish Market. At the intersection just beyond, look left (uphill past the meat market) to see the Fløibanen station. Ahead, on the right, is an unusually classy McDonald's in a 1710 building that was originally a bakery.

But let's look at Norwegian fast food: Across the street, Söstrene Hagelin is a celebration of white and fishy cuisine—very Norwegian. A few steps uphill, the tiny red shack flying the Norwegian flags is the popular 3-Kroneren hot-dog stand (described in "Eating in Bergen," later). Review the many sausage options.

At the McDonald's, wander the length of the cute lane of 200-year-old buildings. Called Hollendergaten, its name comes from a time when the king organized foreign communities of traders into various neighborhoods; this was where the Dutch lived. The curving street marks the former harborfront—these buildings were originally right on the water.

Hooking left, you reach the end of Hollendergaten. Turn right back toward the harborfront. Ahead is the grand stone Børsen building (now Matbørsen, a collection of trendy restaurants), once the stock exchange. Step inside to enjoy its 1920s Art Deco-style murals celebrating Bergen's fishing heritage.

• *Now, cross the street and immerse yourself in Bergen's beloved Fish Market.*

❻ Fish Market (Fisketorget)

A fish market has thrived here since the 1500s, when fishermen rowed in with their catch and haggled with hungry residents. While it's now become a food cir-cus of eateries selling fishy treats to tourists—no local would come here to actually buy fish—this famous market is still worth ▲, offering lots of smelly photo fun and free morsels to taste (June-Aug daily 7:00-19:00, less lively on Sun; Sept-May Mon-Sat 7:00-16:00, closed Sun). Many stands sell premade smoked-salmon *(laks)* sandwiches, fish soup, and other snacks ideal for a light lunch (confirm prices before ordering). To try Norwegian jerky, pick up a bag of dried cod snacks *(torsk)*. The red meat is minke (pronounced mink-ee) whale, caught off the coast of northern Norway. Norwegians, notorious for their whaling, defend it as a traditional livelihood for many of their people. They remind us that they only harvest the minke whale, which is not on an endangered list. In recent years, Norway has assigned itself a quota of nearly 1,300 minke whales a year, with the actual catch coming to a bit over half of that.

• *Watch your wallet: If you're going to get pickpocketed in Bergen, it'll likely be here. When done exploring, with your back to the market, hike a block to the right (note the pointy church spire in the distance and the big blocky stone monument dead ahead) into the modern part of town and a huge, wide square. Pause at the intersection just before crossing into the square, about 20 yards before the blocky monument. Look left to see Mount Ulriken with its TV tower. A cable car called Ulriken643 takes you to its 2,110-foot summit. (Shuttle buses leave from this corner, at the top and bottom of the hour, to its station; for summit details, see page 388.) Now, walk up to that big square monument and meet some Vikings.*

❼ Seafarers' Monument

Nicknamed "the cube of goat cheese" for its shape, this 1950 monument celebrates Bergen's contact with the sea and remembers those

who worked on it and died in it. Study the faces: All social classes are represented. The statues relate to the scenes depicted in the reliefs above. Each side represents a century (start with the Vikings and work clockwise): 10th century—Vikings, with a totem pole in the panel above recalling the pre-Columbian
Norwegian discovery of America; 18th century—equipping Europe's ships; 19th century—whaling; 20th century—shipping and war. For the 21st century, see the real people—a cross-section of today's Norway—sitting at the statue's base. Major department stores (Galleriet, Xhibition, and Telegrafen) are all nearby.

• *The monument marks the start of Bergen's main square...*

❽ Torgallmenningen

Allmenningen means "for all the people." Torg means "square." And, while this is the city's main gathering place, it was actually created as a firebreak. The residents of this wood-built city knew fires were inevitable. The street plan was designed with breaks, or open spaces like this square, to help contain the destruction. In 1916, it succeeded in stopping a fire, which is why it has a more modern feel today.

Walk the length of the square to the angled slab of blue stone (quarried in Brazil) at the far end. This is a monument to King Olav V, who died in 1991, and a popular meeting point: Locals like to say, "Meet you at the Blue Stone." It marks the center of a park-like swath known as...

❾ Ole Bulls Plass

This drag leads from the National Theater (above on right) to a little lake (below on left).

Detour a few steps up for a better look at the **National Theater,** built in Art Nouveau style in 1909. Founded by violinist Ole Bull in 1850, this was the first theater to host plays in the Norwegian language. After 450 years of Danish and Swedish rule, 19th-century Norway enjoyed a cultural awakening, and Bergen became an artistic power. Ole

BERGEN

The Hanseatic League, Blessed by Cod

Middlemen in trade, the clever German merchants of the Hanseatic League ruled the waves of northern Europe for 500 years (c. 1250-1750). These sea-traders first banded together in a Hanse, or merchant guild, to defend themselves against pirates. As they spread out from Germany, they established trading posts in foreign lands, cut deals with local leaders for trading rights, built boats and wharves, and organized armies to protect ships and ports.

By the 15th century, these merchants had organized more than a hundred cities into the Hanseatic League, a free-trade zone that stretched from London to Russia. The League ran a profitable triangle of trade: Fish from Scandinavia was exchanged for grain from the eastern Baltic and luxury goods from England and Flanders. Everyone benefited, and the German merchants—the middlemen—reaped the profits.

At its peak, in the 15th century, the Hanseatic League was the dominant force—economic, military, and political—in northern Europe. This was an age when much of Europe was fragmented into petty kingdoms and dukedoms. Revenue-hungry kings and robber-baron lords levied chaotic and extortionist tolls and duties. Pirates plagued shipments. It was the Hanseatic League, rather than national governments, that brought the stability that allowed trade to flourish.

Bull collaborated with the playwright Henrik Ibsen. Ibsen commissioned Edvard Grieg to compose the music for his play *Peer Gynt*. These three lions of Norwegian culture all lived and worked right here in Bergen.

Head downhill on the square to a delightful fountain featuring a **statue of Ole Bull** in the shadow of trees. Ole Bull was an 1800s version of Elvis. A pop idol and heartthrob in his day, Ole Bull's bath water was bottled and sold by hotels, and women fainted when they heard him play violin. Living up to his name, he fathered over 40 children. Speaking of children, I love to hang out here watching families frolic in the pond, oblivious to the waterfall troll (see the statue with the harp below Ole Bull). According to legend, the troll bestows musical talent on anyone—like old Ole—who gives him a gift (he likes meat).

From here, the park spills farther downhill to a cast-iron pavilion given to the city by Germans in 1889, and on to the little manmade lake (Lille Lungegårdsvann), which is circled by an en-

Bergen's place in this Baltic economy was all about cod—a form of protein that could be dried, preserved, and shipped anywhere. Though cursed by a lack of natural resources, the city was blessed with a good harbor conveniently located between the rich fishing spots of northern Norway and the markets of Europe. Bergen's port shipped dried cod and fish oil southward and imported grain, cloth, beer, wine, and ceramics.

Bryggen was one of four principal Hanseatic trading posts (Kontors), along with London, Bruges, and Novgorod. It was the last Kontor opened (c. 1360), the least profitable, and the final one to close. Bryggen had warehouses, offices, and living quarters. Ships docked here were unloaded by counterpoise cranes. At its peak, as many as a thousand merchants, journeymen, and apprentices lived and worked here.

Bryggen was a self-contained German enclave within the city. The merchants came from Germany, worked a few years here, and retired back in the home country. They spoke German, wore German clothes, and attended their own churches. By law, they were forbidden to intermarry or fraternize with the Bergeners, except on business.

The Hanseatic League peaked around 1500, then slowly declined. Rising nation-states were jealous of the Germans merchants' power and wealth. The Reformation tore apart old alliances. Dutch and English traders broke the Hanseatic monopoly. Cities withdrew from the League and Kontors closed. In 1754, Bergen's Kontor was taken over by the Norwegians. When it closed its doors on December 31, 1899, a sea-trading era was over, but the city of Bergen had become rich...by the grace of cod.

joyable path. This green zone is considered a park and is cared for by the local parks department.

• *If you're up for a lakeside stroll, now's your chance. Also notice that alongside the lake (to the right as you face it from here) is a row of buildings housing the enjoyable **Kode Art Museums**. And to the left of the lake are some fine residential streets (including the picturesque, cobbled Marken); within a few minutes' walk are the **Leprosy Museum** and the **cathedral**.*

Sights in Bergen

Several museums listed here—including the Bryggens Museum, Håkon's Hall, Rosenkrantz Tower, Leprosy Museum, and Gamle Bergen—are part of the Bergen City Museum (Bymuseet) organization. If you buy a ticket to any of them, you can pay half-price at any of the others simply by showing your ticket.

▲Bergenhus Fortress: Håkon's Hall and Rosenkrantz Tower

The tower and hall, sitting boldly out of place on the harbor just beyond Bryggen, are reminders of Bergen's importance as the first permanent capital of Norway. Both sights feel vacant and don't really speak for themselves; the included guided tours, which provide a serious introduction to Bergen's history, are essential for grasping their significance.

Cost and Hours: Hall and tower—90 kr for both (or 60 kr each), includes a guided tour; mid-May-Aug—hall open daily 10:00-16:00, tower open daily 9:00-16:00; Sept-mid-May—hall open daily 12:00-15:00, tower open Sun only 12:00-15:00; tel. 55 31 60 67, free WC.

Visiting the Hall and Tower: The hall and the tower are described in my "Bergen Walk," earlier. Consider them as one sight and start with Håkon's Hall (mid-May-Aug tours leave daily from the building to the right of Håkon's Hall at the top of the hour, last one departs at 15:00; few tours off-season). Tours include both buildings.

Håkon's Hall, dating from the 13th century, is the largest secular medieval building in Norway. Built as a banqueting hall, that's essentially what it is today. While it's been rebuilt, the ceiling's design is modeled after grand wooden roofs of that era. Beneath the hall is a whitewashed cellar.

Rosenkrantz Tower, the keep of a 13th-century castle, is today a stack of barren rooms connected by tight spiral staircases,

with a good history exhibit on the top two floors and a commanding view from its rooftop. In the 16th century, the ruling Danish-Norwegian king enlarged the tower and trained its cannon on the German-merchant district, Bryggen, to remind the merchants of the importance of paying their taxes.

Fortress Museum (Bergenhus Festningmuseum)

This humble museum (which functioned as a prison during the Nazi occupation), set back a couple of blocks from the fortress, will interest historians with its thoughtful exhibits about military history, especially Bergen's WWII experience (look for the Norwegian

Nazi flag). You'll learn about the resistance movement in Bergen (including its underground newspapers), the role of women in the Norwegian military, and Norwegian troops who have served with UN forces in overseas conflicts.

Cost and Hours: Free, daily 11:00-17:00, ask to borrow a translation of the descriptions at the entrance, just behind Thon Hotel Bergen Brygge at Koengen, tel. 55 54 63 87.

▲▲Bryggens Museum

This modern museum explains the 1950s archaeological dig to uncover the earliest bits of Bergen (1050-1500). Brief English explanations are posted. From September through May, when there is no tour, consider buying the good museum guidebook (25 kr).

Cost and Hours: 70 kr; in summer, entry included with Bryggen Walking Tour described earlier; mid-May-Aug daily 10:00-16:00; Sept-mid-May Mon-Fri 11:00-15:00, Sat 12:00-15:00, Sun 12:00-16:00; inexpensive cafeteria; in big, modern building just beyond the end of Bryggen and the Radisson Blu Royal Hotel, tel. 55 58 80 10, www.bymuseet.no.

Visiting the Museum: The manageable, well-presented permanent exhibit occupies the ground floor. First up are the foundations from original wooden tenements dating back to the 12th century (displayed right where they were excavated) and a giant chunk of the hull of a 100-foot-long, 13th-century ship that was found here. Next, an exhibit (roughly shaped like the long, wooden double-tenements outside) shows off artifacts and explains lifestyles from medieval Bryggen. Behind that is a display of items you might have bought at the medieval market. You'll finish with exhibits about the church in Bergen, the town's role as a royal capital, and its status as a cultural capital. Upstairs are two floors of temporary exhibits.

BERGEN

▲▲Hanseatic Museum (Hanseatiske Museum)

This little museum offers the best possible look inside the wooden houses that are Bergen's trademark. Its creaky old rooms—with hundred-year-old cod hanging from the ceiling—offer a time-tunnel experience back to Bryggen's glory days. It's located in an atmospheric old merchant house furnished with dried fish, antique ropes, an old oxtail (used for wringing spilled cod-liver oil back into the bucket), sagging steps, and cupboard beds from the early 1700s—one with a medieval pinup girl. You'll explore two upstairs levels, fully furnished and with funhouse floors. The place still feels eerily lived-in; neatly sorted desks with tidy ledgers seem to be waiting for the next workday to begin.

Cost and Hours: 70 kr; entry included with Bryggen Walking Tour; daily May-Sept 9:00-17:00; Oct-April Tue-Sat 11:00-14:00, Sun 11:00-16:00, closed Mon; Finnegården 7a, tel. 55 54 46 96 or 55 54 46 90, www.museumvest.no.

Tours: There are scant English explanations, but it's much better if you take the good, included 45-minute guided tour (3/day in English—call to confirm, mid-May-mid-Sept only, times displayed just inside door). Even if you tour the museum with the Bryggen Walking Tour, you're welcome to revisit (using the same ticket) and take this longer tour.

Theta Museum

This small museum highlights Norway's resistance movement. You'll peek into the hidden world of a 10-person cell of courageous students, whose group—called Theta—housed other fighters and communicated with London during the Nazi occupation in World War II. It's housed in Theta's former headquarters—a small upstairs room in a wooden Bryggen building.

Cost and Hours: 30 kr, June-Aug Tue, Sat, and Sun 14:00-16:00, closed Mon, Wed-Fri, and Sept-May, Enhjørningsgården.

▲▲Fløibanen Funicular

Bergen's popular funicular climbs 1,000 feet in seven minutes to the top of Mount Fløyen for the best view of the town, surrounding islands, and fjords all the way to the west coast. The top is a popular picnic or pizza-to-go dinner spot, perfect for enjoying the sunset (Peppes Pizza is tucked behind the Hanseatic Museum, a block away from the base of the lift). The Fløien Folkeres-taurant, at the top of the funicular, offers affordable self-service food all day in season. Behind the station, you'll find a playground and a fun giant troll photo op. The top is also the starting point for many peaceful hikes.

You'll buy your funicular ticket at the base of the Fløibanen (notice the photos in the entry hall of the construction of the funicular and its 1918 grand opening).

If you'll want to hike down from the top, ask for the *Fløyen Hiking Map* when you buy your ticket; you'll save 50 percent by purchasing only a one-way ticket up. From the top, walk behind the

station and follow the signs to the city center. The top half of the 30-minute hike is a gravelly lane through a forest with fine views. The bottom is a paved lane through charming old wooden homes. It's a steep descent. To save your knees, you could ride the lift most of the way down and get off at the Promsgate stop to wander through the delightful cobbled and shiplap lanes (note that only the :00 and :30 departures stop at Promsgate).

Cost and Hours: 85 kr round-trip, 43 kr one-way, Mon-Fri 7:30-23:00, Sat-Sun 8:00-23:00, departures 4/hour—on the quarter-hour most of the day, runs continuously if busy, tel. 55 33 68 00, www.floibanen.no.

Cathedral (Domkirke)

Bergen's main church, dedicated to St. Olav (the patron saint of Norway), dates from 1301. Drop in to enjoy its stoic, plain interior with stuccoed stone walls and a giant wooden pulpit. Sit in a hard, straight-backed pew and just try to doze off. Like so many old Norwegian structures, its roof makes you feel like you're huddled under an overturned Viking ship. The church is oddly lopsided, with just one side aisle. Before leaving, look up to see the gorgeous wood-carved organ over the main entrance. In the entryway, you'll see portraits of each bishop dating all the way back to the Reformation.

Cost and Hours: Free; mid-June-mid-Aug Mon-Fri 10:00-16:00, Sun 9:30-13:00, closed Sat; shorter hours off-season.

Leprosy Museum (Lepramuseet)

Leprosy is also known as "Hansen's Disease" because in the 1870s a Bergen man named Armauer Hansen did groundbreaking work in understanding the ailment. This unique museum is in St. Jørgens Hospital, a leprosarium that dates back to about 1700. Up until the 19th century, as much as 3 percent of Norway's population had leprosy. This hospital—once called "a grave-yard for the living" (its last pa-

tient died in 1946)—has a meager exhibit in a thought-provoking dorm for the dying. It's most worthwhile if you read the translation of the exhibit (borrow a copy at the entry) or take the free tour (at the top of each hour). As you leave, if you're interested, ask if you can see the medicinal herb garden out back.

Cost and Hours: 70 kr, mid-May-Aug daily 11:00-15:00, closed Sept-mid-May, between train station and Bryggen at Kong Oscars Gate 59, tel. 55 96 11 55, www.bymuseet.no.

▲Kode Art Museums of Bergen (Kunstmuseene i Bergen)

If you need to get out of the rain (and you enjoyed the National Gallery in Oslo), check out this collection, filling four neighboring buildings facing the lake along Rasmus Meyers Allé. The Lysverket building has an eclectic cross-section of both international and Norwegian artists. The Rasmus Meyer branch specializes in Norwegian artists and has an especially good Munch exhibit. The Stenersen building has installations of contemporary art, while the Permanenten building has decorative arts. Small description sheets in English are in each room.

Cost and Hours: 100 kr, daily 11:00-17:00, closed Mon mid-Sept-mid-May, Rasmus Meyers Allé 3, tel. 55 56 80 00, www.kunstmuseene.no.

Visiting the Museums: Many visitors focus on the **Lysverket** ("Lighthouse"; from outside, enter through Door 4), featuring

an easily digestible collection. Here are some of its highlights: The ground floor includes an extensive display of works by Nikolai Astrup (1880-1928), who depicts Norway's fjords with bright colors and Expressionistic flair. One flight up is a great collection of J. C. Dahl and his students, who captured the majesty of Norway's natural wonders (look for Adelsteen Normann's impressive, photorealistic view of Romsdalfjord). "Norwegian Art 1840-1900" includes works by Christian Krohg, as well as some portraits by Harriet Backer. Also on this floor are icons and various European Old Masters.

Up on the third floor, things get modern. The Tower Hall (Tårnsalen) features Norwegian modernism and a large exhibit of Bergen's avant-garde art (1966-1985), kicked off by "Group 66." The International Modernism section has four stars: Pablo Picasso (sketches, etchings, collages, and a few Cubist paintings), Paul Klee (the Swiss childlike painter), and the dynamic Norwegian duo of Edvard Munch and Ludvig Karisten. Rounding it out are a smattering of Surrealist, Abstract Expressionist, and Op Art pieces.

▲Aquarium (Akvariet)

Small but fun, this aquarium claims to be the second-most-visited sight in Bergen. It's wonderfully laid out and explained in English.

Check out the view from inside the "shark tunnel" in the tropical shark exhibit.

Cost and Hours: 250 kr, kids-150 kr, daily May-Aug 10:00-18:00, Sept-mid-Oct daily 10:00-16:00, mid-Oct-April Tue-Sun 10:00-16:00, closed Mon, feeding times at the top of most hours in summer, cheery cafeteria with light sandwiches, Nordnesbakken 4, tel. 40 10 24 20, www.akvariet.no.

Getting There: It's at the tip of the peninsula on the south end of the harbor—about a 20-minute walk or short ride on bus #11 from the city center. Or hop on the handy little *Vågen* "Akvariet" ferry that sails from the Fish Market to near the aquarium (50 kr one-way, 80 kr round-trip, 2/hour, June-Aug 10:00-17:30, off-season until 16:00).

Nearby: The lovely park behind the aquarium has views of the sea and a popular swimming beach (described later, under "Activities in Bergen"). The totem pole erected here was a gift from Bergen's sister city in the US—Seattle.

▲Gamle Bergen (Old Bergen)

This Disney-cute gathering of 50-some 18th- through 20th-century homes and shops was founded in 1934 to save old buildings from destruction as Bergen modernized. Each of the buildings was moved from elsewhere in Bergen and reconstructed here. Together, they create a virtual town that offers a cobbled look at the old life. It's free to wander through the town and park to enjoy the facades of the historic buildings, but to get into the 20 or so museum buildings, you'll have to join a tour (departing on the hour 10:00-16:00).

Cost and Hours: Free entry, 80-kr tour (in English) required for access to buildings, mid-May-Aug daily 9:00-16:00, closed Sept-mid-May, tel. 55 39 43 04, www.bymuseet.no.

Getting There: Take any bus heading west from Bryggen (such as #6, direction: Lønborglien) to Gamle Bergen (stop: Nyhavnsveien). You'll get off after the tunnel at a freeway pullout and walk 200 yards, following signs to the museum. Any bus heading back into town takes you to the center (buses come by every few minutes). With the easy bus connection, there's no reason to taxi.

ACTIVITIES IN BERGEN
▲Strolling

Bergen is a great town for wandering. Enjoy a little Norwegian paseo. On a balmy Norwegian summer evening, I'd stroll from the castle, along the harborfront, up the main square to Ole Bulls Plass, and around the lake.

Shopping

Most shops are open Mon-Fri 9:00-17:00, Thu until 19:00, Sat 9:00-15:00, and closed Sunday. Many of the tourist shops at the harborfront strip along Bryggen are open daily—even during holidays—until 20:00 or 21:00.

Ting (Things) offers a fun alternative to troll shopping, with contemporary housewares and quirky gift ideas (daily 10:00-22:30, at Bryggen 13, a block past the Hanseatic Museum, tel. 55 21 54 80).

Husfliden is a shop popular for its handmade goodies and reliably Norwegian sweaters (fine variety and quality but expensive, just off Torget, the market square, at Vågsallmenninge 3, tel. 55 54 47 40).

The Galleriet Mall, a shopping center on Torgallmenningen, holds six floors of shops, cafés, and restaurants. You'll find a pharmacy, photo shops, clothing, sporting goods, bookstores, mobile-phone shops, and a basement grocery store (Mon-Fri 9:00-21:00, Sat 9:00-18:00, closed Sun).

Swimming

Bergen has two seaside public swimming areas: one at the aquarium and the other in Gamle Bergen. Each is a great local scene on a hot sunny day. **Nordnes Sjøbad,** near the aquarium, offers swimmers an outdoor heated pool and a protected area of the sea (65 kr, kids-30 kr, mid-May-Aug Mon-Fri 7:00-19:00, Sat 7:00-14:00, Sun 10:00-14:00, Sat-Sun until 19:00 in good weather, closed off-season, Nordnesparken 30, tel. 53 03 91 90). **Sandviken Sjobad,** at Gamle Bergen, is free and open all summer. It comes with changing rooms, a roped-off bit of the bay (no pool), a high dive, and lots of sunbathing space.

SIGHTS NEAR BERGEN
▲Ulriken643 Cable Car

It's amazingly easy and quick to zip up six minutes to the 643-meter-high (that's 2,110 feet) summit of Ulriken, the tallest mountain near Bergen. Stepping out of the cable car, you enter a different

world, with views stretching to the ocean. A chart clearly shows the many well-marked and easy hikes that fan out over the vast, rocky, grassy plateau above the tree line (circular walks of various lengths, a 40-minute hike down, and a 4-hour hike to the top of the Fløibanen funicular). For less exercise, you can simply sunbathe, crack open a picnic, or enjoy the Ulriken restaurant.

Cost and Hours: 150 kr round-trip, 90 kr one-way, 8/hour, daily 9:00-21:00, off-season 9:00-17:00, tel. 53 64 36 43, www. ulriken643.no.

Getting There: It's about three miles southeast of Bergen. From the Fish Market, you can take a blue double-decker shuttle bus that includes the cost of the cable-car ride (250 kr, ticket valid 24 hours, May-Sept daily 9:00-17:00, 2/hour, departs from the corner of Torgallmenningen and Strandgaten, buy ticket as you board or at TI). Alternatively, the public bus stops 200 yards from the lift station.

▲▲Edvard Grieg's Home, Troldhaugen

Norway's greatest composer spent his last 22 summers here (1885-1907), soaking up inspirational fjord beauty and composing many

of his greatest works. Grieg fused simple Norwegian folk tunes with the bombast of Europe's Romantic style. In a dreamy Victorian setting, Grieg's "Hill of the Trolls" is pleasant for anyone and essential for diehard fans. You can visit his house on your own, but it's more enjoyable if you take the included 20-minute tour. The house and adjacent museum are full of memories and artifacts, including the composer's Steinway. The walls are festooned with photos of the musical and literary superstars of his generation. When the hugely popular Grieg died in 1907, 40,000 mourners attended his funeral. His little studio hut near the water makes you want to sit down and modulate.

Cost and Hours: 90 kr, includes guided tour in English, daily May-Sept 9:00-18:00, Oct-April 10:00-16:00, café, tel. 55 92 29 92, www.troldhaugen.com.

Grieg Lunch Concert: Troldhaugen offers a great guided tour/concert package that includes a shuttle bus from the Bergen TI to the doorstep of Grieg's home on the fjord (departs 11:30), an hour-long tour of the home, a half-hour concert (Grieg's greatest piano hits, at 13:00), and the ride back into town (you're back in the center by 14:00). Your guide will narrate the ride out of town as well as take you around Grieg's house (250 kr, daily June-mid-Sept). Lunch isn't included, but there is a café on site, or you could bring a sandwich along. You can skip the return bus ride and spend more time in Troldhaugen. While the tour rarely sells out, it's wise to drop by the TI earlier that day to reserve your spot.

Evening Concerts: Ask at the TI about piano performances in the concert hall at Grieg's home—a gorgeous venue with the fjord stretching out behind the big black grand piano (220 kr, 150 kr with Bergen Card, concerts roughly mid-June-late Aug Sun at 18:00, free round-trip shuttle bus leaves TI at 17:00, show your concert ticket).

Getting to Troldhaugen: It's six miles south of Bergen. The **tram** drops you a long 20-minute walk away from Troldhaugen. Catch the tram in the city center at its terminus near Byparken (between the lake and Ole Bulls Plass), ride it for about 25 minutes, and get off at the stop called Hop. Walk in the direction of Bergen (about 25 yards), cross at the crosswalk, and follow signs to Troldhaugen. Part of the way is on a pedestrian/bike path; you're halfway there when the path crosses over a busy highway. If you want to make the 13:00 lunch-time concert, leave Bergen at 12:00.

To avoid the long walk from the tram stop, consider the Grieg Lunch Concert package (described earlier). If you're driving into Bergen from the east (such as from the Sognefjord), you'll drive right by Troldhaugen on your way into town.

Fantoft Stave Church

This huge, preserved-in-tar stave church burned down in 1992. It was rebuilt and reopened in 1997, but it will never be the same (for more on stave churches, see page 211). Situated in a quiet forest next to a mysterious stone cross, this replica of a 12th-century wooden church is bigger, though no better, than others covered in this book. But it's worth a look if you're in the neighborhood, even after-hours, for its atmospheric setting.

Cost and Hours: 50 kr, mid-May-mid-Sept daily 10:30-18:00, interior closed off-season, no English information, tel. 55 28 07 10, www.fantoftstavkirke.com.

Getting There: It's three miles south of Bergen on E-39 in Paradis. Take the tram (from Byparken, between the lake and Ole Bulls Plass) or bus #83 (from Torget, by the Fish Market) to the Paradis stop (not the "Fantoft" stop). From Paradis, walk uphill to the parking lot on the left, and find the steep footpath to the church.

BERGEN NIGHTSPOTS

With the high latitude, Bergen stays light until 23:00 in the summer. On warm evenings, people are out enjoying the soft light and the mellow scene.

For a selection of cool nightspots, visit the **Pingvinen Pub** and **Café Opera** (both described in "Eating in Bergen," later) and explore the neighboring streets.

For something a little funkier, **Skostredet** ("Shoe Street," recalling the days when cobblers set up shop here) is emerging as the hip, bohemian-chic area. You'll sort through cafés, pubs, and retro shops. There's an American-style Rock and Roll '59er Diner. And **Folk og Røvere** ("People and Robbers") is an unpretentious bar with cheap beer (nightly until late, Skostredet 12).

For candlelit elegance, enjoy a drink at the historic **Dyvekes Wine Cellar.** Named for the mistress of King Christian II of Denmark (her portrait is on the signboard hanging above the door), the atmosphere of the ground-floor bar and the cellar downstairs is hard to beat (daily from 15:00, 80-90 kr for wine by glass, beer on tap, Hollendergaten 7).

For live blues, try **Madam Felle Nightclub** (on the Bryggen strip), which has live music many evenings (often without a cover).

And if you're really drunk at 3:00 in the morning and need a spicy hotdog, the **3-Kroneren** *pølse* stand is open (described in "Eating in Bergen," later).

Sleeping in Bergen

Busy with business travelers and popular with tourists, Bergen can be jammed any time of year. Even with this crush, proud and pricey hotels may be willing to make deals. You might save a bundle by checking the websites of the bigger hotels for their best prices. Otherwise, Bergen has some fine budget alternatives to normal hotels that can save you money.

HOTELS

$$$ Hotel Havnekontoret, with 116 rooms and the best location in town, fills a grand old shipping headquarters dating from the 1920s. It's an especially fine value on weekends and in the summer, for those who eat the included dinner. While part of a chain, it has a friendly spirit. Guests are welcome to climb its historic tower (with a magnificent view) or enjoy its free sauna and exercise room downstairs. If you aren't interested in fancy dining, the room price includes virtually all your food—a fine breakfast, self-service waffles and pancakes in the afternoon, fruit and coffee all day, and a light dinner buffet each evening. If you take advantage of them (and the free loaner bikes for guests), these edible extras are easily

---

Sleep Code

Abbreviations   **(6 kr = about $1, country code: 47)**
S = Single, **D** = Double/Twin, **T** = Triple, **Q** = Quad, **b** = bathroom
Price Rankings
  $$$ Higher Priced—Most rooms 1,400 kr or more.
   $$ Moderately Priced—Most rooms 900-1,400 kr.
    $ Lower Priced—Most rooms 900 kr or less.
Hotel staff speak English, breakfast is included, Wi-Fi is generally free, and credit cards are accepted unless otherwise noted. Prices change; verify current rates online or by email. For the best prices, always book directly with the hotel.

---

worth 600 kr per day per couple, making the cost of this fancy hotel little more than a hostel (Db 1,700-2,300 kr, extra bed-300 kr, book online to save, Wi-Fi, facing the harbor across the street from the Radisson Blu Royal Hotel at Slottsgaten 1, tel. 55 60 11 00, www.choicehotels.no, cc.havnekontoret@choice.no).

$$$ Hotel Park Bergen is classy, comfortable, and in a fine residential neighborhood a 15-minute uphill walk from the town center (10 minutes from the train station). It's tinseled in Old World, lived-in charm, yet comes with all of today's amenities. The 35 rooms are split between two buildings, with 22 in the classy old-fashioned hotel and 13 in the modern annex across the street (Sb-1,110 kr, Db-1,500 kr, extra bed-350 kr, winter weekend discounts, Wi-Fi, Harald Hårfagres Gate 35, tel. 55 54 44 00, www.hotelpark.no, booking@hotelpark.no).

$$$ Thon Hotel Rosenkrantz, with 129 rooms, is one block behind Bryggen, between the Bryggens Museum and the Fløibanen funicular station—right in the heart of Bergen's appealing old quarter. However, the next-door nightclub is noisy on Friday and Saturday nights—be sure to request a quiet room (average rates: Sb-1,295-2,095 kr, Db-1,095-2,295 kr, elevator, guest computer, Wi-Fi, Rosenkrantzgaten 7, tel. 55 30 14 00, www.thonhotels.no/rosenkrantz, rosenkrantz@thonhotels.no).

$$ P-Hotel has 43 basic rooms just up from Ole Bulls Plass. While it's not particularly charming and some rooms come with street noise, it's got a prime location. Ask for a room facing the courtyard in the renovated wing (Sb-975 kr, Db-1,350 kr, prices vary—check online for best deal, credit card only—no cash, box breakfast in your room, elevator, Wi-Fi, Vestre Torggate 9, tel. 80 04 68 35, www.p-hotels.no, bergen@p-hotels.no).

$$ Thon Hotel Bergen Brygge, beyond Bryggen near Håkon's Hall, is part of Thon's cheaper "Budget" chain. However, the 229 spartan rooms can be just about as nice as those in its sister hotels. Because of its relatively good prices and great location, it fills up quickly—book ahead. Light sleepers, beware: Many rooms face the fortress grounds, which sometimes host summer evening concerts. Ask for a room on the quiet side, bring earplugs, or go elsewhere (Db-925-1,500 kr, you save if you book online, elevator, guest computer, Wi-Fi, Bradbenken 3, tel. 55 30 87 00, www.thonhotels.com/bergenbrygge, bergen.brygge@thonhotels.no).

$$ Basic Hotel Victoria is an old hotel turned into a college dorm that becomes a utilitarian, minimalist budget hotel each summer. There are no public spaces, the tiny reception is open only 9:00-23:00, and you won't get your towels changed. But its 43 modern, bright, simple rooms are plenty comfortable for the price (open June-Aug only, Sb-995 kr, Db-1,095 kr, Tb-1,395 kr, Wi-Fi, Kong Oscars Gate 29, tel. 55 31 44 04, www.basichotels.no, victoria@basichotels.no).

$ Citybox is a unique, no-nonsense hotel concept: plain, white, clean, and practical. It rents 55 rooms online and provides you with a confirmation number. Check-in is automated—just punch in your number and get your ticket. The call-in reception is staffed daily 9:00-17:00, except May-Oct until 23:00 (S-600 kr, Sb-700 kr, D-950 kr, Db-1,050 kr, extra bed-150 kr, family room for up to four-1,450 kr, prices fluctuate—check online for best deals, no breakfast, elevator, just away from the bustle in a mostly residential part of town at Nygårdsgaten 31, tel. 55 31 25 00, www.citybox.no, post@citybox.no).

PRIVATE HOMES AND PENSIONS

If you're looking for local character and don't mind sharing a shower, these accommodations—far more quiet, homey, and convenient than hostel beds—might just be the best values in town. Both require guests to climb outdoor stairways, which may be tough for those not packing light.

$ Guest House Skiven is a humble little place beautifully situated on a steep, traffic-free cobbled lane called "the most painted street in Bergen." Alf and Elizabeth Heskja (who live upstairs) rent four bright, non-smoking doubles that share a shower, two WCs, and a kitchen (D-650 kr for Rick Steves readers, no breakfast, Wi-Fi, 4 blocks from train station, at Skivebakken 17, mobile 90 05 30 30, www.skiven.no, rs@skiven.no). From the train station, go down Kong Oscars Gate, uphill on D. Krohns Gate, and up the stairs at the end of the block on the left.

$ Skansen Pensjonat (not to be confused with the nearby Skansen Apartments) is situated 100 yards directly behind the entrance to the Fløibanen funicular. Jannicke Alvær rents seven tastefully decorated rooms with views over town (small non-view

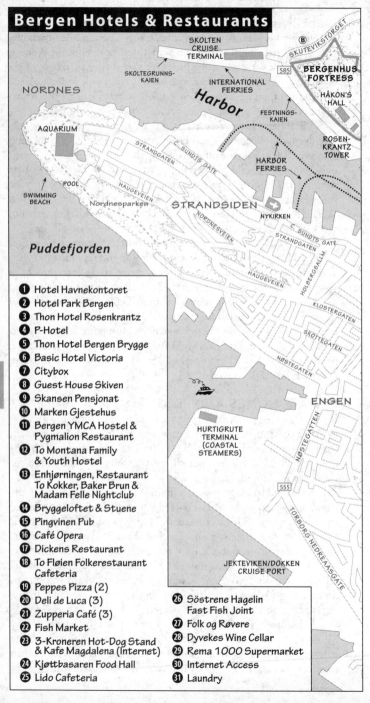

Bergen Hotels & Restaurants

1. Hotel Havnekontoret
2. Hotel Park Bergen
3. Thon Hotel Rosenkrantz
4. P-Hotel
5. Thon Hotel Bergen Brygge
6. Basic Hotel Victoria
7. Citybox
8. Guest House Skiven
9. Skansen Pensjonat
10. Marken Gjestehus
11. Bergen YMCA Hostel & Pygmalion Restaurant
12. To Montana Family & Youth Hostel
13. Enhjørningen, Restaurant To Kokker, Baker Brun & Madam Felle Nightclub
14. Bryggeloftet & Stuene
15. Pingvinen Pub
16. Café Opera
17. Dickens Restaurant
18. To Fløien Folkerestaurant Cafeteria
19. Peppes Pizza (2)
20. Deli de Luca (3)
21. Zupperia Café (3)
22. Fish Market
23. 3-Kroneren Hot-Dog Stand & Kafe Magdalena (Internet)
24. Kjøttbasaren Food Hall
25. Lido Cafeteria
26. Söstrene Hagelin Fast Fish Joint
27. Folk og Røvere
28. Dyvekes Wine Cellar
29. Rema 1000 Supermarket
30. Internet Access
31. Laundry

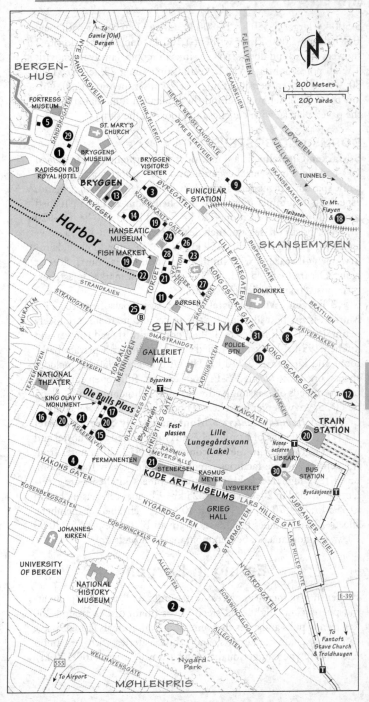

BERGEN

S-500 kr, larger S-550 kr, D-900 kr, fancy D on corner with view and balcony-1,000 kr, apartment-1,100 kr, includes breakfast, 2 showers on ground floor, 2 WCs, sinks in rooms, family room with TV; all non-smoking, Wi-Fi, Vetrlidsalmenning 29, tel. 55 31 90 80, www.skansen-pensjonat.no, post@skansen-pensjonat.no). Follow the switchback road behind the Fløibanen funicular station to the paved plateau with benches, and look for the sign.

DORMS AND HOSTELS

$ Marken Gjestehus is a quiet, tidy, and conveniently positioned 100-bed place between the station and the harborfront. Its rooms, while spartan, are modern and cheery. Prices can rise with demand, especially in summer (dorm bed in 8-bed room-270 kr, in 10-bed room-280 kr, in 4-bed room-320 kr, S-600 kr, D-750 kr, Db-920 kr, lower prices off-season, includes sheets, extra bed-135 kr, towels-15 kr, breakfast voucher-130 kr, Wi-Fi, elevator, kitchen, laundry, open all year but with limited reception hours, fourth floor at Kong Oscars Gate 45, tel. 55 31 44 04, www.marken-gjestehus.com, post@marken-gjestehus.com).

$ Bergen YMCA Hostel, located two blocks from the Fish Market, is the best location for the price, and its rooms are nicely maintained (bunk in 12- to 32-bed dorm with shared shower and kitchen-195 kr, bunk in 4-6-bed family room with private bathroom and kitchen-280-320 kr, Db with kitchen-950 kr, includes sheets, breakfast-65 kr, Wi-Fi, roof terrace, fully open June-Aug, few dorm beds off-season, Nedre Korskirkeallmenningen 4, tel. 55 60 60 55, www.bergenhostel.com, booking@bergenhostel.com).

Away from the Center: **$ Montana Family & Youth Hostel (IYHF),** while one of Europe's best, is high-priced for a hostel and way out of town. Still, the bus connections (#12, 20 minutes from the center) and the facilities—modern rooms, classy living room, no curfew, huge free parking lot, and members' kitchen—are excellent (dorm bed in 20-bed room-225 kr—cheaper off-season, bed in Q-295 kr, Sb-670 kr, Db-850 kr, 10 percent cheaper for members, sheets-70 kr, includes breakfast, 30 Johan Blytts Vei, tel. 55 20 80 70, www.montana.no, bergen.montana@hihostels.no).

Eating in Bergen

Bergen has numerous choices: restaurants with rustic, woody atmosphere, candlelight, and steep prices (main dishes around 300 kr); trendy pubs and cafés that offer good-value meals (100-190 kr); cafeterias, chain restaurants, and ethnic eateries with less ambience where you can get quality food at lower prices (100-150 kr);

and takeaway sandwich shops, bakeries, and cafés for a light bite (50-100 kr).

You can always get a glass or pitcher of water at no charge, and fancy places give you free seconds on potatoes—just ask. Remember, if you get your food to go, it's taxed at a lower rate and you'll save 12 percent.

SPLURGES IN BRYGGEN

You'll pay a premium to eat at these restaurants, but you'll have a memorable meal in a pleasant setting. If they appear to be beyond your budget, remember that you can fill up on potatoes and drink tap water to dine for exactly the price of the dinner plate.

Enhjørningen Restaurant ("The Unicorn") is *the* place in Bergen for fish. With thickly painted walls and no right angles, this dressy-yet-old-time wooden interior wins my "Bryggen Atmosphere" award. The dishes, while not hearty, are close to gour-

met and beautifully presented (320-350-kr main dishes, 580-620-kr multicourse meals, nightly 16:00-22:30, reservations smart, #29 on Bryggen harborfront—look for anatomically correct unicorn on the old wharf facade and dip into the alley and up the stairs, tel. 55 30 69 50, www.enhjorningen.no).

Restaurant To Kokker, down the alley from Enhjørningen (and with the same owners), serves more meat and game. The prices and quality are equivalent, but even though it's also in an elegant old wooden building, I like The Unicorn's atmosphere much better (350-kr mains, 625-750-kr multicourse meals, Mon-Sat 17:00-23:00, closed Sun, tel. 55 30 69 55).

Bryggeloftet & Stuene Restaurant, in a brick building just before the wooden stretch of Bryggen, is a vast eatery serving seafood, vegetarian, and traditional meals. To dine memorably yet affordably, this is your best Bryggen bet. Upstairs feels more elegant and less touristy than the main floor—if there's a line downstairs, just head on up (150-180-kr lunches, 200-350-kr dinners, Mon-Sat 11:00-23:30, Sun 13:00-23:30, try reserving a view window upstairs—no reservations for outside seating, #11 on Bryggen harborfront, tel. 55 30 20 70).

BERGEN

NEAR THE FISH MARKET

Pygmalion Restaurant has a happy salsa vibe, with local art on the walls and a fun, healthy international menu. It's run with creativity and passion by Sissel. Her burgers are a hit, and there are always good vegetarian options, hearty salads, and pancakes (80-kr wraps, 180-kr burgers, 150-200-kr main plates, daily 11:00-22:00, two blocks inland from the Fish Market at Nedre Korskirkealmenning 4, tel. 55 31 32 60).

CHARACTERISTIC PLACES NEAR OLE BULLS PLASS

Bergen's "in" cafés are stylish, cozy, small, and open very late—a great opportunity to experience its yuppie scene. Around the cinema on Neumannsgate, there are numerous ethnic restaurants, including Italian, Middle Eastern, and Chinese.

Pingvinen Pub ("The Penguin") is a homey place in a charming neighborhood, serving traditional Norwegian home cooking to an enthusiastic local clientele. The pub has only indoor seating, with a long row of stools at the bar and five charming, living-room-cozy tables—a great setup for solo diners. After the kitchen closes, the place stays open very late as a pub. For Norwegian fare in a completely untouristy atmosphere, this is a good, affordable option. Their seasonal menu (reindeer in the fall, whale in the spring) is listed on the board (160-220-kr main dishes, nightly until 22:00, Vaskerelven 14 near the National Theater, tel. 55 60 46 46).

Café Opera, with a playful-slacker vibe and chessboards for the regulars, is the hip budget choice for its loyal, youthful following. With two floors of seating and tables out front across from the theater, it's a winner (light 60-80-kr sandwiches until 16:00, 100-200-kr dinners, daily 10:00-24:00, Engen 18, tel. 55 23 03 15).

Dickens is a lively, checkerboard-tiled, turn-of-the-century-feeling place. The window tables in the atrium are great for people-watching, as is the fine outdoor terrace, but you'll pay higher prices for the view (200-kr lunches, 250-300-kr dinners, daily 11:00-23:00, Kong Olav V's Plass 4, tel. 55 36 31 30).

ATOP MOUNT FLØYEN, AT THE TOP OF THE FUNICULAR

Fløien Folkerestaurant Cafeteria offers meals indoors and out with a panoramic view. It's self-service, with sandwiches for around 60 kr and a 139-kr soup buffet (May-Aug daily 10:00-22:00, Sept-April Sat-Sun only 12:00-17:00, tel. 55 33 69 99).

GOOD CHAIN RESTAURANTS

You'll find these chain restaurants in Bergen and throughout Norway. All are open long hours daily. In good weather, enjoy a takeout meal with sun-worshipping locals in Bergen's parks.

Peppes Pizza has cold beer and good pizzas (medium size for 1-2 people-200-220 kr, large for 2-3 people-220-300 kr, takeout possible; consider the Thai Chicken, with satay-marinated chicken, pineapple, peanuts, and coriander). There are six Peppes in Bergen, including one behind the Hanseatic Museum near the Fløibanen funicular station and another inside the Zachariasbryggen harborfront complex, next to the Fish Market (with views over the harbor).

Baker Brun makes 50-70-kr sandwiches, including wonderful shrimp baguettes and pastries such as *skillingsbolle*—cinnamon rolls—warm out of the oven. Their branch in the Bryggen quarter is a prime spot for a simple, inexpensive bite (open from 7:00, seating inside or takeaway).

Deli de Luca is a cut above other takeaway joints, adding sushi, noodle dishes, and calzones to the normal lineup of sandwiches. While a bit more expensive than the others, the variety and quality are appealing (open 24/7, 60-kr sandwiches and calzones, branches in train station and near Ole Bulls Plass at Torggaten 5, branch with indoor seating on corner of Engen and Vaskerelven, tel. 55 23 11 47).

Zupperia is a lively, popular chain that offers burgers, salads, Norwegian fare, and Asian dishes for 75 to 150 kr; their Thai soup is a local favorite. For a lighter meal, order off the lunch menu (120-150 kr) any time of day (daily 12:00-22:00, but Nordahl Bruns location closed Mon). Branches are across from the Fish Market at Market 13, near the National Theater at Vaskerelven 12, and between Ole Bulls Plass and the lake (Nordahl Bruns Gate 9).

BUDGET BETS NEAR THE FISH MARKET

The Fish Market has lots of stalls bursting with salmon sandwiches, fresh shrimp, fish-and-chips, and fish cakes. For a tasty, memorable, and inexpensive Bergen meal, assemble a seafood picnic here (ask for prices first; June-Aug daily 7:00-19:00; Sept-May Mon-Sat 7:00-16:00, closed Sun). Also be sure to peruse the places next door in the ground floor of the TI building, Torghallen.

3-Kroneren, your classic hot-dog stand, sells a wide variety of sausages (various sizes and flavors—including reindeer). The well-described English menu makes it easy to order your choice of artery-clogging guilty pleasures (20-kr tiny weenie, 55-kr medium-size weenie, 75-kr jumbo, open daily from 11:00 until 5:00 in the morning, you'll see the little hot-dog shack a block up Kong Oscars

Gate from the harbor, Kenneht is the boss). Each dog comes with a free little glass of fruit punch.

Kjøttbasaren, upstairs in the restored meat market of 1887, is a genteel-feeling food hall with stalls selling groceries such as meat, cheese, bread, and olives, plus *lefse*, reindeer sausage, and goat cheese—a great opportunity to assemble a bang-up picnic (Mon-Fri 10:00-17:00, Thu until 18:00, Sat 9:00-16:00, closed Sun). You can picnic at the top or bottom of the Fløibanen funicular, just up the street.

Lido Cafeteria offers basic, affordable food with great harbor and market views, better ambience than most self-service places, and a museum's worth of old-town photos on the walls. For cold items (such as 50-100-kr open-face sandwiches and desserts), grab what you want, pay the cashier, and find a table. For hot dishes (120-170-kr Norwegian standards, including one daily special discounted to 110 kr), get a table, order and pay at the cashier, and they'll bring your food to you (120-kr salad bar, Mon-Fri 10:00-19:00, Sat and Sun 10:00-18:00; second floor at Torgallmenningen 1a, tel. 55 32 59 12).

Söstrene Hagelin Fast Fish Joint is an easygoing eatery that's cheerier than its offerings—a dreary extravaganza of Norway's white cuisine. It's all fish here: fish soup, fish burgers, fish balls, fish cakes, and even fish pudding (meals for around 60 kr, Mon-Sat 10:00-22:00, Sun 12:00-18:00, Kong Oscars Gate 2).

Kafe Magdalena, a humble little community center just two blocks off the Fish Market, is run by the church and staffed by volunteers. While it's designed to give Bergen's poor citizens an inviting place to enjoy, everyone's welcome (it's a favorite of local guides). There's little choice here; the menu is driven by what's available to the mission cheap (40-kr daily plate, 70 kr for bigger meal served after 13:30, nice cheap open-face sandwiches, waffles, coffee, Mon-Fri 11:00-16:00, closed Sat-Sun, Kong Oscars Gate 5). They have two computer terminals with Internet access and free Wi-Fi.

PICNICS AND GROCERIES

While you'll be tempted to drop into 7-Eleven-type stores, you'll pay for the convenience. Pick up your groceries for half the price at a real supermarket. The **Rema 1000 supermarket,** just across from the Bryggens Museum and St. Mary's Church, is particularly handy (Mon-Fri 7:00-23:00, Sat 8:00-21:00, closed Sun).

Bergen Connections

Bergen is conveniently connected to **Oslo** by plane and train (trains depart Bergen daily at 7:57, 11:59, 15:59, and 22:59—but no night train on Sat, arrive at Oslo seven scenic hours later, additional departures in summer and fall, confirm times at station, 50-kr seat reservation required—but free with first-class rail pass, book well in advance if traveling mid-July-Aug). From Bergen, you can take the Norway in a Nutshell train/bus/ferry route; for information, see the Norway in a Nutshell chapter. Train info: tel. 81 50 08 88, and then 9 for English, www.nsb.no.

To get to **Stockholm** or **Copenhagen,** you'll go via Oslo (see "Oslo Connections" on page 286). Before buying a ticket for a long train trip from Bergen, look into cheap flights.

By Express Boat to Balestrand and Flåm (on Sognefjord): A handy express boat links Bergen with Balestrand (4 hours) and Flåm (5.5 hours). For details, see page 332.

By Bus to Kristiansand: If you're heading to Denmark on the ferry from Kristiansand, catch the Haukeli express bus (departing Bergen daily at 8:25). After a nearly two-hour layover in Haukeli, take the bus at 14:55, arriving at 19:00 in Kristiansand in time for the evening ferry to Denmark (for boat details, see page 416).

By Boat to Denmark: Fjordline runs a boat from Bergen to Hirtshals, Denmark (18 hours; departs daily at 13:30; boat from Hirtshals departs daily at 20:00; seat in reclining chair around 1,750 kr, tel. 81 53 35 00, www.fjordline.com).

By Boat to the Arctic: Hurtigruten coastal steamers depart nearly daily (June-Oct at 20:00, Nov-May at 22:30) for the seven-day trip north up the scenic west coast to Kirkenes on the Russian border.

This route was started in 1893 as a postal and cargo delivery service along the west coast of Norway. Although no longer delivering mail, their ships still fly the Norwegian postal flag by special permission and deliver people, cars, and cargo from Bergen to Kirkenes. A lifeline for remote areas, the ships call at 34 fishing villages and cities.

For the seven-day trip to Kirkenes, allow from $1,600 and up per person based on double occupancy (includes three meals per day, taxes, and port charges). Prices vary greatly depending on the season (highest June-July), cabin, and type of ship. Their fleet includes those with a bit of brass built in the 1960s, but the majority of the ships were built in the mid-1990s and later. Shorter voyages are possible (including even just a day trip to one of the villages along the route). Cabins should be booked well in advance. Ship services include a 24-hour cafeteria, a launderette on newer boats, and optional port excursions. Check online for senior and off-season (Oct-March) specials at www.hurtigruten.com.

Call Hurtigruten in New York (US tel. 866-552-0371) or in Norway (tel. 81 00 30 30). For most travelers, the ride makes a great one-way trip, but a flight back south is a logical last leg (rather than returning to Bergen by boat—a 12-day round-trip).

BERGEN

SOUTH NORWAY

Stavanger • Setesdal Valley • Kristiansand

South Norway is not about must-see sights or jaw-dropping scenery—it's simply pleasant and pretty. Spend a day in the harborside town of Stavanger. Delve into the oil industry at the surprisingly interesting Norwegian Petroleum Museum. Peruse the Stavanger Cathedral, window-shop in the old town, cruise the harbor, or hoof it up Pulpit Rock for a fine view.

A series of time-forgotten towns stretch across the Setesdal Valley, with sod-roofed cottages and locals who practice fiddles and harmonicas, rose painting, whittling, and gold- and silver-work. The famous Setesdal filigree echoes the rhythmical designs of the Viking era and Middle Ages. Each town has a weekly rotating series of hikes and activities for the regular, stay-put-for-a-week visitor. The upper valley is dead in the summer but enjoys a bustling winter.

In Kristiansand, Norway's answer to a seaside resort, you can promenade along the strand, sample a Scandinavian zoo, or set sail to Denmark.

PLANNING YOUR TIME

Even on a busy itinerary, Stavanger warrants a day. The port town is connected by boat to Bergen (and Hirtshals, Denmark) and by train to Kristiansand.

Frankly, without a car, the Setesdal Valley is not worth the trouble. There are no trains in the valley, bus schedules are as sparse as the population, and the sights are best for joyriding. If you're in Bergen with a car, and want to get to Denmark, this route is more interesting than repeating Oslo. On a three-week Scandinavian trip, I'd do it in one long day, as follows: 7:00—Leave Bergen;

9:00—Catch Kvanndal ferry to Utne; 10:00—Say good-bye to the last fjord at Odda; 13:00—Lunch in Hovden at the top of Setesdal Valley; 14:00—Frolic south with a few short stops in the valley; 16:30—Arrive in Kristiansand for dinner. Spend the night and catch the 9:00 boat to Denmark the next morning.

Kristiansand is not a destination town, but rather a place to pass through, conveniently connecting Norway to Denmark by ferry.

Stavanger

This burg of about 125,000 is a mildly charming (if unspectacular) waterfront city whose streets are lined with unpretentious shiplap cottages that echo its perennial ties to the sea. Stavanger feels more cosmopolitan than most small Norwegian cities, thanks in part to its oil industry—which brings multinational workers (and their money) into the city. Known as Norway's festival city, Stavanger hosts several lively events, including jazz in May (www.maijazz. no), Scandinavia's biggest food festival in July (www.gladmat.no), and chamber music in August (www.icmf.no). With all of this culture, it's no surprise that Stavanger was named a European Capital of Culture for 2008.

From a sightseeing perspective, Stavanger barely has enough to fill a day: The Norwegian Petroleum Museum is the only big-time sight in town, and Gamle Stavanger (the "old town") offers pleasant wandering on cobbled lanes. The city's fine cathedral is worth a peek, but beyond those options, the chief activity is dodging the thousands of cruise passengers routinely dumped here throughout the summer season. For most visitors, the main reason

to come to Stavanger is to use it as a launch pad for side-tripping to Lysefjord and/or the famous, iconic Pulpit Rock: an eerily flat-topped peak thrusting up from the fjord, offering perfect, eagle's-eye views deep into the Lysefjord.

Orientation to Stavanger

The most scenic and interesting parts of Stavanger surround its harbor. Here you'll find the Maritime Museum, lots of shops and restaurants (particularly around the market plaza and along Kirkegata, which connects the cathedral to the Petroleum Museum), the

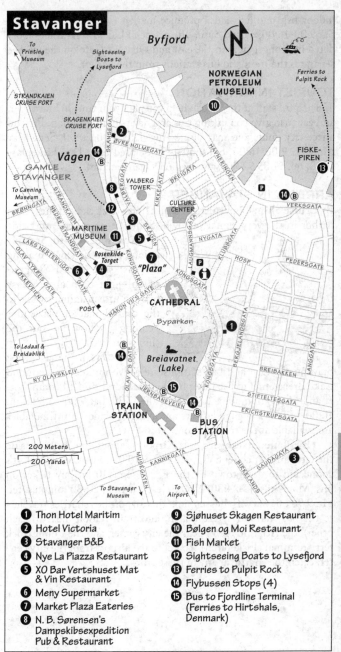

Stavanger

Byfjord

To Printing Museum

Sightseeing Boats to Lysefjord

NORWEGIAN PETROLEUM MUSEUM ❿

STRANDKAIEN CRUISE PORT

Ferries to Pulpit Rock

SKAGENKAIEN CRUISE PORT

Vågen

GAMLE STAVANGER

To Canning Museum

BRØNNGATA

SKANSEGATA ❷

ØVRE HOLMEGATE

⓮ ⓑ

FISKE-PIREN ⓭

VALBERG TOWER

❽ VALBERGGATA

⓬

KIRKEGATA

BREIGATA

HAVNERINGEN

CULTURE CENTER

VERKSGATA

P ⓮ ⓑ

MARITIME MUSEUM

❾

SKAGEN

NEDRE STRANDGATE

⓫

❺

LAUGMANNSGATA

NYGATA

KLUBBGATA

HOSP.

PEDERSGATE

LARS HERTERVIGS

Rosenkilde-Torget

❼ "Plaza"

OLAV KYRRES GATE

STRANDGATE

KONGSGGARD

LØKKEVEIEN

❻

❹

P

HÅKON VII'S GATE

KONGSGATA

P ℹ️

CATHEDRAL ✝

Byparken

POST

KONGSGATA

BERGJELANDSGATA

To Ledaal & Breidablikk

⓮ ⓑ

Breiavatnet (Lake)

❶

BREIBAKKEN

LANGGATA

NY OLAVSKLEIV

OLAV V'S GATE

JERNBANEVEIEN

⓫ ⓑ

STIFTELTESGATA

ERICHSTRUPSGATA

TRAIN STATION

⓮ ⓑ

BUS STATION

SAUDAGATA

BIRKELANDS

KANNIKGATA

❸

MUSÉGATEN

P

200 Meters
200 Yards

To Stavanger Museum

To Airport

SOUTH NORWAY

❶ Thon Hotel Maritim
❷ Hotel Victoria
❸ Stavanger B&B
❹ Nye La Piazza Restaurant
❺ XO Bar Vertshuset Mat & Vin Restaurant
❻ Meny Supermarket
❼ Market Plaza Eateries
❽ N. B. Sørensen's Dampskibsexpedition Pub & Restaurant

❾ Sjøhuset Skagen Restaurant
❿ Bølgen og Moi Restaurant
⓫ Fish Market
⓬ Sightseeing Boats to Lysefjord
⓭ Ferries to Pulpit Rock
⓮ Flybussen Stops (4)
⓯ Bus to Fjordline Terminal (Ferries to Hirtshals, Denmark)

indoor fish market, and a produce market (Mon-Fri 9:00-18:00, Sat 9:00-16:00, closed Sun). The artificial Lake Breiavatnet—bordered by Kongsgaten on the east and Olav V's Gate on the west—separates the train and bus stations from the harbor.

TOURIST INFORMATION
The helpful staff at the TI can help you plan your time in Stavanger, and can also give you hiking tips and day trip information. Pick up a free city guide and map (June-Aug daily 9:00-20:00; Sept-May Mon-Fri 9:00-16:00, Sat 9:00-14:00, closed Sun; Domkirkeplassen 3, tel. 51 85 92 00, www.regionstavanger.com).

ARRIVAL IN STAVANGER
By Cruise Ship: Conveniently, cruise liners dock right at the Vågen harbor in the very center of town. Some tie up on the west side

of the harbor (called **Strandkaien**), and others put in along the east side (called **Skagenkaien**)—but both are an easy five- to fifteen-minute walk to the central market plaza (depending on how far out the ship is docked).

By Train and Bus: Stavanger's train and bus stations are a five-minute walk around Lake Breiavatnet to the inner harbor, cathedral, and TI (train ticket and reservation office Mon-Fri 7:00-17:30, Sat 9:00-16:30, Sun 10:00-16:30). Luggage lockers and Norway-wide train timetables are available at the train station.

By Plane: Stavanger's Sola Airport is about nine miles outside the city (airport code: SVG, tel. 67 03 10 00, www.avinor.no). It's connected to downtown by the Flybussen (110 kr, buy ticket on bus, Mon-Fri 7:45-24:30, 2/hour, less Sat-Sun, 20-30 minutes, tel. 51 59 90 60, www.flybussen.no). This airport bus shuttles travelers to the bus station (Byterminalen) and train station (next to each other), the Atlantic Hotel near the city center, and the Pulpit Rock ferry terminal (Fiskepiren). To get to the airport from the city center, catch the shuttle at any of these stops.

Sights in Stavanger

▲Stavanger Cathedral (Domkirke)

While it's hardly the most impressive cathedral in Scandinavia, Stavanger's top church—which overlooks the town center on a small ridge—has a harmonious interior and a few intriguing details worth lingering over. Good English information throughout the church brings meaning to the place.

Cost and Hours: 30-kr until 15:30, free after 15:30, open June-Aug daily 11:00-19:00, free and open shorter hours off-season, tel. 51 84 04 00, www.kirken.stavanger.no.

Visiting the Church: St. Swithun's Cathedral (its official name) was originally built in 1125 in a Norman style, with basket-handle Romanesque arches. After a fire badly damaged the church in the 13th century, a new chancel was added in the pointy-arched Gothic style. You can't miss where the architecture changes about three-quarters of the way up the aisle. On the left, behind the baptismal font, notice the ivy-lined railing on the stone staircase; this pattern is part of the city's coat of arms. And nearby, appreciate the colorful, richly detailed "gristle Baroque"-style pulpit (from 1658). Notice that the whole thing is resting on Samson's stoic shoulders—even as he faces down a lion.

Stroll the church, perusing its several fine "epitaphs" (tomb markers), which are paintings in ornately decorated frames. Go on a scavenger hunt for two unique features; both are on the second columns from the back of the church. On the right, at the top facing away from the nave, notice the stone carvings of Norse mythological figures: Odin on the left, and a wolf-like beast on the right. Although the medieval Norwegians were Christians, they weren't ready to entirely abandon all of their pagan traditions. On the opposite column, circle around the base and look at ankle level, facing away from the altar. Here you see a grotesque sculpture that looks like a fish head with human hands. Notice that its head has been worn down. One interpretation is that early worshippers would ritualistically put their foot on top of it, as if to push the evil back to the underworld. Mysteriously, both of these features are one-offs—you won't find anything like them on any other column in the church.

▲▲Norwegian Petroleum Museum (Norsk Oljemuseum)

This entertaining, informative museum—dedicated to the discovery of oil in Norway's North Sea in 1969 and the industry built

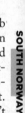

up around it—offers an unapologetic look at the country's biggest moneymaker. With half of Western Europe's oil reserves, the formerly poor agricultural nation of Norway is the Arabia of the North, and a world-class player. It's ranked third among the world's top oil exporters, producing 1.6 million barrels a day.

Cost and Hours: 100 kr; June-Aug daily 10:00-19:00; Sept-May Mon-Sat 10:00-16:00, Sun 10:00-18:00; tel. 51 93 93 00, www.norskolje.museum.no. The small museum shop sells various petroleum-based products. The museum's Bølgen og Moi restaurant, which has an inviting terrace over the water, serves lunch and dinner (see listing under "Eating in Stavanger," later).

Visiting the Museum: The exhibit describes how oil was formed, how it's found and produced, and what it's used for. You'll see models of oil rigs, actual drill bits, see-through cylinders that you can rotate to investigate different types of crude, and lots of explanations (in English) about various aspects of oil. Interactive exhibits cover everything from the "History of the Earth" (4.5 billion years displayed on a large overhead globe, showing how our planet has changed—stay for the blast that killed the dinosaurs), to day-to-day life on an offshore platform, to petroleum products in our lives (though the peanut-butter-and-petroleum-jelly sandwich is a bit much). Kids enjoy climbing on the model drilling platform, trying out the emergency escape chute at the platform outside, and playing with many other hands-on exhibits.

Several included movies delve into specific aspects of oil: The kid-oriented "Petropolis" 3-D film is primitive but entertaining and informative, tracing the story of oil from creation to extraction. Other movies (in the cylindrical structures outside) highlight intrepid North Sea divers and the construction of an oil platform. Each film is 12 minutes long, and runs in English at least twice hourly.

Even the museum's architecture was designed to echo the foundations of the oil industry—bedrock (the stone building), slate and chalk deposits in the sea (slate floor of the main hall), and the rigs (cylindrical platforms). While the museum has its fair share of propaganda, it also has several good exhibits on the environmental toll of drilling and consuming oil.

Gamle Stavanger

Stavanger's "old town" centers on Øvre Strandgate, on the west side of the harbor. Wander the narrow, winding, cobbled back lanes, with tidy wooden houses, oasis gardens, and flower-bedecked en-

tranceways. Peek into a workshop or gallery to find ceramics, glass, jewelry, and more. Many shops are open roughly daily 10:00-17:00, coinciding with the arrival of cruise ships (which loom ominously right next to this otherwise tranquil zone).

Museum Stavanger (M.U.S.T.)

This "museum" is actually 10 different museums scattered around town. The various branches include the **Stavanger Museum,** featuring the history of the city and a zoological exhibit (Muségate 16); the **Maritime Museum** (Sjøfartsmuseum), near the bottom end of Vågen harbor (Nedre Strandgate 17-19); the **Norwegian Canning Museum** (Norsk Hermetikkmuseum—the *brisling*, or herring, is smoked the first Sunday of every month and mid-June-mid-Aug Tue and Thu—Øvre Strandgate 88A); **Ledaal,** a royal residence and manor house (Eiganesveien 45); and **Breidablikk,** a wooden villa from the late 1800s (Eiganesveien 40A). The **Printing Museum** is closed but is slated to reopen by 2016.

Cost: You can buy one 100-kr ticket to cover all of them, or you can pay 70 kr for any individual museum (if doing at least two, the combo-ticket is obviously the better value). Note that a single 70-kr ticket gets you into the Maritime Museum, Canning Museum, and Printing Museum (when open), which are a three-for-one sight. You can get details and buy tickets at any of the museums; handiest is the Maritime Museum right along the harbor.

Hours: Museum hours vary but generally open mid-June-mid-Aug daily 10:00 or 11:00-16:00; off-season Tue-Sun 11:00-16:00, closed Mon, except Ledaal and Breidablikk—these are open Sun only in winter; www.museumstavanger.no.

DAY TRIPS TO LYSEFJORD AND PULPIT ROCK

The nearby Lysefjord is an easy day trip. Those with more time (and strong legs) can hike to the top of the 1,800-foot-high Pulpit Rock (Preikestolen). The dramatic 270-square-foot plateau atop the rock gives you a fantastic view of the fjord and surrounding mountains. The TI has brochures for several boat tour companies and sells tickets.

Boat Tour of Lysefjord

Rødne Clipper Fjord Sightseeing offers three-hour round-trip excursions from Stavanger to Lysefjord (including a view of Pulpit Rock—but no stops). Conveniently, their boats depart from the main Vågen harbor in the heart of town (east side of the harbor, in front of Skansegata, along Skagenkaien; 450 kr; mid-May-mid-

Sept daily at 10:00 and 14:00, also Thu-Sat at 12:00 July-Aug; early May and late Sept daily at 12:00 Oct-April Wed-Sun only at 11:00; tel. 51 89 52 70, www.rodne.no). A different company, **Norled,** also runs similar trips, as well as slower journeys up the Lysefjord on a "tourist car ferry" (www.norled.no).

Ferry and Bus to Pulpit Rock

Hiking up to the top of Pulpit Rock is a popular outing that will take the better part of a day; plan on at least four hours of hiking (two hours up, two hours down), plus time to linger at the top for photos, plus round-trip travel from Stavanger (about an hour each way by a ferry-and-bus combination)—eight hours minimum should do it. The trailhead is easily reached in summer by public transit or tour package. Then comes the hard part: the hike to the top. The total distance is 4.5 miles and the elevation gain is roughly 1,000 feet. Pack a lunch and plenty of water, and wear good shoes.

Two different companies sell ferry-and-bus packages to the trailhead from Stavanger. Ferries leave from the Fiskepiren boat terminal to Tau; buses meet the incoming ferries and head to Pulpit Rock cabin or to Preikestolen Fjellstue, the local youth hostel. Be sure to time your hike so that you can catch the last bus leaving Pulpit Rock cabin for the ferry (confirm time when booking your ticket). These trips generally go daily from mid-May through mid-September; weekends only in April, early May, and late September; and not at all from October to March (when the ferry stops running). As the details tend to change from year to year, confirm schedules with the TI or the individual companies: **Tide Reiser** (240 kr, best options for an all-day round-trip are departures at 8:40 or 9:20, return bus from trailhead corresponds with ferry to Stavanger, tel. 55 23 88 87, www.tidereiser.com) and **Boreal** (150 kr for the bus plus 92 kr for the ferry—you'll buy the ferry ticket separately, best options depart at 8:40 or 9:20, last return bus from trailhead to ferry leaves at 19:55, tel. 51 56 41 00, www.pulpitrock. no).

Rødne Clipper Fjord Sightseeing (listed earlier) may run a handy trip in July and August that begins with a scenic Lysefjord cruise, then drops you off at Oanes to catch the bus to the Pulpit Rock hut trailhead; afterwards, you can catch the bus to Tau for the ferry return to Stavanger. It's similar to the options described above, but adds a scenic fjord cruise at the start. To confirm this is still going and get details, contact Rødne (750 kr plus 46 kr for return ferry to Stavanger, tel. 51 89 52 70, www.rodne.no).

Sleep Code

Abbreviations   **(6 kr = about $1, country code: 47)**
S = Single, **D** = Double/Twin, **T** = Triple, **Q** = Quad, **b** = bathroom
Price Rankings
  $$$ Higher Priced—Most rooms 1,000 kr or more.
   $$ Moderately Priced—Most rooms 600-1,000 kr.
Unless otherwise noted, credit cards are accepted, breakfast is included, and Wi-Fi is generally free. Everyone speaks English. Prices change; verify current rates online or by email. For the best prices, always book directly with the hotel.

Sleeping in Stavanger

$$$ Thon Hotel Maritim, with 223 rooms, is two blocks from the train station near the artificial Lake Breiavatnet. It can be a good deal for a big business-class hotel (flexible rates: Db-1,750-2,245 kr on weekdays, likely 1,150 on weekends, almost as cheap in July, Sb is always 200 kr less, elevator, Wi-Fi, Kongsgaten 32, tel. 51 85 05 00, www.thonhotels.no/maritim, mailto:maritim@thonhotels.no).

$$$ Hotel Victoria has 107 business-class rooms over a stately, high-ceilinged lobby facing the Skagenkaien embankment right on the harbor (in summer and weekends: Sb-890 kr, Db-1,140 kr; weekdays outside of summer: Sb-1,940 kr, Db-2,440 kr; elevator, Wi-Fi, Skansegata 1, tel. 51 86 70 00, www.victoria-hotel.no, victoria@victoria-hotel.no).

$$ Stavanger B&B is Stavanger's best budget option. This large red house among a sea of white houses has tidy, tiny rooms. The lodgings are basic, verging on institutional—not cozy or doily—but they're affordable and friendly. The shared toilet is down the hall; 14 rooms have their own showers, while eight share showers on the hall. Waffles, coffee, and friendly chatter are served up every evening at 21:00 (S-790 kr, D-890 kr, 100 kr less per room for shared shower, extra bed-150 kr, guest computer and Wi-Fi, 10-minute uphill walk behind train station in residential neighborhood, Vikedalsgate 1A, tel. 51 56 25 00, www.stavangerbedandbreakfast.no, post@sbb.no). If you let them know in advance, they may be able to pick you up or drop you off at the boat dock or train station.

Eating in Stavanger

CASUAL DINING

Nye La Piazza, just off the harbor, has an assortment of pasta and other Italian dishes, including pizza, for 150-200 kr (100-kr lunch

SOUTH NORWAY

special, 300-320-kr meat options, Mon-Sat 13:00-23:00, Sun 13:00-22:00, Rosenkildettorget 1, tel. 51 52 02 52).

XO Bar Vertshuset Mat & Vin, in an elegant setting, serves up big portions of traditional Norwegian food and pricier contemporary fare (300-400 kr, light meals-150-190 kr, open Mon-Wed 11:00-23:30, Thu-Sat 11:00-1:30, a block behind main drag along harbor at Skagen 10 ved Prostebakken, mobile 91 00 03 07).

Meny is a large supermarket with a good selection and a fine deli for super-picnic shopping (Mon-Fri 9:00-20:00, Sat until 18:00, closed Sun, in Straen Senteret shopping mall, Lars Hertervigs Gate 6, tel. 51 50 50 10).

Market Plaza Eateries: The busy square between the cathedral and the harbor is packed with reliable Norwegian chain restaurants. If you're a fan of **Deli de Luca, Peppes Pizza,** or **Dickens Pub,** you'll find all of them within a few steps of here.

DINING ALONG THE HARBOR WITH A VIEW

The harborside street of Skansegata is lined with lively restaurants and pubs, and most serve food. Here are a couple options:

N. B. Sørensen's Dampskibsexpedition consists of a lively pub on the first floor (225-340 kr for pasta, fish, meat, and vegetarian dishes; Mon-Wed 11:00-24:00, Sat 11:00-late, Sun 13:00-23:00) and a fine-dining restaurant on the second floor, with tablecloths, view tables overlooking the harbor, and entrées from 300 kr (Mon-Sat 18:00-23:00, closed Sun, Skagenkaien 26, tel. 51 84 38 20). The restaurant is named after an 1800s company that shipped from this building, among other things, Norwegians heading to the US. Passengers and cargo waited on the first floor, and the manager's office was upstairs. The place is filled with emigrant-era memorabilia.

Sjøhuset Skagen, with a woodsy interior, invites diners to its historic building for lunch or dinner. The building, from the late 1700s, housed a trading company. Today, you can choose from local seafood specialties with an ethnic flair, as well as plenty of meat options (180-195-kr lunches, 230-400-kr dinners, Mon-Sat 11:30-23:00, Sun 13:00-21:30, Skagenkaien 16, tel. 51 89 51 80).

Bølgen og Moi, the restaurant at the Petroleum Museum, has fantastic views over the harbor (lunch: 190-kr lunch special, 190-250-kr main dishes, served Mon 11:00-16:00; dinner: 250-kr main dishes, 500 kr three-course meal, served Tue-Sat 18:00-20:00—reservations recommended; Kjeringholmen 748, tel. 51 93 93 53).

Stavanger Connections

From Stavanger by Train to: Kristiansand (4-7/day, 3-3.5 hours), **Oslo** (4/day, 8-8.5 hours, overnight possible).

By Bus to Bergen: Kystbussen operates buses between Stavanger and Bergen (hourly, 5.5 hours, 440 kr one-way, 800 kr round-trip, tel. 52 70 35 26, http://kystbussen.no).

By Boat to Hirtshals, Denmark: For details on this boat, see the "Sailing Between Norway and Denmark" sidebar.

The Setesdal Valley

Welcome to the remote, and therefore very traditional, Setesdal Valley. Probably Norway's most authentic cranny, the valley is a mellow montage of sod-roofed water mills, ancient churches, derelict farmhouses, yellowed recipes, and gentle scenery.

The Setesdal Valley joined the modern age with the construction of the valley highway in the 1950s. All along the valley you'll see the unique two-story storage sheds called *stabburs* (the top floor was used for storing clothes; the bottom, food) and many sod roofs. Even the bus stops have rooftops the local goats love to munch.

In the high country, just over the Sessvatn summit (3,000 feet), you'll see herds of goats and summer farms. If you see an *ekte geitost* sign, that means genuine, homemade goat cheese is for sale. (It's sold cheaper and in more manageable sizes in grocery stores.) To some, it looks like a decade's accumulation of earwax. I think it's delicious. Remember, *ekte* means all-goat—really strong. The more popular and easier-to-eat version is a mix of cow and goat cheese.

For more information on the Setesdal Valley, see www.setesdal.com.

FROM ODDA TO HOVDEN

Attractions from here to Kristiansand are listed roughly from north to south.

Odda

At the end of the Hardanger Fjord, just past the huge zinc and copper industrial plant, you'll hit the industrial town of Odda (well-stocked **TI** for whole region and beyond; in summer daily 9:00-19:00; off-season Mon-Fri 9:00-15:00, closed Sat-Sun; on market square at Torget 2-4, tel. 53 65 40 05, www.visitodda.com). Odda brags that Kaiser Wilhelm came here a lot, but he's dead and I'd drive right through. If you want to visit the tongue of a glacier, drive to Buar and hike an hour to Buarbreen. From Odda, drive

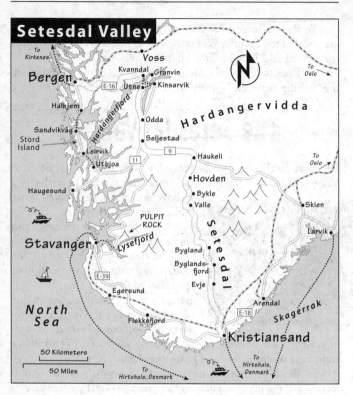

Setesdal Valley

into the land of boulders. The many mighty waterfalls that line the road seem to have hurled huge rocks (with rooted trees) into the rivers and fields. Stop at the giant double waterfall (on the left, pullout on the right, drive slowly through it if you need a car wash).

Røldal

Continue over Røldalsfjellet and into the valley below, where the old town of Røldal is trying to develop some tourism. Drive on by. Its old church isn't worth the time or money. Lakes are like frosted mirrors, making desolate huts come in pairs. Haukeliseter, a group of sod-roofed buildings filled with cultural clichés and tour groups, offers pastries, sandwiches, and reasonable hot meals (from 100 kr) in a lakeside setting. Try the traditional *rømmegrøt* porridge.

Haukeli

This highway and transportation junction has daily bus service to/from Bergen and to/from Kristiansand (Haukeli Motell café open Mon-Fri 11:00-17:00, Sun 11:00-18:00, closed Sat, tel. 35 07 02 14). Turn right over the river onto Route 9, toward Hovden.

Hovden

A ski resort at the top of the Setesdal Valley (2,500 feet), Hovden is barren in the summer and painfully in need of charm. Still, it makes a good home base if you want to explore the area for a couple of days. Locals come here to walk and relax for a week.

Tourist Information: The TI is open all year (Mon-Fri 9:00-16:00, summer Sat 10:00-15:00, July also Sun 10:00-15:00, otherwise closed Sat-Sun, tel. 37 93 93 70, www.hovden.com, post@hovden.com).

Sights and Activities in Hovden

Boat Rental

Hegni Center, on the lake at the south edge of town, rents rowboats, canoes, and kayaks (250-350 kr/day, 195-200 kr/half-day, hourly rentals also possible, cash only, mid-June-mid-Aug daily 11:00-18:00, mid-Aug-mid-Sept Sat-Sun 11:00-15:00, mid-Sept-mid-Oct Sat-Sun only 11:00-16:00, closed mid-Oct-mid-June, tel. 37 93 93 70).

Hikes and Mountain Biking near Hovden

Good walks offer you a chance to see reindeer, moose, arctic fox, and wabbits—so they say. The TI and most hotels stock brochures, maps, and other information about moderate to strenuous hikes in the area as well as biking options. Berry picking is popular in late August, when small, sweet blueberries are in season. A chairlift sometimes takes sightseers to the top of a nearby peak, with great views in clear weather. Bikers can ride the trails downhill (100 kr, 110 kr to bring a bike, June-July daily 11:00-14:00, Aug-mid-Oct Wed and Sat-Sun only). Hunting season starts in late August for reindeer (only in higher elevations) and later in the fall for grouse and moose.

Moose Safari

The TI offers a 2.5-hour *Elg Safari* (*elg* is Norwegian for "moose"). Learn more about this "king of the forest" during a late-night drive through Setesdal's back roads with a stop for moose-meat soup (340 kr, June-Aug only; generally Tue, Fri, and Sun at 22:00—other days on request; 50 percent money-back guarantee if you don't see a moose, tel. 37 93 93 70, post@hovden.com).

Museum of Iron Production (Jernvinnemuseum)

Learn about iron production from the late Iron Age (about 1,000 years ago) with the aid of drawings, exhibits, and recorded narration from a "Viking" (available in English). The museum is about

SOUTH NORWAY

Sailing Between Norway and Denmark

Two companies sail between the tips of Norway and Denmark. **Color Line** and **Fjordline** sail fast boats between Kristiansand, Norway, and Hirtshals, Denmark (2.25-3.25 hours). In addition, Fjordline boats connect Stavanger, Norway, and Hirtshals (11 hours, covered next). They also link Bergen with Hirtshals, though at 18.5 hours, it's a long haul. (For information on an Oslo-Copenhagen cruise—run by a different company—see page 287.)

Both Color Line and Fjordline offer car packages (covering up to 5 people and the car) and have various on-board amenities such as restaurants, coffee bars, duty-free shops, and several classes of travel. I've listed prices in euros, as they appear on the companies' websites.

Sailing Between Kristiansand and Hirtshals, Denmark: Color Line ships generally sail twice daily, all year, with a few more sailings added during summer, but mysteriously they sail only once a day in mid-April. Sailing from Norway to Denmark, Color Line boats usually leave Kristiansand at 8:00 and 16:30, arriving in Hirtshals at 11:15 and 19:45. Going from Denmark to Norway, the boats leave Hirtshals at 12:15 and 20:45, arriving in Kristiansand at 15:30 and midnight. Fares vary with day of week and season (cheaper weekdays and off-season). During the summer, one-way passenger fares start at €20/person mid-week, €40/person on weekends; car packages start at €70 mid-week and €102 on weekends.

Fjordline's seasonal ferry makes the crossing two times a day from late June to mid-August in a speedy 2.25 hours. The schedule is cut back in late spring and early fall, with no ferries

100 yards behind the Hegni Center (look for the sign from the road to *Jernvinnemuseum*).

Cost and Hours: Free, late-June-mid-Aug daily 11:00-19:00, otherwise ask for the key at the TI or Hegni Center.

Swimming Pool

A super indoor spa/pool complex, the Hovden Badeland provides a much-needed way to spend an otherwise dreary and drizzly early evening here.

Cost and Hours: 135-150 kr for 3 hours or more, cheaper for shorter visits, daily 10:00-19:00 in summer, shorter hours off-season, tel. 37 93 93 93, www.badeland.com.

from September to mid-May. In high season, sailing from Norway to Denmark, Fjordline boats leave Kristiansand at 8:30 and 15:00, arriving in Hirtshals at 10:45 and 17:15. Going from Denmark to Norway, the boats leave Hirtshals at 11:45 and 18:00, arriving in Kristiansand at 14:00 and 20:15. One-way passenger fares start at €21/person mid-week; car packages start at €55 mid-week.

Sailing Between Stavanger and Hirtshals, Denmark: Fjordline ships sailing from Norway to Denmark travel overnight, which can save you the cost of a hotel. Enjoy an evening in Stavanger, then sleep (or vomit) as you sail to Denmark. The boat generally sails daily, departing Stavanger at 21:00 and arriving in Hirtshals at 8:00 the next day. Ships also sail daily from Denmark to Norway, departing Hirtshals at 21:00 and arriving in Stavanger at 7:00 in the morning.

Fares vary, depending on how far in advance you book, the time of year, the day of the week, and the type of accommodation you want. Basic one-way fares range from €13 to €102, plus the cost of meals (€17 breakfast, €43 dinner) and accommodations (an airline-type seat or cabin). A seat, referred to as a "sleeperette," starts at €21. But if you're efficient enough to spend a night traveling, you owe yourself the comfort of a private room. Cabins start at around €115 for a basic, two-berth, inside cabin, and go up to €300 or more for a "Fjord Class" cabin with a double bed and ocean view. Car packages range from €100 and up.

Reservations: To get the best fare, book online and early—as soon as you can commit to a firm date (http://fjordline.no and www.colorline.com). This is especially true for Fjordline. Many cheaper fares are nonrefundable and nonchangeable, so be sure to check the details carefully when you book. Days of the week and departure/arrival times can vary—confirm specific schedules when you make your reservations.

Sleeping and Eating in Hovden

$$ Hovden Fjellstoge is a big, old ski chalet renting Hovden's only cheap beds. Even if you're just passing through, their café is a good choice for lunch or an early dinner. Check out the mural in the balcony overlooking the lobby—an artistic rendition of this area's history. Behind the mural is a frightening taxidermy collection (hotel: Sb-from 750 kr, bunk-bed Db-from 990 kr, includes breakfast; cabins: from 890 kr for 2-4 people with bathroom and kitchen; breakfast-110 kr, sheets-100 kr, towel-20 kr; tel. 37 93 95 43, www.hovdenfjellstoge.no, post@hovdenfjellstoge.no).

FROM HOVDEN TO KRISTIANSAND

▲Dammar Vatnedalsvatn

Nine miles south of Hovden is a two-mile side-trip to a 400-foot-high rock-pile dam (look for the *Dammar* signs). Enjoy the great view and impressive rockery. This is one of the highest dams in northern Europe. Read the chart. Sit out of the wind a few rows down the rock pile and ponder the vastness of Norwegian wood.

▲Bykle

The most interesting folk museum and church in Setesdal are in the teeny town of Bykle. The 17th-century church has two balconies—one for men and one for women (free, late June-mid-Aug daily 11:00-17:00, closed off-season, tel. 37 93 63 03, www.setesdalsmuseet.no).

Grasbrokke

On the east side of the main road (at the *Grasbrokke* sign) is an old water mill (1630). A few minutes farther south, at the sign for *Sanden Såre Camping*, exit onto a little road to stretch your legs at another old water mill with a fragile, rotten-log sluice.

Flateland

The **Setesdal Museum** (Rygnestadtunet) offers more of what you saw at Bykle (about 30 kr, two buildings; late June-Aug daily 11:00-17:00; closed off-season; 1 mile east of the road, tel. 37 93 63 03, www.setesdalsmuseet.no). Unless you're a glutton for culture, I wouldn't do both.

Honnevje

Past Flateland is a nice picnic and WC stop, with a dock along the water for swimming...for hot-weather days or polar bears.

▲Valle

This is Setesdal's prettiest village (but don't tell Bykle). In the center, you'll find fine silver- and gold-work, homemade crafts next to the TI, and old-fashioned *lefse* cooking demonstrations (in the small log house by the Valle Motell). The fine suspension bridge attracts kids of any age (b-b-b-b-bounce), and anyone interested in a great view over the river to strange mountains that look like polished, petrified mudslides. European rock climbers, tired of the over-climbed Alps, often entertain spectators with their sport. Is anyone climbing? (TI tel. 37 93 75 29.)

Sleeping in Valle: **$$ Valle Motell** rents basic rooms (Sb-625 kr, Db-790 kr, includes breakfast, cabins with kitchen and bath but no breakfast-725-1195 kr, tel. 37 93 77 00, www.valle-motell.no, post@valle-motell.no).

Nomeland

The Sylvartun silversmith shop, whose owner Hallvard Bjørgum is also a renowned Hardanger fiddle player, sells Setesdal silver in a 17th-century, grass-roofed log cabin next to the main road.

Grendi

The Ardal Church (1827) has a rune stone in its yard. Three hundred yards south of the church is a 900-year-old oak tree.

Evje

A huge town by Setesdal standards (3,500 people), Evje is famous for its gems and mines. Fancy stones fill the shops here. Rock hounds find the nearby mines fun; for a small fee, you can hunt for gems. The TI is by Route 9 in the center of Evje (mid-June-mid-Aug Mon-Fri 10:00-17:00, Sat 10:00-14:00, closed Sun; tel. 37 93 14 00). The **Setesdal Mineral Park** is on the main road, two miles south of town (140 kr, late-June-mid-Aug daily 10:00-18:00, shorter hours off-season, closed mid-Oct-April, tel. 37 93 13 10, www.mineralparken.no).

Kristiansand

This "capital of the south" has 85,000 inhabitants, a pleasant Renaissance grid-plan layout (Posebyen), a famous zoo with Norway's biggest amusement park (6 miles toward Oslo on the main road), a daily bus to Bergen, and lots of big boats going to Denmark. It's the closest thing to a beach resort in Norway. Markensgate is the bustling pedestrian market street—an enjoyable place for good browsing, shopping, eating, and people-watching. Stroll along the Strand Promenaden (marina) to Christiansholm Fortress.

Orientation to Kristiansand

The TI is at Rådhusgata 18, a few blocks from the boat, bus, and train station (mid-June-mid-Aug Mon-Fri 8:00-18:00, Sat 10:00-18:00, Sun 12:00-18:00; mid-Aug-mid-June Mon-Fri 8:00-15:30, Sat 10:00-15:00, closed Sun; tel. 38 12 13 14, www.visitkrs.no). The bank at the Color Line terminal opens for each arrival and departure (even the midnight ones). The Fønix Kino cinema complex is within two blocks of the ferry and TI (110-140 kr, seven screens, movies shown in English, schedules at the entrance, tel. 38 10 42 00).

Sleeping and Eating in Kristiansand

Kristiansand hotels are expensive and nondescript. The otherwise uninteresting harbor area has a cluster of wooden buildings called **Fiskebasaren** ("Fish Bazaar"). The indoor fish market is only open during the day, but numerous restaurants (serving fish, among other dishes) provide a nice atmosphere for dinner. Follow Vester Strandgate past the Fønix movie theater to Østre Strandgate, take a right, and follow the signs to Fiskebrygga.

$$$ Rica Hotel Norge is a modern option (Sb-1,700 kr, Db-1,900 kr, prices are averaged—rates vary with demand, Dronningensgate 5, tel. 38 17 40 00, www.hotel-norge.no, firmapost@hotel-norge.no).

$$$ Thon Hotel Wergeland is inviting for a large chain hotel. It's within earshot of the church bells and busy Kirkegate—ask for a quieter room away from the street (Sb-1,395 kr, Db-1,695 kr, prices are averaged—rates vary with demand, includes breakfast, non-smoking rooms, no elevator, guest computer and Wi-Fi, Kirkegate 15, tel. 38 17 20 40, www.thonhotels.no/wergeland, wergeland@thonhotels.no).

Kristiansand Connections

From Kristiansand by Train to: Stavanger (4-7/day, 3-3.5 hours), **Oslo** (5/day, 4.5 hours).

By Boat to Hirtshals, Denmark: For details on this boat, see the "Sailing Between Norway and Denmark" sidebar.

ROUTE TIPS FOR DRIVERS

Bergen to Kristiansand via the Setesdal Valley (10 hours): Your first key connection is the Kvanndal-Utne ferry (departures hourly 6:00-22:30, fewer on weekends, reservations not possible or even necessary if you get there 20 minutes early, breakfast in cafeteria, www.norled.no). If you make the 9:00, your day will be more relaxed. Driving comfortably, with no mistakes or traffic, it's two hours from your Bergen hotel to the ferry dock. Leaving Bergen is a bit confusing. Pretend you're going to Oslo on the road to Voss (Route E-16, signs for *Nestune, Landås, Nattland*). About a half-hour out of town, after a long tunnel, leave the Voss road and take Route 7 heading for Norheimsund, and then Kvanndal. This road, treacherous for the famed beauty of the Hardanger Fjord it hugs as well as for its skinniness, is faster and safer if you beat the traffic (which you will with this plan).

The ferry drops you in Utne, where a lovely road takes you to Odda and up into the mountains. From Haukeli, turn south on Route 9 and wind up to Sessvatn at 3,000 feet. Enter the

Setesdal Valley. Follow the Otra River downhill for 140 miles south to the major port town of Kristiansand. Skip the secondary routes. The most scenic stretch is between Hovden and Valle. South of Valle, there is a lot more logging (and therefore less scenic). As you enter Kristiansand, pay a 21-kr toll and follow signs for Denmark.

SWEDEN

SWEDEN

Sverige

Scandinavia's heartland, Sweden is far bigger than Denmark and far flatter than Norway. This family-friendly land is home to Ikea, Volvo, WikiLeaks, ABBA, and long summer vacations at red-painted, white-trimmed summer cottages. Its capital, Stockholm, is Scandinavia's grandest city.

Once the capital of blond, Sweden is now home to a growing immigrant population. Sweden is committed to its peoples' safety and security, and proud of its success in creating a society with one of the lowest poverty rates in the world. Yet Sweden has thrown in its lot with the European Union, and locals debate whether to open their economy even further.

Swedes are often stereotyped as sex-crazed, which could not be further from the truth. Several steamy films and film stars from the 1950s and 1960s stuck Sweden with the sexpot stereotype, which still reverberates among male tourists. Italians continue to travel up to Sweden looking for those bra-less, loose, and lascivious blondes...but the real story is that Sweden simply relaxed film censorship earlier than other European countries. The Swedish newspaper ad at right shows typical stereotypes, and asks, "Do you see the world as the world sees you?" Like other Scandinavians, Swedes are frank and open about sexuality. Sex

education in schools is routine, living together before marriage is the norm (and has been common for centuries), and teenagers have easy access to condoms. But Swedes, who are the most unmarried people in the world, choose their partners carefully.

Before the year 2000, Sweden was a Lutheran state, with the Church of Sweden as its official religion. Until 1996, Swedes automatically became members of the Lutheran Church at birth if one parent was Lutheran. Now you need to choose to join the church, and although the culture is nominally Lutheran, few people attend services regularly. While church is handy for Christmas, Easter,

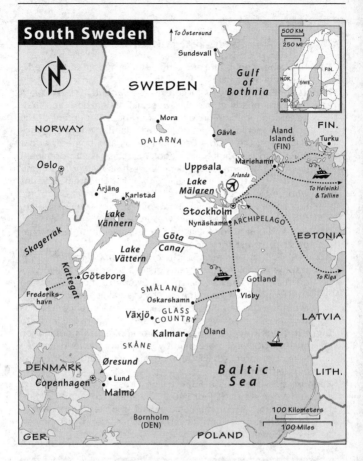

South Sweden

To Östersund

SWEDEN

Gulf of Bothnia

Sundsvall

NORWAY

Mora

DALARNA

Gävle

Åland Islands (FIN)

FIN.

Turku

Oslo

Årjäng

Karlstad

Uppsala

Lake Mälaren

Arlanda

Mariehamn

To Helsinki & Tallinn

Lake Vännern

Stockholm

Nynäshamn

ARCHIPELAGO

ESTONIA

Skagerrak

Göta Canal

Lake Vättern

Kattegat

Göteborg

SMÅLAND

Gotland

To Riga

Frederiks- havn

Oskarshamn

Visby

LATVIA

Växjö

GLASS COUNTRY

Kalmar

Öland

SKÅNE

DENMARK

Øresund

Copenhagen

Lund

Malmö

Baltic Sea

LITH.

Bornholm (DEN)

GER.

POLAND

100 Kilometers

100 Miles

marriages, and burials, most Swedes are more likely to find religion in nature, hiking in the vast forests or fishing in one of the thousands of lakes or rivers.

Sweden is almost 80 percent wilderness, and modern legislation incorporates an ancient common law called *allemans rätt*, which guarantees people the right to move freely through Sweden's natural scenery without asking landowners for permission, as long as they behave responsibly. In summer, Swedes take advantage of the long days and warm evenings for festivals such as Midsummer (in late June) and for crayfish parties in August. Many Swedes have a summer cottage—or know someone who has one—where they spend countless hours swimming, soaking up the sun, and devouring boxes of juicy strawberries.

While Denmark and Norway look westward to Britain and the Atlantic, Sweden has always faced east, across the Baltic Sea. As Vikings, Norwegians went west to Iceland, Greenland, and

Sweden Almanac

Official Name: Konungariket Sverige—the Kingdom of Sweden—or simply Sweden.

Population: Sweden's 9.7 million people (about 56 per square mile) are mostly ethnically Swedish. Foreign-born and first-generation immigrants account for about 15 percent of the population and are primarily from Finland, the former Yugoslavia, and the Middle East. Sweden is also home to about 20,000 indigenous Sami people. Swedish is the dominant language, with most speaking English as well. While immigrants bring their various religions with them, ethnic Swedes who go to church tend to be Lutheran. For great electronic fact sheets on everything in Swedish society from religion to the Sami people, see www.sweden.se.

Latitude and Longitude: 62°N and 15°E, similar latitude to Canada's Northwest Territories.

Area: 174,000 square miles (a little bigger than California).

Geography: A chain of mountains divides Sweden from Norway on the Scandinavian Peninsula. Sweden's mostly forested landscape is flanked to the east by the Baltic Sea, which contributes to the temperate climate. Sweden also encompasses several islands, of which Gotland and Öland are the largest.

Biggest City: Sweden's capital city, Stockholm, has a population of 897,000, with more than two million in the metropolitan area. Göteborg (526,000) and Malmö (307,000) are the next-largest cities.

Economy: Sweden has a $394 billion Gross Domestic Product and a per capita GDP of $40,900—similar to Canada's. Manufacturing, telecommunications, automobiles, and pharmaceuticals rank among its top industries, along with timber, hydropower, and iron ore. The Swedish economy emerged

America; Danes headed south to England, France, and the Mediterranean; and Swedes went east into Russia. (The word "Russia" has Viking roots.) In the early Middle Ages, Swedes founded the Russian cities of Nizhny Novgorod and Kiev, and even served as royal guards in Constantinople (modern-day Istanbul). During the later Middle Ages, German settlers and traders strongly influenced Sweden's culture and language. By the 17th century, Sweden

was a major European power, with one of the largest naval fleets in Europe and an empire extending around the Baltic, including Finland, Estonia, Latvia, and parts of Poland, Russia, and Ger-

from the recent financial crisis as one of the strongest in Europe, helped by its competitive high-tech businesses—and by the government's generally conservative fiscal policies. Eighty percent of Swedish workers belong to a labor union.

Currency: 7 Swedish kronor (kr, officially SEK) = about $1.

Government: King Carl XVI Gustav is the ceremonial head of Sweden's constitutional monarchy. Elected every four years, the 349-member Swedish Parliament (Riksdag) is currently led by Prime Minister Stefan Löfven of the Social Democratic Party (elected in October 2014). *The Economist* magazine—which considered factors such as participation, impact of people on their government, and transparency—ranked Sweden by far the world's most democratic country (followed by the other Scandinavian countries and the Netherlands, with North Korea coming in last).

Flag: The Swedish flag is blue with a yellow Scandinavian cross. The colors are derived from the Swedish coat of arms, with yellow symbolizing the generosity of the people and blue representing vigilance, truth, loyalty, perseverance, and justice.

The Average Swede: He or she is 41 years old, has 1.88 children, and will live to be 82.

many. But by the early 19th century, Sweden's war-weary empire had shrunk. The country's current borders date from 1809.

During a massive wave of emigration from the 1860s to World War II, about a quarter of Sweden's people left for the Promised Land—America. Many emigrants were farmers from the southern region of Småland. The House of Emigrants museum in Växjö tells their story (see the Southeast Sweden chapter), as do the movies *The Emigrants* and *The New Land*, based on the series of books by Vilhelm Moberg.

The 20th century was good to Sweden. While other European countries were embroiled in the two World Wars, neutral Sweden grew stronger, finding a balance between the extremes of communism and the free market. After a recession hit in the early 1990s, and the collapse of Soviet communism reshaped the European political scene, some started to criticize Sweden's "middle way" as extreme and unworkable. But during the late 1990s and early 2000s, Sweden's economy improved, buoyed by a strong lineup of successful multinational companies. Volvo, Scania (trucks and machinery), Ikea, and Ericsson (the telecommunications giant) are leading the way in manufacturing, design, and technology.

The 2008-2009 economic downturn, however, had its impact on Sweden's export-driven economy—its Saab car manufacturer filed for bankruptcy protection in 2011. Unemployment has ticked upward (although it remains enviably low compared to other countries), and Sweden's famously generous welfare systems are feeling the pressure. Although things have rebounded since the crisis, the country's fortunes are dogged by the overall economic weakness of the European Union—Sweden's main export market.

Sweden has come a long way when it comes to accepting immigrants. Less than a century ago, only Swedes who traveled overseas were likely to ever see people of different ethnicities. In 1927 a black man worked in a Stockholm gas station, and people journeyed from great distances to fill up their car there... just to get a look. (Business boomed and his job was secure.)

Since the 1960s, however, Sweden (like Denmark and Norway) has accepted many immigrants and refugees from southeastern Europe, the Middle East, and elsewhere. This praiseworthy humanitarian policy has dramatically—and sometimes painfully—diversified a formerly homogenous country. Many of the service-industry workers you will meet have come to Sweden from elsewhere.

More recently, with refugees flooding in from Syria and Iraq, Swedish social services have been tested as never before. The politics of immigration have become more complex and intense, as Swedes debate the costs (real and societal) of maintaining a culture that wants to be blind to class differences and ethnic divisions.

Though most Swedes speak English, and communication is rarely an issue, a few Swedish words are helpful and appreciated. "Hello" is *"Hej"* (hey) and "Good-bye" is *"Hej då"* (hey doh). "Thank you" is *"Tack"* (tack), which can also double for "please." For a longer list of Swedish survival phrases, see the folllowing page.

Swedish Survival Phrases

Swedish pronunciation (especially the vowel sounds) can be tricky for Americans to say, and there's quite a bit of variation across the country; listen closely to locals and imitate, or ask for help. The most difficult Swedish sound is *sj*, which sounds roughly like a guttural "*h*w" (made in your throat); however, like many sounds, this is pronounced differently in various regions—for example, Stockholmers might say it more like "shw."

English	Swedish	Pronunciation
Hello. (formal)	Goddag!	goh-**dah**
Hi. / Bye. (informal)	Hej. / Hej då.	hey / hey doh
Do you speak English?	Talar du engelska?	**tah**-lar doo **eng**-ehl-skah
Yes. / No.	Ja. / Nej.	yaw / nay
Please.	Snälla. / Tack.*	**snehl**-lah / tack
Thank you (very much).	Tack (så mycket).	tack (soh **mee**-keh)
You're welcome.	Ingen orsak.	**eeng**-ehn **oor**-sahk
Can I help you?	Kan jag hjälpa dig?	kahn yaw **jehl**-pah day
Excuse me.	Ursäkta.	**oor**-sehk-tah
(Very) good.	(Mycket) bra.	(**mee**-keh) brah
Goodbye.	Adjö.	ah-**yew**
one / two	en / två	ehn / tvoh
three / four	tre / fyra	treh / **fee**-rah
five / six	fem / sex	fehm / sehks
seven / eight	sju / åtta	*h*woo / **oh**-tah
nine / ten	nio / tio	**nee**-oh / **tee**-oh
hundred	hundra	**hoon**-drah
thousand	tusen	**too**-sehn
How much?	Hur mycket?	hewr **mee**-keh
local currency: (Swedish) kronor	(Svenske) kronor	(svehn-**skeh**) **kroh**-nor
Where is...?	Var finns...?	var feens
...the toilet	...toaletten	toh-ah-**leh**-tehn
men	man	mahn
women	kvinna	**kvee**-nah
water / coffee	vatten / kaffe	**vah**-tehn / **kah**-feh
beer / wine	öl / vin	url / veen
Cheers!	Skål!	skohl
The bill, please.	Kan jag få notan, tack.	kahn yaw foh **noh**-tahn tack

*Swedish has various ways to say "please," depending on the context. The simplest is *snälla*, but Swedes sometimes use the word *tack* (thank you) the way we use "please."

STOCKHOLM

If I had to call one European city home, it might be Stockholm. One-third water, one-third parks, one-third city, on the sea, surrounded by woods, bubbling with energy and history, Sweden's stunning capital is green, clean, and underrated.

The city is built on a string of islands connected by bridges. Its location midway along the Baltic Sea, behind the natural fortification of its archipelago, made it a fine port, vital to the economy and security of the Swedish peninsula. In the 1500s, Stockholm became a political center when Gustav Vasa established the monarchy (1523). A century later, the expansionist King Gustavus Adolphus made it an influential European capital. The Industrial Revolution brought factories and a flood of farmers from the countryside. In the 20th century, the fuming smokestacks were replaced with steel-and-glass Modernist buildings housing high-tech workers and an expanding service sector.

Today, with more than two million people in the greater metropolitan area (one in five Swedes), Stockholm is Sweden's largest city, as well as its cultural, educational, and media center. It's also the country's most ethnically diverse city. Despite its size, Stockholm is committed to limiting its environmental footprint. Development is strictly monitored, and pollution-belching cars must pay a toll to enter the city. If there's a downside to Stockholm, it's that the city feels super-wealthy (even its Mac-toting hipsters), sometimes snobby, and a bit sure of itself. Stockholm rivals Oslo in expense, and beats it in pretense.

For the visitor, Stockholm offers both old and new. Crawl through Europe's best-preserved old warship and relax on a scenic harbor boat tour. Browse the cobbles and antique shops of the lantern-lit Old Town. Take a trip back in time at Skansen, Europe's first and best open-air folk museum. Marvel at Stockholm's glittering City Hall, slick shopping malls, and art museums. (Even "also ran" museums in this city rank high on the European scale.) Explore the funky vibrancy of the hipster/foodie/design-forward Södermalm district.

While progressive and sleek, Stockholm respects its heritage. In summer, military bands parade daily through the heart of town to the Royal Palace, announcing the Changing of the Guard and turning even the most dignified tourist into a scampering kid.

With extra time, travelers can consider several Stockholm side-trips, including the nearby royal residence, Drottningholm Palace; the cute town of Sigtuna; or the university town of Uppsala, with its grand cathedral and Iron Age mounds (see the Near Stockholm chapter). Stockholm is also an ideal home base for cruising to island destinations in the city's archipelago (see Stockholm's Archipelago chapter).

PLANNING YOUR TIME

On a two- to three-week trip through Scandinavia, Stockholm is worth two days. For the busiest and best two- to three-day plan, I'd suggest this:

Day 1: 10:00—See the *Vasa* warship (movie and tour); 12:00—Visit the Nordic Museum; 13:30—Tour the Skansen open-air museum and grab lunch there; 16:00—Ride the boat (or tram #7) to Nybroplan and follow my self-guided walk through the modern city from  Kungsträdgården; 18:30—Take the Royal Canal boat tour (confirm last sailing time, no boats Jan-March).

Day 2: 10:00—Ride one of the city orientation bus tours (either the hop-on, hop-off or the 1.25-hour bus tour from the Royal Opera House), or take the City Hall tour and climb its tower; 12:15—Catch the Changing of the Guard at the palace (13:15 on Sun); 13:00—Lunch on Stortorget; 14:00—Tour the Royal Armory (and, if time and budget allow, the Nobel Museum and/or Royal Palace sights), and follow my Old Town self-guided walk; 18:30—Explore Södermalm for dinner—it's just across the locks from Gamla Stan—or take a harbor dinner cruise.

Day 3: With an extra day, add a cruise through the scenic island archipelago (easy to do from Stockholm), visit the royal palace at Drottningholm, take a side-trip to charming Sigtuna or Uppsala

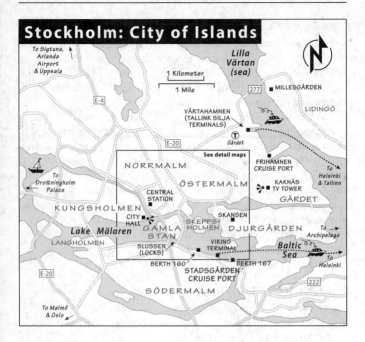

Stockholm: City of Islands

(see next two chapters), or spend more time in Stockholm (there's plenty left to do and experience).

Orientation to Stockholm

Greater Stockholm's two million residents live on 14 islands woven together by 54 bridges. Visitors need only concern themselves with these districts, most of which are islands:

Norrmalm is downtown, with most of the hotels and shopping areas, and the combined train and bus station. **Östermalm,** to the east, is more residential.

Kungsholmen, the mostly suburban island across from Norrmalm, is home to City Hall and inviting lakefront eateries.

Gamla Stan is the Old Town island of winding, lantern-lit streets, antiques shops, and classy cafés clustered around the Royal Palace. The adjacent **Riddarholmen** is similarly atmospheric, but much sleepier. The locks between Lake Mälaren (to the west) and the Baltic Sea (to the east) are at a junction called **Slussen,** just south of Gamla Stan on the way to Södermalm.

Skeppsholmen is the small, central, traffic-free park/island with the Museum of Modern Art and two fine youth hostels.

Djurgården is the park-island—Stockholm's wonderful green playground, with many of the city's top sights (bike rentals just over bridge as you enter island).

Södermalm, just south of the other districts, is sometimes called "Stockholm's Brooklyn"—young, creative, and trendy. Apart from its fine views and some good eateries, this residential island may be of less interest to those on a quick visit.

TOURIST INFORMATION

Stockholm has two TI organizations, one far better than the other. The helpful city-run TI—called **Visit Stockholm**—has two branches. The main office is downtown in the Kulturhuset, facing Sergels Torg (Mon-Fri 9:00-19:00—until 18:00 off-season, Sat 9:00-16:00, Sun 10:00-16:00, Sergels Torg 3, T-bana: T-Centralen, tel. 08/5082-8508, www.visitstockholm.com). They also have a branch at the airport, in Terminal 5, where most international flights arrive (long hours daily, tel. 08/797-6000). The efficient staff provides free city maps, the glossy *Stockholm Guide* booklet that introduces the city, the monthly *What's On* leaflet, Stockholm Cards (described later), transportation passes, day-trip and bus-tour information and tickets, and a room-booking service (small fee). Take a number as you enter, or avoid the wait by looking up sightseeing details on one of the user-friendly computer terminals (they can also give you the code for free Wi-Fi).

Around town, you'll also see the green *i* logo of the other "tourist information" service, **Stockholm Info,** run by a for-profit agency. While less helpful than the official TI, they hand out maps and brochures, sell Stockholm Cards, and may be able to answer basic questions (locations include train station's main hall, Gamla Stan, and Gallerian mall).

Stockholm Card: This 24-hour pass includes all public transit, entry to almost every sight (80 attractions), plus some free or discounted tours for 525 kr—though unfortunately, the card may be discontinued in 2016. A bonus is being able to visit Stockholm's many sights that are worth the time but not the money. The card pays for itself if you use public transportation and see Skansen, the Vasa Museum, and Drottningholm Palace. You can stretch it by entering Skansen on your 24th hour. A child's pass (age 7-17) costs about 60 percent less. The Stockholm Card also comes in 48-hour (675 kr), 72-hour (825 kr), and 120-hour (1,095 kr) versions. Cards are sold at the Visit Stockholm TIs, the unofficial Stockholm Info offices, many hotels and hostels, larger subway stations, and at www.visitstockholm.com.

ARRIVAL IN STOCKHOLM
By Train or Bus

Stockholm's adjacent train (Centralstation) and bus (Cityterminalen) stations, at the southwestern edge of Norrmalm, are a hive of services (including an unofficial Stockholm Info "TI"), eateries, shops, exchange desks, and people on the move. From the train station, the bus station is up the escalators from the main hall and through the glassy atrium (lined with sales desks for bus companies and cruise lines). Those sailing to Finland or Estonia can catch a shuttle bus to the port from the bus terminal. Underground is the T-Centralen subway (T-bana) station—probably the easiest way to reach your hotel. Taxi stands are outside. The best way to connect the city and its airport is via the Arlanda Express shuttle train, which leaves from tracks 1 and 2 (follow

Arlanda Express/airport train signs through the station; see below).

By Plane
Arlanda Airport

Stockholm's Arlanda Airport is 28 miles north of town (airport code: ARN, tel. 08/797-6000, www.arlanda.se). The airport TI (described earlier) can advise you on getting into Stockholm and on your sightseeing plans.

Getting Between the Airport and Downtown: The **airport train,** the Arlanda Express, is the fastest way to zip between the airport and the central train station. Traveling most of the way at 125 mph, it gets you downtown in just 20 minutes—but it's not cheap (260 kr one-way, 490 kr round-trip, free for kids under age 17 with adult, covered by rail pass; generally 4/hour—departing at :05, :20, :35, and :50 past the hour in each direction; toll-free tel. 020-222-224, www.arlandaexpress.com). Buy your ticket either at the window near the track or from a ticket-vending machine, or pay an extra 100 kr to buy it on board. In summer and on weekends, a special fare lets two people travel for nearly half-price (two for 280 kr one-way, available daily mid-June-Aug, Thu-Sun year-round).

Airport shuttle buses (Flygbussarna) run between the airport and Stockholm's train/bus stations (119 kr, 6/hour, 40 minutes, may take longer at rush hour, buy tickets from station kiosks or at airport TI, www.flygbussarna.se).

Taxis between the airport and the city center take 30-40 minutes (about 520 kr, depends on company, look for price printed on side of cab). Establish the price first. Reputable taxis accept credit cards.

The **cheapest airport connection** is to take bus #583 from the airport to Märsta, then switch to the *pendeltåg* (suburban train,

4/hour), which goes to Stockholm's central train station (72 kr, 1 hour total journey time, covered by Stockholm Card).

Skavsta Airport
Some discount airlines use Skavsta Airport, about 60 miles south of Stockholm (airport code: NYO, www.skavsta.se). Flygbussarna shuttle buses connect to the city (159 kr, cheaper if you buy online in advance, about 1-2/hour—generally timed to meet arriving flights, 80 minutes, www.flygbussarna.se).

By Boat
For details on arriving in Stockholm by cruise ship, see page 501. For information on Stockholm's ferry terminals, see page 697 for boats to Tallinn, or page 634 for boats to Helsinki.

By Car
Only a Swedish meatball would drive a car in Stockholm. Park it and use public transit instead. The TI has a *Parking in Stockholm* brochure. Those sailing to Finland or Estonia should ask about long-term parking at the terminal when reserving tickets; to minimize the risk of theft and vandalism, pay extra for the most secure parking garage.

HELPFUL HINTS
Theft Alert: Even in Stockholm, when there are crowds, there are pickpockets (such as at the Royal Palace during the Changing of the Guard). Too-young-to-arrest teens—many from other countries—are hard for local police to control.

Emergency Assistance: In case of an emergency, dial 112.

Medical Help: For around-the-clock medical advice, call 1177. The **C. W. Scheele** 24-hour pharmacy is near the train station at Klarabergsgatan 64 (tel. 08/454-8130).

English Bookstore: The aptly named **English Bookshop,** in Gamla Stan, sells a variety of reading materials (including Swedish-interest books) in English (Mon-Fri 10:00-18:30, Sat 10:00-16:00, Sun 12:00-15:00, Lilla Nygatan 11, tel. 08/790-5510).

Laundry: Tvättomaten is a rare find—the only independent launderette in Stockholm (self-service-100 kr/load, 48-hour full-service-200 kr/load—bring it in early and you can get it back at the end of the day; open Mon-Fri 8:30-18:30—until 17:00 in July-mid-Aug, Sat 9:30-13:00, closed Sun; across from Gustav Vasa church, Västmannagatan 61 on Odenplan, T-bana: Odenplan, tel. 08/346-480, www.tvattomaten.com).

Updates to This Book: For updates to this book, check www.ricksteves.com/update.

GETTING AROUND STOCKHOLM
By Public Transit

Stockholm's fine but pricey public transport network (officially Storstockholms Lokaltrafik—but signed as *SL*) includes subway (Tunnelbana, called "T-bana") and bus systems, and a single handy tram from the commercial center to the sights at Djurgården. It's a spread-out city, so most visitors will need public transport at some point (transit info tel. 08/600-1000, press * for English, www.sl.se/english). The subway is easy to figure out, but many sights are

better served by bus. The main lines are listed on the back of the official city map. A more detailed system map is posted around town and available free from subway ticket windows and SL info desks in main stations. Check out the modern public art in the subway (such as at Kungsträdgården Station).

Tickets: A single ride for subway, tram, or bus costs 36 kr (up to 1.25 hours, including transfers); a 24-hour pass is 115 kr, while a 72-hour pass is 230 kr. Tickets are sold on the tram, but not on board buses—buy one before you board.

You can choose whether to buy paper tickets or get an SL-Access fare card. **Paper tickets** are sold at the Pressbyrån newsstands scattered throughout the city, inside almost every T-bana station, and at some transit-ticket offices (all SL ticket-sellers are clearly marked with a blue flag with the *SL* logo); they are not available at self-service machines.

Locals and savvy tourists carry a blue **SL-Access card,** which you touch against the blue pad to enter the T-bana turnstile or when boarding a bus or tram. If planning to use public transit for more than a few rides, the card can save you money (200 kr for 8 rides, 20-kr deposit for card). You can top up your card at self-service machines (US credit cards work if you know your PIN). Cards are good for several years, so you can pass it along or save it for a return trip.

By Harbor Shuttle Ferry

In summer, ferries let you make a fun, practical, and scenic shortcut across the harbor to Djurgården Island. Boats leave from Slussen (at the south end of Gamla Stan), docking near the Gröna Lund amusement park on Djurgården (45 kr, covered by public-transit passes, 3-4/hour, May-mid-Sept only, 10-minute trip, tel. 08/679-5830, www.waxholmsbolaget.se). On some runs, this ferry also stops near the Museum of Modern Art on Skeppsholmen Island.

The Nybro ferry makes the five-minute journey from Nybroplan to Djurgården, landing next to the Vasa Museum (55 kr, credit cards only, 1/hour, April-Sept daily roughly 9:00-18:00, tel. 08/731-0025, www.ressel.se). While buses and trams run between the same points more frequently, the ferry option gets you out onto the water and can be faster—and certainly more scenic—than overland connections. The hop-on, hop-off boat tour (see page 440) also connects many of these stops.

By Taxi

Stockholm is a good taxi town—provided you find a reputable cab that charges fair rates. Taxis are unregulated, so companies can charge whatever they like. Before hopping in a taxi, look carefully at the big yellow label in the back window, which lists various fares. On the left, you'll see the per-kilometer fares for weekdays, evenings and weekends, and holidays. The largest number, on the right, shows their "highest comparison price" *(högsta järnförpriset)* for a 10-kilometer ride that lasts 15 minutes; this number should be between 290 and 390—if it's higher, move on. (Legally, you're not obligated to take the first cab in line—feel free to compare fares.) Most cabs charge a drop fee of about 45 kr. Taxis with inflated rates tend to congregate at touristy places like the Vasa Museum or in Gamla Stan. I've been ripped off enough by cabs here to know: Take only "Taxi Stockholm" cabs with the phone number (08/150-000) printed on the door. (Other companies that are reportedly honest include Taxi Kurir, tel. 08/300-000, and Taxi 020, tel. 08/850-400 or 020-20-20-20.) Your hotel, restaurant, or museum can call a cab, which will generally arrive within minutes (no extra charge—the meter starts when you hop in).

Tours in Stockholm

The sightseeing company **Strömma** has a lock on most city tours, whether by bus, by boat, or on foot. Their website (www.stromma. se) covers the entire program, much of which is listed next. For more information on their tours, call 08/1200-4000. Tours can be paid for in advance online, or simply as you board. The Stockholm Card provides discounts or even covers some of Strömma's tours, including the Royal Canal or Historic Canal boat trip (free), their orientation bus tour (half-price), and their hop-on, hop-off bus tour (discounted).

BY BUS
Hop-On, Hop-Off Bus Tour
Three hop-on, hop-off buses make a 1.5-hour circuit of the city, orienting riders with a recorded commentary and linking all the essential places from Skansen to City Hall; when cruises are in town,

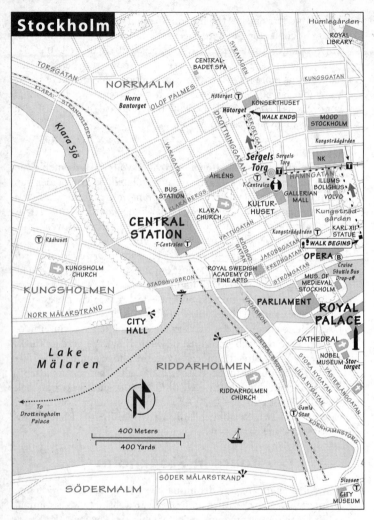

Stockholm

(Map labels:) Humlegården · ROYAL LIBRARY · TORSGATAN · NORRMALM · CENTRAL-BADET SPA · SVEAVÄGEN · KUNGSGATAN · KLARA · STRANDLEDEN · Norra Bantorget · OLOF PALMES · Klara Sjö · Hötorget · KONSERTHUSET · WALK ENDS · MOOD STOCKHOLM · Kungsträdgården · DROTTNINGGATAN · VASAGATAN · SERGELGATAN · NK · Sergels Torg · HAMNGATAN · ÅHLÉNS · ILLUMS BOLIGHUS · BUS STATION · T-Centralen · GALLERIAN MALL · VOLVO · KLARABERGS · KULTUR-HUSET · Kungsträd-gården · CENTRAL STATION · KLARA CHURCH · VATTUGATAN · Kungsträdgården · KARL XII STATUE · T-Centralen · RÅDBODO-GATAN · JAKOBSGATAN · WALK BEGINS · Rådhuset · KUNGSHOLMS CHURCH · FREDSGATAN · OPERA · ROYAL SWEDISH ACADEMY OF FINE ARTS · STRÖMGATAN · Cruise Shuttle Bus Drop-off · KUNGSHOLMEN · STADSHUSBRON · MUS. OF MEDIEVAL STOCKHOLM · NORR MÄLARSTRAND · CITY HALL · VASABRON · PARLIAMENT · ROYAL PALACE · Lake Mälaren · CENTRALBRON · CATHEDRAL · NOBEL MUSEUM · Stor-torget · RIDDARHOLMEN · STORA NYGATAN · LILLA NYGATAN · VÄSTERLÅNGGATAN · To Drottningholm Palace · RIDDARHOLMEN CHURCH · Gamla Stan · KÖRNHAMNSTORG · 400 Meters · 400 Yards · N · Slussen · CITY MUSEUM · SÖDER MÄLARSTRAND · SÖDERMALM

they also stop at both cruise ports (Stadsgården and Frihamnen). **Open Top Tours'** green buses and **City Sightseeing's** red buses both cooperate with Strömma (260 kr/24 hours, 350 kr/72 hours, ticket covers both buses; May-Sept 2/hour daily 10:00-16:00, fewer off-season, none mid-Jan–mid-Feb, www.stromma.se). **Red Sightseeing** offers a similar hop-on, hop-off itinerary for the same price (3/hour, www.redbuses.se). All bus companies offer free Wi-Fi.

Quickie Orientation Bus Tour

Several different city bus tours leave from the Royal Opera House on Gustav Adolfs Torg. Strömma's Stockholm Panorama tour provides a good overview—but, as it's the same price as the 24-hour

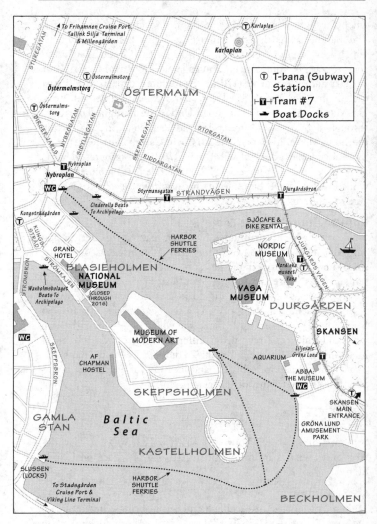

hop-on, hop-off ticket, I'd take this tour only if you want a quick and efficient loop with no unnecessary stops (260 kr, 4-6/day, fewer in Oct-May, 1.25 hours).

BY BOAT
▲City Boat Tours

For a good floating look at Stockholm and a pleasant break, consider a sightseeing cruise. I enjoy these various boat tours at the end of the day,

when the light is warm and the sights and museums are closed. The handiest are the Strömma/Stockholm Sightseeing boats, which leave from Strömkajen, in front of the Grand Hotel, and also stop at Nybroplan five minutes later. The **Royal Canal Tour** is short and informative (170 kr, 50 minutes, departs at :30 past each hour May-Aug 10:30-18:30, less frequent off-season, none Jan-March). The nearly two-hour **Under the Bridges Tour** goes through two locks and under 15 bridges (225 kr, departures on the hour May-mid-Sept). The **Historic Canal Tour** leaves from the Stadshusbron dock at City Hall (170 kr, 50 minutes, departs at :30 past each hour June-Aug). You'll circle Kungsholmen island while learning about Stockholm's history from the early Industrial Age to modern times.

Hop-On, Hop-Off Boat Tour

Stockholm is a city surrounded by water, making this boat option enjoyable and practical. Strömma/Royal Sightseeing offers the same small loop, stopping at key spots such as Djurgården (Skansen and Vasa Museum), Gamla Stan (near Slussen and again near Royal Palace), the Viking Line dock next to the cruise terminal at Stadsgården, and Nybroplan. Use the boat strictly as transport from Point A to Point B, or make the whole one-hour, eight-stop loop and enjoy the recorded commentary (Strömma-160 kr/24 hours, Royal Sightseeing-120 kr/24 hours, 2-3/hour May-mid-Sept, pick up map for schedule and locations of boat stops, www.stromma.se or www.royalsightseeing.com).

ON FOOT
Old Town Walk

Strömma offers a 1.25-hour Old Town walk (150 kr, 2/day July-Aug only, departs from obelisk next to Royal Palace on Gamla Stan).

Local Guides

Håkan Fränden is an excellent guide who brings Stockholm to life (mobile 070-531-3379, hakan.franden@hotmail.com). You can also hire a private guide through the Association of Qualified Tourist Guides of Stockholm (www.guidestockholm.com, info@guidestockholm.com). The standard rate is about 1,500 kr for up to three hours. **Marita Bergman** is a teacher and a licensed guide who enjoys showing visitors around during her school breaks (1,650 kr/half-day tour, mobile 073-511-9154, maritabergman@bredband.net).

BY BIKE

To tour Stockholm on two wheels, you can either use one of the city bikes or rent your own.

Using City Bikes: Stockholm's City Bikes program is a good option for seeing this bike-friendly town. While you'll find similar bike-sharing programs all over Europe, Stockholm's is the most usable and helpful for travelers. It's easy, the bikes are great, and the city lends itself to joy-riding.

Purchase a 165-kr, three-day City Bike card at the TI, at the SL Center (Stockholm Transport) office at Sergels Torg, or at many hotels and hostels. The card allows you to grab a bike from one of the more than 90 City Bike racks around the city. You must return it within three hours (to any rack), but if you want to keep riding, just check out another bike. You can do this over and over for three days (available April-Oct only, www.citybikes.se).

The downside: Unless you have a lock, you can't park your bike as you sightsee. You'll need to return it to a station and get another when you're ready to go—which sounds easy enough, but in practice many stations are full (without an empty port in which to leave a bike) or have no bikes available. To overcome this problem, download the fun, easy, and free app from the website, which can help you find the nearest racks and bikes.

Renting a Bike: You can also rent bikes (and boats) at **Sjö-caféet,** next to Djurgårdsbron bridge near the Vasa Museum. It's ideally situated as a springboard for a pleasant bike ride around the park-like Djurgården island—use their free and excellent bike map/guide. For details, see page 467.

Stockholm Walks

This section includes two different self-guided walks to introduce you to Stockholm, both old (Gamla Stan) and new (the modern city).

▲▲OLD TOWN (GAMLA STAN) WALK

Stockholm's historic island core is charming, photogenic, and full of antiques shops, street lanterns, painted ceilings, and surprises. Until the 1600s, all of Stockholm fit in Gamla Stan. Stockholm traded with other northern ports such as Amsterdam, Lübeck, and Tallinn. German culture influenced art, building styles, and even the language, turning Old Norse into modern Swedish. With its narrow alleys and stairways, Gamla Stan mixes poorly with cars and modern economies. Today, it's been given over to the Royal Palace and to the tourists, who throng Gamla Stan's main drag,

Stockholm's Gamla Stan Walk

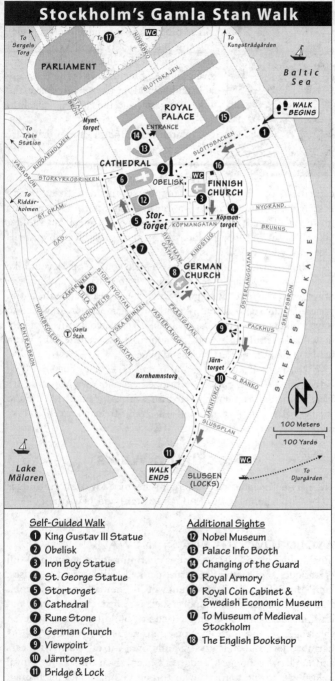

Self-Guided Walk

1. King Gustav III Statue
2. Obelisk
3. Iron Boy Statue
4. St. George Statue
5. Stortorget
6. Cathedral
7. Rune Stone
8. German Church
9. Viewpoint
10. Järntorget
11. Bridge & Lock

Additional Sights

12. Nobel Museum
13. Palace Info Booth
14. Changing of the Guard
15. Royal Armory
16. Royal Coin Cabinet & Swedish Economic Museum
17. To Museum of Medieval Stockholm
18. The English Bookshop

STOCKHOLM

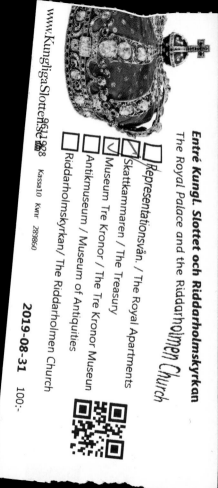

www.KungligaSlotten.se

Kassa10 Kvnr 289860

Entré Kungl. Slottet och Riddarholmskyrkan
The Royal Palace and the Riddarholmen Church

- [ ] Representationsvån. / The Royal Apartments
- [ ] Skattkammaren / The Treasury
- [✓] Museum Tre Kronor / The Tre Kronor Museun
- [ ] Antikmuseum / Museum of Antiquities
- [ ] Riddarholmskyrkan/ The Riddarholmen Church

2019-08-31 100:-

Västerlånggatan, seemingly unaware that most of Stockholm's best attractions are elsewhere. While you could just happily wander, this quick walk gives meaning to Stockholm's Old Town.

• *Our walk begins along the harborfront. Start at the base of Slottsbacken (the Palace Hill esplanade) leading up to the...*

Royal Palace: Along the water, check out the ❶ **statue of King Gustav III** gazing at the palace, which was built on the site of Stockholm's first castle (described later, under "Sights in Stockholm"). Gustav turned Stockholm from a dowdy Scandinavian port into a sophisticated European capital, modeled on French culture. Gustav loved the arts, and he founded the Royal Dramatic Theater and the Royal Opera in Stockholm. Ironically, he was assassinated at a masquerade ball at the Royal Opera House in 1792, inspiring Verdi's opera *Un Ballo in Maschera*.

Walk up the broad, cobbled boulevard to the crest of the hill. Stop, look back, and scan the harbor. The grand building across

the water is the National Museum, which is often mistaken for the palace. Beyond that, in the distance, is the fine row of buildings on Strandvägen street. Until the 1850s, this area was home to peasant shacks, but as Stockholm entered its grand stage, it was cleaned up and replaced by fine apartments, including some of the city's smartest addresses. The blocky gray TV tower—a major attraction back in the 1970s—stands tall in the distance. Turn to the palace facade on your left (finished in 1754, replacing one that burned in 1697). The niches are filled with Swedish bigwigs (literally) from the mid-18th century.

As you crest the hill, you're facing the ❷ **obelisk** that honors Stockholm's merchant class for its support in a 1788 war against Russia. In front of the obelisk are tour buses (their drivers worried about parking cops) and a sand pit used for *boules*. The royal family took a liking to the French game during a Mediterranean vacation, and it's quite popular around town today. Behind the obelisk stands Storkyrkan, Stockholm's cathedral (which we'll visit later in this walk). From this angle you can see its Baroque facade, which was added to better

match the newer palace. Opposite the palace (dark orange building on left) is the Finnish church (Finska Kyrkan), which originated as the royal tennis hall. When the Protestant Reformation hit in 1527, church services could at last be said in the peoples' languages rather than Latin. Suddenly, each merchant community needed its own church. Finns worshiped here, the Germans built their own church (coming up on this walk), and the Swedes got the cathedral.

Stroll up the lane to the right of the Finnish church into the shady churchyard where you'll find the fist-sized ❸ *Iron Boy,* the tiniest

public statue (out of about 600 statues) in Stockholm. Swedish grannies knit caps for him in the winter. Local legend says the statue honors the orphans who had to transfer cargo from sea ships to lake ships before Stockholm's locks were built. Some people rub his head for good luck (which the orphans didn't have). Others, likely needy when it comes to this gift, rub his head for wisdom. The artist says it's simply a self-portrait of himself as a child, sitting on his bed and gazing at the moon.

• *Continue through the yard, turn left onto Trädgårdsgatan, then bear right with the lane until you pop out at...*

Köpmangatan: Take a moment to explore this street from one end to the other. With its cobbles and traditional pastel facades, this is a quintessential Gamla Stan lane—and one of the oldest in town. The mellow yellow houses are predominantly from the 18th century; the red facades are mostly 17th century. Once merchants' homes, today these are popular with antique dealers. Back when there was comfort living within a city's walls, Gamla Stan streets like this were densely populated.

Head left, and you'll emerge on Köpmantorget square, with the breathtaking ❹ **statue of St. George** slaying the dragon. About 10 steps to the right of that is a maiden (representing Stockholm), looking on with thanks and admiration. At the other (top) end of the lane is old Stockholm's main square, our next stop.

❺ **Stortorget, Stockholm's Oldest Square:** Colorful old buildings topped with gables line this square, which was the heart of medieval Stockholm (pop. 6,000 in 1400). This was where the many tangled lanes intersected, becoming the natural center for shopping and the town well. Today Stortorget is home to lots of tourists—including a steady storm of cruise groups following the numbered Ping-Pong paddle

of their guides on four-hour blitz tours of the city (300 ships call here between June and September each year). The square also hosts concerts, occasional demonstrators, and—in winter—Christmas shoppers at an outdoor market.

The grand building on the right is the **Stock Exchange.** It now houses the noble Nobel Museum (described later, under "Sights in Stockholm"). On the immediate left is the social-services agency **Stockholms Stadsmission** (offering the cheapest and best lunch around at the recommended Grillska Huset). If you peek into the adjacent bakery, you'll get a fine look at the richly decorated ceilings characteristic of Gamla Stan in the 17th century—the exotic flowers and animals implied that the people who lived or worked here were worldly. You'll also spy some tempting marzipan cakes (a local favorite) and *kanelbullar* (cinnamon buns). There's a cheap sandwich counter in the back and lots of picnic benches in the square.

The town well is still a popular meeting point. This square long held the town's pillory. Scan the fine old facades. The site of the **Stockholm Bloodbath** of 1520, this square has a notorious history. During a Danish power grab, many of Stockholm's movers and shakers who had challenged Danish rule—Swedish aristocracy, leading merchants, and priests—were rounded up, brought here, and beheaded. Rivers of blood were said to have flowed through the streets. Legend holds that the 80 or so white stones in the fine red facade across the square symbolize the victims. (One victim's son escaped, went into hiding, and resurfaced to lead a Swedish revolt against the Danish rulers. Three years later, the Swedes elected that rebel, Gustav Vasa, as their first king. He went on to usher in a great period in the country's history—the Swedish Renaissance.)

• *At the far end of the square (under the finest gables), turn right and follow Trångsund toward the cathedral.*

❻ **Cathedral (Storkyrkan):** Just before the church, you'll see my personal phone booth (Rikstelefon) and the gate to the churchyard—guarded by statues of Caution and Hope. Enter the yellow-brick church—Stockholm's oldest, from the 13th century (40 kr; daily 9:00-16:00, open later Mon-Fri in summer—until 17:00 or 18:00). Signs explain events (busy with tours and services in summer).

When buying your ticket, pick up the free, worthwhile English-language flier. Exploring the cathedral's interior, you'll find many

STOCKHOLM

styles, ranging from medieval to modern. The front of the nave is paved with centuries-old **tombstones.** At one time, more than a thousand people were buried under the church. The tombstone of the Swedish reformer Olaus Petri is appropriately simple and appropriately located—under the finely carved and gilded pulpit. A witness to the Stockholm Bloodbath, Petri was nearly executed himself. He went on to befriend Gustav Vasa and guide him in Lutheranizing Sweden (and turning this cathedral from Catholic to Protestant). The fine 17th-century altar is made of silver and ebony. Above it, the silver Christ stands like a conquering general evoking the 1650s, an era of Swedish military might.

Opposite the pulpit, find the **bronze plaque** in the pillar. It recalls the 1925 Swedish-led ecumenical meeting of all Christian leaders—except the pope—that encouraged the Church to speak out against the type of evil that resulted in World War I's horrific death toll.

The **royal boxes** (carved wood, between the pulpit and the altar) date from 1684. In June of 2010, this church hosted a royal wedding (Crown Princess Victoria, heir to the throne, married Daniel Westling, her personal trainer). Imagine the pomp and circumstance as the nation's attention was drawn to this spot.

The remarkably detailed **statue** to the left of the altar, *Saint George and the Dragon* (1489)—a copy of which you saw outside a few minutes ago—is carved of oak and elk horn. To some, this

symbolizes the Swedes' overcoming the evil Danes (commemorating a military victory in 1471). In a broader sense, it's an inspiration to take up the struggle against even non-Danish evil. Regardless, it must be the gnarliest dragon's head in all of Europe.

Return to the back of the church to find the exit. Before leaving, just to the left of the door, notice the **painting** that depicts Stockholm in the early 1500s, showing a walled city filling only today's Gamla Stan. It's a 1630 copy of the 1535 original. The church with its black spire dominated the town back then. The strange sun and sky predicted big changes in Sweden—and as a matter of fact, that's what happened. Gustav Vasa brought on huge reforms in religion and beyond. (The doors just to the left and right of the painting lead to a free WC.)

Heading outside, you'll emerge into the kid-friendly churchyard, which was once the cemetery.

• *With your back to the church's front door, turn right and continue down*

Trångsund. At the next corner, turn left and go downhill on Storkyrko-brinken and take the first left on...

Prästgatan: Enjoy a quiet wander down this peaceful 15th-century "Priests' Lane." Västerlånggatan, the touristy drag, parallels this lane one block over. (While we'll skip it now, you can

walk back up it from the end point of this walk.) As you stroll Prästgatan, look for bits of its past: hoists poking out horizontally from gables (merchants used these to lift goods into their attics), tie bolts (iron bars necessary to bind the timber beams of tall buildings together), small coal or wood hatches (for fuel delivery back in the good old days), and flaming gold phoenixes under red-crown medallions (telling firefighters which houses paid insurance and could be saved in case of fire—for example, #46). Like other Scandinavian cities, Stockholm was plagued by fire until it was finally decreed that only stone, stucco, and brick construction (like you see here) would be allowed in the town center.

After a few blocks (at Kåkbrinken), a cannon barrel on the corner (look down) guards a Viking-age ❼ **rune stone.** In case you can't read the old Nordic script, it says: "Torsten and Frogun erected this stone in memory of their son."

• *Continue one block farther down Prästgatan to Tyska Brinken and turn left. You will see the powerful brick steeple of the German Church.*

❽ **German Church** (Tyska Kyrkan): The church's carillon has played four times a day since 1666. Think of the days when German merchants worked here. Today, Germans come to Sweden not to run the economy, but to enjoy its pristine nature (which is progressively harder to find in their own crowded homeland). Sweden formally became a Lutheran country even before the northern part of Germany—making this the very first German Lutheran church (free, Mon-Sat 11:00-15:00, Sun 12:30-17:00).

• *Wander through the churchyard (past a cute church café) and out the back. Exit right onto Svartmangatan and follow it to the right, ending at an iron railing overlooking Österlånggatan.*

❾ **Viewpoint:** From this perch, survey the street below to the left and right. Notice how it curves. This marks the old shoreline. In medieval times, piers stretched out like fingers into the harbor. Gradually, as land was reclaimed and developed, these piers were extended, becoming lanes leading to piers farther away. Behind you is a cute shop where elves can actually be seen making elves.

• *Walk right along Österlånggatan to...*

❿ **Järntorget:** A customs square in medieval times, this was the home of Sweden's first bank back in 1680 (the yellow building with the bars on the windows). The Co-op Nära supermarket on this square offers picnic fixings. From here, Västerlånggatan—the eating, shopping, and commercial pedestrian mall of Gamla Stan—leads back across the island. You'll be there in a minute, but first finish this walk.

• *Continue out of the square (opposite where you entered) down Järntorgsgatan, walk (carefully) out into the traffic hell, passing an equestrian statue of Jean-Baptiste Bernadotte—the French son of a lawyer invited to establish the current Swedish royal dynasty in the early 1800s. Continue ahead 50 yards until you reach a viewpoint overlooking a lock.*

⓫ Bridge Overlooking Slussen: This area is called Slussen, named for the locks between the salt water of the Baltic Sea (to your left) and the fresh water of the huge Lake Mälaren (to your right). In fact, Stockholm exists because this is where Lake Mälaren meets the sea. Traders would sail their goods from far inland to this point, where they'd meet merchants who would ship the goods south to Europe. In the 13th century, the new Kingdom of Sweden needed revenue, and began levying duty taxes on all the iron, copper, and furs shipped through here. From the bridge, you may notice a current in the water, indicating that the weir has been lowered and water is spilling from Lake Mälaren (about two feet above sea level) into the sea. Today, the locks are nicknamed "the divorce lock" because this is where captains and first mates learn to communicate under pressure and in the public eye.

Survey the view. Opposite Gamla Stan is the island of **Södermalm**—bohemian, youthful, artsy, and casual—with its popular Katarina viewing platform (see sidebar on page 465). Moored on the saltwater side are the cruise ships, which bring thousands of visitors into town each day during the season. Many of these boats are bound for Finland. The towering white syringe is the Gröna Lund amusement park's free-fall ride. The revolving *Djurgården Färjan* sign, along the embankment to your left, marks the ferry that zips from here directly to Gröna Lund and Djurgården.

You could catch bus #2, which heads back downtown (the stop is just beyond Bernadotte, next to the waterfront). But better yet, linger longer in Gamla Stan—day or night, it's a lively place to enjoy. Västerlånggatan, Gamla Stan's main commercial drag, is a touristy festival of distractions that keeps most visitors from seeing the historic charms of the Old Town—which you just did. Now you're free to window-shop and eat (see page 452). Or, if it's late, find some live music (see page 480).

• *For more sightseeing, consider the other sights in Gamla Stan or at the Royal Palace (all described later, under "Sights in Stockholm"). If you continue back up Västerlånggatan (always going straight), you'll reach the Parliament building and cross the water back over onto Norrmalm*

Fika: Sweden's Coffee Break

Swedes drink more coffee per capita than just about any other country in the world. The Swedish coffee break—or *fika*—is a ritual. *Fika* is to Sweden what tea-time is to Britain. The typical *fika* is a morning or afternoon break in the workday, but can happen any time, any day. It's the perfect opportunity (and excuse) for tourists to take a break as well.

Fika fare is coffee with a snack—something sweet or savory. Your best bet is a *kanelbulle*, a Swedish cinnamon bun, although some prefer *pariserbulle*, a bun filled with vanilla cream. These can be found nearly everywhere coffee is sold, including just about any café or *konditori* (bakery) in Stockholm. A coffee and a cinnamon bun in a café will cost you about 40 kr. (Most cafés will give you a coffee refill for free.) But at Pressbyrån, the Swedish convenience stores found all over town, you can satisfy your *fika* fix for 25 kr by getting a coffee and bun to go. Grab a park bench or waterside perch, relax, and enjoy.

(where the street becomes Drottninggatan). This pedestrian street leads back into Stockholm's modern, vibrant new town.

From here it's also a 10-minute walk to Kungsträdgården, the starting point of my Modern City self-guided walk (described next). You can either walk along the embankment and take the diagonal bridge directly across to the square, or you can walk back through the middle of Gamla Stan, taking the stately walkway past the Parliament, then turning right when you cross the bridge. On the way there, you'll pass the Royal Opera House and (tucked behind it) Gustav Adolfs Torg, with its imposing statue of Gustavus Adolphus. He was the king who established the Swedish empire. Considered by many to be the father of modern warfare for his innovative tactics, he was a Protestant hero of the Thirty Years' War.

STOCKHOLM'S MODERN CITY WALK

On this walk, we'll use the park called Kungsträdgården as a springboard to explore the modern center of Stockholm—a commercial zone designed to put the focus not on old kings and mementos of superpower days, but on shopping. For the route, see the map on page 438.

• *Find the statue of King Karl XII, facing the waterfront at the harbor end of the park.*

Kungsträdgården: Centuries ago, this "King's Garden" was the private kitchen garden of the king, where he grew his cabbage salad. Today, this downtown people-watching center, worth ▲, is considered Stockholm's living room, symbolizing the Swedes' freedom-loving spirit. While the name implies that the garden is a private royal domain, the giant clump of elm trees just behind the statue reminds locals that it's the people who rule now. In the 1970s, demonstrators chained themselves to these trees to stop the

building of an underground train station here. They prevailed, and today, locals enjoy the peaceful, breezy ambience of a teahouse instead. Watch the AstroTurf zone with "latte dads" and their kids, and enjoy a summer concert at the bandstand. There's always something going on. High above is a handy reference point—the revolving NK clock.

Kungsträdgården—surrounded by the harborfront and tour boats, the Royal Opera House, and shopping opportunities (including a welcoming Volvo showroom near the top-left side of the square, showing off the latest in Swedish car design)—is *the* place to feel Stockholm's pulse (but always ask first: *"Kan jag kanna på din puls?"*).

Kungsträdgården also throws huge parties. The Taste of Stockholm festival runs for a week in early June, when restaurateurs show off and bands entertain all day. Beer flows liberally—a rare public spectacle in Sweden.

• *Stroll through Kungsträdgården, past the fountain and the Volvo store, and up to Hamngatan street. From here, we'll turn left and walk the length of the NK department store (across the street) as we wade through...*

Stockholm's Urban Shopping Zone (Hamngatan): In just a couple of blocks, we'll pass some major landmarks of Swedish consumerism. First, at the top of Kungsträdgården on the left, look for the gigantic **Illums Bolighus** design shop. (You can enter from the square and stroll all the way through it, popping out at Hamngatan on the far end.) This is a Danish institution, making its play for Swedish customers with this prime location. Across the street (on your right as you walk down Hamngatan), notice the giant gold *NK* marking the **Nordiska Kompaniet** department store (locals joke that the NK stands for "no kronor left"). It's located in an elegant early 20th-century building that dominates the top end of Kungsträdgården. If it feels like an old-time American department store, that's because its architect was inspired by grand stores he'd seen in the US (circa 1910).

Another block down, on the left, is the sleeker, more modern

Gallerian mall. Among this two-story world of shops, upstairs you'll find a Clas Ohlson hardware and electronics shop (a men's favorite, as most Stockholmers have a cabin that's always in need of a little DIY repair). And there are plenty of affordable little lunch bars and classy cafés for your *fika* (Swedish coffee-and-bun break). You may notice that American influence (frozen yogurt and other trendy food chains) is challenging the entire notion of the traditional *fika*.

• *High-end shoppers should consider heading into the streets behind NK, with exclusive designer boutiques and the chichi Mood Stockholm mall (see page 479). Otherwise, just beyond the huge Gallerian mall, you'll emerge into Sergels Torg. (Note that the handy tram #7 goes from here directly to Skansen and the other important sights on Djurgården; departures every few minutes, tickets sold on board.)*

Sergels Torg and Kulturhuset: Sergels Torg square, worth ▲, dominates the heart of modern Stockholm with its stark 1960s-era functionalist architecture. The glassy tower in the middle of the fountain plaza is ugly in daylight but glows at night, symbolic of Sweden's haunting northern lights.

Kulturhuset, the hulking, low-slung, glassy building overlooking the square (on your left) is Stockholm's "culture center." Inside, just past the welcoming info desk, you'll find a big model of the city that locals use to check in on large infrastructure projects. Push a few buttons and see what's happening. In this lively cultural zone, there's a space for kids, a library (with magazines and computer terminals), chessboards, fun shops, fine art cinema, art exhibits, and a venue for new bands (tel. 08/5083-1508, www.kulturhuset.stockholm.se).

I like to take the elevator to the top and explore each level by riding the escalator back down to the ground floor. On the rooftop, choose from one of two recommended eateries with terrific city views: Cafeteria Panorama has cheap meals and a salad bar while the Mat and Bar café is trendier and pricier (see page 498).

Back outside, stand in front of the Kulturhuset (across from the fountain) and survey the expansive square nicknamed "Plattan" (the platter). Everything around you dates from the 1960s and 1970s, when this formerly run-down area was reinvented as an urban "space of the future." In the 1970s, with no nearby residences, the desolate Plattan became the domain of junkies. Now the city is actively revitalizing it, and the Plattan is becoming a people-friendly heart of the commercial town.

DesignTorget (enter from the lower level of Kulturhuset) is a place for independent Swedish designers to showcase and sell their clever products. (Local designers submit their creations, and the DesignTorget staff votes on and carries their favorites—perhaps you need a banana case?) Nearby are the major boutiques and department stores, including, across the way, H&M and Åhléns.

Sergelgatan, a thriving pedestrian and commercial street, leads past the five uniform white towers you see beyond the fountain. These office towers, so modern in the 1960s, have gone from seeming hopelessly out-of-date to being considered "retro," and are now quite popular with young professionals.

· *Walk up Sergelgatan past the towers, enjoying the public art and people-watching, to the market at Hötorget.*

Hötorget: "Hötorget" means "Hay Market," but today its stalls feed people rather than horses. The adjacent indoor market, Hötorgshallen, is fun and fragrant.

It dates from 1914 when, for hygienic reasons, the city forbade selling fish and meat outdoors. Carl Milles' statue of *Orpheus Emerging from the Underworld* (with seven sad Muses) stands in front of the city concert hall (which hosts the annual Nobel Prize award ceremony). The concert house, from 1926, is Swedish Art Deco (a.k.a. "Swedish Grace"). The lobby (open through much of the summer, 70-kr tours) still evokes Stockholm's Roaring Twenties. If the door's open, you're welcome to look in for free.

Popping into the Hötorget T-bana station provides a fun glimpse at local urban design. Stockholm's subway system was inaugurated in the 1950s, and many stations are modern art installations in themselves.

· *Our walk ends here. For more shopping and an enjoyable pedestrian boulevard leading back into the Old Town, cut down a block to Drottninggatan and turn left. This busy drag leads straight out of the commercial district, passes the Parliament, then becomes the main street of Gamla Stan.*

Sights in Stockholm

GAMLA STAN (OLD TOWN)

The best of Gamla Stan is covered in my self-guided "Old Town Walk," earlier. But here are a few ways to extend your time in the Old Town.

On Stortorget
▲Nobel Museum (Nobelmuseet)

Opened in 2001 for the 100-year anniversary of the Nobel Prize, this wonderful little museum tells the story of the world's most prestigious prize. Pricey but high-tech and eloquent, it fills the grand old stock exchange building that dominates Gamla Stan's main square, Stortorget.

Cost and Hours: 100 kr, free Tue after 17:00; open June-Aug daily 10:00-20:00; Sept-May Tue 11:00-20:00, Wed-Sun 11:00-17:00, closed Mon; audioguide-20 kr, free 30-minute orientation tours in English: 6/day in summer, fewer off-season; on Stortorget in the center of Gamla Stan a block from the Royal Palace, tel. 08/5348-1800, www.nobelmuseum.se.

Background: Stockholm-born Alfred Nobel was a great inventor, with more than 300 patents. His most famous invention: dynamite. Living in the late 1800s, Nobel was a man of his age. It was a time of great optimism, wild ideas, and grand projects. His dynamite enabled entire nations to blast their way into the modern age with canals, railroads, and tunnels. It made warfare much more destructive. And it also made Alfred Nobel a very wealthy man. Wanting to leave a legacy that celebrated and supported people with great ideas, Alfred used his fortune to fund the Nobel Prize. Every year since 1901, laureates have been honored in the fields of physics, chemistry, medicine, literature, and peacemaking.

Visiting the Museum: Inside, portraits of all 700-plus prize-winners hang from the ceiling—shuffling around the room like shirts at the dry cleaner's (miss your favorite, and he or she will come around again in six hours). Behind the ticket desk are video screens honoring the six Nobel Prize categories, each running a clip about the most recent laureate in that category.

Flanking the main hall beyond that—where touchscreens organized by decade invite you to learn more about the laureates of your choice—two video rooms run a continuous montage of quick programs (three-minute bios of various winners in one program, five-minute films celebrating various intellectual environments—from Cambridge to Parisian cafés—in the other).

To the right of the ticket desk, find "The Gallery," with an endearingly eccentric collection of items that various laureates have cited as important to their creative process, from scientific equip-

Stockholm at a Glance

▲▲▲**Skansen** Europe's first and best open-air folk museum, with more than 150 old homes, churches, shops, and schools. **Hours:** Park—daily May-late-June 10:00-19:00, late-June-Aug 10:00-22:00, Sept 10:00-18:00, Oct and March-April 10:00-16:00, Nov-Feb 10:00-15:00; historical buildings—generally 11:00-17:00, late June-Aug some until 19:00, most closed in winter. See page 468.

▲▲▲**Vasa Museum** Ill-fated 17th-century warship dredged from the sea floor, now the showpiece of an interesting museum. **Hours:** Daily June-Aug 8:30-18:00; Sept-May 10:00-17:00 except Wed until 20:00. See page 470.

▲▲**Military Parade and Changing of the Guard** Punchy pomp starting near Nybroplan and finishing at Royal Palace outer courtyard. **Hours:** Mid-May-mid-Sept daily, mid-Sept-April Wed and Sat-Sun only, start time varies with season but always at mid-day. See page 456.

▲▲**Royal Armory** A fine collection of ceremonial medieval royal armor, historic and modern royal garments, and carriages, in the Royal Palace. **Hours:** May-June daily 11:00-17:00; July-Aug daily 10:00-18:00; Sept-April Tue-Sun 11:00-17:00, Thu until 20:00, closed Mon. See page 457.

▲▲**City Hall** Gilt mosaic architectural jewel of Stockholm and site of Nobel Prize banquet, with tower offering the city's best views. **Hours:** Required tours daily generally June-Aug every 30 minutes 9:30-16:00, off-season hourly 10:00-15:00. See page 462.

▲▲**Nordic Museum** Danish Renaissance palace design and five fascinating centuries of traditional Swedish lifestyles. **Hours:** Daily 10:00-17:00, Wed until 20:00 Sept-May. See page 473.

ment to inspirational knickknacks. The randomness of the items offers a fascinating and humanizing insight into the great minds of our time. Beyond that are a room dedicated to Alfred Nobel and a small children's area.

The Viennese-style Bistro Nobel is the place to get creative with your coffee...and sample the famous Nobel ice cream. All Nobel laureates who visit the museum are asked to sign the bottom of a chair in the café. Turn yours over and see who warmed your chair. And don't miss the lockable hangers, to protect your fancy, furry winter coat. The Swedish Academy, which awards the Nobel Prize for literature each year, is upstairs.

▲**Nobel Museum** Star-studded tribute to some of the world's most accomplished scientists, artists, economists, and politicians. **Hours:** June-Aug daily 10:00-20:00; Sept-May Tue 11:00-20:00, Wed-Sun 11:00-17:00; closed Mon. See page 453.

▲**Royal Palace Museums** Complex of Swedish royal museums, the two best of which are the Royal Apartments and Royal Treasury. **Hours:** Mid-May-mid-Sept daily 10:00-17:00; mid-Sept-mid-May Tue-Sun 12:00-16:00, closed Mon. See page 458.

▲**Royal Coin Cabinet** Europe's best look at the history of money, with a sweep through the evolution of the Swedish economy to boot. **Hours:** Daily June-Aug 11:00-17:00, Sept-May 10:00-16:00. See page 460.

▲**Kungsträdgården** Stockholm's lively central square, with life-size chess games, concerts, and perpetual action. **Hours:** Always open. See page 449.

▲**Sergels Torg** Modern square with underground mall. **Hours:** Always open. See page 451.

▲**ABBA: The Museum** A super-commercial and wildly-popular-with-ABBA-fans experience. **Hours:** Daily 10:00-20:00, shorter hours off-season. See page 474.

▲**Thielska Galleriet** Enchanting waterside mansion with works of Scandinavian artists Larsson, Zorn, and Munch. **Hours:** Tue-Sun 12:00-17:00, closed Mon. See page 476.

▲**Millesgården** Dramatic cliffside museum and grounds featuring works of Sweden's greatest sculptor, Carl Milles. **Hours:** Daily 11:00-17:00 except closed Mon in Oct-April. See page 478.

Royal Palace Complex (Kungliga Slottet)

Although the royal family beds down at Drottningholm (see next chapter), this complex in Gamla Stan is still the official royal residence. The palace, designed in Italian Baroque style, was completed in 1754 after a fire wiped out the previous palace—a much more characteristic medieval/Renaissance complex. This blocky Baroque replacement, which houses various museums, is big and (frankly) pretty dull. Note two of the sights—the Royal Armory and the Royal Coin Cabinet—are operated by different organizations, so they have separate entrances and tickets.

Planning Your Time: Visiting the several sights in and near

STOCKHOLM

the palace could fill a day, but Stockholm has far better attractions elsewhere. Prioritize. The Changing of the Guard and the awesome Royal Armory are the highlights.

The Royal Palace ticket includes four museums. Of these, the Royal Treasury is worth a look; the Royal Apartments are not much as far as palace rooms go; the Museum of Three Crowns gets you down into the medieval cellars to learn about the more interesting earlier castle; and Gustav III's Museum of Antiquities is skippable. The chapel is nice enough (and the only interior that's free to enter). The Royal Coin Cabinet—which requires a separate ticket—fascinates coin collectors.

Visitors in a rush should see the Changing of the Guard, pay to enter the Royal Armory, and skip the rest. The information booth in the semicircular courtyard (at the top, where the guard changes) gives out a list of the day's guided tours and an explanatory brochure/map that marks the entrances to the different sights. The main entrance to the Royal Palace (including the apartments, chapel, and treasury) faces the long, angled square and obelisk.

Tours: In peak season, the main Royal Palace offers a full slate of English tours covering the different sights (included in the admission)—allowing you to systematically cover nearly the entire complex. If you're paying the hefty price for a ticket, you might as well try to join at least one of the tours—otherwise, you'll struggle to appreciate the place. Some tours are infrequent, so be sure to confirm times when you purchase your admission (for more on tours, see the individual listings below).

Expect Changes: Since the palace is used for state functions, it is sometimes closed to tourists. And, as the exterior is undergoing a 20-year renovation, don't be surprised if parts are covered in scaffolding.

▲▲Military Parade and Changing of the Guard

Starting two blocks from Nybroplan (in front of the Army Museum at Riddargatan 13), Stockholm's daily military parade marches over Norrbro bridge, in front of the Parliament building, and up to the Royal Palace's outer courtyard, where the band plays and the guard changes. Smaller contingents of guards spiral in from other parts of the palace complex, eventually convening in the same place.

The performance is fresh and spirited, because the soldiers are visiting Stockholm just like you—and it's a chance for young soldiers from all over Sweden in every branch of the service to show their stuff in the big city. Pick

your place at the palace courtyard, where the band arrives at about 12:15 (13:15 on Sun). The best spot to stand is along the wall in the inner courtyard, near the palace information and ticket office. There are columns with wide pedestals for easy perching, as well as benches that people stand on to view the ceremony (arrive early). Generally, after the barking and goose-stepping formalities, the band shows off for an impressive 30-minute marching concert. Though the royal family now lives out of town at Drottningholm, the palace guards are for real. If the guard by the cannon in the semicircular courtyard looks a little lax, try wandering discreetly behind him.

Cost and Hours: Free; mid-May-mid-Sept Mon-Sat parade begins at 11:45 (reaches palace at 12:15), Sun at 12:45 (palace at 13:15); April-mid-May and mid-Sept-Oct Wed and Sat at 11:45 (palace at 12:15), Sun at 12:45 (palace at 13:15); Nov-March starts at palace Wed and Sat at 12:15, Sun at 13:15. Royal appointments can disrupt the schedule; confirm times at TI. In summer, you might also catch the mounted guards (but they do not appear on a regular schedule).

▲▲Royal Armory (Livrustkammaren)

The oldest museum in Sweden is both more and less than an armory. Rather than dusty piles of swords and muskets, it focuses on royal clothing: impressive ceremonial armor (never used in battle) and other fashion through the ages (including a room of kidswear), plus a fine collection of coaches. It's an engaging slice of royal life. Everything is displayed under sturdy brick vaults, beautifully lit, and well-described in English and by the museum's evocative audioguide.

Cost and Hours: 90 kr, half-price if you've already bought your Royal Palace ticket—so if you're touring both sights, buy your palace ticket before you come here; May-June daily 11:00-17:00; July-Aug daily 10:00-18:00; Sept-April Tue-Sun 11:00-17:00, Thu until 20:00, closed Mon; 20-kr audioguide is excellent—romantic couples can share it if they crank up the volume, information sheets in English available in most rooms; entrance at bottom of Slottsbacken at base of palace, tel. 08/402-3010, www.livrustkammaren.se.

Visiting the Museum: Buy your ticket and begin with the ground-floor collection. The first room (A) is almost a shrine for Swedish visitors. It contains the clothes **Gustavus Adolphus** wore—and even the horse he was riding, when he was killed in the

Thirty Years' War. Continue through Room B into Rooms C and D, where the exquisite workmanship on the **ceremonial armor** is a fine example of weaponry as an art form. Also in Room D are **royal suits and gowns** through the ages. The 1766 wedding dress of Queen Sofia is designed to cleverly show off its fabulously rich fabric (the dress seems even wider when compared to her 20-inch corseted waist). There are some modern dresses here as well. The **royal children** get a section for themselves (Room E), featuring a cradle that has rocked heirs to the throne since the 1650s; eventually it will leave the armory to rock the next royal offspring as well. It's fun to imagine little princes romping around their 600-room home with these toys. A century ago, one prince treasured his boxcar and loved playing cowboys and Indians. At the end of the main hall is a children's area.

The easy-to-miss **mezzanine level** (overlooking these main rooms) is typically filled with good temporary exhibits.

Backtrack to the entrance and find the stairs down to the basement, filled with lavish **royal coaches.** The highlight (last coach on the right, with purple and blue accents) is a plush coronation coach made in France in about 1700 and shipped to Stockholm, ready to be assembled Ikea-style. It last rolled a king to his big day—with its eight fine horses and what was then the latest in suspension gear—in 1869. At the end of the hall, the display of luggage over the centuries makes it obvious that Swedish royalty didn't know how to pack light.

▲Royal Palace

The Royal Palace consists of a chapel and four museums. Compared to many grand European palaces, it's underwhelming and flooded with cruise-excursion groups who don't realize that Stockholm's best sightseeing is elsewhere. It's worth a quick walk-through if you have a Stockholm Card (and, as a bonus, cardholders can go straight into each museum, bypassing the ticket office).

Cost and Hours: 150-kr combo-ticket covers all four museums and the chapel, includes guided tour; mid-May-mid-Sept daily 10:00-17:00; mid-Sept-mid-May Tue-Sun 12:00-16:00, closed Mon; tel. 08/402-6130, www.royalcourt.se.

Orientation: I've listed the museums in order of sightseeing worthiness. But if you want to see them all with minimal backtracking, follow this plan: Begin at the main entrance. Head up to the chapel for a peek, then descend to the treasury. Tour the Royal Apartments, exiting at the far side of the building—where you can head straight into the Museum of Three Crowns. Exiting there, you'll find the final sight (Museum of Antiquities) to your right.

Royal Apartments: The stately palace exterior encloses 608 rooms (one more than Britain's Buckingham Palace) of glittering

18th-century Baroque and Rococo decor. Clearly the palace of Scandinavia's superpower, it's steeped in royal history. You'll enter into the grand main hall (cheapskates can get a free look at this first room before reaching the ticket checkpoint), then walk the long halls through four sections. On the main level are the Hall of State (with an exhibit of fancy state awards) and the lavish Bernadotte Apartments (some fine Rococo interiors and portraits of the Bernadotte dynasty); upstairs you'll find the State Apartments (with rooms dating to the 1690s—darker halls, faded tapestries, and a wannabe hall of mirrors) and the Guest Apartments (with less lavish quarters, where visiting heads of state still crash). Guided 45-minute **tours** in English run twice daily.

Royal Treasury (Skattkammaren): Refreshingly compact compared to the sprawling apartments, the treasury gives you a good, up-close look at Sweden's crown jewels. Climbing down into the super-secure vault, you'll see 12 cases filled with fancy crowns, scepters, jeweled robes, the silver baptismal font of Karl XI, and plenty of glittering gold. It's particularly worthwhile with an English guided **tour** (daily at 13:00) or the included **audioguide** (which covers basically the same information). The first room holds the crowns of princes and princesses, while the second shows off the more serious regalia of kings and queens. For more than a century, these crowns have gone unworn: The last Swedish coronation was Oskar II's in 1873; in 1907 his son and successor—out of deference for the constitution (and living in a Europe that was deep in the throes of modernism)—declined to wear the crown, so he was "enthroned" rather than "coronated." The crowns still belong to the monarchs and are present in the room on special occasions—but they are symbols rather than accessories.

Museum of Three Crowns (Museum Tre Kronor): This museum shows off bits of the palace from before a devastating 1697 fire. The models, illustrations, and artifacts are displayed in vaulted medieval cellars that are far more evocative than the run-of-the-mill interior of today's palace. But while the stroll through the cellars is atmospheric, it's basically just more old stuff, interesting only to real history buffs (guided tours in English offered on summer afternoons).

Chapel: If you don't want to spring for a ticket, but would like a little taste of palace opulence, climb the stairs inside the main entrance for a peek into the chapel—the only free sight at the palace. It's standard-issue royal Baroque: colorful ceiling painting, bubbly altars, and a giant organ.

Gustav III's Museum of Antiquities (Gustav III's Antikmuseum): In the 1700s, Gustav III traveled through Italy and brought home an impressive gallery of classical Roman statues. These are displayed exactly as they were in the 1790s. This was a huge deal for those who had never been out of Sweden (English tour at 16:00).

▲Royal Coin Cabinet (Kungliga Myntkabinettet)

More than your typical royal coin collection, this is the best money museum I've seen in Europe. A fine exhibit tells the story of money from crude wampum to credit cards, and traces the development of the modern Swedish economy. The mellow but informative included audioguide helps make sense of the collection (which has only some English descriptions).

Cost and Hours: 70 kr, free on Mon, open daily June-Aug 11:00-17:00, Sept-May 10:00-16:00, Slottsbacken 6, tel. 08/5195-5304, www.myntkabinettet.se.

Visiting the Museum: You'll begin on the ground floor, with a chronological sweep through the history of money, starting with the first-ever coin (look for the tiny, easy-to-miss golden pellet labeled *det första myntet*, dating from 625 B.C.). The gang's all here: the ancient Greek drachma, the Roman dinarius, Charlemagne's denier, Florence's florin, ducats, pesos...and the German taler, where our dollar got its name. Banknotes finally arrived on the scene in 1661.

The upper floors are less engaging: The first floor up is heavy on Swedish economic history, including an interesting exhibit on "plate money"—from a time when, rather than bags of small coins, merchants carried around 40-pound slabs of copper (try to lift one). The second floor has the small royal coin collection and a large exhibit on ceremonial medals—including an actual Nobel Prize. The "Tally Up!" exhibit examines the role of money in our contemporary world, where the gulf between rich and poor seems greater than ever.

More Gamla Stan Sights

These first two sights sit on the Gamla Stan islet of Helgeandsholmen (just north of the Royal Palace), which is dominated by the Swedish Parliament. Also at the edge of Gamla Stan is the stately island of Riddarholmen.

Parliament (Riksdag)

For a firsthand look at Sweden's government, tour the Parliament buildings. Guides enjoy a chance to teach a little Swedish poli-sci along the standard tour of the building and its art. It's also possible to watch the Parliament in session.

Cost and Hours: Free one-hour tours go in English late June-late Aug, usually 4/day Mon-Fri (when Parliament is not in session). The rest of the year tours run 1/day Sat-Sun only; you're also welcome to join Swedish citizens in the viewing gallery (free); enter at Riksgatan 3a, call 08/786-4862 between 9:00 and 11:00 to confirm tour times, www.riksdagen.se.

Museum of Medieval Stockholm (Medeltidsmuseet)

This modern, well-presented museum offers a look at medieval Stockholm. When the government was digging a parking garage near the Parliament building in the 1970s, workers uncovered a major archaeological find: parts of the town wall that King Gustav Vasa built in the 1530s, as well as a churchyard. This underground museum preserves these discoveries and explains how Stockholm grew from a medieval village to a major city, with a focus on its interactions with fellow Hanseatic League trading cities. Lots of artifacts, models, life-size dioramas, and sound and lighting effects—all displayed in a vast subterranean space—help bring the story to life.

The museum does a particularly good job of profiling individuals who lived in medieval Stockholm; their personal stories vividly set the context of the history. You'll also see the preserved remains of a small cannon-ship from the 1520s and a reconstructed main market square from 13th-century Stockholm.

Cost and Hours: 100 kr ticket normally includes Stockholm City Museum in Södermalm, but that's closed for restoration through 2017, so ticket price may change; Tue-Sun 12:00-17:00, Wed until 19:00, closed Mon; English audioguide-20 kr, enter museum from park in front of Parliament—down below as you cross the bridge, tel. 08/5083-1790, www.medeltidsmuseet.stockholm.se.

Nearby: The museum sits in **Strömparterren** park. With its café and Carl Milles statue of the *Sun Singer* greeting the day, it's a pleasant place for a sightseeing break (pay WC in park, free WC in museum).

Literally the "Knights Isle," Riddarholmen is the quiet and stately far side of Gamla Stan, with a historic church, private palaces, and a famous view. The knights referred to in its name were the nobles who built their palaces on this little island to be near the Royal Palace, just across the way. The island, cut off from the rest of Gamla Stan by a noisy highway, is pretty lifeless, with impersonal government agencies filling its old mansions. Still, a visit is worthwhile for a peek at its church and to enjoy the famous view of City Hall and Lake Mälaren from its far end.

A statue of Birger Jarl (considered the man who founded Stockholm in 1252) marks the main square. Surrounding it are 17th-century private palaces of old noble families (now government buildings). And towering high above is the spire of the Riddarholmen Church. Established in the 13th century as a Franciscan church, this has been the burial place of nearly every Swedish royal since the early 1600s. If you're looking for a Swedish Westminster Abbey, this is it (50 kr, daily 10:00-17:00, shorter hours off-season). An inviting, shady café at the far end of the island is where people (and TV news crews) gather for Riddarholmen's iconic Stockholm view.

DOWNTOWN STOCKHOLM

I've organized these sights and activities in the urban core of Stockholm by island and/or neighborhood.

On Kungsholmen, West of Norrmalm
▲▲City Hall (Stadshuset)

The Stadshuset is an impressive mix of eight million red bricks, 19 million chips of gilt mosaic, and lots of Stockholm pride. While churches dominate cities in southern Europe, in Scandinavian capitals, city halls seem to be the most impressive buildings, celebrating humanism and the ideal of people working together in community. Built in 1923, this is still a functioning city hall. The members of the city council—101 people (mostly women) representing the 850,000 people of Stockholm—are hobby legislators with regular day jobs. That's why they meet in the evening. One of Europe's finest public buildings, the site of the annual Nobel Prize banquet, and a favorite spot for weddings (they do two per hour on Saturday after-

noons, when some parts of the complex may be closed), City Hall is particularly enjoyable and worthwhile for its entertaining and required 50-minute tour.

Cost and Hours: 100 kr; English-only tours offered daily, generally June-Aug every 30 minutes 9:30-16:00, off-season hourly 10:00-15:00; schedule can change due to special events—call to confirm; 300 yards behind the central train station—about a 15-minute walk from either the station or Gamla Stan, bus #3 or #62, tel. 08/5082-9059, www.stockholm.se/cityhall. City Hall's cafeteria, which you enter from the courtyard, serves complete lunches for 95 kr (Mon-Fri 11:00-14:00, closed Sat-Sun).

Visiting City Hall: On the tour, you'll see the building's sumptuous National Romantic style interior (similar to Britain's Arts and Crafts style), celebrating Swedish architecture and craftwork, and created almost entirely with Swedish materials. Highlights include the so-called Blue Hall (the Italian piazza-inspired, loggia-lined courtyard that was originally intended to be open air—hence the name—where the 1,300-plate Nobel banquet takes place); the City Council Chamber (with a gorgeously painted wood-beamed ceiling that resembles a Viking longhouse—or maybe an overturned Viking boat); the Gallery of the Prince (lined with frescoes executed by Prince Eugene of Sweden); and the glittering, gilded, Neo-Byzantine-style, and aptly named Golden Hall, where the Nobel recipients cut a rug after the banquet.

In this over-the-top space, a glimmering mosaic Queen of Lake Mälaren oversees the proceedings with a welcoming but

watchful eye, as East (see Istanbul's Hagia Sophia and the elephant, on the right) and West (notice the skyscrapers with the American flag, on the left) meet here in Stockholm. Above the door across the hall is Sweden's patron saint, Erik, who seems to have lost his head (due to some sloppy mosaic planning). On the tour, you'll find out exactly how many centimeters each Nobel banquet attendee gets at the table, why the building's plans were altered at the last minute to make the tower exactly one meter taller, where the prince got the inspiration for his scenic frescoes, and how the Swedes reacted when they first saw that Golden Hall (hint: they weren't pleased).

▲City Hall Tower

This 348-foot-tall tower rewards those who make the climb with the classic Stockholm view: The old church spires on the atmo-

spheric islands of Gamla Stan pose together, with the rest of the green and watery city spread-eagle around them.

Cost and Hours: 40 kr, daily June-Aug 9:15-17:15, May and Sept 9:15-15:55, closed Oct-April.

Crowd-Beating Tips: Only 30 people at a time are allowed up into the tower, every 40 minutes throughout the day. To ascend, you'll need a timed-entry ticket, which you can only get in person at the tower ticket office on the same day (no phone or Internet orders). It can be a long wait for the next available time, and tickets can sell out by mid-afternoon. If you're touring City Hall, come to the tower ticket window first to see when space is available. Ideally an appointment will coincide with the end of your tour.

Visiting the Tower: A total of 365 steps lead to the top of the tower, but you can ride an elevator partway up—leaving you only 159 easy steps to the top.

First you'll climb up through the brick structure, emerging at an atmospheric hall filled with models of busts and statues that adorn City Hall and a huge, 25-foot-tall statue of St. Erik. The patron saint of Stockholm, Erik was supposed to be hoisted by cranes up through the middle of the tower to stand at its top. But plans changed, big Erik is forever parked halfway up the structure, and the tower's top is open for visitors to gather and enjoy the view.

From Erik, you'll twist gradually up ramps and a few steps at a time through the narrow, labyrinthine brick halls with peek-a-boo views of the city. Finally you'll emerge into the wooden section of the tower, where a spiral staircase brings you up to the roof terrace. Enjoy the view from there, but also take some time to look around at the building's features. Smaller statues of Erik, Klara, Maria Magdalena, and Nikolaus, all patron saints, face their respective parishes. Look up: You're in the company of the tower's nine bells.

On Blasieholmen and Skeppsholmen

The peninsula of Blasieholmen pokes out from downtown Stockholm, and is tethered to the island of Skeppsholmen by a narrow bridge (with great views and adorned with glittering golden crowns). While not connected to the city by T-bana or tram, you can reach this area by bus #65 or the harbor shuttle ferry. Although Skeppsholmen is basically a "dead end" from a transportation perspective, it offers a peaceful break from the bustling city, with glorious views of Gamla Stan on one side and Djurgården on the other.

▲National Museum of Fine Arts (Nationalmuseum)

Stockholm's 200-year-old art museum, though mediocre by European standards, owns a few good pieces. Highlights include several canvases by Rembrandt and Rubens, a fine group of Impressionist works, and a sizeable collection of Russian icons. Seek out the exquisite paintings by the Swedish artists Anders Zorn and Carl Larsson.

Cost and Hours: The museum is

Stockholm's Best Views

For a bird's-eye perspective on this wonderful urban mix of water, parks, concrete, and people, consider these viewpoints.

City Hall Tower: The top of the tower comes with the classic city view (see listing on page 463).

Katarina: This viewing platform—offering fine views over the steeples of Gamla Stan—rises up from Slussen (the busy transit zone between Gamla Stan and Södermalm). You can get to the platform via a pedestrian bridge from Mosebacke Torg, up above in Södermalm. In good summer weather, you'll have to wade through the swanky tables of Eriks restaurant to reach the (free and public) viewpoint.

Himlen: Rising above Södermalm's main drag, the Skrapan skyscraper has a free elevator to the 25th-floor restaurant, called Himlen. While they're hoping you'll buy a meal (200-kr starters, 350-kr main courses) or nurse a 150-kr cocktail in the lounge, it's generally fine to take a discreet peek at the 360-degree views—just march in the door at #78 and ride the elevator up to 25 (daily 14:00-late, Götgatan 78, tel. 08/660-6068, www.restauranghimlen.se).

Kaknäs Tower: This bold, concrete, 500-foot-tall TV tower—looming above the eastern part of the city, and visible from just about everywhere—was once the tallest building in Scandinavia (55 kr, June-Aug Mon-Sat 9:00-22:00, Sun until 19:00, shorter hours off-season, restaurant on 28th floor, east of downtown—bus #69 from Nybroplan or Sergels Torg to Kaknästornet Södra stop, tel. 08/667-2105, www.kaknastornet.se).

closed for an extensive renovation (reopening in 2017); for the latest, see www.nationalmuseum.se.

Museum of Modern Art (Moderna Museet)

This bright, cheery gallery on Skeppsholmen island is as far out as can be. For serious art lovers, it warrants ▲▲. The impressive permanent collection includes modernist all-stars such as Picasso, Braque, Dalí, Matisse, Munch, Kokoschka, and Dix; lots of goofy Dada art (including a copy of Duchamp's urinal); Pollock, Twombly, Bacon, and other postmodern works; and plenty of excellent contemporary stuff as well (don't miss the beloved Rauschenberg *Goat with Tire*).

The curator draws from this substantial well of masterpieces to assemble changing exhibits. The building also houses the Architec-

ture and Design Center, with changing exhibits on those topics (www.arkdes.se, covered by a separate ticket). All of the exhibits are illuminated by an excellent, free audioguide that makes modern art meaningful to visitors who might not otherwise appreciate it (download the audioguide app using the museum's Wi-Fi).

Cost and Hours: Museum-120 kr, Architecture and Design Center-80 kr, 180 kr for both, free on Fri from 18:00; Tue and Fri 10:00-20:00, Wed-Thu and Sat-Sun 10:00-18:00, closed Mon; fine bookstore, harborview café, T-bana: Kungsträdgården plus 10-minute walk, or take bus #65, tel. 08/5202-3500, www.modernamuseet.se.

Östermalm

What this ritzy residential area lacks in museums, it makes up for in posh style. Explore its stately streets, dine in its destination restaurants, and be sure to explore the delightful, upscale Saluhall food market right on Östermalmstorg (see page 499). Östermalm's harborfront is hemmed in by the pleasant park called Nybroplan; from here, ferries lead to various parts of the city and beyond (as this is the jumping-off point for cruises into Stockholm's archipelago). If connecting to the sights in Djurgården, consider doing Östermalm by foot.

Waterside Walk

Enjoy Stockholm's ever-expanding shoreline promenades. Tracing the downtown shoreline while dodging in-line skaters and ice-cream trolleys (rather than cars and buses), you can walk from Slussen across Gamla Stan, all the way to the good ship *Vasa* in Djurgården. Perhaps the best stretch is along the waterfront Strandvägen street (from Nybroplan past weather-beaten old boats and fancy facades to Djurgården). As you stroll, keep in mind that there's free fishing in central Stockholm, and the harbor waters are restocked every spring with thousands of new fish. Locals tell of one lucky lad who pulled in an 80-pound salmon. The waterside lanes are extremely bike-friendly here and throughout Stockholm.

DJURGÅRDEN

Four hundred years ago, Djurgården was the king's hunting ground (the name means "Animal Garden"). You'll see the royal gate to the island immediately after the bridge that connects it to the mainland. Now this entire lush island is Stockholm's fun center, protected as a national park. It still has a smattering of animal life among its biking paths, picnicking families, art galleries, various amusements, and museums, which are some of the best in Scandinavia.

Orientation: Of the three great sights on the island, the Vasa and Nordic museums are neighbors, and Skansen is a 10-minute walk away (or hop on any bus or tram—they come every couple of minutes). Several lesser or special-interest attractions (from the ABBA museum to an amusement park) are also nearby.

To get around more easily, consider **renting a bike** as you enter the island. You can get one at Sjöcaféet, a café just over the Djurgårdsbron bridge; they also rent boats (bikes-80 kr/hour, 275 kr/day; canoes-150 kr/hour, kayaks-125 kr/hour; open May-Oct daily 9:00-21:00, closed off-season and in bad weather; handy city cycle maps, tel. 08/660-5757, www.sjocafeet.se).

In the concrete building upstairs from the café, you'll find a **Djurgården visitors center,** with free maps, island bike routes, brochures, and information about the day's events (you can also buy ABBA museum tickets here; center open daily in summer 8:00-20:00, shorter hours off-season).

Getting There: Take tram #7 from Sergels Torg (the stop is right under the highway overpass) or Nybroplan (in front of the gilded theater building) and get off at one of these stops: Nordic Museum (used also for Vasa Museum), Liljevalc Gröna Lund (for ABBA museum), or Skansen. In summer, you can take a ferry from Nybroplan or Slussen (see "Getting Around Stockholm," earlier). Walkers enjoy the harborside Strandvägen promenade, which leads from Nybroplan directly to the island (described under "Waterside Walk," earlier).

Major Museums on Djurgården

▲▲▲Skansen

Founded in 1891, Skansen was the first in what became a Europe-wide movement to preserve traditional architecture in open-air

museums. It's a huge park gathering more than 150 historic buildings (homes, churches, shops, and schoolhouses) transplanted from all corners of Sweden. Other languages have borrowed the Swedish term "Skansen" (which originally meant "the Fort") to describe an "open-air museum." Today, tourists enjoy exploring this Swedish-culture-on-a-lazy-Susan, seeing folk crafts in action and wonderfully furnished old interiors. Kids love Skansen, where they can ride a life-size wooden *Dala*-horse and stare down a hedgehog, visit Lill-Skansen (a children's zoo), and take a mini-train or pony ride. While it's lively June through August before about 17:00, at other times of the year it can seem pretty dead; consider skipping it if you're here off-season.

Cost and Hours: 160 kr, kids-60 kr, less off-season; park open daily May-late-June 10:00-19:00, late-June-Aug 10:00-22:00, Sept 10:00-18:00, Oct and March-April 10:00-16:00, Nov-Feb 10:00-15:00; historical buildings generally open 11:00-17:00, late June-Aug some until 19:00, most closed in winter. Check their excellent website for "What's Happening at Skansen" during your visit

(www.skansen.se) or call 08/442-8000 (press 1 for a live operator).

Music: Skansen does great music in summer. There's fiddling (30-minute performances June-Aug Tue-Fri at 18:15), folk dancing (June-Aug Tue-Fri at 19:00, also Sat-Sun at 16:00), and public dancing to live bands (Mon-Sat from

20:00, call for that evening's theme—big band, modern, ballroom, folk). Confirm performance times before you go.

Visiting Skansen: Skansen isn't designed as a one-way loop; it's a sprawling network of lanes and buildings, yours to explore.

For the full story, invest in the 75-kr museum guidebook. With the book, you'll understand each building you duck into and even learn about the Nordic animals awaiting you in the zoo. Check the live crafts schedule at the information stand by the main entrance to make a smart Skansen plan. Guides throughout the park are happy to answer your questions—but only if you ask them. The old houses come alive when you take the initiative to get information.

From the entrance, bear left to find the escalator, and ride it up to **"The Town Quarter"** (Stadskvarteren), where shoemakers, potters, and glassblowers are busy doing their traditional thing (daily 10:00-17:00) in a re-created Old World Stockholm. Continuing deeper into the park—past the bakery, spice shop/grocery, hardware store, and a cute little courtyard café—you'll reach the central square, **Bollnästorget** (signed as "Central Skansen" but labeled on English maps as "Market Street"), with handy food stands. The rest of Sweden spreads out from here. Northern Swedish culture and architecture is in the north (top of park map), and southern Sweden's in the south (bottom of map). Various homesteads—each one clustered protectively around an inner courtyard—are scattered around the complex.

Poke around. Follow signs—or your instincts. It's worth stepping into the old, red-wood Seglora Church (just past Bollnästorget), which aches with atmosphere under painted beams. The park has two different zoos: Lill-Skansen is a children's petting zoo. Beyond the big brick spa tower and carnival rides sprawls the Scandinavian Animals section, with bears, wolves, moose ("elk"), seals, reindeer (near the Sami camp), and other animals.

Eating at Skansen: The park has ample eating options to suit every budget. The most memorable—and affordable—meals are at the small folk food court on the main square, **Bollnästorget.** Here, among the duck-filled lakes, frolicking families, and peacenik local toddlers who don't bump on the bumper cars, kiosks dish up "Sami slow food" (smoked reindeer), waffles, hot dogs, and more. There are lots of picnic benches—Skansen encourages **picnicking.** (A small grocery store is tucked away across the street and a bit to the left of the main entrance.)

For a sit-down meal, the old-time **Stora Gungan Krog,** right at the top of the escalator in the craftsmen's quarter, is a cozy inn (100-180-kr indoor or outdoor lunches—meat, fish, or veggie—with a salad-and-cracker bar). Another snug spot is **Gubbhyllan,** on the ground floor and fine porch of an old house (90-kr sandwiches, 130-160-kr meals, at base of escalator, just past main entrance). For a less atmospheric choice, consider one of three restaurants that share a modern building facing the grandstand (just up the hill inside the main entrance), all with nice views over the city: the simple **Skansen Terrassen** cafeteria (100-170-kr meals); **Tre Byttor Taverne,** with 18th-century pub ambience (140-kr lunches, 170-240-kr main courses); and, upstairs, the fussy **Solliden** restaurant, with a dated blue-and-white dining hall facing a wall of windows; the main reason to eat here is the big *smörgåsbord* lunch (370 kr, served 12:00-16:00).

Aquarium: The "aquarium"—featuring lemurs, meerkats, baboons, Gila monsters, giant anacondas, rattlesnakes, geckos, crocodiles, colorful tree frogs, and small sharks...but almost no fish—is located within Skansen, but is not covered by your Skansen ticket. Only animal lovers find it worth the steep admission price, but if you have a Stockholm Card, it's a fun and free walk-through (120 kr, Sept-May daily 10:00-16:00, tel. 08/660-1082, www.skansenakvariet.se).

▲▲▲Vasa Museum (Vasamuseet)

Stockholm turned a titanic flop into one of Europe's great sightseeing attractions. The glamorous but unseaworthy warship *Vasa*—top-heavy with an extra cannon deck—sank 40 minutes into her 1628 maiden voyage when a breeze caught the sails and blew her over. After 333 years at the bottom of Stockholm's harbor, she rose again from the deep with the help of marine archaeologists. Rediscovered in 1956 and raised in 1961, this Edsel of the sea  is today the best-preserved ship of its age anywhere—housed since 1990 in a brilliant museum. The masts perched atop the roof—best seen from a distance—show the actual height of the ship.

Cost and Hours: 130 kr, includes film and tour; daily June-Aug 8:30-18:00; Sept-May 10:00-17:00 except Wed until 20:00; WCs on level 3, good café, Galärvarvet, Djurgården, tel. 08/5195-4800, www.vasamuseet.se.

Getting There: The *Vasa* is on the waterfront immediately behind the stately brick Nordic Museum (described later), a 10-minute walk from Skansen. Or you can take tram #7 from downtown.

To get from the Nordic Museum to the Vasa Museum, face the Nordic Museum and walk around to the right (going left takes you into a big dead-end parking lot).

Crowd-Beating Tips: The museum can have very long lines, but they generally move quickly—you likely won't wait more than 15-20 minutes. If crowds are a concern, get here either right when it opens, or after about 16:00 (but note that the last tour starts at 16:30).

Tours: The free 25-minute **tour** is worthwhile. Because each guide is given license to cover whatever he or she likes, no two tours are alike—if you're fascinated by the place, consider taking two different tours to pick up new details. In summer, English tours run on the hour and half-hour (last tour at 16:30); off-season (Sept-May) tours go 3/day Mon-Fri, hourly Sat-Sun (last tour at 15:30). Listen for the loudspeaker announcement, or check at the info desk for the next tour. Alternatively, you can access the **audioguide** by logging onto the museum's Wi-Fi (www.vasamuseet.se/audioguide).

Film: The excellent 17-minute film digitally re-creates *Vasa*-era Stockholm (and the colorfully painted ship itself), dramatizes its sinking, and documents the modern-day excavation and preservation of the vessel. It generally runs three times per hour; virtually all showings are either in English or with English subtitles.

Visiting the Museum: For a thorough visit, plan on spending at least an hour and a half—watch the film, take a guided tour, and

linger over the exhibits (this works in any order). After buying your ticket, head inside. Sort out your film and tour options at the information desk to your right.

Upon entry, you're prow-to-prow with the great ship. The *Vasa*, while not quite the biggest ship in the world when launched in 1628, had the most firepower, with two fearsome decks of cannons. The 500 carved wooden statues draping the ship—once painted in bright colors—are all symbolic of the king's power. The 10-foot lion on the magnificent prow is a reminder that Europe considered the Swedish King Gustavus Adolphus the "Lion from the North." With this great ship, Sweden was preparing to establish its empire and become more engaged in European power politics. Specifically, the Swedes (who already controlled much of today's Finland and Estonia) wanted to push south to dominate the whole of the Baltic Sea, in order to challenge their powerful rival, Poland.

Designed by a Dutch shipbuilder, the *Vasa* had 72 guns of the same size and type (a rarity on mix-and-match warships of the age), allowing maximum efficiency in reloading—since there was no need to keep track of different ammunition. Unfortunately, the king's unbending demands to build it high (172 feet tall) but skinny made it extremely unstable; no amount of ballast could weigh the ship down enough to prevent it from tipping.

Now explore the **exhibits,** which are situated on six levels around the grand hall, circling the ship itself. All displays are well described in English. You'll learn about the ship's rules (bread can't be older than eight years), why it sank (heavy bread?), how it's preserved (the ship, not the bread), and so on. Best of all is the chance to do slow laps around the magnificent vessel at different levels. Now painstakingly restored, 98 percent of the *Vasa*'s wood is original (modern bits are the brighter and smoother planks).

On **level 4** (the entrance level), right next to the ship, you'll see a 1:10 scale model of the *Vasa* in its prime—vividly painted and fully rigged with sails. Farther along, models show how the *Vasa* was salvaged; a colorful children's section re-creates the time period; and a 10-minute multimedia show explains why the *Vasa* sank (alternating between English and Swedish showings). Heading behind the ship, you'll enjoy a great view of the sculpture-slathered stern of the *Vasa*. The facing wall features full-size replicas of the carvings, demonstrating how the ship was originally colorfully painted.

Several engaging displays are on **level 5.** "Life On Board" lets you walk through the gun deck and study cutaway models of the hive of activity that hummed below decks (handy, since you can't enter the actual ship). Artifacts—including clothes actually worn by the sailors—were salvaged along with the ship. "Battle!" is a small exhibit of cannons and an explanation of naval warfare.

Level 6 features "The Sailing Ship," with models demonstrating how the *Vasa* and similar vessels actually sailed. You'll see the (very scant) remains of some of the *Vasa*'s actual riggings and sails. **Level 7** gives you even higher views over the ship.

Don't miss **level 2**—all the way at the bottom (ride the handy industrial-size elevator)—with some of the most interesting exhibits. "The Shipyard" explains how this massive and majestic vessel was brought into being using wood from tranquil Swedish forests. Tucked under the ship's prow is a laboratory where today's scientists continue with their preservation efforts. The "Objects" exhibit shows off actual items found in the shipwreck, while "Face to Face" introduces you to some of those who perished when the

Vasa sunk—with faces that were re-created from skeletal remains. Nearby, you'll see some of the skeletons found in the shipwreck.

As you exit, you'll pass a hall of (generally excellent) temporary exhibits.

▲▲Nordic Museum (Nordiska Museet)

Built to look like a Danish Renaissance palace, this museum offers a fascinating peek at 500 years of traditional Swedish lifestyles. The exhibits insightfully place everyday items into their social/historical context in ways that help you really grasp various chapters of Sweden's past. It's arguably more informative than Skansen. Take time to let the excellent, included audioguide enliven the exhibits.

Cost and Hours: 100 kr, free Wed after 17:00 Sept-May; daily 10:00-17:00, Wed until 20:00 Sept-May; Djurgårdsvägen 6-16, at Djurgårdsbron, tram #7 from downtown, tel. 08/5195-6000, www.nordiskamuseet.se.

Visiting the Museum: Entering the museum's main hall, you'll be face-to-face with Carl Milles' huge painted-wood statue of Gustav Vasa, father of modern Sweden. The rest of this floor is usually devoted to temporary exhibits.

Highlights of the permanent collection are on the top two floors. Head up the stairs, or take the elevator just to the left of

Gustav. Begin on floor 4 and work your way down.

On **floor 4,** four different exhibits ring the grand atrium. The "Homes and Interiors" section displays 400 years of home decor. As you travel through time—from dark, heavily draped historical rooms to modern living rooms, and from rustic countryside cottages to aristocratic state bedrooms—you'll learn the subtle meaning behind everyday furniture that we take for granted. For example, the advent of television didn't just change entertainment—it gave people a reason to gather each evening in the living room, which, in turn, became a more-used (and less formal) part of people's homes. You'll learn about the Swedish designers who, in the 1930s, eschewed stiff-backed traditional chairs in favor of sleek perches that merged ergonomics and looks—giving birth to functionalism.

Also on this floor, the "Folk Art" section shows off colorfully painted furniture and wood carvings; vibrant traditional costumes; and rustic Bible-story illustrations that adorned the walls of peasants' homes. The "Sápmi" exhibit tells the fascinating and often overlooked story of the indigenous Sami people (formerly called "Lapps"), who lived in the northern reaches of Norway, Sweden, Finland, and Russia centuries before Europeans created those modern nations. On display are shoes, ceremonial knives, colorful hats and clothing, and other features of Sami culture. You'll learn how their nomadic lifestyle—following their herds of grazing reindeer—allowed them to survive so far north, and how the Sami (who still number around 20,000) have had an impact on greater Swedish society. Finally, tucked behind the stairwell, the "Small Things" collection shows off timepieces, ceramics, and tobacco pipes, among other items.

Floor 3 has several smaller exhibits. The most interesting are "Table Settings" (with carefully set tables from the last century, representing different time periods, social classes, and occasions—from an elegant tea party to a rowdy pub) and "Traditions" (showing and describing each old-time celebration of the Swedish year—from Christmas to Midsummer—as well as funerals, confirmations, and other life events). Also on display: 300 years of Swedish clothing illustrating how we define ourselves through our attire; jewelry and textile exhibits; a dollhouse and toy collection; and a photo exhibition pulled from the museum's archive.

▲ABBA: The Museum

The Swedish pop group ABBA was, for a time, a bigger business than Volvo. After bursting on the scene in 1974 by winning the Eurovision Song Contest with "Waterloo," and increasing their fame by serenading Sweden's newly minted queen with "Dancing Queen" in 1976, they've sold more than 380 million records, and the musical based on their many hits, *Mamma Mia!*, has been enjoyed by 50 million people. It was only a matter of time before Stockholm opened an ABBA museum, which is conveniently located just across the street from Skansen and next to Gröna Lund amusement park. Like everything ABBA, it is aggressively for-profit and slickly promoted, with the steepest ticket price in town (not covered by Stockholm Card). True to its subject, it's bombastic, glitzy, and highly interactive. If you like ABBA, it's lots of fun; if you love ABBA, it's ▲▲▲ nirvana.

Cost and Hours: 195 kr, 500-kr family ticket covers two adults and up to four kids, cash not accepted, daily 10:00-20:00, shorter hours off-season—likely until 18:00, Djurgårdsvägen 68, bus #44 or tram #7 to Liljevalc Gröna Lund stop, tel. 08/1213-2860, www.abbathemuseum.com.

Audioguide: ABBA aficionados will happily fork over 40 kr extra for the intimate audioguide, in which Agnetha, Benny, Björn, and Anni-Frid share their memories, in their own words.

Getting In: To control the crowds, only 75 people are let in every 15 minutes with timed-entry tickets. The museum strongly encourages getting tickets in advance from their website or at the TI. In fact, they'll charge you 20 kr extra per ticket to book one in person (but computer terminals are standing by if you want to "pre-book" on the spot). It can be crowded on summer weekends, in which case you may have to wait for a later time.

Visiting the Museum: The museum is high-tech, with plenty of actual ABBA artifacts, re-created rooms where the group did its composing and recording (including their famous "Polar Studio" and their rustic archipelago cottage), a room full of gold and platinum records, plenty of high-waisted sequined pantsuits, and lots of high-energy video screens. Everything is explained in English.

Included in the ticket is a "digital key" that lets you take advantage of several interactive stations. For example, you can record a music video karaoke-style as a fifth member of the group—with virtual ABBA members dancing around you—and pick up the production from their website. A small wing features the Swedish Music Hall of Fame, but apart from that, it's all ABBA.

Waterfront Sights

While the tram zips sightseers between the Vasa Museum and Skansen, it's a short, enjoyable, and very scenic walk along the waterfront—a delight on a nice day. You'll see food stands, boats bobbing in the harbor, and sunbathing Swedes.

You'll also pass several sights. Between the Vasa Museum and the Djurgårdsbron bridge is **Junibacken,** a fairy-tale house based on the writings of Astrid Lindgren, who created *Pippi Longstocking.* While oriented toward Swedish kids, American children may enjoy it, too (entry fee, www.junibacken.se). The pier directly in front of the Vasa Museum is actually part of the **Maritime Museum** (Sjöhistoriska), where historic ships are moored (typically big icebreakers from the Arctic, and sometimes military boats). Farther south, near the amusement park, is the Maritime Museum's boat hall #2 (Båthall 2), filled with more boats and exhibits (free entry to all Maritime Museum sights, www.sjohistoriska.se). And halfway along the waterfront is the following odd but endearing museum that offers a weird but welcome break from heavier sightseeing.

Spiritmuseum

The museum's highly conceptual permanent exhibit considers the role of alcohol—and specifically, flavored vodkas—in Swedish society. While Sweden got a reputation for its "loose morals" in the 1970s (mostly surrounding sex and nudity), at the same time it was extremely puritanical when it came to alcohol; the government actively tried to get Swedes to stop drinking (hence the liquor-store system and sky-high alcohol taxes that still exist). In the exhibit's season-themed rooms, you'll be able to smell different types of flavored liquors (orange in the spring, elderflower in the summer, and so on); upstairs, you can ace a virtual pub quiz, recline (or nap) in the boozy drunk-simulator room, and step into a garishly lit, buzzing room that simulates a hangover. The temporary exhibits here are also quite good.

Cost and Hours: 100 kr, 200-kr ticket adds a taster kit of flavored vodkas; daily June-Aug 10:00-18:00, Sept-May 10:00-17:00, Tue until 20:00 year-round, Djurgårdsvägen 38, tel. 08/1213-1300, www.spritmuseum.se.

Other Djurgården Sights
Gröna Lund Amusement Park

Stockholm's venerable and lowbrow Tivoli-type amusement park still packs in the local families and teens on cheap dates. It's a busy venue for local pop concerts.

Cost and Hours: 110 kr, late April-late Sept daily 12:00-23:00, closed off-season, www.gronalund.com.

▲Thielska Galleriet

If you liked the Larsson and Zorn art in the National Gallery, and/or if you're a Munch fan, this charming mansion on the water at the far end of the Djurgården park is worth the trip.

Cost and Hours: 100 kr, Tue-Sun 12:00-17:00, closed Mon, bus #69 (not #69K) from downtown, tel. 08/662-5884, www.thielska-galleriet.se.

▲Biking the Garden Island

In all of Stockholm, Djurgården is the most natural place to enjoy a bike ride. There's a good and reasonably priced bike-rental place just over the bridge as you enter the island (see page 440), and a world of park-like paths and lanes with harbor vistas to enjoy.

Ask for a free map and route tips when you rent your bike. Figure about an hour to pedal around Djurgården's waterfront perimeter; it's mostly flat, but with some short,

steeper stretches that take you up and over the middle of the island. Those who venture beyond the Skansen park find themselves nearly all alone in the lush and evocative environs.

At the summit of the island you'll come upon Rosendal's Garden, with a bakery and café (daily 11:00-17:00). You can sit in the greenhouse or in the delightful orchard or flower garden, where locals come to pick a bouquet and pay by the weight. (The garden is fertilized by the horse pies from adjacent Skansen.) Just beyond is the **Rosendals Slott,** the cute mini-palace of Karl Johans XIV, founder of the Bernadotte dynasty. This palace, in the so-called Karl Johans style ("Empire style"), went together in prefabricated sections in the 1820s. The story is told on a board in front, and a 9-ton porphyry vase graces the backyard.

A garden café at the eastern tip of the island offers a scenic break midway through your pedal. For a longer ride, you can cross the canal to the Ladugårdsgärdet peninsula ("Gärdet" for short), a swanky, wooded residential district just to the north.

SÖDERMALM

Just south of Gamla Stan, the Södermalm district is the downscale antidote to the upscale, ritzy areas where most tourists spend their time (Norrmalm, Östermalm, Djurgården, and Gamla Stan). Södermalm recently has been in vogue thanks to Stieg Larsson's *Girl with the Dragon Tattoo* novels, in which Lisbeth Salander and her cohorts represent the "real," hardscrabble Stockholm (all the villains come from the posh north side). While the area has few tourist sights (aside from the Stockholm City Museum, which is closed for renovation through 2017), it offers fine views and is a fun place to eat (for recommendations, see page 494). Towering over Södermalm's main road is the Skrapan building, with the Himlen view terrace on its 25th floor (see sidebar on page 465). The big white sphere on the horizon is the Ericsson Globe, a hockey arena.

With newfound popularity comes investment, and Södermalm is gentrifying quickly—giving it something of a split personality. While the often-repeated comparison to "Stockholm's Brooklyn" is a stretch (this relatively sterile area lacks the loosey-goosey hipster charm of many such neighborhoods in the US and other parts of Europe), it does have a nice variety of shops, squares, restaurants, and bars where locals outnumber tourists. The most interesting areas to explore are along Götgatan and the zone south of Folkungagatan street—nicknamed "SoFo."

Getting There: To stroll this area, simply head from Gamla Stan through the confusing Slussen transit mess. Facing the big P-hus Slussen tunnel, turn right one block into the pedestrian area (uphill, passing the T-bana station on your left and the Stockholm City Museum on your right), then left onto colorful Götgatan, and head on up the hill. Alternatively, you can ride the T-bana to Medborgarplatsen, which puts you right on the area's main market square (but misses the interesting shops along Götgatan). Medborgarplatsen itself is a wonderful workaday plaza that feels like the center of a big urban neighborhood. Ringed by fun eateries, it's great for people-watching.

ON THE OUTSKIRTS

The home and garden of Carl Milles, Sweden's greatest sculptor, is less than an hour from the city center. For sights farther outside Stockholm (all reachable by public transportation), see the next chapter.

▲Millesgården

The villa and garden of Carl Milles is a veritable forest of statues by Sweden's greatest sculptor. Millesgården is dramatically situated on a bluff overlooking the harbor in Stock-holm's upper-class suburb of Lidingö. While the art is engaging and enjoyable, even the curators have little to say about it from an interpretive point of view—so your visit is basically without guidance. But in Milles' house, which dates from the 1920s, you can see his north-lit studio and get a sense of his creative genius.

Carl Milles spent much of his career teaching at the Cranbrook Academy of Art in Michigan. But he's buried here at his villa, where he lived and worked for 20 years, lovingly designing this sculpture garden for the public. Milles wanted his art to be displayed on pedestals...to be seen "as if silhouettes against the sky." His subjects—often Greek mythological figures such as Pegasus or Poseidon—stand out as if the sky was a blank paper. Yet unlike silhouettes, Milles' images can be enjoyed from many angles. And Milles liked to enliven his sculptures by incorporating water features into his figures. *Hand of God,* perhaps his most famous work, gives insight into Milles' belief that when the artist created, he was—in a way—divinely inspired.

Cost and Hours: 100 kr; daily 11:00-17:00 except closed Mon in Oct-April; English booklet explains the art, restaurant and café, tel. 08/446-7590, www.millesgarden.se.

Getting There: Catch the T-bana to Ropsten, then take bus #207 to within a five-minute walk of the museum; several other #200-series buses also get you close enough to walk (allow about 45 minutes total each way).

Shopping in Stockholm

Sweden offers a world of shopping temptations. Smaller stores are open weekdays 10:00-18:00, Saturdays until 17:00, and Sundays 11:00-16:00. Some of the bigger stores (such as NK, H&M, and Åhléns) are open later on Saturdays and Sundays.

Fun Chain Stores

These chains have multiple branches around town; the most convenient are marked on the map on pages 484-485.

DesignTorget, dedicated to contemporary Swedish design, receives a commission for selling the unique works of local designers (generally Mon-Fri 10:00-19:00, Sat 10:00-18:00, Sun 11:00-17:00, big branch underneath Sergels Torg—enter from basement level of Kulturhuset, other branches are at Nybrogatan 23 and at the airport, www.designtorget.se).

Systembolaget is Sweden's state-run liquor store chain. A sample of each bottle of wine or liquor sits in a display case. A card in front explains how it tastes and suggests menu pairings. Look for the item number and order at the counter. Branches are in Hötorget underneath the movie theater complex, in Norrmalm at Vasagatan 21, and just up from Östermalmstorgat Nybrogatan 47 (Mon-Wed 10:00-18:00, Thu-Fri 10:00-19:00, Sat 10:00-15:00, closed Sun, www.systembolaget.se).

Hamngatan

The main shopping zone between Kungsträdgården and Sergels Torg (described in "Stockholm's Modern City Walk" on page 449) has plenty of huge department stores. At the top of Kungsträdgården, **Illums Bolighus** is a Danish design shop. Across the street, **Nordiska Kompaniet** (NK) is elegant and stately; the Swedish design (downstairs) and kitchenware sections are particularly impressive. The classy **Gallerian** mall is just up the street from NK and stretches seductively nearly to Sergels Torg. The **Åhléns** store, kitty-corner across Sergels Torg, is less expensive than NK and has two cafeterias and a supermarket. Affordable clothing chain **H&M** has a store right across the street.

Mood Stockholm

The city's most exclusive mall is a downtown block filled with big-name Swedish and international designers, plus a pricey food court and restaurants. The preciously upscale decor and mellow music give it a Beverly Hills vibe (Mon-Fri 10:00-20:00, Sat 10:00-18:00, Sun 11:00-17:00, Regeringsgatan 48). This mall anchors a ritzy, pedestrianized shopping zone; for additional trendy and exclusive shops, browse the nearby streets Jakobsbergsgatan and Biblioteksgatan.

Södermalm

When Swedes want the latest items by local designers, they skip the downtown malls and head for funky Södermalm. **Götgatan,** the main drag that leads from Slussen up to this neighborhood, is a particularly good choice, with shop after shop of mostly Swedish designers. Boutiques along here—some of them one-offs, others belonging to Swedish chains—include Weekday (jeans and dressed-up casual), Filippa K (smart casual and business attire), and Tiogruppen (bold bags and fabrics).

Nybrogatan

This short and pleasant traffic-free street, which connects Östermalmstorg with the Nybroplan waterfront, is lined with small branches of interesting design shops, including Nordiska Galleriet (eye-catching modern furniture, at #11), DesignTorget (described earlier, at #16), and Hemslöjden (Swedish handicrafts, at #23). It also has shoe and handbag stores, and an enticing cheese shop and bakery.

Flea Markets

For a *smörgåsbord* of Scanjunk, visit the **Loppmarknaden,** northern Europe's biggest flea market, at Vårberg Center (free entry weekdays and Sat-Sun after 15:00, 15 kr on weekends—when it's busiest; open Mon-Fri 11:00-18:00, Sat 10:00-16:00, Sun 11:00-16:00; T-bana: Vårberg, tel. 08/710-0060, www.loppmarknaden.se). Hötorget, the produce market, also hosts a Sunday flea market in summer (see page 497).

Nightlife and Entertainment in Stockholm

Bars and Music in Gamla Stan

The street called Stora Nygatan, with several lively bars, has perhaps the most accessible and reliable place for live jazz in town: Stampen. Several pubs here offer live Irish traditional music sessions or bluegrass several times each week; they tend to share musicians, who sometimes gather at one of these pubs for impromptu jam sessions (ask around, or stroll this street with your ears peeled). While it may seem odd to listen to Irish or bluegrass music in Stockholm, these venues are extremely popular with locals.

Stampen Jazz & Rhythm 'n' Blues Pub has two venues under one roof: a stone-vaulted cellar below and a fun-loving saloon-like bar upstairs (check out the old instruments and antiques hanging from the ceiling). From Monday through Thursday, there's live music in the saloon. On Friday and Saturday, bands alternate sets in both the saloon and the cellar (160-kr cover Fri-Sat only, open

Mon-Thu 17:00-late, Fri-Sun 20:00-late, special free jam session Sat 14:00-18:00, Stora Nygatan 5, tel. 08/205-793, www.stampen. se). For the location, see the map on page 492.

Several other lively spots are within a couple of blocks of Stampen on Stora Nygatan. Your options include **Wirströms Pub** (live blues bands play in crowded cellar Tue-Sat 21:00-24:00, no cover, 62-kr beers, open daily 11:00-late, Stora Nygatan 13, www. wirstromspub.se); **O'Connells Irish Pub** (a lively expat sports bar with music—usually Tue-Sat at 21:00, open daily 12:00-late, Stora Nygatan 21, www.oconnells.se); and **The Liffey** (classic Irish pub with 150-180-kr pub grub, live music Wed and Fri-Sun at 21:30, open daily 11:00-late, Stora Nygatan 40-42, www.theliffey.se).

Icebar Stockholm

If you just want to put on a heavy coat and gloves and drink a fancy vodka in a modern-day igloo, consider the fun, if touristy,

Icebar Stockholm. Everything's ice—shipped down from Sweden's far north. The bar, the glasses, even the tip jar are made of ice. You get your choice of vodka drinks and 45 minutes to enjoy the scene (online booking-185 kr, drop-ins pay 10 kr more—on weekends drop-ins only allowed after 21:45, additional drinks-95 kr, reservations smart; daily June-Aug 11:15-24:00, Sept-May 15:00-24:00; in the Nordic C Hotel adjacent to the main train station's Arlanda Express platform at Vasaplan 4, tel. 08/5056-3124, www.icebarstockholm.se). If you go too early, it can be really dead—you'll be all alone. At busy times, people are let in all at once every 45 minutes. That means there's a long line for drinks, and the place goes from being very crowded to almost empty as people gradually melt away. At first everyone's just snapping photos. While there are ice bars all over Europe now, this is the second one (after the Ice Hotel in Lapland). And it really is pretty cool...a steady 23°F.

Cinema

In Sweden, international movies are shown in their original language with Swedish subtitles. Swedish theaters sometimes charge more for longer films, and tickets come with assigned seats (drop by to choose seats and buy a ticket, box offices generally open 11:00-22:00 daily). The Hötorget and Drottninggatan neighborhoods have many theaters.

Swedish Massage, Spa, and Sauna

To treat yourself to a Swedish spa experience—maybe with an authentic "Swedish massage"—head for the elegant circa-1900 **CentralBadet Spa.** It's along downtown's main strolling street, Drottninggatan, tucked back inside a tranquil and inviting garden courtyard. Admission includes entry to an extensive gym, "bubble-pool," sauna, steam room, "herbal/crystal sauna," and an elegant Art Nouveau pool. Most areas are mixed, with men and women together, but some areas are reserved for women. If you won't make it to Finland, enjoy a sauna here (for more on saunas, see page 611). Bring your towel into the sauna—not for modesty, but for hygiene (to separate your body from the bench). The steam room is mixed; bring two towels (one for modesty and the other to sit on). The pool is more for floating than for jumping and splashing. The leafy courtyard restaurant is a relaxing place to enjoy affordable, healthy, and light meals (220 kr, increases to 320 kr on Sat, towels and robes available for rent; slippers are required—20 kr to buy, 10 kr to rent; open Mon-Fri 7:00-20:30, Sat 9:00-20:30, Sun 9:00-17:30, last entry one hour before closing, ages 18 and up, Drottninggatan 88, 10 minutes up from Sergels Torg, tel. 08/5452-1300, reservation tel. 08/218-821, www.centralbadet.se).

Sleeping in Stockholm

Between business travelers and the tourist trade, demand for Stockholm's hotels is healthy but unpredictable, and most hotels' rates vary from day to day. For each hotel (for comparison's sake), I've listed the average price for a standard double room in high season (mid-June-mid-Aug)—but your rate will almost certainly be higher or lower, depending on the timing of your visit. Use my descriptions to determine which hotels interest you, then check the specific rates online; it's easiest to do this on a comparison booking site (but once you see the rates, book directly with the hotel, which may net you a lower price). For more booking tips, see page 728.

A program called **Destination Stockholm** is, for many (especially families), the best way to book a big hotel on weekends or during the summer. When you reserve a hotel room through this service, it includes a free Stockholm à la Carte card, which covers public transportation, most major sights, and lots of tours for the duration of your visit (even better than the Stockholm Card). Kids sleep free (and also get the card). Reserve by phone or online; be sure to review the cancellation policy before you commit (tel. 08/663-0080, www.destination-stockholm.com).

Consider hostels. Stockholm's hostels are among Europe's best, offering good beds in simple but interesting places for about

---

Sleep Code

Abbreviations   (7 kr = about $1, country code: 46, area code: 08)
S = Single, **D** = Double/Twin, **T** = Triple, **Q** = Quad, **b** = bathroom
Price Rankings
 $$$ **Higher Priced**—Most rooms 1,800 kr or more
  $$ **Moderately Priced**—Most rooms 800-1,800 kr
   $ **Lower Priced**—Most rooms 800 kr or less
Unless otherwise noted, English is spoken, credit cards are accepted, breakfast is included, and Wi-Fi is generally free. Prices change; verify current rates online or by email. For the best prices, always book directly with the hotel.

---

300 kr per night for a dorm bed. Each has helpful English-speaking staff, pleasant family rooms, and good facilities.

NEAR THE TRAIN STATION

$$$ Freys Hotel is a Scan-mod, four-star place, with 127 compact, smartly designed rooms. It's well-situated for train travelers, located on a dead-end pedestrian street across from the central station. While big, it works hard to be friendly and welcoming. Its cool, candlelit breakfast room becomes a bar in the evening, popular for its selection of Belgian microbrews (Sb-1,750 kr, Db-2,470 kr, check website for specials as low as Db-1,750 kr, air-con, guest computer, Wi-Fi, Bryggargatan 12, tel. 08/5062-1300, www.freyshotels.com, freys@freyshotels.com).

$$$ Scandic Kungsgatan, central but characterless, fills the top floors of a downsized department store with 270 rooms. If the Starship *Enterprise* had a low-end hotel, this would be it. Save about 100 kr by taking a "cabin" room with no windows—the same size as other rooms, quiet, and well-ventilated (Db-2,000 kr, air-con, guest computer, Wi-Fi, Kungsgatan 47, tel. 08/723-7220, www.scandichotels.com, kungsgatan@scandichotels.com).

$$ HTL Kungsgatan, jamming modernity into a classic old building a few blocks from the station, takes a futuristic approach to providing just what travelers really need—and nothing else. You reserve online, then check in at a self-service kiosk on arrival. Roving receptionists are standing by in the coffee bar for any needs. The 274 rooms are small and functional (no desk or chairs) but trendy and comfortable. Everything surrounds a stylish, glassy atrium boasting a hip lounge/restaurant with a youthful party vibe and live music until 24:00 on most weekends (Sb/Db-1,700 kr, can be much lower—around 700 kr—in slow times, 100 kr less for windowless but well-ventilated "sleeper" room, breakfast-75 kr,

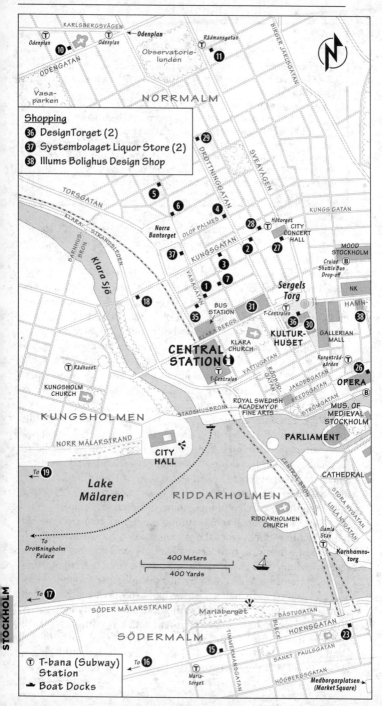

Shopping

- 36 DesignTorget (2)
- 37 Systembolaget Liquor Store (2)
- 38 Illums Bolighus Design Shop

T-bana (Subway) Station

➤ Boat Docks

STOCKHOLM

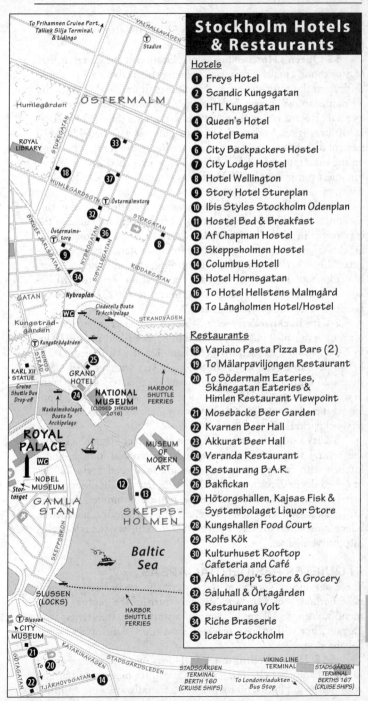

Stockholm Hotels & Restaurants

Hotels

1. Freys Hotel
2. Scandic Kungsgatan
3. HTL Kungsgatan
4. Queen's Hotel
5. Hotel Bema
6. City Backpackers Hostel
7. City Lodge Hostel
8. Hotel Wellington
9. Story Hotel Stureplan
10. Ibis Styles Stockholm Odenplan
11. Hostel Bed & Breakfast
12. Af Chapman Hostel
13. Skeppsholmen Hostel
14. Columbus Hotell
15. Hotel Hornsgatan
16. To Hotel Hellstens Malmgård
17. To Långholmen Hotel/Hostel

Restaurants

18. Vapiano Pasta Pizza Bars (2)
19. To Mälarpaviljongen Restaurant
20. To Södermalm Eateries, Skånegatan Eateries & Himlen Restaurant Viewpoint
21. Mosebacke Beer Garden
22. Kvarnen Beer Hall
23. Akkurat Beer Hall
24. Veranda Restaurant
25. Restaurang B.A.R.
26. Bakfickan
27. Hötorgshallen, Kajsas Fisk & Systembolaget Liquor Store
28. Kungshallen Food Court
29. Rolfs Kök
30. Kulturhuset Rooftop Cafeteria and Café
31. Åhléns Dep't Store & Grocery
32. Saluhall & Örtagården
33. Restaurang Volt
34. Riche Brasserie
35. Icebar Stockholm

Map labels: To Frihamnen Cruise Port, Tallink Silja Terminal, & Lidingo · VALHALLAVÄGEN · Stadion · ÖSTERMALM · Humlegården · ROYAL LIBRARY · STUREGATAN · HUMLEGÅRDSGTN · Östermalmstorg · BIRGER JARLSGATAN · STORGATAN · NYBROGATAN · SIBYLLEGATAN · Östermalms-torg · RIDDARGATAN · GATAN · Nybroplan · Cindatella Boats To Archipelago · WC · STRANDVÄGEN · Kungsträd-gården · Kungsträdgården · KUNGS STRÅG · KARL XII STATUE · Cruise Shuttle Bus Drop-off · GRAND HOTEL · Waxholmsbolaget Boats To Archipelago · NATIONAL MUSEUM (CLOSED THROUGH 2016) · HARBOR SHUTTLE FERRIES · ROYAL PALACE · WC · MUSEUM OF MODERN ART · NOBEL MUSEUM · Stor-torget · GAMLA STAN · SKEPPS-HOLMEN · SKEPPSBRON · Baltic Sea · SLUSSEN (LOCKS) · Slussen · CITY MUSEUM · HARBOR SHUTTLE FERRIES · KATARINAVÄGEN · GÖTAGATAN · To · STADSGÅRDSLEDEN · TJÄRHOVSGATAN · VIKING LINE TERMINAL · STADSGÅRDEN TERMINAL BERTH 160 (CRUISE SHIPS) · To Londonviadukten Bus Stop · STADSGÅRDEN TERMINAL BERTHS 167 (CRUISE SHIPS)

STOCKHOLM

air-con, elevator, Wi-Fi, Kungsgatan 53, tel. 08/4108-4150, www. htlhotels.com, htlkungsgatan@htlhotels.com).

$$ Queen's Hotel enjoys a great location at the quiet top end of Stockholm's main pedestrian shopping street (about a 10-minute walk from the train station, or 15 minutes from Gamla Stan). The 59 rooms are well worn, but reasonably priced for the convenient location. Rooms facing the courtyard are quieter (Sb-1,100 kr, Db-1,300 kr, bigger "superior" Db with pull-out sofa bed-1,900, 10 percent discount for readers who book direct—ask for it; if booking online enter rate code "RICKS" in all caps, extra bed-250 kr, elevator, guest computer, Wi-Fi, Drottninggatan 71A, tel. 08/249-460, www.queenshotel.se, info@queenshotel.se).

$$ Hotel Bema, a bit farther out than the others listed in this section, is a humble place that rents 12 fine rooms for some of the best prices in town (S-900 kr, Db-1,100 kr, extra person-250 kr, breakfast served at nearby café, bus #65 from station to Upplandsgatan 13—near the top of the Drottninggatan pedestrian street, or walk about 15 minutes from the train station—exit toward *Vasagatan* and head straight up that street, tel. 08/232-675, www.hotelbema.se, info@hotelbema.se).

$ City Backpackers, with 140 beds a quarter-mile from the station, is youthful but classy (bunk in 8- to 12-bed room-230 kr, in 6-bed room-290 kr, in 4-bed room-320 kr; bunk-bed D-740 kr, 40 percent more for Fri- or Sat-night stay without weeknight; sheets-25 kr, free cook-it-yourself pasta, breakfast-55 kr, pay laundry, guest computer, Wi-Fi, movies, tours, sauna, lockers, Upplandsgatan 2A, tel. 08/206-920, www.citybackpackers.se, info@citybackpackers.se).

$ City Lodge Hostel, on a quiet side street just a block from the central train station, has 68 beds, a convivial lounge, and a kitchen with free cooking staples (bunk in 18-bed dorm-220 kr, in 6-bed dorm-275 kr, in quad-315 kr; a few tiny bunk-bed doubles-640 kr, bigger D-820 kr, cheaper outside of summer; sheets-50 kr, breakfast-60-kr, guest computer, Wi-Fi, laundry, no curfew, Klara Norra Kyrkogata 15, tel. 08/226-630, www.citylodge.se, info@citylodge.se).

IN QUIETER RESIDENTIAL AREAS

These options in Norrmalm and Östermalm are in stately, elegant neighborhoods of five- and six-story turn-of-the-century apartment buildings. All are too long of a walk from the station with luggage, but still in easy reach of downtown sights and close to T-bana stops.

$$$ Hotel Wellington, two blocks off Östermalmstorg, is in a less handy but charming part of town. It's modern and bright, with hardwood floors, 60 rooms, and a friendly welcome. While it may seem pricey, it's a cut above in comfort, and its great amenities—such as a very generous buffet breakfast, free coffee all day long, and free buffet dinner in the evening—add up to a good value (prices range widely, but in summer generally Db-1,820 kr, smaller Db for 200 kr less, mention this book when you book direct for a 10 percent discount, guest computer, Wi-Fi, free sauna, old-fashioned English bar, garden terrace bar, T-bana: Östermalmstorg, exit to Storgatan and walk past big church to Storgatan 6; tel. 08/667-0910, www.wellington.se, cc.wellington@choice.se).

$$$ Story Hotel Stureplan is a colorful boutique hotel with a creative hipster vibe. Conveniently located near a trendy dining zone between Östermalmstorg and the Nybroplan waterfront, it has 83 rooms above a sprawling, cleverly decorated, affordably priced restaurant. You'll book online, check yourself in at the kiosk, and receive a text message with your door key code (tight bunk-bed Db-1,700 kr, standard Db-2,000 kr, more for bigger rooms, elevator, free minibar drinks, Wi-Fi, Riddargatan 6, tel. 08/5450-3940, www.storyhotels.com).

$$$ Ibis Styles Stockholm Odenplan rents 76 cookie-cutter rooms on several floors of a late-19th-century apartment building (Db-1,950 kr, about 300 kr cheaper with nonrefundable "advance saver" rate, Wi-Fi, T-bana: Odenplan, Västmannagatan 61, reservation tel. 08/1209-0000, reception tel. 08/1209-0300, www.ibisstyles.se, odenplan@uniquehotels.se).

$ Hostel Bed and Breakfast is a tiny, woody, and easygoing independent hostel renting 36 beds in various dorm-style rooms. Many families stay here (bed in 4-bed room-320 kr, Sb-550 kr, Db-780 kr, sheets-50 kr, kitchen, laundry, Wi-Fi, across the street from T-bana: Rådmansgatan, just off Sveavägen at Rehnsgatan 21, tel. 08/152-838, www.hostelbedandbreakfast.com, info@hostelbedandbreakfast.com).

IN GAMLA STAN

These options are in the midst of sightseeing, a short bus or taxi ride from the train station. For locations, see the map on page 485.

$$$ Scandic Gamla Stan offers Old World elegance in the heart of Gamla Stan (a 5-minute walk from Gamla Stan T-bana station). Its 52 small rooms are filled with chandeliers and hardwood floors (Sb-1,400 kr, Db-2,000 kr, 200 kr extra for larger room, elevator, Wi-Fi, Lilla Nygatan 25, tel. 08/723-7250, www.scandichotels.com, gamlastan@scandichotels.com).

$$$ Lady Hamilton Hotel, classic and romantic, is shoehorned into Gamla Stan on a quiet street a block below the cathedral and Royal Palace. The centuries-old building has 34 small but plush and colorfully decorated rooms. Each one is named for a Swedish flower and is filled with antiques (Db-2,200 kr, a few hundred kronor more for a bigger "corner" room with a better view, elevator, guest computer, Wi-Fi, Storkyrkobrinken 5, tel. 08/5064-0100, www.ladyhamiltonhotel.se, info@ladyhamiltonhotel.se).

$$ Urban Hostel Old Town is a sane and modern hostel conveniently located in an untrampled part of Gamla Stan, just a few steps off the harbor. Conscientiously run, with 135 beds in small but tidy modern rooms, it's not a party hostel—grown-ups will feel comfortable here (bunk in 16-bed dorm-295 kr, S-695 kr, D-900 kr, Db-1,500 kr, T-1,100 kr, Q-1,400 kr, Qb-2,200 kr, breakfast-75 kr, air-con, elevator, Wi-Fi, Nygränd 5, tel. 08/1214-0444, www.urbanhostels.se, info@urbanhostels.se).

$$ The Ånedin Hostel is a floating hotel, moored near the foot of the Royal Palace. Once a cruise boat, the classic liner MS *Birger Jarl* has 130 cabins, varying from small simple rooms to superior cabins with private baths (Db-600 kr, Qb-900 kr, prices vary by size of room and berth configuration, breakfast-90 kr, Wi-Fi in public spaces, Skeppsbron Tullhus 1, tel. 08/6841-0130, www.anedinhostel.com, info@anedinhostel.com).

ON SKEPPSHOLMEN

This relaxing island—while surrounded by Stockholm—feels a world apart, both in terms of its peacefulness and its somewhat less convenient transportation connections (you'll rely on bus #65, the shuttle ferry, or your feet—it's about a 20-minute walk from the train station). For locations, see the map on page 485.

$ Af Chapman Hostel, a permanently moored 100-year-old schooner, is Europe's most famous youth hostel and has provided a berth for the backpacking crowd for years. Renovated from keel to stern, the old salt offers 120 bunks in four- to six-bed rooms (bunk-375 kr, D-850 kr, fancier "navigational" or "captain's" cabins-1,240 kr/1,030 kr, 50 kr less for members, Wi-Fi, see next listing for contact information). Reception and breakfast are at the Skeppsholmen Hostel (next).

$ Skeppsholmen Hostel, just ashore from the *Af Chapman*, has 160 beds (bunk in 17-bed dorm-265 kr, in 3- to 6-bed room-310 kr, D-690 kr, 50 kr less for members; includes sheets, breakfast-80 kr, laundry service, no lockout, Wi-Fi, tel. 08/463-2266, chapman@stfturist.se).

ON OR NEAR SÖDERMALM

Södermalm is residential and hip, with Stockholm's best café and bar scene. You'll need to take the bus or T-bana to get here from the train station.

$$$ Columbus Hotell—located in a 19th-century building that formerly housed a brewery, a jail, and a hospital—has 69 quiet rooms facing a big courtyard in the heart of Södermalm (Sb-1,600 kr, Db-1,850 kr, Tb-2,100 kr, rates may increase with planned renovation—which may also add an elevator; T-bana: Medborgarplatsen or bus #53 from train station to Tjärhovsplan, then a 5-minute walk to Tjärhovsgatan 11; tel. 08/5031-1200, www.columbushotell.se, info@columbushotell.se).

$$ Hotel Hornsgatan is a tidy, welcoming, nicely decorated B&B upstairs in an old townhouse facing a busy but elegant-feeling boulevard. Four of the 17 small rooms have private baths; the others share five modern bathrooms. Thoughtfully run by Clara and Scott, this is a good value for the location (S-900 kr, Sb-1,300 kr, D-1,100 kr, Db-1,500 kr, elevator, Wi-Fi, reception staffed until 22:00—make arrangements if arriving late, Hornsgatan 66B, T-bana: Mariatorget plus a short walk, 15-minute walk from Slussen/Gamla Stan, tel. 08/658-2901, www.hotelhornsgatan.se, info@hotelhornsgatan.se).

$$ Hotel Hellstens Malmgård is an eclectic collage of 50 rooms crammed with antiques in a circa-1770 mansion. No two rooms are alike, but all have modern baths and quirky touches such as porcelain stoves or four-poster beds. Unwind in its secluded cobblestone courtyard, and you may forget what century you're in (Db-1,600 kr, elevator, Wi-Fi; T-bana: Zinkensdamm, then a 5-minute walk to Brännkyrkagatan 110; tel. 08/4650-5800, www.hellstensmalmgard.se, hotel@hellstensmalmgard.se).

$$ Långholmen Hotel/Hostel is on Långholmen, a small island off Södermalm that was transformed in the 1980s from Stockholm's main prison into a lovely park. Rooms are converted cells in the old prison building. You can choose between hostel- and hotel-standard rooms at many different price levels (hostel rooms: dorm bed-260 kr, bunk-bed twin D-630 kr, Db-750 kr, Tb-900 kr, Q-1,040 kr, Qb-1,160 kr, 50 kr less for members, sheets-65 kr, breakfast-98 kr; hotel rooms: Db-2,050 kr, extra bed-250 kr, includes breakfast, about 100 kr cheaper for nonrefundable booking, Wi-Fi, laundry room, kitchen, cafeteria, free parking, on-site swimming; T-bana: Hornstull, walk 10 minutes down and cross small bridge to Långholmen island, follow hotel signs 5 minutes farther; tel. 08/720-8500, www.langholmen.com, hotel@langholmen.com).

Eating in Stockholm

To save money, eat your main meal at lunch, when cafés and restaurants have 95-kr daily special plates called *dagens rätt* (generally Mon-Fri only). Most museums have handy cafés (with lots of turnover and therefore fresh food, 100-kr lunch deals, and often with fine views). Convenience stores serve gas station-style food (and often have seats). As anywhere, department stores and malls are eager to feed shoppers and can be a good, efficient choice. If you want culturally appropriate fast food, stop by a local hot dog stand. Picnics are a great option—especially for dinner, when restaurant prices are highest. There are plenty of park-like, harborside spots to give your cheap picnic some class. I've also listed a few splurges—destination restaurants that offer a good sample of modern Swedish cooking.

IN GAMLA STAN

Most restaurants in Gamla Stan serve the 95-kr weekday lunch special mentioned above, which comes with a main dish, small salad, bread, and tap water. Choose from Swedish, Asian, or Italian cuisine. Several popular places are right on the main square (Stortorget) and near the cathedral. Järntorget, at the far end, is another fun tables-in-the-square scene. Touristy places line Västerlånggatan. You'll find more romantic spots hiding on side lanes. I've listed my favorites below (for locations, see the adjacent map).

Grillska Huset is a cheap and handy cafeteria run by Stockholms Stadsmission, a charitable organization helping the poor. It's grandly situated right on the old square, with indoor and outdoor seating (tranquil garden up the stairs and out back), fine daily specials, a hearty salad bar, and a staff committed to helping others. You can feed the hungry (that's you) and help house the homeless at the same time. The 95-kr daily special gets you a hot plate, salad, and coffee, or choose the 90-kr salad bar—both available Mon-Fri 11:00-14:00 (also 100-kr meals, café serves sandwiches and salads daily 10:00-18:00, Stortorget 3, tel. 08/787-8605). They also have a fine little bakery *(brödbutik)* with lots of tempting cakes and pastries (30-40-kr premade sandwiches, closed Sun).

Kryp In, a small, cozy restaurant (the name means "hide away") tucked into a peaceful lane, has a stylish hardwood and candlelit interior, great sidewalk seating, and an open kitchen letting you in on Vladimir's artistry. If you dine well in Stockholm once (or twice), I'd do it here. It's gourmet without pretense. They serve delicious, modern Swedish cuisine with a 475-kr three-course dinner. In the good-weather months, they serve weekend lunches, with specials starting at 120 kr. Reserve ahead for dinner (200-290-kr plates, daily 17:00-23:00, May-Oct Sat-Sun from 12:30, a block off Stortorget at Prästgatan 17, tel. 08/208-841, www. restaurangkrypin.se).

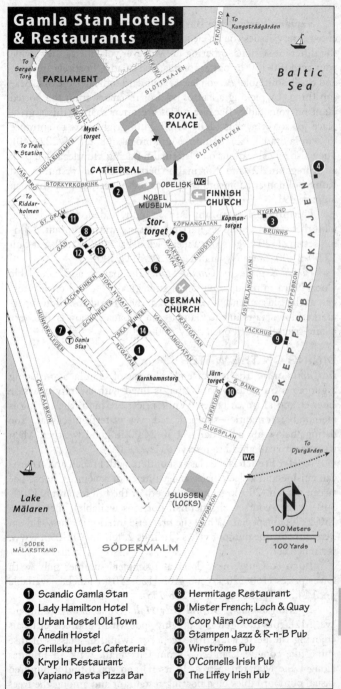

Gamla Stan Hotels & Restaurants

To Kungsträdgården

Baltic Sea

To Sergels Torg

PARLIAMENT

ROYAL PALACE

Mynt-torget

To Train Station

RIDDARHOLMEN

CATHEDRAL

SLOTTSBACKEN

STORKYRKOBRINK

OBELISK   WC

NOBEL MUSEUM

FINNISH CHURCH

To Riddar-holmen

ST. GRÄM.

Stor-torget

KÖPMANGATAN

Köpman-torget

NYGRÄND

GÅS.

BRUNNS.

Svartman Gätan

KINDSTU.

GERMAN CHURCH

KÅCK BRINKEN

LILLA NYGATAN

STORA NYGATAN

SCHÖNFELTS

TYSKA BRINKEN

VÄSTERLÅNGGATAN

PRÄSTGATAN

Gamla Stan

NYGATAN

Kornhamnstorg

PACKHUS

Järn-torget

S. BANKO.

JÄRNTORG.

SLUSSPLAN

WC

To Djurgården

SLUSSEN (LOCKS)

SKEPPSBRON

Lake Mälaren

100 Meters

100 Yards

SÖDER MÄLARSTRAND

SÖDERMALM

❶ Scandic Gamla Stan	❽ Hermitage Restaurant
❷ Lady Hamilton Hotel	❾ Mister French; Loch & Quay
❸ Urban Hostel Old Town	❿ Coop Nära Grocery
❹ Ånedin Hostel	⓫ Stampen Jazz & R-n-B Pub
❺ Grillska Huset Cafeteria	⓬ Wirströms Pub
❻ Kryp In Restaurant	⓭ O'Connells Irish Pub
❼ Vapiano Pasta Pizza Bar	⓮ The Liffey Irish Pub

STOCKHOLM

Vapiano Pasta Pizza Bar, a bright, high-energy, family-oriented eatery, issues you an electronic card as you enter. Circulate to the different stations, ordering up whatever you like as they swipe your card (80-150-kr pastas, pizzas, and salads). Portions are huge and easily splittable. As you leave, your card indicates the bill. Season things by picking a leaf of basil or rosemary from the potted plant on your table. Because tables are often shared, this a great place for solo travelers (daily 11:00-24:00, right next to entrance to Gamla Stan T-bana station, Munkbrogatan 8, tel. 08/222-940). They also have locations on Östermalm (facing Humlegården park at Sturegatan 12) and Norrmalm (between the train station and Kungsholmen at Kungsbron 15)—for these locations, see the map on page 491.

Hermitage Restaurant is a friendly, faded, hippie-feeling joint that serves a tasty vegetarian buffet in a warm communal dining setting (120 kr gets you a meal, Mon-Fri 11:00-21:00, Sat-Sun 12:00-21:00, Stora Nygatan 11, tel. 08/411-9500).

Picnic Supplies in Gamla Stan: The handy and affordable **Coop Nära** mini supermarket is strategically located on Järntorget, at the Slussen end of Gamla Stan; the **Munkbrohallen** supermarket downstairs in the Gamla Stan T-bana station is also very picnic-friendly (both open daily 7:00-22:00).

DINING ON THE WATER

In Gamla Stan: The harbor embankment of Gamla Stan, facing a gorgeous Stockholm panorama, is lined with swanky quayside eateries and al fresco tables. While prices are high, the setting is memorably romantic—sophisticated, yet waterfront-casual. The listings below are open daily 11:30-24:00 in good weather, when it's smart to call ahead to reserve a view table.

Mister French is the classiest option, with French and American cuisine and a sleek black-and-white color scheme. Choose between the bar (200-kr simple bar food) or the full restaurant (200-300-kr main courses, cheaper half-portions available). They serve a 150-kr lunch special. While the brasserie interior is classy, I'd eat here only for the outdoor views (Tullhus 2, tel. 08/202-095, www.mrfrench.se).

Loch & Quay, next door, is a simpler "summer pub" with lower prices (160-220-kr pub grub, 120-150-kr lunches available until 14:30, Tullhus 2, tel. 08/225-755).

In Kungsholmen, Behind City Hall: On a balmy summer's eve, **Mälarpaviljongen** is a dreamy spot with hundreds of locals enjoying the perfect lakefront scene, as twinkling glasses of rosé shine like convivial lanterns. From City Hall, walk 15 minutes along Lake Mälaren (a treat in itself) and you'll find a hundred casual outdoor tables on a floating restaurant and among the trees

Swedish Cuisine

Most people don't travel to Sweden for the food. Though potatoes and heavy sauces are a focus of the country's cuisine, its variety of meat and fish dishes can be surprisingly satisfying. If you don't think you'll like Swedish or Scandinavian food, be sure to splurge at a good-quality place before you pass final judgment.

Every region of Sweden serves different specialties, but you'll always find *svenska köttbullar* on the menu (Swedish meatballs made from beef and pork in a creamy sauce). This Swedish favorite is topped with lingonberry jam, which is served with many meat dishes across Scandinavia. Potatoes, seemingly the only vegetable known to Sweden, make for hearty *kroppkakor* dumplings filled with onions and minced meat. The northern variation, *pitepalt*, is filled with pork. Southern Sweden takes credit for *pytt i panna*, a medley of leftover meat and diced potatoes that's fried and served with an egg yolk on top. And it seems that virtually every meal you'll eat here includes a side of boiled, small new potatoes.

Though your meals will never be short on starch, be sure to try Sweden's most popular baked good, *kanelbulle*, for a not-so-light snack during the day. This pastry resembles a cinnamon roll, but it's made with cardamom and topped with pearl sugar. Enjoy one during *fika*, the daily Swedish coffee break so institutionalized that many locals use the term as a verb (see page 449).

Like those of its Nordic neighbors, Sweden's extensive coastline produces some of the best seafood in the world. A light, tasty appetizer is *gravad lax*, a dill-cured salmon on brown bread or crackers. You'll also likely encounter *Toast Skagen*. This appetizer-spread is made from shrimp, dill, mayonnaise, and Dijon mustard, and is eaten on buttered toast.

For a main course, the most popular seafood dish is crayfish. Though eaten only by the aristocracy in the 16th century, these shellfish have since become a nationwide delicacy; they're cooked in brine with dill and eaten cold as a finger food. Traditional crayfish parties take place outdoors on summer evenings, particularly in August. Friends and family gather around to indulge in this specialty with rye bread and a strong cheese. The Swedes also love Baltic herring; try *stekt strömming*, a specialty of the east coast, which is herring fried with butter and parsley. As usual, it's served with potatoes and lingonberry jam. Adventurous diners can have their herring pickled or fermented—or order more unusual dishes like reindeer.

As for beer, the Swedes classify theirs by alcohol content. The higher the number, the higher the alcohol content—and the price. *Klass 1* is light beer—very low-alcohol. *Klass 2* is stronger, but still mild. And *Klass 3* has the most body, the most alcohol, and the highest price.

STOCKHOLM

on shore. Line up at the cafeteria to order a drink, snack, or complete meal. When it's cool, they have heaters and blankets. The walk along the lake back into town caps the experience beautifully (60-kr beer, 130-kr cocktails, 110-kr lunch plates, 180-240-kr evening meals, open in good weather April-Sept daily 11:00-late, easy lakeside walk or T-bana to Fridhemsplan plus a 5-minute walk to Nörr Mälarstrand 63, no reservations, tel. 08/650-8701).

In Djurgården: **Sjöcaféet,** beautifully situated and greedily soaking up the afternoon sun, fills a woody terrace stretching along the harbor just over the Djurgårdsbron bridge. In summer, this is a fine place for a meal or just a drink before or after your Skansen or *Vasa* visit. They have affordable lunch plates (105 kr, Mon-Fri 11:00-13:00 only); after 14:00, you'll pay 130-180 kr per plate (also 12-kr pizzas, order at the bar, daily 8:00-20:00, often later in summer, closed off-season, tel. 08/661-4488). For the location, see the map on page 467.

Oaxen Slip Bistro, a trendy harborfront place 200 yards below the main Skansen gate, serves creative Nordic cuisine with sturdy local ingredients in a sleek interior or on its delightfully woody terrace. Overlooking a canal in what feels like an old shipyard, and filled with in-the-know locals, this place is a real treat. Reservations are smart (200-kr plates, game and seafood, daily 12:00-14:00 & 17:00-21:30, Beckholmsvägen 26, tel. 08/5515-3105, www.oaxen. com). For location, see the map on page 467.

Dinner Cruises on Lake Mälaren: The big sightseeing company Strömma sells a variety of lunch and dinner cruises that allow you to enjoy the delightful waterways of Stockholm and the archipelago while you eat. Options include shorter dinner cruises to Drottningholm Palace (2.5 hours round-trip), longer ones to the outer archipelago (up to 5 hours), and *smörgåsbord* cruises around Lake Mälaren. For prices, details, and booking, check www. stromma.se; see also their other options, including a shrimp cruise and a jazz cruise.

SÖDERMALM STREETS AND EATS

This quickly gentrifying, working-class district, just south of Gamla Stan (steeply uphill from Slussen), has some of Stockholm's most enticing food options—especially for beer lovers. It's also a bit less swanky, and therefore more affordable, than many of the city's more touristy neighborhoods. Combine dinner here with a stroll through a side of Stockholm many visitors miss. For more on Södermalm, see page 477.

Götgatan and Medborgarplatsen

The neighborhood's liveliest street is the artery called Götgatan, which leads from Slussen (where Södermalm meets Gamla Stan) steeply up into the heart of Södermalm. Here, mixed between the boutiques, you'll find cafés tempting you to join the Swedish coffee break called *fika*, plus plenty of other eateries. Even if you don't dine in Södermalm, it's worth a stroll here just for the window-shopping fun.

At the top of the street, you'll pop out into the big square called Medborgarplatsen. This neighborhood hang-out is a great scene, with almost no tourists and lots of options—especially for Swedish fast food. (My favorite, Melanders Fisk, is listed next.) Outdoor restaurant and café tables fill the square, which is fronted by a big food hall. (There's also a T-bana stop here for an easy return home after dinner.) The recommended Kvarnen beer hall (see later) is just around the corner to the left.

Melanders Fisk, facing the square, has only outside tables (and is therefore an option only in warm weather). You order at the bar and join locals in this classic scene. *Skagenröra,* shrimp with mayo on toast or filling a baked potato, is the signature dish—and dear to the Swedish heart (115 kr; also 90-kr lunch plates daily, 130-150-kr fish plates served daily until 21:00, after 21:00 it's only *skagenröra,* Medborgarplatsen 3, tel. 08/644-4040).

Skånegatan and Nytorget

A bit farther south, these cross-streets make another good spot to browse among fun and enticing restaurants, particularly for ethnic cuisine.

Nytorget Urban Deli is the epitome of Södermalm's trendy-hipster vibe and an amazing scene. It's half fancy artisanal delicatessen—with all manner of ingredients—and half white-subway-tile-trendy eatery, with indoor and outdoor tables filled with Stockholm yuppies eating well. If it's busy—as it often is—they'll scrawl your name at the bottom of the long butcher-paper waiting list (no reservations). If it's full, you can grab a place at the bar and eat there (international and Swedish modern dishes, 100-190-kr light meals, 190-225-kr bigger meals, daily 8:00-23:00, at the far end of Skånegatan at Nytorget 4, tel. 08/5990-9180).

Nytorget Urban Deli Picnic: The upscale grocery store attached to the deli seems designed for picnickers, with lots of creative boxed meals and salads to go (same address and hours—see listing above). The park across the street has lots of benches and picnic tables.

Kohphangan, with an almost laughably over-the-top island atmosphere that belies its surprisingly good Thai food, has been a hit for 20 years. (Thailand is to Swedes what Mexico is to Americans—the sunny "south of the border" playground.) The ambience? Mix a shipwreck, Bob Marley, and a Christmas tree and you've got it (160-220-kr dishes, daily 12:00-24:00, Skånegatan 57, tel. 08/642-5040).

Gossip is a mellow, unpretentious hole-in-the-wall serving Bangladeshi street food (120-160-kr dishes, Mon-Fri 11:00-23:00, Sat-Sun 13:00-23:00, Skånegatan 71, tel. 08/640-6901).

Beer and Pub Grub in Södermalm

Södermalm cultivates the most interesting beer scene in this beer-crazy city.

Beer Garden with a View: **Mosebacke,** perched high above town, is a gravelly beer garden with a grand harbor view. The beer garden (open only on warm summer evenings) prides itself on its beer rather than its basic grub (read: bar snacks). It's a good place to mix with a relaxed young crowd. As each of the beer kiosks has its own specialties, survey all of them before making your choice (a block inland from the top of the Katarina viewing platform, look for the triumphal arch at Mosebacke Torg 3, tel. 08/556-09890, www.sodrateatern.com). The adjacent restaurant serves fine 250-kr plates.

Classic Swedish Beer Halls: Two different but equally traditional Södermalm beer halls serve well-executed, hearty Swedish grub in big, high-ceilinged, orange-tiled spaces with rustic wooden tables.

Kvarnen ("The Mill") is a reliable choice with a 1908 ambience. As it's the home bar for the supporters of a football club, it can be rough. Pick a classic Swedish dish from their fun and easy menu (100-130-kr starters, 140-200-kr main courses, daily 17:00-24:00, Tjärhovsgatan 4, tel. 08/643-0380).

Pelikan, an old-school beer hall, is less sloppy and has nicer food. It's a bit deeper into Södermalm (120-230-kr starters, 190-270-kr main courses, Mon-Thu 16:00-23:00, Fri-Sun 13:00-23:00, Blekingegatan 40, tel. 08/5560-9290).

Trendier "Craft Beer" Pub: **Akkurat** has a staggering variety of microbrews—both Swedish and international (on tap and bottled)—as well as whisky. It's great if you wish you were in England with a bunch of Swedes (short menu of 190-240-kr pub grub, Mon-Fri 11:00-24:00, Sat 15:00-24:00, Sun 18:00-24:00, Hornsgatan 18, tel. 08/644-0015).

IN NORRMALM
At or near the Grand Hotel

Royal Smörgåsbord: To stuff yourself with all the traditional Swedish specialties (a dozen kinds of herring, salmon, reindeer, meatballs, lingonberries, and shrimp, followed by a fine table of cheeses and desserts) with a super harbor view, consider splurging at the Grand Hotel's dressy **Veranda Restaurant.** While very touristy, this is considered the finest *smörgåsbord* in town. The Grand Hotel, where royal guests and Nobel Prize winners stay, faces the harbor across from the palace. Pick up their English flier for a good explanation of the proper way to enjoy this grand buffet (and read about *smörgåsbords* on page 732). Reservations are often necessary (485 kr in evening, 445 kr for lunch, drinks extra, open nightly 18:00-22:00, also open for lunch Sat-Sun 13:00-16:00 year-round and Mon-Fri 12:00-15:00 in May-Sept, no shorts after 18:00, Södra Blasieholmshamnen 8, tel. 08/679-3586, www.grandhotel.se)

Restaurang B.A.R. has a fun energy, with diners surveying the meat and fish at the ice-filled counter, talking things over with the chef, and then choosing a slab. Prices are on the board, and everything's grilled (250-300-kr meals, open daily except closed Sun-Mon in July, behind the Grand Hotel at Blasieholmsgatan 4, tel. 08/611-5335).

At the Royal Opera House

The Operakällaren, one of Stockholm's most exclusive restaurants, runs a little "hip pocket" restaurant called **Bakfickan** on the side, specializing in traditional Swedish quality cooking at reasonable prices. It's ideal for someone eating out alone, or for anyone wanting an early dinner. Choose from two different daily specials or pay 180-280 kr for main dishes from their regular menu (160-180-kr specials served daily from 12:00 until they run out—which can be early or as late as 20:00, no specials in July). Sit inside—at tiny private side tables or at the big counter with the locals—or, in good weather, grab a table on the sidewalk, facing a cheery red church (Mon-Sat 12:00-22:00, closed Sun, on the inland side of Royal Opera House, tel. 08/676-5809).

At or near Hötorget

Hötorget ("Hay Market"), a vibrant outdoor produce market just two blocks from Sergels Torg, is a fun place to picnic-shop. The outdoor market closes at 18:00, and many merchants put their unsold produce on the push list (earlier closing and more desperate merchants on Sat).

Hötorgshallen, next to Hötorget (in the basement under the modern cinema complex), is a colorful indoor food market with an old-fashioned bustle, plenty of exotic and ethnic edibles, and—in the tradition of food markets all over Europe—some great little eateries (Mon-Fri 10:00-18:00, Sat 10:00-15:00, closed Sun). The best is **Kajsas Fisk,** hiding behind the fish stalls. They serve delicious fish soup to little Olivers who can hardly believe they're getting... more. For 95 kr, you get a big bowl of hearty soup, a simple salad, bread and crackers—plus one soup refill. Their *stekt strömming* (traditional fried herring and potato dish) is a favorite (90-150-kr daily fish specials, Mon-Fri 11:00-18:00, Sat 11:00-16:00, closed Sun,

Hötorgshallen 3, tel. 08/207-262). There's a great kebab and falafel place a few stalls away.

Kungshallen, an 800-seat indoor food court across the square from Hötorget, has more than a dozen eateries. The main floor is a bit more upscale, with sit-down places and higher prices, while the basement is a shopping-mall-style array of fast-food counters, including Chinese, sushi, pizza, Greek, and Mexican. This is a handy place to comparison-shop for a meal at lower prices (Mon-Fri 9:00-22:00, Sat-Sun 12:00-22:00).

On or near Drottninggatan

The pleasant, pedestrianized shopping street called Drottning-gatan, which runs from the train station area up into Stockholm's suburbs, is a fine place to find a forgettable meal but with memorable people-watching. Several interchangeable eateries with sidewalk tables line the street (and don't miss the delightful, leafy park courtyard of Centralbadet, at #88, with several outdoor cafés). None of them merits a special detour, except the next listing.

Rolfs Kök, a vibrant neighborhood favorite, is worth the pleasant five-minute stroll up from the end of Drottninggatan. The long bar up front fades into an open kitchen hemmed in with happy diners at counters, and tight tables fill the rest of the space before spilling out onto the sidewalk. Trendy, casual, and inviting, this bistro features international fare with a focus on Swedish classics and a good wine list. Reservations are smart (100-160-kr starters, 220-300-kr main courses, Mon-Fri 11:30-24:00, Sat-Sun 17:00-24:00, closed in July and sometimes early Aug—confirm it's open before making the trip, Tegnérgatan 41, tel. 08/101-696, www.rolfskok.se).

Near Sergels Torg

Kulturhuset Rooftop Eateries: Two places (one cheap and the other trendy) are handy for simple meals with great city views. **Cafeteria Panorama,** offering cheap eats and a salad bar, has both inside and outside seating with jaw-dropping vistas (90-kr lunch specials with salad bar, Sat-Mon 11:00-18:00, Tue-Fri 11:00-20:00). The more stylish **Mat and Bar café** has a pleasant garden setting with pricier food (daily until 21:00).

The many modern shopping malls and department stores around Sergels Torg all have appealing, if pricey, eateries catering to the needs of hungry local shoppers. **Åhléns** department store has a Hemköp supermarket in the basement (daily until 21:00) and two restaurants upstairs with 80-110-kr daily lunch specials (Mon-Fri 11:00-19:30, Sat 11:00-18:30, Sun 11:00-17:30).

IN ÖSTERMALM

Saluhall, on Östermalmstorg (near recommended Hotel Wellington), is a great old-time indoor market with top-quality artisanal

producers and a variety of sit-down and
takeout eateries. While it's nowhere near
"cheap," it's one of the most pleasant market halls I've seen, oozing with upscale
yet traditional Swedish class. Inside you'll
find Middle Eastern fare, sushi, classic
Scandinavian open-face sandwiches, seafood salads, healthy wraps, cheese counters, designer chocolates, gourmet coffee
stands, and a pair of classic old sit-down
eateries (Elmqvist and Tystamare). This is
your chance to pull up a stool at a lunch
counter next to well-heeled Swedish
yuppies (Mon-Thu 9:30-18:00, Fri until
19:00, Sat until 16:00, closed Sun).

Örtagården, upstairs from the Saluhall, is primarily a vegetarian restaurant and serves a 145-kr buffet weekdays until 17:00
and a larger 155-kr buffet evenings and weekends (Mon-Fri 11:00-
22:00, Sat-Sun 11:00-21:00, entrance on side of market building at
Nybrogatan 31, tel. 08/662-1728).

Restaurang Volt is a destination restaurant for foodies looking to splurge on "New Nordic" cooking: fresh, locally sourced ingredients fused into bold new recipes with fundamentally Swedish
flavors. Owners Fredrik Johnsson and Peter Andersson fill their
minimalist black dining room with just 31 seats, so reservations
are essential (550 kr/four courses, 700 kr/six courses, no à la carte,
Tue-Sat 18:00-24:00, closed Sun-Mon, Kommendörsgatan 16, tel.
08/662-3400, www.restaurangvolt.se).

Riche, a Parisian-style brasserie just a few steps off Nybroplan at Östermalm's waterfront, is a high-energy environment
with a youthful sophistication. They serve up pricey but elegantly
executed Swedish and international dishes in their winter garden,
bright dining room, and white-tile-and-wine-glass-chandeliered
bar (140-230-kr starters, 200-340-kr main courses, 175-kr plat du
jour, Mon-Fri 7:30-24:00, Sat-Sun 12:00-24:00, Birger Jarlsgatan
4, tel. 08/5450-3560).

Stockholm Connections

BY BUS

Unless you have a rail pass, long-distance buses are cheaper than
trains, such as from Stockholm to Oslo or Kalmar. Buses usually
take longer, but have more predictable pricing, shorter ticket lines,

and student discounts. Swebus is the largest operator (tel. 0771-21-8218, www.swebus.se); Nettbuss also has lots of routes (www.nettbuss.se). Some bus companies offer discounts with advance purchase.

From Stockholm by Bus to: Copenhagen (about 3/day with change in Malmö, 9.5 hours, longer for overnight trips), **Oslo** (3/day, 8 hours), **Kalmar** (4/day, fewer on weekends, 6 hours).

BY TRAIN

The easiest and cheapest way to book train tickets is online at www.sj.se. Simply select your journey and pay for it with a credit card. When you arrive at the train station, print out your tickets at a self-service ticket kiosk (bring your purchase confirmation code). You can also buy tickets at a ticket window in a train station, but this comes with long lines and a 5 percent surcharge. For timetables and prices, check online, call 0771/757-575, or use one of the self-service ticket kiosks.

As with airline tickets and hotel rooms, Swedish train ticket prices vary with demand. The cheapest are advance-purchase, nonchangeable, and nonrefundable.

For rail-pass holders, seat reservations are required on express (such as the "SJ high-speed" class) and overnight trains, and they're recommended on some longer routes (to Oslo, for example). Second-class seat reservations to Copenhagen cost 65 kr (150 kr in first class). If you have a rail pass, make your seat reservation at a ticket window in a train station, by phone (at the number above), or online (under "Buy Tickets," choose "pass 2cl" from the "customer card" menu).

From Stockholm by Train to: Uppsala (4/hour, 40 minutes; also possible on slower suburban *pendeltåg*—2/hour, 55 minutes, covered by local transit pass plus small supplement), **Växjö** (every 2 hours, 3.5 hours, change in Alvesta, reservations required), **Kalmar** (hourly, 4.5-5 hours, transfer in Alvesta, reservations required), **Copenhagen** (almost hourly, 5-6 hours on high-speed train, some with a transfer at Lund or Hässleholm, reservations required; overnight train requires a change in Malmö or Lund; all trains stop at Copenhagen airport before terminating at the central train station), **Oslo** (2/day direct Intercity trains, 6 hours; 2/day with change, 6-7.5 hours).

BY OVERNIGHT BOAT

Ferry boat companies run shuttle buses from the train station to coincide with each departure; check for details when you buy your ticket. When comparing prices between boats and planes, remember that the boat fare includes a night's lodging.

From Stockholm to: Helsinki and **Tallinn** (daily/nightly boats, 16 hours, see Helsinki and Tallinn chapters), **Turku** (daily/nightly boats, 11 hours). St. Peter Line connects Stockholm to **St. Petersburg,** but the trip takes two nights—you'll sail the first night to Tallinn, then a second night to St. Petersburg; returning, you'll sail the first night to Helsinki, and the second night to Stockholm (www.stpeterline.com). Note: To visit Russia, American and Canadian citizens need a visa (arrange weeks in advance); for details on the visa requirement and the company, see page 640 in the Helsinki chapter.

BY CRUISE SHIP

For many more details on Stockholm's ports, and other cruise destinations, pick up my *Rick Steves Northern European Cruise Ports* guidebook.

Stockholm has two cruise ports: the more central **Stadsgården** port, used mainly by ships that are just passing through, is in Södermalm; the **Frihamnen** port, used primarily by ships that are beginning or ending a cruise, is three miles northeast of the city center.

Getting Downtown: Most cruise lines offer a convenient **shuttle bus** (about 100 kr round-trip) that drops you in downtown Stockholm near the Opera House. From there it's an easy walk or public bus/tram ride to various points of interest. It's not a bad value in this expensive city, where a single one-way ticket on public transit costs over $5. **Taxis** from each port are also available (depending on your destination, figure 115-190 kr from Stadsgården and 150-235 kr from Frihamnen). Other options, including a hop-on, hop-off bus or boat from Stadsgården or the public bus from Frihamnen, are explained next.

Port Details: TI kiosks (with bus tickets, city guides, and maps) open at both ports when ships arrive.

Stadsgården is a long embankment, with cruises arriving at areas that flank the busy Viking Line Terminal (used by boats to Helsinki). The nearest transportation hub (with bus and T-bana stops) is Slussen, which sits beneath the bridge connecting the Old Town/Gamla Stan and the Södermalm neighborhood. Berth 160 is an easy 10-minute **walk** to Slussen; berths 165/167 are farther out but still walkable (about 25 minutes to Slussen).

From Stadsgården, a good option is the handy **hop-on, hop-off harbor boat** tour, which departs from right next to the cruise dock and connects several worthwhile downtown areas for a reasonable price (120-160 kr for 24 hours, tickets often discounted from cruise port; for more details, see page 440). A taxi stand is next to the TI kiosk just outside the port gate. Near the taxi stand is the departure point for **hop-on, hop-off tour buses** (for details, see page 437). The public bus from Stadsgården is not a convenient option.

Frihamnen is a sprawling, drab industrial port zone used by cruise liners as well as overnight Baltic boats. Cruises typically use one of three berths—634, 638, or 650. Berth 638 is the main dock and has the only dedicated terminal building (with a TI desk and gift shops). Along the main harborfront road you'll find a TI kiosk; hop-on, hop-off bus tours (pricey but convenient; for details see page 437); and a public **bus** stop—a good option. Bus #76 zips you to several major sights, including Djurgårdsbron, Nybroplan, Kungsträdgården, Räntmästartrappan, and Slussen (4-7/hour Mon-Fri, 2-3/hour Sat, none on Sun). On weekends, you may be better off taking the less convenient but more frequent bus #1, which cuts across the top of Östermalm and Norrmalm to the train station (runs daily). You can't buy bus tickets on board—get one at the TI inside the terminal, at the booth near the bus stop, or from the ticket machine at the bus stop.

BY PLANE

For information on arriving at Stockholm's airports, see "Arrival in Stockholm," earlier in this chapter.

To Helsinki and Tallinn: Many low-fare airlines are offering flights across the Baltic. For flights from Stockholm to Helsinki, check www.flysas.com/fi; to Tallinn, also visit www.norwegian.com and www.estonian-air.com.

ROUTE TIPS FOR DRIVERS

Stockholm to Oslo: It's an eight-hour drive from Stockholm to Oslo. **Årjäng,** just before the Norwegian border, is a good place for a rest stop. At the border, change money at the little TI kiosk (on right side). Pick up the Oslo map and *What's On in Oslo,* and consider buying your Oslo Card here.

NEAR STOCKHOLM

Drottningholm Palace • Sigtuna • Uppsala

At Stockholm's doorstep is a variety of fine side-trip options—all within an hour of the capital. Drottningholm Palace, on the city's outskirts, was the summer residence—and most opulent castle—of the Swedish royal family, and has a uniquely well-preserved Baroque theater, to boot. The adorable town of Sigtuna is a cutesy, cobbled escape from the big city, studded with history and rune stones. Uppsala is Sweden's answer to Oxford, offering stately university facilities and museums, the home and garden of scientist Carl Linnaeus, as well as a grand cathedral and the enigmatic burial mounds of Gamla Uppsala on the outskirts of town. Note that another side-trip option is to visit a few of the islands in Stockholm's archipelago (described in the next chapter).

Drottningholm Palace

The queen's 17th-century summer castle and current royal residence has been called "Sweden's Versailles." While that's a bit of a stretch, Drottningholm Palace (Drottningholms Slott) is worth ▲▲. It's enjoyable to explore the place where the Swedish royals bunk and to stroll their expansive gardens. Just as worthwhile is touring the nearby **Baroque-era theater** (also rated ▲▲), which preserves 18th-century stage sets and special-effects machinery. You can likely squeeze everything in with half a day here, or linger for an entire day.

GETTING THERE

The castle is an easy boat or subway-plus-bus ride from downtown Stockholm. Consider approaching by water (as the royals tradition-

ally did) and then returning by bus and subway (as a commoner).

Boats depart regularly from near City Hall for the relaxing hour-long trip (145 kr one-way, 195 kr round-trip, discount with Stockholm Card, departs from Stadshus-bron across from City Hall on the hour through the day, likely additional departures at :30 past the hour on weekends or any day in July-Aug, fewer departures Sept-April, tel. 08/1200-4000, www.stromma.se). It can be faster (30-45 minutes total) to take **public transit:** Ride the T-bana about 20 minutes to Brommaplan, where you can catch any #300-series bus for the five-minute ride to Drottningholm (as you leave the Brommaplan Station, check monitors to see which bus is leaving next—usually from platform A, E, or F; 54 kr one-way).

ORIENTATION TO DROTTNINGHOLM PALACE

Cost and Hours: 120 kr, May-Aug daily 10:00-16:30, Sept daily 11:00-15:30, Oct and April Fri-Sun only 11:00-15:30, Nov-March Sat-Sun only 12:00-15:30, closed last two weeks of Dec, tel. 08/402-6280, www.royalcourt.se.

Tours: You can explore the palace on your own, but with sparse posted explanations and no audioguide, it's worth the 20 kr extra for the 30-minute English guided tour, which brings the rooms to life. Tours are offered June-Aug usually at 10:00, 12:00, 14:00, and 16:00 (fewer tours off-season). Alternatively, you could buy the inexpensive palace guidebook.

Services: The gift shop/café at the entrance to the grounds (near the boat dock and bus stop) acts as a visitors center; Drottning-holm's only WCs are in the adjacent building. The café serves light meals. A handy Pressbyrån convenience store is also nearby (snacks, drinks, and transit tickets), and taxis are usually standing by.

BACKGROUND

"Drottningholm" means "Queen's Island." When the original castle mysteriously burned down in 1661 immediately after a visit from Queen

Near Stockholm

Gamla Uppsala ● / To Gävle
Uppsala
E-4
55
10 Kilometers
10 Miles
To Nörrtälje
Litslena
Arlanda ✈
E-18
To Västerås & Oslo
E-18
Sigtuna ● Märsta
E-4
See Archipelago detail map
To Turku (11 hrs)
To Helsinki (16 hrs)
Lake Mälaren
E-18
Vaxön ●
Vaxholm
See Stockholm detail maps
Nacka
Strängnäs ●
DROTTNINGHOLM ●
Stockholm
222
GRIPSHOLM CASTLE
E-4
73
Baltic Sea
E-3
To Kalmar, Malmö & Copenhagen ▼
Södertälje ● Haninge ●
To Nynäshamn ▼

Hedvig Eleonora, she (quite conveniently) had already commissioned plans for a bigger, better palace.

Built over 40 years—with various rooms redecorated by centuries of later monarchs—Drottningholm has the air of overcompensating for an inferiority complex. While rarely absolute rulers, Sweden's royals long struggled with stubborn parliaments. Perhaps this made the propaganda value of the palace decor even more important. Touring the palace, you'll see art that makes the point that Sweden's royalty is divine and belongs with the gods. Portraits and prominently displayed gifts from fellow monarchs attempt to legitimize the royal family by connecting the Swedish blue bloods with Roman emperors, medieval kings, and Europe's great royal families. The portraits you'll see of France's Louis XVI and Russia's Catherine the Great are reminders that Sweden's royalty was related to or tightly networked with the European dynasties.

Of course, today's monarchs are figureheads ruled by a constitution. The royal family makes a point to be as accessible and as "normal" as royalty can be. King Carl XVI Gustaf (b. 1946)—whose main job is handing out Nobel Prizes once a year—is a car nut who talks openly about his dyslexia. He was the first Swedish king not to be crowned "by the grace of God." The popular Queen Silvia is a businessman's daughter. At their 1976 wedding festivities, ABBA serenaded her with "Dancing Queen." Their daughter and heir to the throne, Crown Princess Victoria, studied political science at Yale and interned with Sweden's European Union delegation. In 2010, she married gym owner Daniel Westling—the first royal wedding in Sweden since her parents' marriage. Victoria and Daniel's first child, Princess Estelle, was born on February 23, 2012—and instantly became the next heir to the throne. The king and queen still live in one wing of Drottningholm, while other members of the royal family attempt to live more "normal" lives elsewhere.

VISITING THE PALACE

While not the finest palace interior in Europe (or even in Scandinavia), Drottningholm offers a chance to stroll through a place where a monarch still lives. You'll see two floors of lavish rooms, where Sweden's royalty did their best to live in the style of Europe's divine monarchs.

Ascend the grand staircase (decorated with faux marble and relief-illusion paintings) and buy your ticket on the first floor. Entering the state rooms on the **first floor,** admire the craftsmanship of the walls, with gold leaf shimmering on expertly tooled leather. Then pass through the Green Cabinet and hook right into Hedvig Eleonora's State Bed Chambers. The richly colored Baroque decor here, with gold embellishments, is representative of what the entire interior once looked like. Hedvig Eleonora was a "dowager queen," meaning that she was the widow of a king—her husband, King Karl X, died young at age 24—after they had been married just six years. Looking around the room, you'll see symbolism of this tragic separation. For example, in the ceiling painting, Hedvig Eleonora rides a cloud, with hands joined below her—suggesting that she will be reunited with her beloved in heaven.

This room was also the residence of a later monarch, Gustav III. That's why it looks like (and was) more of a theater than a place for sleeping. In the style of the French monarchs, this is where the ceremonial tucking-in and dressing of the king would take place.

Backtrack into the golden room, then continue down the other hallway. You'll pass through a room of royal portraits with very consistent characteristics: pale skin with red cheeks; a high forehead with gray hair (suggesting wisdom); and big eyes (windows to the soul). At the end of the hall is a grand library, which once held some 7,000 books. The small adjoining room is filled by a large model of a temple in Pompeii; Gustav III—who ordered this built—was fascinated by archaeology, and still today, there's a museum of antiquities named for him at the Royal Palace in Stockholm.

On the **second floor,** as you enter the first room, notice the faux doors, painted on the walls to create symmetry, and the hidden doors for servants (who would scurry—unseen and unheard—through the walls to attend to the royal family). In the Blue Drawing Room is a bust of the then-king's cousin, Catherine the Great. This Russian monarch gave him—in the next room, the Chinese Drawing Room—the (made-in-Russia) faux "Chinese" stove. This dates from a time when exotic imports from China (tea, silk, ivory, Kung Pao chicken) were exciting and new. (Around the same time, in the mid-18th century, the royals built the Chinese Pavilion on Drottningholm's grounds.) The Gobelins tapestries in this room were also a gift, from France's King Louis XVI. In the next room, the darker Oskar Room, are more tapestries—these a gift from England's King Charles I. (Sensing a trend?) You'll pass through Karl XI's Gallery (overlooking the grand staircase)—which is still used for royal functions—and into the largest room on this floor, the Hall of State. The site of royal weddings and receptions, this room boasts life-size paintings of very important Swedes in golden frames and a bombastically painted ceiling.

Drottningholm Palace Park: Like so many European "summer palaces," the Drottningholm grounds are graced with sprawling gardens. Directly behind the palace is the rigid and geometrical Baroque Garden, with angular hedges, tidy rows of trees, fountains, and outdoor "rooms" at the far end. To the right is the English Garden, which has rugged, naturalistic plantings and is speckled with statues. And at the far end of

the grounds, surrounding the Chinese Pavilion, are the Rococo Gardens. While charming, these gardens aren't grand on a European scale—but they are a pretty place for a stroll.

NEAR THE PALACE: DROTTNINGHOLM COURT THEATER

This 18th-century theater (Drottningholms Slottsteater) has miraculously survived the ages—complete with its instruments, hand-operated sound-effects machines for wind, thunder, and clouds; and original stage sets. Visit it on a 40-minute guided tour, which some find more enjoyable than the palace tour.

Cost and Hours: 100 kr for guided tour, English tours about hourly May-Aug 11:00-16:30, Sept 12:00-15:30—these are first and last tour times, shop open before and after, may be limited tours on weekends in April and Oct-Dec, no tours Jan-March, tel. 08/759-0406, www.dtm.se.

Performances: Check their schedule for the rare opportunity to see perfectly authentic operas (about 25 performances each summer). Tickets for this popular time-travel musical and theatrical experience cost 300-1,000 kr and go on sale each March; purchase online (www.ticnet.se), at the theater shop, or by phone (from the US, call +46-77-170-7070; see www.dtm.se for details).

Background: Built by a Swedish king to impress his Prussian wife—who found Sweden dreadfully provincial—this is one of two such historic theaters remaining in Europe (the other is in the town of Český Krumlov, in the Czech Republic). Their son, King Gustav III, loved the theater (some say more than he loved ruling Sweden): Besides ordering Stockholm's Royal Opera to be built, he also wrote, directed, and acted in several theatrical presentations (including the first-ever production in the Swedish language, rather than French). He even died in a theater, assassinated at a masquerade ball in the very opera house he had built. When he died, so too did this flourishing of culture—the theater became a warehouse until it was rediscovered in 1921. Soon thereafter, it began producing plays once again.

Visiting the Theater: On the tour, you'll see the bedrooms where famous actors would sleep while performing here, then enter the theater itself, lit only with (now simulated) candles. You'll see the extremely deep stage (with scenery peeking in from the edges), the royal boxes where the king and queen entered, and doors and curtains that were painted onto walls to achieve perfect symmetry. Be ready to volunteer to try out the old equipment used to make thunder and wind noises. It's fascinating to think that the system of pulleys, trap doors, and actors floating in from the sky isn't so different from the techniques employed on stages today.

Sigtuna

Sigtuna, the oldest town in Sweden (established in the 970s), is the country's cutest town as well. Worth ▲, it sits sugary sweet on Lake Mälaren, about 30 miles inland from Stockholm (reachable by train/bus or sightseeing boat). A visit here affords a relaxed look at an open-air folk museum of a town, with ruined churches, ancient rune stones, and a cobbled lane of 18th-century buildings—all with English info posts. It also offers plenty of shopping and eating options in a park-like lakeside setting. If you're looking for stereotypical Sweden and a break from the big city, Sigtuna is a fun side-trip.

Getting There: By **public transport** from Stockholm, it's a one-hour trip out (take the *pendeltåg* suburban train from Stockholm to Märsta and then change to bus #570). Guided two-hour **sightseeing cruises** run to Sigtuna in summer (350 kr round-trip, Wed-Sun morning departures from Stockholm's Stadshusbron dock, www.stromma.se). If traveling by **car** to Uppsala or Oslo, Sigtuna is a short detour.

Tourist Information: The helpful TI is on the main street and eager to equip you with a town map and info (daily 10:00-18:00, Storagatan 33, tel. 08/5948-0650).

Sights in Sigtuna

Main Street: Storagatan

Sigtuna's main street provides the town's spine. Along it, besides the TI, you'll find the town hall from 1744, with a nicely preserved interior (free, daily 12:00-16:00), and the Sigtuna History Museum, with archaeological finds from the Viking culture here (may be closed for renovation). As you stroll the street, read the historical signs posted along the way and poke into shops and cafés. The most charming place for lunch, a snack, or a drink is Tant Brun ("Auntie Brown's") Café, tucked away just around the corner from the TI in a super-characteristic 17th-century home with a cozy garden.

Churches

Before the Reformation came along, Sigtuna was an important political and religious center, and the site of the country's archbishopric. Along with powerful monastic communities, the town had seven churches. When the Reformation hit, that was the end of the monasteries, and there was a need for only one church—the Gothic Mariakyrkan. It survived, and the rest fell into ruins. Mariakyrkan, or Mary's Church, built by the Dominicans in the 13th century, is decorated with pre-Reformation murals and is worth a look (free, daily 9:00-17:00).

The stony remains of St. Olaf's Church stand in the Mary's Church cemetery. This 12th-century ruin is evocative, with stout vaults and towering walls that served the community as a place of last refuge when under attack.

NEAR STOCKHOLM

Rune Stones

Sigtuna is dotted with a dozen rune stones. Literally "word stones," these memorial stones are carved with messages in an Iron Age runic language. Sigtuna has more of these than any other Swedish town. Those here generally have a cross, indicating that they are from the Christian era (11th century). Each is described in English. I like Anund's stone, which says, "Anund had this stone erected in memory of himself in his lifetime." His rune carver showed a glimpse of personality and that perhaps Anund had no friends. (It worked. Now he's in an American guidebook, and 10 centuries later, he's still remembered.)

Uppsala

Uppsala, Sweden's fourth-largest city, is a rather small town with a big history. A few blocks in front of its train station, an inviting commercial center bustles around the main square and along a scenic riverfront. Towering across the river are its historic cathedral and a venerable university. For visitors, the university features a rare 17th-century anatomical theater, an exhibit of its prestigious academic accomplishments, and a library with literary treasures on display. Uppsala is home to the father of modern botany, Carl Linnaeus, whose garden and house—now a museum—make for a fascinating visit. And, just outside town stands Gamla Uppsala, the site of a series of majestic burial mounds where Sweden buried its royalty back in the 6th century. While Gamla Uppsala is a short bus ride away, everything else is within delightful walking distance. If you're not traveling anywhere else in Sweden other than Stockholm, Uppsala (less than an hour away) makes a pleasant day trip. While buzzing during the school year, this university town is sleepy during summer vacations.

GETTING THERE

Take the train from Stockholm's central station (4/hour, 40 minutes, 85 kr; also possible on slower suburban *pendeltåg*—2/hour, 55 minutes, covered by local transit pass plus small supplement). Since the Uppsala station has lockers and is in the same direction from Stockholm as the airport, you could combine a quick visit here with an early arrival or late departure.

Orientation to Uppsala

TOURIST INFORMATION

The helpful TI, across the street from the train station, has the informative *What's On Uppsala* magazine, which includes the best map of the center and a list of all sights (Mon-Fri 10:00-18:00, Sat 10:00-15:00, Sun July-Aug only 11:00-15:00, Kungsgatan 59, tel. 018/727-4800, www.destinationuppsala.se). They sell the **Uppsala Card** (150 kr, covers all attractions in the city plus bus fare and admission to Gamla Uppsala).

ARRIVAL IN UPPSALA

From the train station (pay lockers), cross the busy street and find the TI on the right (pick up the *What's On* magazine). Walk two blocks to Kungsängsgatan, turn right, and walk to the main square, Stora Torget. The spires of the cathedral mark two of the top three sights (the cathedral itself and the adjacent university buildings). The Linnaeus Garden and Museum is a few blocks up the river, and the bus to Gamla Uppsala is a couple of blocks away (see map, above).

Sights in Uppsala

▲▲UPPSALA CATHEDRAL (UPPSALA DOMKYRKAN)

One of Scandinavia's largest, most historic cathedrals feels as vital as it does impressive. While the building was completed in 1453, the spires and interior decorations are from the late 19th century. The cathedral—with a fine Gothic interior, the relics of St. Erik, memories of countless Swedish coronations, and the tomb of King Gustav Vasa—is well worth a visit.

Cost and Hours: Free, daily 8:00-18:00; guided 45-minute English tours go 1-2 times/day in season (mid-June-mid-Aug Mon-Sat at 11:00 and 14:00, Sun at 15:00), or pick up brochure from gift shop; tel. 018/187-177, www.uppsaladomkyrka.se.

Visiting the Cathedral: Grab a seat in a pew and take in the graceful Gothic lines of the longest nave in Scandinavia (130

yards). The gorgeously carved, gold-slathered Baroque pulpit is a reminder of the Protestant (post-Reformation) focus on preaching the word of God in the people's language. Look high above in the choir area to enjoy fine murals, restored in the 1970s. For ages, pilgrims have come here to see the relics of St. Erik. All around you are important side chapels, tombs, and memorials (each with an English description).

Near the entrance is the tomb and memorial to scientist Carl Linnaeus, the father of modern botany, who spent his career at the university here (for more on him, see the Linnaeus Garden and Museum listing, later).

In the chapel at the far east end of the church is the tomb of King Gustav Vasa and his family. This chapel was originally dedicated to the Virgin Mary. But Gustav Vasa brought the Reformation to Sweden in 1527 and usurped this prized space for his own tomb. In good Swedish style, the decision was affirmed by a vote in parliament, and bam—the country was Lutheran. (A few years later, England's King Henry VIII tried a similar religious revolution—and had a much tougher time.) Notice that in the tomb sculpture, Gustav is shown flanked by two wives—his first wife died after suffering a fall; his second wife bore him 10 children. High above are murals of Gustav's illustrious life.

Speaking of Mary, notice the modern statue of a common-rather-than-regal Protestant Mary outside the chapel looking in.

This eerily lifelike statue from 2005, called *Mary (The Return)*, captures Jesus' mother wearing a scarf and timeless garb. In keeping with the Protestant spirit here, this new version of Mary is shown not as an exalted queen, but as an everywoman, saddened by the loss of her child and seeking solace—or answers—in the church.

Cathedral Treasury: By the gift shop, you can pay to ride the elevator up to the treasury collection. Here (with the help of a loaner flashlight and English translations), you'll find medieval textiles (tapestries and vestments), swords and crowns found in Gustav's grave, and the Nobel Peace Prize won by Nathan Söderblom, an early-20th-century archbishop here (40 kr, daily 10:00-17:00, until 16:00 in off-season). In this same narthex area, notice the debit-card machine for offerings.

UNIVERSITY ATTRACTIONS AND NEARBY

Scandinavia's first university was founded in Uppsala in 1477. Two famous grads are Carl Linnaeus (the famous botanist) and Anders Celsius (the scientist who developed the temperature scale that bears his name). The campus is scattered around the cathedral part of town, and two university buildings are particularly interesting and welcoming to visitors: the Gustavianum and the library.

▲▲Gustavianum

Facing the cathedral is the university's oldest surviving building, with a bulbous dome that doubles as a sundial (notice the gold numbers). Today it houses a well-presented museum that features an anatomical theater, a cabinet filled with miniature curiosities, and Celsius' thermometer. The collection is curiously engaging for the glimpse it gives into the mindset of 17th-century Europe.

Cost and Hours: 50 kr, June-Aug Tue-Sun 10:00-16:00, Sept-May Tue-Sun 11:00-16:00, closed Mon, Akademigatan 3, tel. 018/471-7571, www.gustavianum.uu.se.

Visiting the Gustavianum: Ride the elevator (near the gift shop/ticket desk) up to the fourth floor. Then, see the exhibits as you walk back down.

Up top is a collection of **Viking artifacts** discovered at Valsgärde, a prehistoric site near Uppsala used for burials for more than 700 years. Archaeologists have uncovered 15 boat graves here (dating from A.D. 600-1050—roughly one per generation), próviding insight on the Viking Age. The recovered artifacts on display here show fine Viking workmanship and a society more refined than many might expect.

Next you'll find the **anatomical theater** (accessible from the fourth and third floors). This theater's only show was human dissection. In the mid-1600s, as the enlightened ideas of the Renaissance swept far into the north of Europe, scholars began to consider dissection of the human body the ultimate scientific education. Corpses of hanged criminals were carefully sliced and diced here, under a dome in an almost temple-like atmosphere, demonstrating the lofty heights to which science had risen in society. Imagine 200 students standing tall all around and leaning in to peer intently at the teacher's scalpel. Notice the plaster death masks of the dissected in a case at the entry.

On the second floor is a fascinating exhibit on the **history of the university.** The Physics Chamber features a collection of instruments from the 18th and 19th centuries that were used by university teachers. The Augsburg Art Cabinet takes center stage here with a dizzying array of nearly a thousand miniscule works of art and other tidbits held in an ornately decorated oak cabinet. Built in the 1620s for a bigwig who wanted to impress his friends, the cabinet once held the items shown in display cases all around. Find the interactive video screen, where you can control a virtual tour of the collection. Just beyond the cabinet is a thermometer that once belonged to Celsius (in his handwriting, notice how 0 and 100 were originally flip-flopped, with water boiling at 0 degrees Celsius rather than 100).

On the first floor is the university's **classical antiquities collection** from the Mediterranean. These ancient Greek and Roman artifacts and Egyptian sarcophagi were used to bring classical culture and art to students unable to travel abroad.

▲University Library (Universitetsbiblioteket)

Uppsala University's library, housed in a 19th-century building called the Carolina Rediviva, is a block uphill from the cathedral and Gustavianum. Off the entry hall (to the right) is a small but exquisite exhibit of treasured old books. Well-displayed and well-described in English, the carefully selected collection is surprisingly captivating.

Cost and Hours: Free, daily 9:00-18:00, Dag Hammarskjölds väg 1, tel. 018/471-3941, www.ub.uu.se.

Visiting the Library: With precious items like Mozart scores in the composer's own hand and a map of Mexico City dating from 1555, the display cases here feel like the Treasures room at the British Library.

The most valuable item is the **Silver Bible,** a translation from Greek of the four Gospels into the now-extinct Gothic language. Written in Ravenna in the 6th century, Sweden's single most precious book is so named for its silver-ink writing on purple-colored calfskin vellum. Booty from a 1648 Swedish victory in Prague, it ended up at Uppsala University in 1669.

Another rarity is the **Carta Marina,** the first more-or-less accurate map of Scandinavia, printed in Venice in 1539 from nine woodblocks. Compare this 16th-century understanding of the region with your own travels.

▲Linnaeus Garden and Museum (Linnéträdgården)

Carl Linnaeus, famous for creating the formal system for naming different species of plants and animals, spent his career in Uppsala as a professor. This home, office, greenhouse, and garden is the ultimate Linnaeus sight, providing a vivid look at this amazing scientist and his work.

Cost and Hours: 60 kr for museum and garden; May-Sept Tue-Sun 11:00-17:00, garden open until 20:00, closed Mon and off-season; daily 45-minute English tour at 14:30; after 17:00, when the museum closes, the garden becomes a free public space—enter on Svartbäcksgatan at #27; tel. 018/471-2874, www.linnaeus.uu.se.

Visiting the Garden and Museum: While Linnaeus (whose noble name was Carl von Linné) was professor of medicine and botany at the University of Uppsala, he lived and studied here. From 1743 until 1778, he ran this botanical garden and lived on site to study the plant action—day and night, year-round—of about 3,000 different species. When he moved in, the university's department of medicine and botany moved in as well.

It was in this garden (the first in Sweden, originally set up in 1655) that Linnaeus developed a way to classify the plant kingdom. Wandering the garden where the most famous of all botanists did his work, you can pop into the orangery, built so temperate plants could survive the Nordic winters.

The museum, in Linnaeus' home (which he shared with his wife and seven children), is filled with the family's personal possessions and his professional gear. You'll see his insect cabinet, herbs cabinet, desk, botany tools, and notes. An included audioguide helps bring the exhibit to life.

More Sights near the University

Uppsala has a range of lesser sights, all within walking distance of the cathedral. The **Uppland Museum** (Upplandsmuseet), a regional history museum with prehistoric bits and folk-art scraps, is on the river by the waterfall, near the TI (free, Tue-Sun 12:00-17:00, closed Mon). Uphill from the university library is the 16th-century **Uppsala Castle,** which houses an art museum and runs slice-of-castle-life tours (required 80-kr tour, offered in English only a few weeks each summer Tue-Sun at 13:00 and 15:00, tel. 018/727-2485).

▲GAMLA UPPSALA

This site on the outskirts of town gives historians goose bumps. Gamla Uppsala—literally, "Old Uppsala"—includes nine large royal burial mounds circled by a walking path. Fifteen hundred years ago, when the Baltic Sea was higher and it was easy to sail all the way to Uppsala, the pagan Swedish kings had their capital here. Old Uppsala is where the petty Swedish kingdoms came together and a nation coalesced.

Cost and Hours: The **mounds** are free and always open. The **museum** is 70 kr and open April-Aug daily 11:00-17:00; shorter hours in off-season (generally 12:00-15:00 and closed Tue and Fri); closed in Dec. In summer your museum admission includes a 40-minute guided English tour of the mounds (July-Aug daily at 15:00, tel. 018/239-300, www.raa.se/gamlauppsala). The **church** is free and open daily April-Aug 9:00-18:00, Sept-March 9:00-16:00 (tiny church museum across the lane is free and open Sat-Sun only 12:00-15:00).

Getting There: A direct city bus stops right at the site. From the Uppsala train station, go to the bus stop at Vaksalagatan 7-13 (a block and a half away) and take bus #2, marked *Gamla Uppsala*, to the last stop (30 kr, buy ticket at nearby Pressbyrån kiosk, 2-4/hour, 15-minute trip). All the Gamla Uppsala sights are within 200 yards of each other, making it an easy visit.

Eating: Gamla Uppsala is great for picnics, or you can drop by the rustic and half-timbered Odinsborg café, which serves sandwiches, mead, and daily plates (daily 10:00-18:00, tel. 018/323-525).

Visiting Gamla Uppsala: The highlight of a visit is to climb the evocative mounds, which you're welcome to wander. Also at the site is a small but interesting museum and a 12th-century church.

The Mounds: The focus of ritual and religious activities from the 6th through 13th centuries, the mounds are made meaningful with the help of English info boards posted around.

Imagine the scene over a thousand years ago, when the democratic tradition of this country helped bring the many small Swedish kingdoms together into one nation. A *ting* was a political assembly where people dealt with the issues of the day. Communities would gather here at the rock that marked their place, and then the leader, standing atop the flat mound (nearest today's café), would address the crowd as if in a natural amphitheater. It was here that Sweden became Christianized a thousand years ago. In 1989 Pope John Paul II gave a Mass right here to celebrate the triumph of Christianity over paganism in Sweden. (These days, this is a pretty secular society and relatively few Swedes go to church.)

Museum: Gamla Uppsala's museum gives a good overview of early Swedish history and displays items found in the mounds. While humble, it is instructive, with plenty of excavated artifacts.

Church: Likely standing upon a pagan holy site, the church dates from the 12th century and was the residence of the first Swedish archbishop. An 11th-century rune stone is embedded in the external wall. In the entryway, an iron-clad oak trunk with seven locks on it served as the church treasury back in the 12th century. In the nave, a few Catholic frescoes, whitewashed over in the 16th century with the Reformation, have been restored.

Eating in Uppsala

Survey the many eateries on or near the main square or along the river below the cathedral. The **Cathedral Café** (a few steps to the right as you exit the cathedral) is charming, reasonable, and handy—and your money supports the city's mission of helping the local homeless population (100-kr lunch specials, soup and sandwich menus, Mon-Fri 10:00-17:00, Sat-Sun 11:00-16:00).

STOCKHOLM'S ARCHIPELAGO

Vaxholm • Grinda • Svartsö • Sandhamm

Some of Europe's most scenic islands stretch 80 miles out into the Baltic Sea from Stockholm. If you're cruising to (or from) Finland, you'll get a good look at this island beauty. If you have more time and want to immerse yourself in all that simple Swedish nature, consider spending a day or two island-hopping.

The Swedish word for "island" is simply *ö*, but the local name for this area is Skärgården—literally, "garden of skerries," which are unforested rocks sticking up from the sea. That stone is granite, carved out and deposited by glaciers. The archipelago closer to Stockholm is rockier, with bigger islands and more trees. Farther out (such as at Sandhamn), the glaciers lingered longer, slowly grinding the granite into sand and creating smaller islands.

Locals claim there are more than 30,000 of these islands, and as land here is rising slowly, more pop out every year. Some 150 are inhabited year-round, and about 100 have ferry service. There's an unwritten law of public access in the archipelago: Technically you're allowed to pitch your tent anywhere for up to two nights, provided the owner of the property can't see you from his or her house. It's polite to ask first and essential to act responsibly.

With thousands of islands to choose from, every Swede seems to have a favorite. This chapter covers four very different island destinations that offer an overview of the archipelago. Vaxholm, the gateway to the archipelago, comes with an imposing fortress, a charming fishermen's harbor, and the easiest connections to Stockholm. Rustic Grinda feels like—and used to be—a Swedish summer camp. Sparsely populated Svartsö is another fine back-to-nature experience. And swanky Sandhamn thrills the sailboat set, with a lively yacht harbor, a scenic setting at the far edge of the archipelago, and (true to its name) sandy beaches.

The flat-out best way to experience the magic of the archipelago is simply stretching out comfortably on the rooftop deck

of your ferry. The journey truly is the destination. Enjoy the charm of lovingly painted cottages as you glide by, sitting in the sun on delicate pairs of lounge chairs that are positioned to catch just the right view, with the steady rhythm of the ferries lacing this world together, and people savoring quality time with each other and nature.

ARCHIPELAGO

PLANNING YOUR TIME

On a Tour: For the best quick look, consider one of the many half- or full-day package boat trips from downtown Stockholm to the archipelago. **Strömma** runs several options, including the three-hour Archipelago Tour (2-4/day, 250 kr), or the all-day Thousand Island Cruise (departs daily in summer at 9:30, 1,150 kr includes lunch and dinner; tel. 08/1200-4000, www.stromma.se).

On Your Own: For more flexibility, freedom, and a better dose of the local vacation scene, do it on your own. Any one of the islands in this chapter is easily doable as a single-day side-trip from Stockholm. And, because all boats to and from Stockholm pass through Vaxholm, it's easy to tack on that town to any other one. For general information about the archipelago, see www.visitskargarden.se.

For a very busy all-day itinerary that takes in the two most enjoyable island destinations (Grinda and Sandhamn), consider this plan: 8:00—Set sail from Stockholm; 9:30—Arrive in Grinda for a quick walk around the island; 10:50—Catch the boat to Sandhamn; 11:45—Arrive in Sandhamn, have lunch, and enjoy the town; 17:00—Catch boat to Stockholm (maybe have dinner on board); 19:05—Arrive back in Stockholm. Or you could craft a route tailored to your interests: For example, for a back-to-nature experience, try Stockholm-Grinda-Svartsö-Stockholm. For an urban mix of towns, consider Stockholm-Vaxholm-Sandhamn-Stockholm.

Overnighting on an island really lets you get away from it all and enjoy the island ambience. I've listed a few island accommodations, but note that midrange options are few; most tend to be either pricey and top-end or very rustic (rented cottages with minimal plumbing).

Don't struggle too hard with the "which island?" decision. The

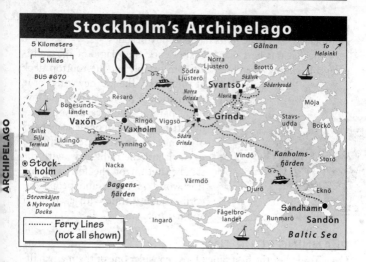

Stockholm's Archipelago

main thing is to get well beyond Vaxholm, where the scenery gets more striking. I'd sail an hour or two past Vaxholm, have a short stop on an island, then stop in Vaxholm on the way home. Again, the real joy is the view from your ferry.

GETTING AROUND THE ARCHIPELAGO

A few archipelago destinations (including Vaxholm) are accessible overland, thanks to modern bridges. For other islands, you'll take a boat. Two major companies run public ferries from downtown Stockholm to the archipelago: the bigger Waxholmsbolaget and the smaller Cinderella Båtarna.

Tickets: Regular tickets are sold on board. Simply walk on, and at your convenience, stop by the desk to buy your ticket before you disembark (or wait for them to come around and sell you one). Waxholmsbolaget offers a deal that's worthwhile if you're traveling with a small group or doing a lot of island-hopping. You can save 25 percent by buying a 1,000-kr ticket credit for 750 kr (sold only on land; use the splittable credit to buy tickets on the boat). If you're staying in the archipelago for a few days and want to island-hop, consider the Boat Hopper Pass. This five-day, all-inclusive pass is good on either boat line (420 kr, plus a 20-kr smartcard fee). Buy the card at the Waxholmsbolaget office.

Schedules: Check both companies' schedules when planning your itinerary; you might have to mix and match to make your itinerary work. A single, confusing schedule booklet mixes times for both lines. Ferry schedules are complex even to locals, especially outside of peak season.

Note that the departures mentioned below are for summer (mid-June-mid-Aug); the number of boats declines off-season.

Waxholmsbolaget: Their ships depart from in front of Stockholm's Grand Hotel, at the stop called Stromkäjen (tel. 08/679-5830, www.waxholmsbolaget.se). Waxholmsbolaget boats run from Stockholm to these islands: **Vaxholm** (at least hourly, 1.5 hours, 75 kr), **Grinda** (nearly hourly, 2 hours, 90 kr), **Svartsö** (3/day, 2.5 hours, 110 kr), and **Sandhamn** (1/day, Sat-Sun only, 3.5 hours, 150 kr). These destinations and their timetables are listed in the "Visitor" section of Waxholmsbolaget's website. The same company has routes and schedules throughout the archipelago.

Cinderella Båtarna: This company focuses its coverage on the most popular destinations. Their ships—generally faster, more comfortable, and a little pricier than their rivals'—leave from near Stockholm's Nybroplan, along Strandvägen (tel. 08/1200-4000, www.cinderellabatarna.com). Cinderella boats sail frequently (4/day Mon-Thu, 5/day Fri-Sun) from Stockholm to **Vaxholm** (50 minutes, 110 kr) and **Grinda** (1.5 hours, 145 kr). After Grinda, the line splits, going either to **Sandhamn** (from Stockholm: 1/day Mon-Thu, 2/day Fri-Sun, 2.5 hours, 165 kr), or Finnhamn, with a stop en route at **Svartsö** (from Stockholm: 2/day, 2.5 hours, 165 kr). These fares are for peak season (mid-June-mid-Aug); Cinderella's fares are slightly cheaper off-season.

On Board: When you board, tell the conductor which island you're going to. Boats don't land at all of the smaller islands unless passengers have requested a stop. Hang on to your ticket, as you'll have to show it to disembark. Some boats have luggage-storage areas (ask when you board).

You can usually access the outdoor deck; if you can't get to the front deck (where the boats load and unload), head to the back. Or nab a window seat inside. For the best seat, with less sun and nicer views, I'd go POSH: Port Out, Starboard Home (on the left side leaving Stockholm, on the right side coming back). As you sail, a monitor on board shows the position of your boat as it motors through the islands.

Food: You can usually buy food on board, ranging from simple fare at snack bars to elegant sea-view dinners at fancy restaurants. If your boat has a top-deck restaurant and you want to combine your cruise with dinner, make a reservation as soon as you board. Once you have a table, it's yours for the whole trip, so you can simply claim your seat and enjoy the ride, circling back later to eat. You can also try calling ahead to reserve a table for a specific cruise (for Waxholmsbolaget, call 08/243-090; for Cinderella, call 08/1200-4000).

HELPFUL HINTS

Opening Times: Any opening hours I list in this chapter are reliable only for peak season (mid-June-mid-Aug). During the rest of the tourist year ("shoulder season"—late May, early June, late August, and September), hours are flexible and completely weather-dependent; more services tend to be open on weekends than weekdays. Outside the short summer season, many places close down entirely.

Money: Bring cash. The only ATMs are in Vaxholm; farther out, you'll wish you'd stocked up on cash in Stockholm, though most vendors do accept credit cards.

Signal for Stop: At the boat landings or jetties on small islands, you'll notice a small signal tower (called a semaphore) that's used to let a passing boat know you want to be picked up. Pull the cord to spin the white disc and make it visible to the ship. Be sure to put it back before boarding the boat. At night, you signal with light—locals just use their mobile phones.

Weather: The weather on the islands is often better than in Stockholm. For island forecasts, check Götland's (the big island far to the south) instead of Stockholm's.

Local Drink: A popular drink here is *punsch,* a sweet fruit liqueur. Stately old buildings sometimes have *punsch-verandas,* little glassed-in upstairs porches where people traditionally would imbibe and chat.

Vaxholm

The self-proclaimed "gateway to the archipelago," Vaxholm is more developed and less charming than the other islands. Connected by bridge to Stockholm, it's practically a suburb, and not the place to commune with Swedish nature. But it also has an illustrious history as the anchor of Stockholm's naval defense network, and it couldn't be easier to reach (constant buses and boats from Stockholm). While Vaxholm isn't the rustic archipelago you might be looking for, you're almost certain to pass through here at some point on your trip. If you have some extra time, hop off the boat for a visit.

Getting There: Boats constantly shuttle between Stockholm's waterfront and Vaxholm (1-2/hour, 50 minutes-1.5

hours, 75-110 kr depending on boat company). **Bus #670** runs regularly from the Tekniska Högskolan T-bana stop in northern Stockholm to the center of Vaxholm (3/hour Mon-Fri, 2/hour Sat-Sun, 40-minute trip, 75 kr one-way—three zones). Unless you're on a tight budget, I'd take the boat for the scenery.

Orientation to Vaxholm

Vaxholm, with about 11,000 people, is on the island of Vaxön, connected to the mainland (and Stockholm) by a series of bridges. Everything of interest is within a five-minute walk of the boat dock.

TOURIST INFORMATION
Vaxholm's good TI is well-stocked with brochures about Vaxholm itself, Stockholm, and the archipelago, and can help you with boat schedules (June-Aug Mon-Fri 10:00-18:00, Sat-Sun 10:00-16:00, shorter hours off-season; in the Town Hall building on Rådhustorget, tel. 08/5413-1480, www.vaxholm.se).

ARRIVAL IN VAXHOLM
Ferries stop at Vaxholm's south harbor (Söderhamnen). The **bus** from Stockholm arrives and departs at the bus stop called Söderhamnsplan, a few steps from the boats. To get your bearings, follow my Vaxholm Walk. Luggage lockers are in the Waxholmsbolaget building on the waterfront. The handy electronic departure board (*Nasta Avgang* means "next departure") near the ticket office shows when boats are leaving. For more help, confirm your plans with the person at the ticket office.

Vaxholm Walk

This 30-minute, self-guided, two-part loop will take you to the most characteristic corners of Vaxholm. Begin at the boat dock—you can even start reading as you approach.

Waterfront: Dominating Vaxholm's waterfront is the big Art Nouveau Waxholms Hotell, dating from the early 20th century.

Across the strait to the right is Vaxholm's stout fortress, a reminder of this town's strategic importance over the centuries.

With your back to the water, turn left and walk with the big hotel on your right-hand side. Notice the Waxholmsbolaget office building. Inside you can buy tickets, confirm boat schedules, or stow your bag in a locker. After the hamburger-and-hot-dog stand, you'll reach a roundabout. Just to your left is the stop for bus #670, connecting Vaxholm to Stockholm. Beyond that, a wooden walkway follows the seafront to the town's private boat harbor (Västerhamnen, or "west harbor"), where you can count sailboats and rent a bike.

But for now, continue straight up Vaxholm's appealing, shop-lined main street, Hamngatan. After one long block (notice the handy Coop/Konsum grocery store across the street), turn right up Rådhusgatan (following signs to *Rådhustorget*) to reach the town's main square. The TI is inside the big, yellow Town Hall building on your left. Continue kitty-corner across the square (toward the granite slope) and head downhill on a street leading to the...

Fishermen's Quarter: This Norrhamnen ("north harbor") is ringed by former fishermen's homes. Walk out to the dock and  survey the charming wooden cottages. In the mid-19th century, Stockholmers considered Vaxholm's herring, called *strömming*, top-quality. Caught fresh here, the herring could be rowed into the city in just eight hours and eaten immediately, while herring caught farther out on the archipelago, which had to be preserved in salt, lost its flavor.

As you look out to sea, you'll see a pale green building protruding on the left. This is the charming Hembygdsgården homestead museum, with a pleasant indoor-outdoor café. It's worth heading to this little point (even if the museum is closed, as it often is): As you face the water, go left about one block, then turn right down the gravel lane called Trädgårdsgatan (also marked for *Hembygdsgården*). At this corner, look for the *Strömmingslådan* ("herring shop") sign for the chance to buy what herring connoisseurs consider top-notch fish (summer only).

Continuing down Trädgårdsgatan lane, you'll run right into the **Hembygdsgården homestead.** The big house features an endearing museum showing the simple, traditional fisherman's lifestyle (pop in if it's open; free but donation requested). Next door is a fine café serving sweets and light meals with idyllic outdoor seating (both in front of and behind the museum—look around for your favorite perch, taking the wind direction into consideration). This is the best spot in town for coffee or lunch (see listing under "Sleeping and Eating in Vaxholm," later). From here, look across the inlet at the tiny beach (where we're heading next).

Backtrack to the fishermen's harbor, then continue straight uphill on Fiskaregatan road, and take the first left up the tiny gravel lane marked *Vallgatan*. This part of the walk takes you back

in time, as you wander among old-fashioned wooden homes. At the end of the lane, head left. When you reach the water, go right along a path leading to a thriving little **sandy beach.** In good weather, this offers a fun chance to commune with Swedes at play. (In bad weather, it's hard to imagine anyone swimming or sunning here.)

When you're done relaxing, take the wooden stairs up to the top of the rock and **Battery Park** (Batteripark)—where giant artillery helped Vaxholm flex its defensive muscles in the late 19th century. As you crest the rock and enjoy the sea views, notice (on your right) the surviving semicircular tracks from those old artillery guns. With a range of 10 kilometers, the recoil from these powerful cannons could shatter glass in nearby houses. Before testing them, they'd play a bugle call to warn locals to stow away their valuables. More artifacts of these defenses are dug into the rock.

To head back to civilization, turn right before the embedded bunker (crossing more gun tracks and passing more fortifications on your left). As you leave the militarized zone, take a left at the fork, and the road will take you down to the embankment—just around the corner from where the boat docks, and our starting point. From along this stretch of embankment, you can catch a boat across the water to Vaxholm Fortress.

Sights in Vaxholm

Vaxholm Fortress and Museum (Vaxholms Kastell/ Vaxholms Fästnings Museum)

Vaxholm's only real attraction is the fortification just across the strait. While the town feels sleepy today, for centuries it was a crucial link in Sweden's nautical defense because it presided over the most convenient passage between Stockholm and the outer archipelago (and, beyond that, the Baltic Sea, Finland, and Russia). The name "Vaxholm" means "Island of

the Signal Fire," emphasizing the burg's strategic importance. In 1548, King Gustav Vasa decided to pin his chances on this location, ordering the construction of a fortress here and literally filling in other waterways, effectively making this the only way into or out of Stockholm...which it remained for 450 years. A village sprang up across the waterway to supply the fortress, and Vaxholm was born. The town's defenses successfully held off at least two major invasions (Christian IV of Denmark in 1612, and Peter the Great of Russia in 1719). Vaxholm's might gave Sweden's kings the peace of mind they needed to expand their capital to outlying islands—which means that the pint-size powerhouse of Vaxholm is largely to thank for Stockholm's island-hopping cityscape.

Cost and Hours: 60 kr, July-Aug daily 11:15-17:00, June daily 12:15-16:00, first Sat-Sun in Sept 11:15-17:00, closed off-season, tel. 08/5417-1890, www.vaxholmsfastning.se.

Getting There: A ferry shuttles visitors back and forth from Vaxholm (50 kr round-trip, every 20 minutes when museum is open, catch the boat just around the corner and toward the fortress from where the big ferries put in). Once on the island, hike into the castle's inner courtyard and look to the left to find the museum entrance.

Visiting the Fortress: The current, "new" fortress dates from the mid-19th century, when an older castle was torn down and replaced with this imposing granite behemoth. During the 30 years it took to complete the fortress, the tools of warfare changed. Both defensively and offensively, the new fortress was obsolete before it was even completed. The thick walls were no match for the invention of shells (rather than cannonballs), and the high hatches used for attacking tall sailing vessels were useless against new, low-lying, *Monitor*-style attack boats.

Today, the fortress welcomes guests to wander its tough little island and visit its museum. Presented chronologically on two floors (starting upstairs), the modern exhibit traces the military history of this fortress and of Sweden in general. It uses lots of models and mannequins, along with actual weaponry and artifacts, to tell the story right up to the 21st century. There's no English posted, but you can pick up good English translations as you enter. It's as interesting as a museum about Swedish military history can be.

Sleeping and Eating in Vaxholm

Since Vaxholm is so close to Stockholm, there's little reason to sleep here. But in a pinch, Waxholms is the only hotel in town.

Sleeping: **$$$ Waxholms Hotell**'s stately Art Nouveau facade dominates the town's waterfront. Inside are 42 pleasant rooms with classy old-fashioned furnishings (peak-season Sb-1,450 kr, Db-1,750 kr; weekends/July Sb-1,150 kr, Db-1,495 kr; Wi-Fi, loud music some nights in summer—ask what's on and request a

Sleep Code

Abbreviations (7 kr = about $1, country code: 46, area code: 08)
S = Single, **D** = Double/Twin, **T** = Triple, **Q** = Quad, **b** = bathroom
Price Rankings
  $$$ Higher Priced—Most rooms 1,500 kr or more
   $$ Moderately Priced—Most rooms 1,000-1,500 kr
    $ Lower Priced—Most rooms 1,000 kr or less
Unless otherwise noted, English is spoken, credit cards are accepted, breakfast is included, and Wi-Fi is generally free. Prices change; verify current rates online or by email. For the best prices, always book directly with the hotel.

quiet room if necessary, Hamngatan 2, tel. 08/5413-0150, www. waxholmshotell.se, info@waxholmshotell.se). The hotel has a grill restaurant outside in summer and a fancy dining room inside.

Eating: **Hembygdsgården ("Homestead Garden") Café** is Vaxholm's most tempting eatery, serving "summer lunches" (salads and sandwiches) and homemade sweets, with delightful outdoor seating around the Homestead Museum in Vaxholm's characteristic fishermen's quarter. Anette's lingonberry muffins are a treat (light lunches served daily May-Aug, closed Sept-April, tel. 08/5413-1980).

Grinda

The rustic, traffic-free isle of Grinda—half retreat, half resort—combines back-to-nature archipelago remoteness with easy proximity to Stockholm. The island is a tasteful gaggle of hotel buildings idyllically situated amid Swedish nature—walking paths, beaches, trees, and slabs of glacier-carved granite sloping into the sea. Since Grinda is a nature preserve (owned by the Stockholm Archipelago Foundation, or Skärgårdsstiftelsen), only a few families actually live here. There's no real town. But in the summer, Grinda becomes a magnet  for day-tripping urbanites, which can make it quite crowded. Adding to its appeal is the nostalgia it holds for many Stockholmers, who fondly recall when this was a summer camp island. In a way, with red-and-white cottages bunny-hopping up its gentle hills and a stately old inn anchoring its center, it retains that vibe today.

Orientation to Grinda

Grinda is small and easy to manage. It's a little wider than a mile in each direction; you can walk from end to end in a half-hour. Its main settlement—the historic **Wärdshus building** (a busy hub of tourist activities), hotel, and related amenities—sits next to its harbor, where private yachts and sailboats put in. Everything on the island is owned and operated by the same company; fortunately, it does a tasteful job of managing the place to keep the island's relaxing personality intact.

Major points of interest are well-signposted in Swedish: *Södra Bryggan* (south dock), *Norra Bryggan* (north dock), *Värdshus* (hotel at the heart of the island), *Gästhamn* (guest harbor); *Affär* (general store); *stuga/stugby* (cottage/s); *Grindastigen* (nature trail); and *Tältplats* (campground).

TOURIST INFORMATION

The red cottage marked *Expedition* greets arriving visitors just up the hill from the Södra Grinda ferry dock. The staff answers questions, and the cottage serves as a small shop, a place to rent kayaks or saunas, and a reception desk for the island's cottages and hostel (open daily in season; general info tel. 08/5424-9491, www.archipelagofoundation.se).

ARRIVAL IN GRINDA

Public ferries use one of two docks, at opposite ends of the island: Most use Södra Grinda to the south (nearest the hostel and cottages), while a few use Norra Grinda to the north (closer to the campground). From either of these, it's about a 10- to 15-minute walk to the action.

Sights in Grinda

Grinda is made to order for strolling through the woods, taking a dip, picnicking, and communing with Swedish nature. Watch the

boats bob in the harbor and work on your Baltic tan. You can simply stick to the gravel trails connecting the island's buildings, or for more nature, take the Grindastigen trail, which loops to the far end of the island and back in less than an hour (signposted from near the Wärdshus).

You can also rent a kayak or rent the private little sauna hut bobbing in the harbor. There's no bike rental here—and the island is a bit too small to keep a serious biker busy—but you could bring one on the boat from Stockholm.

As you stroll, you might spot a few haggard-looking tents through the trees. The right to pitch a tent here was established by the Swedish government during World War II, to give the downtrodden a cheap place to sleep. Those permissions are still valid, inherited, bought, and sold, which means that Grinda has a thriving community of tent-dwelling locals who camp out here all summer long (April-Oct). While some may be the descendants of those original hobos, these days they choose this lifestyle and live as strange little barnacles attached to Grinda. Once each summer they have a progressive tent-crawl bender before heading to the Wärdshus to blow a week's food budget on a fancy meal.

The island just across from the Södra Grinda dock (to the right) is Viggsö, where the members of ABBA have summer cottages and wrote many of their biggest hits.

Sleeping in Grinda

You have various options, in increasing order of rustic charm: hotel, hostel, and cottages. You can reserve any of these through the Grinda Wärdshus. This hub of operations has a restaurant, bar, Wi-Fi, and conference facilities (tel. 08/5424-9491, www.grinda. se, info@grinda.se).

Grinda is busiest in the summer, when tourists fill its hotel; in spring and fall, it mostly hosts conferences. If sleeping at the hostel or cottages, arrange arrival details (you'll probably pick up your keys at the *Expedition* shed near the dock). The hostel and cottages charge extra for bed linens. If you have a tent, you can pitch it at the basic campsite near the north jetty for a small fee.

$$$ Grinda Hotel rents 30 rooms (each named for a local bird or fish) in four buildings just above the Wärdshus. These are modern, comfortable, and made for relaxing, intentionally lacking distractions such as TVs or phones (Sb-1,600 kr, Db-2,000 kr, larger suite-2,600 kr, 120 kr less/person if you skip breakfast, extra bed-400 kr, if dining at the restaurant the "Wärdshus package" will save you a few kronor).

$ The 27 **cottages**—most near the Södra Grinda ferry dock— are rentable, offering a rustic retreat (kitchenettes but no running water, shared bathroom facilities outside). From mid-June to mid-August, these come with a one-week minimum and cost more (2-bed cottage-3,000 kr/week, 4-bed cottage-3,500 kr/week, 6-bed cottage-4,000 kr; at other times rentable by the night: 2-bed-1,000 kr, 4-bed-1,200 kr, 6-bed-1,500 kr).

$ Grinda Hostel (Vandrarheim) is the place to sleep if you wish you'd gone to Swedish summer camp as a kid. The 44 bunks are in simple two- and four-bed cottages, surrounding a pair of fire pits (300 kr/bed regardless of room size, great shared kitchen/dining hall). A small pebbly beach and a basic sauna are nearby.

Eating in Grinda

All your options (aside from bringing your own picnic from Stockholm) are run by the hotel, with choices in each price range.

Grinda Wärdshus, the inn at the center of the complex, has a good restaurant that combines rural island charm with fine food. You can choose between traditional Swedish meals and contemporary international dishes. Servings are small but thoughtfully designed to be delicious. Eat in the woody dining room or on the terrace out front (1,395 kr/person covers dinner and double room, 140-170-kr starters, 190-300-kr main dishes; open late June-Aug daily 12:00-24:00; weekends only—and some Fri—in off-season).

Grindas Framfickan ("Grinda's Front Pocket") is a pleasant bistro that serves up basic but tasty food (such as fish burgers and grilled shrimp) right along the guest harbor. Order at the counter, then choose a table to wait for your food (140-200-kr dishes, early June-mid-Aug daily 11:00-22:00, otherwise sporadically open in good weather—especially weekends).

The **general store and café** (Lanthandel) just below the Wärdshus is the place to rustle up some picnic fixings. You'll also find coffee to go, ice cream, "one-time grills" for a disposable barbecue, and kayak rentals (open long hours daily early June-mid-Aug, Fri-Sun only in shoulder season).

Svartsö

The remote and lesser-known isle of Svartsö (svert-show, literally "Black Island"), a short hop beyond Grinda, is the "Back Door" option of the bunch. Unlike Grinda, Svartsö is home to a real community; islanders have their own school and library. But with only 80 year-round residents, the old generation had to specialize. Each person learned a skill to fill a niche in the community—one guy was a carpenter, the next was a plumber, the next was an electrician, and so on. While the island is less trampled than the others in this chapter (just one B&B and a great restaurant), it is reasonably well-served by ferries. Svartsö feels remote and potentially even boring for those who aren't wowed by simply strolling through meadows. But it's ideal for those who want to slow down and immerse themselves in nature.

Svartsö hosts the school for this part of the archipelago. Because Swedish law guarantees the right to education, even kids living on remote islands are transported to class. A school boat trundles from island to island each morning to collect kids headed for the school on Svartsö. If the weather is bad, a hovercraft retrieves them. If it's really bad, and all of the snow days have been used up, a helicopter takes the kids to school.

Orientation to Svartsö: The island, about five miles long and a half-mile wide, has three docks. The main one, at the southwestern tip, is called Alsvik (with the general store and restaurant). Halfway up is Skälvik (near the B&B), and at the northeastern end is Söderboudd. Most boats stop at Alsvik, but if you want to go to a different dock, you can request a stop (ask the conductor on board, or use the semaphore signal at the dock).

At the **Alsvik dock,** the great little general store, called Svartsö Lanthandel, sells anything you could need and also acts as the town TI, post office, and liquor store (open daily mid-May–mid-Aug, more sporadic in off-season but open year-round, tel. 08/5424-7325). You can rent bikes here; in busy times, call ahead to reserve one. The little café on the dock sells drinks and light food, and rents cottages (shared outdoor toilets, tel. 08/5424-7110).

The island has a few paved lanes and almost no traffic. Residents own three-wheeled utility motorbikes for hauling things to and from the ferry landing. The interior consists of little more than trees. With an hour or so, you can bike across the island and back, enjoying the mellow landscape and chatting with the friendly big-city people who've found their perfect escape.

Eating in Svartsö: If you leave the Alsvik dock to the right and walk five minutes up the hill, you'll find the excellent **Svartsö Krog** restaurant. Opened by a pair of can-do foodies who also run a top-end butcher shop at a Stockholm market hall, this place has a deep respect for the sanctity of meat. Specializing in well-constructed, ingredient-driven dishes, the restaurant brings Stockholm culinary sophistication to a castaway island. Choose one of the three eating zones (each with the same menu): outside, the upscale dining room, or in the original pub interior (an Old West-feeling tavern that the new owner has kept as-is to respect the old-timers). The menu is pricey but good (100-200-kr starters, 175-300-kr main dishes). Their specialty is "golden entrecôte," grilled steak that's been aged for eight weeks (open for lunch and dinner daily June-Aug; May and Sept open Thu-Sun for dinner, as well as lunch on Sat-Sun; closed Oct-April; tel. 08/5424-7255).

Sandhamn

Out on the distant fringe of the archipelago—the last stop before Finland—sits the proud village of Sandhamn (on the island of Sandön). Literally "Sand Harbor," this is where the glacier got hung up and kept on churning away, grinding stone into sand. The town has a long history as an important and posh place. In 1897, the Royal Swedish Sailing Society built its clubhouse here, putting Sandhamn on the map as the yachting center of the Baltic—

Sweden's answer to Nantucket. It remains an extremely popular stop for boaters—from wealthy yachties to sailboat racers—as well as visitors simply seeking a break from the big city.

The island of Sandön feels stranded on the edge of the archipelago, rather than immersed in it. Sandhamn is on its sheltered side. Though it's far from Stockholm, Sandhamn is very popular. During the peak of summer (mid-June through late August), it's extremely crowded. Expect to stand in line, and call ahead for restaurant reservations. But even during these times, the Old Town is relatively peaceful and pleasant to explore. If the weather's decent, shoulder season is delightful (though it can be busy on weekends).

Orientation to Sandhamn

You'll find two halves to Sandhamn: In the shadow of that still-standing iconic yacht clubhouse is a ritzy resort/party zone throbbing with big-money nautical types. But just a few steps away, around the harbor, is an idyllic time-warp Old Town of colorfully painted shiplap cottages tucked between tranquil pine groves. While most tourists come here for the resort, the quieter part of Sandhamn holds the real appeal.

Sandhamn has a summer-only **TI** (open June-mid-Aug) in the harbor area (www.destinationsandhamn.se.)

Sandhamn Walk

To get your bearings from the ferry dock, take this self-guided walk. Begin by facing out to sea.

As you look out to the little point across from the dock, notice the big yellow building. In the 18th century, this was built as the

pilot house. Because the archipelago is so treacherous to navigate—with its tens of thousands of islands and skerries, not to mention untold numbers of hidden underwater rocks—locals don't trust outsiders to bring their boats here. So passing ships unfamiliar with these waters were required to pick up a local captain (or "pilot") to take them safely all the way to Stockholm. The tradition continues today. The orange boats marked *pilot*, moored below the house, ferry loaner captains to oncoming ships. And, since this is the point of entry into Sweden, foreign ships can also be processed by customs here.

The little red shed just in front of the pilot house is home to a humble **town museum** that's open sporadically in the summer, featuring exhibits on Sandhamn's history and some seafaring tales. Just below that, notice the waterfront red barn with the *T* sign. The owner of this boat-repair shop erected this marker for Stockholm's T-bana just for fun.

Just above the barn, look for the yellow building with the blue letters spelling **Sandhamns Värdshus.** This traditional inn, built in the late 17th century, housed sailors while they waited here to set out to sea. During that time, Stockholm had few exports, so ships that brought and unloaded cargo there came to Sandhamn to load up their holds with its abundant sand as ballast. Today the inn still serves good food (see "Eating in Sandhamn," later).

Stretching to the left of the inn are the quaint storefronts of most of Sandhamn's **eateries** (those that aren't affiliated with the big hotel)—bakery, deli, and grocery store, all of them humble but just right for a simple bite or picnic shopping. Local merchants enjoy a pleasantly symbiotic relationship. Rather than try to compete with each other, they attempt to complement what the next shop sells—each one finding just the right niche.

The area stretching beyond these storefronts is Sandhamn's **Old Town**—a maze of wooden cottages that's an absolute delight to explore (and easily the best activity in town). Only 50 of Sandhamn's homes (of around 450) are occupied by year-rounders. The rest are summer cottages of wealthy Stockholmers, or bunkhouses for seasonal workers in the tourist industry. Most locals live at the farthest-flung (and therefore least desirable) locations. Imagine the impact of 100,000 annual visitors on this little town.

Where the jetty meets the island, notice (on the right) the old-fashioned telephone box with the fancy *Rikstelefon* logo. It con-

tains the island's lone working pay phone. Just to the right of the phone box, you can see the back of the town's bulletin board, where locals post their classified ads. To the left at the base of the dock is Sandhamns Kiosk, a newsstand selling local and international publications (as well as candy and ice cream). A bit farther to the left, the giant red building with the turret on top is the **yacht clubhouse** that put Sandhamn on the map, and still entertains the upper crust today with a hotel, several restaurants, spa, mini-golf course, outdoor pool, and more (see page 532). You'll see its proud SSS-plus-crown logo (standing for Svenska Segelsällskapet—Swedish Sailing Society) all over town. In the 1970s, the building was owned by a notorious mobster who made meth in the basement, then smuggled it out beneath the dock to sailboats moored in the harbor.

Spinning a bit farther to the left, back to where you started, survey the island across the strait (Lökholmen). Just above the trees, notice the copper dome of an observatory that was built by this island's eccentric German oil-magnate owner in the early 20th

century. He also built a small castle (not quite visible from here) for his kids to play in.

For a narrated stroll to another fine viewpoint, walk into town and turn left along the water. After about 50 yards, a sign on the right points up a narrow lane to *Post*. This unassuming gravel path is actually one of Sandhamn's most important streets, with the post office, police department (which handles only paperwork—real crimes are deferred to the Stockholm PD), and doctor (who visits town every second Wednesday). While Sandhamn feels remote, it's served—like other archipelago communities—by a crack emergency-response network that can dispatch a medical boat or, in extreme cases, a helicopter. With top-notch hospitals in Stockholm just a 10-minute chopper ride away, locals figure that if you have an emergency here, you might just make it to the doctor faster than if you're trying to make it through congested city streets in an ambulance. At the end of this lane, notice the giant hill of the town's namesake sand.

Continuing along the main tree-lined harborfront strip, you can't miss the signs directing yachters to the *toalett* (toilet) and *sopor* (garbage dump). Then you'll pass the Sandhamns Guiderna office, a **travel agency** where you can rent bikes, kayaks, and fishing gear (tel. 08/640-8040). Just after that is the barn for the volunteer fire department (Brandstation). With all the wooden buildings in town, fire is a concern—one reason why Sandhamn restricts camping (and campfires).

Go beneath the skyway connecting the big red hotel to its modern annex. Then veer uphill (right) at the *Badstranden Trouville* sign, looking down at the mini-golf course. After you crest the top of the hill, on the left is a big, flat expanse of rock nicknamed Dansberget ("Dancing Rock") because it once hosted community dances with a live orchestra. Walk out to enjoy fine **views** of the Baltic

Sea—from here, boaters can set sail for Finland, Estonia, and St. Petersburg, Russia. Looking out to the horizon, notice the three lighthouse towers poking up from the sea, used to guide ships to this gateway to the archipelago. The finish line for big boat races stretches across this gap (from the little house on the point to your left). In summer, this already busy town gets even more jammed with visitors, thanks to the frequent sailing races that end here. The biggest annual competition is the Götlandrunt, a round-trip from here to the island of Götland. In 2009, Sandhamn was proud to be one of just 10 checkpoints on the Volvo Ocean Race, a nine-month race around the world that called mostly at bigger cities (such as Boston, Singapore, and Rio).

Our walk is finished. You can head back into town. Or, to hit the beach, continue another 15 minutes to Trouville beach (explained below).

Sights in Sandhamn

Beaches (Stränder)

True to its name, Sandön ("Sandy Island") has some of the archipelago's rare sandy beaches. The closest, and local favorite, is the no-name beach tucked in a cove just behind the Old Town (walk through the community from the main boat dock, then follow the cove around to the little sandy stretch).

The most popular—which can be quite crowded in summer—is Trouville beach, at the opposite end of the island from Sandhamn (about a 20-minute walk). To find it, walk behind the big red hotel and take the right, uphill fork (marked with the low-profile *Badstranden Trouville* sign) to the "Dancing Rock," then proceed along the road. Take a left at the fork by the tennis courts, then walk about 10 minutes through a mysterious-feeling forest until you reach a little settlement of red cottages. Take a right at the fork (look up for the *Till Stranden* sign), and then, soon after, follow the middle fork (along the plank walks) right to the beach zone: two swathes of sand marked off by rocks, stretching toward Finland.

Sleeping in Sandhamn

Sandhamn has a pair of very expensive top-end hotels, a basic but comfortable B&B, and little else. If you're sleeping on Sandhamn, the B&B is the best choice.

$$$ Sands Hotell is a stylish splurge sitting proudly at the top of town. While oriented mostly to conferences and private parties, its 19 luxurious rooms also welcome commoners in the summer (Sb-2,100 kr, Db-2,500 kr, Wi-Fi, elevator, spa, tel. 08/5715-3020, www.sandshotell.se, info@sandshotell.se).

$$$ Sandhamns Seglarhotellet rents 79 nautical-themed rooms in a modern annex behind the old yacht club building (where you'll find the reception). The rooms are fine, but the prices are sky-high (Db-2,390 kr, 200 kr more for balcony, extra bed-400 kr, small apartment-2,590 kr, large apartment-2,890 kr, suite-4,090 kr, Wi-Fi, loud music from disco inside the clubhouse—light sleepers should ask for a quieter back room, great gym and pool area, tel. 08/5745-0400, www.sandhamn.com, reception@sandhamn.com).

$ Sandhamns Värdshus B&B rents five rustic but tasteful, classically Swedish rooms in an old mission house buried deep in the colorful Old Town. To melt into Sandhamn and get away from the yachties, sleep here (S-930 kr, D-1,350 kr, mostly twins, all rooms share WC and shower, tiny cottage with its own bathroom for same price, includes breakfast, reception is at the restaurant—see below, tel. 08/5715-3051, www.sandhamns-vardshus.se, info@sandhamns-vardshus.se). The rooms are above a reception hall that is rented out for events, but after 22:00, quiet time kicks in.

Eating in Sandhamn

IN THE OLD TOWN

Sandhamn's most appealing eateries are along the Old Town side of the harbor.

Sandhamns Värdshus, right on the water, is the town's best eatery. They serve traditional Swedish food in three separate dining zones (which mostly share the same menu, but each also has its own specials): out on an inviting deck overlooking the water; upstairs in a salty dining room with views; or downstairs in a simple pub (open daily for lunch and dinner nearly year-round, tel. 08/5715-3051).

To grab a bite or assemble a picnic, browse through these smaller eateries (listed in the order you'll reach them from the boat dock): **Westerbergs Livsmedel** grocery store has basic supplies (open sporadic hours daily). **Dykarbaren Café** serves lunches and dinners with indoor and outdoor seating (open daily mid-June-mid-Aug, Wed-Sun only in shoulder season, closed off-season; tel. 08/5715-3554). **Monrads Deli** is a bright, innovative shop where you can buy sandwiches and salads, a wide array of meats for grilling, cheeses, cold cuts, drinks, fresh produce, and other high-quality picnic fixings (open long hours daily in summer, mobile 0709-650-300). Just around the corner (uphill from the harbor and behind the

Värdsgasthus), **Sandhamns Bageriet,** a popular bakery/café serving coffee, sweet rolls, and sandwiches, is a great early-morning venue (daily in summer).

AMONG THE YACHTIES

Sandhamn Seglarhotell has several eateries, open to guests and non-guests. Out on the dock is the Seglargrillen, an American-style grill with a takeout window and outdoor tables (85-kr dishes, open in summer in good weather only). Upstairs in the building's main ballroom is an eatery serving good but pricey Swedish and international food (150-200-kr starters, 185-300-kr main courses, traditional daily lunch special for 145 kr). The restaurant enjoys fine sea views and has a bar/dance hall zone (with loud disco music until late, nearly nightly in summer). Down on the ground floor is a pub/nightclub (tel. 08/5745-0421).

SOUTHEAST SWEDEN

Växjö • Glass Country • Kalmar • Öland

Ranking Sweden's sights, Stockholm is tops, but the southeastern province of Småland is a worthy runner-up. More Americans came from this densely forested area than any other part of Scandinavia, and the House of Emigrants in Växjö tells the story well. Between Växjö and Kalmar is Glass Country, a 70-mile stretch of forest sparkling with glassworks that welcome guests to tour and shop. Historic Kalmar has a rare Old World ambience and the most magnificent medieval castle in Scandinavia. From Kalmar, you can cross one of Europe's longest bridges to hike through the Stonehenge-like mysteries of the strange island of Öland.

PLANNING YOUR TIME

By train, on a three-week Scandinavian trip, I'd skip this area in favor of taking the direct, high-speed train from Copenhagen to Stockholm, or the night train from Malmö (just over the Øresund Bridge from Copenhagen) to Stockholm. Side-trips from Stockholm to Helsinki and Tallinn merit more time than this part of Sweden.

But if you have at least three weeks in Scandinavia and a car, the sights described in this section are an interesting way to spend a couple of days. While I'm not so hot on the Swedish countryside (OK, blame my Norwegian heritage), you can't see only Stockholm and say you've seen Sweden. Växjö and Kalmar give you the best possible dose of small-town Sweden. (I find Lund and Malmö, both popular side-trips from Copenhagen, relatively dull. And I'm not old or sedate enough to find a sleepy boat trip along the much-loved Göta Canal appealing.)

By Car

Drivers can spend three days getting from Copenhagen to Stockholm this way:

Day 1: Leave Copenhagen after breakfast, drive over the bridge to Sweden and on to Växjö, tour Växjö's House of Emigrants, drive into Glass Country, tour Kosta Boda and Transjö glassworks, and arrive in Kalmar in time for dinner.

Day 2: Spend the day in Kalmar touring the castle and Kalmar County Museum, and browsing its people-friendly streets. If you're restless, cross the bridge for a joyride on the island of Öland.

Day 3: 8:00—Begin five-hour drive north along the coast to Stockholm; 10:30—Break in Västervik; 12:00—Stop in Söderköping for picnic lunch and a walk along the Göta Canal; 13:30—Continue drive north; 16:00—Arrive in Stockholm.

Shorten your stops on Day 3 and you'll arrive in Stockholm in time to make the overnight boat to Tallinn or Helsinki. This is an especially good plan on Sunday through Wednesday in the off-season, when boat fares are cheaper. You can see Stockholm on the way back.

By Public Transit

Växjö and Kalmar are easy to visit by train. Without a car, I'd skip Glass Country and Öland, but if you wouldn't, take the bus (from

Växjö to Kosta Boda glassworks, and from Kalmar to Öland; see "Växjö Connections," later).

Växjö

A pleasant, sleepy town of almost 85,000, Växjö (locals say VEK-hwuh; Stockholmers pronounce it VEK-shuh) is in the center of Småland. An important trading town for centuries, its name loosely means "where the road meets the lake." Coming in by train or car, you'd think it might mean "buried in a vast forest." Today an enjoyable three-mile path encircles that lake, and a farmers market enlivens the otherwise too-big and too-quiet main square on Wednesday and Saturday mornings.

My favorite activity in Växjö is to simply enjoy browsing through quintessential, small-town Sweden without a tourist in sight. While there isn't much heavy-duty sightseeing in Växjö, it does have a trio of worthwhile attractions: the earnest House of Emigrants, chronicling the plight of Swedes who fled to North America; the Smålands Museum, offering a convenient look at the region's famous glass without a trip to Glass Country; and the cathedral, decorated with fine modern glass sculptures.

In 1996, Växjö set itself the goal of becoming a fossil-fuel-free city by the year 2050. Now a single biomass power plant provides nearly all the community's heat and hot water, half of its energy comes from renewable sources, and carbon dioxide emissions are down considerably. Växjö earned the title "Greenest City in Europe" when it received the EU's first award for sustainable development in 2007.

Orientation to Växjö

Växjö's town center is compact and pedestrian-friendly; the train station, main square, and two important museums are all within two blocks of each other. Blocks here are short; everything I mention is within about a 15-minute walk of everything else. Tourists are so rare that a polite English-speaking visitor will find locals generous, warm, and helpful.

For a delightful three- or four-hour stopover, I'd do this loop from the station: Cross the tracks on the overpass to tour the glass and history museums (Smålands Museum and House of Emigrants). A block away is the lovely lake (encircled by a path), next to a pretty park and the cathedral. A block in front of the cathedral is the town square, Stortorget (with the TI); from there it stretches the main commercial drag, Storgatan. Browse this orderly street before heading back to the station.

ARRIVAL IN VÄXJÖ

Växjö's modern train station has snack stands and coin-op lockers (an ATM is a block away to the right as you leave). Pick up a city map at the information desk. The station faces the heart of town; walk a few steps straight ahead, and you'll be in the pedestrian shopping zone. Everything in town is in front of you except the two main museums, which are behind the station; to reach these, cross the tracks using the pedestrian overpass. Drivers will find several parking lots near the station.

TOURIST INFORMATION

The **TI** is inside the municipal building facing the main town square, about a 10-minute walk from the train station. With your back to the station, go straight two blocks and turn right on Linnégatan (June-Aug Mon-Fri 9:30-18:00, Sat 10:00-14:00, closed Sun; Sept-May Mon-Fri 9:30-16:30, closed Sat-Sun; room-booking service, good *Växjö Town Park* brochure in English, Kronobergsgatan 7, tel. 0470/733-280, www.turism.vaxjo.se).

Internet Access: Everlast Internet café, two blocks in front of the train station (Mon-Sat 12:00-18:00, closed Sun; Sandgärdsgatan 12, next to recommended Ali Baba restaurant).

Sights in Växjö

Växjö's attractions cluster around the north end of its pleasant lake and the surrounding park. The glass and history museums are on the hill just behind the train station (take the overpass).

Smålands Museum/Swedish Glass Museum (Sveriges Glasmuseum)

This instructive museum, while humble, celebrates the region of Småland and its glassmaking tradition. On the ground floor, the "Six Centuries of Swedish Glass" exhibit traces the history of the product that still powers the local economy. Upstairs you'll find more on glass, along with displays on the region's prehistory, and a look at Kronoberg County (which includes Växjö) in the 19th century. Temporary exhibits round out your visit. The collection is well-described in English, so this is a handy place to learn a bit about glass if you're not headed deeper into Glass Country. Who knew that the person who designed the original Coca-Cola bottle in 1915 was a Swede?

Cost and Hours: 70-kr combo-ticket includes House of Emigrants; June-Aug daily 10:00-17:00; Sept-May Tue-Fri 10:00-17:00, Sat-Sun 11:00-16:00, closed Mon; café with 100-kr light meals, immediately in front of train-station overpass at Södra Järnvägsgatan 2, tel. 0470/704-200, www.smalandsmuseum.se.

▲House of Emigrants (Utvandrarnas Hus)

If you have Swedish roots, this tidy museum is exciting. Even if you don't, it's an interesting stop for anyone with immigrant ances-

tors. While modest, the well-presented, inspiring "Dream of America" exhibit offers powerful insight into the experience of more than one million Swedes who sought refuge in North America in the late 19th and early 20th centuries.

Cost and Hours: Same ticket and hours as Swedish Glass Museum; 50 yards down the hill behind the glass museum, Vilhelm Mobergs Gata 4, tel. 0470/20120, www.smalandsmuseum.se.

Background: As economic woes wracked Sweden from the 1850s to the 1920s (even a potato famine hit at one point), the country was caught up in an "American Fever." Nearly 1.3 million mostly poor Swedes endured long voyages and culture shock to find prosperity and freedom in the American promised land. In that period, one in six Swedes went to live in the US. So many left the country that Swedish authorities were forced to rethink their social policies and to institute reforms.

Visiting the Museum: In the "Dream of America" exhibit, displays (thoughtfully translated into English) explain various aspects of the immigrant experience.

One display vividly recounts how 3.8 million new arrivals from around the world entered the US through Manhattan's Castle Garden processing center between 1886 and 1890. Firsthand accounts recall the entry procedure, including medical evaluations and an uncomfortable eye exam.

The model of a poor, potato-famine-stricken village demonstrates why so many Swedes were forced to emigrate. The Swedes formed enclaves across North America: on farms and prairies, from

New York to Texas, from Maine to Seattle—and, of course, in Chicago's "Swede Town" (the world's second-biggest Swedish town in the world in 1900). The life-size *Snusgatan* re-creates the main street in a Swedish neighborhood—called "Snoose Boulevard," for Swedish snuff. Other displays trace immigrant lifestyles, religion, treatment in the press, women's experiences, and the Swedish cultural societies that preserved the traditions of the Old World in the New. Rounding out the exhibit, homage is paid to prominent Swedish-Americans, including Charles Lindbergh and the second man on the moon, Buzz Aldrin.

Don't miss the display about the *Titanic*, which takes pains to point out that—after Americans—Swedes were the second-largest group to perish on that ill-fated vessel. On view are a few items that went to the bottom of the Atlantic with one of those Swedes.

The Moberg Room celebrates local writer Vilhelm Moberg (1898-1973), who put the Swedish immigrant experience on the map with his four-novel series *The Emigrants*. (These books—and two Max von Sydow/Liv Ullmann films based on them, *The Emigrants* and *The New Land*—are essential pretrip reading and viewing for Swedish-Americans.) Here you'll see a replica of Moberg's "writer's hut," his actual desk, and some original manuscripts.

Växjö Town Park (Växjö Stadspark)

Directly downhill from the House of Emigrants, you'll reach the big lake called Växjösjön. This is a fine place to relax with a picnic or go for a stroll. The pleasant three-mile park path around the lake takes you from manicured flower gardens through forested areas. The top part of the lake borders the inviting Linnéparken next to the cathedral (both described next).

A 10-minute walk around the top of the lake from the House of Emigrants is the town's modern **swimming hall** (*Simhall*, 80-kr base price includes sauna; extra fee if you want to tan, use the exercise room, or rent a towel or locker; family ticket available, call or check online for open-swim hours, tel. 0470/41204, www. medley.se/vaxjosimhall).

Cathedral (Domkyrka)

Växjö's striking orange church, with its distinctive double-needle steeple, features fine sacred art—in glass, of course. Its austere, bright-white interior is enlivened by gorgeous, colorful, and highly symbolic glass sculptures.

Cost and Hours: Free entry, daily 9:00-18:00.

Visiting the Cathedral: Pick up the

well-written 15-kr brochure, which offers a detailed and evangelical self-guided tour. Near the back-left corner, the *Tree of Life and Knowledge* is a fantastically detailed candelabra shaped like a tree. On one side, find Adam and Eve reaching for a very tempting apple with the clever snake egging them on from below. On the other, Jesus and Mary welcome the faithful with arms outstretched. Notice the thematically parallel design—the snake opposite the dove (representing the Holy Spirit); the snake's tempting apple opposite the bunch of grapes (symbolizing the wine of the Eucharist). At the front of the church, the main altar stands before a glass-decorated triptych showing the subtle interplay between light and dark. Explore the other pieces of glass art around the church, and take in its trio of pipe organs. In the back, notice the ATM-like machine that accepts offerings from your debit or credit card.

Linnéparken

This peaceful park beside the cathedral is dedicated to the great Swedish botanist Carl von Linné (a.k.a. Carolus Linnaeus). It has an arboretum, lots of well-categorized perennials, a cactus garden, and a children's playground.

▲Strolling Storgatan

Växjö's main pedestrian shopping boulevard offers a fun way to cap your visit. From the main square (Stortorget), Storgatan stretches several blocks west. Walk the entire length of the street to observe small-town Sweden without any tourists. (You could make the popular Askelyckan bakery and café, at #24, your goal.) Imagine growing up or raising a family here: safe but boring, friendly but traditional, pleasant but predictable. The community seems super-content and super-conformist; it's very blond but also multiethnic. Feel the order and the quiet, like there's Valium in the air. Sweden is among the most highly taxed, least church-going, affluent, and satisfied societies in the world. This region lost more to emigration than any other, and it's thought-provoking to consider what impact that had on the character of those who remained behind (and their descendants).

Sleep Code

Abbreviations   (7 kr = about $1, country code: 46, area code: 0470)
S = Single, **D** = Double/Twin, **T** = Triple, **Q** = Quad, **b** = bathroom
Price Rankings
  $$$ Higher Priced—Most rooms 1,200 kr or more
   $$ Moderately Priced—Most rooms 700-1,200 kr
    $ Lower Priced—Most rooms 700 kr or less
Unless otherwise noted, English is spoken, credit cards are accepted, breakfast is included, and Wi-Fi is free. Prices change; verify current rates online or by email. For the best prices, always book directly with the hotel.

Sleeping in Växjö

$$$ Elite Stadshotell is a big, modern, business-class hotel with all the comforts in its 163 rooms. It's in a royal setting on the town's main square (very flexible prices; in peak season usually Sb-1,000 kr, Db-1,400 kr; summer/weekends Sb-550 kr, Db-900 kr; , about a block from the train station's main entrance at Kungsgatan 6, tel. 0470/13400, www.elite.se, info.vaxjo@elite.se).

$$ Hotell Värend is friendly, comfortable, and inexpensive. It has 24 worn but workable rooms at the edge of a residential neighborhood six blocks from the front of the train station along Kungsgatan (Sb-550-700 kr, Db-650-850 kr, Tb-795-1,000 kr, elevator, Wi-Fi, free parking, a block beyond N. Esplanaden at Kungsgatan 27, tel. 0470/776-700, mobile 076-769-0700, www.hotellvarend.se, info@hotellvarend.se).

$$ Hotel Esplanad, nearby on a busy street, is a bit more modest, with 25 less-expensive rooms, some with private baths on the hall (S-650 kr, Sb-850 kr, D-900 kr, Db-1,050 kr, free parking, N. Esplanaden #21A, tel. 0470/22580, www.hotellesplanad.com, info@hotellesplanad.com, Anna). From the train station, walk five blocks up Klostergatan and turn left on N. Esplanaden.

$ Hostel: Växjö's fine **Evedal Hostel** is near a lake three miles outside town (250 kr/bed in 4-bed rooms, D-600 kr, breakfast-70 kr, sheets-75 kr, confirm reception hours before you arrive, tel. 0470/63070, www.vaxjovandrarhem.nu, vaxjo.vandrarhem@telia.com). From Växjö's train station, catch bus #7 (about hourly, 15 minutes). A taxi from the station costs about 200 kr.

Eating in Växjö

After-hours Växjö is not very exciting. Consider livening things up by dining out.

Kafe De Luxe, about a block from the station, is a hip and funky hangout with live music many nights. They serve lunches and dinners daily in a cozy Old World interior or under a happy tent outside (burgers, *tarte flambée*, 200-kr dinners, daily 11:30-24:00, Sandgärdsgatan 19, tel. 0470/740409).

Ali Baba's, one of the best places in town to eat cheap, has a glitzy, Lebanese-casino vibe and a fun stalactite ceiling. All dishes, including their 70-kr pizzas and pastas, include a salad bar (120-kr Lebanese plates, daily 12:00-22:00, about a block from the station at Sandgärdsgatan 10, tel. 0470/27900).

Askelyckan Bakery Café, with an inviting terrace under a tree by a fountain on the city's main commercial drag, is a delightful place for a drink, cake, or light lunch on a sunny day (cakes, pastries, salads and sandwiches at lunch, daily 7:30-18:30, Storgatan 25, tel. 0470/12311).

PM & Vänner is a trendy eatery where a younger crowd stands in line to see and be seen. They have good international cuisine with Swedish flair, a mod black-and-white interior, and nice outdoor tables on the pedestrian mall. Their menu changes to feature seasonal and local ingredients (115-kr lunch special, 200-300-kr main dishes, Mon-Sat 11:30-23:00, closed Sun, Storgatan 22 at corner of Västergatan, tel. 0470/759711).

Ethnic Eateries on and near Storgatan: If you're looking to save money, or if it's a Sunday—when other restaurants are closed—visit one of downtown Växjö's dozen or so Asian restaurants and kebab-and-pizza shops. The **Rose Garden** serves "Neo-Asian" and is a cut above most (Storgatan 33).

Groceries: Visit the **ICA supermarket** at the corner of Sandgärdsgatan and Klostergatan, one block from the front of the train station (Mon-Sat 7:00-21:00, Sun 11:00-20:00).

Växjö Connections

From Växjö by Bus to: Kosta (2-4/day, 1 hour, bus #218 from Växjö bus station; for schedules see www.lanstrafikenkron.se/en).

By Train to: Copenhagen (hourly, 2.5 hours), **Stockholm** (every 2 hours, 3.5 hours, change in Alvesta, reservations required), **Kalmar** (12/day, 60-70 minutes). See the Stockholm chapter (page 500) for information on taking trains in Sweden.

Glass Country

Filling the remote-feeling woods between Växjö and Kalmar with busy glassmaking workshops, Sweden's famous Glasriket ("Kingdom of Crystal") is worth ▲▲ for drivers. It's touristy, yes—but it also wins over skeptics. There's something to please everybody here: Shoppers thrill at the chance to pick up deeply discounted factory seconds, art-lovers enjoy seeing all of the creative uses for glass, and engineers are fascinated by the skilled glassblowers who persuade glowing globs of molten glass to become fine pieces of tableware or art.

Visiting a glassworks *(glasbruk)* has three parts: the shop; an exhibition of attractive pieces by local artists; and the hot shop, or *hytta,* where glassblowers are hard at work. At most glassworks, it's possible to walk through the hot shop—close enough to feel the heat from the globs of glass as they're being worked (arrive before the midafternoon quitting time). The shops and exhibitions are usually free, but some collect a token fee. Most hot shops charge admission—but at smaller glassworks you can usually just stroll through. Taking a guided tour of at least one hot shop is a must to really understand the whole process. (For starters, read the "Glassmaking in Sweden" sidebar.)

The glassworks I describe in this chapter are a representative mix of the 15 or so that you can visit in Glass Country, ranging from big corporate factories to charming artistic workshops. On the corporate side, the Kosta company dominates; its flagship Kosta Boda complex is the biggest and most accessible of all the glassworks. But round out your look at the region with at least one smaller, independent producer as well (Transjö Glashytta is the most appealing, but I also describe Bergdala and Mats Jonasson Målerås). For more tips on which glassworks to visit—and which to skip—see "Planning Your Time."

For a change of pace, you can learn about traditional papermaking (at the Lessebo mill) and the local moose population (at the Moose Park).

Information: The *Glasriket/Kingdom of Crystal* magazine (available at any TI) and the region's official website (www. glasriket.se) describe the many glassworks that welcome the public. The 95-kr **Glasriket Pass** includes free entry to exhibitions and hot shops, and discounts on tours, shopping, and *hyttsill* dinners (explained on page 555). The pass, sold at glassworks, local TIs, and online, is worthwhile only if you're visiting several hot shops and doing some serious shopping (10 percent discount at certain shops, some with a 500-kr minimum purchase). Note that in Swedish, *glas* is glass, while *glass* is ice cream.

PLANNING YOUR TIME

Though you can take a bus from Växjö to Kosta (see "Växjö Connections"), the glassworks aren't worth the time and trouble unless you have a car. Train travelers should instead take a careful look at the glass exhibit in Växjö's Smålands Museum, and then go straight to Kalmar.

By Car

With a car, the drive from Växjö to Kalmar is a 70-mile joy—light traffic with endless forest-and-lake scenery punctuated by numerous glassworks. The driving time between Växjö and Kosta is 45 minutes; it's another 45 minutes between Kosta and Kalmar.

Looking at a map, you'll notice the glassworks are scattered around the center of the region. While it would take the better part of a day to loop around and visit them all, distances are relatively short and roads are good. Still, it's smart to be selective. On a tight schedule, I'd visit Kosta and Transjö, possibly Bergdala, and maybe the Lessebo paper mill, skipping the rest.

If you're visiting Glass Country en route from Växjö to Kalmar, consider this driving plan: Head southeast from Växjö on highway 25, following signs for *Kalmar*. If you want to visit Bergdala, turn off after Hovmantorp; to skip it, head straight to Lessebo (and its paper mill). In Lessebo, turn north for Kosta and tour the big Kosta Boda glassworks there. Then, if you'd like to visit the Moose Park, detour slightly east (it's just on the outskirts of Kosta, toward Orrefors). From here you can also detour much farther to the Mats Jonasson glassworks, to the northeast in Målerås. Otherwise, from Kosta, head south on highway 28, watching for signs to *Transjö* for the best of the smaller, artsy glassworks. Pick up highway 25 again when you're ready to make a beeline east to Kalmar.

Sights in Glass Country

These attractions are tied together by the driving tour described above. Don't forget the historic paper mill and Moose Park, described after the glassworks.

GLASSWORKS (GLASBRUKS)

These are listed in the order you'll reach them, from Växjö to Kalmar. Many glassworks charge admission to watch the hot shop at work, but most aren't set up to actually collect this fee at the door—so curious tourists can simply poke around and might not even have to pay (the entrance fee is waived if you have the 95-kr Glasriket Pass; described earlier in "Information"). Also note that many workshops take a lunch break sometime between 10:00 and 11:00, and stop working entirely after about 15:00 or 15:30.

Glassmaking in Sweden

In the mid-16th century, King Gustav Vasa decided he wanted more fine glass to decorate his palace, so he invited German glassmakers to train his subjects, and the trend took off. It's no surprise that glassmaking caught on here in Sweden. The resources needed for glass are abundant: vast forests to fire the ovens, and lakes with an endless supply of sand. By the difficult 19th century—when a sixth of Sweden's population emigrated to North America—the iron mills had closed, leaving behind unemployed workers who were highly skilled at working with materials at high temperatures. Glassmaking was their salvation, and by the early 1900s, this region had more than 100 glassworks.

While glassmaking was important throughout Sweden, it was in the dense forest between Växjö and Kalmar that it took hold the strongest, and lasted the longest. When other materials became cheaper than glass (for example, paper cartons instead of glass bottles), the industry was hit hard, and it dried up in other parts of Sweden. But here in Glass Country, workers refocused their efforts: They still make some everyday items, but their emphasis is on high-quality art pieces that command top kronor. An Ikea wine glass made in China costs 10 kr, while a handmade Swedish one might cost 150 kr—but consumers interested in quality are willing to pay that premium.

The glassmaking process is fascinating—and hasn't changed much over the centuries. The glass begins as little white pellets that are about 70 percent sand. Soda and potash are added to lower the melting point, and limestone and zinc are added to minimize boiling (and the resulting bubbles). The final qualities of the glass are determined by other additives—glassmakers use a different mix for a thin champagne flute than for a thick platter.

You'll see two different types of glass being created: everyday tableware and art pieces. The mass-produced tableware—such as wine glasses—is created by small teams of glassblowers who use an assembly-line system, supervised by a "master," who monitors quality control. Art-glass pieces, however, are never the same. The region has a passel of big-name designers, each with its own aesthetic and all considered local celebrities. Most glass artists conceptualize the design, but leave the actual grunt work to their assistants—you might see the artist hovering off to the side, directing the glassblowers.

As you watch these masters at work, keep in mind they're working with a molten medium that can melt skin. First, a worker places the glassblowing rod into the furnace (notice the foot pedals used to open and close the doors) and grabs a blob of molten

glass. Glassblowers have to move quickly—before the glass hardens too much—but carefully, to avoid shattering the medium or burning their colleagues. After rolling the glass out on a heat-resistant graphite table to give it the desired shape, they blow into the end of the rod to open a space inside. If creating a mass-produced item, they generally stick it into a mold to ensure the correct dimensions. Other appendages are added; for example, if it's a wineglass with a stem and foot, separate pieces of glass are stretched out to the appropriate shape and stuck on the bottom.

For this entire process, the glass is at about 2,100 degrees Fahrenheit. If it gets too hot, glassblowers cool it down with water or air; if the glass needs to be reheated, they use a blowtorch or poke it momentarily back into the furnace. All glass begins clear. To make colored glass, they either add powdered dye during production, or paint the finished piece and then refire it. Finally, the area where the glass was attached to the rod is cut with an industrial diamond, broken off, and ground and polished smooth. When the piece is finished, it's set in a special oven to cool gradually—over a few hours for smaller pieces, or a day or more for large items.

The workday ends around 15:00, when the raw materials for the next day's glass are dumped into giant, custom-made clay pots and placed in the ovens. Overnight, these will gradually melt down to the molten medium the glassblowers will need the next morning at 7:00.

The last stop is quality control. Only the best pieces are deemed "first quality" (*1:A Sortering*)—you'll pay a premium for these flawless items. Some items, deemed "second quality" (*2:A Sortering*), have minor imperfections that bring the price down substantially. When shopping, pay close attention to these labels; if you don't need your glass perfect, you can save by looking for second quality. Quite a few items are simply too imperfect—these are dumped into a bin and disposed of. Sorry, budget travelers—these "factory thirds" are trashed, not sold.

▲Bergdala Studioglas

The small, independent Bergdala glassworks, in a village of the same name, has an enjoyably artsy hot shop. Its well-stocked shop is full of its trademark blue-rimmed tableware, and the engaging gallery upstairs shows off a different sampling of local artists every year.

Cost and Hours: Hot shop—20 kr, mid-June-Aug Mon-Thu 7:00-15:30, Fri until 13:30, closed Sat-Sun; gallery—free, mid-June-Aug Mon-Fri 10:00-18:00, Sat-Sun 10:00-16:00; shorter hours off-season, tel. 0478/31650, www.bergdalastudioglas.se/start/.

▲▲Kosta (a.k.a. Kosta Boda)

About an hour east of Växjö, the village of Kosta boasts the oldest of the *glasbruks*, dating back to 1742. Today, the sprawling Kosta complex—the only real jolt of civilization in this otherwise remote-feeling landscape—includes a modern outlet mall, a factory store, a fancy new art hotel...and, of course, the glassworks.

The highlight here is unquestionably watching the **glassworks** in action. In what is arguably the best hot-shop viewing in the region, you'll look over the shoulders of glassblowers crafting both mass-produced, crank-'em-out tableware and high art fit to be shown in a museum. You can visit the glassworks and its gallery on your own, but it's worth calling or emailing ahead to reserve a spot on a 30-minute English tour. In the surprisingly modest **exhibition gallery,** each piece is identified with a photo and brief bio (in English) of its designer, which personalizes the art (often offered for sale).

Cost and Hours: Free, 50 kr for tour; usually open Mon-Fri 8:30-15:30, Sat-Sun 10:00-16:00. From early July to early Aug, when the glassblowers are on vacation, there's less glassblowing and more tourists—and the complex is open daily 10:00-16:00. To reserve a tour and confirm times, call 0478/34529 or email info@kostaboda.se (www.kostaboda.se).

Shopping: In the Kosta **factory outlet shop,** crystal "seconds" (with tiny bubbles or sets that don't quite match) and discontinued pieces are sold at good prices. This is duty-free shopping, and they'll happily mail your purchases home. Don't confuse this with the big outlet mall across the street (Mon-Fri 10:00-18:00, Sat-Sun 10:00-17:00).

Sleeping and Eating: I ate well at the **cafeteria** inside the outlet mall, which features thrifty lunch specials. Nearby is the pricey **$$$ Kosta Boda Art Hotel,** designed to impress. Everything's decorated to the hilt with (of course) artistic glass, created in the hot shop across the street. With Växjö and Kalmar so close, there's little reason to sleep here (rooms start at Db-2,500 kr, tel. 0478/34830, www.kostabodaarthotel.se). But if you have a few extra minutes, poke around this over-the-top, world-of-glass complex, which includes a "glass bar," a mind-bending indoor swimming pool, and a restaurant where, on most evenings, you can watch an actual glassblower at work while you dine.

▲▲Transjö Hytta

Set up in an old converted farm 10 minutes south of Kosta, this tiny glassworks does expensive but unique fine-art pieces. From

the main shop, a canal-like pond (with glass art pieces suspended overhead) leads back to the hopping hot shop. Transjö—started by a pair of highly regarded glass designers—uses up-and-coming artists as apprentices; they imbue it with a youthful vigor. You can feel the art oozing out of the ovens. The tiny glassworks is funkier and less predictable than the big boys; it's most worthwhile if you catch the artists in action.

The gift shop out front sells one-of-a-kind (expensive) art pieces and limited-run production items made on-site (the *elevarbete*/apprentice works are cheaper). Unfortunately the hot shop is often closed (they don't do much work in warmer weather), but if you follow the canal back to the workshop, you might find the glassblowers in action. If the shop is closed, the glassblowers will often take a break and open it for you.

Cost and Hours: Free, shop usually open early June-mid-Sept daily 9:00-17:00, hot shop hours unpredictable, smart to call or email ahead—tel. 0478/50700, www.transjohytta.com, info@transjohytta.com. To find it, look for *Transjö* signs just south of Kosta.

Mats Jonasson Målerås

In the town of Målerås northeast of Kosta, Mats Jonasson's glassworks specializes in engraving, mixed metal-and-glass sculptures, and necklaces. While it started small, the facility has grown quite big, giving the glassworks a less personal atmosphere. The "design arena" shows off works by other local glass artists.

Cost and Hours: Free; watch glassmaking Mon-Fri 11:00-15:00; shop/gallery open June-Aug Mon-Fri 10:00-18:00, Sat 10:00-17:00, Sun 11:00-17:00, shorter hours off-season; tel. 0481/31401, www.matsjonasson.com.

Orrefors

Once a glassworks with its own proud history, Orrefors (OH-reh-fohs) is now part of the Kosta empire and plays second fiddle to the flagship brand. While Kosta does more handmade pieces, Orrefors focuses on machine-made mass production, much of which has moved abroad. Orrefors feels drearily industrial and sadly neglected, but might be worth visiting if you know your glass and have a special affinity for their works.

The dazzling **museum** displays its historic art pieces chronologically (from early-20th-century pieces with Art Nouveau flair through works from the 1940s) and includes a "crystal bar." Like Kosta, Orrefors' **shop** sells nearly perfect crystal seconds at deep discounts.

Cost and Hours: Gift shop—Mon-Fri 10:00-18:00, Sat 10:00-16:00, Sun 12:00-16:00; museum—June-Aug only, same hours as gift shop; tel. 0481/34189, www.orrefors.com.

OTHER ATTRACTIONS

▲Lessebo Hand Paper Mill (Handpappersbruket)

The town of Lessebo has a 300-year-old paper mill (tucked next to a giant modern one) that's kept working for visitors to enjoy. If you've never seen handmade paper produced, this mill is worth a visit. Cotton linters (fibers) are soaked, packed into a frame, pressed, dried, glazed, and hand-torn into the perfect size and shape. This paper is coveted for special purposes: top-of-the-line stationery (for wedding invitations), impossible-to-forge embossed document paper (for certificates or important examinations), and long-lasting archival use (the cotton fibers ensure the paper will stay pristine for decades).

You can pick up the English brochure and visit on your own, but to see papermaking in action, join a 45-minute English tour with one of the craftsmen who still run the place. Watercolor paper and stationery are available for purchase.

Cost and Hours: Free, late June-late Aug Mon-Fri 9:10-17:00, closed Sat-Sun, off-season closes at 16:00 and for lunch 12:00-13:00; 95-kr guided tours depart 5/day in summer; look for black-and-white *Handpappersbruk* sign just after the Kosta turnoff, Storgatan 79, tel. 0478/47691, www.lessebopapper.se.

Grönåsen's Moose Park (Älgpark)

This offbeat attraction, just outside Kosta, demonstrates the love-hate relationship Swedes feel toward their moose population. (The

Swedish word *älg* can be translated both as "moose" and "elk," but these are the same Bullwinkle-type moose you'll find in the northern latitudes of North America.) A third of a million of these giant, majestic beasts live in Sweden. They're popular with hunters but unpopular with drivers. At this attraction, you'll walk through the moose-happy gift shop before taking a mile-long stroll around the perimeter of a pen holding live moose. Periodic museum exhibits—life-size dioramas with stuffed moose (including one plastered to the hood of a car)—round out the attraction. You can even buy moose sausage. Sure it's a hokey roadside stop, and will hardly be a hit with animal-rights activists, but for many the park is an enjoyable place to learn about Swedish moose.

Cost and Hours: 60 kr, Easter-mid-Nov daily 10:00-18:00, closed off-season, just outside Kosta on the road to Orrefors, tel. 0478/50770, www.moosepark.net.

Eating in Glass Country

You'll find plenty of simple eateries designed for day-trippers. For example, the cafeteria in the outlet mall at the big Kosta complex is the perfect place for fast and cheap, Ikea-style Swedish grub.

If you'd like to linger over a more serious dinner, consider joining one of the special *hyttsill* **dinners** at various glass workshops. Traditionally, a hot shop's fires made it a popular place to convene after hours on frigid winter nights. People would huddle around the ovens and be entertained by wandering minstrel-type entertainers called *luffar*. The food was nothing special (*hyttsill* literally means "hot shop herring," usually served with crispy pork, potatoes, and other stick-to-your-ribs fare), but it was a nice opportunity for a convivial rural community to get together. Today modern glassworks carry on the tradition, inviting tourists on several nights through the summer. They usually have live music and glassblowers working while you dine (figure around 400 kr per person; for more information, see www.glasriket.se).

Kalmar

Kalmar feels like it used to be of strategic importance. In its hey-day—back when the Sweden/Denmark border was just a few miles to the south—they called Kalmar Castle the "Key to Sweden." But today Denmark is distant, and Kalmar is a bustling small city of 64,000 (with 9,000 students in its university and maritime academy). Kalmar's salty old center, classic castle, and busy waterfront give it a wistful sailor's charm.

History students may remember Kalmar as the place where the treaty establishing the 1397 Kalmar Union was signed. This "three crowns" treaty united Norway, Sweden, and Denmark against their common enemy: German Hanseatic traders. It created a huge kingdom, dominated by Denmark, that lasted a bit more than a hundred years. But when the Swede Gustav Vasa came to power in 1523, Kalmar was rescued from the Danes, the union was dissolved...and even the European Union hasn't been able to reunify the Scandinavian Peninsula since.

Kalmar town was originally next to the castle. But that put the townsfolk directly in the line of attack whenever the castle was besieged. So, after a huge fire in 1647, they relocated the town on Kvarnholmen, an adjacent, easier-to-defend island. There it was encircled by giant 17th-century earthworks and bastions, parts of which still survive.

The town center of Kvarnholmen, the charming Old Town, the castle, and the nearby vacation island of Öland are all enjoyable to explore, making Kalmar Sweden's most appealing stop after Stockholm. Its tourist season is boom-or-bust, busiest from mid-June through mid-August.

Orientation to Kalmar

Kalmar is easily walkable and fun by bike. The mostly pedestrianized core of the town is on the island of Kvarnholmen, walled and with a grid street plan. The Old Town district is between Kvarnholmen and Kalmar Castle, which is on a little island of its own (a 10-minute walk from Kvarnholmen). The train station, TI, and ugly industrial "new harbor" are on a manmade extension just south of Kvarnholmen.

Additional islands make up Kalmar (including charming Ängö and mod Varvsholmen), but most visitors stick to Kvarnholmen, the Old Town, and the castle. If your time is limited, your top priorities should be a town walk, the castle, and the public beach just beyond the castle.

TOURIST INFORMATION

The TI is in the big, modern building next to the marina (summer Mon-Fri 9:00- 21:00, Sat-Sun 10:00- 17:00; shorter hours off-season and generally closed Sat-Sun Oct-April; Ölandskajen 9, tel. 0480/417-700, www.kalmar.com).

The TI has guest computers and Wi-Fi, and can book you a room in a hotel or B&B. Ask about live music and entertainment; for example, there are free concerts on Larmtorget, in Kvarnholmen (Tue and Thu in the summer).

Biking: Many hotels have loaner or rental bikes for guests. The Baltic Shop (across from TI, closed Sun) rents bikes for 120 kr per day. Consider riding the ferry from the harbor to the island of Öland (45 kr, about hourly, 30 minutes), which is made to order for a Swedish country bike ride. (Note you cannot ride a bike over the Öland Bridge.)

ARRIVAL IN KALMAR

Arriving at the combined train and bus station couldn't be easier (train ticket office open Mon-Fri 6:40-18:00, Sat 8:40-15:00, Sun 10:30-17:00; lockers available). As you walk out the front door, the town center (Kvarnholmen) is dead ahead. The TI is 100 yards to your right, across the busy street on the harbor. Kalmar Castle and the Old Town are behind you (follow the tracks to your left until the first crosswalk, then follow the big tree-lined boulevard to the castle; with more time, take my scenic "Back-Streets Walk" to the castle—see page 563).

Sights in Kalmar

▲▲KALMAR CASTLE (KALMAR SLOTT)

This moated castle is one of Europe's great medieval experiences. The imposing exterior, anchored by stout watchtowers and cuddled

by a lush park, houses a Renaissance palace interior. Built in the 12th century, the castle was enlarged and further fortified by the great King Gustav Vasa (r. 1523-1560) and lived in by two of his sons, Erik XIV and Johan III. In the 1570s, Johan III redecorated the castle in the trendy Renaissance style, giving it its present shape. Kalmar Castle remained a royal hub until 1658, when the Swedish frontier shifted south and the castle lost its strategic importance. Kalmar Castle was neglected, then used as a prison, distillery, and granary. Finally, in the mid-19th century, a newfound respect for history led to the castle's renovation. Today,

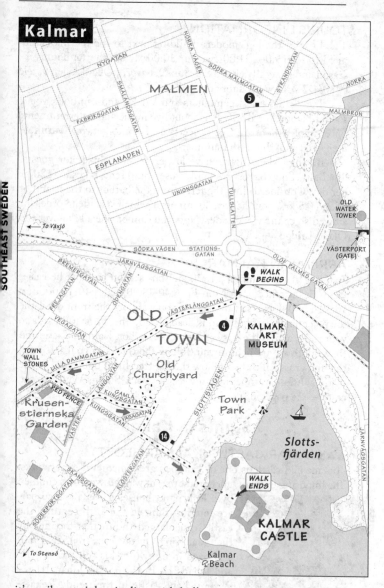

it's a vibrant sight giggling with kid's activities, a new restaurant, park-like ramparts, and well-described historic rooms.

Cost and Hours: 120 kr, late June-Aug daily 10:00-18:00, May and Sept daily 10:00-16:00, Oct-April generally Sat-Sun only 10:00-16:00, tel. 0480/451-490, www.kalmarslott.se.

Tours: Catch the one-hour English tour to hear about the

SOUTHEAST SWEDEN

1 Calmar Stadshotell
2 Frimurare Hotellet
3 Kalmar Sjömanshem Vandrarhem Hostel
4 Slottshotellet
5 Hotell Hilda
6 To Hotell Svanen
7 Källaren Kronan Restaurant
8 Hamnkrog Restaurant
9 Grill Brygghuset
10 Kullzénska Café
11 Ernesto Restaurante
12 O'Reilly's Irish Pub
13 Co-op Grocery
14 Söderportcafé
15 Bike Rental

goofy medieval antics of Sweden's kings (included in admission price, offered 3/day late June-mid-Aug).

Visiting the Castle: Each room has a printed English description. The floor plan is tough to follow, so be sure to pick up and use the castle map. You can try to follow my proposed route, or just read it in advance and then ramble, reading plaques as you go.

Approaching the castle, you'll cross a wooden drawbridge.

Peering into the grassy, filled-in moat, look for sunbathers, who enjoy soaking up rays while the ramparts protect them from cool winds. To play "king of the castle," scramble along these outer ramparts.

In the central **courtyard** is the canopied Dolphin Well, a fine work of Renaissance craftsmanship. (If you haven't bought your ticket yet, do so in the gift shop on the left.)

Access to most of the rooms is from the main courtyard. To the right of the gift shop, you'll find models and drawings in the **Governor's Quarters** that illustrate the evolution of the castle over time. Notice the bulky medieval shape of the towers, before they were capped by fancy Renaissance cupolas; and the Old Town that once huddled in the not-protective-enough shadow of the castle.

In the adjoining **Prisoners' Tower,** you can peer down into the dungeon pit. The room was later converted into a kitchen (notice the big fireplace), and the pit became a handy place to dump kitchen waste.

Go through the labyrinth of rooms to the right that show daily life at the castle: a reconstruction of the castle kitchen, a room being "painted" by medieval workers in anticipation of a royal visit, and more. Check out the touch-screen terminals with information about the castle and Kalmar.

Then head back toward the gift shop and (at the red banner marked *Codex*) climb into the **Women's Prison,** with a grim 19th-century chapter of the castle's history (English explanation of the entire section is in the corner). Modern black-and-white photographs interpret the prison experience of women incarcerated during the Middle Ages and Renaissance. Images of women in stocks, or of an accused "witch" undergoing trial by water, will stay in your mind long after the royal rooms fade away.

Then climb the **Queen's Staircase,** up steps made of Catholic gravestones. While this simply might have been an economical way to recycle building materials, some speculate that it was a symbolic move in support of King Gustav Vasa's Reformation, after the king broke with the pope in a Henry VIII-style power struggle.

At the top of the stairs, go through the wooden door into the **Queen's Suite.** The ornate Danish bed (captured from the Danes after a battle) is the only surviving original piece of furniture in the castle. The faces decorating the bed have had their noses chopped off, as superstitious castle-dwellers believed that potentially troublesome spirits settled in the noses. This bed could easily be disassembled ("like an Ikea bed," as my guide put it) and moved from place to place—handy for medieval kings and queens, who were forever traveling throughout their realm. Smaller servants' quarters adjoin this room.

Proceed into the **Checkered Hall.** You'll see copies of a king's coronation robe and a queen's royal dress. Examine the intricately inlaid wall panels, which make use of 17 different types of wood—each a slightly different hue. Appreciate the faded Renaissance frescoes throughout the palace.

Continue into the **dining room** (a.k.a. Gray Hall, for the frescoes of Samson and Delilah high on the wall). The table is set for an Easter feast (based on a detailed account by a German visitor to one particular Easter meal held here). For this holiday event, the whole family was in town—including Gustav Vasa's two sons, Erik XIV and Johan III. Erik's wife, Katarzyna Jagiellonka, was a Polish Catholic (their marriage united Sweden, Poland, and Lithuania into a grand empire); for her, Easter meant an end to Lenten abstinences. Notice the diverse savories on the table, including fish patties with egg, elaborate pies, and chopped pike in the shape of pears. The giant birds are for decoration, not for eating. Logically, forks (which resembled the devil's pitchfork) were not used—just spoons, knives, and hands.

The door in the far corner with the faded sun above it leads to the **King's Chamber.** Notice the elaborate lock on the door, installed by King Erik XIV because of constant squabbles about succession. The hunting scenes inside have been restored a bit too colorfully, but the picture of Hercules over the left window is original—likely painted by Erik himself. Examine more of the inlaid panels. To see the king's toilet, peek into the little room to the left of the fireplace, with a fine castle illustration embedded in its hidden door (if closed, ask a museum wench to open it). Also in here was a secret escape hatch the king could use in case of trouble. Perhaps King Erik XIV was right to be so paranoid; he eventually died under mysterious circumstances, perhaps poisoned by his brother Johan III, who succeeded him as king.

Backtrack through the dining room and continue into the **Golden Hall,** with its gorgeously carved (and painstakingly restored) gilded ceiling. The entire ceiling is suspended from the true ceiling by chains. If you visually trace the ceiling,

the room seems crooked—but it's actually an optical illusion to disguise the fact that it's not perfectly square. Ponder the portraits of the royal family: Gustav Vasa, one of his wives, sons Erik XIV and Johan III, and Johan's son Sigismund. Imagine the reality-show-level dysfunction that carbonated the social scene here back then.

Peek into **Agda's Chamber,** the bedroom of Erik's consort. The replica furniture re-creates how it looked when the king's kept woman lived here. Later, the same room was used for a different type of captivity: as a prison cell for female inmates.

Cut across to the top of the King's Staircase (also made of gravestones like the Queen's Staircase, and topped by a pair of lions). The big door leads to the grand **Green Hall,** once used for banquets and now for concerts.

At the end of this hall, the **chapel** is one of Sweden's most popular wedding venues (up to four ceremonies each Saturday). As

reflected by the language of the posted Bible quotations, the sexes sat separately: men, on the warmer right side, were more literate and could read Latin; women, on the cooler left side, read Swedish. The fancy pews at the front were reserved for the king and queen.

At the far end, near the altar, a door leads to a stairwell with a model ship, donated by a thankful sailor who survived a storm. In the next room is Anita, the stuffed body of the last horse who served with the Swedish military (until 1937); beyond that you might find some temporary exhibits.

The rest of the castle complex includes the vast **Burned Hall,** which—true to its name—feels stripped-down and is not as richly decorated. In summer you may find a temporary art exhibit here: The curators usually choose a modern theme to give visitors a refreshing break from the Renaissance.

▲THE OLD TOWN

The original Kalmar town burned (in 1647) and is long gone. But the cute, garden-filled residential zone that now fills the park-like space between the castle and the modern town center is worth a look.

It's a toy village of colorfully painted wooden homes, tidy yards, and perfect picket fences. Locals still call it the Old Town (Gamla

Stan), even though almost everything here is newer than the buildings on Kvarnholmen, now the heart of town.

Back-Streets Walk to the Castle

Consider a slight detour strolling through the Old Town on your way from the train station to the castle. Rather than give directions, I've just listed the sights in a convenient order, knowing you can refer to the map on page 558 (and its dotted lines) to locate them. Begin where the pleasant, tree-shaded Slottsvägen boulevard intersects with Västerlånggatan, the cobbled street angling to the right.

Västerlånggatan: Wandering down this cobbled lane, enjoy the time-passed cottages as you peek over fences into private gardens. You'll pass behind the grand mansion (now the recommended **Slottshotellet**) that belonged to the prestigious Jeansson family, who donated the parkland near the castle to the town.

At the first intersection, continue straight, then follow the path through the middle of the big park. As you cross the road on the far side of the park, you'll pass two lines of stones, a small surviving remnant of Kalmar's town wall (on the right).

Krusenstiernska Gården: Watch on the left for the entrance to this relaxed, kid-friendly garden, with its breezy café selling traditional homemade cakes. Poke inside to discover a manicured world of charming plantings clustered around a well, and peek into timewarp workshops. On summer evenings, this garden is a venue for top Swedish comedy acts, which pack the place (park free, daily 11:00-18:00 in summer, shorter hours on weekends and off-season).

Leaving the garden, follow the red fence to the right. Where the fence ends, jog left and squeeze between the yellow and red houses.

Gamla Kungsgatan and the Old Churchyard: Immerse yourself in this Swedish village world. On the left, watch for the Old Churchyard (Gamla Kyrkogården), dating from the 13th century and scattered with headstones. It's virtually all that remains of the original Old Town. Look for the monument topped by a statue of a man carrying a boy (St. Christopher, patron of traders and seafarers). Circling this slab, you'll see the floor plan of the original cathedral, an image looking down the cathedral's nave, and a rendering of the town before it was destroyed. The cathedral tower—which had partially survived the 1647 fire—was torn down in 1678 by the Swedes themselves, who wanted to ensure that their enemies (the Danes) couldn't use the tower to launch an attack on the castle.

About 50 yards farther into the yard, the stone slab on the pedestal (marked *Kalmarunionen 600 år*) commemorates the 600th anniversary of the 1397 Kalmar Union, which united the Nordic states. On June 14, 1997, the contemporary leaders of those same nations—Sweden, Norway, Denmark, Finland, and Iceland—came here to honor that union. You can see their signatures etched in the stone.

Exit the churchyard the way you came in, turn right on the paved street, and take the first left (down Kungsgatan) to the main boulevard. You'll be facing the town park (described next) and the castle; on your left is the appealing, recommended Söderportcafé (with an inviting terrace and an economical buffet-lunch deal, described below).

Town Park (Stadsparken): Unfurling along the waterfront between the castle and the city, this entertaining English-style garden is Kalmar's playground. While thoughtfully planned, it's also rugged, with surprises around each corner. Locals brag that their region is a "banana belt" that enjoys a milder climate than most of Sweden; some of the plants here grow nowhere else in the country. This diversity of foliage, and the many sculptures and monuments, make the park a delight to explore. The modern art museum stands in an appropriately modern building in the center of the park (constantly changing contemporary exhibits).

▲Kalmar Beach (Kalmarsundsbadet)

Kalmar's best beach is at the edge of the Old Town, just beyond the castle. On a hot summer day, this is a festive and happy slice of Swedish life—well worth a stroll even if you're not "going to the beach." With snack stands, showers, sand castles, wheelchair beach access, and views of the castle and the island of Öland, the beach has put Kalmar on the fun-in-the-sun map. It's quite popular with RVers and the yachting crowd. And if you enjoy people-watching, it's a combination Swedish beauty pageant/tattoo show. For some extra views and kid-leaping action, be sure to walk to the end of the long pier.

The beach stretches a mile south. Beyond it is the charming little seafront community of **Stensö**, with its own pocket-size harbor and charming fishing cottages.

▲KVARNHOLMEN TOWN CENTER

Today, downtown Kalmar is on the island of Kvarnholmen. Get your bearings with the following walk, which basically just cuts straight through the length of town. Then dig into its museums.

Kvarnholmen Self-Guided Walk

Most action centers on the lively, restaurant-and-café-lined square called **Larmtorget**, a few steps uphill from the train station. This is the most inviting square in town for outdoor dining—scout your options for dinner later tonight. It's also the nightlife center of town, especially on Tuesday and Thursday evenings in summer, when it's packed for free concerts. The

many cafés bordering the square are a reminder that this is a college town, with lots of students. The fountain depicts David standing triumphantly over the slain Goliath—a thinly veiled allusion to King Gustav Vasa, who defeated the Danes (the fountain's reliefs depict his arrival in Kalmar in 1520).

The area just to the north, up Larmgatan, is a charming old quarter with the historic Västerport gate and a restored old water tower. The tower, dating from 1900, was turned into a modern apartment building, winning an award for the architect who successfully maintained the tower's historic design.

But for now, we'll stroll straight through town on the main pedestrian shopping street, **Storgatan.** Kvarnholmen is a planned Renaissance town, laid out on a regular grid plan (after the devastating 1647 fire consumed the Old Town). While a 1960s push to "modernize" stripped away much of the Old World character, surviving historic buildings and the lack of traffic on most of its central streets make Kvarnholmen a delightful place to stroll.

The first major cross-street, Kaggensgatan, leads (to the right, past a fine row of 17th-century stone houses) down to the harbor; a block to the left, on the right-hand side (at #26), is the landmark Kullzénska Café, whose owners refused to let this charming 18th-century merchant's house be torn down to make way for "progress." (It remains a good place for a drink or light meal in a genteel setting—see "Eating in Kalmar," later.)

Continue down Storgatan. On the right, just before the big square (after #20), look for the building marked *1667*, with the cannonballs decorating the doorway. This was the home of a war profiteer—a lucrative business in this military-minded town (now an inviting gift shop with local products, teas, chocolates, and cheese).

Storgatan leads to the town's main square, **Stortorget.** Built in the 17th century in a grand style befitting a European power, the "big square" tries a little too hard to show off—today it feels too big and too quiet (locals prefer hanging out on the cozier Larmtorget).

The **cathedral** *(domkyrkan)* dominating the square is the biggest and (some say) finest Baroque church in Sweden. Its interior,

which contains a gigantic 17th-century pulpit and bells from the earlier town cathedral, has been elegantly restored to its original glory. Its architect was inspired by the great Renaissance churches of Rome. The interior is all very high-church (for such a Lutheran country), with a fine Baroque altar, carved tombstones used for flooring, and homogeneous white walls (free, Mon-Fri 8:00-20:00, Sat-Sun 9:00-20:00, shorter hours off-season, free noon "Lunch Music" organ concerts daily in summer). Facing the cathedral is the decorated facade of the **Town Hall** *(rådhuset)*.

From here, go straight through the square and stroll down Storgatan. Notice the fine old houses, all lovingly cared for. At the end of town, the area beyond Östra Vallgatan (the old eastern wall of the city) has a pleasant **park** and small **swimming beach.** You may notice dads out with their babies—most Scandinavians get over a year of paid leave for the mom and dad to split as they like. (Use it or lose it, so dads are pushing strollers as never before. They're nicknamed "Latte Dads," and cafés complain that they clog their floor space with too many carriages.)

This park area is called Kattrumpan (literally, "cat's rear end") because of the widely held and disturbing notion that Kvarnholmen looks like a cat's skin splayed out.

To the left, on a little pier in the water (just out of sight), stands the last remaining *klapphus*—laundry building—in Kalmar (and Scandinavia). In the mid-1800s, four of these small, wooden structures with floating floors stood at the seaside. Washers would stand in barrels inset around the central laundry pool for a better working position. Today the *klapphus* is still occasionally used for washing rugs and carpets. The Baltic seawater is considered good for carpet health.

Across the water is the island neighborhood of Varvsholmen, which once housed an eyesore shipyard but has been converted into a futuristic residential development.

To the left of Varvsholmen is the sleepy island neighborhood of Ängö, traditionally home to sailors and fishermen, now one of Kalmar's most desirable residential areas. To the right stretches the Öland Bridge. When built in 1972 to connect Öland Island with the mainland, it was Europe's longest bridge.

• *Your walk is finished. Hooking around*

to the right, you first reach the former city bathhouse (in a 1909 Art Nouveau building), which faces the tiny Maritime History Museum (described below). A block beyond that, the waterfront is dominated by giant red-brick buildings—steam mills once used to grind flour. Today this complex houses the fascinating Kalmar County Museum, described next.

▲▲Kalmar County Museum (Kalmar Läns Museum)

This museum is worth a visit for its excellent exhibit on the royal ship *Kronan*, a shipwrecked 17th-century warship that still sits on the bottom of the Baltic just off the island of Öland. Soggy bits and rusted pieces, well-described in English, give visitors a here's-the-buried-treasure thrill. It's a more intimate look at life at sea than Stockholm's grander Vasa Museum, though this exhibit lacks the boat's actual hull.

Cost and Hours: 100 kr; mid-June-mid-Aug daily 10:00-18:00, off-season daily 10:00-16:00, included 45-minute English tours daily in season at noon; kid-friendly café on Floor 4, Skeppsbrogatan 51, tel. 0480/451-300, www.kalmarlansmuseum.se.

Visiting the Museum: While the museum has plenty of exhibits, your visit will focus mostly on the third floor with the *Kronan* shipwreck artifacts.

Beyond the entry, the first floor has temporary exhibits and shows off the cannons recovered from the *Kronan* wreckage. In those days, cannons were so valuable they were prized the way a Rolls Royce would be today, so each one has its own story (described in English). In the years following the ship's sinking, these cannons were the only artifacts considered worth recovering.

From the first floor, I'd skip the temporary exhibits on Floor 2 and head directly to Floor 3, which displays salvage from the **Kronan**. Twice the size of Stockholm's famous *Vasa*, this warship was a floating palace and the most heavily armed vessel in the world. But it exploded and sank about three miles beyond the island of Öland in 1676. The painted wall at the elevator shows the dramatic event: The *Kronan*'s admiral misjudged conditions and harnessed too much wind, causing the vessel to tip and its gun ports to fill with water. As the ship began to list into the water, a fallen lantern ignited explosives in the hold, and...BLAM! The ship went right down. Its Danish and Dutch foes—who hadn't fired a shot—happily watched it sink into the deep. Of the 850 people on board, only about 40 were rescued. The wreck's whereabouts were forgotten until 1980, when it was rediscovered by the same oceanographer who found the *Vasa*.

Head into the exhibit, where you'll view a model of the shipwreck site (press the button for a short English explanation). You'll see a cross-section of the mighty vessel and a recovered carving of

SOUTHEAST SWEDEN

the potbellied Swedish king (one of many such carvings that decorated the ship). The small theater plays a 15-minute film about the ship (English subtitles).

The replica of the middle gun deck leads to the exhibit's most interesting section, which explains everyday life on board. The 850 sailors who manned the ship (about the population of a midsized town of that age) represented all walks of life, "all in the same boat." Engaging illustrations, eyewitness accounts, and actual salvage items bring the story to life. You'll see guns, musical instruments, a medicine chest, dishes, and clothing—items that emphasize the nautical lifestyles of the simple, common people who worked and perished on the ship. A treasure chest contains coins from all around the known world at the time, each one carefully identified.

The final exhibit (with another short film) reminds us that the *Kronan* still rests on the sea floor, awaiting funding to be raised to the surface. You'll see a replica of the diving bell used in 1680 to retrieve the cannons, and the modern diving bell from very early explorations of the site. Today a dedicated crew of scientists and enthusiasts—including, at times, Sweden's King Carl XVI Gustav—continue to dive to recover bits and pieces.

For extra credit, head up to Floor 4 for its exhibit on **Jenny Nyström**, an early-1900s Kalmar artist who gained fame for her cute Christmas illustrations featuring elves and pixies. You'll see some of her children's books and textbooks, as well as some less commercial, more artistic portraits (with a touch of Art Nouveau flair). Ponder Nyström's status as a proto-feminist icon: She was one of the first female artists to support her family by selling her paintings.

Maritime History Museum (Sjöfartsmuseum)

This humble, dusty little exhibit sits a long block beyond the Kalmar County Museum. It's a jumble of photos of vessels, model boats, charts, and other seafaring bric-a-brac that traces the nautical story of Kalmar up to modern times. The collection is displayed in four rooms of a former apartment, shuffled between beautiful porcelain stoves left behind by a previous owner. (These were display models for his stove retail business.) While it's explained by an English booklet (that you can borrow or buy), the volunteers love to talk and are eager to show you around.

Cost and Hours: 50 kr, mid-June-Aug daily 11:00-16:00, off-season open only Sun 12:00-16:00, Södra Långgatan 81, tel. 0480/15875.

Sleeping in Kalmar

IN KVARNHOLMEN TOWN CENTER

$$$ Calmar Stadshotell is a 126-room business hotel filling a historic shell right on Kalmar's too-big main square, Stortorget (standard Sb-1,000-1,200 kr, standard Db-1,100-1,500 kr, deluxe "superior" rooms 200-kr extra; elevator, Wi-Fi, Stortorget 14, tel. 0480/496-900, www.profilhotels.se, calmarstadshotell@profilhotels.se).

$$ Frimurare Hotellet fills a grand old building overlooking inviting Larmtorget square, just steps from the train station.

Warmly run, the place has soul and a disarmingly friendly staff. Rich public areas, broad hardwood halls, and chandeliers give it a 19th-century elegance. Guests can help themselves to coffee, tea, juice, fruit, and cookies in the lounge anytime. The 35 rooms provide modern comfort amid period decor. Because it's squeezed between a café-packed square and a park that's popular for concerts, it can come with some noise (Sb-950 kr, Db-1,140 kr, Tb-1,340, these special rates for peak season are promised when you book directly with hotel with this book, elevator, Wi-Fi, free sauna, free loaner bikes for Rick Steves travelers, 50 yards in front of train station, Larmtorget 2, tel. 0480/15230, www.frimurarehotellet.com, info@frimurarehotellet.se).

Kalmar Sjömanshem Vandrarhem, a charming place built in 1910 for sailors and now used for student housing, opens to travelers in the summer (mid-June-mid-Aug only). While its 13 rooms are very simple and bathrooms are down the hall, it has an inviting TV lounge, handy guest kitchen, and a peaceful garden behind a white picket fence facing the harbor (S-400 kr, D-500 kr, T-700 kr, Q-800 kr, sheets and towels-80 kr, no breakfast, free parking, Ölandsgatan 45, tel. 0480/10810, www.kalmarsjomanshem.se, info@kalmarsjomanshem.se).

OUTSIDE THE TOWN CENTER

$$$ Slottshotellet ("Castle Hotel") is an enticing splurge in the atmospheric Old Town. It's the nicely upgraded but still homey former mansion of a local big shot. The 70 rooms—some in the mansion, others sprinkled throughout nearby buildings—sit across a leafy boulevard from Kalmar's Town Park, just up the street from the castle (rough prices: standard Sb-1,300 kr, standard Db-1,500 kr, bigger "superior" Db-1,700 kr, Wi-Fi, Slottsvägen 7, tel. 0480/88260, www.slottshotellet.se, info@slottshotellet.se).

$$ Hotell Hilda has eight good rooms in an updated old house, located in a modern residential zone just over the canal from the town center (Sb-795 kr, Db-1,095 kr, elevator, Wi-Fi in breakfast room, free parking, Esplanaden 33, tel. 0480/54700, www. hotellhilda.se, info@hotellhilda.se). The ground-floor Kallskänken café, which doubles as the reception, serves good salads and sandwiches (Mon-Fri 8:00-18:00, Sat 8:00-14:00, Sun 10:00-11:00; if checking in outside of these times, call ahead for the door code).

$$ Hotell Svanen, a 15-minute walk or short bus ride from the center in the Ängö neighborhood, is a new breed of budget hotel with a mix of nicer hotel rooms with private bath, cheaper rooms with shared bath, and hostel beds (no more than six beds per room). Services include laundry and kitchen facilities, a TV room, Wi-Fi, a pay Internet terminal, a sauna, and rental bikes and canoes. While it's a bit institutional, you can't argue with the value (hotel: S-615 kr, Sb-725-815 kr, D-870 kr, Db-970-1050 kr, price depends on size, includes sheets and breakfast; hostel: dormitory bed-195 kr, D-510 kr, Db-640 kr, T-735 kr, Q-960 kr, sheets-60 kr, no member discount, breakfast-80 kr; reception open daily 7:30-21:00, elevator, Rappegatan 1, tel. 0480/25560, www. hotellsvanen.se, info@hotellsvanen.se). You'll see a blue-and-white hotel sign and a hostel symbol at the edge of town on Ängöleden street, a mile from the train station. Catch bus #405 at the station to Ängöleden (2-3/hour, 5 minutes), or take a taxi for about 70 kr.

Eating in Kalmar

Kalmar has a surprising number of good dining options for a small city. For lunch, look for the *dagens rätt* (daily special) for 80-100 kr, which gets you a main dish, salad, bread, and usually coffee or a soft drink.

IN KVARNHOLMEN TOWN CENTER

Källaren Kronan, open only for dinner, is a candlelit cellar restaurant with romantic tables under low stone arches. They serve old-time Swedish dishes, including elk, as well as modern cuisine (100-140-kr starters, 150-300-kr main dishes, 250-kr two-course meals, 300-kr three-course meals, nightly 18:00-23:00, Ölandsgatan 7, tel. 0480/411-400).

Hamnkrog is *the* place for a dressy harborview meal among the Swedish sailing set. Its mod white interior and yacht-deck outdoor tables create a cool, elegant showcase for their French cuisine with plenty of seafood. The self-service 250-kr shrimp-and-mussels buffet, served summer evenings, is a hit (160-240-kr main dishes, Mon-Sat 11:30-14:00 & 18:00-22:00, closed Sun; just beyond the Baronen mall, surrounded by boats at Skeppsbrogatan 30, tel. 0480/411-020).

Grill Brygghuset, open only in summer, seems made to order for visiting yachters. Right on the dock, casual yet stylish, it grills everything, serving traditional and modern dishes with local ingredients (100-200-kr plates, mid-June-mid-Aug Tue-Sun from 17:00, closed Mon, at the marina next to the TI and train station at Ölandskajen, mobile 073-354-0333).

Kullzénska Café, a cozy, antique-filled eatery in a historic building, specializes in sandwiches and pastries. Locals adore its always-fresh berry cobblers (with vanilla sauce or ice cream). While it has street seating, the dining rooms upstairs are what it's all about (Mon-Fri 10:00-18:30, Sat-Sun 12:00-16:00, Kaggensgatan 26 at the corner of Norra Långgatan, go up the stairs, tel. 0480/28882).

Ernesto Restaurante is driven by Ernesto, who came here from Naples nearly 30 years ago. This local favorite for Italian food is a high-energy, dressy place with good indoor and outdoor seating (140-kr pasta and pizza, great selection of Italian wines, daily from 16:00, Södra Långgatan 5, tel. 0480/24100).

O'Reilly's Irish Pub brags that it's the most Irish Irish pub in this part of Sweden. Eamonn runs it and provides the live music on weekends (popular burgers, closed Sun-Mon, Larmgatan 6, tel. 0480/23040).

Supermarket: In the pedestrian district, you'll find the **Co-op,** which has everything you need for a good picnic, including a salad bar (daily 6:00-23:00, Södra Långgatan 8).

NEAR THE CASTLE

The castle lawn cries out for a picnic (buy one in the town center before your visit). Or you can grab a bite in the café inside the castle itself. Otherwise, consider:

Söderportcafé, just across the street from the castle, offers quick, light lunches (tiny self-service sandwich bar in back) and all-you-can-eat buffets (lunch-115 kr, daily 11:30-14:00; dinner-245 kr, daily 17:00-22:00, Slottsvägen 1, tel. 0480/12501). They're well-regarded locally for their live music (Wed-Sat evenings).

Kalmar Connections

From Kalmar by Train to: Växjö (12/day, 60-70 minutes), **Copenhagen** and its airport (hourly, 4 hours, some transfer in Alvesta), **Stockholm** (12/day, 4.5-5 hours, transfer in Alvesta, reservations required; some prefer the slower but more scenic coastal route via Linköping).

By Bus to Stockholm: The bus to Stockholm is much cheaper but slower than the train (4/day, fewer on weekends, 6 hours).

ROUTE TIPS FOR DRIVERS

Kalmar to Copenhagen: See "Route Tips for Drivers" at the end of the Near Copenhagen chapter.

Kalmar to Stockholm (230 miles, 6 hours): Leaving Kalmar, follow *E-22 Lindsdal* and *Nörrköping* signs. Sweden did a cheap widening job, paving the shoulders of the old two-lane road to get 3.8 lanes. Fortunately, traffic is polite and sparse. There's little to see, so stock the pantry, set the compass on north, and home in on Stockholm. Make two pleasant stops along the way: Västervik and the Göta Canal.

Västervik is 90 miles north of Kalmar, with an 18th-century core of wooden houses (3 miles off the highway, *Centrum* signs lead you to the harbor). Park on the waterfront near the great little smoked-fish market (Mon-Sat).

Sweden's famous **Göta Canal** consists of 190 miles of canals that cut the country in half, with 58 locks *(slussen)* that work up to a summit of 300 feet. It was built 150 years ago at a low ebb in the country's self-esteem—with more than seven million 12-hour man-days (60,000 men working about 22 years)—to show her industrial might. Today it's a lazy three- or four-day tour, which shows Sweden's zest for good living.

Take just a peek at the Göta Canal over lunch, in the medieval town of **Söderköping:** Stay on E-22 past where you'd think you'd exit for the town center, then turn right at the *Kanalbåtarna/ Slussen.* Look for the *Kanal P* signs leading to a handy canalside parking lot. From there, walk along the canal into the action. The TI on Söderköping's Rådhustorget (a square about a block off the canal) has good town and Stockholm maps, a walking brochure, and canal information (www.ostergotland.info). On the canal is the Kanalbutiken, a yachters' laundry, shower, shop, and WC, with idyllic picnic grounds just above the lock. From the lock, stairs lead up to the Utsiktsplats pavilion (commanding view).

From Söderköping, E-22 takes you to Nörrköping. Follow *E-4* signs through Nörrköping, past a handy rest stop, and into Stockholm. The *Centrum* is clearly marked.

The Island of Öland

The island of Öland—90 miles long and only 8 miles wide—is a pleasant resort known for its windmills, wildflowers, old limestone buildings, happy birdwatchers, prehistoric sights, roadside produce stands on the honor system, and Swede-filled beaches. This castaway island, with only about 25,000 permanent residents, attracts some 2.5 million visitors annually. It's a top summer vacation destination for Swedes—even the king and queen have their summer home here—due to its climate and tony Martha's Vineyard vibe. Because of its relatively low rents, better weather, and easy bridge access to the mainland, Öland is also a popular bedroom community for Kalmar. If you've got a car, good weather, and some time to kill—and if the place isn't choked with summer crowds—Öland is a fine destination for a quick joyride. (For a basic map of Öland, see page 540.)

Dubbed the "Island of Sun and Wind," Öland enjoys an even warmer climate than already-mild Kalmar, along with a steady sea breeze. And, because its top layer of soil was scraped off by receding glaciers, it has a completely different landscape than the pines-and-lakes feel of mainland Sweden. The island's chalky limestone, rich soil, and lush vegetation make it feel almost more Mediterranean than Baltic. Öland is one of Sweden's premier agricultural zones. Some call it "Sweden's Provence." While that's a stretch, skeptical visitors are pleasantly surprised by its colorful spring wildflowers and by the bright sunshine, which works like a magnet both on holidaymakers and on artists.

Centuries ago, the entire island was the king's private hunting ground. Because local famers were not allowed to fell trees, they made their simple houses from limestone. The island's 34 limestone churches, which were also used for defense, have few windows. Stone walls demarcate property and were used to contain grazing livestock.

When built in 1972, the **Öland Bridge** from Kalmar to the island was Europe's longest (free, 3.7 miles). The channel between Kalmar and Öland is filled with underwater rocks, making passage here extremely treacherous—but ideal for the Vikings' flat-bottomed boats. (In fact, "Kalmar" comes from the phrase "stones in water.") The little town of Färjestaden, near the island end of the bridge, was once the "ferry town" where everyone came and went; today it sits sad and neglected.

GETTING THERE

Public transportation is tricky but workable (buses accept credit cards—but no cash); the island is most worthwhile if you have a car and at least three extra hours to explore. **Drivers** simply head north from Kalmar a few minutes on highway 137 to the Öland Bridge. Once across, highway 136 is the island's main north-south artery. **Buses** regularly connect Kalmar with the town of Borgholm (56 kr, nearly hourly in summer, off-season every 2 hours, 50-60 minutes) and, with less frequency, to other Öland destinations (check www.klt.se). **Bikers** who are in shape might enjoy biking to and around Öland, but note that you're not allowed to ride your bike on the bridge; instead, take the ferry that carries bikers across from

Kalmar to Öland (45 kr, about hourly, 30 minutes). It's possible to rent bikes on Öland (try Ölands Cykeluthyrning, with shops on the island in Borgholm and Mörbylånga, tel. 076-103-9879).

Sights on Öland

Visitors can (and do) spend days exploring this giant island's pleasures. But on a quick visit of a few hours, you'll want to narrow your focus. Your basic choices are center/north Öland (more developed and resorty, with royal sights, and easier to reach on a quick visit) or south Öland (more rugged and remote-feeling, with prehistoric sites, and demanding more time). I've outlined a few basic ideas for each area below, but these are just the beginning—there's much more to discover on Öland.

CENTRAL/NORTH ÖLAND

On a quick spin to the island, I'd stick with the strip of Öland just north of the bridge. As you drive north along highway 136, keep an eye out for some of Öland's characteristic, old-fashioned windmills. Occasional stone churches dot the landscape (including the one in Räpplinge—just off the main road—where the royals worship when in town).

The island's main town is **Borgholm** (BOY-holm), about a 30-minute drive north of the bridge. Borgholm itself isn't much to see, unless you enjoy watching Swedes at play. It's got a smattering of turn-of-the-century wooden villas, erected here after the royal palace was built nearby (described below). Notice that many of these have a humble shack in the garden: Locals would move into these cottages so they could rent the main villas to vacationing Stockholmers in the summer and make a killing. The traffic-free main drag, Storgatan, is lined with tacky tourist shops and ice-cream parlors (Ölandsglass, at #10, is tops). At the handy **TI,** right on the town's main street, you can get maps and advice for your visit (generally Mon-Fri 9:00-17:00, in summer until 18:00 and also 10:00-16:00 on Sat and sometimes Sun, Storgatan 1, tel. 0485/89000, www.olandsturist.se).

A pair of interesting sights sits on the hill just above Borgholm (to reach them, you can either drive or hike—get details at TI). **Borgholm Castle** (Borgholms Slott), which looks like Kalmar Castle with its top blown off, broods on the bluff above town, as if to remind visitors of the island's onetime strategic function. Its hard-fought history has left it as the empty shell you see today—impressive, but not worth the entry fee (www.borgholmsslott.se).

From near the castle, you can hike down to a more recent and appealing royal sight, the current royal summer residence, **Solliden Palace** (Sollidens Slott). It was built in 1906 in an Italian villa style, after the tastes of the Austrian-import queen, who hated Sweden. The palace interior is off-limits, but its sprawling, gorgeously landscaped garden is open to us commoners. Divided into Italian (geometrical and regimented), English

(wild), and Dutch (flowers) sections, the Solliden garden complex is well worth a wander (95 kr, mid-May–mid-Sept daily 11:00-18:00, last entry at 17:00, closed off-season, on-site café open the same hours, tel. 0485/15356, www.sollidensslott.se).

Swedish royalty is smart about not testing the patience of their subjects: The palace and garden complex is financially self-sufficient. And locals brag that when the royals come down from Stockholm, they fly commercial. If the first two rows are open when you board your Stockholm-Kalmar flight, you know they'll soon be filled by a royal backside.

SOUTH ÖLAND

A 60-mile loop south of the bridge will give you a good dose of the island's more remote, windy rural charm. Head south on highway 136 to experience the savannah-like limestone plain, old graveyards, and mysterious prehistoric monuments.

Gettlinge Gravfält (off the road about 10 miles up from the south tip, just south of Smedby) is a wonderfully situated, boat-

shaped, Iron Age graveyard littered with monoliths and overseen by a couple of creaky old windmills. It offers a commanding view of the windy and mostly treeless island.

Farther south is the **Eketorp Prehistoric Fort** (Eketorps Borg), a reconstructed fifth-century stone fort that, as Iron Age forts go, is fairly interesting. Several evocative huts and buildings are designed in what someone imagined was the style back then, and the huge rock fort is surrounded by runty Linderöd pigs, a native breed that was common in Sweden 1,500 years ago. A sign reads: "For your convenience and pleasure, don't leave your children alone with the animals" (120 kr, mid-June–mid-Aug daily 10:30-18:00, free English tours daily—call for times, closed off-season, tel. 0485/662-000, www.eketorp.se). It's near the southern tip of the island, on the eastern side: When you approach Grönhögen on the main road from the north, look for signs on the left.

FINLAND

FINLAND

Suomi

Finland is a fun, fascinating, sadly overlooked corner of Europe. Its small population fills a sprawling, rocky, forested land that shares a long border with Russia. The Finns have often been overshadowed by their powerful neighbors, the Swedes and the Russians. And yet, they've persevered magnificently, with good humor, a zest for architecture and design, a deep love of saunas, and an understandable pride in things that are uniquely Finnish.

For much of their history, the Finns embraced a simple agrarian and fishing lifestyle. They built not cities, but villages—easy pickings for their more ambitious neighbors. From medieval times to 1809, Finland was part of Sweden. Destructive city fires left little standing from this period, but Finland still has a sizeable Swedish-speaking minority, bilingual street signs, and close cultural ties to Sweden.

In 1809, Sweden lost Finland to Russia. Under the next century of relatively benign Russian rule, the "Grand Duchy of Finland" began to industrialize, and Helsinki grew into a fine and elegant city. Still, at the beginning of the 1900s, the rest of Finland was mostly dirt-poor and agricultural, and its people were eagerly emigrating to northern Minnesota. (Read Toivo Pekkanen's *My Childhood* to learn about the life of a Finnish peasant in the early 1900s.)

In 1917, Finland and the Baltic States won their independence from Russia, fought brief but vicious civil wars against their pro-Russian domestic factions, and then enjoyed two decades of prosperity... until the secret Nazi-Soviet pact of August 1939 assigned them to the Soviet sphere of influence. When Russia invaded, only Finland resisted successfully. White-camouflaged Finnish ski troops won the Winter War against the Soviet Union in

1939-1940 and held off the Russians in what's called the Continuation War from 1941 to 1944.

After World War II, Finland was made to suffer for having

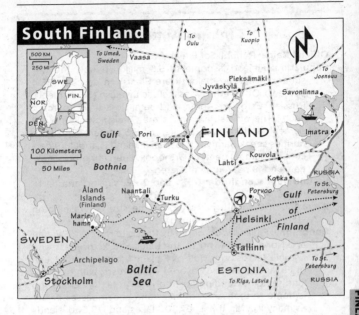

allied itself for a time with Nazi Germany and for having fought
against one of the Allied Powers. The Finns were forced to cede
Karelia (eastern Finland) and part of Lapland to the USSR, to accept a Soviet naval base on Finnish territory, and to pay huge repa-
rations to the Soviet government. Still, Finland's bold, trendsetting
modern design and architecture blossomed, and it built up successful timber, paper, and electronics industries. All through the Cold
War, Finland teetered between the West and the Soviet Union,
trying to be part of Western Europe's strong economy while treading lightly and making nice with her giant neighbor to the east.

The collapse of the Soviet Union has done to Finland what a
good long sauna might do to you. When Moscow's menace van-
ished, so did about 20 percent of Finland's trade. After a few years
of adjustment, Finland bounced back quickly, joining the European Union and adopting the euro currency. In the past, Finns
would move to Sweden (where they are still the biggest immigrant
group), looking for better jobs in Stockholm. Some still nurse an
inferiority complex, thinking of themselves as poor cousins to the
Swedes. But now Finland is the most technologically advanced
country in Europe, and its talented young people are more likely to
seek their fortunes here. Home to the giant mobile-phone company
Nokia, Finland has more mobile-phone numbers than fixed ones,
and ranks fourth among European nations (15th globally) in the
number of Internet users per capita.

We think of Finland as Scandinavian, but it's better to call it
"Nordic." Technically, the Scandinavian countries are Denmark,

Finland Almanac

Official Name: Republic of Finland.

Population: Finland is home to 5.3 million people (40 per square mile). The majority are Finnish in descent (93.4 percent). Other ethnicities include Swedish (5.6 percent), Russian, Estonian, Roma, and Sami (less than 1 percent each). The official languages are Finnish, spoken by 91 percent, and Swedish, spoken by 5.5 percent. Small minorities speak Sami and Russian. Finland is about 79 percent Lutheran, 1 percent Orthodox, 1 percent other Christian, and 19 percent unaffiliated.

Latitude and Longitude: 64°N and 26°E, similar latitude to Nome, Alaska.

Area: 130,500 square miles (about the size of Washington state and Oregon combined).

Geography: Finland is bordered by Russia to the east, Sweden and Norway to the north, the Baltic Sea to the west, and Estonia (across the Gulf of Finland) to the south. Much of Finland is flat and covered with forests, with the Lapland region extending north of the Arctic Circle. Finland is home to thousands of lakes and encompasses nearly as many islands: It has 187,800 lakes and 179,500 islands (the last time I counted).

Biggest City: Helsinki is the capital of Finland and has a population of 604,000; 1.3 million people—about one in four Finns—live in the Helsinki urban area.

Economy: Finland's Gross Domestic Product is $195 billion and its per-capita GDP is $35,900. Manufacturing, timber, engineering, electronics, and telecommunications are its chief industries, with mobile phones among its top exports.

Currency: €1 (euro) = about $1.40.

Government: Finland has both a president, responsible for foreign policy, and a prime minister, who—along with the 200-member Parliament (Eduskunta)— is responsible for domestic legislation. President Sauli Niinistö began his six-year term in March of 2012. Alexander Stubb was appointed prime minister in June of 2014.

Flag: The Finnish flag is white with a blue Scandinavian cross. The blue represents the lakes of Finland, and the white its winter snow.

The Average Finn: He or she is 43 years old, has 1.73 children, will live to be 80, and is tech savvy; the United Nations' Technology Achievement Index ranks Finland first in the world (the US ranks second).

Sweden, and Norway—all constitutional monarchies with closely related languages. Add Iceland, Finland, and maybe Estonia—former Danish or Swedish colonies that speak separate languages—and you have the "Nordic countries." Iceland, Finland, and Estonia are also republics, not monarchies. In 1906, Finnish women were the first in Europe to vote. The country's president from 2000 to 2012 was a woman, and today, 40 percent of the Finnish parliament is female.

Finnish is a difficult-to-learn Uralic language whose only relatives in Europe are Estonian (closely) and Hungarian (distantly). Finland is officially bilingual, and about 1 in 20 residents speaks Swedish as a first language. You'll notice that Helsinki is called *Helsingfors* in Swedish. Helsinki's street signs list places in both Finnish and Swedish. Nearly every educated young person speaks effortless English—the language barrier is just a speed bump. But to get you started, I've included a selection of Finnish survival phrases on the following page.

The only essential word needed for a quick visit is *kiitos* (KEE-tohs)—that's "thank you," and locals love to hear it. *Hei* (hey) means "hi" and *hei hei* (hey hey) means "goodbye." *Kippis* (KIHP-pihs) is what you say before you down a shot of Finnish vodka or cloudberry liqueur *(lakka)*.

Finnish Survival Phrases

In Finnish, the emphasis always goes on the first syllable. Double vowels (e.g., *ää* or *ii*) sound similar to single vowels, but are held a bit longer. The letter *y* sounds like the German *ü* (purse your lips and say "oh"). In the phonetics, *ī* sounds like the long *i* in "light," and bolded syllables are stressed.

English	Finnish	Pronunciation
Good morning. (formal)	Hyvää huomenta.	**hew**-vaah **hwoh**-mehn-tah
Good day. (formal)	Hyvää päivää.	**hew**-vaah **pī**-vaah
Good evening. (formal)	Hyvää iltaa.	**hew**-vaah **eel**-taah
Hi. / Bye. (informal)	Hei. / Hei-hei.	hey / hey-hey
Do you speak English?	Puhutko englantia?	**poo**-hoot-koh **ehn**-glahn-tee-yah
Yes. / No.	Kyllä. / Ei.	**kewl**-lah / ay
Please.	Ole hyvä.	**oh**-leh **hew**-vah
Thank you (very much).	Kiitos (paljon).	**kee**-tohs (**pahl**-yohn)
You're welcome.	Kiitos. / Ei kestä.	**kee**-tohs / ay **kehs**-tah
Can I help you?	Voinko auttaa?	**voin**-koh **owt**-taah
Excuse me.	Anteeksi.	**ahn**-teek-see
(Very) good.	(Oikein) hyvä.	(**oy**-kayn) **hew**-vah
Goodbye.	Näkemiin.	**nah**-keh-meen
one / two	yksi / kaksi	**ewk**-see / **kahk**-see
three / four	kolme / neljä	**kohl**-meh / **nehl**-yah
five / six	viisi / kuusi	**vee**-see / **koo**-see
seven / eight	seitsemän / kahdeksan	**sayt**-seh-mahn / **kah**-dehk-sahn
nine / ten	yhdeksän / kymmenen	**ew**-dehk-sahn / **kewm**-meh-nehn
hundred	sata	**sah**-tah
thousand	tuhat	**too**-haht
How much?	Paljonko?	**pahl**-yohn-koh
local currency: euro	euro	**ay**-oo-roh
Where is...?	Missä on...?	**mee**-sah ohn
...the toilet	...WC	**vay**-say
men	miehet	**mee**-ay-heht
women	naiset	**nī**-seht
water / coffee	vesi / kahvi	**veh**-see / **kah**-vee
beer / wine	olut / viini	**oh**-luht / **vee**-nee
Cheers!	Kippis!	**kip**-pis
The bill, please.	Saisinko laskun, kiitos.	**sī**-seen-koh **lahs**-kuhn **kee**-tohs

HELSINKI

The Finnish capital (Europe's youngest) feels like an outpost of both the Nordic and European worlds—it's the northernmost capital of the EU, and a short train ride from Russia. Yet against all odds, this quirky metropolis thrives, pleasing locals and tickling tourists. While it lacks the cutesy cobbles of Copenhagen, the dramatic setting of Stockholm, or the futuristic vibe of Oslo, Helsinki holds its own among Nordic capitals with its endearing Finnish personality. It's a spruce-and-stone wonderland of stunning 19th- to 21st-century architecture, with a bustling harborfront market, a lively main boulevard, fine museums, a scintillating design culture, dueling cathedrals (Lutheran and Orthodox), a quirky east-meets-west mélange of cultures...and a welcoming Finnish spirit to tie it all together.

Gusting winds swirl crying seagulls against a perfectly azure sky scattered with cotton-ball clouds. Rock bands and folk-dancing troupes enliven the Esplanade from the stage in front of Café Kappeli, sunny days lure coffee sippers out onto the sidewalks, and joyous festivals fill the summer (when the sky is still bright after midnight). And in this capital of a country renowned for design, window-

shopping the Design District—with unique home decor, clever kitchen gadgets, eye-grabbing prints, delicately handmade jewelry, and unique clothes that make a fashion statement with a Finnish accent—has a funny way of turning browsers into buyers.

While budget flights affordably connect Helsinki to the other Scandinavian capitals (and beyond), for many travelers, the next best thing to being in Helsinki is getting there on Europe's most enjoyable overnight boat. The trip from Stockholm starts with dramatic archipelago scenery, a setting sun, and a royal *smörgåsbord* dinner. Dance until you drop and sauna until you drip. Budget travel rarely feels this hedonistic. Sixteen hours after you depart, it's "Hello Helsinki." You can also cross—much more quickly—by boat to or from Tallinn, Estonia. For details on these options, see "Helsinki Connections," near the end of this chapter.

PLANNING YOUR TIME

On a three-week trip through Scandinavia, Helsinki is worth at least the time between two successive nights on the overnight boat—about seven hours. To do the city justice, two days is ideal. (Wear layers; Helsinki can be windy and cold.)

For a quick one-day visit, start with the 1.75-hour orientation bus tour that meets the boat at the dock. Then take my self-guided walking tour through the compact city center from the harbor—enjoying Helsinki's ruddy harborfront market and getting goose bumps in the churches—ending at the underground Temppeliaukio Church.

With more time, explore the Design District, dive into Finnish culture in the open-air folk museum, or take a walk in Kaivopuisto Park. If the weather's good, head for Suomenlinna, the island fortress where Helsinki was born. If it's bad, go for a sauna. Enjoy a cup of coffee at the landmark Café Kappeli before sailing away.

Orientation to Helsinki

Helsinki (pop. 604,000) has a compact core. The city's natural gateway is its main harbor, where ships from Stockholm and Tallinn dock. At the top of the harbor is Market Square (Kauppatori), an outdoor food and souvenir bazaar. Nearby are two towering, can't-miss-them landmarks: the white Lutheran Cathedral and the red-brick Orthodox Cathedral.

Helsinki's grand pedestrian boulevard, the Esplanade, begins right at Market Square, heads up past the TI, and ends after a few blocks in the central shopping district. At the top end of the Esplanade, the broad, traffic-filled Mannerheimintie avenue veers north through town past the train and bus stations on its way to

Helsinki History

Helsinki is the only European capital with no medieval past. Although it was founded in the 16th century by the Swedes in hopes of countering Tallinn as a strategic Baltic port, it stayed a village until the 18th century. Then, in 1746, Sweden built a huge fortress on an island outside its harbor, and Helsinki boomed as it supplied the fortress. After taking over Finland in 1809, the Russians decided to move Finland's capital and university closer to St. Petersburg—from Turku to Helsinki. They hired a young German architect, Carl Ludvig Engel, to design new public buildings for Helsinki and told him to use St. Petersburg as a model. This is why the oldest parts of Helsinki (around Market Square and Senate Square) feel so Russian—stone buildings in yellow and blue pastels with white trim and columns. Hollywood used Helsinki for the films *Gorky Park* and *Dr. Zhivago*, because filming in Russia was not possible during the Cold War.

Though the city was part of the Russian Empire in the 19th century, most of its residents still spoke Swedish, which was the language of business and culture. In the mid-1800s, Finland began to industrialize. The Swedish upper class in Helsinki expanded the city, bringing in the railroad and surrounding the old Russian-inspired core with neighborhoods of four- and five-story apartment buildings, including some Art Nouveau masterpieces. Meanwhile, Finns moved from the countryside to Helsinki to take jobs as industrial laborers. The Finnish language slowly acquired equal status with Swedish, and eventually Finnish speakers became the majority in Helsinki (though Swedish remains a co-official language).

Since downtown Helsinki didn't exist until the 1800s, it was more conscientiously designed and laid out than other European capitals. With its many architectural overleafs and fine Neoclassical and Art Nouveau buildings, Helsinki often turns guests into students of urban design and planning. Good neighborhoods for architecture buffs to explore are Katajanokka, Kruununhaka, and Eira.

All of this makes Helsinki sound like a very dry place. It's not. Despite its sometimes severe cityscape and chilly northern latitude, splashes of creativity and color hide around every corner. With a shorter (and, admittedly, less riveting) history than this book's other big cities, it helps to approach Helsinki as a city of today. Ogle its fine architecture, and delve into the boutiques of the Design District for some of Scandinavia's most eye-pleasing fashion and home decor. As you browse, remember that for the past several decades, global trends—from Marimekko's patterned fabrics to Nokia's sleek cell phones to the Angry Birds gaming empire—have been born right here in Helsinki.

many of Helsinki's museums and architectural landmarks. For a do-it-yourself orientation to town along this route, follow my self-guided walk on page 594. The "Helsinki Tram #2/#3 Tour" (see page 605) also provides a good drive-by introduction to the main sights, and takes you into outlying neighborhoods that most tourists miss.

Linguistic Orientation: Finnish is completely different from the Scandinavian languages of Norwegian, Danish, and Swedish. That can make navigating a bit tricky. Place names ending in -*katu* are streets, -*tie* is "road" or "way," and -*tori* or -*aukio* means "square." Complicating matters, Finland's bilingual status means that most street names, tram stops, and map labels appear in both Finnish and Swedish. The two names often look completely different (for example, the South Harbor—where many overnight boats arrive—is called Eteläsatama in Finnish and Södra Hamnen in Swedish; the train station is Rautatieasema in Finnish, Järnvägsstationen in Swedish). The Swedish names can be a little easier to interpret than the Finnish ones. In any event, I've rarely met a Finn who doesn't speak excellent English.

TOURIST INFORMATION

The friendly, energetic **main TI,** just off the harbor, offers great service, and its brochure racks are fun to graze through. It's located a half-block inland from Market Square, on the right just past the fountain, at the corner of the Esplanade and Unioninkatu (May-Sept Mon-Fri 9:00-20:00, Sat-Sun 9:00-18:00, Oct-April closes two hours earlier, free Wi-Fi, guest computer, tel. 09/3101-3300, www.visithelsinki.fi). Pick up a city map, a public-transit map, and the free *Helsinki This Week* magazine (nicely illustrated, with articles on what to do in town as well as lists of sights, hours, concerts, and events). Ask about the scenic #2/#3 tram route/map. If interested in design, ask for publications about the local design culture; if music's your thing, ask about concerts—popular venues are Kallio Church and the Lutheran Cathedral.

The tiny **train station TI,** which consists of a one-person desk inside the Helsinki Expert office, provides many of the same services and publications.

Helsinki Expert: This private service, owned by Strömma/Sightseeing Helsinki, sells the Helsinki Card (described next), ferry tickets (€8 booking fee), and sightseeing tours by bus and boat. They have one branch in the train station hall, another occupying the front desks in the main TI on Market Square, and small, summer-only sightseeing kiosks on the Esplanade and by the harbor (all branches open Mon-Fri 9:00-15:00, Sat 10:00-14:00, closed Sun, tel. 09/2288-1600, www.stromma.fi).

Helsinki Card: If you're planning to visit a lot of museums in

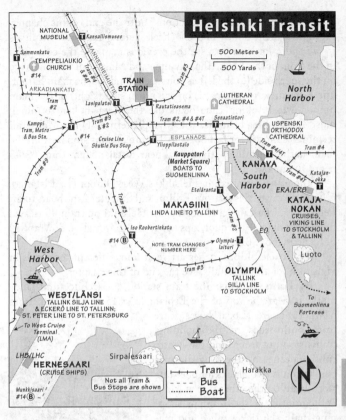

Helsinki Transit

NATIONAL MUSEUM · *Kansallismuseo*

Sammonkatu

TEMPPELIAUKIO CHURCH · #14

ARKADIANKATU

TRAIN STATION

Tram #2

Lasipalatsi

Kamppi Tram, Metro & Bus Stn.

Tram #9 & #2 · #14

Cruise Line Shuttle Bus Stop

LUTHERAN CATHEDRAL

Rautatieasema

Tram #2, #4 & #4T · *Senaatintori*

North Harbor

USPENSKI ORTHODOX CATHEDRAL

ESPLANADE · *Ylioppilastalo*

Kauppatori (Market Square) BOATS TO SUOMENLINNA

KANAVA · South Harbor

Tram #4/4T · Tram #4 · *Katajan-okka*

Eteläranta

MAKASIINI LINDA LINE TO TALLINN

Iso Roobertinkatu

#14

NOTE: TRAM CHANGES NUMBER HERE

ERA/ERB

KATAJA-NOKAN CRUISES, VIKING LINE TO STOCKHOLM & TALLINN

EO

Olympia-laituri

Tram #2

Luoto

West Harbor

Tram #3

OLYMPIA TALLINK SILJA LINE TO STOCKHOLM

To Suomenlinna Fortress

WEST/LÄNSI TALLINK SILJA LINE & ECKERÖ LINE TO TALLINN; ST. PETER LINE TO ST. PETERSBURG

To West Cruise Terminal (LMA)

LHB/LHC **HERNESAARI** (CRUISE SHIPS)

Sirpalesaari

Munkkisaari #14

Not all Tram & Bus Stops are shown

Harakka

500 Meters · 500 Yards

Tram
Bus
Boat

HELSINKI

Helsinki, this card can be a good deal. The card includes free entry to over 50 museums, fortresses, and other major sights; free use of buses, trams, and the ferry to Suomenlinna; a free city bus tour or harbor cruise (your choice—plus a discount on the other, plus a discount on the hop-on, hop-off bus); and a 72-page booklet (€44/24 hours, €54/48 hours, €64/72 hours, €3 less if bought online and picked up on arrival at the main TI's Helsinki Expert desk; sold at all Helsinki Expert locations, most hotels, and both Viking Line and Tallink Silja ferry terminals, www.helsinkicard.com).

For a cheaper alternative, you could buy a public-transit day ticket (see "Getting Around Helsinki," later), take my self-guided walk or tram tour, visit the free churches (Temppeliaukio Church, Lutheran Cathedral, Uspenski Orthodox Cathedral, and Kamppi Chapel of Silence), and stop by the free Helsinki City Museum.

ARRIVAL IN HELSINKI

By Boat: For details on taking the overnight boat from Stockholm to Helsinki, or the boat across the Gulf of Finland from Tallinn to

Helsinki, see "Helsinki Connections" near the end of this chapter. Helsinki's main South Harbor (Eteläsatama) has four terminals *(terminaali)*; for locations, see the previous map and the color map in the front of this book. The Olympia and Makasiini terminals are on the south side (to the left as you face inland) of the main harbor. The Katajanokan terminal is on the north side (right) of the main harbor. Most Viking Line boats use the Katajanokan terminal; most Tallink Silja boats use the Olympia terminal. The Makasiini terminal is mostly for fast boats to Tallinn. Trams stop near all the main-harbor terminals (tram #4T near Katajanokan, tram #2/#3 near Olympia).

The Länsi terminal, in Helsinki's West Harbor (Länsistama), is for large car ferries to/from Tallinn and St. Peter Line boats to St. Petersburg. You can get to downtown Helsinki on tram #9 (leaves from right outside the door, zips you to the train station downtown) or by taxi (about €15).

By Cruise Ship: Cruises arrive at four different terminals in Helsinki; for all the details, see the end of this chapter.

By Train and Bus: The train station, an architectural landmark, is near the top of the Esplanade, a 15-minute walk from Market Square. Local buses leave from both sides of the building, trams stop out front, and the Metro runs underneath. The long-distance bus station is two blocks (or one tram stop) away, on the other side of Mannerheimintie, at the Kamppi shopping mall; the ticket office and machines are on the ground floor, with bus platforms below.

By Plane: Helsinki Airport is about 10 miles north of the city (airport code: HEL, www.helsinki-vantaa.fi). To get between the airport and downtown Helsinki, take the Finnair bus (€6.30, 3/hour, 35-minute trip, www.finnair.com; stops at some downtown hotels on request; return buses leave for airport from platform 30 at Elielinaukio on west side of train station) or public bus #615 (€5, pay driver, not covered by transit tickets or Helsinki Card, 3-6/hour, 45-minute trip, also stops at Hakaniemi; return buses leave for airport from platform 3 at Rautatientori on east side of train station). Or take the Yellow Line door-to-door shared van service (€20 for 1-2 people, €30 for 3-4 people, €40 for 5-6 people, tel. 010-00700 or toll tel. 0600-555-555, www.yellowline.fi). An ordinary taxi from the airport runs about €35-40.

HELPFUL HINTS

Time: Finland and Estonia are one hour ahead of Sweden and the rest of Scandinavia.

Money: Finland's currency is the euro. ATM machines are labeled *Otto.*

Telephones: Finland's phone system generally uses area codes, but has some national or mobile numbers (starting with 010 or 020) that must be dialed in full when you're calling from anywhere in the country.

Internet Access: For the tourist, Helsinki is one of Europe's handiest cities for free Wi-Fi; along the Esplanade and throughout the city center, look for the "Helsinki City Open" network. Most hotels, cafés, and museums also have hot spots. The **City Hall,** facing Market Square and the harbor, has six free, fast terminals and speedy Wi-Fi in its inviting lobby (get code for terminal from desk, Mon-Fri 9:00-19:00, Sat-Sun 10:00-16:00).

Pharmacy: A **24-hour pharmacy**—*apteekki*—is located at Mannerheimintie 96 (at Kansaneläkelaitos stop for tram #2, #4/4T, or #10, tel. 020-320-200).

Laundry: PesuNet, primarily a dry-cleaning shop, welcomes travelers to use its half-dozen self-service machines. It's within a few blocks of recommended hotels, and the Iso Roobertinkatu stop for tram #3 is around the corner. Multitaskers can browse the nearby Design District to pass waiting time (€10/load, not coin-op—pay staff who will help, Mon-Thu 8:00-19:00, Fri 8:00-18:00, Sat 10:00-15:00, closed Sun, Punavuorenkatu 3, tel. 09/622-1146).

Bike Rental: Try **Greenbike** (one-speed bike-€5/hour or €20/all day; three-speed bike-€30/all day; May-Aug daily 10:00-18:00, shorter hours and closed Sun-Mon off-season, Bulevardi 32—but entrance is just around the corner on Albertinkatu, mobile 050-550-1020, www.greenbike.fi). Another option is at the locksmith shop just inside the Metro station facing the **Kamppi plaza**—but they have higher prices and less helpful service (€24/4 hours, €30/all day, €35/24 hours, Mon-Fri 7:00-21:00, Sat 9:00-18:00, Sun 12:00-18:00, tel. 09/739-010); Greenbike sometimes has a temporary location set up on this plaza, as well.

Best View: The **Torni Tower's Ateljee Bar** offers a free panorama view. Ride the elevator from the lobby of the venerable Torni Hotel (built in 1931) to the 12th floor, where you can browse around the perch or sit down for a pricey drink (€5 coffee, €8-10 alcohol, Sun-Thu 14:00-24:00, Fri-Sat 12:00-24:00, Yrjönkatu 26, tel. 020-123-4604).

Meet the Finns: With **Cozy Finland's** "Meet the Finns" program, you can match your hobbies with a local—and suddenly, you're searching out classic comics at the flea market with a new Finnish friend. Their most popular service involves arranging dinner at a local host's home (around €60); contact Cozy Finland for exact prices (www.cosyfinland.com).

What's With the Slot Machines? Finns just have a love affair with lotteries and petty gambling. You'll see coin-operated games of chance everywhere, including restaurants, supermarkets, and the train station.

Updates to This Book: For updates to this book, check www.ricksteves.com/update.

GETTING AROUND HELSINKI

In compact Helsinki, you won't need to use public transportation as much as in Stockholm.

By Bus and Tram: With the public-transit route map (available at the TI, also viewable on the Helsinki Region Transport website—www.hsl.fi) and a little mental elbow grease, the buses and trams are easy, giving you Helsinki by the tail. The single Metro line is also part of the system, but is not useful unless you're traveling to my recommended sauna.

Single tickets are good for an hour of travel (€3 from driver, €2.50 at ticket machines at a few larger bus and tram stops). A day ticket (€8/24 hours of unlimited travel, issued on a plastic card you'll touch against the card reader when entering the bus or tram) pays for itself if you take four or more rides; longer versions are also available (€4 per extra 24 hours, 7-day maximum). Day tickets can be bought at the ubiquitous yellow-and-blue R-Kiosks (convenience stores), as well as at TIs, the train station, Metro stations, ticket machines at a handful of stops, and on some ferries, but not from drivers. The Helsinki Card also covers public transportation. All of these tickets and cards are only valid within the city of Helsinki, not the suburbs; for example, you pay extra for the public bus to the airport.

Tours in Helsinki

As in Stockholm, the big company Strömma (also called Sightseeing Helsinki and Helsinki Expert) has a near monopoly on city tours, whether by bus, boat, or foot. For a fun, cheap tour, take public tram #2/#3—it makes the rounds of most of the town's major sights in an hour. Use my self-guided "Helsinki Tram #2/#3

Tour" (described later and rated ▲▲) to follow along with what you see, and also pick up the helpful tram #2/#3 explanatory brochure—free at TIs and often on board.

▲▲▲Orientation Bus Tours

These 1.75-hour "Helsinki Panorama" bus tours give an ideal city overview with a look at all of the important buildings, from the remodeled Olympic Stadium to Embassy Row. You stay on the bus the entire time, except for a 10-minute stop or two (when possible, they try to stop at the Sibelius Monument and/or Temppeliaukio Church). You'll learn strange facts, such as how Finns took down the highest steeple in town during World War II so that Soviet bombers flying in from Estonia couldn't see their target. Tours get booked up, so it's wise to reserve in advance online or ask your hotelier to help (€31, free with Helsinki Card, tel. 09/2288-1600, www.stromma.fi, sales@stromma.fi).

Bus Tours Departing from Boat Dock: Conveniently, tours depart from the Viking Line and Tallink Silja boat docks at 10:30, soon after the boats arrive from Stockholm. Tours end back at the dock they started from, though you can get off downtown near the end of the tour. If you want to take the bus tour and end up downtown for an overnight stay, stow your bag on the bus, and get off in the city center before the end of the tour (cost-effectively using the tour for transportation as well as for information). Viking Line tours usually have recorded commentary, while Tallink Silja tours typically have a live guide in the summer (June-Aug).

Bus Tour Departing from the Center: The same 1.75-hour bus tour (usually with recorded commentary) leaves later in the day from the corner of Fabianinkatu and the Esplanade. The 11:00 tour goes daily year-round (additional departures possible April-Aug).

Hop-On, Hop-Off Bus Tours

If you'd enjoy the tour described above, but want the chance to hop on and off at will, consider **Open Top Tours** (owned by Strömma/Helsinki Sightseeing, green buses), with a 1.5-hour loop that connects downtown Helsinki, several outlying sights—including the Sibelius Monument and Olympic Stadium—as well as the Hernesaari cruise terminal. Buses run every 30-45 minutes and make 13 stops (€27, €39 combo-ticket also includes harbor tour—see next, all tickets good for 24 hours, mid-May-late Sept daily 10:00-16:00, www.stromma.fi). A different company, **Sightseeing City Tour** (red buses), offers a similar route for similar prices, but has fewer departures (www.citytour.fi).

Harbor Tours

Three boat companies compete for your attention along Market Square, offering snoozy cruises around the harbor and its islands

HELSINKI

Helsinki at a Glance

▲▲▲**Temppeliaukio Church** Awe-inspiring, copper-topped 1969 "Church in the Rock." **Hours:** June-Sept Mon-Sat 10:00-17:45, Sun 11:45-17:45; closes one hour earlier off-season. See page 614.

▲▲**Uspenski Orthodox Cathedral** Orthodoxy's most prodigious display outside of Eastern Europe. **Hours:** Tue-Fri 9:30-20:00, Sat 10:00-15:00, Sun 12:00-15:00, closed Mon. See page 608.

▲▲**Lutheran Cathedral** Green-domed, 19th-century Neoclassical masterpiece. **Hours:** June-Aug Mon-Sat 9:00-24:00, Sun 12:00-24:00; Sept-May Mon-Sat 9:00-18:00, Sun 12:00-18:00. See page 609.

▲▲**Suomenlinna Fortress** Helsinki's harbor island, sprinkled with picnic spots, museums, and military history. **Hours:** Museum daily May-Sept 10:00-18:00, Oct-April 10:30-16:30. See page 617.

▲▲**Seurasaari Open-Air Folk Museum** Island museum with 100 historic buildings from Finland's farthest corners. **Hours:** June-Aug daily 11:00-17:00; late May and early Sept Mon-Fri 9:00-15:00, Sat-Sun 11:00-17:00, buildings closed mid-Sept-mid-May. See page 620.

▲**Senate Square** Consummate Neoclassical square, with Lutheran Cathedral. **Hours:** Always open. See page 595.

roughly hourly from 10:00 to 18:00 in summer (typically 1.5 hours for €17-24; www.royalline.net, www.ihalines.fi, www.stromma.fi). The narration is slow-moving—often recorded and in as many as four languages. I'd call it an expensive nap. Taking the ferry out to Suomenlinna and back gets you onto the water for much less money (€5 round-trip, covered by day ticket or Helsinki Card). If you do take a harbor cruise, here's how the competing companies differ: **Helsinki Sightseeing/Strömma** (yellow-and-white boats) offers the best and priciest route, going through a narrow channel in the east to reach sights that the other cruises miss. The other companies focus on the harbor itself and Suomenlinna fortress; of these, **Royal Line** (green-and-white boats) has the best food service on board, while **IHA** (blue-and-white boats) is more likely to have a live guide (half their boats have live guides, the others have recorded commentary).

▲**Helsinki City Museum** Tells the city's history well and in English. **Hours:** Mon-Fri 9:00-17:00, Thu until 19:00, Sat-Sun 11:00-17:00. See page 610.

▲**Ateneum, The National Gallery of Finland** Largest collection of art in Finland, including local favorites plus works by Cézanne, Chagall, Gauguin, and Van Gogh. **Hours:** Tue and Fri 10:00-18:00, Wed-Thu 9:00-20:00, Sat-Sun 10:00-17:00, closed Mon. See page 610.

▲**National Museum of Finland** The scoop on Finland, featuring folk costumes, an armory, czars, and thrones; the prehistory and 20th-century exhibits are best. **Hours:** Tue-Sun 11:00-18:00, closed Mon. See page 613.

▲**Sibelius Monument** Stainless-steel sculptural tribute to Finland's greatest composer. **Hours:** Always open. See page 615.

▲**Design Museum** A chronological look at Finland's impressive design pedigree, plus cutting-edge temporary exhibits. **Hours:** June-Aug daily 11:00-18:00; Sept-May Tue 11:00-20:00, Wed-Sun 11:00-18:00, closed Mon. See page 615.

HELSINKI

Pub Tram

In summer, this antique red tram makes a 50-minute loop through the city while its passengers get looped on the beer for sale on board (€9 to ride, €6 beer, mid-May-Aug Tue-Sat 14:00-20:00, no trams Sun-Mon, leaves at the top of each hour from in front of the Fennia building, Mikonkatu 17, across from train-station tower, www.koff.net).

Local Guides

Helsinki Expert can arrange a private guide (book at least three days in advance, €204/2 hours, tel. 09/2288-1222, sales@stromma.fi). **Christina Snellman** is a good, licensed guide (mobile 050-527-4741, chrisder@pp.inet.fi). **Archtour** offers local guides who specialize in Helsinki's architecture (tel. 09/477-7300, www.archtours.com).

Helsinki Walk

This self-guided walk—worth ▲▲▲—offers a convenient spine for your Helsinki sightseeing. I've divided the walk into two parts: On a quick visit, focus on Part 1 (which takes about an hour). To dig deeper into the city's architectural landmarks—and reach some of its museums—continue with Part 2 (which adds about another 45 minutes). Note that several points of interest on this walk are described in more detail later, under "Sights in Helsinki."

PART 1: THE HARBORFRONT, SENATE SQUARE, AND ESPLANADE

• *Start at the obelisk in the center of the harborfront market.*

❶ Market Square

At the square's heart is the **Czarina's Stone,** with its double-headed eagle of imperial Russia. It was the first public monument in Helsinki, designed by Carl Ludvig Engel and erected in 1835 to celebrate the visit by Czar Nicholas I and Czarina Alexandra. Step over the chain and climb to the top step for a clockwise spin-tour:

Begin by facing the **harbor.** The big, red Viking ship and white Silja ship are each floating hotels for those making the 40-hour Stockholm-Helsinki round-trip. Now pan to the right. The brick-and-tan building along the harborfront is the Old Market Hall, with some enticing, more upscale options than the basic grub at the outdoor market (for a rundown on both options, see "Eating in Helsinki," later). Between here and there, a number of harbor cruise boats vie for your business. Farther to the right, the trees mark the beginning of Helsinki's grand promenade, the Esplanade (where we're heading). Hiding in the leaves is the venerable iron-and-glass Café Kappeli. The yellow building across from the trees is the TI. From there, a string of Neoclassical buildings face the harbor. The blue-and-white City Hall building was designed by Engel in 1833 as the town's first hotel, built to house the czar and czarina. The Lutheran Cathedral is hidden from view behind this building (we'll go there soon). Next, after the short peach-colored building, is the Swedish Embassy (flying the blue-and-yellow Swedish flag and designed to look like Stockholm's Royal Palace). Then comes the Supreme Court and, tucked back in the far corner, Finland's Presidential Palace. Finally, standing proud, and reminding Helsinki of the Russian behemoth to its east, is the Uspenski Orthodox Cathedral.

Explore the colorful **outdoor market**—part souvenirs and crafts, part fruit and veggies, part fish and snacks. Sniff the stacks of trivets, made from cross-sections of juniper twigs—an ideal, fragrant, easy-to-pack gift for the folks back home (they smell even nicer when you set something hot on them).

Done exploring? With your back to the water, walk left to the end of Market Square and cross the street (tiptoeing over tram tracks) to reach the fountain, *Havis*

Amanda. Designed by Ville Vallgren and unveiled here in 1908, the fountain has become the symbol of Helsinki, the city known as the "Daughter of the Baltic"— graduating students decorate her with a school cap. The voluptuous figure, modeled after the artist's Parisian mistress, was a bit too racy for the conservative town, and Vallgren had trouble getting paid. But as artists often do, Vallgren had the last laugh: For more than a hundred years now, the city budget office (next to the Sasso restaurant across the street) has seen only her backside.

• *Follow Havis Amanda's right cheek across the street, go right one block (toward the harborfront), then turn left up Sofiankatu street (passing, on your right, the City Hall—with free Wi-Fi, Internet terminals, huge public WCs in the basement, and free exhibits on Helsinki history— often photography). Near the end of the block, on the left, you may see the free* **Helsinki City Museum** *(unless it's 2016 or later, in which case it will have moved one block east). You'll pop out right in the middle of...*

❷ Senate Square

This was once a simple town square with a church and City Hall— but its original buildings were burned when Russians invaded in 1808. Later, after Finland became a grand duchy of the Russian Empire, the czar sent in architect Carl Ludvig Engel (a German who had lived and worked in St. Petersburg) to give the place some Neo-class. The result: the finest Neoclassical square in Europe. Engel represents the paradox of Helsinki: The city as we know it was built by Russia, but with an imported European architect, in a very intentionally "European" style. So Helsinki is, in a sense, both entirely Russian...and not Russian in the slightest.

The statue in the center of the square honors **Russian Czar Alexander II.** While he wasn't popular in Russia (he was assassinated), he was well-liked by the Finns. That's because he gave Finland more autonomy in 1863 and never pushed the "Russification" of Finland. The statue shows him holding the Finnish constitution,

HELSINKI

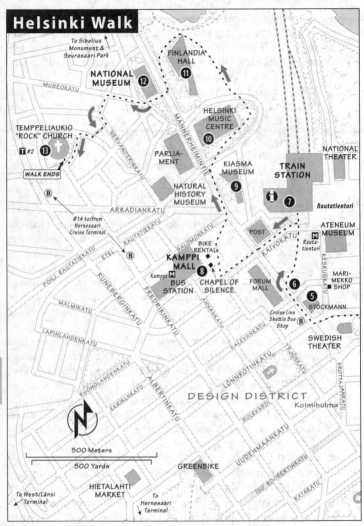

Helsinki Walk

To Sibelius
Monument &
Seurasaari Park

FINLANDIA
HALL **11**

MUSEOKATU

NATIONAL
MUSEUM **12**

HELSINKI
MUSIC
CENTRE **10**

NATIONAL
THEATER

TEMPPELIAUKIO
"ROCK" CHURCH

T #2 **13**

PARLIA-
MENT

KIASMA
MUSEUM **9**

TRAIN
STATION

WALK ENDS

B

NATURAL
HISTORY
MUSEUM

7

Rautatientori

#14 to/from
Hernesaari
Cruise Terminal

ARKADIANKATU

POST

ATENEUM
MUSEUM

B

SALOMONKATU

BIKE
RENTAL

KAMPPI
MALL **8**

Rauta-
tientori

M

KESKUSKATU

MARI-
MEKKO
SHOP

Kamppi **M**

BUS
STATION

CHAPEL OF
SILENCE

FORUM
MALL

6

POHJ. RAUTATIEKATU

ETEL. RAUTATIEKATU

5

STOCKMANN

MALMIKATU

RUNEBERGINKATU

FREDRIKINKATU

ANNANKATU

KALEVANKATU

Cruise Line
Shuttle Bus
Shop

B

SWEDISH
THEATER

LAPINLAHDENKATU

LÖNNROTINKATU

DESIGN DISTRICT

Kolmihulma

EROTAJANKATU

RUOHOLAHDENKATU

EERIKINKATU

ALBERTINKATU

ISO ROOBERTINKATU

BULEVARDI

UUDENMAANKATU

N

500 Meters

500 Yards

GREENBIKE

HIETALAHTI
MARKET

To West/Länsi
Terminal

To
Hernesaari
Terminal

KATAKATU

HELSINKI

which he supported. It defined internal independence and affirmed
autonomy.

The huge **staircase** leading up to the **Lutheran Cathedral** is a
popular meeting (and tanning) spot in Helsinki. This is where students from the nearby university gather...and romances are born.

Head up those stairs and survey Senate Square from the top.
Scan the square from left to right. First, 90 degrees to your left is
the **Senate building** (now the prime minister's office). The small,
blue, stone building with the slanted mansard roof in the far-left
corner, from 1757, is one of just two pre-Russian-conquest build-

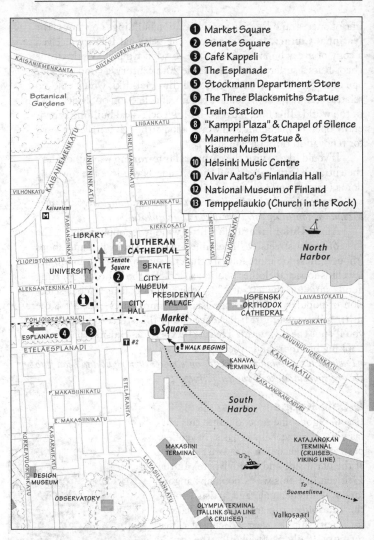

1. Market Square
2. Senate Square
3. Café Kappeli
4. The Esplanade
5. Stockmann Department Store
6. The Three Blacksmiths Statue
7. Train Station
8. "Kamppi Plaza" & Chapel of Silence
9. Mannerheim Statue & Kiasma Museum
10. Helsinki Music Centre
11. Alvar Aalto's Finlandia Hall
12. National Museum of Finland
13. Temppeliaukio (Church in the Rock)

ings remaining in Helsinki. **Café Engel** (opposite the cathedral at Aleksanterinkatu 26) is a fine place for a light lunch or cake and coffee. The café's winter lighting seems especially designed to boost the spirits of glum, daylight-deprived Northerners.

Continue looking right. Facing the Senate directly across the square is its twin, the **University of Helsinki's** main building (36,000 students, 60 percent female). Symbolically (and physically), the university and government buildings are connected via the cathedral, and both use it as a starting point for grand ceremonies.

Farther to the right, and tucked alongside the cathedral, the line of once-grand Russian administration buildings now house the **National Library.** In czarist times, the National Library received a copy of every book printed in the Russian Empire. With all the chaos Russia suffered throughout the 20th century, a good percentage of its Slavic texts were destroyed. But Helsinki, which enjoyed relative stability, claims to have the finest collection of Slavic books in the world. This fine, purpose-built Neoclassical building is generally open to the public and worth a look (though it may be closed for renovation through late 2015).

If you'd like to visit the **cathedral interior,** now's your chance; the entrance is tucked around the left side as you face the towering dome (see page 609 for a description).

• *When you're ready, head back down the stairs and angle right through the square, continuing straight down Unioninkatu.*

Along **Unioninkatu,** do a little window-shopping; this is the first of many streets we'll see lined with made-in-Finland shops (though these are more touristy than the norm). In addition to the jewelry shops and clothes boutiques, look for the Schröder sporting goods store (on the left, at #23), which shows off its famous selection of popular Finnish-made Rapala fishing lures—ideal for the fisher folk on your gift list. At the end of this street (on the right), you'll spot the TI, with a Helsinki Expert desk inside (handy for booking bus tours and other activities).

• *Facing Havis Amanda's backside once more, turn right and head into the grassy median, with the delightful...*

❸ Café Kappeli

If you've got some time, dip into this old-fashioned, gazebo-like oasis of coffee, pastry, and relaxation (get what you like at the bar inside and sit anywhere). In the 19th century, this was a popular hangout for local intellectuals and artists. Today the café offers romantic tourists waiting for their ship a great €3-cup-of-coffee memory (daily 9:00-24:00). The bandstand in front hosts nearly daily music and dance performances in summer.

• *Beyond Café Kappeli stretches...*

❹ The Esplanade

Helsinki's top shopping boulevard sandwiches a park in the middle (another Engel design from the 1830s). The grandiose street names Esplanadi and Bulevardi, while fitting today, must have been bombastic and almost comical in rustic little 1830s Helsinki. To help you imagine this elegant promenade in the 19th century, informative signs (in English) explain Esplanade Park's background and its many statues.

The north side (on the right, with the TI) is interesting for window-shopping, people-watching, and sun-worshipping. In fact, after the first block, browsers may want to leave the park and cross over to that side of the street. In just a few steps, you'll pass flagship stores for several household-name Finnish designers.

First up, at #25B, **Iittala** displays dishes and other glassware, both decorative and functional. Popping into the shop, you'll see Alvar Aalto's signature wavy-mouthed vases, which haven't gone out of fashion since 1936; Oiva Toikka's iconic "dew drop"-patterned chalices and pedestal bowls, from 1964, as well as his bird sculptures; and a mini-museum of glass art in the back (Art & Design Studio).

Back on the Esplanade, a few doors down at #27C, **Kalevala Jewelry** sells quality made-in-Finland jewelry. Some pieces look modern, while others are inspired by old Scandinavian, Finnish, and Sami themes. Next door (also at #27C), **Aarikka** is more affordable and casual, with costume jewelry, accessories, and home decor made mostly from big, colorful spheres of wood.

In the next block, the hulking, ornately decorated **Hotel Kämp** (#29) is a city landmark. **Galleria Esplanad** (entrance at #31) is a super-exclusive mall with big-name Finnish and international fashion stores. Then, after the recommended **Strindberg Café** (one of many fine spots along the Esplanade to nurse a drink), at the corner, is perhaps Finland's most famous export: **Marimekko,** whose mostly floral patterns adorn everything from purses to shower curtains to iPhone cases (two more Marimekko branches—specializing in clothes and kids' stuff—are within a block of here).

Directly across the Esplanade's park median from Marimekko is another landmark of world design, **Artek.** Founded by designers Alvar and Elissa Aalto, this shop showcases expensive, high-end housewares in the modern, practical style that Ikea commercialized successfully for the mass market.

In the block after Marimekko, at #39, is the huge **Academic Bookstore** (Akateeminen Kirjakauppa), designed by Alvar Aalto, with an extensive map and travel section, periodicals, English books, and Café Aalto.

At the very top of the Esplanade, the park dead-ends at the **Swedish Theater.** Built under Russian rule to cater to Swedish residents of a Finnish city, this building encapsulates Helsinki's complex cultural mix. (The theater's recommended Teatterin Grilli is handy for a drink or meal out in the park.) The Finnish National Theater—catering to the other segment of the city's bilingual population—is nearby, close to the train station.

• At the end of the Esplanade, on the right, you'll reach...

❺ Stockmann Department Store

This prestigious local institution is Finland's answer to Harrods or Macy's. Stockmann is the biggest, best, and oldest department store in town, with a great gourmet supermarket in the basement. Just beyond is Helsinki's main intersection, where Esplanade and Mannerheimintie meet.

• Turn right on Mannerheimintie. At the far side of Stockmann, you'll see a landmark statue, the...

❻ Three Blacksmiths

While there's no universally accepted meaning for this statue (from 1932), most say it celebrates human labor and cooperation

and shows the solid character of the Finnish people. On the base, note the rare, surviving bullet damage from World War II. The Soviet Union used that war as an opportunity to invade Finland—which it had lost just 20 years prior—to try to reclaim their buffer zone. In a two-part war (the "Winter War," then the "Continuation War"), Finland held fast and emerged with its freedom—and relatively little damage.

Stockmann's entrance on Aleksanterinkatu, facing the *Three Blacksmiths*, is one of the city's most popular meeting points. Everyone in Finland knows exactly what it means when you say: "Let's meet under the Stockmann's clock." Tram #2/#3 makes a stop around the corner from the clock, on Mannerheimintie. Across the street from the clock, the Old Student Hall is decorated with mythic Finnish heroes.

• For a shortcut to our next stop, duck through the passage (marked City-Käytävä) directly across the street from Stockmann's clock. This will take you through a bustling commercial zone. You'll enter—and continue straight through—the City Center shopping mall. Emerging on the far side, you're face-to-face with the harsh (but serene) architecture of the...

❼ Train Station

This Helsinki landmark was designed by Eliel Saarinen (see sidebar). The four people on the facade symbolize peasant farmers with lamps coming into the Finnish capital. Duck into the main hall and the Eliel Restaurant inside to catch the building's ambience.

Exiting, with your back to the train station, look to the left; diagonally across the square is Finland's National Gallery, the

Ateneum (with works by obscure but talented Finns, as well as better-known international artists). Directly across the square (and not visible from here), it faces the **Finnish National Theater**—the counterpoint to the Swedish Theater we saw earlier.

• *We've worked our way through the central part of town. Now, if you're ready to explore some interesting buildings and monuments, continue with...*

PART 2: MANNERHEIMINTIE AND HELSINKI'S ICONIC ARCHITECTURE

The rest of this walk follows the boulevard called Mannerheimintie, which serves as a showcase for much of Helsinki's iconic architecture; this walk also helps you reach some of the city's farther-flung sights. (Details on many of these appear later, under "Sights in Helsinki.")

• *With your back to the station, turn right and follow the tram tracks (along Kaivokatu street) back out to the busy boulevard called Mannerheimintie. Cross the street and the tram tracks, and continue straight ahead, toward what looks like a giant wood block. You'll pop out the bustling plaza in front of the Kamppi shopping mall, called...*

❽ "Kamppi Plaza" (Narinkkatori) and the Chapel of Silence

This is a hub of Helsinki—both for transportation (with a Metro stop and bus station nearby) and for shopping (with the towering Kamppi Center shopping mall). Turn your attention to the round, wooden structure at the corner of the plaza nearest the Esplanade. This is one of Helsinki's newest and most surprising bits of architecture: the Kamppi **Chapel of Silence.** Enter through the doorway in the black building just to the right, and enjoy a moment or three of total serenity. (For more on the chapel, see page 612.)

• *Leaving the chapel, cut through the middle of the big plaza, with the shopping mall on your left and the low-lying yellow building on your right. Through the gap at the end of the square, you'll see an equestrian statue. Go meet him.*

❾ Carl Gustaf Mannerheim and the Kiasma Museum

The busy street's namesake was a Finnish war hero who frustrated the Soviets both in Finland's "Civil War" for independence, and again later, in World War II. Mannerheim and his fellow Finns put up a fierce resistance, and the Soviets finally gave up and redirected their efforts to the race to Berlin. While the Baltic States—across the Gulf of Finland—were "liberated" by the Red Army, dooming them to decades under the Soviet system, the Finns managed to refuse this assistance. Mannerheim became Finland's first postwar

Two Men Who Remade Helsinki

Eliel Saarinen (1873-1950)

At the turn of the 20th century, architect Eliel Saarinen burst on the scene by pioneering the Finnish National Romantic style. Inspired by peasant and medieval architectural traditions, his work was fundamental in creating a distinct—and modern—Finnish identity. The château-esque National Museum of Finland, de-signed by Saarinen and his two partners after winning a 1902 architectural com-petition, was his first major success (see page 613). Two years later, Saarinen won the contract to construct the Helsinki train station (completed in 1919). Its de-sign marks a transition into the Art Nou-

veau style of the early 1900s. The landmark station—charac-terized by massive male sculptures flanking its entrance, ornate glass and metalwork, and a soaring clock tower—pres-ently welcomes over 300,000 travelers each day.

In the early 1920s, Saarinen and his family emigrated to the US where his son, Eero, would become the architect of such iconic projects as the Gateway Arch in St. Louis and the main terminal at Dulles International Airport near Washington, DC.

Alvar Aalto (1898-1976)

Alvar Aalto was a celebrated Finnish architect and designer working in the Modernist tradition; his buildings used abstract

forms and innovative materials without sacrificing functional-ity. Finlandia Hall in Helsinki is undoubtedly Aalto's most fa-mous structure, but that's just the beginning. A Finnish Frank Lloyd Wright, Aalto concerned himself with nearly every as-pect of design, from furniture to light fixtures. Perhaps most notable of these creations was his sinuous Savoy Vase, a mas-

terpiece of simplicity and sophistication that is emblematic of the Aalto style. His designs became so popular that in 1935 he and his wife opened Artek, a company that manufactures and sells his furniture, lamps, and textiles to this day (see page 622).

president, and thanks to his
efforts (and those of countless
others), Finland was allowed
to chart its own democratic,
capitalist course after the war.
(Even so, Finland remained
officially neutral through the
Cold War, providing both East
and West a political buffer
zone.)

Mannerheim is standing in front of the glassy home of the
Kiasma Museum, with changing exhibits of contemporary art. A
bit farther along and across the street from Kiasma, with its stoic
row of Neoclassical columns, stands the Finnish **Parliament.**

From Mannerheim and Kiasma, head down into the grassy,
sloping park. At the lowest point, watch out—you're crossing a
busy **bicycle highway** that cuts right through the middle of the city
center. Look left under the tunnel to see how they turned a disused
old rail line into a subterranean pedalers' paradise.

• *The glassy building dominating the end of the park is the...*

⑩ Helsinki Music Centre (Musiikkitalo)

Completed in 2011, this structure is even bigger than it looks: two-
thirds of it is underground, and the entire complex houses seven

separate venues. It's decorated, inside
and out, with bold art (such as the gigantic pike on tiptoes that stands in
the middle of the park). As you approach the bottom of the building,
step into the atrium (Mon-Fri 8:00-
22:00, Sat 10:00-22:00, Sun 10:00-
20:00) and look up to ogle the shim-
mering silver sculpture. While you're there, consider stopping by
the ticket desk (on the lower floor) to ask about performances while
you're in town; unfortunately, the season is September through
April—low time for tourists. Upstairs is a music store. The interior
features a lot of pine and birch accents, which warm up the space
and improve the (Japanese-designed) acoustics. It didn't take long
for the Music Centre to become an integral part of the city's cultural life; in the first season of performances alone, some 400,000
people attended events here. They also offer English tours of the
facility (see "Sights in Helsinki," later).

Back outside, circle around the back side of the Music Centre.
Follow the straight, flat promenade that runs alongside a grassy
park used for special events, and a former industrial zone that's
slated for further redevelopment; the train tracks are just beyond.

• Crossing the street, you'll see (on the left) perhaps the most important work of Finnish architecture...

⓫ Alvar Aalto's Finlandia Hall

While famous, this big, white building can be a bit difficult for nonarchitects to appreciate. Walk through the long parking lot

all the way to the far end, and look back for a more dramatic view. The building—entirely designed by Aalto, inside and out—opened in 1971 and immediately became a national icon. Notice how Aalto employs geometric shapes and sweeping lines to create a striking concert hall, seating up to 1,700 guests. Aalto designed the inclined roof to try to maximize the hall's acoustics—imitating the echo chamber of an old-fashioned church tower—with marginal success.

Turn to face shimmering **Töölönlahti Bay** (not a lake, but an inlet of the Baltic Sea)—ringed by a popular walking and jogging track. From here, you can see more Helsinki landmarks: across the lake and a bit to the left, the white tower marks the Olympic Stadium that hosted the world in 1952. And to the right are the rides of Helsinki's old-time amusement park, Lenininpuisto.

• If you'd like to extend this walk with a leisurely stroll, join the natives on the waterfront path (which offers even better views of Finlandia Hall). Otherwise, consider...

More Helsinki Sights

To reach two more major sights, go up the stairs immediately to the right of Finlandia Hall, then continue all the way up to the main road. Directly across the street stands what looks like a château with a steeple. This building houses the fine ⓬ **National Museum of Finland,** which tells this country's story with lots of artifacts.

There's one more great architectural treasure in Helsinki, about a 10-minute walk behind the National Museum: the sit-and-wipe-a-tear beautiful "Church in the Rock," ⓭ **Temppeliaukio.** Once inside, sit. Enjoy the music. It's a wonderful place to end this walk.

To continue on to the **Sibelius Monument,** located in a lovely park setting, take bus #24 (direction: Seurasaari) from nearby Arkadiankatu street. The same ticket is good for your return trip (within one hour), or ride it to the end of the line for the bridge to Seurasaari Island and Finland's open-air folk museum. From there, bus #24 returns to the top of the Esplanade.

All three of these sights are explained in more detail later, under "Sights in Helsinki."

Helsinki Tram Tour

Of Helsinki's many tram routes, #2/#3 seems made-to-order for a tourist's joyride, and is worth ▲▲. In fact, the TI hands out a free little map with the described route, making this self-guided tour easier to follow.

If you buy a single ticket, just stay on the tram for the entire circuit (€3 from driver, €2.50 from ticket machines at a few major stops, good for one hour). Using a day ticket (see "Getting Around Helsinki," earlier) or a Helsinki Card allows you to hop off to tour a sight, then catch a later tram (runs every 10 minutes).

You can't get lost because the route makes a figure-eight, and an hour after you start, you end up back at the beginning. The only confusing thing is that the tram has different names during different parts of the figure-eight; the top-left and bottom-right lobes are #2, the other lobes are #3, and the letter on the tram's sign changes at the north and south ends of the route. A few departures circle only the top or bottom loop, so confirm with the driver before boarding that your tram will make the entire figure-eight.

❶ **Market Square:** While you can hop on anywhere, it's most convenient to start—and end—at Market Square by the TI. Stand at the tram stop that is between the fountain and the market, and wait for one of the frequent #2 trams. Since the tracks split here briefly, it's hard to get on in the wrong direction; still, confirm that the destination listed on the front of the tram is *Eläintarha*, not *Kaivopuisto*. From Market Square, you'll first pass **Senate Square** (with the gleaming white Lutheran Cathedral, a statue of Alexander II—Finland's favorite czar, and many of the oldest buildings in town) and then head up Aleksanterinkatu street. It's Helsinki's Fifth Avenue-type main shopping drag (tram stop: Aleksanterinkatu).

❷ **Finnish National Theater/Train Station:** After the Mikonkatu stop, you'll pass a big square. Fronting it is Finland's granite National Theater, in Art Nouveau style. The statue in the square honors Aleksis Kivi, the father of Finnish literature, who in 1870 wrote *The Seven Brothers,* the first great novel in Finnish. The mid-19th century was a period of national awakening. By elevating the language to high culture, Kivi helped inspire his countrymen to stand strong and proud during a period of attempted "Russification." On the left is the **Ateneum,** Finland's national art gallery. From there (on the right), you'll pass the striking train station—with its iconic countrymen stoically holding their lamps—designed by the great Finnish architect, Eliel Saarinen.

HELSINKI

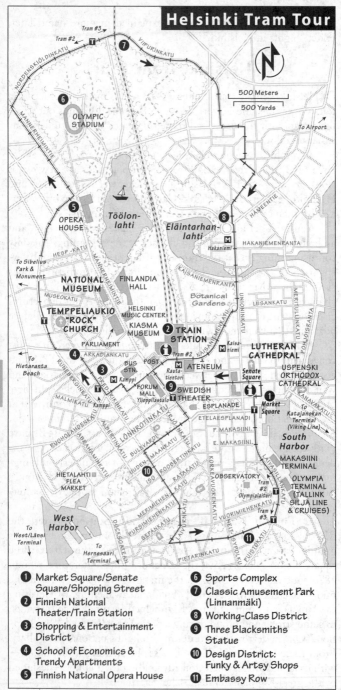

Helsinki Tram Tour

Tram #3
Tram #2

VIIPURINKATU

NORDENSKIÖLDINKATU

500 Meters
500 Yards

To Airport

6 OLYMPIC STADIUM

MANNERHEIMINTIE

7

Töölön-lahti

5 OPERA HOUSE

HESP.-KATU

Eläintarhan-lahti

HÄMEENTIE

8

Hakaniemi

HAKANIEMENRANTA

To Sibelius Park & Monument

NATIONAL MUSEUM

MUSEOKATU

FINLANDIA HALL

MANNERHEIMINTIE

KAISANIEMENRANTA

Botanical Gardens

UNIONINKATU

LIISANKATU

MERITULLINKATU

TEMPPELIAUKIO "ROCK" CHURCH

HELSINKI MUSIC CENTER

KIASMA MUSEUM

PARLIAMENT

ARKADIANKATU

4

To Hietaranta Beach

3

BUS STN.

POST

Kamppi

Rauta-tientori

2 TRAIN STATION

Kaisa-niemi

Tram #2

KAISANIEMENKATU

ATENEUM

Senate Square

LUTHERAN CATHEDRAL

USPENSKI ORTHODOX CATHEDRAL

RUNEBERGINKATU

FREDRIKINKATU

Kamppi

FORUM MALL

Ylioppilastalo

9 SWEDISH THEATER

ESPLANADE

1 Market Square

To Katajanokan Terminal (Viking Line)

MALMIKATU

ALBERTINKATU

ABRAHAMINKATU

LÖNNROTINKATU

BULEVARDI

UUDEN MAANKATU

YRJÖNKATU

ETELÄESPLANADI

F. MAKASIINI

E. MAKASIINI

South Harbor

HIETALAHTI FLEA MARKET

10

ROOBERTINKATU

RATAKATU

KORKEAVUORENKATU

OBSERVATORY

Tram #2

Olympialaituri

MAKASIINI TERMINAL

OLYMPIA TERMINAL (TALLINK SILJA LINE & CRUISES)

West Harbor

DOCKSGATAN

MERIMIEHEN KATU

PURSIMIEHENKATU

SEPÄNKATU

TEHTAANKATU

KAPTEENINKATU

LAIVASILLANKATU

11

Tram #3

PUISTOKATU

To West/Länsi Terminal

To Hernesaari Terminal

PIETARINKATU

① Market Square/Senate Square/Shopping Street
② Finnish National Theater/Train Station
③ Shopping & Entertainment District
④ School of Economics & Trendy Apartments
⑤ Finnish National Opera House
⑥ Sports Complex
⑦ Classic Amusement Park (Linnanmäki)
⑧ Working-Class District
⑨ Three Blacksmiths Statue
⑩ Design District: Funky & Artsy Shops
⑪ Embassy Row

❸ **Shopping and Entertainment District:** Crossing the busy Mannerheimintie boulevard, you'll pass the Kamppi mall, with the bus station in its basement and the wood-cylinder Kamppi Chapel of Silence in front (tram and Metro stop: Kamppi). The adjacent Tennis Palace is a cultural zone with galleries and movie theaters.

❹ **School of Economics and Trendy Apartments:** After passing the yellow brick buildings of the School of Economics (on your left, note facade—Kauppakorkeakoulut stop), you'll enter a neighborhood with lots of desirable 1920s-era apartments. Young couples start out here, move to the suburbs when they have their kids, and return as empty-nesters. The Temppeliaukio Church (a.k.a. "Church in the Rock"), while out of sight, is just a block uphill from the next stop (Sammonkatu).

❺ **Finnish National Opera House:** Built in 1993, the National Opera House is the white, sterile, shower-tile building on the right (tram stop: Ooppera). The next stop (Töölön halli) is a short walk from the Sibelius Monument and its pretty park (detour along a street called Sibeliuksenkatu).

❻ **Sports Complex:** A statue honors long-distance runner Paavo Nurmi (early 20th-century Finn who won a slew of Olympic gold medals, on left). The white building with the skinny tower (in the distance on the right) marks the Olympic Stadium, used for the summer games in 1952. After the Auroran sairaala stop, you'll see skateboarders enjoying a park of their own (on the right). At the next stop, Eläintarha, the tram may pause as it changes to become #3 (stay seated).

❼ **Classic Amusement Park: Linnanmäki,** Helsinki's low-end, Tivoli-like amusement park is by far the most-visited sight in town (on the right, free admission to park, rides cost €4-6, open daily until late, tram stop: Alppila, www.linnanmaki.fi). Roller-coaster nuts enjoy its classics from the 1950s.

❽ **Working-Class District:** Next you'll enter an old working-class neighborhood. Its soccer fields (on your left) are frozen into ice rinks for hockey in the winter. You'll pass the striking granite **Kallio Church** (Art Nouveau, on your right) and **Hakaniemi** square, with a big indoor/outdoor market (on your left). Crossing a saltwater inlet, you'll pass Helsinki's **Botanical Gardens** (on the right), and then head back toward the town center. As you return to the train station with its buff lamp-holders, you've completed the larger, top loop of the figure-eight.

❾ **The *Three Blacksmiths* Statue:** After turning left on big, busy Mannerheimintie, you'll pass the most famous statue in town, the *Three Blacksmiths* (on your left), which honors hard work and cooperation. Towering above the smiths is the Stockmann department store. Then (at the Ylioppilastalo stop), the round, white Swedish Theater marks the top of the town's graceful park—the

Esplanade—which leads back down to the harbor (where you began this tour). From here, you'll loop through the colorful and artsy Design District.

⓾ **Design District—Funky and Artsy Shops:** The cemetery of the church (which dates from 1827) on the right was cleaned out to make a park. It's called the "Plague Park," recalling a circa-1700 plague that killed more than half the population. Coming up, funky small boutiques, cafés, and fun shops line the streets (stops: Fredrikinkatu, Iso Roobertinkatu, and Viiskulma). After the Art Deco brick church (on your right), the tram makes a hard left (at the Eiran sairaala stop, for a hospital) and enters a district with Art Nouveau buildings. Look down streets on the right for facades and decorative turrets leading to the Baltic Sea.

⓫ **Embassy Row and Back to Market Square:** After the Neitsytpolku stop, spy the Russian Embassy (on left), still sporting its hammer and sickle; it was built to look like London's Buckingham Palace. Across the street is the Roman Catholic church, and beyond that (on the right), a street marked "no entry" leads to a fortified US Embassy. Returning to the harbor, you'll likely see the huge Tallink Silja ship that leaves at 17:00 each evening for Stockholm. Its terminal (the appropriately named Olympiaterminaali) was built for the 1952 Olympics, which inundated Helsinki with visitors. Across the harbor stands the Uspenski Orthodox Cathedral. Then, after passing the cute brick Old Market Hall (with several great little eateries), you'll arrive back at Market Square, where you started.

Sights in Helsinki

NEAR THE SOUTH HARBOR
▲▲Uspenski Orthodox Cathedral

This house of worship was built for the Russian military in 1868 (at a time when Finland belonged to Russia). *Uspenski* is Russian for the Assumption of Mary. It hovers above Market Square and faces the Lutheran Cathedral, just as Russian culture faces Europe.

Cost and Hours: Free; Tue-Fri 9:30-20:00, Sat 10:00-15:00, Sun 12:00-15:00, closed Mon, Kanavakatu 1 (about a 5-minute walk beyond the harborfront market).

Visiting the Cathedral: Before heading inside, view the exterior. The uppermost "onion dome" represents the "sacred heart of Jesus," while the smaller ones represent the hearts of the 12 apostles.

The cathedral's interior is a potentially emotional icon experience. Its rich images are a stark contrast to the sober Lutheran Cathedral. While commonly called the "Russian church," the cathedral is actually Finnish Orthodox, answering to the patriarch in Constantinople (Istanbul). Much of eastern Finland (parts of the Karelia region) is Finnish Orthodox.

The cathedral's Orthodox Mass is beautiful, with a standing congregation, candles, incense, icons in action, priests behind the iconostasis (screen), and timeless music (human voices only—no instruments). In the front left corner, find the icon featuring the Madonna and child, surrounded by rings and jewelry (under glass), given in thanks for prayers answered. Across from the icon is a white marble table with candle holes and a dish of wheat seeds, representing recent deaths. Wheat seeds symbolize that death is not the end, it's simply a change.

Though the cathedral is worthwhile, the one in Tallinn is more richly decorated; skip this one if you're visiting both cities and are short on time.

▲▲Lutheran Cathedral

With its prominent green dome, gleaming white facade, and the 12 apostles overlooking the city and harbor, this church is Carl Ludvig Engel's masterpiece.

Cost and Hours: Free; June-Aug Mon-Sat 9:00-24:00, Sun 12:00-24:00; Sept-May Mon-Sat 9:00-18:00, Sun 12:00-18:00; sometimes closes for events; on Senate Square, www.helsinginseurakunnat.fi. In summer, free organ concerts are held on Sundays at 20:00.

Visiting the Cathedral: Enter the building around the left side. Finished in 1852, the interior is pure architectural truth.

Open a pew gate and sit, surrounded by the saints of Protestantism, to savor Neo-classical nirvana. Physically, this church is perfectly Protestant—austere and unadorned—with the emphasis on preaching (prominent pulpit) and music (huge organ). Statuary is limited to the local Reformation big shots: Martin Luther, Philipp Melanchthon (Luther's Reformation sidekick), and the leading Finnish reformer, Mikael Agricola. A follower of Luther at Wittenberg, Agricola brought the Reformation to Finland. He also translated the Bible into Finnish and is considered the father of the modern Finnish language. Agricola's Bible is to Finland what the Luther Bible is to Germany and the King James Bible is to the English-speaking world.

▲Helsinki City Museum

This interesting museum, a few steps off of Senate Square, gives an excellent, accessible overview of the city's history in English. At the beginning of 2016, they are scheduled to move one block east, to Katariinankatu. But until then, they'll be showing off the enjoyable "Mad About Helsinki" exhibit. The ground floor is a sentimental look at some of the people of Helsinki's favorite places: seafront gardens, the cathedral steps, amusement park attractions, and home sweet home (with a mock-up of a typical Helsinki kitchen). The upstairs exhibit traces the history of the city from the 1550s, taking the novel approach of zooming in on individual, everyday people—from different historical periods and social classes—to better understand why each of them chose to call Helsinki home. While this specific exhibit may not make the move to the new location, it's an indication of the clever, intimate, and affectionate approach the museum brings to its subject.

Cost and Hours: Free, Mon-Fri 9:00-17:00, Thu until 19:00, Sat-Sun 11:00-17:00, Sofiankatu 4—or one block east on Katariinankatu beginning in 2016, www.helsinkicitymuseum.fi.

BEYOND THE ESPLANADE

These sights are scattered in the zone west of the Esplanade, listed roughly in the order you'll reach them from the city center (and in the order they appear on my self-guided walk, earlier).

▲Ateneum, The National Gallery of Finland

This museum showcases Finnish artists (mid-18th to 20th century) and has a fine international collection, including works by Cézanne, Chagall, Gauguin, and Van Gogh. They also have good temporary exhibits. However, as the building is being renovated through late 2015, many of their star canvases are out on loan, and the "greatest hits" of their Finnish collection has been condensed on the ground floor. Before buying your ticket, be clear on what's on view today. Either way, the collection is hard to appreciate without the €3 audioguide (though the laminated English information sheets in a few rooms are helpful).

Cost and Hours: €12, Tue and Fri 10:00-18:00, Wed-Thu 9:00-20:00, Sat-Sun 10:00-17:00, closed Mon, near train station at Kaivokatu 2, tel. 0294-500-401, www.ateneum.fi.

Visiting the Museum: The Finnish section provides the opportunity to be introduced to talented artists who aren't well known outside their homeland. Get swept up in the lyrical, romantic canvases of Akseli Gallen-Kallela (1865-1931), who illustrated scenes from the Finnish national epic, *Kalevala*. (In 1835, Elias Lünnrot collected folkloric tales from humble, rural Finnish peasants and assembled them into this romantic poem, which was designed to be

Sauna

Finland's vaporized fountain of youth is the sauna—Scandinavia's answer to support hose and facelifts. A traditional sauna  is a wood-paneled room with wooden benches and a blistering-hot wood-fired stove topped with rocks. Undress entirely before going in. Lay your towel on the bench, and sit or lie on it (for hygienic reasons). Ladle water from the bucket onto the rocks to make steam. Choose a higher bench for hotter temperatures. Let yourself work up a sweat, then, just before bursting, go outside to the shower for a Niagara of liquid ice. Suddenly your shower stall becomes a Cape Canaveral launch pad, as your body scatters to every corner of the universe. A moment later you're back together and can re-enter the steam room. Repeat as necessary. The famous birch branches are always available for slapping your skin. Finns claim this enhances circulation while emitting a refreshing birch aroma that opens your sinuses. For more on the history of saunas, see www.sauna.fi.

Your hostel, hotel, or cruise ship may have a sauna, which may be heated only at specific times. Some saunas are semi-public (separate men's and women's hours), while others are for private use (book a 45- to 60-minute time slot; to save money, split the cost with a group of friends, either mixed or same-sex). Public saunas are a dying breed these days, because most Finns have private saunas in their homes or cabins. But some public saunas survive in rougher, poorer neighborhoods.

For a good, traditional sauna with a coarse and local crowd, try the **Kotiharjun Sauna.** Pay €12 plus €3 for a towel (cash only), find a locker, strip (keep the key on your wrist), and head for the steam. Cooling off is nothing fancy—just a bank of cold showers. A woman in a fish-cleaner's apron will give you a wonderful scrub with Brillo pad-like mitts (€9, only on Tue and Fri-Sat 16:00-19:00). Regulars relax with beers on the sidewalk just outside (open Tue-Sun 14:00-21:30, closed Mon, last entry 1.5 hours before closing; men—ground floor, women—upstairs; 200 yards from Sörnäinen Metro stop, Harjutorinkatu 1, tel. 09/753-1535, www.kotiharjunsauna.fi).

The **Kulttuurisauna** sits in a little park along the Baltic—to cool off, take a dip in the sea. Designed and operated by a husband-and-wife, Finnish-Japanese, artist-and-architect team, it's both modern and traditional. This is a *savusauna* (smoke sauna, without a chimney)—and, while the room is ventilated before bathers arrive, the smoky atmosphere lingers (€15, towel rental-€4, all nude and gender-segregated, Wed-Sun 16:00-21:00, closed Mon-Tue, last entry at 20:00, just north of downtown at Hakaniemenranta 17, nearest tram/bus stop is Hakaniemi—about a 10-minute walk away, www.kulttuurisauna.fi).

HELSINKI

sung—a very important cultural touchstone for the Finnish people, during a time when their culture and language were subordinated by Sweden and Russia.) Gallen-Kallela's scenes tapped into the spirit of the burgeoning Finnish National Revival. Also appreciate the stylized, gauzy, Impressionistic portraits by Helene Schjerfbeck.

▲Kamppi Chapel of Silence (Kampin Kappeli)

Sitting unassumingly on the busy, commercialism-crazy plaza in front of the Kamppi shopping mall/bus-station complex, this restful space was opened by the city of Helsinki in 2012 to give residents and visitors a place to escape the modern world. The teacup-shaped wooden structure, clad in spruce and with an oval footprint, encloses a 38-foot-tall cylinder of silence. Indirect light seeps in around the edges of the ceiling, bathing the clean, curved, alder-wood paneling in warmth and tranquility. Does it resemble Noah's Ark? The inside of an egg? The architects left it intentionally vague—up to each visitor's interpretation. Although it's a church, there are no services; the goal is to keep it open for anyone needing a reflective pause. Locals drop by between their shopping chores to sit in a pew and ponder their deity, wrestle with tough issues...or just get a break from the chaos of urban life. Along with the Church in the Rock, it's one more example of a poignant and peaceful spot where secular modern architecture and spiritual sentiment converge beautifully.

Cost and Hours: Free, Mon-Fri 7:00-20:00, Sat-Sun 10:00-18:00, Simonkatu 7, enter through adjacent low-profile black building.

Kiasma Museum

Finland's museum of contemporary art, designed by American architect Steven Holl, hosts temporary exhibitions and doesn't have a permanent collection. Ask at the TI or check online to find out what's showing.

Cost and Hours: €10, Tue 10:00-17:00, Wed-Fri 10:00-20:30, Sat 10:00-18:00, Sun 10:00-17:00, closed Mon, Mannerheiminaukio 2, near train station, tel. 0294-500-501, www.kiasma.fi.

Natural History Museum

Run by the University of Helsinki, this museum has about eight million animal specimens, the largest collection of its kind in Finland. Displays range from spiders to dinosaurs, all with English descriptions.

Cost and Hours: €10; June-Aug Tue-Sun 10:00-17:00, closed Mon; Sept-May Tue-Fri 9:00-16:00 except Thu until 18:00, Sat-Sun 10:00-16:00, closed Mon; up the street behind the Parliament at Pohjoinen Rautatiekatu 13, www.luomus.fi.

Helsinki Music Centre (Musiikkitalo)

This modern facility, open since 2011, provides a home for the arts in Helsinki. Containing seven different venues, its biggest draw may be the park that surrounds it, decorated with wildly creative contemporary art. While you can stop in anytime it's open to look around, music lovers can also consider taking in a performance (season runs Sept-April), and architecture fans may want to take an English tour.

Cost and Hours: Building open Mon-Fri 8:00-22:00, Sat 10:00-22:00, Sun 10:00-20:00; English tours offered most days in summer for €12, check website for schedule; Mannerheimintie 13A, tel. 020-707-0400, www.musiikkitalo.fi.

Finlandia Hall (Finlandia-Talo)

Alvar Aalto's most famous building in his native Finland means little to the nonarchitect without a tour. To see the building from

its best angle, view it from the seaside parking lot, not the street—where nearly everyone who looks at the building thinks, "So what?" (For the answer to that question, see page 604 of my self-guided walk, earlier.)

Cost and Hours: €12.50 for a tour, call ahead or visit website to check times; hall information shop open Mon-Fri 9:00-19:00, closed Sat-Sun; Mannerheimintie 13e, tel. 09/40241, www.finlandiatalo.fi.

▲National Museum of Finland (Kansallismuseo)

This pleasant, easy-to-handle collection is in a grand building designed by three of this country's greatest architects—including Eliel Saarinen—in the early 1900s. Divided into four sections, the exhibit chronologically traces the land of the Finns from prehistory to the 20th century. The Neoclassical furniture, folk costumes, armory, and other artifacts are interesting, but the highlights are Finland's largest permanent archaeological collection (covering the prehistory of the country) and the 20th-century exhibit,

which brings Finland's story up to the modern day. While the collection is impressive and well-described in English, those descriptions are quite dry, and the museum is a bit hard to appreciate. The interactive top-floor workshop is worth a look for its creative teaching.

Cost and Hours: €8, free on Fri 16:00-18:00; open Tue-Sun 11:00-18:00, closed Mon; Mannerheimintie 34, tel. 09/4050-9552, www.nba.fi. The museum café, with a tranquil outdoor courtyard, has light meals and Finnish treats such as lingonberry juice and reindeer quiche (open until 17:00). It's just a five-minute walk from Temppeliaukio Church.

Visiting the Museum: Following the clear English-language descriptions, visit each of the museum's four parts, in chronological order. First, straight ahead from the ticket desk is the **Prehistory of Finland,** where you'll learn how Stone, Bronze, and Iron Age tribes in this area lived. You'll see lots of early stone tools (ax and arrow heads), pottery, human remains, and—at the end of the exhibit—Iron Age weapons and jewelry.

You'll proceed into **The Realm,** which picks up the story with the Middle Ages (represented by the 14th-century St. Birgitta, Sweden's top saint). You'll pass through dimly lit halls of mostly wood-carved church art—from roughly hewn Catholic altarpieces to brightly painted, post-Reformation, Lutheran pulpits—then learn about Finland's time as part of Sweden (the introduction of the Renaissance). Continuing upstairs, you'll find out about the different social classes in historical Finland—the nobility, the peasants, the clergy, the rulers and monarchs, and the burghers (craftsmen and guild members). You'll see a Rococo-period drawing room and—transitioning from Swedish to Russian rule—portraits of Russia's last czars around an impressive throne.

From there, temporary exhibits lead back to the main hall, where you can continue into **A Land and Its People.** In this display of Finnish peasant traditions, you'll see farming and fishing tools, a thought-provoking exhibit about the indigenous Sami people (distributed across the northern reaches of Finland, Sweden, Norway, and Russia), and a particularly fine collection of beautifully decorated tools used for spinning—folk art used to make folk art.

From the folk furniture, find the stairs back down to the ground floor and the **SF-1900** exhibit (that's Suomi/Finland from 1900), starting with the birth of modern Finland in 1917 and its 1918 civil war. A six-minute loop of archival footage shows you early-20th-century Finland. Touchscreen tables help tell the story of the fledgling nation, as do plenty of well-presented artifacts (including clothing, household items, vehicles, and a traditional outhouse).

▲▲▲Temppeliaukio Church

A more modern example of great church architecture (from 1969), this "Church in the Rock" was blasted out of solid granite. It was designed by architect brothers Timo and Tuomo Suomalainen, and built within a year's time. Barren of decor except for a couple of simple crosses, the church is capped with a copper-and-skylight dome; it's normally filled with live or recorded music and awestruck visitors. Grab a pew. Gawk upward at a 13-mile-long coil of copper ribbon. Look at the bull's-eye and ponder God. Forget your camera. Just sit in the middle, ignore the crowds, and be thankful for peace...under your feet is an air-raid shelter that can accommodate 6,000 people.

Cost and Hours: Free, June-Sept Mon-Sat 10:00-17:45, Sun 11:45-17:45, closes one hour earlier off-season and for special events and concerts, Lutherinkatu 3, tel. 09/2340-6320, www.helsinginseurakunnat.fi.

Getting There: The church is at the top of a gentle hill in a residential neighborhood, about a 15-minute walk north of the bus station or a 10-minute walk behind the National Museum (or take tram #2 to Sammonkatu stop).

▲Sibelius Monument

Six hundred stainless-steel pipes called "Love of Music"—built on solid rock, as is so much of Finland—shimmer in a park to honor Finland's greatest composer, Jean Sibelius. It's a for-
est of pipe-organ pipes in a forest of trees. The artist, Eila Hiltunen, was forced to add a bust of the composer's face to silence critics of her otherwise abstract work. City orientation bus tours stop here for 10 min-
utes—long enough. Bus #24 stops here (30 minutes until the next bus, or catch a quick glimpse on the left from the bus) on its way to the Seurasaari Open-Air Folk Museum. The #2 tram, which runs more frequently, stops a few blocks away.

THE DESIGN DISTRICT, SOUTHWEST OF THE ESPLANADE

Exploring Helsinki's Design District—described in detail under "Shopping in Helsinki," later—can be a sightseeing highlight for many visitors. A good starting point is the Design Museum, which sits just a few blocks south of the Esplanade.

▲Design Museum

Design is integral to contemporary Finnish culture, and this fine museum—with a small but insightful permanent collection and well-presented temporary exhibits—offers a good overview. Worth

▲▲▲ to those who came to Finland just for the design, it's interesting to anybody.

Cost and Hours: €10; June-Aug daily 11:00-18:00; Sept-May Tue 11:00-20:00, Wed-Sun 11:00-18:00, closed Mon; Korkeavuorenkatu 23, www.designmuseum.fi.

Visiting the Museum: From the ticket desk on the ground floor, turn left and enter the permanent exhibit, called **Finnish Form.** Several actual items and good English descriptions trace the evolution of domestic design from the 1870s, when "applied arts"—merging artistic aesthetics and function—first caught on throughout Europe. You'll see how a fine line separated design and industrial production in those early days, and learn how the Finland pavilion at the 1900 World's Fair in Paris first thrust this nation onto the world design map.

In the post-WWI era (peaking in the 1930s), Functionalism focused on stripping away needless and cumbersome decoration—the goal was to boil an item down to its structural parts, and to celebrate those parts in a way that maximized both usefulness and beauty. You'll see early works by the first and last name in Finnish design, Alvar Aalto, who designed elegantly streamlined furnishings for a tuberculosis sanatorium (1929-1933). In 1935, Aalto founded the home decor company Artek—sort of a proto-Ikea—which still stands on the Esplanade (see page 622).

After World War II, Finland entered a Golden Age of design. The 1950s and 1960s saw a population boom, and the majority of Finns shifted from rural to urban lifestyles, resulting in lots of new homes that needed to be furnished. You'll see some recognizable objects here, from the characteristic "dew drop" dishes to items you may have in a drawer at your house (such as Olof Bäckströms's orange-handled scissors).

Design hit some challenges with the environmentalism and the oil crisis of the 1960s and 1970s, when the mass-production of plastics became both economically and ethically more challenging. Finnish designers recalibrated their focus to over-the-top ergonomics rather than mass production. Some of these innovations wound up as little more than quirky footnotes (such as Eero Aarnio's egg-shaped "Pallo" chair, from 1966) while others eventually went mainstream: Esko Pajamies' "Koivutaru" chair, from 1974, suspiciously resembles the Ikea "Poäng" chair that furnishes every college dorm room in America.

The present-day exhibits more or less match what you'll see in shop windows around Helsinki today, and remind us that many fixtures of contemporary American life—such as Nokia cell phones (see them evolve from huge to tiny)—were born in this tiny, obscure, chilly little European country.

Upstairs and downstairs, you'll find typically excellent **temporary exhibits** that allow individual Finnish designers to take center stage.

OUTER HELSINKI

A weeklong car trip up through the Finnish lakes and forests to Mikkeli and Savonlinna would be relaxing, but you can actually enjoy Finland's green-trees-and-blue-water scenery without leaving Helsinki. Here are three great ways to get out and go for a walk on a sunny summer day. If you have time, do at least one of them during your stay.

▲▲Suomenlinna Fortress

The island guarding Helsinki's harbor served as a strategic fortress for three countries: Finland, Sweden, and Russia. It's now a popular park, with delightful paths, fine views, and a visitors center. On a sunny day, it's a delightful place to stroll among hulking buildings with recreating Finns. The free Suomenlinna guidebooklet (stocked at the Helsinki TI, ferry terminal, and the visitors center) cov-

ers the island thoroughly. The island has one good museum (the Suomenlinna Museum, at Suomenlinna Centre—described later) and several skippable smaller museums, including a toy museum and several military museums (€3-4 each, open summer only).

Getting There: Catch a ferry to Suomenlinna from Market Square. Walk past the high-priced excursion boats to the public HKL ferry (€5 round-trip, covered by day ticket and Helsinki Card, 15-minute trip, May-Aug 2-3/hour—generally at :00, :20, and :40 past the hour, but pick up schedule to confirm; Sept-April every 40-60 minutes). If you'll be taking at least two tram rides within 24 hours of visiting Suomenlinna, it pays to get a day ticket instead of a round-trip ticket. A private ferry, JT Line, also runs a "water bus" to Suomenlinna from Market Square in summer (€7 round-trip, May-Sept 2/hour, tel. 09/534-806, www.jt-line.fi). As it costs a bit more and runs less frequently, the JT Line is only worthwhile if you're in a rush to get to the Suomenlinna Centre and museum (since the water bus uses a dock here instead of the northern port used by the public ferry).

Tours: The one-hour English-language island tour departs

Suomenlinna Timeline

1748—Construction began on Sveaborg ("Sweden Fortress").

1788—The fort was used as a base for a Swedish war against Russia.

1808—It was surrendered by Sweden to Russia.

1809—Finland became part of the Russian Empire, and the fort was used as a Russian garrison for 108 years.

1855—French and British navies bombarded the fort during the Crimean War, inflicting heavy damage.

1917—Finland declared independence.

1918—The fort was annexed by Finland and renamed Suomenlinna ("Finland Fortress").

1939—The fort served as a base for the Finnish navy.

1973—The Finnish garrison moved out, the fort's administration was transferred to the Ministry of Education, and the fort was opened to the public.

from the Suomenlinna Centre (€10, free with Helsinki Card; June-Aug daily at 11:00, 12:30, and 14:30; Sept-May 1/day Sat-Sun only). The tour is fine if you're a military history buff, but it kind of misses the point of what's now essentially a giant playground for all ages.

Background: The fortress was built by the Swedes with French financial support in the mid-1700s to counter Russia's rise to power. (Russian Czar Peter the Great had built his new capital, St. Petersburg, on the Baltic and was eyeing the West.) Named Sveaborg ("Fortress of Sweden"), the fortress was Sweden's military pride and joy. With five miles of walls and hundreds of cannons, it was the second strongest fort of its kind in Europe after Gibraltar. Helsinki, a small community of 1,500 people before 1750, soon became a boomtown supporting this grand "Gibraltar of the North."

The fort, built by more than 10,000 workers, was a huge investment and stimulated lots of innovation. In the 1760s, it had the world's biggest and most modern dry dock. It served as a key naval base during a brief Russo-Swedish war in 1788-1790. But in 1808, the Russians took the "invincible" fort without a fight—by siege—as a huge and cheap military gift.

Today, Suomenlinna has 1,000 permanent residents, is home to Finland's Naval Academy, and is most appreciated by locals for its fine scenic strolls. The island is large—actually, it's six islands connected by bridges—and you and your imagination get free run of the fortifications and dungeon-like chambers. When it's time to eat, you'll find a half-dozen cafés and plenty of picnic opportunities.

Visiting Suomenlinna: Across from the public ferry landing are the Jetty Barracks, housing a small information desk (a good place to pick up the free island map/booklet, if you haven't already), convenient WC, free modern art exhibit, and the pricey Panimo brewpub/restaurant. From here, start your stroll of the island. You'll wander on cobbles past dilapidated shiplap cottages that evoke a more robust time for this once-strategic, now-leisurely island. The garrison church on your left, which was Orthodox until its 20th-century conversion to Lutheranism, doubled as a lighthouse.

A five-minute walk from the ferry brings you to the **Suomenlinna Centre,** which houses the worthwhile Suomenlinna Museum. Inside the (free) lobby, you'll find an information desk, gift shop, café, and giant model of all six islands that make up Suomenlinna—handy for orientation. The exhibits themselves are well-presented but dryly explained: fragments of old walls, cannons, period clothing, model ships, and so on; the upstairs focuses on the site's transition from a fortress to a park. The main attraction is the fascinating 25-minute "multivision" show, presenting the island's complete history, which runs twice hourly and has a headphone soundtrack in English (€6.50 for museum and film, daily May-Sept 10:00-18:00, Oct-April 10:30-16:30, tel. 09/684-1850, www.suomenlinna.fi).

From the Suomenlinna Centre, cross the bridge—noticing the giant, rusted seaplane hall on the right, housing the Regatta Club, with a fun sailboat photo exhibition and shop. On the far side of the hall, peer into the gigantic dry dock.

Back on the main trail, climb five minutes uphill to the right into **Piper Park** (Piperin Puisto). Hike up past its elegant 19th-

century café (with rocky view tables), and continue up and over the ramparts to a surreal swimming area. From here, follow the waterline—and the ramparts—to the south. You'll walk above bunkers burrowed underground, like gigantic molehills (or maybe Hobbit houses). Periodic ladders let you scramble down onto the rocks. Imposing cannons, now used as playsets and photo-op props for kids, are still aimed ominously at the Gulf of Finland—in case, I imagine, of Russian invasion...or if they just get fed up with all of those cruise ships. Reaching the southern tip of the island, called King's Gate, peek out through the cannon holes. Then make your walk a loop by circling back to the Suomenlinna Centre and, beyond that, the ferry dock for the ride home.

HELSINKI

Peninsula Promenade

For a breezy, salty seaside walk, consider this promenade around the Kaivopuisto Park peninsula. Allow 1.5 hours at a leisurely pace. From Market Square, wander past the brick Old Market Hall and Tallink Silja terminal (with its huge ship likely at the dock) and follow the shoreline pedestrian path. The first island you come to, Valkosaari, hosts the local yacht club—NJK—the oldest in Scandinavia, with a classy restaurant (daily 17:00-24:00). The next island, Luoto, is home to the posh Palace Kämp by the Sea restaurant (with shuttle boat service). During a typical winter, the bay freezes (18 inches of ice is strong enough to allow cars to drive to the islands—in the past there was even a public bus route that extended to an island during the winter). The fortress island of Suomenlinna is in the distance. The hill you're circling (on the right) is home to several embassies; ahead, Ursula Café, with its fine harbor views, is good for a coffee break.

Around the corner, the next island, Uunisaari, belonged to the military until the 1980s. Its unique plant life (much studied by local students) is believed to have hitched a ride all the way to Finland from Siberia on the boots of Russian soldiers. The odd-looking pier nearby is a station for washing rugs (those are not picnic tables). Saltwater brightens the rag rugs traditionally made by local grandmas. While American men put on aprons and do the barbecue, Finnish men wash the carpets. After the scrub, the rugs are sent through big mechanical wringers and hung on nearby racks to dry in the wind. The posted map shows 11 such stations scattered around Helsinki. Buy an ice cream at the nearby stand and watch the action (best in the morning).

In the distance looms Helsinki's big new West Harbor port, hosting 300 cruise ships a year. From here you can follow Neitsyt-polku street back to the town center, keeping an eye out for fun Art Nouveau buildings.

▲▲Seurasaari Open-Air Folk Museum

Inspired by Stockholm's Skansen, also on a lovely island on the edge of town, this is a collection of 100 historic buildings from every corner of Finland. It's wonder-

fully furnished and gives rushed visitors an opportunity to sample the far reaches of Finland without leaving the capital city. If you're not taking a tour, get the €1.20 map or the helpful €6 guidebook. You're welcome to bring a picnic, or you can have a light lunch (snacks and cakes) in the Antti farmstead at the center of the park.

Off-season, when the buildings are closed, the place is empty and not worth the trouble.

Cost and Hours: Free park entry, €8 to enter buildings; June-Aug daily 11:00-17:00; late May and early Sept Mon-Fri 9:00-15:00, Sat-Sun 11:00-17:00; buildings closed mid-Sept-mid-May; tel. 09/4050-9660, www.seurasaari.fi.

Tours: English tours are free with €8 entry ticket, offered mid-June-mid-Aug generally at 15:00, and take one hour (confirm times on their website).

Getting There: To reach the museum, ride bus #24 (from the top of the Esplanade, 2/hour) to the end (note departure times for your return) and walk across the quaint footbridge.

NEAR HELSINKI

Porvoo, the second-oldest town in Finland, has wooden architecture that dates from the Swedish colonial period. This coastal town can be reached from Helsinki by bus (one hour) or by excursion boat from Market Square.

Turku, the historic capital of Finland, is a two-hour bus or train ride from Helsinki. Overall, Turku is a pale shadow of Helsinki, and there is little reason to make a special trip. It does have a handicraft museum in a cluster of wooden houses (the only part of town to survive a devastating fire in the early 1800s), an old castle, a fine Gothic cathedral (this was the first part of Finland to be Christianized, in the 12th century), and a market square. Viking and Tallink Silja boats sail from Turku to Stockholm every morning and evening, passing through the especially scenic Turku archipelago.

Naantali, a cute, commercial, well-preserved medieval town with a quaint harbor, is an easy 20-minute bus ride from Turku.

Shopping in Helsinki

Helsinki may be the top shopping town in the Nordic countries. Even in this region that prides itself on its creative design culture, Helsinki is a trendsetter; many Finnish designers are household names worldwide. Plus, the city's rather chilly architecture and weather often force people inside, making browsing in the shops a productive thing to do while escaping from a passing squall. The easiest place to get a taste of Finnish design is along the Esplanade, but with even a little more time, it's worth delving into the nearby Design District.

Opening Times: Most shops are open all day long Mondays through Fridays (generally 10:00 until 17:00 or 18:00), and often have shorter hours on Saturday (likely opening at 10:00 or 12:00 and closing around 16:00), and most are closed on Sundays. Larger shops have longer hours, including brief opening hours on Sundays. While specific hours are not listed for each shop below, I have noted those that seriously buck these trends (and you can find complete hours for any shop online).

ALONG THE ESPLANADE

Helsinki's elegant main drag, the Esplanade, is a coffee-sipper's and window-shopper's delight. Practically every big name in Finn-

ish design (and there are lots of them) has a flagship store along this people-pleasing strip. These tend to be open a bit longer than the hours noted above; most are open until 19:00 (or even 20:00) on weekdays, until 17:00 on Saturdays, and even on Sundays (typically 12:00-16:00 or 17:00).

On my self-guided walk, earlier, I pointed out several Esplanade shops worth dipping into: Consider the purses, scarves, clothes, and fabrics from **Marimekko,** the well-known Finnish fashion company famous for striped designs (at #33A, www.marimekko. com). Two more Marimekko branches are a short walk away: one specializing in children's items halfway up the cross-street, Mikonkatu, at #2D; and another specializing in clothing one block farther up the Esplanade, then right up Keskuskatu to the intersection with Aleksanterinkatu. **Aarikka** (#27C, www.aarikka.com) and **Iittala** (#25B, www.iittala.com) have Finnish housewares and ceramics, while **Kalevala** (at #27C, along with Aarikka) sells finely crafted, handmade jewelry (www.kalevalakoru.com).

Across the street, on the south side of the Esplanade, are more shops: **Artek,** Alvar and Elissa Aalto's flagship store (#18, www. artek.fi); **Finlayson** is a more affordable option for Finnish home decor and design (one block closer to the harbor at #14, www. finlayson.fi).

The Esplanade is capped by the enormous, eight-floor **Stockmann** department store, arguably Scandinavia's most impressive (Mon-Fri 9:00-21:00, Sat 9:00-18:00, Sun 12:00-18:00, great basement supermarket, Aleksanterinkatu 52B, www.stockmann. fi). Bookworms enjoy the impressive **Academic Bookstore** just downhill from Stockmann (#39, same hours as Stockmann).

Fans of Tove Jansson's Moomin children's stories will enjoy the **Moomin Shop,** on the second floor of the Forum shopping mall at Mannerheimintie 20, across the busy tram-lined street from Stockmann (Mon-Fri 9:00-21:00, Sat 9:00-18:00, Sun 12:00-18:00, www.moomin.fi).

THE DESIGN DISTRICT

Helsinki's Design District is a several-block cluster of streets that are lined with a dizzying array of one-off boutiques, galleries, and other shops highlighting local designers. From high fashion to comfy everyday clothes, and from lovingly handcrafted jewelry to clever kitchen doodads, this is an engaging zone to explore. For a handy orientation to the options in this ever-changing area, visit www.designdistrict.fi, and get tips at the TI—they often hand out maps or brochures illustrating your options.

While the Design District sprawls—roughly southwest of the Esplanade nearly all the way to the waterfront—the following sub-areas are most worthy of exploration.

Kolmikulma Park and Nearby

Just a block south of the Esplanade's top end (down Erottajanka-tu), the park called Kolmikulma (literally "Triangular," also called Diana Park for its spear-throwing statue centerpiece) is a handy epicenter of Design District liveliness. From here, streets fan out to the west. A few choices ring the park itself, while several more line the streets that stretch southwest.

Uudenmaankatu has the highest concentration of shops, especially fashion boutiques of local designers. **Nounou** (on the left, at #2) has very colorful glass pieces (open only Tue, Thu, and Sat); the recommended **Café Bar No. 9,** across the street, is a popular place to grab a filling meal. Farther along, **Astra Taivas** (on the right, at #13) is a hole-in-the-wall crammed with precarious shelves of secondhand glassware—causing even the most cautious visitor to feel like the proverbial bull in a china shop. At the end of the block, **Ivana Helsinki** (at #15, on the right) has pattered casual dresses. A detour to the right up the next street (Annankatu) takes you to **Momono,** a tight and endearing shop highlighting Finnish design (on the left at Annankatu 12).

Back on Uudenmaankatu, it's just one more (less interesting) block to Fredrikinkatu, with a lot more choices (described next).

Meanwhile, a block south, pedestrianized **Iso Roobertinkatu** has a few more less interesting choices, and also has lots of cheap eateries. **Formverk,** at the corner with Annankatu, has fun home decor and kitchenware (Annankatu 5).

Fredrikinkatu

This street, which crosses Uudenmaankatu two blocks west of the park, is one of the most engaging streets in town. (For a sneak peek of the many shops lining this street—only a few of which are noted here—see www.fredashops.fi.)

At the corner with Uudenmaankatu, **C. Hagelstam** is an antiquariat with cool vintage prints and antique books, while across the street, **Peroba** (at Uudenmaankatu 33) displays bold Scan design. From here, head north along Fredrikinkatu, which is lined with mostly fashion designers, plus **Kauniste** (on the left at #24, uniquely patterned fabrics and prints) and, at the end of the block on the left, **Chez Marius** (#26, a world of fun kitchen gadgets and cooking gear). This shop also marks the pleasant intersection with the tree- and tram-lined Bulevardi. **Day,** kitty-corner from the Chez Marius, has funky, quirky home decor and gifts (Bulevardi 11).

Continuing north across Bulevardi and along Fredrikinkatu, the next block has several home decor shops, including **Casuarina** (on the left at #30, with a spare, rustic, reclaimed aesthetic), and **Primavera Interiors** (across the street at #41, with a more artistic and funky style).

Browse your way two more blocks up Fredrikinkatu to the cross-street, **Eerikinkatu,** which also has lots of inviting little galleries and boutiques; two are at the same address, just around the corner to the left (at Eerikinkatu 18): **DesiPeli,** with a variety of home decor, including some very cool, Marimekko-type fabrics (closed Sun-Mon); and **Napa & Paja,** a collective gallery of three jewelry designers, showcasing their beautiful, unique, delicate designs. They also stock casual handbags and books about Finland.

Near the Design Museum

The Design Museum—a worthwhile stop in its own right (see "Sights in Helsinki," earlier), three long blocks south of the middle of the Esplanade on Korkeavuorenkatu—anchors an appealing area of boutiques. Continuing south of the museum about one block on **Korkeavuorenkatu,** you'll find vintage shops, kitchenware, antiques, pop-up stores, fashion boutiques, hair salons, and cafés. In particular, keep an eye out for **Pore Helsinki** (at #3), with casual fashion and accessories; and **Fasaani** (at #5). Fasaani (a.k.a. Helsinki Secondhand) is particularly worth a detour for bargain-hunters. It's a sprawling warren of an antique shop, with more than 10,000 square feet crammed with affordable pre-owned versions of many of the same home-decor items you'll see in galleries around town—furniture, dishes, glassware, and more. This place would be equally perfect for furnishing a Helsinki hipster flat or a remote cottage in the Finnish wilds (Mon-Fri 10:00-18:00, Sat 10:00-16:00, closed Sun, Korkeavuorenkatu 5, www.fasaani.fi).

OTHER SHOPPING OPTIONS

Market Square: This harborfront square is packed not only with fishmongers and producers, but also with stands selling Finnish souvenirs and more refined crafts (roughly Mon-Fri 6:30-17:00—or until 18:00 in summer, Sat 6:30-16:00, only tourist stalls open on Sun 10:00-16:00).

Modern Shopping Mall: For less glamorous shopping needs, the **Kamppi** mall above and around the bus station is good.

Flea Market: If you brake for garage sales, Finland's biggest flea market, the outdoor **Hietalahti Market,** is worth the 15-minute walk from the harbor or a short ride on tram #6 from Mannerheimintie to the Hietalahdentori stop (June-Aug Mon-Fri 9:00-19:00, Sat 8:00-16:00, Sun 10:00-16:00; less action,

shorter hours, and closed Sun off-season). The adjacent red-brick indoor Hietalahti Market Hall houses food stands (described later, under "Eating in Helsinki").

Sleeping in Helsinki

I've listed a wide range of accommodations in Helsinki, from fancy, well-located big hotels, to modest but cozy smaller hotels, to some unusually comfortable hostels that rent plenty of twin-bedded rooms. Also remember that some of the cheapest beds in Helsinki are on the overnight boats to Stockholm.

Every hotel in Helsinki employs "dynamic pricing," which means that rates for a room can fluctuate wildly from day to day. Peak-season months (with lots of business travel, as well as lots of tourism) are May, June, August, and September. July tends to be a bit slower (little to no domestic business travel), but it can still be busy with the tourist trade. The once-predictable patterns of deeply discounted rooms on weekends and in July and August no longer hold true.

This makes it tricky to give specific rates here. I've tried to list what you can expect, on average, for a standard double room in high season—but prices can range dramatically above and below what I list. Check hotel websites for exact rates. Better yet, plug your dates into a room-finding website (like Booking.com) to see what a variety of hotels are offering for the specific date(s) you're in town, then use my listings to decide which suits your style the best. Once you've determined the best deal, book directly with the hotel (which cuts out the middleman and could snare you an even better price).

HOTELS
On Friday and Saturday nights and from late June to early August, Helsinki's more expensive hotels (the ones denoted with **$$$**) usu-

---

Sleep Code

Abbreviations   **(€1 = about $1.40, country code: 358)**
S = Single, **D** = Double/Twin, **T** = Triple, **Q** = Quad, **b** = bathroom
Price Rankings

  $$$ **Higher Priced**—Most rooms €150 or more.

   $$ **Moderately Priced**—Most rooms €80-150.

    $ **Lower Priced**—Most rooms €80 or less.

Unless otherwise noted, credit cards are accepted, English is spoken, breakfast is included, and Wi-Fi is generally free. Public areas of all hotels are non-smoking, though a few still have rooms designated for smokers—if you're not one, you can request a non-smoking room. Prices change; verify current rates online or by email. For the best prices, always book directly with the hotel.

---

ally have great deals. Checking the hotel's own website can save you a bundle; the best deals are for a nonrefundable reservation.

$$$ Hotel Haven, with 77 elegantly appointed, comfortable rooms and a lobby that artfully mingles class and rustic comfort, owns a convenient location near both the harbor and the Esplanade. "Standard" rooms face the back, with some street noise; quieter "style" rooms face the harbor (but with no views). It's worth a splurge, particularly if you can snare a deal (rates change constantly but typically Db-€219 on weekdays or €184 on weekends, €30 more for a non-view "style" room, €80 more for a "deluxe" seaview room, air-con, Wi-Fi, elevator, Unioninkatu 17, tel. 09/681-930, www.hotelhaven.fi).

$$$ Hotel Rivoli Jardin is a cozy place with a handy location, tucked away just off the middle of the Esplanade and above the harbor. Warm and personal, it has an inviting lounge and 55 rooms with classic Finnish comfort and a few classy flourishes (Db-about €190, discounted to around €110 in summer and on weekends, bigger "superior" room for €20 extra also includes Wi-Fi—otherwise pay Wi-Fi, extra bed-€30, elevator, air-con, Kasarmikatu 40, tel. 09/681-500, www.rivoli.fi, rivoli.jardin@rivoli.fi). They also have 13 apartments (figure €150 for a 1-bedroom, €190 for a 2-bedroom).

$$$ Hotel Fabian, Hotel Haven's sister property a few blocks from the Esplanade, has 58 spacious and comfortable rooms with a black-and-white color scheme (standard "comfort" Db-€200 but can be as low as €130 in slow times, €30 more for bigger and sleeker "style" room, €60 more for "luxe" room with kitchenette, air-con, elevator, Wi-Fi, Fabianinkatu 7, tel. 09/6128-2000, www.hotelfabian.fi, sales@hotelfabian.fi).

$$$ Hotel Katajanokka is a former red-brick prison built in

1888. Its last prisoner checked out in 2002, and it was converted in 2007 into a four-star, business-class hotel. Its 106 rooms are very quiet—the walls are so thick that the hotel provides free Internet cables rather than Wi-Fi. While the windows no longer have bars (thanks to the local fire code) and walls have been removed so that two or three cells make a room, you can still imagine the guards strolling up and down the corridors. Check out the two original cells in the restaurant (Db-€170, around €110 in slow times, €10 more for a twin room, elevator, gym, bike rental, by Vyökatu stop of tram #4 near the Viking cruise ship terminal, Merikasarminka-tu 1A, tel. 09/686-450, www.bwkatajanokka.fi, reception@bwkatajanokka.fi).

$$$ Scandic Grand Marina, a huge 462-room, impersonal four-star hotel filling a big, brick warehouse building near the Viking cruise ship terminal, discounts its doubles from about €190 down to €105 (air-con, elevator, Wi-Fi, Katajanokanlaituri 7, tel. 09/16661, www.scandichotels.com/grandmarina, grandmarina@scandichotels.com).

$$$ GLO Hotel Art has 171 modern rooms behind a striking Art Nouveau facade that makes it feel like a stony medieval château has landed in the middle of Helsinki (Db-€150, elevator, air-con, Wi-Fi, Lönnrotinkatu 29, tel. 010-344-4100, www.glohotels.fi, art@glohotels.fi).

$$$ GLO Hotel Kluuvi, which has 184 rooms and a well-designed spa-type quality, gives you an appreciation for how an extremely wealthy society manages to survive a long, dark winter. This temping splurge is quite trendy and a bit snobby. Perfectly situated just north of the Esplanade, it's worth considering if you prize elegance and location—especially if you can get a good discount (Db-€264, €10 less for a "small" room or €20 more for a "large" room, air-con, elevator, Wi-Fi, Kluuvikatu 4, tel. 010-3444-400, www.glohotels.fi).

$$ Hotel Anna is conscientiously run, reasonably priced, and feels like home. Its 64 well-worn rooms help raise funds for the Finnish Free Church (it's actually attached to a church—ask them to show you the shortcut to the choir loft). For more air in the rooms, ask at the desk for a key to open the larger windows (Sb-€110, Db-€145, extra bed-€15, reserve directly by email and mention this book for best prices—generally a 10 percent discount off prevailing rate, worth checking website for deals, 2-room Qb and family rooms available, elevator, guest computer, Wi-Fi, 4 blocks south of the top of the Esplanade—take tram #2/#3 to Iso Roober-tinkatu, Annankatu 1, tel. 09/616-621, www.hotelanna.fi, info@hotelanna.fi).

$$ Hotelli Finn is inexpensive and wonderfully central. Its 35 rooms are stowed quietly on the sixth floor of an office building

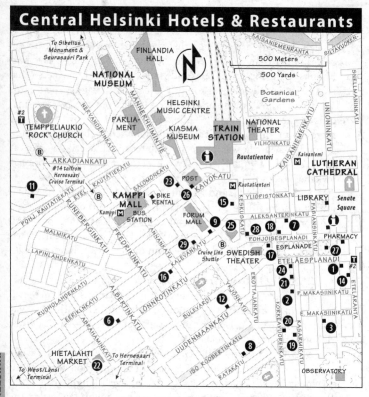

Central Helsinki Hotels & Restaurants

near the top of the Esplanade. It's also consciously short on amenities: no shower curtains in the tiny bathrooms, no desks or chairs in
the rooms, no breakfast (though a nearby bakery offers a €7 buffet
spread), and no real lobby or common space—just a dark, somewhat gloomy hallway. The price and location are right, though, and
it's worth considering for a quick stay when other places aren't dis-
counting (Sb-€69, Db-€79-99—up to €129 at busy times, third or
fourth person-about €15, best to reserve on website, elevator, Wi-
Fi, Kalevankatu 3B, tel. 09/684-4360, www.hotellifinn.fi, info@
hotellifinn.fi).

$ Essex Home is a good budget alternative. Sweet Seija Lap-
palainen rents 13 apartments (all with kitchenettes) scattered
around the residential streets of the Katajanokka peninsula (rates
vary but generally studio Db-€69, 1-bedroom Db-€125, expect
lots of stairs, Wi-Fi, Luotsikatu 9A, mobile 040-516-2714, www.
essexhome.fi, info@essexhome.fi). The two "Essex Studio" rooms
are a bit farther out.

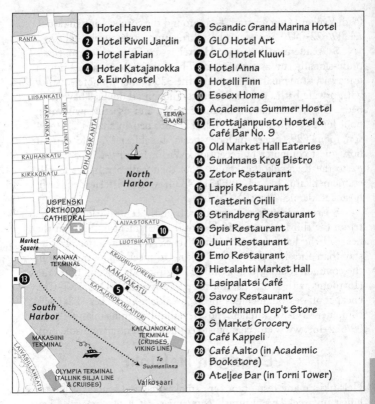

① Hotel Haven
② Hotel Rivoli Jardin
③ Hotel Fabian
④ Hotel Katajanokka & Eurohostel
⑤ Scandic Grand Marina Hotel
⑥ GLO Hotel Art
⑦ GLO Hotel Kluuvi
⑧ Hotel Anna
⑨ Hotelli Finn
⑩ Essex Home
⑪ Academica Summer Hostel
⑫ Erottajanpuisto Hostel & Café Bar No. 9
⑬ Old Market Hall Eateries
⑭ Sundmans Krog Bistro
⑮ Zetor Restaurant
⑯ Lappi Restaurant
⑰ Teatterin Grilli
⑱ Strindberg Restaurant
⑲ Spis Restaurant
⑳ Juuri Restaurant
㉑ Emo Restaurant
㉒ Hietalahti Market Hall
㉓ Lasipalatsi Café
㉔ Savoy Restaurant
㉕ Stockmann Dep't Store
㉖ S Market Grocery
㉗ Café Kappeli
㉘ Café Aalto (in Academic Bookstore)
㉙ Ateljee Bar (in Torni Tower)

HOSTELS

Helsinki's hostels are unusually comfortable. While they offer €3 discounts for those with hostel cards, all ages are welcome with or without a hostel membership. Eurohostel and Academica are more like budget hotels than hostels.

$ Eurohostel, a modern hostel with 255 beds in 35 rooms, is 400 yards from the Viking ferry terminal and a 10-minute walk from Market Square. The more expensive rooms come with TVs. It's packed with facilities, including a laundry room, a members' kitchen with unique refrigerated safety-deposit boxes for your caviar and beer, a restaurant, and plenty of good budget-travel information. While generally fully booked in advance, they release no-show beds at 18:00. In the following rates, the lower price is for the older "backpacker" rooms, while the higher price is for the newer "Eurohostel" rooms (S-€47/€53, D-€56/€63, T-€75/€85, family room with up to 4 kids under age 15-€66/€74, shared twins available, includes sheets; breakfast-€9, free morning sauna, evening sauna-€7.50, private lockable closets, pay Wi-Fi, laundry-€3/

load, Vyökatu stop for tram #4 is around the corner, Linnankatu 9, tel. 09/622-0470, www.eurohostel.fi, eurohostel@eurohostel.fi).

$ Academica Summer Hostel is a university dorm that's professionally run as a hostel from June through August. Finnish university students have it good—the 326 rooms are hotel-quality with private baths and kitchenettes, though all doubles have twin beds. Guests can have a morning sauna and use the swimming pool for free (Sb-€49, Db-€62, Tb-€85, bed in shared 2-3-person room-€29, prices include sheets, breakfast-€7, safe deposit box, guest computer by reception, Wi-Fi, laundry-€5/load; tram #2 to the Kauppakorkeakoulut stop, then walk 5 minutes to Hietaniemenkatu 14, tel. 09/1311-4334, www.hostelacademica.fi, hostel.academica@hyy.fi).

$ Erottajanpuisto is a smaller, friendly, centrally located hostel on the third floor of a 19th-century apartment building in the heart of the happening Design District. This is a better place to stay than Eurohostel if you're looking to meet fellow travelers in the common room and don't mind lugging your bags up the stairs (15 rooms with 2-8 beds, dorm bed-€30, S-€60, D-€75, T-€99, cheaper off-season, includes sheets, breakfast-€7, lockers-€2, guest computer, Wi-Fi, kitchen, no elevator, Uudenmaankatu 9, tel. 09/642-169, www.erottajanpuisto.com, info@erottajanpuisto.com).

Eating in Helsinki

Helsinki's many restaurants are smoke-free and a good value for lunch on weekdays. Finnish companies get a tax break if they distribute lunch coupons (worth €9) to their employees. It's no surprise that most downtown Helsinki restaurants offer weekday lunch specials that cost exactly the value of the coupon. These low prices evaporate in the evenings and all day Saturday and Sunday, when picnics and Middle Eastern kebab restaurants are the only budget options. Dinner reservations are smart at nicer restaurants.

FUN HARBORFRONT EATERIES

Stalls on Market Square: Helsinki's delightful and vibrant square is magnetic any time of day...but especially at lunchtime. This really is the most memorable, casual, quick-and-cheap lunch place in town. A half-dozen orange tents (erected to shield diners from bird bombs) serve fun food on paper plates until 18:00. It's not unusual for the Finnish president to stop by here with visiting dignitaries. There's a crêpe place, and at the far end—my favorites—several salmon grills (€10-13 for a good meal). The only real harborside dining in this part of town is picnicking. While these places provide picnic tables, you can also have your food foil-wrapped to go and grab benches right on the water down near Uspenski Orthodox Cathedral.

Old Market Hall (Vanha Kauppahalli): Just beyond the harborside market is a cute, red-brick, indoor market hall. It's beautifully renovated with upscale-feeling woodwork, and quite tight inside (Mon-Sat 8:00-18:00, closed Sun). Today, along with produce stalls, it's a hit for its fun, inexpensive eateries. You'll find lots of enticing coffee shops with tempting pastries; various grilled, smoked, or pickled fish options (you'll smell it before you see it); mounds of bright-yellow paella; deli counters with delectable open-face sandwiches; a handy chance to sample reindeer meat; and an array of ethnic eats, from Middle Eastern and Lebanese meals to Vietnamese banh mi sandwiches. In the market hall, **Soppakeittiö** ("Soup Kitchen") serves big bowls of filling, tasty seafood soup for €9.50, including bread and water (Mon-Fri 11:00-16:00, Sat 11:00-15:00—except closed Sat in summer, closed Sun year-round).

Sundmans Krog Bistro is sedate and Old World but not folkloric, filling an old merchant's mansion facing the harbor. As it's the less fussy and more affordable (yet still super-romantic) little sister of an adjacent, posh, Michelin-rated restaurant, quality is assured. A rare and memorable extra is their Baltic fish buffet—featuring salmon, Baltic sprat, and herring with potatoes and all the toppings—€15 as a starter, €25 as a main course. The €19 lunch special (Mon-Fri 11:00-15:00) includes the buffet plus the main dish of the week—often more fish (€23-25 main courses, €40 three-course dinners, Mon-Fri 11:00-23:00, Sat 12:00-23:00, Sun 13:00-23:00, Eteläranta 16, tel. 09/6128-5450).

FINNISH-THEMED DINING: TRACTORS AND LAPP CUISINE

Zetor, the self-proclaimed *traktor* restaurant, mercilessly lampoons Finnish rural culture and cuisine (while celebrating it deep down). It's the kitschy Finnish answer to the Cracker Barrel. Sit next to a cow-crossing sign at a tractor-turned-into-a-table, in a "Finnish Western" atmosphere reminiscent of director Aki Kaurismäki's movies. For lunch or dinner, main courses run €17-23 and include reindeer, vendace (small freshwater fish), and less exotic fare. This place, while touristy and tacky, can be fun. It gets loud after 20:00 when the dance floor gets going (daily 12:00-24:00, 200 yards north of Stockmann department store, across street from McDonald's at Mannerheimintie 3, tel. 010-766-4450).

Lappi Restaurant is a fine place for Lapp cuisine, with an entertaining menu (they smoke their own fish) and creative decor that has you thinking you've traveled north and lashed your reindeer to the hitchin' post. The friendly staff serves tasty Sami dishes in a snug and very woody atmosphere. Dinner reservations are strongly recommended (€24-39 main courses, Mon-Fri 16:00-24:00, Sat 13:00-24:00, closed Sun, off Bulevardi at Annankatu 22, tel. 09/645-550, www.lappires.com).

VENERABLE ESPLANADE CAFÉS

Highly competitive restaurants line the sunny north side of the Esplanade—offering creative lunch salads and light meals in their cafés (with fine sidewalk seating), plush sofas for cocktails in their bars, and fancy restaurant dining upstairs.

Teatterin Grilli, attached to the landmark Swedish Theater, has several interconnected eateries inside and fine, park-side seating indoors and out. Order a salad from the café counter in the "Wine & Deli & Juice" bar, facing the Academic Bookstore (€10 with bread, choose two meats or extras to add to crispy base, Caesar salad option). The long cocktail bar is popular with office workers yet comfortable for baby-boomer tourists. Whether you order a meal or a drink, you're welcome to find a seat out on the leafy Esplanade terrace (café counter open Mon-Fri 9:00-20:30, Sat 11:00-20:30, Sun 12:00-20:30 except closed Sun in winter, at the top of the Esplanade, Pohjoisesplanadi 2, tel. 09/6128-5000). There's also a fancy restaurant.

Strindberg, near the corner of the Esplanade and Mikonkatu, has several parts—each one oozing atmosphere and class. Downstairs is an elegant café with outdoor and indoor tables great for people-watching (€8-15 sandwiches and salads). The upstairs cocktail lounge—with big sofas and bookshelves giving it a den-like coziness—attracts the after-work office crowd. Also upstairs, the inviting restaurant has huge main dishes for €20-30, with fish, meat, pasta, and vegetarian options; reserve in advance to try to get a window seat overlooking the Esplanade (restaurant open Mon 11:00-23:00, Tue-Sat 11:00-24:00, closed Sun; café open Mon 9:00-23:00, Tue-Sat 9:00-24:00, Sun 10:00-22:00, Pohjoisesplanadi 33, tel. 09/681-2030).

TRENDY EATERIES IN AND NEAR THE DESIGN DISTRICT

Predictably, several creative eateries cluster in the Design District, a short stroll south and west of the Esplanade. While these aren't for budget diners, they do offer a fresh and updated take on the cuisine of Finland. Many of these highlight the exciting "New Nordic" school of cooking, featuring fresh, seasonal, local ingredients—often foraged—with modern presentation (for more on New Nordic, see page 114).

Spis is your best Helsinki bet for splurging on Finnish New Nordic. Reserve ahead for one of the prized tables in its tiny, peeling-plaster, rustic-chic dining room (tasting menus only: €57/4 courses, €77/6 courses, Tue-Sat from 17:30, last seating at 20:30, closed Sun-Mon, Kasarmikatu 26, mobile 045-305-1211, www. spis.fi).

Juuri has a trendy, casual interior and serves a variety of "sapas" (Suomi tapas)—small plates highlighting Finland's culinary bounty. It's lunch-only on weekdays, but open for dinner on weekends (€5 small plates, €28 main courses, Mon-Fri 11:00-14:30 only, Sat 12:00-22:00, Sun 16:00-22:00, Korkeavuorenkatu 27, tel. 09/635-732).

Emo Restaurant is a pleasantly unpretentious, blue-jeans wine bar in a sleepy zone just a block off of the Esplanade. They serve up €10 small plates; most patrons share several (lunch Tue-Thu 11:30-14:30; dinner Mon-Sat 17:00-24:00, closed Sun; Kasarmikatu 44, mobile 010-505-0900, www.emo-ravintola.fi).

Pub Grub: **Café Bar No. 9** is a simpler, cheaper choice right in the heart of the Design District. Tucked between design shops, its borderline-divey bar vibe attracts a loyal local following, who enjoy digging into plates of unpretentious pub food (€10-16 meals, Uudenmaakatu 9, tel. 09-621-4059).

Market Hall: Hiding in a nondescript neighborhood at the edge of the Design District, the **Hietalahti Market Hall** is a fun place to browse for a meal. It's similar to the Old Market Hall along the South Harbor, but far less touristy. The elegantly renovated old food hall is filled with an enticing array of vendors, with delightful seating upstairs (Mon-Fri 8:00-18:00, Sat 8:00-17:00, closed Sun).

FUNCTIONAL EATING

Lasipalatsi, the renovated, rejuvenated 1930s Glass Palace, is on Mannerheimintie between the train and bus stations. The café (with a youthful terrace on the square out back) offers a self-service buffet (€10 weekday lunch before 15:00, €17 weekend brunch, €13 dinner after 15:00 any day); there are always €5 sandwiches and cakes (Mon-Fri 7:30-22:00, Sat 9:00-23:00, Sun 11:00-22:00, more expensive restaurant upstairs—closed Sun, across from post office at Mannerheimintie 22, tel. 09/612-6700).

DRESSY SPLURGE DINNERS

Savoy Restaurant, where locals go for special occasions, is expensive, formal, and drenched in Alvar Aalto design. Everything—from the chairs and lampshades to the doors—is 1937 original. The food is Continental with a Finnish touch. While the glassed-in terrace offers a great eighth-floor, rooftop view, the interior is where you'll experience a classic Finnish atmosphere. Reservations are advised (€42-47 main courses, €70 three-course lunch, €110-120 four- to five-course dinner, Mon-Fri 11:30-14:30 & 18:00-22:30,

Sat 18:00-22:30, closed Sun, Eteläesplanadi 14, tel. 09/6128-5300, www.ravintolasavoy.fi).

PICNICS
In supermarkets, buy the semi-flat bread (available dark or light) that Finns love—every slice is a heel. Finnish liquid yogurt is also a treat (sold in liter cartons). Karelian pasties, filled with rice or mashed potatoes, make a good snack. A beautiful, upscale super-market is in the basement of the **Stockmann** department store—follow the *Delikatessen* signs downstairs (Mon-Fri 9:00-21:00, Sat 9:00-18:00, open most Sun 12:00-18:00, Aleksanterinkatu 52B). Two blocks north, a more workaday, inexpensive supermarket is **S Market,** under the Sokos department store next to the train station (Mon-Sat 7:00-22:00, Sun 10:00-22:00).

Helsinki Connections

BY BUS OR TRAIN
From Helsinki, it's easy to get to **Turku** (hourly, 2 hours by ei-ther bus or train) or **St. Petersburg, Russia** (see options later). For train info, visit www.vr.fi. For bus info in English, consult www.matkahuolto.fi.

BY OVERNIGHT BOAT BETWEEN STOCKHOLM AND HELSINKI

Two fine and fiercely competitive lines, Viking Line and Tallink Silja, connect the capitals of Sweden and Finland. Each line offers state-of-the-art, 2,700-bed ships with luxu-rious *smörgåsbord* meals, reasonable cabins, plenty of entertainment (dis-cos, saunas, gambling), and enough duty-free shopping to sink a ship.

The fares are reasonable—when you consider that they include both international transportation and accommodations—because

many locals sail to shop and drink tax-free. It's a huge oper-ation. The boats are filled with about 45 percent Finns, 45 per-cent Swedes, and 10 percent cruisers from other countries. The average passenger spends as much on booze and tax-free items as on the boat fare. To main-tain their tax-free status, the boats make a midnight stop in the Åland Islands—a self-governing, Swedish-speaking province of

Finland that's exempt from the European Union's value-added tax (VAT).

The Pepsi and Coke of the Scandinavian cruise industry vie to outdo each other with bigger and fancier boats. Of the two, Viking Line has the reputation as the party boat. Tallink Silja is considered more elegant. But both lines—used mostly by locals for a quick getaway and duty-free booze run—have their share of noisy, sometimes-irritating passengers. (See "Arrival in Helsinki" for terminal locations.)

Schedules and Tickets

Schedules: Both Viking Line (www.vikingline.fi) and Tallink Silja (www.tallinksilja.com) sail nightly between Stockholm and Helsinki year-round. In both directions, the boats leave between 16:30 and 17:30, and arrive the next morning around 10:00.

Cost: As with Scandinavian hotels, cruise fares vary by season, by day of the week, and by cabin class. Check both lines' websites to see the options for your itinerary. Mid-June to mid-August is most crowded and expensive. Off-season, Friday is the most expensive night to travel, while Sunday through Wednesday nights are the cheapest. In summer, a one-way ticket per person for the cheapest bed that has a private bath (in a tight, windowless, below-car-deck "C"-class stateroom shared with other travelers) costs €35-80; for a similar cabin, couples will pay a total of about €120-130 in peak times. Of course, the more you're willing to pay, the plusher your options. Travelers with rail passes that include Sweden or Finland get 20 to 40 percent discounts on both lines. There also may be discounts for early booking, seniors, and families (look for family-cabin rates). Note that the lines may not permit travel on some Stockholm-Finland routes by those ages 18-20 who are not accompanied by a parent or guardian; for details, check websites or contact the cruise lines.

Itinerary Options: "Round-trip" fares (across and back on **successive nights,** leaving you access to your bedroom throughout the day) generally cost less than two one-way trips. The drawback is that this itinerary leaves you with only a few hours on land. But you may be able to get the round-trip fare on **nonsuccessive nights** if you book a hotel through the cruise line for every intervening night. If it fits your schedule, this can be a good deal.

Reservations: *For summer or weekend sailings, reserve well in advance.* Book online with a credit card—you'll get a reservation number and pick up your boarding card at the port. You can also book by phone or in person, but you may be charged an extra fee (likely €5); however, they are typically happy to answer questions for no charge. **Viking Line's** Swedish number is tel. 08/452-4000, and its Finnish number is tel. 0600-41577 (a pricey toll line). For **Tallink Silja,** the customer service line is a German phone number: +49-40-547-541-222; their Swedish number is tel. 08/222-140, and their Finnish number is tel. 0600-15700 (a pricey toll line). Any travel agent in Scandinavia can also sell you a ticket (with a small booking fee).

Terminals in Stockholm and Helsinki

Terminal buildings are well-organized, with cafés, lockers, tourist information desks, lounges, and phones. Remember, 2,000-plus passengers come and go with each boat. Boats open 1.5 hours before departure, and you must be checked in 20 minutes before departure. Both lines offer safe and handy parking in Stockholm. Ask for details when you reserve your ticket.

In Stockholm: Viking Line has its own terminal (squeezed between cruise ships) along the Stadsgården embankment on Södermalm (facing the Old Town/Gamla Stan). To get there, it's easiest to ride Viking Line's shuttle bus from Stockholm's bus station right to the terminal (10 kr, departs according to boat schedule). You can also ride public bus #53 (from the train station or Gamla Stan) or #71 (from the Opera House or Gamla Stan) to the Londonviadukten stop, then hike five minutes down to the terminal. A taxi from the train station will cost you around 150 kr.

Tallink Silja's boats leave from the Frihamnen port, about three miles northeast of the city center. At Frihamnen, Tallink Silja boats use the terminal called Värtahamnen (at the northern end of the sprawling industrial port). To reach the terminal, it's simplest to catch the Tallink Silja shuttle bus from Stockholm's bus station (50 kr, departs according to boat schedule). By public transportation, you can either ride the T-bana to the Gärdet station, then walk about 10 minutes; or you can take public bus #76 all the way from downtown (Mon-Sat only, direction Ropsten, get off at Färjeterminalen stop). Figure about 230-250 kr for a taxi from Gamla Stan, the train station, or other downtown areas.

For Stockholm public transport information, see www.sl.se.

In Helsinki: Both lines are perfectly central, on opposite sides of the main harbor, a 10-minute walk from the center. See the map on page 587.

Tips on Board

Meals: While ships have cheap, fast cafeterias as well as classy, romantic restaurants, they are famous for their *smörgåsbord* dinners. If you want the *smörgåsbord* experience, board the ship hungry. Dinner is self-serve in two sittings, one at about 17:30, the other around 20:00. You'll pay extra for both the dinner *smörgåsbord* (usually around €35-40) and for the breakfast buffet (€10); you can get discounts for prebooking both together. If you board without a reservation, go to the restaurant and make one. Make sure to reserve your table, not just your meal; window seats are highly sought after. The key to eating a *smörgåsbord* is to take small portions and pace yourself. (For more tips, see page 732.) The price includes free beer, wine, soft drinks, and coffee. Of course, you can also bring a picnic and eat it on deck, or eat at one of the ship's other restaurants.

Scenery: During the first few hours out of Stockholm, your ship passes through the *Skärgården* (archipelago). The third hour features the most exotic island scenery—tiny islets with cute red huts and happy people. I'd have dinner at the first sitting (shortly after departure) and be on deck for sunset. But you can also take other factors into consideration: As the cruise progresses, it gets colder outside, and the ride can get choppier (as the ship leaves the protected archipelago and enters the open sea).

Time Change: Finland is one hour ahead of Sweden. Sailing from Stockholm to Helsinki, operate on Swedish time until you're ready to go to bed, then reset your watch. Morning schedules are Finnish time, and vice versa when you return. The cruise-schedule flier in English makes this clear—pick it up as you board.

Other Services: Many ships have saunas and massages (both for an extra charge, reserve as you board), and typically offer racks of *Stockholm* or *Helsinki This Week* magazines. For purchases, ships take credit cards, euros, and Swedish kronor. Ships have exchange desks, but not on-board ATMs; you'll find those in the terminals at each end.

Adding Other Destinations

Tallinn: The Estonian capital can be spliced into your Helsinki itinerary in a number of ways: as a side-trip from Helsinki (or vice-versa), or as a triangle trip (Stockholm-Helsinki-Tallinn-Stockholm, must be booked as three one-ways). For details on the boats connecting Tallinn to Helsinki and to Stockholm, see "Tallinn Connections" on page 697.

Turku: Both Viking Line and Tallink Silja also sail from Stockholm to Turku in Finland, a shorter crossing (11 hours, departing daily at about 7:00-9:00 and 19:30-21:00). Turku, a "mini-Helsinki" with more medieval charm but less urban bustle, is two hours from Helsinki by bus or train. The cheaper fare saves you enough to pay for the train trip from Turku to Helsinki.

BY CRUISE SHIP

For more details on the following ports, and other cruise destinations, pick up my *Rick Steves Northern European Cruise Ports* guidebook.

Cruises arrive in Helsinki at various ports circling two large harbors—West Harbor (Länsistama) and South Harbor (Eteläsatama). Each individual cruise berth is designated by a three-letter code (noted in this section, along with each terminal's name in both Finnish and Swedish). For a map, see www.portofhelsinki.fi.

Getting Downtown: In addition to the public transit and/or walking options outlined later, many cruise lines offer a **shuttle bus** into downtown (likely €8 one-way, €12 round-trip; especially worth considering if you arrive at the farther-flung West Harbor). This bus usually drops you off across the street from Stockmann department store (near the corner of Mannerheimintie and Lönnrotinkatu). To reach the top of the Esplanade, cross the busy Mannerheimintie boulevard and proceed down the street between the huge, red-brick Stockmann and the white, round Swedish Theater (Svenska Teatern). Another option is to take a **hop-on, hop-off bus tour;** these meet arriving ships at Hernesaari terminal, and are easy to find around the South Harbor (for details, see "Tours in Helsinki," earlier).

West Harbor (Länsistama/Västra Hamnen)

This ugly industrial port is about two miles west of downtown. From either of the two cruise ports here, it's about a €15-20 taxi ride into town.

Hernesaari Terminal (Ärtholmen in Swedish): The primary cruise port for Helsinki sits on the eastern side of West Harbor. It has two berths (Quay B, code: LHB; and Quay C, code: LHC) and a tiny-but-handy TI kiosk where you can pick up free maps and brochures, buy a day ticket for public transit (€8, credit cards only), or use the free Wi-Fi. It's a five-minute walk to the stop for **bus #14,** which takes you downtown: Head through the parking lot, turn left at the street, take the next right, and look for the bus stop marked *Pajamäki/Smedjebacka* (3-6/hour). From here, ride bus #14 to Kamppi (a 10-minute walk from the train station area and the Esplanade) or continue to Kauppakorkeakoulut (near Temppeliaukio, the Church in the Rock—get off the bus, walk straight ahead one block, then turn right up Luthernikatu to find the church). In summer, there's also a **ferry** that goes from Hernesaari to Market Square (€7 one-way, €10 all day, only 3/day starting at 9:30, late June-early Aug daily, early-late June and early-late Aug Sat-Sun only, 30 minutes, mobile 040-736-2329, www.seahelsinki. fi).

West Terminal (Länsiterminaali/Västra Terminalen): From the cruise berth at Melkki Quay (code: LMA), you'll walk 10 minutes through dull shipyards (follow the green line on the pavement) to the Länsiterminaali building, with ATMs and other services. From right in front of this terminal, tram #9 zips into town (6/hour, handiest downtown stop is Rautatieasema, at the train station).

South Harbor (Eteläsatama/Södra Hamnen)

This centrally located harbor, which fans out from Market Square, is an easy walk from downtown (taxis are unnecessary here, but if you take one, figure €10-15 to most points in the city center). Ringing this harbor are several terminals for both cruises and overnight boats; two are most commonly used by cruise ships.

Katajanokan Terminal (Skatudden in Swedish): The harbor's northern embankment has two cruise berths (codes: ERA and ERB). A third berth (code: EKL), used more by overnight boats than cruise ships, is closer to town. The Viking Line terminal in this area has ATMs, other services, and—across the street—the stop for **tram #4T,** which zips you right into town (stops at City Hall, Senate Square, Lasipalatsi near the train station, and National Museum). Or you can simply **walk** 15 minutes to Market Square (stroll between brick warehouses, with the harbor on your left, toward the white-and-green dome).

Olympia Terminal: Smaller cruise ships use this terminal (code: EO), along the southern embankment. Inside the terminal are ATMs and other services; out front is a stop for **tram #2,** which takes you to Senate Square, then the train station (Rautatieasema stop), then the Sammonkatu stop near Temppeliaukio (the Church in the Rock). It's also easy to **walk** into town from here—figure about 15 minutes (head around the harbor, with the water on your right, toward the white-and-green dome).

The South Harbor berths that are closest to downtown

(**Kanava terminal** and **Makasiini terminal**) are used mostly by overnight boats, though occasionally overflow cruise ships may end up there. Either one is an easy five-minute walk to Market Square.

CONNECTING HELSINKI AND ST. PETERSBURG

Many visitors use Helsinki as a launch pad for a visit to St. Petersburg, Russia—just 240 miles east. For more details on St. Petersburg, consider my *Rick Steves Snapshot St. Petersburg, Helsinki & Tallinn.*

Visa Requirements: American and Canadian travelers to Russia need a visa, which must be arranged weeks in advance. You'll need to secure an official "invitation" in St. Petersburg and mail your passport to the Russian consulate (for details, US citizens should see www.russianembassy.org; Canadians can consult www.rusembassy.ca). Given the logistical headaches, it's smart to enlist an agency to help obtain an invitation and process your paperwork (I've had a good experience with www.passportvisasexpress.com). It's not cheap: Plan on at least $350 per person to cover the visa, service fee, and secure shipping.

Visa Exceptions: If you arrive in St. Petersburg **on a cruise,** the visa requirement is waived provided you contract with a local tour operator (or join one of your cruise line's excursions) for a guided visit around the city—you'll have no free time. But there is an exception that gives you time on your own: If you go to St. Petersburg on a St. Peter Line ship (see below), then pay for a "shuttle service" from the dock into the city (typically €25 round-trip), you can technically stay up to 72 hours before returning with a St. Peter Line shuttle and boat. Although this is not a guided visit, it's treated as the "cruise exception" explained above—at least, it is as of this writing (in early 2015). **Important:** As this loophole may well be closed in the future—and all aspects of the Russian visa situation change frequently—carefully confirm these details before planning your trip.

By Land: You have two options. The **bus** is slower and cheaper (3-5/day, including overnight options; 8-9 hours, €35-40, less for students, www.matkahuolto.fi, arrives at Baltiisky Vokzal train station near the Baltiiskaya Metro stop); the Allegro **train,** operated by Finnish Railways, is much faster (4/day, 3.5 hours, €70-105 depending on demand, no student discount, www.vr.fi, book ahead online, arrives at Finlyandsky train station near Ploshchad Lenina Metro stop). There's also a daily overnight train to **Moscow.** Rail passes are not valid on the international trains to Russia.

By Sea: Many Baltic Sea **cruises** include a stop in St. Petersburg. But if you're on your own, **St. Peter Line** can take you there from Helsinki. Their *Princess Maria* sails every other day (3-4/ week), departing from Helsinki's West Harbor (from the West/ **Länsi terminal**) at 18:00; 14.5 hours later, it reaches St. Petersburg (where it turns around and, at 19:00, heads back to Helsinki). In high season (July-late Aug), the cheapest bunk in a shared four-bed cabin costs €27 one-way; a round-trip "cruise" starts at €150. St. Peter Line's ship *Anastasia* connects St. Petersburg to Tallinn about once weekly, then continues on to Stockholm. For details, see www.stpeterline.com; Helsinki Expert also has information.

ESTONIA

ESTONIA

Eesti

 The most accessible part of the former USSR, Estonia is shaped by its eclectic past and inspired by the prospect of an ever-brighter future. In the European Union, only three micro-states (Cyprus, Luxembourg, and Malta) have a smaller population than Estonia. But like its fellow Baltic countries (Latvia and Lithuania), Estonia has an endearing enthusiasm for the things that make it unique—proving that you don't have to be big to have a clear cultural identity.

Estonians are related to the Finns and have a similar history—first Swedish domination, then Russian (1710-1918), and finally independence after World War I. In 1940, Estonians were at least as affluent and as advanced as the Finns, but they could not preserve their independence from Soviet expansion during World War II. As a result, Estonia sank into a nearly 50-year period of communist stagnation. Since then, the country has made great strides in its recovery; it joined the EU and NATO in 2004, adopted the euro currency in 2011, and today feels pretty much as "Western" as its Nordic neighbors.

EU membership seemed like a natural step to many Estonians; they already thought of themselves as part of the Nordic world. Language, history, religion, and twice-hourly ferry departures connect Finns and Estonians. Only 50 miles separate Helsinki and Tallinn, and Stockholm is just an overnight boat ride away. Finns visit Tallinn to eat, drink, and shop more cheaply than at home. While some Estonians resent how Tallinn becomes a Finnish nightclub on summer weekends, most people on both sides are happy since the end of the Cold War to have friendly new neighbors.

You'd be wrong to think of this "former USSR" country as backward. Thanks to visionary and aggressive development policies implemented soon after independence—including the designation of Internet access as a basic human right—Estonia is now a global trendsetter in technology. By 1998, every school in Estonia was already online. The country has some of the fastest broadband speeds in the world, Estonians vote and file their taxes electronically, and

Estonia Almanac

Official Name: Eesti Vabariik—the Republic of Estonia—or simply Estonia.

Population: Estonia is home to 1.3 million people (77 per square mile). Nearly three in four are of Estonian heritage, and about one-quarter are of Russian descent, with smaller minorities of Ukrainians, Belarusians, and Finns. About 70 percent speak the official language—Estonian—and nearly 30 percent speak Russian. The majority of Estonians are unaffiliated with any religion. About 10 percent are Lutheran and 16 percent are Orthodox.

Latitude and Longitude: 59°N and 26°E, similar latitude to Juneau, Alaska.

Area: 17,500 square miles, about the size of New Hampshire and Vermont combined.

Geography: Between Latvia and Russia, Estonia borders the Baltic Sea and Gulf of Finland. It includes more than 1,500 islands and islets, and has the highest number of meteorite craters per land area in the world.

Biggest City: The capital of Estonia, Tallinn, has 400,000 people (500,000 in the metropolitan area).

Economy: Estonia's transition to a free-market system included joining the World Trade Organization and the European Union. In recent years, it's had one of the highest per capita income levels in Central Europe and boasts a per-capita GDP of $22,400. Its four major trading partners are Finland, Sweden, Russia, and Germany; the strengths of "E-stonia" are electronics and telecommunications.

Currency: €1 (euro) = about $1.40.

Government: Estonia is a parliamentary democracy, with a president elected by parliament and a prime minister. The 101-member parliament (Riigikogu) is elected by popular vote every four years.

Flag: The pre-1940 Estonian flag was restored in 1990. It has three equal horizontal bands with blue at the top, black in the middle, and white on the bottom. The blue represents Estonia's lakes and sea, and the loyalty and devotion of the  country to its people. The black symbolizes the homeland's rich soil and the hardships the people have suffered. The white represents hope and happiness.

The Average Estonian: He or she is 41 years old, has 1.4 children, and will live to be 74. About 58 percent of the population are women (they live longer), and when she sings the national anthem, she uses the same melody as Finland.

Skype—used by travelers worldwide to keep in touch—was invented right here. The multibillion-dollar windfall from Skype's 2005 sale to eBay kickstarted a whole new venture-capital industry that is still paying dividends today.

And yet, despite its modernity, Estonian culture can be romantic—sometimes shaded with a tinge of darkness. This little

land has a long, jagged, hauntingly beautiful coastline, and over a thousand lakes. Fifty percent of the landscape is forest, while marshlands and bogs cover another twenty percent. Traditional folk music buoys the national spirit—especially at the Song Festival every five years, where a significant portion of the population convenes to pour out their souls in song. Some of Estonia's traditions may strike you as quirky. Estonians snack on nearly black rye bread slathered in garlic and bury their dead in evocative pine forests—where skinny trunks recede into the infinite heavens.

Even as Estonia will always face West, across the Baltic, it also faces East, into the Russian hinterlands. One difficult legacy of the Soviet experience is Estonia's huge Russian population. Most Estonian Russians' parents and grandparents were brought to Estonia in the 1950s and 1960s to work in now-defunct factories in Tallinn and the northeastern cities. Twenty-five percent of Estonia's population is now ethnically Russian. Under Vladimir Putin, Russia has demanded better treatment of Estonia's Russian-speaking population. After Putin declared he would "protect" Russian speakers in Ukraine and fostered a separatist revolt there, some Estonians wondered if something similar could happen here. Making Russians feel at home in Estonia while building a distinctly Estonian culture and identity is one of independent Estonia's biggest challenges.

Most Estonians speak English—it's the first choice these days at school. About half can carry on a normal conversation in English. Estonian is similar to Finnish and equally difficult; only a million people speak it worldwide. Two useful phrases to know are *"Tänan"* (TAH-nahn; "Thank you") and *"Terviseks!"* (TEHR-vee-sehks; "Cheers!"). If you'd like to learn a few more phrases, see the Estonian survival phrases on the following page. The farther you go beyond the touristy zones, the more you see that Russian is still Estonia's second language. If you know some Russian, use it. It's the mother tongue of about 40 percent of Tallinners (many of whom have no intention of learning Estonian).

ESTONIA

Estonian Survival Phrases

Estonian has a few unusual vowel sounds. The letter *ä* is pronounced "ah" as in "hat," but *a* without the umlaut sounds more like "aw" as in "hot." To make the sound *ö*, purse your lips and say "oh"; the letter *õ* is similar, but with the lips less pursed. Listen to locals and imitate.

In the phonetics, ī sounds like the long *i* in "light," and bolded syllables are stressed.

English	Estonian	Pronunciation
Hello. (formal)	Tervist.	**tehr**-veest
Hi. / Bye. (informal)	Tere. / Nägemist.	**teh**-reh / **nah**-geh-meest
Do you speak English?	Kas te räägite inglise keelt?	kahs teh **raah**-gee-teh **een**-glee-seh kehlt
Yes. / No.	Jah. / Ei.	yah / ay
Please. / You're welcome.	Palun.	**pah**-luhn
Thank you (very much).	Tänan (väga).	**tah**-nahn (**vah**-gaw)
Can I help you?	Saan ma teid aidata?	saahn mah tayd ī-dah-tah
Excuse me.	Vabandust.	**vaw**-bahn-doost
(Very) good.	(Väga) hea.	(**vah**-gaw) **hey**-ah
Goodbye.	Hüvasti.	**hew**-vaw-stee
one / two	üks / kaks	ewks / kawks
three / four	kolm / neli	kohlm / **nay**-lee
five / six	viis / kuus	vees / koos
seven / eight	seitse / kaheksa	**sayt**-seh / **kaw**-hehk-sah
nine / ten	üheksa / kümme	**ew**-hehk-sah / **kew**-meh
hundred	sada	**saw**-daw
thousand	tuhat	**too**-hawt
How much?	Kui palju?	kwee **pawl**-yoo
local currency: (Estonian) crown	(Eesti) krooni	(**eh**-stee) **kroo**-nee
Where is...?	Kus asub...?	koos ah-**soob**
...the toilet	...tualett	**too**-ah-leht
men	mees	mehs
women	naine	**nī**-neh
water / coffee	vesi / kohvi	**vay**-see / **koh**-vee
beer / wine	õlu / vein	**oh**-loo / vayn
Cheers!	Terviseks!	**tehr**-vee-sehks
The bill, please.	Arve, palun.	**ahr**-veh **pah**-luhn

ESTONIA

TALLINN

Tallinn is a rewarding detour for those who want to spice up their Scandinavian travels with a Baltic twist. Among Nordic medieval cities, there's none nearly as well-preserved as Tallinn. Its mostly intact city wall includes 26 watchtowers, each topped by a pointy red roof. Baroque and choral music ring out from its old Lutheran churches. I'd guess that Tallinn (with 400,000 people) has more restaurants, cafés, and surprises per capita and square inch than any city in this book—and the fun is comparatively cheap. Yes, Tallinn's Nordic Lutheran culture and language connect it with Scandinavia, but two centuries of czarist Russian rule and 45 years as part of the Soviet Union have blended in a distinctly Russian flavor. Overlying all of that, however, is the vibrancy of a free nation that's just a generation old. Estonian pride is in the air...and it's catching.

As a member of the Hanseatic League, the city of Tallinn was a medieval stronghold of the Baltic trading world. (For more on the Hanseatic League, see the sidebar on page 380.) In the 19th and early 20th centuries, Tallinn industrialized and expanded beyond its walls. Architects encircled the Old Town, putting up broad streets of public buildings, low Scandinavian-style apartment buildings, and single-family wooden houses. Estonia's brief period of independence ended in World War II, and after 1945, Soviet planners ringed the city with stands of now-crumbling concrete high-rises where many of Tallinn's Rus-

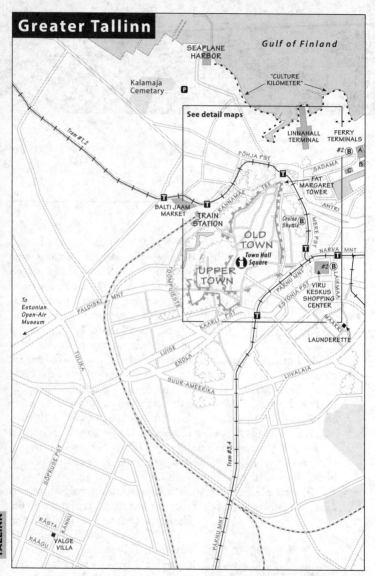

Greater Tallinn

Gulf of Finland

SEAPLANE HARBOR

"CULTURE KILOMETER"

Kalamaja Cemetery **P**

Tram #1,2

See detail maps

LINNAHALL TERMINAL

FERRY TERMINALS

PÕHJA PST

#2 **B** A
B

SADAMA

T

FAT MARGARET TOWER

AHTRI

BALTI JAAM MARKET

RANNAMÄE TEE

TRAIN STATION

T

Cruise Shuttle **B**

MERE PST

OLD TOWN

Town Hall Square **i**

UPPER TOWN

T

NARVA MNT

#2 **B**

LAIKMAA

TOOMPUIESTEE

To Estonian Open-Air Museum

PALDISKI MNT

KAARLI PST

PÄRNU MNT

ESTONIA PST

VIRU KESKUS SHOPPING CENTER

T

MAAKRI

LAUNDERETTE

LUISE

ENDLA

SUUR-AMEERIKA

LIIVALAIA

SOPRUSE PST

TULIKA

Tram #3,4

PÄRNU MNT

RASTA

KANNU

RÄÄGU

VALGE VILLA

sian immigrants settled. The city still struggles to more effectively incorporate its large Russian minority.

The post-communist chapter has been a success story. Since independence in 1991, Tallinn has westernized at an astounding rate. The Old Town has been scrubbed into a pristine Old World theme park—a fascinating package of pleasing towers, ramparts, facades, *striptiis* bars, churches, shops, and people-watching. Meanwhile,

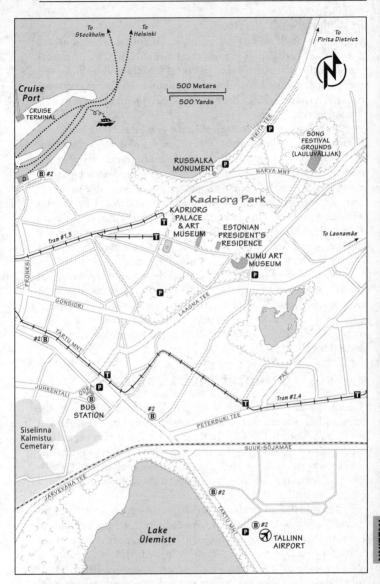

the outlying districts (such as the Rotermann Quarter) are a Petri dish of architectural experimentation. Cruise ships have discovered Tallinn, and cruisers mob its cobbles at midday. Given its compact scale, Tallinn can be easily appreciated as a side-trip (from Helsinki, or from a cruise ship). But the city rewards those who spend the night. More time gives you the chance to explore some of the more colorful slices of life outside the Old Town walls.

PLANNING YOUR TIME

On a three-week tour of Scandinavia, Tallinn is certainly worth a day. Most people find it works best as a full-day side-trip from Helsinki. Or take overnights in both Helsinki and Tallinn—either as a triangular detour from Stockholm, or on the way between Stockholm and St. Petersburg. And, of course, many come to Tallinn on a cruise ship.

Day-Trippers or Cruisers: Hit the ground running by following my self-guided walk right from the port. Enjoy a nice restaurant in the Old Town for lunch. Then spend the afternoon shopping and browsing (or choose one of the outlying sights: Seaplane Harbor for boats and planes, Rotermann Quarter for cutting-edge architecture, Estonian Open-Air Museum for folk culture, or Kumu Art Museum for Estonian art and a walk in nearby Kadriorg Park). Remember to bring a jacket—Tallinn can be chilly even on sunny summer days. And, given that locals call their cobbled streets "a free foot massage," sturdy shoes are smart, too.

With More Time: Start off with the self-guided walk, but slow things down a bit. Because Tallinn can be inundated midday with cruise passengers and day-trippers, it makes sense to tour the Old Town early or late, then get out of town when it's crowded to hit some outlying sights. Check concert schedules if you'll be around for the evening.

Orientation to Tallinn

Tallinn's walled Old Town is an easy 15-minute walk from the ferry and cruise terminals, where most visitors land (see "Arrival in Tallinn," later). The Old Town is divided into two parts (historically, two separate towns): the upper town (Toompea) and the lower town (with Town Hall Square). A remarkably intact medieval wall surrounds the two towns, which are themselves separated by another wall.

Town Hall Square (Raekoja Plats) marks the heart of the medieval lower town. The main TI is nearby, as are many sights and eateries. Pickpockets are a problem in the more touristy parts of the Old Town, so keep valuables carefully stowed. The area around the Viru Keskus mall and Hotel Viru, just east of the Old Town, is useful for everyday shopping (bookstores and supermarkets), practical services (laundry), and public transport.

TOURIST INFORMATION

The hardworking TI has maps, concert listings, and free brochures (May-Aug Mon-Fri 9:00-19:00—until 20:00 mid-June-Aug, Sat-Sun 9:00-17:00—until 18:00 mid-June-Aug; Sept-April Mon-Fri 9:00-18:00, Sat-Sun 9:00-15:00; a block off Town Hall Square at

Kullassepa 4, tel. 645-7777, www.tourism.tallinn.ee, visit@tallinn.ee). Look for the helpful *Tallinn in Your Pocket*, a booklet with restaurant, hotel, and sight listings (€2.50 at the TI and elsewhere around town, but you may find free copies at your hotel, and you can download it for free at www.inyourpocket.com).

Tallinn Card: This card—sold at the TIs, airport, train station, travel agencies, ferry ports, and big hotels—gives you free use of public transport and entry to more than 40 museums and major sights (€24/24 hours, €32/48 hours, €40/72 hours, comes with good info booklet, www.tallinncard.ee). It includes one tour of your choice (orientation walk or one of two hop-on, hop-off bus routes), plus a 50 percent discount on any others (see "Tours in Tallinn," later, for specifics). If you're planning to take one of these tours and to visit several sights, this card will likely save you money—do the math.

ARRIVAL IN TALLINN

For advice on taking taxis, and more details on the public transportation and ticket options mentioned below, see "Getting Around Tallinn," later.

By Boat or Cruise Ship: Tallinn has four terminals lettered A through D, a fifth one called Linnahall (used only by the fast Linda Line boat), and a dedicated cruise terminal. A-Terminal, B-Terminal, and C-Terminal are clustered together; the cruise terminal is just to the north; D-Terminal is a 10-minute walk to the east (and the farthest from Old Town); the Linnahall terminal is a 10-minute walk to the west (just over the large stairway). Each terminal offers baggage storage. Be sure to confirm which terminal your return boat will use. The main cruise pier can accommodate two large ships; when more are in town, they may use one of the other terminals.

If you have no luggage, you can **walk** 15 minutes to reach the center of town—just follow signs to the city center and set your sights on the tallest spire in the distance (or follow my self-guided walk, later). (If you'd rather first visit the Seaplane Harbor, described on page 679, look for a red-gravel path—straight ahead as you leave the cruise port, marked *Kultu-urikilomeeter*—which takes you

there on a long, scenic, mostly seaside stroll.)

If you have bags, it's best to grab a **taxi**—otherwise your rolling suitcase will take a pounding on the Old Town's cobbled streets and gutter-ridden sidewalks. While the legitimate taxi fare to anywhere in or near the Old Town should be less than €5, unscrupulous cabbies may try to charge double or triple.

To get into town by bus, you have several options: Public **bus #2** goes from A-Terminal and D-Terminal directly to the A. Laikmaa stop—behind Hotel Viru and the Viru Keskus mall, just south of the Old Town—then continues to the airport (2/hour, buy Ühiskaart smartcard from R-Kiosk shops in terminals, or pay €1.60 for a ticket on board). Cruise lines sometimes offer a shuttle bus into town (to the Russian Cultural Center, near Hotel Viru), but—since it's so easy to just stroll from the port into town—this isn't worth paying for.

By Plane: The convenient Tallinn airport (Tallinna Lennujaam), just three miles southeast of downtown, has a small info desk (airport code: TLL, www.tallinn-airport.ee, tel. 605-8888). A **taxi** to the Old Town should cost €8-10. Public **bus #2** runs every 20-30 minutes from the lower entrance (floor 0) into town; the seventh stop, A. Laikmaa, is behind the Viru Keskus mall, a short walk from the Old Town (buy Ühiskaart smartcard from R-Kiosk store in terminal—or pay €1.60 for a single ticket on board; to reach the bus stop, follow bus signs down the escalator, go outside, and look left).

By Train and Bus: While Tallinn has a sleepy and cute little train station (called Balti Jaam), few tourists will need to use it. The station, a five-minute walk across a busy road from the Old Town (use the pedestrian underpass), is adjacent to the big, cheap Hotel Shnelli and the colorful Balti Jaam Market. Tallinn's long-distance bus station *(autobussijaam)* is midway between downtown and the airport, and served by bus #2 and trams #2 and #4.

HELPFUL HINTS

Money: Estonia uses the euro. You'll find ATMs (sometimes marked *Otto*) at locations around Tallinn.

Time: Estonia is one hour ahead of continental Europe, which means it's generally seven/ten hours ahead of the East/West Coasts of the US.

Telephones: In case of a medical emergency, dial 112. For police, dial 110. Most Estonian phone numbers are seven to eight digits with no area codes. Tallinn numbers begin with 6, and mobile phones (more expensive to call) begin with 5. (From outside Estonia, you'll first dial the country code: 372; for more on dialing, see page 735.)

Internet Access: Every hotel I list offers free Wi-Fi, and some have a computer for guests to use. Public Wi-Fi is easy to find around Tallinn; look for the free "Tallinn WiFi" network. The **main TI** has one terminal where you can briefly check your email for free.

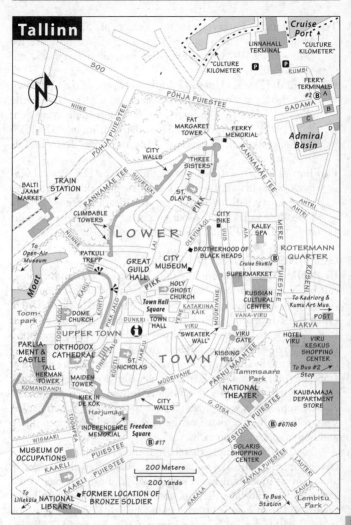

Tallinn

Cruise Port

"CULTURE KILOMETER"

LINNAHALL TERMINAL

"CULTURE KILOMETER"

SOO

RUMBI

PÕHJA PUIESTEE

FERRY TERMINALS #2 A

SADAMA B

NIINE

PÕHJA PUIESTEE

Admiral Basin

FAT MARGARET TOWER

FERRY MEMORIAL

RANNAMÄE TEE

CITY WALLS

"THREE SISTERS"

AHTRI

BALTI JAAM MARKET

TRAIN STATION

RANNAMÄE TEE

SUURTUKI

LAI

PIKK

ST. OLAV'S

CITY BIKE

KALEV SPA

MERE PUIESTEE

AHTRI

CLIMBABLE TOWERS

OLEVIMÄGI

UUS

AIA

ROTERMANN QUARTER

To Open-Air Museum

NUNNE

L O W E R

LAI

BROTHERHOOD OF BLACK HEADS

ROSENI

PATKULI TREPP

RABU

KOHTU

GREAT GUILD HALL

CITY MUSEUM

Cruise Shuttle

SUPERMARKET

To Kadriorg & Kumu Art Mus.

Moat

PIKK

HOLY GHOST CHURCH

RUSSIAN CULTURAL CENTER

Toom-park

TOOM-KOOLI

DOME CHURCH

PIKK JALG

DUNKRI

Town Hall Square

KATARIINA KÄIK

VEHE

VANA-VIRU

POST

NARVA

U P P E R   T O W N

ORTHODOX CATHEDRAL

TOOM

LOSSI PLATS

KOHTU

TOWN HALL

VIRU

MÜÜRIVAHE

VIRU GATE

HOTEL VIRU

VIRU KESKUS SHOPPING CENTER

PARLIA-MENT & CASTLE

ST. NICHOLAS

RÜÜTLI

HARJU

"SWEATER WALL"

T O W N

KISSING HILL

PÄRNU MAANTEE

To Bus #2 Stop

TALL HERMAN TOWER

LOKHARJU

MÜÜRIVAHE

Tammsaare Park

KOMANDANDI

MAIDEN TOWER

TOOMPEA

KIEK IN DE KÖK

Harjumägi

CITY WALLS

G. OTSA

NATIONAL THEATER

KAUBAMAJA DEPARTMENT STORE

WISMARI

INDEPENDENCE MEMORIAL

Freedom Square

#17

ESTONIA PUIESTEE

#67/68

MUSEUM OF OCCUPATIONS

PUIESTEE

KAARLI

200 Meters

200 Yards

SOLARIS SHOPPING CENTER

RÄVALA PUIESTEE

LAUTERI

To Lilleküla

KAARLI   PUIESTEE

NATIONAL LIBRARY

FORMER LOCATION OF BRONZE SOLDIER

SAKALA

To Bus Station

KAUKA

Lembitu Park

Laundry: The Viru Keskus mall has a handy **Top Clean** laundry drop-off service downstairs (Mon-Fri 8:00-20:00, Sat 10:00-20:00, closed Sun; underground facing bus stalls 1 and 2, tel. 610-1405, www.puhastuskeskus.ee).

Otherwise, **Pesumaja Sol** is just beyond the Viru Keskus mall and Kaubamaja department store (just walkable from the Old Town, or take tram #2 or #4 to the Paberi stop, a few blocks away—see map on page 655). Choose between self-serve (€6/load, ask staff to interpret Estonian-only instructions) or full-service (€16/load, Mon-Fri 7:00-20:00, Sat 8:00-16:00, closed Sun, Maakri 23, tel. 677-1551).

Travel Agency: Estravel, at the corner of Suur-Karja and Müürivähe, is handy and sells boat tickets for no extra fee (Mon-Fri 9:00-18:00, closed Sat-Sun, Suur-Karja 15, tel. 626-6233).

Bike Rental: Head for **City Bike,** at the north end of the Old Town near the ferry terminals (€10/6 hours, €13/24 hours; electric bikes—€5/hour, €20/6 hours, €25/24 hours; daily May-Sept 9:00-19:00, Oct-April 9:00-17:00, Uus 33, mobile 511-1819, www.citybike.ee). They also do bike tours (see "Tours in Tallinn," later).

Parking: The Port of Tallinn has a cheap lot by D-Terminal (€5/day, www.portoftallinn.com). Old Town parking is very expensive; try parking in the lot underneath Freedom Square (Vabaduse väljak), at the southern tip of the Old Town, a short walk from the TI and Town Hall Square (€3/hour).

GETTING AROUND TALLINN

By Public Transportation: The Old Town and surrounding areas can be explored on foot, but use public transit to reach outlying sights (such as Kadriorg Park, Kumu Art Museum, or the Estonian Open-Air Museum). Tallinn has buses, trams, and trolley buses (buses connected to overhead wires)—avoid mistakes by noting that they reuse the same numbers (bus #2, tram #2, and trolley bus #2 are totally different lines). Maps and schedules are posted at stops, or visit http://soiduplaan.tallinn.ee (for an overview of transit stops useful to visitors, see the "Greater Tallinn" map on page 650). As you approach a station, you'll hear the name of the impeding stop, followed by the name of the next stop—don't get confused and hop off one stop too early.

You can buy a **single ticket** from the driver for €1.60 (exact change appreciated). If you'll be taking more than three rides in a day, invest in an **Ühiskaart smartcard.** You can buy one for €2 at any yellow-and-blue R-Kiosk convenience store (found all over town), and then load it up with credit, which is deducted as you travel (€1.10 for any ride up to 1 hour, €3/24 hours, €5/72 hours, €6/120 hours). The card is shareable by multiple people for single rides, but you'll need separate cards for the multiride options.

Bus #2 (Moigu-Reisisadam) is helpful on arrival and departure, running every 20-30 minutes between the ferry port's A-Terminal and the airport. En route it stops at D-Terminal; at A. Laikmaa, next to the Viru Keskus mall (a short walk south of the Old Town); and at the long-distance bus station.

By Taxi: Taxis in Tallinn are handy, but it's easy to get ripped off. The safest way to catch a cab is to order one by phone (or ask a trusted local to call for you)—this is what Estonians usually do. **Tulika** is the largest company, with predictable, fair prices

(€3.35 drop charge plus €0.69/kilometer, €0.80/kilometer from 23:00-6:00, tel. 612-0001 or 1200, check latest prices at www.tulika.ee). **Tallink Takso** is another reputable option with similar fares (tel. 640-8921 or 1921). Cabbies are required to use the meter and give you a meter-printed receipt. If you don't get a receipt, it's safe to assume you're being ripped off and legally don't need to pay. Longer rides around the city (e.g., from the airport to the Old Town) should run around €8-10.

If you must catch a taxi off the street, go to a busy taxi stand where lots of cabs are lined up. Before you get in, take a close look at the yellow price list on the rear passenger-side door; the base fare should be €3-4 and the per-kilometer charge under €1. If it's not, keep looking. Glance inside—a photo ID license should be attached to the middle of the dashboard. Don't negotiate or ask for a price estimate; let the driver use the meter. Rates must be posted by law, but are not capped or regulated, so the most common scam— unfortunately widespread and legal—is to list an inflated price on the yellow price sticker (as much as €3/kilometer), and simply wait for a tourist to hop in without noticing. Singleton cabs lurking in tourist areas are usually fishing for suckers, as are cabbies who flag you down ("Taxi?")—give them a miss. It's fun to play spot-the-scam as you walk around town.

Tours in Tallinn

Bus and Walking Tour

This enjoyable, narrated 2.5-hour tour of Tallinn comes in two parts: first by bus for an overview of sights outside the Old Town, such as the Song Festival Grounds and Kadriorg Park, then on foot to sights within the Old Town (€20, pay driver, covered by Tallinn Card, in English; daily morning and early afternoon departures from A-Terminal, D-Terminal, and major hotels in city center; tel. 610-8616, www.traveltoestonia.com).

Local Guides

Mati Rumessen is a top-notch guide, especially for car tours inside or outside town (€35/hour driving or walking tours, price may vary with group size, mobile 509-4661, www.tourservice.ee, matirumessen@gmail.com). Other fine guides are **Antonio Villacis** (mobile 5662-9306, antonio.villacis@gmail.com) and **Miina Puusepp** (€20/hour, mobile 551-7028, miinap@hot.ee).

Tallinn Traveller Tours

These student-run tours show you the real city without the political and corporate correctness of official tourist agencies. Check www.traveller.ee to confirm details for their ever-changing lineup, and to

Tallinn at a Glance

Central Tallinn

▲▲▲**Tallinn's Old Town** Well-preserved medieval center with cobblestoned lanes, gabled houses, historic churches, and turreted city walls. **Hours:** Always open. See page 660.

▲▲**Russian Orthodox Cathedral** Accessible look at the Russian Orthodox faith, with a lavish interior. **Hours:** Daily 8:00-19:00, icon art in gift shop. See page 667.

▲**Museum of Estonian History** High-tech exhibits explain Estonia's engaging national narrative. **Hours:** May-Aug daily 10:00-18:00, same hours off-season except closed Wed. See page 672.

▲**Museum of Occupations** Estonia's tumultuous, sometimes secret history under Soviet and Nazi occupiers from 1940 to 1991. **Hours:** June-Aug Tue-Sun 10:00-18:00, Sept-May Tue-Sun 11:00-18:00, closed Mon year-round. See page 674.

St. Nicholas Church Art museum displaying Gothic art in a restored old church. **Hours:** Wed-Sun 10:00-17:00, closed Mon-Tue. See page 665.

Town Hall and Tower Gothic building with history museum and climbable tower on the Old Town's main square. **Hours:** Museum—July-Aug Mon-Sat 10:00-16:00, closed Sun and rest of year; tower—May-mid-Sept daily 11:00-18:00, closed rest of year. See page 672.

---

reserve (or call mobile 5837-4800). The **City Introductory Walking Tour** is free, but tips are encouraged (around €5/person if you enjoy yourself, daily at 12:00, 2 hours). They also typically offer a two-hour **Old Town Walking Tour** (€15, daily at 10:00, similar to the free tour but generally a much smaller group), a **ghost walk** (€15, 2/week at 20:00), and a **pub crawl** (€20, 1/week at 20:00), and can also arrange private tours. They have a variety of **bike tours**, including a 2.5-hour "Welcome to Tallinn" overview (€16, daily at 11:00). And they offer minibus excursions that get you into the Estonian countryside, including one to the **Coastal Cliffs** and the Soviet military town of Paldiski (€45, daily in summer at 10:00, 3/week off-season, 7 hours), and one to **Lahemaa National Park** (€49, daily at 10:00, 9 hours). If you're heading to **Rīga, Latvia,** consider the excellent value they provide: a 12-hour sightseeing shuttle trip between Tallinn and Rīga, with several stops on route to experience the Estonian and Latvian countrysides (€49). These excursions go year-round, but require at least two people to run.

Outside of the Core

▲▲**Kumu Art Museum** The best of contemporary Estonian art displayed in a strikingly modern building. **Hours:** May-Sept Tue-Sun 11:00-18:00, Wed until 20:00, closed Mon; same hours off-season except closed Mon-Tue. See page 676.

▲▲**Seaplane Harbor** Impressive museum of boats and planes—including a WWII-era submarine—displayed in a cavernous old hangar along the waterfront. **Hours:** May-Sept daily 10:00-19:00; same hours off-season except closed Mon. See page 679.

▲**Kadriorg Park** Vast, strollable oasis with the palace gardens, Kumu Art Museum, and a palace built by Czar Peter the Great. **Hours:** Park always open. See page 675.

▲**Song Festival Grounds** National monument and open-air theater where Estonians sang for freedom. **Hours:** Open long hours daily. See page 680.

▲**Estonian Open-Air Museum** Authentic farm and village buildings preserved in a forested parkland. **Hours:** Late April-Sept—park open daily 10:00-20:00, buildings open until 18:00; Oct-late April—park open daily 10:00-17:00 but many buildings closed. See page 684.

You can also book any one of these tours—or others, all well-described on their website—for your own small group for the same per-person price (4-person minimum). All tours start from in front of the main TI.

Hop-On, Hop-Off Bus Tours

Tallinn City Tour offers three different one-hour bus tours—you can take all three (on the same day) for one price. Aside from a stop near Toompea Castle, the routes are entirely outside the Old Town, and the frequency is low (just 6-8/day, May-Sept only—so you'll need to coordinate your sightseeing to the infrequent departures). But if you want to rest your feet and listen to a fairly good recorded commentary, the tours do get you to outlying sights such as Kadriorg Park and the towering Russalka Monument. You can catch the bus at the port terminals and near the Viru Turg clothing market (€19/24 hours, free with Tallinn Card, tel. 627-9080, www.citytour.ee). **CitySightseeing Tallinn** also runs three similar

TALLINN

routes, with a similarly sparse frequency (€18 for all three lines, €15 for just one line, www.citysightseeing.ee).

City Bike Tours

City Bike offers a two-hour, nine-mile **Welcome to Tallinn** bike tour that takes you outside the city walls to Tallinn's more distant sights: Kadriorg Park, Song Festival Grounds, the beach at Pirita, and more (€16, 50 percent discount with Tallinn Card, daily at 11:00 year-round, departs from their office at Uus 33 in the Old Town). They can also arrange multiday, self-guided bike tours around Estonia (mobile 511-1819, www.citybike.ee).

Tallinn Walk

This self-guided walk, worth ▲▲▲, explores the "two towns" of Tallinn. The city once consisted of two feuding medieval towns separated by a wall. The upper town—on the hill, called Toompea—was the seat of government for Estonia. The lower town was an autonomous Hanseatic trading center filled with German, Danish, and Swedish merchants who hired Estonians to do their menial labor. Many of the Old Town's buildings are truly old, dating from the boom times of the 15th and 16th centuries. Decrepit before the 1991 fall of the Soviet Union, the Old Town has been slowly revitalized, though there's still plenty of work to be done.

Two steep, narrow streets—the "Long Leg" and the "Short Leg"—connect the upper town (Toompea) and the lower town. This two-part walk—"Part 1" focusing on the lower town, and "Part 2" climbing up to the upper town—goes up the short leg and down the long leg. Allow about two hours for the entire walk (not counting time to enter museums along the way).

PART 1: THE LOWER TOWN

• *The walk starts at the port—where cruise ships and ferries from Helsinki arrive. If you're coming from elsewhere in Tallinn, take tram #1 or #2 to the Linnahall stop, or just walk out to the Fat Margaret Tower from anywhere in the Old Town.*

❶ To Fat Margaret Tower and Start of Walk

From the port, hike toward the tall tapering spire, go through a small park, and enter the Old Town through the archway by the squat Fat Margaret Tower.

Just outside the tower, on a bluff overlooking the harbor, is

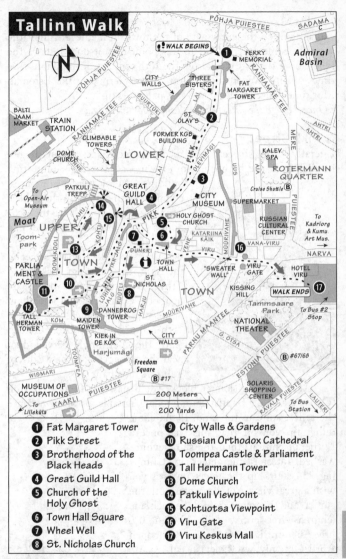

Tallinn Walk

1. Fat Margaret Tower
2. Pikk Street
3. Brotherhood of the Black Heads
4. Great Guild Hall
5. Church of the Holy Ghost
6. Town Hall Square
7. Wheel Well
8. St. Nicholas Church
9. City Walls & Gardens
10. Russian Orthodox Cathedral
11. Toompea Castle & Parliament
12. Tall Hermann Tower
13. Dome Church
14. Patkuli Viewpoint
15. Kohtuotsa Viewpoint
16. Viru Gate
17. Viru Keskus Mall

half of a **black arch.** (The other half of the arch sits in the park just below the hill.) This is a memorial to 852 people who perished in September of 1994 when the *Estonia* passenger-and-car ferry sank in stormy conditions during its Tallinn-Stockholm run. The ship's bow visor came off, and water flooded into the car deck, throwing the boat off-balance. Only 137 people survived. The crew's maneuvering of the ship after it began taking on water is thought to have caused its fatal list and capsizing.

Fat Margaret Tower (Paks Margareeta, so called for its thick walls) guarded the entry gate of the town in medieval times (the sea once came much closer to this point than it does today). The relief above the gate dates from the 16th century, during Hanseatic times, when Sweden took Estonia from Germany. The Estonian Maritime Museum in the tower is paltry—skip it.

• *Once through the gate, head up Tallinn's main drag...*

❷ Pikk Street

Literally "Long Street," the medieval merchants' main drag—leading from the harbor up into town—is lined with interesting

buildings. Many were warehouses, complete with cranes on the gables. Strolling here, you'll feel the economic power of those early German trading days.

One short block up the street on the right, the buildings nicknamed **"Three Sisters"** (now a hotel) are textbook examples of a merchant home/warehouse/office from the 15th-century Hanseatic Golden Age. The charmingly carved door near the corner evokes the wealth of Tallinn's merchant class.

After another, longer block, you'll pass **St. Olav's Church** (Oleviste Kirik, a Baptist church today), notable for what was once

the tallest spire in the land. If the name didn't tip you off that this was once a Lutheran church, then the stark, white-washed interior guarantees it. Climbing 234 stairs up the tower rewards you with a great view. You can enter both the church and the tower around the back side (church—free entry, daily 10:00-18:00, July-Aug until 20:00; tower—€2, open April-Oct only; www.oleviste.ee).

While tourists see only a peaceful scene today, locals strolling this street are reminded of dark times under Moscow's rule. The KGB used the tower at St. Olav's Church to block Finnish TV signals. The once-handsome building at **Pikk #59** (the second house after the church, on the right) was, before 1991, the sinister local headquarters of the KGB. "Creative interrogation methods" were used here. Locals well knew that the road of suffering started here, as Tallinn's troublemakers were sent to Siberian gulags. The ministry building was called the "tallest" building in town (because "when you're in the basement, you can already see Siberia"). Notice the bricked-up windows at foot level and the commemorative plaque (in Estonian only).

• *A few short blocks farther up Pikk (after the small park), on the left at #26, is the extremely ornate doorway of the...*

❸ Brotherhood of the Black Heads

Built in 1440, this house was used as a German merchants' club for nearly 500 years (until Hitler invited Estonian Germans back to their historical fatherland in the  1930s). Before the 19th century, many Estonians lived as serfs on the rural estates of the German nobles who dominated the economy. In Tallinn, the German big shots were part of the Great Guild (which we'll see farther up the street), while the German little shots had to make do with the Brotherhood of the Black Heads. This guild, or business fraternity, was limited to single German men. In Hanseatic towns, when a fire or battle had to be fought, single men were deployed first, because they had no family. Because single men were considered unattached to the community, they had no opportunity for power in the Hanseatic social structure. When a Black Head member married a local woman, he automatically gained a vested interest in the town's economy and well-being. He could then join the more prestigious Great Guild, and with that status, a promising economic and political future often opened up.

Today the hall is a concert venue (and, while you can pay to tour its interior, I'd skip it—it's basically an empty shell). Its namesake "black head" is that of St. Maurice, an early Christian soldier-martyr, beheaded in the third century A.D. for his refusal to honor the Roman gods. Reliefs decorating the building recall Tallinn's Hanseatic glory days.

Keep going along Pikk street. Architecture fans enjoy several **fanciful facades** along here, including the boldly Art Nouveau #18 (on the left, reminiscent of the architectural bounty of fellow Baltic capital Rīga; appropriately enough, today this building houses one of Tallinn's leading cutting-edge architecture firms) and the colorful, eclectic building across the street (with the pointy gable).

On the left, at #16 (look for *Kalev* awnings), the famous and recommended **Maiasmokk** ("Sweet Tooth") coffee shop, in business since 1864, remains a fine spot for a cheap coffee-and-pastry break.

• *Just ahead, pause at the big yellow building on the right (at #17).*

❹ Great Guild Hall (Suurgildi Hoone)

With its wide (and therefore highly taxed) front, the Great Guild Hall was the epitome of wealth. Remember, this was the home of the most prestigious of Tallinn's Hanseatic-era guilds. Today it houses the worthwhile **Museum of Estonian History,** offering a concise, engaging, well-presented survey of this country's story (for details, see "Sights in Tallinn," later).

• *Across Pikk street from the Great Guild Hall is the...*

❺ Church of the Holy Ghost (Pühavaimu Kirik)

Sporting an outdoor clock from 1633, this pretty medieval church is worth a visit. (The plaque on the wall just behind the ticket desk is in Estonian and Russian, but not English; this dates from before 1991, when things were designed for "inner tourism"—within the USSR.) The church retains its 14th-century design. Flying from the back pillar, the old flag of Tallinn—the same as today's red-and-white Danish flag—recalls 13th-century Danish rule. (The name "Tallinn" means "Danish Town.") The Danes sold Tallinn to the German Teutonic Knights, who lost it to the Swedes, who lost it to the Russians. The windows are mostly from the 1990s (€1, Mon-Sat 9:00-18:00, closes earlier in winter, closed most of Sun to non-worshippers, Pühavaimu 2, tel. 646-4430, www.eelk.ee). The church hosts English-language Lutheran services Sundays at 15:00 (maybe earlier in summer).

• *If you were to go down the street to the left as you face the church, it's a three-minute walk to the **Tallinn City Museum** (described later, under "Sights in Tallinn").*

  Leading alongside the church, tiny Saiakang lane (meaning "White Bread"—bread, cakes, and pies have been sold here since medieval times) takes you to...

❻ Town Hall Square (Raekoja Plats)

A marketplace through the centuries, with a cancan of fine old buildings, this is the focal point of the Old Town. The square was the center of the autonomous lower town, a merchant city of Hanseatic traders. Once, it held criminals chained to pillories for public humiliation and knights showing off in chivalrous tournaments; today it's full of Scandinavians and Russians savoring cheap beer, children singing on the bandstand, and cruise-ship groups following the numbered paddles carried high by their well-scrubbed local guides.

The 15th-century **Town Hall** (Raekoda) dominates the square; it's now a museum, and climbing its tower earns you a commanding

view (see photo; for details, see page 672).

On the opposite side of the square, across from #12 in the corner, the **pharmacy** (Raeapteek) dates from 1422 and claims—as do many—to be Europe's oldest. With decor that goes back to medieval times, the still-operating pharmacy welcomes visitors with painted ceiling beams, English descriptions, and long-expired aspirin. Past the functioning counter is a room of display cases with historical exhibits (free entry, Tue-Sat 10:00-18:00, closed Sun-Mon).

Town Hall Square is ringed by inviting but touristy eateries, a few of which are still affordable, such as Troika and the Kehrwieder cafés. The TI is a block away (behind Town Hall).

• *Facing the Town Hall, head right up Dunkri street—lined with several more eateries—one long block to the* ❼ *wheel well, named for the "high-tech" wheel, a marvel that made fetching water easier.*

Turn left on Rataskaevu street (which soon becomes Rüütli) and walk two short blocks to...

❽ St. Nicholas Church (Niguliste Kirik)

This 13th-century Gothic church-turned-art-museum served the German merchants and knights who lived in this neighborhood 500 years ago. On March 9, 1944, while Tallinn was in German hands, Soviet forces bombed the city, and the church and surrounding area—once a charming district, dense with medieval buildings—were burned out; only the church was rebuilt.

The church's interior houses a fine collection of mostly Gothic-era ecclesiastical art (€3.50, Wed-Sun

10:00-17:00, last entry 30 minutes before closing, closed Mon-Tue; organ concerts Sat and Sun at 16:00 included in admission).

You'll enter the church through the modern cellar, where you can see photos of the WWII destruction of the building (with its toppled steeple). Then make your way into the vast, open church interior. Front and center is the collection's highlight: a retable (framed altarpiece) from 1481, by Herman Rode—an exquisite example of the northern Germanic late-Gothic style. Along with scenes from the life of St. Nicholas and an array of other saints, the altarpiece shows the skyline of Lübeck, Germany (Rode's home-town, and—like Tallinn—a Hanseatic trading city). The intricate symbolism is explained by a nearby touchscreen. Also look for another work by a Lübeck master, Bernt Notke's *Danse Macabre* ("Dance of Death"). Once nearly 100 feet long, the surviving frag-ment shows sinister skeletons approaching people from all walks of life. This common medieval theme reminds the viewer that life is fleeting, and no matter who we are, we'll all wind up in the same place.

• *As you face the church, if you were to turn left and walk downhill on Rüütli street, you'd soon pass near* **Freedom Square**—*for a taste of modern Tallinn (described on page 673).*

But for now, let's continue our walk into the upper town.

PART 2: THE UPPER TOWN (TOOMPEA)

• *At the corner opposite the church, climb uphill along the steep, cobbled, Lühike Jalg ("Short Leg Lane"), home to a few quality craft shops. At the top of the lane, pause at the giant stone tower, noticing the original oak door—one of two gates through the wall separating the two cities. This passage is still the ritual meeting point of the mayor and prime minister whenever there is an important agreement between town and country.*

Facing that tower and door, turn left and go through the café court-yard to its far end. You'll emerge into a beautiful view terrace in front of the...

❾ City Walls and Gardens

The imposing city wall once had 46 towers, of which 26 still stand. The gravel-and-grass strip that runs in front of the wall offers a fun stroll and fine views. If you have interest and energy, you can also climb some of the towers and ramparts. (While the views from the towers are nice, keep in mind that we'll be reaching some even more dramatic viewpoints—overlooking different parts of town—later on this walk.)

The easiest option is to simply scramble up the extremely steep and tight steps of the **Dannebrog restaurant tower;** you can buy a drink or a cheap meal here (€5 soups, €7 pastas), but they generally don't charge those who just want a quick look at the view.

To reach a higher vantage point—or if Dannebrog is charging admission—you can pay €3 to enter the nearby **Maiden Tower** (Neitsitorn). It has a few skippable exhibits, an overpriced café, and great views—particularly from the top floor, where a full glass wall reveals panoramic town views (tower and café open daily 10:30-22:00, exhibits open until 19:00, shorter hours Oct-April).

With more time, add a visit to the **Kiek in de Kök**—the stout, round tower that sits farther along the wall (with extremely tight,

twisty, steep stone staircases inside). While fun to say, the name is Low German for "Peek in the Kitchen"—so called because it's situated to allow guards to literally peek into townspeople's homes. This tower is bigger than the Maiden Tower, with more impressive exhibits—not a lot of real artifacts, but plenty of cannons, mannequins, model ships, movies, and models of the castle to give you a taste of Tallinn's medieval heyday. The €7 combo-ticket with the Maiden Tower lets you walk along the scenic rampart between the two towers (find the door marked *Väljapääs* on the second floor of the Maiden Tower, and open it with your wristband ticket; also possible to enter just Kiek in de Kök with €4.50 ticket; extra for tour of tunnels below the tower).

• *When you're finished with the towers and ramparts, go through the hole in the wall, and head uphill into the upper town.*

Circle around the left side of the big, onion-domed church; as you stroll, on your left is the so-called **"Danish King's Garden."** Tallinn is famous among Danes as the birthplace of their flag. According to legend, the Danes were losing a battle here. Suddenly, a white cross fell from heaven and landed in a pool of blood. The Danes were inspired and went on to win. To this day, their flag is a white cross on a red background.

• *Complete your circle around to the far side of the church (facing the pink palace) to enjoy a great view of the cathedral, and to find the entrance.*

⑩ Russian Orthodox Cathedral

The Alexander Nevsky Cathedral—worth ▲▲—is a gorgeous building. But ever since the day it was built (in 1900), it has been a jab in the eye for Estonians. The church went up near the end of the two centuries when Estonia was part of the Russian Empire. And, as throughout Europe in the late 19th century, Tallinn's oppressed ethnic groups—the Estonians and the Germans—were caught up in national revival movements, celebrating their own culture, language, and history rather than their Russian overlords'. So the Russians flexed their cultural muscle by building this church in this location, facing the traditional Estonian seat of power, and over the supposed grave of a legendary Estonian hero, Kalevipoeg. They also tore down a statue of Martin Luther to make room.

The church has been exquisitely renovated inside and out. Step inside for a sample of Russian Orthodoxy (church free and open daily 8:00-19:00, icon art in gift shop). It's OK to visit discreetly during services (daily at 9:00 and 18:00), when you'll hear priests singing the liturgy in a side chapel. Typical of Russian Orthodox churches, it has glittering icons (the highest concentration fills the big screen—called an iconostasis—that shields the altar from the congregation), no pews (worshippers stand through the service), and air that's heavy with incense. All of these features combine to create a mystical, otherworldly worship experience. Notice the many candles, each representing a prayer; if there's a request or a thank-you in your heart, you're welcome to buy one at the desk by the door. Exploring this space, keep in mind that about 40 percent of Tallinn's population is ethnic Russian.

• *Across the street is the...*

⓫ Toompea Castle (Toompea Loss)

The pink palace is an 18th-century Russian addition onto the medieval Toompea Castle. Today, it's the Estonian Parliament (Riigigoku) building, flying the Estonian flag—the flag of both the first (1918-1940) and second (1991-present) Estonian republics. Notice the Estonian seal: three lions for three great battles in Estonian history, and oak leaves for strength and stubbornness. Ancient pagan Estonians, who believed spirits lived in oak trees, would walk through forests of oak to toughen up. (To this day, Estonian cemeteries are in forests. Keeping some of their pagan sensibilities, they believe the spirits of the departed live on in the trees.)

• *Facing the palace, go left through the gate into the park to see the...*

⓬ Tall Hermann Tower (Pikk Hermann)

This tallest tower of the castle wall is a powerful symbol here. For 50 years, while

Estonian flags were hidden in cellars, the Soviet flag flew from Tall Hermann. As the USSR was unraveling, Estonians proudly and defiantly replaced the red Soviet flag here with their own black, white, and blue flag.

• *Backtrack and go uphill, passing the Russian church on your right. Climb Toom-Kooli street to the...*

⓭ Dome Church (Toomkirik)

Estonia is ostensibly Lutheran, but few Tallinners go to church. A recent Gallup Poll showed Estonia to be the least religious country

in the European Union—only 14 percent of respondents identified religion as an important part of their daily lives. Most churches double as concert venues or museums, but this one is still used for worship. Officially St. Mary's Church—but popularly called the Dome Church—it's a perfect example of simple Northern European Gothic, built in the 13th century during Danish rule, then rebuilt after a 1684 fire. Once the church of Tallinn's wealthy German-speaking aristocracy, it's littered with more than a hundred coats of arms, carved by local masters as memori-

als to the deceased and inscribed with German tributes. The earliest dates from the 1600s, the latest from around 1900. For €5, you can climb 140 steps up the tower to enjoy the view (church entry free, daily 9:00-18:00, www.eelk.ee/tallinna.toom).

• *Leaving the church, turn left and hook around the back of the building. You'll pass a slanted tree, then the big, green, former noblemen's clubhouse on your right (at #1, vacated when many Germans left Estonia in the 1930s). Head down cobbled Rahukohtu lane (to the right of the yellow, pyramid-shaped house). Strolling the street, notice the embassy signs: Government offices and embassies have moved into these buildings and spruced up the neighborhood. Continue straight under the arch and belly up to the grand...*

⓮ Patkuli Viewpoint

Survey the scene. On the far left, the Neoclassical facade of the executive branch of Estonia's government enjoys the view. Below you, a bit of the old moat remains. The *Group* sign marks Tallinn's tiny train station, and the clutter of stalls

behind that is the rustic market. Out on the water, ferries shuttle to and from Helsinki (just 50 miles away). Beyond the lower town's medieval wall and towers stands the green spire of St. Olav's Church, once 98 feet taller and, locals claim, the world's tallest tower in 1492. Far in the distance is the 1,000-foot-tall TV tower, the site of a standoff between Soviet paratroopers and Estonian patriots in 1991 (see page 681).

During Soviet domination, Finnish TV was even more important, as it gave Estonians their only look at Western lifestyles. Imagine: In the 1980s, many locals had never seen a banana or a pineapple—except on TV. People still talk of the day that Finland broadcast the soft-porn movie *Emmanuelle*. A historic migration of Estonians purportedly flocked from the countryside to Tallinn to get within rabbit-ear's distance of Helsinki and see all that flesh onscreen. The TV tower was recently refurbished and opened to visitors.

• *Go back through the arch, turn immediately left down the narrow lane, turn right (onto Toom-Rüütli), take the first left, and pass through the trees to the...*

⓯ Kohtuotsa Viewpoint

Scan the view from left to right. On the far left is St. Olav's Church, then the busy cruise port and the skinny white spire of the Church

of the Holy Ghost. The narrow gray spire farther to the right is the 16th-century Town Hall tower. On the far right is the tower of St. Nicholas Church. Below you, visually trace Pikk street, Tallinn's historic main drag, which winds through the Old Town, leading from Toompea Castle down the hill (from right to left), through the gate tower, past the Church of the Holy Ghost, behind St. Olav's, and out to the harbor. Less picturesque is the clutter of Soviet-era apartment blocks on the distant horizon. The nearest skyscraper (white) is Hotel Viru, in Soviet times the biggest hotel in the Baltics, and infamous as a clunky, dingy slumbermill. Locals joke that Hotel Viru was built from a new Soviet wonder material called "micro-concrete" (60 percent concrete, 40 percent microphones). Underneath the hotel is the modern Viru Keskus, a huge shopping mall and local transit center, where this walk will end. To the left of Hotel Viru, between it and the ferry terminals, is the Rotermann

Quarter, where old industrial buildings are being revamped into a new commercial zone.

• *From the viewpoint, descend to the lower town. Go out and left down Kohtu, past the Finnish Embassy (on your left). Back at the Dome Church, the slanted tree points the way, left down Piiskopi ("Bishop's Street"). At the onion domes, turn left again and follow the old wall down Pikk Jalg ("Long Leg Lane") into the lower town. Go under the tower, then straight on Pikk street, and after two doors turn right on Voorimehe, which leads into Town Hall Square.*

⓰ Through Viru Gate

Cross through the square (left of the Town Hall's tower) and go downhill (passing the kitschy medieval Olde Hansa Restaurant, with its bonneted waitresses and merry men). Continue straight down Viru street toward Hotel Viru, the blocky white skyscraper in the distance. Viru street is old Tallinn's busiest and kitschiest shopping street. Just past the strange and modern wood/glass/stone mall, Müürivahe street leads left along the old wall, called the "Sweater Wall." This is a colorful and tempting gauntlet of women selling knitwear (anything with images and bright colors is likely machine-made). Katariina Käik, a lane with glassblowing shops, leads left, beyond the sweaters. Back on Viru street, pass the golden arches and walk through the medieval arches—Viru Gate—that mark the end of old Tallinn. Outside the gates, opposite Viru 23, above the flower stalls, is a small park on a piece of old bastion known as the Kissing Hill (come up here after dark and you'll find out why).

• *Use the crosswalk to your right to reach the...*

⓱ Viru Keskus Mall

Here, behind Hotel Viru, at the end of this walk, you'll find the real world: basement supermarket, ticket service, bookstore, and many bus and tram stops. If you still have energy, you can cross the busy street by the complex and explore the nearby Rotermann Quarter (see page 675).

Sights in Tallinn

IN OR NEAR THE OLD TOWN

Central Tallinn has dozens of small museums, most suitable only for specialized tastes. The following sights are the ones I'd visit first.

TALLINN

▲Museum of Estonian History (Eesti Ajaloomuuseum)

The Great Guild Hall on Pikk street (described on my self-guided walk, earlier) houses this modern, well-presented-in-English exhibit. The museum's "Estonia 101" approach—combining lots of actual artifacts (from prehistory to today) and high-tech interactive exhibits—is geared toward educating first-time visitors about this obscure but endearing little country.

Cost and Hours: €5, May-Aug daily 10:00-18:00, same hours off-season except closed Wed, tel. 696-8690, www.ajaloomuuseum. ee.

Visiting the Museum: As you enter, download the free smartphone audioguide to navigate the collection. Pondering the question of what it means to be an Estonian, you'll view a coin collection of past currencies (including the Soviet ruble and the pre-euro krooni), then head into the whitewashed vaulted hall to see the "Spirit of Survival" exhibit, which traces 11,000 years of Estonian history. Steep steps lead down into the cellar, with an armory, ethnographic collection, items owned by historical figures, an exhibit about the Great Guild Hall itself, and a fun "time capsule" that lets you insert your face into videos illustrating episodes in local history.

Town Hall (Raekoda) and Tower

This museum facing Town Hall Square is open to the general public only in the summer. It has exhibits on the town's administration and history, along with an interesting bit on the story of limestone. The tower, the place to see all of Tallinn, rewards those who climb its 155 steps with a wonderful city view.

Cost and Hours: Museum—€5, entrance through cellar, July-Aug Mon-Sat 10:00-16:00, closed Sun and Sept-June; audioguide-€4.75; tower—€3, May-mid-Sept daily 11:00-18:00, closed rest of year; tel. 645-7900, www.tallinn.ee/raekoda.

Tallinn City Museum (Tallinna Linnamuuseum)

This humble museum, filling a 14th-century townhouse, features Tallinn history from 1200 to the 1950s. It displays everyday items through history. Even though there are basic English explanations, it's not enough; the museum is a loose collection of artifacts that offers a few intimate peeks at local lifestyles.

Cost and Hours: €3.20, March-Oct Wed-Mon 10:30-18:00, Nov-Feb Wed-Mon 10:00-17:30, closed Tue year-round, last entry 30 minutes before closing, Vene 17, at corner of Pühavaimu, tel. 615-5183, www.linnamuuseum.ee.

Visiting the Museum: You'll begin on the ground floor, at a model of circa-1825 Tallinn—looking much like it does today. Then you'll head up through three more floors, exploring exhibits on the port (with model ships), guilds (tools and products), advertising in the 1920s and 30s (chronicling the rise of modern local industries in pre-Soviet times), Tallinn's Estonian identity (with recreated rooms from the early 20th century), and the Soviet period (displaying propaganda, including children's art that celebrated the regime).

Freedom Square (Vabaduse Väljak)

Once a USSR-era parking lot at the southern tip of the Old Town, this fine public zone was recently revamped: The cars were moved underground, and now a glassy new plaza invites locals (and very few tourists) to linger. The recommended **Wabadus café,** with tables out on the square, is a popular hangout. The space, designed to host special events, feels a bit stern and at odds with the cutesy cobbles just a few steps away. But it's an easy opportunity to glimpse a contrast to the tourists' Tallinn.

The towering **cross** monument facing the square (marked *Eesti Vabadussõda 1918-1920*) honors the Estonian War of Independence.

Shortly after the Bolshevik Revolution set a new course for Russia, the Estonians took advantage of the post-WWI reshuffling of Europe to rise up and create—for the first time ever—an independent Estonian state. The "cross of liberty" on top of the pillar represents a military decoration from that war (and every war since). The hill behind the cross has more monuments, and fragments of past fortifications.

Across the busy street from the square, the hulking, red-brick building houses the **office of Tallinn's mayor.** Edgar Savisaar, a former prime minister, has been mayor of this city twice (most recently since 2007). Criticized by some for his authoritarian approach and his coziness with Russia, Savisaar is adored by others for his aggressive legislation. For example, in 2013, he made all public transit completely free to anyone living within the city limits—a move designed to cut commuting costs (and carbon emissions) and to lure suburbanites to move into the town center. Younger locals grumble about what they jokingly term *"Homo soveticus"*—a different species of Estonian who was raised in Soviet times and is accustomed to a system where everything is free. To this day, governmental giveaways are the easiest way to boost approval ratings.

If you're interested in Estonia's 20th- and 21st-century history, it's an easy five-minute walk from this square to the next sight.

TALLINN

▲Museum of Occupations (Okupatsioonide Muuseum)

Locals insist that Estonia didn't formally lose its independence from 1939 to 1991, but was just "occupied"—first by the Soviets (for one year), then by the Nazis (for three years), and then again by the USSR (for nearly 50 years). Built with funding from a wealthy Estonian-American, this compact museum tells the history of Estonia during its occupations.

Cost and Hours: €5, June-Aug Tue-Sun 10:00-18:00, Sept-May Tue-Sun 11:00-18:00, closed Mon year-round, skip the amateurish €4 audioguide, Toompea 8, at corner of Kaarli Puiestee, tel. 668-0250, www.okupatsioon.ee.

Visiting the Museum: Entering, you'll walk past a poignant monument made of giant suitcases—a reminder of people who fled the country. After buying your ticket, pick up the English descriptions and explore. (The ticket desk also sells a well-chosen range of English-language books on the occupation years.)

The exhibit is organized around seven TV monitors screening 30-minute **documentary films** (with dry commentary, archival footage, and interviews)—each focusing on a different time period. At each screen, use the mouse to select English. Surrounding each monitor is a display case crammed with artifacts of the era. The footage of the Singing Revolution is particularly stirring.

Before settling into the film loop, take a quick clockwise spin from the ticket desk to see the larger **exhibits,** which illustrate how the Soviets kept the Estonians in line. First you'll see a rustic boat that a desperate defector actually rowed across the Baltic Sea to the Swedish island of Gotland. Look for the unsettling surveillance peephole, which will make you want to carefully examine your hotel room tonight. Surrounded by a lot more of those symbolic suitcases, the large monument with a swastika and a red star is a reminder that Estonia was occupied by not one, but two different regimes in the 20th century. You'll also see vintage cars, phone boxes, and radios that give a flavor of that era. Near the center of the exhibit, somber prison doors evoke the countless lives lost to detention and deportation.

Near those prison doors, take the red-velvet staircase down to the **basement.** There, near the WCs, is a collection of Soviet-era statues of communist leaders—once they lorded over the people, now they're in the cellar guarding the toilets.

Nearby: One of Tallinn's most famous recent sights *can't* be seen in its original location, in front of the National Library (just south of the Museum of Occupations). Called simply **The Bronze Sol-**

dier, this six-foot-tall statue of a Soviet solider marked the graves of Russians who died fighting to liberate Tallinn in 1944. In 2007, the Estonian government exhumed those graves and moved them—along with the statue—from this very central location to the Tallinn Military Cemetery, on the city's southern outskirts. Estonia's sizeable Russian minority balked at this move, and—through a series of protests and clashes—grabbed the world's attention. The Kremlin took note, furious protestors surrounded the Estonian embassy in Moscow for a week (essentially laying siege to the building), and mysterious "cyberattacks" from Russian IP addresses crippled Estonian governmental websites. When the dust settled, The Bronze Soldier stayed in its new home—but Estonians of all stripes were confronted with a bitter reminder that even a generation after independence, tensions between ethnic Russians and ethnic Estonians have not been entirely resolved.

▲Rotermann Quarter (Rotermanni Kvartal)

Sprawling between Hotel Viru and the port, just east of the Old Town, this 19th-century industrial zone is being redeveloped into

shopping, office, and living space. Characteristic old brick shells are being topped with visually striking glass-and-steel additions. For those interested in the gentrification of an aging city—and even for those who aren't—it's worth a quick stroll to see the cutting edge of old-meets-new Nordic architecture. While construction is ongoing, and the area still feels a bit soulless (only a few shops and restaurants are open), developers are setting the stage for the creation of a vital new downtown district. I've recommended two good restaurants that give you an excuse to walk five minutes across the street from the Old Town to take a look around; see "Eating in Tallinn," later. To see the first completed section, start at Hotel Viru, cross busy Narva Maantee and walk down Roseni street. At #7 you'll find the hard-to-resist Kalev chocolate shop, selling Estonia's best-known sweets (Mon-Sat 10:00-20:00, Sun 11:00-18:00).

KADRIORG PARK AND THE KUMU MUSEUM

▲Kadriorg Park

This expansive seaside park, home to a summer royal residence and the Kumu Art Museum, is just a five-minute tram ride or a 25-minute walk from Hotel Viru. After Russia took over Tallinn in 1710, Peter the Great built the cute, pint-sized Kadriorg Palace for Czarina Catherine (the palace's name means "Catherine's Valley"). Stately, peaceful, and crisscrossed by leafy paths, the park has a rose garden, duck-filled pond, playground and benches, and old czarist guardhouses harkening back to the days of Russian rule. It's a delightful place for a stroll or a picnic. If it's rainy, duck into one of the cafés in the park's art museums (described below).

Getting There: Reach the park on tram #1 or #3 (direction: Kadriorg; catch at any tram stop around the Old Town). Get off at the Kadriorg stop (the end of the line, where trams turn and head back into town), and walk 200 yards straight ahead and up Weizenbergi, the park's main avenue. Peter's summer palace is on the left; behind it, visit the formal garden (free). At the end of the avenue is the Kumu Art Museum, the park's most important sight. A taxi from Hotel Viru to this area should cost €5 or less. If you're returning from here directly to the port to catch your cruise ship or boat to Helsinki, use tram #1—it stops at the Linnahall stop near the main cruise port and Terminals A, B, and C (a bit father from Terminal D).

Visiting Kadriorg Park: The palace's manicured **gardens** (free to enter) are a pure delight; on weekends, you'll likely see a steady parade of brides and grooms here, posing for wedding pictures. The summer palace itself is home to the **Kadriorg Art Museum** (Kadrioru Kunstimuuseum), with very modest Russian and Western European galleries (€4.80; May-Sept Tue-Sun 10:00-17:00, Wed until 20:00, closed Mon; same hours off-season except closed Mon-Tue; Weizenbergi 37, tel. 606-6400, www.kadriorumuuseum.ee).

The fenced-off yard directly behind the garden is where you'll spot the local "White House" (although it's pink)—home of **Estonia's president.** Walk around to the far side to find its main entrance, with the seal of Estonia above the door, flagpoles flying both the Estonian and the EU flags, and stone-faced guards.

A five-minute walk beyond the presidential palace takes you to the Kumu Art Museum, described next. For a longer walk from here, the rugged park rolls down toward the sea.

▲▲Kumu Art Museum
(Kumu Kunstimuuseum)

This main branch of the Art Museum of Estonia brings the nation's best art together in a striking modern building designed by an international (well, at least Finnish) architect, Pekka Vapaavuori. The entire collec-

tion is accessible, well-presented, and engaging, with a particularly thought-provoking section on art from the Soviet period. The museum is well worth the trip for art lovers, or for anyone intrigued by the unique spirit of this tiny nation—particularly when combined with a stroll through the nearby palace gardens (described earlier) on a sunny day.

Cost and Hours: €5.50, or €4.20 for just the permanent collection; May-Sept Tue-Sun 11:00-18:00, Wed until 20:00, closed Mon; same hours off-season except closed Mon-Tue; audioguide-€3.20; trendy café, tel. 602-6000, www.kumu.ee.

Getting There: To reach the museum, follow the instructions for Kadriorg Park, explained earlier; Kumu is at the far end of the park. To get from the Old Town to Kumu directly without walking through the park, take bus #67 or #68 (each runs every 10-15 minutes, #68 does not run on Sun); both leave from Teatri Väljak, on the far side of the pastel yellow theater, across from the Solaris shopping mall. Get off at the Kumu stop, then walk up the stairs and across the bridge.

Visiting the Museum: Just off the ticket lobby (on the second floor), the **great hall** has temporary exhibits; however, the permanent collection on the third and fourth floors is Kumu's main draw. While you can rent an audioguide, I found the free laminated sheets in most rooms enough to enjoy the collection. The maze-like layout on each floor presents the art chronologically.

The **third floor** displays a concise "Treasury of Estonian Art" through the mid-20th century. It starts with 18th-century por-

traits of local aristocrats, then moves through 19th-century Romanticism (including some nice views of Tallinn, scenes of Estonian nature, and idealized images of Estonian peasant women in folk costumes). Eduard von Gebhardt's engaging *Sermon on the Mount* (1904) includes a wide variety of Estonian portraits—some attentive, others distracted—listening to Jesus' most famous address. You'll see the Estonian version of several Modernist styles: Pointillism (linger over the lyrical landscapes of Konrad Mägi and the recently rediscovered works of Herbert Lukk), Cubism, and Expressionism. In the 1930s, the Pallas School provided a more traditional, back-to-nature response to the wild artistic trends of the time. By the dawn of World War II, you can see the art growing even more conservative, and the final canvases, from the war years, convey an unmistakable melancholy. In the corner, one very high-ceilinged room has a wall lined with dozens of expressive busts by sculptor Villu Jaanisoo.

The **fourth-floor exhibit,** called "Difficult Choices," is a fascinating survey of Estonian art from the end of World War II until "re-independence" in 1991. Some of the works are mainstream (read: Soviet-style), while others are by dissident artists.

Estonian art parted ways with Western Europe with the Soviet takeover in 1945. The Soviets insisted that artworks actively promote the communist struggle, and to that end, Estonian artists were forced to adopt the Stalinist formula, making paintings that were done in the traditional national style but that were socialist in content—in the style now called **Socialist Realism.**

Socialist Realism had its roots in the early 20th-century Realist movement, whose artists wanted to depict the actual conditions of life rather than just glamour and wealth—in America, think of John Steinbeck's novels or Walker Evans' photographs of the rural poor. In the Soviet Union, this artistic curiosity about the working class was perverted into an ideology: Art was supposed to glorify labor and the state's role in distributing its fruits. In a system where there was ultimately little incentive to work hard, art was seen as a tool to motivate the masses, and to support the Communist Party's hold on power.

In the collection's first room, called "A Tale of Happiness," you'll see syrupy images of what Soviet leadership imagined to be the ideal of communist Estonia. In *Agitator Amongst the Voters* (1952), a stern portrait of Stalin in the hazy background keeps an eye on a young hotshot articulating some questionable ideas; his listeners' reactions range from shudders of horror to smirks of superiority. *The Young Aviators* (1951) shows an eager youngster wearing a bright-red neckerchief (indicating his membership in the Pioneers, the propaganda-laden communist version of Scouts) telling his enraptured schoolmates stories about a model airplane.

The next room shows canvases of miners, protesters, speechifiers, metalworkers, tractor drivers, and more all doing their utmost for the communist society. You'll also see paintings of industrial achievements (like bridges) and party meetings. Because mining was integral to the Estonian economy, miners were portrayed as local heroes, marching like soldiers to their

TALLINN

glorious labor. Women were depicted toiling side by side with men, as equal partners. (Though they're not always on display here, posters were a natural fit, with slogans exhorting laborers to work hard on behalf of the regime.)

While supposedly a reflection of "real" life, Socialist Realism art was formulaic and showed little creative spirit. Though some Estonian artists flirted with social commentary and the avant-garde, a few ended up in Siberia as a result. Stroll through a few more rooms, noticing a handful of artists who attempted some bolder compositions. Also keep an eye out for a sly portrait of the "great leader"—Stalin.

Later, in the Brezhnev years, Estonian artists managed to slip Surrealist, Pop, and Photorealist themes into their work (for example, Rein Tammik's large painting *1945-1975*, which juxtaposes an old tractor with the flower children of the Swingin' Sixties). Estonia was the only part of the USSR that recognized Pop Art. As the Soviets would eventually learn, change was unstoppable.

The rest of the museum is devoted to temporary exhibits, with contemporary art always on the **fifth floor** (where there's a nice view back to the Old Town from the far gallery). It's also worth admiring the mostly successful **architecture**—the building is partly dug into the limestone hill, and the facade is limestone, too (for the big picture, look for the model of the building, just inside the main doors).

ALONG THE HARBORFRONT
▲▲Seaplane Harbor (Lennusadam)

One of Tallinn's newest and most ambitious sights, this nautical, aviation, and military museum fills a gigantic old hangar along the waterfront north of downtown. It has loads of hands-on activities for kids, and thrills anyone interested in transportation, while others find it off-puttingly militaristic. (The many Russian tourists who enjoy posing with its machine-gun simulators don't help matters.)

Cost and Hours: €10; May-Sept daily 10:00-19:00; same hours off-season except closed Mon; last entry one hour before closing, Vesilennuki 6, tel. 620-0550, www.seaplaneharbour.com.

Getting There: It's along the waterfront, about a mile north of the Old Town. It's a long but doable **walk,** made more enjoyable if you follow the red-gravel "Culture Kilometer" (Kultuurikilomeeter) seaside path from near the cruise terminals. While there's no handy tram or bus to the museum, a one-way **taxi** from the town center shouldn't cost much more than €5. The **hop-on, hop-off buses** also stop here.

Visiting the Museum: When you buy your ticket, you'll be issued an electronic card, which you can use at terminals posted throughout the exhibit to email yourself articles on topics that interest you. The entire collection is enlivened by lots of interactive screens, giant movies, and simulators (such as huge-scale shoot-'em-up video games with life-sized artillery). Touchscreens explain everything in three languages: Estonian, Russian, and English...in that order.

The cavernous old **seaplane hangar** cleverly displays exhibits on three levels: the ground floor features items from below the sea (such as a salvaged 16th-century shipwreck, plus a cinema that shows films subtitled in English); catwalks halfway up connect exhibits dealing with the sea surface (the impressive boat collection—from buoys to sailboats to the massive *Lembit* sub); and airplanes are suspended overhead. Touchscreens provide more information in English; just take your time exploring the collection. The star of the show is the 195-foot-long *Lembit* submarine from 1937: Estonian-commissioned and British-built, this vessel saw fighting in World War II and later spent several decades in the service of the USSR's Red Fleet. You can climb down below decks to see how the sailors lived, peek through the periscope, and even stare down the torpedo tubes. A cool café on the top level (above the entrance) overlooks the entire space, which feels endless.

Outside, filling the old harbor, is the maritime museum's collection of **historic ships,** from old-fashioned tall ships to modern-day military boats. The highlight is the steam-powered icebreaker *Suur Tõll*, from 1914. Sometimes you can pay to go out on a brief trip on one of the sailboats (ask at the ticket desk when you enter).

On the opposite side of the building, facing the main entrance, is a collection of **military vehicles.**

OUTER TALLINN
▲Song Festival Grounds (Lauluväljak)

At this open-air theater, built in 1959 and resembling an oversized Hollywood Bowl, the Estonian nation gathers to sing. Every five years, these grounds host a huge national song festival with 25,000 singers and 100,000 spectators. During the festival, the singers rehearse from Monday through Thursday, and then, on Friday morning, dress up in their traditional outfits and march out to the Song Festival Grounds from Freedom Square. While it hosts big pop-music acts, too, it's a national monument for the compelling role it played in Estonia's fight for independence.

Since 1988, when locals sang patriotic songs here in defiance of Soviet rule, these grounds have taken on a symbolic importance to the nation. Locals vividly recall putting on folk costumes knitted by their grandmothers (some of whom later died in Siberia) and coming here with masses of Estonians to sing. Overlooking the grounds from the cheap seats is a statue of Gustav Ernesaks, who directed the Estonian National Male Choir for 50 years through the darkest times of Soviet rule. He was a power in the drive for independence, and lived to see it happen.

Estonia's Singing Revolution

When you are a humble nation of just a million people lodged between Russia and Germany (and tyrants such as Stalin and Hitler), simply surviving is a challenge. Estonia was free from 1920 to 1939. The country then had a 50-year Nazi/Soviet nightmare. Estonians say, "We were so few in numbers that we had to emphasize that we exist. We had no weapons. Being together and singing together was our power." Singing has long been a national form of expression in this country; the first Estonian Song Festival occurred in 1869, and has been held every five years since then.

Estonian culture was under siege during the Soviet era. Moscow wouldn't allow locals to wave their flag or sing patriotic songs. Russians and Ukrainians were moved in, and Estonians were shipped out in an attempt to dilute the country's identity. But as cracks began to appear in the USSR, the Estonians mobilized—by singing.

In 1988, 300,000 Estonians—imagine...a third of the population—gathered at the Song Festival Grounds outside Tallinn to sing patriotic songs. On August 23, 1989—the 50th anniversary of a notorious pact between Hitler and Stalin—the people of Latvia, Lithuania, and Estonia held hands to make "the Baltic Chain," a human chain that stretched 360 miles from Tallinn to Vilnius in Lithuania. Some feared a Tiananmen Square-type bloodbath, but Estonians kept singing.

In February of 1990, the first free parliamentary elections took place in all three Baltic states, and pro-independence candidates won majorities. In 1991, hardline communists staged a coup against Soviet leader Mikhail Gorbachev, and Estonians feared a violent crackdown. The makeshift Estonian Parliament declared independence. Then, the coup in Moscow failed. Suddenly, the USSR was gone, and Estonia was free.

Watch the documentary film *The Singing Revolution* before your visit (www.singingrevolution.com) to tune into this stirring bit of modern history and to draw inspiration from Estonia's valiant struggle for freedom.

Cost and Hours: Free, open long hours, bus #1A, #5, #8, #34A, or #38 to Lauluväljak stop.

▲Pirita Neighborhood

Several gently fascinating sights cluster in the Pirita neighborhood, just a few miles northeast of the Song Festival Grounds. If you have a car (or a local guide with a car), or have the time to lace things together with public transportation, this can be a fun way to escape the city and see some different facets of Estonia.

Getting There: It's easy to lace these sights together: You'll take the waterfront Pirita Tee highway north (passing behind the Song Festival Grounds, described earlier) to Pirita, then turn right to cut through the forest to the TV Tower. Buses #34A and #38 follow exactly this same route—departing from the underground bus platforms at Viru Keskus mall—and conveniently link all of the places listed here.

Sights in Pirita: Coming from central Tallinn on Pirita Tee, you'll pass two starkly different memorials. First, as you skirt behind Kadriorg Park, watch on the left for the **Russalka Monument** (Russalka Mälestusmärk). An angel on a pedestal commemorates the 1893 sinking of the Russian warship *Russalka* ("Mermaid"). Farther along—after passing the Song Festival Grounds—look on the right for the towering **World War II Memorial** (Maarjamäe Memoriaal)—a 115-foot-tall obelisk erected to honor those who died defending the Soviet Union, and now the centerpiece of Estonia's war memorial.

Just after crossing the Pirita River and the little marina (with the yachting center built for the 1980 Olympics), watch on the right for the **ruins of St. Bridget's Convent** (Pirita Klooster; bus stop: Pirita). This early 15th-century convent, which housed both monks and nuns (in separate quarters, of course), was destroyed in 1577 by Ivan the Terrible. Its stones were quarried to build Baltic manor houses, but today you can pay a small fee to tour the evocative Gothic ruins (www.piritaklooster.ee).

Down along the water from here, **Pirita Beach** is one of the most popular in Tallinn. On a sunny summer day, Estonians are out enjoying sand, sun, and the Baltic Sea.

At the first traffic light after the convent ruins, turn right  on Kloostrimetsa Tee, which cuts through a forest—and through the **Forest Cemetery** (Metsakalmistu), offering a poignant look at unique Estonian burial customs (bus stop: Metsakalmistu, then continue about 200 yards down the road, following *Teletorn* signs to the gate). Traditionally, Estonians bury the departed not in fields or parks, but in forests—thanks to a deeply rooted belief that their spirit will live on in the trees. This particular cemetery is one of Estonia's best-known, and is the eternal resting place both of commoners and of VIPs—athletes, chess champions, musicians, writers, and politicians. Exploring here, find the "Hill of Celebrities" (Kuulsuste Küngas). Among the illustrious Estonians buried here is Konstantin Päts (1847-1956), the first president of independent Estonia, who later died in a Siberian mental institution. After freedom, his remains were located and moved here to be re-interred. Lydia Koidula (1843-1886, marked by a red stone) was Estonia's premier 19th-century poet and wrote the first play in Estonian.

Just past the Forest Cemetery, the **TV tower** (Teletorn)—with its antenna copping 1,000 feet tall—was built for the 1980 Moscow Olympics (the sailing regatta took place in Tallinn). You can ride up to the 550-foot-high observation deck for sweeping views over Estonia (and, on a clear day, all the way to Finland) and the endearing "Estonian Hall of Fame," celebrating Estonian contributions to the world (www.teletorn.ee).

In front of the tower, you'll see a monument to the brave Estonians who faced off against a potential Soviet counterattack. On August 19, 1991, a coup by generals in Moscow created confusion and panic across the USSR. The next day, on August 20—still celebrated today as Estonia's national holiday—the Declaration of Independence was signed. On August 21, Russian military forces moved to take this national broadcast tower and cut off Estonian communications. But two policemen and some radio operators cleverly prevented them from entering the tower's control station, by jamming the door and threatening to engage the fire-exhaust system. Eventually a ragtag gang of Estonian civilians showed up to defend the tower and stare down the troops. By late afternoon, it became clear that Boris Yeltsin had gained control in Moscow, and the Russian troops were told to stand down. Estonia had its tower—and a few weeks later, Russia recognized this little country's right to exist.

Lasnamäe Neighborhood

In its attempt to bring Estonia into the Soviet fold, Moscow moved tens of thousands of Russian workers into Tallinn, using the promise of new apartments as an incentive. Today, two generations later, Tallinn has a huge Russian minority (about 40 percent of the city's population) and three huge, charmless suburbs of ugly, Soviet-built apartments: Mustamäe, Õismäe, and Lasnamäe.

Sights in Lasnamäe: Today, about one of every two Tallinners lives in one of these Brezhnev-era suburbs of massive, cookie-cutter apartment blocks (many now privatized). About eighty percent of the residents who live in Lasnamäe are Russian-speaking. Some parts are poor, rough, and edgy (not comfortable after dark), with blue lights in the public toilets so that junkies can't see their veins. Other sections are nicer, and by day, you can visit here without fear. Some zones are finally being upgraded with a spare-no-expense local pride; a new Russian Orthodox cathedral opened here in 2013 (built with the support of Tallinn's mayor to curry favor with ethnic-Russian voters). Some "social apartment" buildings—owned by the city—were also recently built in this area.

Forging Russians and Estonians into a single society, with the Estonian language dominant, was an optimistic goal in the early 1990s. Ethnic Russians grumbled, but knew they probably had a brighter economic future in Estonia than in Russia. Now, with a new generation of children learning both languages in school and most enjoying reasonable prosperity, peaceful ethnic coexistence (like between Swedes and Finns in Helsinki) may be achievable.

Getting There: For a quick look at Lasnamäe, hop on bus #67 or #68 (each runs every 10-15 minutes); both leave from Teatri Väljak, on the far side of the pastel yellow theater from the Old Town, across from the Solaris shopping mall. You'll see carefully dressed young women, track-suited men, grass that needs mowing, cracked paving stones, grandmothers pushing strollers, and lots of new, boxy shops. Ride to the last stop (about 25 minutes), then return to town.

▲Estonian Open-Air Museum (Vabaõhumuuseum)

Influenced by their ties with Nordic countries, Estonians are enthusiastic advocates of open-air museums. For this one, they sal-

vaged farm buildings, windmills, and an old church from rural areas and transported them to a park-like setting just outside town (4 miles west of the Old Town). The goal: to both save and share their heritage. Attendants are posted in many houses, but to really visualize life in the old houses, rent the audioguide (€7/3 hours). The park's Kolu Tavern serves traditional dishes. You can rent a bike (€3/hour) for a breezy roll to quiet, far-away spaces in the park.

Cost and Hours: Late April-Sept: €7, park open daily 10:00-20:00, historic buildings until 18:00; Oct-late April: €5, park open daily 10:00-17:00 but many buildings closed; tel. 654-9100, www.evm.ee.

Getting There: Take bus #21 or #21B from the train station to the Rocca al Mare stop. Because buses back to Tallinn run in-frequently, check the departure schedule as soon as you arrive, or ask staff how to find the Zoo stop, with more frequent service, a 15-minute walk away.

Lahemaa National Park (Lahemaa Rahvuspark)

This vast, flat, forested coastal preserve on the Gulf of Finland is only a one-hour drive east of Tallinn. While it is a popular tour destination and the nature is pristine, the park's charms are mod-est. I had a great guide, and it was a fascinating day out. But with an average guide, it could be a snore. Highlights include the thick forest (including cemeteries, because Estonians bury their dead in the woods), bog walks, rich berry and mushroom picking, rebuilt manor homes, and peaceful fishing villages surrounded by the evocative ruins of Soviet occupation. Tallinn Traveller Tours or-ganizes day trips to the national park (see "Tours in Tallinn," page 657). For hiking and cycling trail descriptions, check online (www.keskkonnaamet.ee) or stop at the park's visitor center when you arrive (open daily in summer, Mon-Fri off-season, tel. 329-5555).

Shopping in Tallinn

With so many cruise-ship tourists inundating Tallinn, the Old Town is full of trinkets, but it is possible to find good-quality stuff. Wooden goods, like butter knives and juniper-wood trivets, are a good value. Marvel at the variety of booze on sale in Tallinn's li-quor stores, popular with visiting Scandinavians. Tucked into the Old Town are many craft and artisan shops where prices are lower than in Nordic countries.

The **"Sweater Wall"** is a fun place to browse sweaters and woolens, though few are hand-knitted by grandmothers these

days. Find the stalls under the wall on Müürivahe street (daily 10:00-17:00, near the corner of Viru street, described on page 671). From there, explore **Katariina Käik,** a small alley between Müürivahe and Vene streets, which has several handicraft stores and workshops selling pieces that make nice souvenirs.

The cheery **Navitrolla Gallerii** is filled with work by the well-known Estonian artist who goes just by the name Navitrolla. His whimsical, animal-themed prints are vaguely reminiscent of *Where the Wild Things Are* (Mon-Fri 10:00-18:00, Sat 10:00-17:00, Sun 10:00-16:00, Sulevimägi 1, tel. 631-3716, www.navitrolla.ee).

The **Rahva Raamat** bookstore in the Viru Keskus mall (floors 3-4, high up in the glass atrium) has English-language literature on the main floor, and a huge wall of travel books upstairs (daily 9:00-21:00).

Balti Jaam Market, Tallinn's bustling traditional market, is behind the train station and has little of touristic interest besides

wonderful photo ops. That's why I like it. It's a great time-warp scene, fragrant with dill, berries, onions, and mush-rooms. You'll hear lots of Russian. The indoor sections sell meat, clothing, and gadgets. You could also assemble a very rustic picnic here. To find the market from the train station, just walk across the head of the train platforms (following *Jaama Turg* signs) and keep going (Mon-Fri 8:00-18:00, Sat-Sun 8:00-17:00, better early).

For something tamer, the **Viru Turg outdoor market,** a block outside the Old Town's Viru Gate, has a lively, tourist-oriented collection of stalls selling mostly clothing, textiles, and flowers (daily May-Sept 9:00-17:00, Oct-April 10:00-16:00, north of Viru street at Mere Puiestee 1).

Entertainment in Tallinn

Music

Tallinn has a dense schedule of classical music performances, especially during the annual Old Town Days, generally at the beginning of June (www.vanalinnapaevad.ee). Choral singing became a symbol of the struggle for Estonian independence after the first Estonian Song Festival in 1869 (still held every five years—next one in 2019).

Even outside of festival times, you'll find many performances in Tallinn's churches and concert halls, advertised on posters around town or at the TI. Tickets are usually available at the door or through the Piletilevi booth in the Viru Keskus mall (daily 9:00-21:00, www.piletilevi.ee). Watch for performances by Hortus Musicus, one of Estonia's finest classical ensembles, or concerts featuring the work of Arvo Pärt, Veljo Tormis, or Erkki-Sven Tüür, who are among Estonia's best modern choral composers and arrangers. Estonian groups have put out a lot of good CDs; you'll find a good music shop on the top floor (A5) of the Kaubamaja department store (daily 9:00-21:00, behind Viru Keskus mall).

Swimming

The indoor water park and 50-meter pool at the **Kalev Spa** is lots of fun. Many Finns come here on fitness travel packages. It's centrally located, between the Old Town and the modern shopping zone (€11.90/2.5 hours, €9.90/1.5 hours, cheaper on weekday mornings; open Mon-Fri 6:45-21:30, Sat-Sun 8:00-21:30; swimsuit rental available, Aia 18, tel. 649-3370, www.kalevspa.ee).

Sleeping in Tallinn

In general, real hotel options are surprisingly sparse and expensive, particularly in the Old Town; many people prefer rental apartments found online (such as at Booking.com or Airbnb.com). While I've focused my listings on places in or near the Old Town, you'll have more options and pay less if you're willing to stay a short walk or bus ride away.

As in Scandinavia, it's important to start your search on hotel websites. Room prices vary with current demand. Many hotels, especially the bigger ones, list their best price on the website and offer walk-in individuals only the inflated rack rates—the bulk of their business comes from agencies anyway.

Summer is high season (Tallinn has more tourists than business travelers), and prices almost always drop from October to April, except around Christmas and New Year's. I've listed high-season, summer prices here. When I give a range, expect the higher rate during busy times (typically Friday and Saturday nights) and the lower price on slow days. All of my listings offer free Wi-Fi.

Use a taxi to get to your hotel when you arrive, and then figure out public transportation later.

IN AND NEAR THE OLD TOWN

$$$ Baltic Hotel Imperial is a fine four-star hotel set in a lovely park-like spot under the Old Town wall. Its 32 rooms are modern and small, while the public spaces have a spacious, professional ambience. Though it feels like a chain (and is), when it's discounted, it's the best Old Town, top-end value I've found (inflated official rates—Sb-€140, Db-€180; deals are often cheaper—website shows best rates; elevator, air-con, pay sauna, kids' playroom, Nunne 14, tel. 627-4800, www.imperial.ee, imperial@baltichotelgroup.com).

$$$ My City Hotel fills a handsome 1950s building on the south edge of the Old Town with 68 rooms and a spacious, classy lobby lounge. Along with the Sõprus cinema across the street, it's done in the Stalinist Classical style—Soviet stars and sheaves of wheat still adorn the facade (typically Db-€90 on weekdays—a great deal—or €140 on weekends, more for larger "superior" room, extra bed-€25, children 12 and under free in parents'

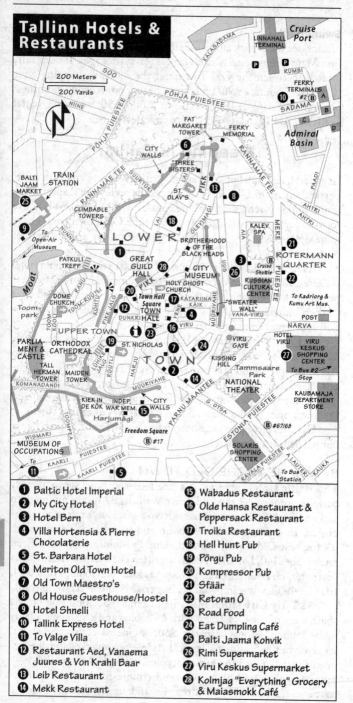

Tallinn Hotels & Restaurants

200 Meters
200 Yards

1. Baltic Hotel Imperial
2. My City Hotel
3. Hotel Bern
4. Villa Hortensia & Pierre Chocolaterie
5. St. Barbara Hotel
6. Meriton Old Town Hotel
7. Old Town Maestro's
8. Old House Guesthouse/Hostel
9. Hotel Shnelli
10. Tallink Express Hotel
11. To Valge Villa
12. Restaurant Aed, Vanaema Juures & Von Krahli Baar
13. Leib Restaurant
14. Mekk Restaurant
15. Wabadus Restaurant
16. Olde Hansa Restaurant & Peppersack Restaurant
17. Troika Restaurant
18. Hell Hunt Pub
19. Põrgu Pub
20. Kompressor Pub
21. Sfäär
22. Retoran Ö
23. Road Food
24. Eat Dumpling Café
25. Balti Jaama Kohvik
26. Rimi Supermarket
27. Viru Keskus Supermarket
28. Kolmjag "Everything" Grocery & Maiasmokk Café

---

room, elevator, air-con, guest computer, sauna-€20-30/hour,
Vana-Posti 11/13, tel. 622-0900, www.mycityhotel.ee, booking@
mycityhotel.ee).

$$$ Hotel Bern, tucked at the edge of the Old Town, is an
endearing place with 50 businesslike rooms in a new brick building
(Db-€98, but can be less in slow times, air-con, elevator, Aia 10,
tel. 680-6630, www.tallinnhotels.ee, bern@tallinnhotels.ee).

$$ Villa Hortensia rents six simple, creaky-floored rooms
with kitchenettes above a sophisticated little café in a courtyard
close to Town Hall Square. The three twin-bed rooms and one
single-bed room are furnished sparsely, with beds in a sleeping loft.
The "deluxe" room comes with a double bed and a small balcony.
The suite is on two floors, with a double bed upstairs and a fold-
out sofa bed in the living room. Named after the home of a group
of down-and-outs in a famous Estonian novel, the hotel is creatively run by jewelry designer Jaan Pärn. It's a decent, inexpensive
choice if you don't mind the ramshackle feeling and the fact that
the rooms aren't serviced every day. Jaan's jewelry shop, across the
courtyard, serves as the reception (Sb-€45, Db-€65, deluxe Db-
€90, suite Db-€120 or Tb-€140, no breakfast, no elevator, 50 yards
from the corner of Vene and Viru streets at Vene 6, look for *Masters'
Courtyard* sign, mobile 504-6113, www.hoov.ee, jaan.parn@gmail.
com).

$$ St. Barbara Hotel, a stylish and affordable choice, fills
a former hospital from 1904 just beyond the ring road from Tal-
linn's Freedom Square (at the edge of the Old Town)—about a
10-minute walk from Town Hall Square. This old building is filled
with 53 modern, fairly simple rooms and an atmospheric beer cel-
lar that gives the place a Germanic vibe (Db-€79 on weekdays or
€87 on weekends—but prices are flexible, elevator, free parking,
Roosikrantsi 2A—just take the pedestrian underpass from Free-

TALLINN

dom Square under the busy road, tel. 640-0040, www.stbarbara. ee, reservations@stbarbara.ee).

$$ Meriton Old Town Hotel sits grandly (for a hotel in its category) at the tip of the Old Town, near Fat Margaret Tower and not far from the ferry terminals. Its 41 small, slightly dated rooms are mostly doubles with twin beds and showers, and—as it faces a busy street—some could be noisy if you sleep with the window open. But the price is right and the location convenient. Don't let them move you to the nearby, similarly named, more expensive Meriton Old Town Garden Hotel (very fluid rates, Db-€85-110 depending on demand, much less off-season, can be cheaper if you skip breakfast, elevator, guest computer, Lai 49, tel. 614-1300, www.meritonhotels.com, reservations@meritonhotels.com).

$$ Old Town Maestro's is a simple budget choice with 23 modern rooms tucked in the heart of the Old Town. While the prices are right, it comes with a catch: It sits along one of Tallinn's rowdiest nightlife streets, so try requesting a quieter courtyard room (Sb-€55, Db-€65, elevator, Suur-Karja 10, tel. 626-2000, www.maestrohotel.ee, maestro@maestrohotel.ee).

$ Old House Guesthouse and Hostel is your small-and-snug, cheap-and-basic option, split between two buildings halfway between Town Hall Square and the ferry terminals. There's street noise in many rooms, so bring earplugs (bed in 6-person dorm-€15, S-€30, twin D-€44, D with one big bed-€48, T-€63, Q-€84, see their website for deals, includes sheets and towel, breakfast-€4, no lockout, shared shower and WC, kitchen facilities, unsecured free parking—reserve ahead, Uus 26, tel. 641-1464, www.oldhouse. ee, info@oldhouse.ee). They also rent apartments around the Old Town.

SLEEPING MORE AFFORDABLY, AWAY FROM THE OLD TOWN

Near the Train Station: **$$ Hotel Shnelli,** a big, high-rise "efficiency hotel" adjacent to the sleepy little train station (a 5-minute walk from the Old Town in a neighborhood that feels a bit seedy at night), rents 137 Ikea-mod rooms. It fronts a noisy street, so request a quiet room in the back—these overlook the tracks, but no trains run at night (Db-€60-65, sometimes €10-20 more on weekends, connecting family rooms, apartment-€130, you can save a few euros if you skip breakfast, elevator, Toompuiestee 37, tel. 631-0100, www.gohotels.ee, reservations@gohotels.ee).

Near the Port: Given how compact Tallinn is (and how inexpensive honest taxis are), there's little reason to sleep near the ferry terminals—other than low prices. But if you're in a pinch, **$$ Tallink Express Hotel** is a few steps from the A, B, and C ferry terminals, close to Linnahall terminal, and a short walk from the Old

Town. It's a modern, cheery Motel 6-type place with excellent prices and 163 comfortable, colorful, cookie-cutter rooms. The rooms can be stuffy in hot weather, as windows don't open very far and there's no air-conditioning. Walk-in rates are much higher than the website prices I give here (Sb/Db-€70-80 but can vary dramatically—less in winter and more on busy weekends, extra bed-€25, children under 17 sleep free on sofa beds in family rooms, elevator, free guest computer, free parking, Sadama 9, tel. 630-0808, www. hotels.tallink.com, hotelbooking@tallink.ee).

In Lilleküla, Outside the Center: Lilleküla is a quiet, green, and peaceful residential area of single-family houses, small Soviet-era apartment blocks, and barking dogs. For a clearer understanding of Estonian life, stay here. You'll save money without sacrificing comfort. The downside: It's a 15-minute, €1.10 bus ride into the center.

$ Valge Villa ("White Villa"), a homey guesthouse set in a great garden run by Anne and Andres Vahtra and their family, does everything right. It's worth the commute for its competitive prices and 10 spacious, wood-paneled, well-furnished rooms. They like you to book and pay a 10 percent advance deposit on their website (Sb-€39, Db-€45, small suite-€60, larger suite-€70, suite-apartments-€80, extra bed-€16, every fifth night free, guest computer, free parking, bikes-€15/day, sauna-€20, laundry-€12/load; take bus #17 to Räägu stop, or trolley bus #2, #3, or #4 to Tedre stop; Kännu 26/2, between Rästa and Räägu streets—see map on page 688, tel. 654-2302, www.white-villa.com, villa@white-villa.com). I'd take a taxi here to check in (about €15 from the ferry port), and figure out the public-transit options later.

Eating in Tallinn

Tallinn's Old Town has a wide selection of largely interchangeable, mostly tourist-oriented eateries. Don't expect bargains here—you'll pay near-Scandinavian prices (average main dishes can cost €15-20). For a better value, roam at least a block or two off the main drags, where you can find great food at what seems like fire-sale prices. At most of my listings, you can assemble a three-course meal for around €20. Some restaurants have good-value lunch specials on weekdays (look for the words *päeva praad*). As a mark of quality, watch for restaurants with an *Astu Sisse!* label in the window; this Estonian equivalent of a Michelin star is awarded to just 50 res-

taurants each year. Tipping is not required, but if you like the service, round your bill up by 5-10 percent when paying. Reserving ahead for dinner is a smart idea.

A few years ago it was hard to find authentic local cuisine, but now Estonian food is trendy—a hearty Northern mixture of meat, potatoes, root vegetables, mushrooms, dill, garlic, bread, and soup. Pea soup is a local specialty. You usually get a few slices of bread as a free, automatic side dish. A typical pub snack is Estonian garlic bread *(küüslauguleivad)*—deep-fried strips of dark rye bread smothered in garlic and served with a dipping sauce. Estonia's Saku beer is good, cheap, and on tap at most eateries. Try the nutty, full-bodied Tume variety.

ESTONIAN CUISINE IN THE OLD TOWN

Restorant Aed is an elegant, almost gourmet, health-food eatery calling itself "the embassy of pure food." While not vegetarian, it is passionate about serving organic, seasonal, modern Estonian cuisine in a woody, romantic setting. Take your pick from four dining options: under old beams, in the cellar, out front on the sidewalk, or out back on the garden terrace (€10-15 main dishes, daily 12:00-23:00, Rataskaevu 8, tel. 626-9088, www.vonkrahl.ee/aed).

Vanaema Juures ("Grandma's Place"), an eight-table cellar restaurant, serves homey, traditional Estonian meals, such as pork roast with sauerkraut and horseradish. This is a fine bet for local cuisine, and dinner reservations are strongly advised. No tacky medieval stuff here—just good food at fair prices in a pleasant ambience, where you expect your waitress to show up with her hair in a bun and wearing granny glasses (€8-17 main dishes, daily 12:00-22:00, Rataskaevu 10/12, tel. 626-9080, www.vonkrahl.ee/vanaemajuures).

At **Leib** ("Back Bread"), just outside the walls at the seaside end of the Old Town, you enter up steps into a fun garden under the medieval ramparts, and can sit indoors or out. Peruse the classy and engaging menu, which changes with the seasons—their food has Estonian roots, but with international influences (€10-16 main courses, daily 12:00-15:00 & 18:00-23:00, Uus 31, tel. 611-9026, www.leibresto.ee/en).

Mekk is a small, fresh, upscale place whose name stands for "modern Estonian cuisine." While their à la carte prices are a bit higher than at my other listings, they offer artful weekday lunch specials for just €7 (not available July-Aug), and a €35 four-course fixed-price meal for serious eaters. Young, elegant locals take their lunch breaks here (€12-25 main dishes, Mon-Sat 12:00-23:00, closed Sun, Suur-Karja 17/19, tel. 680-6688, www.mekk.ee).

Modern Cuisine on Freedom Square: **Wabadus,** facing the vast and modern square, turns its back on old Tallinn. This sleek, urbane café/restaurant—which has been the town meeting place since 1937—serves coffee, cocktails, and international fare. To escape the cobbles and crowds of the Old Town, walk a few minutes to enjoy a moment of peace—ideally at one of the terrace tables on the square, if the weather's good (€5 weekday lunch specials, €7-10 salads, €7-18 main courses, Mon-Tue 11:00-19:00, Wed-Thu 11:00-21:00, Fri-Sat 11:00-24:00, closed Sun, Vabaduse Väljak 10, tel. 601-6461, www.wabadus.ee).

TOURIST TRAPS ON AND NEAR TOWN HALL SQUARE

Tallinn's central square is a whirlpool of tacky tourism, where aggressive restaurant touts (some dressed as medieval wenches or giant *matryoshka* dolls) accost passersby to lure them in for a drink or meal. While a bit off-putting, some of these restaurants have surprisingly good (if expensive) food. Of the many options ringing the square and surrounding streets, these are the ones most worth considering.

"Medieval" Estonian Cuisine: Two well-run restaurants just below Town Hall Square specialize in re-creating medieval food (from the days before the arrival of the potato and tomato from the New World). They are each grotesquely touristy, complete with gift shops where you can buy your souvenir goblet. Both have street seating, but you'll get all the tourists and none of the atmosphere.

Olde Hansa, filling three creaky old floors and outdoor tables with tourists, candle wax, and scurrying medieval waitresses, can be quite expensive. And yet, the local consensus is that the food here is far better than it has any right to be (€14-30 main dishes, daily 10:00-24:00, musicians circulate Tue-Sun after 18:00, a belch below Town Hall Square at Vana Turg 1, reserve in advance, tel. 627-9020, www.oldehansa.ee).

Peppersack, across the street, tries to compete in the same price range, and feels marginally less circus-like (Vana Turg 6, tel. 646-6800).

Russian Food: As more than a third of the local population is enthusiastically Russian, there are plenty of places serving Russian cuisine (see also "Budget Eateries," described later). **Troika** is my choice for Russian food. Right on Town Hall Square, with a folkloric-costumed waitstaff, they serve €7-11 *bliny* (pancakes) and *pelmeni* (dumplings), and €11-20 main dishes. Sit out on the square (reserve for dinner); in the more casual, Russian-village-themed tavern; or under a fine vault in the trendy, atmospheric cellar (which has slightly cheaper prices). A balalaika player usually strums and strolls after 19:00 (open daily 10:00-23:00, Raekoja Plats 15, tel. 627-6245, www.troika.ee).

PUBS IN THE OLD TOWN

Young Estonians eat well and affordably at pubs. In some pubs, you go to the bar to look at the menu, order, and pay. Then find a table, and they'll bring your food out when it's ready.

Hell Hunt Pub ("The Gentle Wolf") was the first Western-style pub to open after 1991, and it's still going strong, attracting a mixed expat and local crowd with its tasty food. Five of their own microbrews are on tap. Consider making a meal from the great pub snacks (€3-6) plus a salad (€5-6). Choose a table in its convivial, rustic-industrial interior or on the garden terrace across the street (€6 pastas, €10 main dishes, daily 12:00-24:00, Pikk 39, tel. 681-8333).

Von Krahli Baar serves cheap, substantial Estonian grub—such as potato pancakes *(torud)* stuffed with mushrooms or shrimp—in a big, dark space that doubles as a center for Estonia's alternative theater scene; there's also seating in the tiny courtyard where you enter. It started as the bar of the theater upstairs, then expanded to become a restaurant, so it has a young, avant-garde vibe. You'll feel like you're eating backstage with the stagehands (€6-7 main dishes, Mon-Sat 12:00-24:00, Sun 12:00-15:00, Rataskaevu 10/12, a block uphill from Town Hall Square, near Wheel Well, tel. 626-9090).

Põrgu is particularly serious about its beer, with a wide variety of international and Estonian brews on tap—including some microbrews. Its simple, uncluttered cellar feels like less of a tourist trap than the others listed here (€3-7 bar snacks and salads, €8-13 main dishes, Mon-Sat 12:00-24:00, closed Sun, Rüütli 4, tel. 644-0232).

Kompressor, a big, open-feeling beer hall, is in all the guidebooks for its cheap, huge, and filling €5 pancakes—savory or sweet (daily 11:00-24:00, Rataskaevu 3, tel. 646-4210).

IN THE ROTERMANN QUARTER

This modern, up-and-coming district (described on page 675), just across the busy road from Tallinn's Old Town, is well worth exploring for a jolt of cutting-edge architecture and hipster edginess. It's an antidote to the central area's ye-olde aura. As more and more buildings in this zone are being renovated, this is a fast-changing scene. But these two choices, in a long brick building facing the Old Town, are well-established and a good starting point.

Sfäär (Sphere), which combines an unpretentious bistro with a design shop, is a killing-two-birds look at the Rotermann Quarter. In this lively, cheery place, tables are tucked between locally designed clothes and home decor. The menu is bold but accessible and affordable, featuring Estonian and international fare with a hint of molecular flair (€6-10 starters and pastas, €12-16 main dishes,

Mon-Wed 8:00-22:00, Thu-Fri 8:00-24:00, Sat 10:00-24:00, Sun 10:00-22:00, shop open daily 12:00-21:00, Mere Puiestee 6E, mobile 5699-2200, www.sfaar.ee).

Retoran Ö (Swedish for "Island"), just a few doors down in the same building, is your Rotermann Quarter splurge. The dressy, trendy, retrofitted-warehouse interior feels a sophisticated world away from the Old Town's tourist traps. The cuisine tries to highlight an Estonian approach to "New Nordic" cooking—small dishes carefully constructed with seasonal, local ingredients. Reservations are smart (€19-24 main courses, €70 tasting *menu*, Mon-Sat 18:00-23:00, closed Sun, Mere Puiestee 6E—enter from the parking lot around back, tel. 661-6150, www.restoran-o.ee).

BUDGET EATERIES

Road Food, tucked on a tiny lane immediately behind the Town Hall Tower, has some of the best cheap eats in the city. A branch of the Olde Hansa food empire, this sandwich shop serves up an excellent, quick taste of Estonia, stuffing its €4-5 sandwiches with local meats and sauces. It's attached to a well-stocked beer and wine shop, making it easy to browse for the perfect drink to wash things down (daily 11:00-24:00, shorter hours off-season, Vanaturo kael 8).

Eat, a laid-back, cellar-level student hangout with a big foosball table and a book exchange, serves the best-value lunch in town. Its menu is very simple: three varieties of *pelmeenid* (dumplings), plus sauces, beet salad, and pickles. You dish up what you like and pay by weight (€2-3/big bowl). Ask for an education in the various dumplings and sauces and then go for the complete experience. Enjoy with abandon—you can't spend much money here, and you'll feel good stoking their business (Mon-Sat 11:00-21:00, closed Sun, Sauna 2, tel. 644-0029).

At the Outdoor Market: **Balti Jaama Kohvik,** at the end of the train station near the Balti Jaam Market, is an unimpressive-looking 24-hour diner with no real sign (look for a faded red awning and *Kohvik avatud 24 tundi*—"café open 24 hours"—on the door; it's actually built into the train-station building). The bustling stainless-steel kitchen cranks out traditional Russian/Estonian dishes—the cheapest hot food in town. While you won't see or hear a word of English here, the glass case displays the various offerings and prices (€3 meals, €1.60 soups, dirt-cheap-yet-wonderful savory pancakes for less than €1, and tasty *beljaš*—a kind of pierogi). Unfortunately, the area feels sketchy after dark.

Supermarkets: For picnic supplies, try the **Rimi** supermarket just outside the Old Town at Aia 7, near the Viru Gate (daily 8:00-22:00). A larger, more upscale supermarket in the basement of the **Viru Keskus** mall (directly behind Hotel Viru) has convenient, inexpensive takeaway meals (daily 9:00-21:00). The handy little **Kol-mjag "Everything"** grocery is a block off Town Hall Square (daily 24 hours, Pikk 11, tel. 631-1511).

BREAKFAST AND PASTRIES

The **Maiasmokk** ("Sweet Tooth") café and pastry shop, founded in 1864, is the grande dame of Tallinn cafés—ideal for dessert or breakfast. Even through the Soviet days, this was *the* place for a good pastry or a glass of herby Tallinn schnapps ("Vana Tallinn"). Point to what you want from the selection of classic local pastries at the counter, and sit down for breakfast (€3 omelets) or coffee on the other side of the shop. Everything's reasonable (Mon-Fri 8:00-21:00, Sat 9:00-21:00, Sun 9:00-20:00, Pikk 16, across from church with old clock, tel. 646-4079). They also have a marzipan shop (separate entrance).

Pierre Chocolaterie at Vene 6 has scrumptious fresh pralines, sandwiches, and coffee in a courtyard filled with craft shops (also €5-8 light meals, daily 8:30-late, tel. 641-8061).

Tallinn Connections

BY BUS OR TRAIN

The bus is usually the best way to travel by land from Tallinn (for domestic bus schedules, see www.tpilet.ee). The largest operator, with the most departures, is Lux Express (tel. 680-0909, www.luxexpress.ee); there's also Ecolines (tel. 614-3600 or mobile 5637-7997, www.ecolines.net) and the spiffy Hansabuss (with onboard Wi-Fi, tel. 627-9080, www.hansabuss.ee). The bus station *(auto-bussijaam)* is at Lastekodu 46, a short taxi ride from the Old Town, or a few stops on trams #2 or #4 to the Autobussijaam stop (direction: Ülemiste). Not much English is spoken at the station; reserving online is recommended.

From Tallinn to: Rīga (12 buses/day, 4.5 hours, no train option; consider Tallinn Traveller Tours' "sightseeing shuttle" between these cities, a full-day, 12-hour journey with sightseeing stops en route—see "Tours in Tallinn," earlier), **Vilnius** (3 buses/day departing in the morning, plus 3/day overnight, 10 hours), **St. Petersburg** (buses nearly hourly, 6.5-8 hours; also possible by overnight cruise—about 1/week, 14.5 hours, www.stpeterline.com; for cruise details, see page 640), **Moscow** (take the overnight train—daily at 15:30, 19-hour trip, www.gorail.ee—or fly). Americans and Canadians must obtain a visa to travel to Russia and need to plan long in advance (for more information on visa requirements, see page 640 in the Helsinki chapter; www.russianembassy.org or www.rusembassy.ca).

For the latest bus and train schedules, see the h
at the TI or consult *Tallinn in Your Pocket*.

BY BOAT

You have two basic options: A slow overnight boat ride from Stockholm, or a fast daytime boat from Helsinki.

Sailing Overnight Between Stockholm and Tallinn

Tallink Silja's overnight cruise ships leave Stockholm at 17:30 or 17:45 every evening and arrive in Tallinn at 10:00 or 10:45 the next morning. Return trips leave Tallinn at 18:00 and arrive in Stockholm at 10:00 or 10:15. All times are local (Tallinn is an hour ahead of Stockholm). As with hotels, these cruises use "dynamic pricing" that flexes with demand. Fares vary by the day and season. The highest rates are typically for Friday and Saturday nights, and for the peak of summer (July-mid-Aug); outside of peak season, Sunday through Thursday nights tend to be cheaper. A one-way berth in a four-person, sex-segregated cabin with a private bath costs around €50; couples can travel in a private cabin for about €150-200. The *smörgåsbord* dinner and buffet breakfast cost extra (prebook these meals and reserve a table when buying your ticket). Book online (www.tallinksilja.com); booking by phone or in person may come with an extra charge, but they can answer questions for free (Swedish tel. 08/222-140, Estonian tel. 640-9808). Note that travelers below age 20 are not allowed on this cruise without a parent or guardian (for details, see the website).

Terminals: In **Stockholm**, Tallink Silja ships leave from the Värtahamnen harbor. To get there from downtown Stockholm, take the Tallink Silja shuttle bus from the train station (50 kr, departs according to boat schedule), or take the T-bana (subway) to the Gärdet station, then walk 10 minutes to the harbor. On Mondays through Saturdays, public bus #76 (direction: Ropsten) takes you directly to the terminal (leaves from several downtown locations, including Kungsträdgården; get off at Färjeterminalen stop). For Stockholm public transit information, see page 436 and www.sl.se. In **Tallinn**, Tallink Silja ships dock at D-Terminal (see "Arrival in Tallinn," earlier).

Speeding Between Helsinki and Tallinn

Four different companies—shown in the table on the next page—offer ferry trips between Helsinki and Tallinn. Fares run €20-55 one-way (evening departures from Helsinki and morning departures from Tallinn tend to be cheaper; student and senior discounts available). Their websites have all the latest information and prices. Advance reservations aren't essential, but usually save a litt' money, ensure your choice of departure, and provide peace of m

Helsinki/Tallinn Connections

Company	Website	Terminal in Helsinki	Terminal in Tallinn
Tallink Silja	www.tallinksilja.com	Länsi	D
Linda Line (fast catamarans)	www.lindaline.ee	Makasiini	Linnahall
Eckerö Line	www.eckeroline.fi	Länsi	A/B
Viking Line	www.vikingline.fi	Katajanokan	A/B

Note: All of these lines also have phone numbers and brick-and-mortar offices, both in Estonia and in Finland (find them on the websites); but in most cases, you'll pay an extra fee to book by phone or in person. Booking online is easy and free.

If you travel round-trip on the same day, your ticket will cost barely more than a one-way fare, but you'll have just a few hours on shore. Prices differ only slightly from company to company—base your choice on the most convenient departure times and ferry terminal locations. Make sure you know which terminal your boat leaves from and how to get to it (for descriptions of Helsinki's terminals, see page 636; for Tallinn's, see "Arrival in Tallinn," earlier).

Unless you're bringing a car, the Linda and Viking lines are usually the most convenient, as their docks in Helsinki and Tallinn are easy to reach by foot or public transport. **Linda Line** uses 400-passenger, Australian-made catamarans that zip across the Gulf of Finland in just 1.5 hours (6-7/day March-Oct, 3-5/day Nov-Feb). Boats leave from the Makasiini terminal in Helsinki's South Harbor (Eteläsatama), just five minutes' walk from Market Square, and arrive in Tallinn at the Linnahall terminal. Catamarans lack the spacious party atmosphere of larger boats, and are slightly more expensive. Cancellations, which can occur in stormy conditions, rarely happen in summer; still, if you have a plane to catch, play it safe and take a regular ferry. **Viking Line** leaves from the other side of Helsinki's South Harbor (Katajanokan terminal), and arrives at Tallinn's A/B-Terminal. Viking offers a more traditional experience on a big ferry with restaurants and shops (2/day, 2.5-hour crossing, generally a few euros less than Linda Line).

Tallink Silja and **Eckerö Line** leave from the relatively inconvenient Länsi terminal at Helsinki's West Harbor (Länsistama), which you can reach on tram #9 (catch it at Kamppi mall in downtown Helsinki; the terminal is the end of the line). At the other end of the journey, Tallink Silja uses Tallinn's D-Terminal—the farthest from the Old Town, making it a bit less convenient but still walkable. On the other hand, Tallink Silja's ferries are frequent and fast (6-7/day, 2-hour crossing). Eckerö Line has just two slow, inexpensive sailings per day (3.5-hour crossing).

Slower boats—all except Linda Line—have *smörgåsbord* buffets. The slower the boat, the more likely it is to be filled with "four-legged Finns" crazy about cheap booze, slot machines, and karaoke.

SCANDINAVIAN HISTORY

On your trip, you'll see reminders everywhere of Scandinavia's long history. Eerie graves, carved rune stones, and horned helmets bring to mind *Lord of the Rings*-style warriors of old who worshipped Thor and Odin. You'll see the ships and weapons of their descendants—the Vikings—who terrorized Europe with their fierce, pagan culture. Evocative wooden-stave churches show how Christianity slowly seeped into the region.

You'll visit the harbors of these seafaring peoples and tour the stark castles of nobles who fought for control of Baltic trade. As modern nations emerged, absolute monarchs built luxurious palaces intended to rival Versailles. Today's streets and main squares are studded with statues and monuments honoring great kings and their battles, great patriots who lobbied for national independence, and great writers and musicians who enriched Scandinavian culture. Scandinavian museums are filled with paintings that capture the beauty of the landscape and celebrate its people. You'll hear bittersweet stories of the millions of 19th-century Scandinavians who left their homes for better lives in America. You'll learn about those who suffered under WWII Nazi occupation, and the heroes who organized resistance and sheltered Jewish people. And you'll experience the richness of Scandinavia today—its wealth, its liberal policies, and its global outlook.

Want to hear more of the Scandinavian story? Read on.

PREHISTORY AND HUNTERS WITH SPEARS (C. 8000 B.C.-A.D. 1)

Scandinavia became habitable when the glaciers receded at the end of the last ice age. Stone Age hunters moved north, chasing valuable deer, moose, and fish. Among these were the forebears of the Sami—or Laplanders—of northern Scandinavia, some of whom continue to herd reindeer and live a nomadic lifestyle today. For more on the Sami, visit Oslo's National Historical Museum (page 249) or Norwegian Folk Museum (page 255), or Stockholm's Nordic Museum (page 473). The early Scandinavians began farming (c. 4000 B.C.) and eventually developed tools and weapons made of bronze (c. 1800 B.C.). We know these people mainly by their graves—either burial mounds (as on the island of Öland, Sweden, page 572) or the heavy stone tombs called dolmens (as on Denmark's isle of Ærø, page 147).

IRON-AGE WARRIORS WITH HORNED HELMETS (A.D. 1-800)

Isolated from the Continent and unconquered by the Romans, Scandinavia kept close to its prehistoric past. The 2,000-year-old

Grauballe Man—whose corpse was preserved in a peat bog (and is now displayed at the Moesgård Museum just outside Aarhus, page 191)—was a contemporary of Julius Caesar. But in his world, people spoke not Latin but a Germanic language, wore animal-horned helmets, and used ceremonial curvy-shaped *lur* horns. They forged iron implements decorated with the gods of their pagan religion (such as the Gundestrup Cauldron displayed in Copenhagen's National Museum, page 70). They commemorated heroic deeds with large stones carved with the angular alphabet known as runes (see the rune stones at Copenhagen's National Museum, page 70, and at Jelling, Denmark, page 201). One of their most sacred sites is at Gamla Uppsala near Stockholm (page 516), where mighty chieftains were buried along with their worldly possessions—weapons, jewels, dogs, horses, and even slaves. This distinct, pre-Christian Scandinavian culture thrived in the first centuries A.D. and continued even as the rest of Europe fell under the sway of Rome's Latin culture and, later, Christianity.

Though isolated, the Scandinavians made fleeting contact with Roman Europe, trading furs and amber (a petrified tree sap, used in jewelry) for crucial tool-making metals from the Continent. Eventually, the Scandinavians learned to extract their own bronze and iron. With better tools, they became productive farmers and shipbuilders. The population boomed due to a warmer climate and better nutrition. The Scandinavians were soon eyeing Europe and the North Atlantic as a source for new resources, and for potential expansion of their clans.

VIKINGS WITH SHIPS (800-1000)

Scandinavia's entrance onto the European stage was swift, dramatic, and unforgettable. On January 8, 793, a fleet of Scandinavian pirates came ashore on the northeast coast of England and sacked the Lindisfarne monastery, slaughtering monks, burning buildings, and plundering sacred objects. Word spread like wildfire of brutal pirates who seemed to come from nowhere, looted and pillaged with extreme prejudice, then moved on. Their victims called them *Normanni, Dani, Rus,* or worse, but the name they gave themselves came from the inlets and bays *(vik)* where they lived: the Vikings.

For the next 200 years, hardy Viking sailors plundered and explored the coasts of northern Europe. Vikings from Norway primarily went west to the British Isles and settled Iceland, Greenland, and beyond; Swedes ventured east to the Baltic states, navigated the Russian rivers, and reached Constantinople; and Danes headed south (to England, France, Spain, and Italy).

The Vikings attacked in fleets of sleek, narrow, open-topped ships a hundred feet long, called *drakkars*. (See them for yourself at the Viking Ship Museums in Oslo, page 256, or Roskilde, page 130.) Rigged with square sails and powered by dozens of men at the oars, they could attack at 15 miles an hour and land right on the beach, where they would pour out, brandishing their weapons.

Each Viking was decked out with a coat of mail, a small shield, and a helmet (though not one with horns, which by Viking times were merely ceremonial). Each warrior specialized in a particular kind of warfare: sword, spear, battle-axe, or bow-and-arrow. At the battle's crucial moment, the Vikings might send in their secret weapon—the so-called *berserkers*. These warriors attacked with a seemingly superhuman (and possibly drug-induced) frenzy, scaring the leotards off their enemies and giving us our English word "berserk."

Despite their reputation as ruthless pirates, most Vikings were settlers who established towns, married the locals, farmed the land, hunted in the forests, and traded with their neighbors. They spread Scandinavian culture and rune stones far and wide. In Northern France, the region of "Normandy" was settled by the "North-men." Eric the Red, a Norwegian Viking, was an early settler in Iceland, and his son Leif Eriksson sailed as far as the coast of North America around A.D. 1000.

To the dismay of Roman Catholic bishops, while the rest of Europe became Christian, the Vikings held onto their pagan gods, many of whom were, like themselves, warriors: Odin, the king of the gods (who gave us our word for Wednesday), and Thor with his hammer, the god of war (and of Thursday). Believing in an afterlife, the Vikings buried their dead ceremonially along with their possessions. Some were interred beneath large mounds of dirt (such as the Gamla Uppsala burial mounds described on page 516). Others were laid to rest in ships that were buried underground, or in graves marked with stones placed upright in the shape of a full-size ship.

By the year 1000, Scandinavian society was gradually changing—unifying, Christianizing, and assimilating into European culture. Scattered Nordic peoples coalesced into kingdoms, united under the banner of Christianity. In Norway, there was King (later "Saint") Olav II (c. 1020). Among the Svea people (Sweden), King Olof Skotkonung (c. 968-1020) unified and Christianized the land. The Danes were united by King Harald Bluetooth (c. 980), who commemorated Denmark's Christian conversion on a now-famous rune stone (located in Jelling, page 201)—although in reality, Bluetooth's "conversion" was a ploy to keep the German-Catholic bishops and missionaries at bay. Under Harald's grandson, King Canute, Denmark ruled a large empire that included parts of southern England (c. 1020). One of Canute's battles there inspired the nursery song "London Bridge Is Falling Down."

By 1100, the last pagans were gathering at Gamla Uppsala to put on their ceremonial horned helmets, worship the sun, bury fallen heroes, and retell the sagas of their ancestors. Viking culture blended into the European mainstream, but we still see traces of it today—in rune stones and burial sites; in surviving tools, weapons, and jewelry; and in the dragon-prowed designs found on Christian stave churches and even on contemporary Scandinavian coins.

MEDIEVAL CHRISTIANS, BICKERING NOBLES, AND GERMAN BUSINESSMEN (1000-1400)

In the Middle Ages, three separate (if loosely united) kingdoms emerged: Denmark, Sweden, and Norway. They were Christian

and feudal, with land worked by peasants who owed allegiance to a petty noble sworn to the king. Towns sprang up, including what would become the main cities: Oslo (1048), Copenhagen (1165), and Stockholm (1255). Rulers began flying flags featuring a cross, which eventually became the main motif in each country's national flag.

Christianity dominated. Some of the region's oldest churches (especially in Norway) are wooden stave,

Typical Castle Architecture

Castles were fortified residences for medieval nobles. Castles come in all shapes and sizes, but knowing a few general terms will help you understand them.

Barbican: A fortified gatehouse, sometimes a stand-alone building located outside the main walls.

Crenellation: A gap-toothed pattern of stones atop the parapet.

Drawbridge: A bridge that could be raised or lowered, using counterweights or a chain-and-winch.

Great Hall: The largest room in the castle, serving as throne room, conference center, and dining hall.

Hoardings (or Gallery): Wooden huts built onto the upper parts of the stone walls. They served as watch towers, living quarters, and fighting platforms.

The Keep (or Donjon): A high, strong stone tower in the center of the complex; the lord's home and refuge of last resort.

Loopholes (or Embrasures): Narrow wall slits through which soldiers could shoot arrows.

Machicolation: A stone ledge jutting out from the wall, with holes through which soldiers could drop rocks or boiling oil onto wall-scaling enemies below.

Moat: A ditch encircling the wall, sometimes filled with water

Parapet: Outer railing of the wall walk.

Portcullis: An iron grille that could be lowered across the entrance.

made with vertical planks and ornamented with dragons and other semi-pagan figures to ward off evil and ease the transition to Christianity (see page 211). Devout Christians laid the cornerstones for huge cathedrals, such as the skyscraping Uppsala Cathedral in 1287, Aarhus Cathedral in 1201, and Stockholm Cathedral in 1306.

Finland entered the Scandinavian sphere when zealous Swedes launched a series of crusades to forcibly convert their pagan neighbors to the east, farm their lands, and fish in their lakes. They conquered and assimilated the region (c. 1200), making it a part of their own country for the next 600 years. Even today, Swedish is spoken on Finland's southern coast. Danish and German "warrior monks" fought a similar crusade against the loosely organized Estonian people, divvying up that region between themselves.

The many castles that dot Scandinavia attest to the civil warfare between nobles. A strong central government headed by a dominant king was still centuries away.

Sea trade between the Scandinavian neighbors boomed. The lucrative trade was controlled by enterprising German businessmen

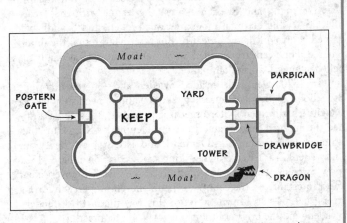

Postern Gate: A small, unfortified side or rear entrance. In wartime, it became a "sally-port" used to launch surprise attacks, or as an escape route.

Towers: Square or round structures with crenellated tops or conical roofs serving as lookouts, chapels, living quarters, or the dungeon.

Turret: A small lookout tower rising from the top of the wall.

Wall Walk (or Allure): A pathway atop the wall where guards could patrol and where soldiers stood to fire at the enemy.

The Yard (or Bailey): An open courtyard inside the castle walls.

who organized Scandinavia's ports into a free-trade zone known as the Hanseatic League (c. 1200-1400). Under German direction, Scandinavia became a powerful player in overseas commerce with the Continent. Cities such as Bergen, Norway, reaped big rewards under the Hanse (see Håkon's Hall on page 382). German settlers emigrated to Scandinavia, influencing the culture and language. By 1370, these German businessmen were so rich that they wielded more actual power than any Scandinavian king. It took a queen to break them.

DOMINANT DANES: WARS AND REFORMATION (1400-1600)

When Margrethe I of Denmark married the Norwegian king in 1363, Norway came under Danish control (where it would remain for the next 450 years). Denmark emerged as the region's main power.

In 1397, Margrethe took on the Hanseatic League by uniting Norway, Denmark, and Sweden against the league with the Treaty of Kalmar. The German monopoly was broken, and Scandinavia gained control of its own wealth. But after Margrethe, the union faltered. For a century, Swedish nobles chafed and occasionally rebelled against Danish domination.

In 1520, Denmark invaded Sweden and—in the notorious Stockholm Bloodbath—massacred 80 rebellious Swedish nobles in the city's main square, Stortorget (see page 441). Gustav Vasa rallied the enraged Swedes and drove out Denmark's King Christian (known as Christian II in Denmark and as Christian the Tyrant in Sweden). Vasa was crowned king of Sweden on June 6, 1523 (now Sweden's flag day). He centralized the Swedish government and Protestantized the country, seizing church property to form a strong nation-state. In many ways, this was the birth of modern Sweden (and the origin of the name for Wasa flatbread).

By the 1500s, all of Scandinavia had converted to Lutheran-style Protestantism. They'd been primed by the influence of German Hanseatic traders and preachers. And their kings jumped at the chance to confiscate former church property and authority.

For the next century, Denmark and Sweden—the region's two powerhouses—battled for control of the Baltic's lucrative trade routes, particularly for the Øresund, the crucial strait between Denmark and Sweden that connects the Baltic with the North Sea (and is now spanned by a modern bridge—see sidebar on page 143). It was during this period that much of Estonia fell under control of the Swedish empire.

SWEDISH SUPERIORITY: ABSOLUTE MONARCHS (1600-1800)

By 1600, Denmark-Norway was still the region's superpower, but Sweden-Finland-Estonia was rising fast. Denmark's one-eyed, high-living King Christian IV was spending centuries' worth of acquired wealth building lavish castles—including Rosenborg and Frederiksborg—and putting a Renaissance face on Copenhagen and Oslo (see page 80 and the sidebar on page 34). Meanwhile, his wars with Sweden and others were slowly sapping the country, emptying its coffers, and undermining Danish superiority. Christian IV even sold the Orkney and Shetland Islands to England to raise funds.

Sweden emerged under the inspired military leadership of King Gustavus Adolphus (1594-1632). The "Lion of the North"

roared southward, conquering large chunks of Russia, Poland, Germany, and Denmark during the Thirty Years' War. The vast *Vasa* ship in Stockholm, which the king commissioned in 1628, trumpeted the optimism of the era—but sank ignominiously in the middle of Stockholm harbor on its maiden voyage (see page 430).

Sweden's supreme moment came under Gustavus' great-grandson, Karl X Gustav (1622-1660). In 1657, Karl invaded Denmark through the back door—from the south. The winter was extremely cold, and the seas froze between several of Denmark's islands. In one of the most daring maneuvers in military history, Karl X Gustav led his armies across the ice between the islands—from Funen to Langeland to Lolland to Zealand—then sped toward Copenhagen. The astonished Danes surrendered, signing the humiliating Treaty of Roskilde (1658). The treaty gave Sweden a third of Danish territory, plus shared control of the Øresund Strait. Denmark would never again dominate, while Sweden became a major European power, with an imposing fleet and a Baltic empire that included Finland, Estonia, Latvia, and parts of Poland, Russia, and Germany.

In the 1660s, the kings of Denmark-Norway and Sweden-Finland-Estonia—following the trend set by Louis XIV in France—declared themselves to be absolute, divinely ordained monarchs. For the next 50 years, these kings scuffled with each other (and neighboring countries) for superiority in the Baltic. By 1720, the wars had drained both countries, at the very time that France and England were on the rise. Sweden ceded Estonia to the Russians, and Scandinavia sank back into relative obscurity.

For the rest of the 1700s, Denmark-Norway and Sweden-Finland mostly avoided war while trying to modernize and expand their economies. But the French Revolution (1789) and the Europe-wide wars that followed stirred up this relative peace, awakening a desire for democracy, ethnic recognition, and national independence.

PATRIOTS, ARTISTS, INDUSTRIALISTS, AND EMIGRANTS (1800S)

As Europe's monarchs ganged up on Revolutionary France under Napoleon, Scandinavia was forced to take sides. Through a series of complicated alliances, Denmark ended up backing the loser (France), while Sweden backed the winners (Britain and others). At war's end, Denmark was forced to cede Norway to Sweden in the 1814 Treaty of Kiel. Meanwhile, Sweden had just lost Finland to Russia in 1809. Thus began the nation-building process that, a century later, would result in the five independent countries we have today.

The wars also gave Sweden a new king—a French soldier

who spoke not a word of Swedish, was not Scandinavian, and had not a drop of noble blood. But Jean-Baptiste Bernadotte, a career military man in Napoleon's army, was loved by Sweden's childless king, admired by Sweden's soldiers for his fighting prowess, and popular with the people for treating Swedish prisoners well during the wars. The bizarre choice of a French commoner was a surprise, but everyone said *oui-oui*, and Jean-Baptiste was crowned Sweden's King Karl Johan XIV (and Karl Johan III in Norway). During his reign (1818-1844), Bernadotte brought peace, prosperity, and fresh DNA, founding the royal dynasty that would produce the current monarchs of Sweden—and, by intermarriage, of Norway and Denmark.

The French Revolution (and Napoleon) spread the idea throughout Europe that people should embrace their ethnic roots and demand self-rule. Norwegians—having been ruled for centuries by Danes, and now Swedes—met at Eidsvoll Manor (outside Oslo—see page 269), drafted a constitution with a parliament, elected a king, and demanded independence. Though the country was still too weak to make this a political reality, the date of May 17, 1814, has become the country's Fourth of July, celebrated today with plenty of flag-waving and folk costumes by Norwegians both in and out of Norway.

Culturally (if not politically), nationalism flourished, producing artists like J. C. Dahl, who captured the beauty of the Norwegian countryside and the simple dignity of its people. (You can see his works at Oslo's National Gallery, page 242.) Playwright Henrik Ibsen realistically portrayed the complexities of a changing Norwegian society. And composer Edvard Grieg used music to convey the majesty of the landscape near his home in Bergen (Troldhaugen, page 389).

In Denmark, nationalism inspired the German-speaking majority in the provinces of Schleswig and Holstein to call for autonomy (1848-1851). The region was finally taken by force from Denmark by Prussia (1864) and incorporated into the new state of Germany. The resulting nationwide sense of humiliation and self-critique actually spurred a cultural golden age. Philosopher Søren Kierkegaard captured the angst of an age when traditional certainties were crumbling. Storyteller Hans Christian Andersen (*The Ugly Duckling*, *The Emperor's New Clothes*, *The Little Mermaid*, and others) gained a Europe-wide reputation. And sculptor Bertel Thorvaldsen, who studied and worked in Rome, decorated Copenhagen with his realistic, Neoclassical statues (at Copenhagen's Cathedral of Our Lady, page 55; and the Thorvaldsen's Museum, page 75).

Throughout the 1800s, Scandinavia was modernizing. The Industrial Revolution brought trains, factories, and larger cities. While some got rich, millions of poor farmers were forced to emigrate from Sweden, Norway, and Finland to America between 1850 and 1920, due to the changing economy, overpopulation, and famine. (The House of Emigrants museum in Växjö, Sweden, tells their story—see page 543.) As in other European countries, Scandinavia saw the steady advance of democracy, parliaments, labor unions, and constitutional monarchies. The 20th century would quicken that pace.

INDEPENDENCE AND WORLD WARS (1900-1945)

In 1905—after five and a half centuries of Danish and Swedish rule—Norway finally was granted independence when it voted overwhelmingly to break from Sweden. National pride ran high, as Oslo's own Roald Amundsen became the first person to reach the South Pole (in 1911—for more, see the Fram Museum on page 258). In 1919, Finland and Esto-

nia—after centuries of Swedish and Russian rule—won their independence while Russia was distracted by the Bolshevik Revolution.

The Scandinavian nations remained neutral through World War I. But when Hitler's Nazi Germany began its European conquest in World War II, it was impossible for Scandinavians—try as they might—to remain uninvolved. While officially neutral, Sweden allowed Nazi troops "on leave" to march through. (Sweden's neutrality later provided a safe haven for Danish Jews and a refuge for the Danish and Norwegian resistance movements.)

Germany invaded Denmark and Norway on April 9, 1940, with Operation Weserübung. Scattered fighting at the Danish border was quickly put down, and Denmark capitulated and officially cooperated with the Nazis until 1943, when the Germans took over the government. Danish resistance groups harried the Nazis and provided intelligence to the Allies (see the Museum of Danish Resistance, page 80). In 1943, a German diplomat informed Copenhagen's rabbi that the Jews were about to be deported. Danish citizens quickly hid and eventually evacuated all but 500 of Denmark's Jews to neutral Sweden.

Norway's army held out a few weeks longer, allowing time for King Håkon VII to flee and organize a vital resistance movement (memorialized at Oslo's Norwegian Resistance Museum, page 241). Norway spent the war chafing under a Nazi puppet government headed by Vidkun Quisling, whose surname has become synonymous with "traitor."

Denmark, Sweden, and Norway came out of the war without

the horrendous damage and loss of life suffered elsewhere in Europe—in part, probably, because Hitler wanted to turn the Scandinavian countries into model states. After all, these were the people Germany was trying to emulate: tall, blond, blue-eyed symbols of the Aryan race.

Finland and Estonia's fates were more complicated. During the war, the Finns valiantly battled Russian invaders, at one point allying with Hitler against the Russians. By war's end, Finland had fought both the Soviets and the Nazis. Estonia, meanwhile, was occupied first by the Soviets and later by the Nazis.

As postwar Europe was divvied up between the communist East and the democratic West, Estonia wound up in the Soviet sphere of influence. Finland avoided this fate through a compromise policy called "Finlandization." The Finns paid lip service to Soviet authority, censored their own media, acted as a buffer against military invasion from the West, rejected rebuilding money from the US (the Marshall Plan), and avoided treaties with the West. In return, Finland remained a self-ruling capitalist democracy and a firm part of the Nordic world. They imported raw materials from the Soviets, then shipped them back as manufactured products, in a mutually beneficial trade agreement.

Meanwhile, Norway and Denmark stood with the West, joining NATO and participating in the Marshall Plan. Sweden took a more neutral approach, and Swede Dag Hammarskjöld served as the UN's Secretary General from 1953 to 1961. Estonia was submerged into the Soviet Union as one of the 15 "republics" of the USSR, only regaining its independence with the breakup of the Soviet Union in 1991.

THE SOCIAL WELFARE STATE (1946-PRESENT)

In the decades since World War II, the Scandinavian countries have made themselves quite wealthy following a mixed capitalist-

socialist model. In the late 1960s, Norway discovered oil in the North Sea, almost instantly transforming itself into a rich nation. Citizens across Scandinavia have come to take for granted cradle-to-grave security—health care, education, unemployment benefits, welfare, and so on—all financed with high taxes. In social policies, Scandinavia has often led the way in liberal attitudes toward sexuality, drug use, and gay rights. For more on current-day Scandinavia, see page 18.

Little Maria...or Metallica?

Scandinavia is viewed as one of the most liberal corners of Europe, so Americans are often surprised to learn there are  government restrictions on what parents can name their children. Historically, parents in Denmark, Norway, Sweden, and Finland were required to choose their child's name from a published list of acceptable monikers. Any variations had to be approved by a government board. One intent of the rules was to prevent commoners from using royal names and to ban names considered ridiculous, inappropriate, potentially harmful to the child, or just not Scandinavian enough. A Norwegian mom even spent two days in jail in the '90s for naming her son Gesher (it means "bridge" in Hebrew). But following a recent series of court rulings, Scandinavian countries are relaxing parts of their naming laws. Denmark has allowed some Legolases and Gandalfs, and in Sweden there's a little girl named Metallica and a little boy named Q.

Estonia took a different approach: In the 1930s it encouraged its citizens to change their Swedish-sounding names to the Estonian equivalents.

Immigration in the late 20th century brought many citizens from non-European nations. While adding diversity, it also threatened the homogenous fabric of a society whose roots have traditionally been white, Christian, European, democratic, and blond. Far-right parties gained support with anti-immigration platforms, but reaction to the July 2011 massacre in Norway (see page 270) weakened those movements, at least in the short term. In September of 2013, however, a new right-wing government came to power in Norway, with the victorious Conservative Party forming a coalition with the anti-immigration Progress Party.

Today, Finland, Sweden, Denmark, and Estonia are all members of the European Union. Norway has stayed outside (a decision still hotly debated by Norwegians, though an association agreement gives the country most of the benefits of membership). While Finland and Estonia have embraced the euro, Norway, Sweden, and Denmark have preserved their own currencies (though Denmark's is pegged to the euro).

As the Scandinavian people forge into the 21st century, they are adamant about preserving their culture, traditions, and high standard of living while competing in a global economy.

PRACTICALITIES

Contents

This chapter covers the practical skills of European travel: how to get tourist information, pay for purchases, sightsee efficiently, find good-value accommodations, eat affordably but well, use technology wisely, and get between destinations smoothly. To study ahead and round out your knowledge, check out "Resources" for a summary of recommended books and films.

Tourist Information

The Scandinavian Tourist Board's office in **the US** is a wealth of information on Norway, Denmark, Sweden, and Finland. Before your trip, download brochures and request any specifics you want (such as regional and city maps and festival schedules). Call 212/885-9700 or visit www.goscandinavia.com (info@goscandinavia.com). Estonia doesn't have a tourist office in the US, but you can check their website (www.visitestonia.com, tourism@eas.ee).

In Scandinavia, your best first stop in every town is generally the tourist information office (abbreviated **TI** in this book). Throughout Scandinavia, you'll find TIs are usually well-organized and always have an English-speaking staff. Most TIs are run by the government, which means their information isn't colored by a drive for profit. (The big exception is the commercially operated Copenhagen TI, which dubs itself "Wonderful Copenhagen.")

TIs are good places to get a city map and information on public transit (including bus and train schedules), walking tours, special events, and nightlife. Many TIs have information on the entire country or at least the region, so try to pick up maps for destinations you'll be visiting later in your trip. If you're arriving in town after the TI closes, call ahead or pick up a map in a neighboring town.

Most big cities publish a *This Week in...* or *What's On...* guide (to Oslo, Bergen, Stockholm, Helsinki, and Tallinn, but not Copenhagen). These are free, found all over town or online, and packed with all the details about each city (24-hour pharmacy, embassies, tram/bus fares, restaurants, sights with hours/admissions/phone numbers), plus a useful calendar of events and a map of the town center.

While TIs are eager to book you a room, they're a good deal only if you're in search of summer and weekend deals on business hotels. A TI can help you find small pensions and private homes, but you'll save yourself and your host money by going direct with the listings in this book.

Travel Tips

Emergency and Medical Help: In all the countries in this book, dial 112 for medical or other emergencies. If you get sick, go to a pharmacist for advice. Or ask at your hotel for help—they'll know the nearest medical and emergency services.

For police, dial 112 in Denmark, Norway, Finland, and Sweden—but in Estonia, dial 110.

Theft or Loss: To replace a passport, you'll need to go in person to an embassy (see page 765). If your credit and debit cards disappear, cancel and replace them (see "Damage Control for Lost Cards" on page 718). File a police report, either on the spot or within a day or two; you'll need it to submit an insurance claim for lost or stolen rail passes or travel gear, and it can help with replacing your passport or credit and debit cards. For more information, see www.ricksteves.com/help. Precautionary measures can minimize the effects of loss—back up photos and other files frequently.

Time Zones: Norway, Sweden, and Denmark, which share the same time zone as continental Europe, are generally six/nine hours ahead of the East/West Coasts of the US. Finland and Estonia are one hour ahead of Norway, Sweden, and Denmark. The exceptions are the beginning and end of Daylight Saving Time: Europe "springs forward" the last Sunday in March (two weeks after most of North America) and "falls back" the last Sunday in October (one week before North America). For a handy online time converter, try www.timeanddate.com/worldclock.

Business Hours: Banks are generally open weekdays from 9:00 to 15:00 or 16:00, with retail shops open an hour or two later. Saturdays are virtually weekdays, with earlier closing hours and no rush hour. Sundays have the same pros and cons as they do for travelers in the US: Sightseeing attractions are generally open, while shops and banks are closed, public transportation options are fewer (for example, no bus service to or from the smaller towns), and there's no rush hour. Rowdy evenings are rare on Sundays. Many museums in Scandinavia are closed on Mondays.

Watt's Up? Europe's electrical system is 220 volts, instead of North America's 110 volts. Most newer electronics (such as laptops, battery chargers, and hair dryers) convert automatically, so you won't need a converter, but you will need an adapter plug with two round prongs, sold inexpensively at travel stores in the US. Avoid bringing older appliances that don't automatically convert voltage; instead, buy a cheap replacement in Europe.

Discounts: While discounts are generally not listed in this book, note that liberal Scandinavia is Europe's most generous corner when it comes to youths (under 18), students (with International Student Identity Cards, www.isic.org), seniors, and families. Children usually sleep and sightsee for half-price or free.

Online Translation Tip: You can use Google's Chrome browser (available free at www.google.com/chrome) to instantly translate websites. With one click, the page appears in (very rough) English translation. You can also paste the URL of the site into the translation window at www.google.com/translate.

Money

This section offers advice on how to pay for purchases on your trip (including getting cash from ATMs and paying with plastic), dealing with lost or stolen cards, VAT (sales tax) refunds, and tipping.

WHAT TO BRING
Bring both a credit card and a debit card. You'll use the debit card at cash machines (ATMs) to withdraw local cash for most purchases, and the credit card to pay for larger items. Some travelers carry a third card, in case one gets demagnetized or eaten by a temperamental machine.

Exchange Rates

I've priced things in local currencies throughout the book. Here are the rough exchange rates for each country. (Check www.oanda.com for the latest rates.)

$1 equals about...
6 Danish kroner (1 krone equals about $0.17)
6 Norwegian kroner (1 krone equals about $0.17)
7 Swedish kronor (1 krona equals about $0.15)
0.72 euro in Finland and Estonia (€1 equals about $1.40)

Kroner are decimalized: 100 øre = 1 krone. Kroner from one Scandinavian country are not accepted in the next (except at foreign-exchange bureaus and banks, and then only bills). Standard abbreviations are Danish krone, DKK; Swedish krona, SEK; and Norwegian kroner, NOK. I'll keep it simple. For all three countries, I'll use the krone abbreviation "kr." Finland and Estonia's currency is the euro (€).

To roughly convert Danish and Norwegian prices into US dollars, multiply by two, then drop a zero (e.g., 15 kr = about $3, 100 kr = about $20). In Sweden, divide prices by 7 (100 kr = about $14). So, that 1,000-kr Norwegian sweater is about $200, and your 360-kr dinner in Stockholm is about $50. To roughly convert prices in euros to dollars, add 40 percent (€20 = about $28).

For an emergency stash, bring several hundred dollars in hard cash in $20 bills.

Because Scandinavian countries have different currencies, you'll likely wind up with leftover cash when you're leaving a country. Coins can't be exchanged once you leave the country, so try to spend them before you cross the border. But bills are easy to convert to the "new" country's currency. When changing cash, use exchange bureaus rather than banks. The Forex desks (easy to find at major train stations and airports) are considered reliable and fair.

CASH

Cash is just as desirable in Europe as it is at home. Small businesses

(B&Bs, mom-and-pop cafés, shops, etc.) prefer that you pay your bills with cash. Some vendors will charge you extra for using a credit card, and some won't take credit cards at all. Cash is the best—and sometimes only—way to pay for cheap food, bus fare, taxis, and local guides.

Throughout Europe, ATMs are the standard way for travelers to get cash. To withdraw money from an ATM, you'll need a debit card (ideally with a Visa or MasterCard logo for maximum usability), plus a PIN code. Know your PIN code in numbers; there are only numbers—no letters—on European keypads. For increased security, shield the keypad when entering your PIN code, and don't use an ATM if anything on the front of the machine looks loose or damaged (a sign that someone may have attached a "skimming" device to capture account information). Try to withdraw large sums of money to reduce the number of per-transaction bank fees you'll pay.

When possible, use ATMs located outside banks—a thief is less likely to target a cash machine near surveillance cameras, and if your card is munched by a machine, you can go inside for help. Stay away from "independent" ATMs such as Travelex, Euronet, Moneybox, Cardpoint, and Cashzone, which charge huge commissions, have terrible exchange rates, and may try to trick users with "dynamic currency conversion" (described at the end of "Credit and Debit Cards," next).

Although you can use a credit card for an ATM transaction, it only makes sense in an emergency, because it's considered a cash advance (borrowed at a high interest rate) rather than a withdrawal.

While traveling, if you want to monitor your accounts online to detect any unauthorized transactions, be sure to use a secure connection (see page 745).

Pickpockets target tourists. To safeguard your cash, wear a money belt—a pouch with a strap that you buckle around your waist like a belt and tuck under your clothes. Keep your cash, credit cards, and passport secure in your money belt, and carry only a day's spending money in your front pocket.

CREDIT AND DEBIT CARDS

For purchases, Visa and MasterCard are more commonly accepted than American Express. Just like at home, credit or debit cards work easily at larger hotels, restaurants, and shops. I typically use my debit card to withdraw cash to pay for most purchases. I use my credit card only in a few specific situations: to book hotel reservations by phone, to buy advance tickets for events or sights, to cover major expenses (such as car rentals, plane tickets, and long hotel stays), and to pay for things near the end of my trip (to avoid another visit to the ATM). While you could use a debit card to make most large purchases, using a credit card offers a greater degree of fraud protection (because debit cards draw funds directly from your account).

Ask Your Credit- or Debit-Card Company: Before your trip, contact the company that issued your debit or credit cards.

• Confirm that your **card will work overseas,** and alert them that you'll be using it in Europe; otherwise, they may deny transactions if they perceive unusual spending patterns.

• Ask for the specifics on transaction **fees.** When you use your credit or debit card—either for purchases or ATM withdrawals—you'll often be charged additional "international transaction" fees of up to 3 percent (1 percent is normal) plus $5 per transaction. If your card's fees seem too high, consider getting a different card just for your trip: Capital One (www.capitalone.com) and most credit unions have low-to-no international fees.

• If you plan to withdraw cash from ATMs, confirm your daily **withdrawal limit,** and if necessary, ask your bank to adjust it. Some travelers prefer a high limit that allows them to take out more cash at each ATM stop (saving on bank fees), while others prefer to set a lower limit in case their card is stolen. Note that foreign banks also set maximum withdrawal amounts for their ATMs. Also, remember that you're withdrawing local currency, not dollars—so, for example, in Finland and Estonia, if your daily limit is $300, withdraw just €200. Many frustrated travelers walk away from ATMs thinking their cards have been rejected, when actually they were asking for more cash in the local currency than their daily limit allowed.

• Get your bank's emergency **phone number** in the US (but not its 800 number, which isn't accessible from overseas) to call collect if you have a problem.

• Ask for your credit card's **PIN** in case you need to make an emergency cash withdrawal or encounter Europe's "chip-and-PIN" system; the bank won't tell you your PIN over the phone, so allow time for it to be mailed to you.

Chip and PIN: Europeans are increasingly using chip-and-PIN cards, which are embedded with an electronic security chip (in addition to the magnetic stripe found on American-style cards). To make a purchase with a chip-and-PIN card, the cardholder inserts the card into a slot in the payment machine, then enters a PIN (like using a debit card in the US) while the card stays in the slot. The chip inside the card authorizes the transaction; the cardholder doesn't sign a receipt. Your American-style card might not work at payment machines using this system, such as those at train and subway stations, toll roads, parking garages, luggage lockers, bike-rental kiosks, and self-serve gas pumps. If you have problems using your American card in a chip-and-PIN machine, here are some suggestions: For either a debit card or a credit card, try entering that card's PIN when prompted. (Note that your credit-card PIN may not be the same as your debit-card PIN; you'll need to ask your bank for your credit-card PIN.) If your cards still don't work, look for a machine that takes cash, seek out a clerk who might be able to process the transaction manually, or ask a local if you can pay them cash to run the transaction on their card.

And don't panic. Most travelers who carry only magnetic-stripe cards don't run into problems. Still, it pays to carry plenty of cash; remember, you can always use an ATM with your magnetic-stripe debit card.

If you're still concerned, you can apply for a chip card in the US (though I think it's overkill). One option is the no-annual-fee GlobeTrek Visa, offered by Andrews Federal Credit Union in Maryland (open to all US residents; see www.andrewsfcu.org). In the future, chip cards should become standard issue in the US: Visa and MasterCard have asked US banks and merchants to use chip-based cards by late 2015.

Dynamic Currency Conversion: If merchants offer to convert your purchase price into dollars (called dynamic currency conversion, or DCC), refuse this "service." You'll pay even more in fees for the expensive convenience of seeing your charge in dollars. "Independent" ATMs (such as Travelex and Moneybox) may try to confuse customers by presenting DCC in misleading terms. If an ATM offers to "lock in" or "guarantee" your conversion rate, choose "proceed without conversion." Other prompts might state, "You can be charged in dollars: Press YES for dollars, NO for kroner." Always choose the local currency in these situations.

Damage Control for Lost Cards

If you lose your credit, debit, or ATM card, you can stop people from using it by reporting the loss immediately to the respective global customer-assistance centers. Call these 24-hour US numbers collect: Visa (tel. 303/967-1096), MasterCard (tel. 636/722-7111), and American Express (tel. 336/393-1111). European toll-free numbers (listed by country) can be found at the websites for Visa (usa.visa.com) and Mastercard (www.mastercard.us).

Providing the following information will allow for a quicker cancellation of your missing card: full card number, whether you are the primary or secondary cardholder, the cardholder's name exactly as printed on the card, billing address, home phone number, circumstances of the loss or theft, and identification verification (your birth date, your mother's maiden name, or your Social Security number—memorize this, don't carry a copy). If you are the secondary cardholder, you'll also need to provide the primary cardholder's identification-verification details. You can generally receive a temporary card within two or three business days in Europe (see www.ricksteves.com/help for more).

If you report your loss within two days, you typically won't be responsible for any unauthorized transactions on your account, although many banks charge a liability fee of $50.

TIPPING

Tipping in Europe isn't as automatic and generous as it is in the US—and Scandinavia is one part of Europe where tips are less common. For special service, tips are appreciated, but not expected. As in the US, the proper amount depends on your resources, tipping philosophy, and the circumstances, but some general guidelines apply.

Restaurants: Tipping is an issue only at restaurants that have table service. If you order your food at a counter, don't tip.

Throughout Scandinavia, a service charge is typically included in your bill, and you aren't required to leave an additional tip. But don't assume that the service charge goes to your server—often it goes right to the restaurant owner. In fancier restaurants or whenever you enjoy great service, round up the bill (about 5-10 percent of the total check). Rounding up for good service is especially common in Estonia (though never more than 10 percent).

Taxis: To tip the cabbie, round up. For a typical ride, round up your fare a bit (for instance, if the fare is 85 kr, pay 90 kr). If the cabbie hauls your bags and zips you to the airport to help you catch your flight, you might want to toss in a little more. But if you feel like you're being driven in circles or otherwise ripped off, skip the tip.

Special Services: In general, if someone in the service industry does a super job for you, a small tip (the equivalent of a euro or two) is appropriate...but not required. If you're not sure whether (or how much) to tip for a service, ask your hotelier or the TI.

GETTING A VAT REFUND

Wrapped into the purchase price of your Scandinavian souvenirs is a Value-Added Tax (VAT) of 20-25 percent (among the highest rates in Europe). You're entitled to get most of that tax back if you purchase goods worth more than a certain amount (300 kr in Denmark, 315 kr in Norway, 200 kr in Sweden, €40 in Finland, and €38 in Estonia) at a store that participates in the VAT refund scheme (look for signs in store windows—VAT is called MVA in Norway and MOMS in Denmark, Finland, and Sweden). Typically, you must ring up the minimum at a single retailer—you can't add up your purchases from various shops to reach the required amount.

Getting your refund is usually straightforward and, if you buy a substantial amount of souvenirs, well worth the hassle. If you're lucky, the merchant will subtract the tax when you make your purchase. (This is more likely to occur if the store ships the goods to your home.) Otherwise, you'll need to:

Get the paperwork. Have the merchant completely fill out the necessary refund document. You'll have to present your passport.

Get the paperwork done before you leave the store to ensure you'll have everything you need (including your original sales receipt).

Get your stamp at the border or airport. If you've made purchases in Denmark, Sweden, Finland, and/or Estonia, process your VAT document at your last stop in the European Union (such as at the airport) with the customs agent who deals with VAT refunds. If you've shopped hard in Norway (a non-EU country), get your document(s) stamped at the border or at your point of departure from Norway.

Arrive an additional hour before you need to check in for your flight to allow time to find the local customs office—and to stand in line. It's best to keep your purchases in your carry-on. If they're too large or dangerous to carry on (such as knives), pack them in your checked bags and alert the check-in agent. You'll be sent (with your tagged bag) to a customs desk outside security, which will examine your bag, stamp your paperwork, and put your bag on the belt. You're not supposed to use your purchased goods before you leave. If you show up at customs wearing your new Norwegian sweater, officials might look the other way—or deny you a refund.

Collect your refund. You'll need to return your stamped document to the retailer or its representative. Many merchants work with services, such as Global Blue or Premier Tax Free, that have offices at major airports, ports, or border crossings (either before or after security, probably strategically located near a duty-free shop). These services, which extract a 4 percent fee, can usually refund your money immediately in cash, or credit your card (within two billing cycles). If the retailer handles VAT refunds directly, it's up to you to contact the merchant for your refund. You can mail the documents from home, or more quickly, from your point of departure (using an envelope you've prepared in advance or one that's been provided by the merchant). You'll then have to wait—it can take months.

CUSTOMS FOR AMERICAN SHOPPERS

You are allowed to take home $800 worth of items per person duty-free, once every 30 days. You can take home many processed and packaged foods: vacuum-packed cheeses, dried herbs, jams, baked goods, candy, chocolate, oil, vinegar, mustard, and honey. Fresh fruits and vegetables and most meats are not allowed, with exceptions for some canned items.

As for alcohol, you can bring in one liter duty-free (it can be packed securely in your checked luggage, along with any other liquid-containing items). To bring alcohol (or liquid-packed foods) in your carry-on bag on your flight home, buy it at a duty-free shop at the airport. You'll increase your odds of getting it onto a connecting flight if it's packaged in a "STEB"—a secure, tamper-evident bag. But stay away from liquids in opaque, ceramic, or metallic containers, which usually cannot be successfully screened (STEB or no STEB).

For details on allowable goods, customs rules, and duty rates, visit www.cbp.gov.

Sightseeing

Sightseeing can be hard work. Use these tips to make your visits to Scandinavia's finest sights meaningful, fun, efficient, and painless.

PLAN AHEAD

Set up an itinerary that allows you to fit in all your must-see sights. For a one-stop look at opening hours in the bigger cities, see the "At a Glance" sidebars for Copenhagen, Oslo, Bergen, Stockholm, Helsinki, and Tallinn. Most sights keep stable hours, but you can easily confirm the latest by checking with the TI or visiting museum websites.

Don't put off visiting a must-see sight—you never know when a place will close unexpectedly for a holiday, strike, or restoration. Many museums are closed or have reduced hours at least a few days a year, especially on holidays such as Christmas, New Year's, and Labor Day (May 1). A list of holidays is on page 766; check museum websites for possible closures during your trip. In summer, some sights may stay open late. Off-season, many museums have shorter hours.

Going at the right time helps avoid crowds. This book offers tips on the best times to see specific sights. Try visiting popular sights very early or very late. Evening visits are usually peaceful, with fewer crowds.

Study up. To get the most out of the sight descriptions in this book, read them before your visit.

AT SIGHTS

Here's what you can typically expect:

Entering: Be warned that you may not be allowed to enter if you arrive 30 to 60 minutes before closing time. And guards start ushering people out well before the actual closing time, so don't save the best for last.

Some important sights have a security check, where you must open your bag or send it through a metal detector. Some sights require you to check daypacks and coats. (If you'd rather not check your daypack, try carrying it tucked under your arm like a purse as you enter.)

Photography: If the museum's photo policy isn't clearly posted, ask a guard. Generally, taking photos without a flash or tripod is allowed. Some sights ban photos altogether.

Temporary Exhibits: Museums may show special exhibits in addition to their permanent collection. Some exhibits are included in the entry price, while others come at an extra cost (which you may have to pay even if you don't want to see the exhibit).

Expect Changes: Artwork can be on tour, on loan, out sick, or shifted at the whim of the curator. To adapt, pick up a floor plan as you enter, and ask museum staff if you can't find a particular item.

Audioguides: Many sights rent audioguides, which generally offer excellent recorded descriptions in English (about $8 or less). If you bring your own earbuds, you can enjoy better sound and avoid holding the device to your ear. To save money, bring a Y-jack and share one audioguide with your travel partner. Increasingly, museums are offering apps (often free) that you can download to your mobile device.

Services: Important sights may have an on-site café or cafeteria (usually a handy place to rejuvenate during a long visit). The WCs at sights are free and nearly always clean.

Before Leaving: At the gift shop, scan the postcard rack or thumb through a guidebook to be sure that you haven't overlooked something that you'd like to see.

Every sight or museum offers more than what is covered in this book. Use the information in this book as an introduction—not the final word.

Sleeping

Accommodations in Scandinavia are fairly expensive, but normally very comfortable and come with breakfast. When budgeting, plan on spending about $180 per hotel double in big cities, and $100 in towns and in private homes.

I favor hotels and restaurants that are handy to your sightseeing activities. Rather than list hotels scattered throughout a city, I choose two or three favorite neighborhoods and recommend the best accommodation values in each, from dorm beds to fancy doubles with all the comforts.

A major feature of this book is its extensive and opinionated listing of good-value rooms. I like places that are clean, central, relatively quiet at night, reasonably priced, friendly, small enough to have a hands-on owner and stable staff, run with a respect for Scandinavian traditions, and not listed in other guidebooks. (In Scandinavia, for me, six out of these eight criteria means it's a keeper.) I'm more impressed by a convenient location and a fun-loving philosophy than flat-screen TVs and a pricey laundry service. I've also thrown in a few hostels, private rooms, and other cheap options for budget travelers.

Book your accommodations well in advance, especially if you'll be traveling during busy times. See page 766 for a list of major holidays and festivals in Scandinavia; for tips on making reservations, see page 728.

Some people make reservations as they travel, calling hotels a few days to a week before their arrival. If you'd rather travel without any reservations at all, you'll have greater success snaring rooms if you arrive at your destination early in the day. If you anticipate crowds (weekends are worst) on the day you want to check in, call hotels at about 9:00 or 10:00, when the receptionist knows who'll be checking out and which rooms will be available. If you encounter a language barrier, ask the fluent receptionist at your current hotel to call for you.

To get the most sleep for your dollar at these northern latitudes, pull the dark shades (and even consider bringing your own night shades) to keep out the early-morning sun.

RATES AND DEALS

I've described my recommended accommodations using a Sleep Code (see sidebar). Prices listed are for one-night stays in peak season, include breakfast, and assume you're booking directly with the hotel (not through an online-booking engine or TI). Booking services extract a commission from the hotel, which logically closes the door on special deals. Book direct.

Each of my recommended hotels has a website (often with a built-in booking form) and an email address; you can expect a response in English within a day (and often sooner).

If you're on a budget, it's smart to email several hotels to ask for their best price. Comparison-shop and make your choice. This is especially helpful when dealing with the larger hotels that use "dynamic pricing," a computer-generated system that predicts the demand for particular days and sets prices accordingly: High-demand days will often be more than double the price of low-demand days. This makes it impossible for a guidebook to list anything more accurate than a wide range of prices. I regret this trend. While you can assume that hotels listed in this book are good, it's very difficult to say which ones are the better value unless you email to confirm the price.

As you look over the listings, you'll notice that some accommodations promise special prices to Rick Steves readers. To get these rates, you must book direct (that is, not through a booking site like TripAdvisor or Booking.com), mention this book when you reserve, and then show the book upon arrival. Rick Steves discounts apply to readers with ebooks as well as printed books. Be-

Sleep Code

Price Rankings

To help you easily sort through my hotel listings, I've divided the accommodations into three categories, based on the highest price for a standard double room with bath during high season:

$$$	**Higher Priced**
$$	**Moderately Priced**
$	**Lower Priced**

Prices can change without notice; verify the hotel's current rates online or by email. For the best prices, always book directly with the hotel.

Abbreviations

To pack maximum information into minimum space, I use the following code to describe accommodations in this book. Prices listed are per room, not per person. When a price range is given for a type of room (such as double rooms listed for 1,050-1,250 kr), it means the price fluctuates with the season, size of room, or length of stay; expect to pay the upper end for peak-season stays.

S = Single room (or price for one person in a double).

D = Double or twin room. "Double beds" can be two twins sheeted together and are usually big enough for nonromantic couples.

T = Triple (generally a double bed with a single).

Q = Quad (usually two double beds; adding an extra child's bed to a T is usually cheaper).

b = Private bathroom with toilet and shower or tub.

According to this code, a couple staying at a "Db-1,050 kr" hotel in Sweden would pay a total of 1,050 kr (about $150) for a double room with a private bathroom. Unless otherwise noted, breakfast is included, hotel staff speak basic English, and credit cards are accepted.

There's almost always Wi-Fi and/or a guest computer available, either free or for a fee.

cause I trust hotels to honor this, please let me know if you don't receive a listed discount. Note, though, that discounts understandably may not be applied to promotional rates.

In general, prices can soften if you do any of the following: offer to pay cash, stay at least three nights, or mention this book. You can also try asking for a cheaper room or a discount, or offer to skip breakfast.

Many places keep an odd misfit room (100 kr cheaper than the others) lashed to a bedpost in the attic, but will only tell you if you ask. Backpacker places have a range of rooms, blurring the distinction between "hotel" and "hostel." Money-conscious travelers should consider doubles in hostels and rooms in simple hotels with shared baths—a respectable option in clean and wholesome Scandinavia.

A triple is much cheaper than a double and a single. While hotel singles are most expensive, private accommodations have a flat per-person rate. Hostels and dorms always charge per person. Families can get a price break; normally a child can sleep free or for very little in the parents' room.

TYPES OF ACCOMMODATIONS
Hotels

Hotels are expensive ($150-250 doubles), with some exceptions. Even though most hotels in Scandinavia base their prices on de-

mand, it is possible to find lower prices during the summer and on weekends. Check hotel websites for deals. When a classy, modern $200 place has a $150 summer special that includes two $10 buffet breakfasts, the dumpy $100 hotel room without breakfast becomes less exciting.

Many modern hotels have "combi" rooms (singles with a sofa that turns the room into a perfectly good double), which are cheaper than a full double. And if a hotel is not full, any day can bring out summer discounts.

If you're arriving early in the morning, your room probably won't be ready. You can drop your bag safely at the hotel and dive right into sightseeing.

Hoteliers can be a great help and source of advice. Most know their city well, and can assist you with everything from public transit and airport connections to finding a good restaurant, the nearest launderette, or a Wi-Fi hotspot.

Even at the best places, mechanical breakdowns occur: Air-conditioning malfunctions, sinks leak, hot water turns cold, and toilets gurgle and smell. Report your concerns clearly and calmly at the front desk. For more complicated problems, don't expect instant results.

If you suspect night noise will be a problem (if, for instance, your room is over a nightclub), ask for a quieter room in the back or on an upper floor. To guard against theft in your room, keep valuables out of sight. Some rooms come with a safe, and other hotels have safes at the front desk. I've never bothered using one.

Checkout can pose problems if surprise charges pop up on your bill. If you settle up your bill the afternoon before you leave,

The Good and Bad of Online Reviews

User-generated travel review websites—such as TripAdvisor, Booking.com, and Yelp—have quickly become a huge player in the travel industry. These sites give you access to actual reports—good and bad—from travelers who have experienced the hotel, restaurant, tour, or attraction.

My hotelier friends in Europe are in awe of these sites' influence. Small hoteliers who want to stay in business have no choice but to work with review sites—which often charge fees for good placement or photos, and tack on commissions if users book through the site instead of directly with the hotel.

While these sites work hard to weed out bogus users, my hunch is that a significant percentage of reviews are posted by friends or enemies of the business being reviewed. I've even seen hotels "bribe" guests (for example, offer a free breakfast) in exchange for a positive review. Also, review sites can become an echo chamber, with one or two flashy businesses camped out atop the ratings, while better, more affordable, and more authentic alternatives sit ignored further down the list. (For example, I find review sites' restaurant recommendations skew to very touristy, obvious options.)

Remember that a user-generated review is based on the experience of one person. That person likely stayed at one hotel and ate at a few restaurants, and doesn't have much of a basis for comparison. A guidebook is the work of a trained researcher who has exhaustively visited many alternatives to assess their relative value. I recently checked out some top-rated TripAdvisor listings in various towns; when stacked up against their competitors, some are gems, while just as many are duds.

Both types of information have their place, and in many ways, they're complementary. If a hotel or restaurant is well-reviewed in a guidebook or two, and also gets good ratings on one of these sites, it's likely a winner.

you'll have time to discuss and address any points of contention (before 19:00, when the night shift usually arrives).

Above all, keep a positive attitude. Remember, you're on vacation. If your hotel is a disappointment, spend more time out enjoying the city you came to see.

Private Rooms

Throughout Scandinavia, people rent rooms in their homes to travelers for about $85 per double (or about $95 for a double with private bath). You'll get your own key to a clean, comfortable, but usually simple private room (sometimes without a sink), with access to the family shower and WC if the room doesn't have its own bath.

While some put out a *Værelse, Rom, Rum,* or *Hus Rum* sign, and some can be booked through the local TI (which occasionally keeps these B&Bs a secret until all hotel rooms are taken), you'll most likely find them online through sites such as Airbnb or Roomorama. When possible, I've listed direct contact information for B&Bs—booking direct saves both you and your host the cut the TI takes. The TIs are very protective of their lists. If you enjoy a big-city private home that would like to be listed in this book, I'd love to hear from you.

Other Accommodation Options: If you want a place to sleep that's free, Couchsurfing.org is a vagabond's alternative to Airbnb. It lists millions of outgoing members, who host fellow "surfers" in their homes. And websites such as HomeAway and its sister sites VRBO and GreatRentals are good resources for finding apartments or houses to rent.

Hostels

Scandinavian hostels, Europe's finest, are open to travelers of all ages. They offer classy facilities, members' kitchens (making your own meals is a great way to save money), cheap hot meals (often breakfast buffets), plenty of doubles (for a few extra kroner), guest computers, Wi-Fi, self-service laundries, and great people experiences. Nowadays, concerned about bedbugs, hostels are likely to provide all bedding, including sheets. Family and private rooms may be available on request. Hostels are also a tremendous source of local and budget travel information. Note that many hostels close in the off-season.

You'll find lots of Volvos in hostel parking lots, as Scandinavians know that hostels provide the best (and usually only) $35 beds in town. Hosteling is ideal for families who fit into two sets of bunk beds (4-bed rooms, kitchens, washing machines, discount family memberships). Pick up each country's free hostel directory at any hostel or TI.

Independent hostels tend to be easygoing, colorful, and informal (no membership required); www.hostelworld.com is the standard way backpackers search and book hostels these days, but also try www.hostelz.com and www.hostels.com.

Official hostels are part of Hostelling International (HI) and share an online booking site (www.hihostels.com). HI hostels typically require that you either have a membership card or pay extra per night. Many hostels in Norway regularly promote nonmember prices—if you have a membership card, be sure to ask about a discount.

Camping

Scandinavian campgrounds are practical, comfortable, and cheap (about $10/person with $20 camping card, available on the spot).

Making Hotel Reservations

Reserve your rooms several weeks in advance—or as soon as you've pinned down your travel dates. Note that some national holidays merit your making reservations far in advance (see page 766).

Requesting a Reservation: It's easiest to book your room through the hotel's website. (For the best rates, always use the hotel's official site and not a booking agency's site.) If there's no reservation form, or for complicated requests, send an email (see sample request). Most recommended hotels take reservations in English. The hotelier wants to know:

- the number and type of rooms you need
- the number of nights you'll stay
- your date of arrival (use the European style for writing dates: day/month/year)
- your date of departure
- any special needs (such as bathroom in the room or down the hall, cheapest room, twin beds vs. double bed, and so on)

Mention any discounts—for Rick Steves readers or otherwise—when you make the reservation.

Confirming a Reservation: Most places will request your credit-card number to hold the room. If they don't have a secure online reservation form—look for the *https*—you can email it (I do), but it's safer to share that confidential info via a phone call or two emails (splitting your number between them).

Canceling a Reservation: If you must cancel, it's courteous—and smart—to do so with as much notice as possible, especially

This is the middle-class Scandinavian family way to travel: safe, great social fun, and no reservation problems. Campgrounds are friendly, safe, more central and convenient than rustic, and rarely full.

The national tourist office websites have campground listings, but for more comprehensive guides, visit these websites: www.camping.se (Sweden), www.camping.dk (Denmark), and www.camping.no (Norway). Your hometown travel bookstore should also have guidebooks on camping in Europe. You'll find campgrounds just about everywhere you need them.

Most campgrounds provide **huts** *(hytter)* for wannabe campers with no gear. Huts normally sleep four to six in bunk beds, come with blankets and a kitchenette, and charge one fee (about 500 kr or more, plus extra if you need sheets). The toilet and shower may

From:	rick@ricksteves.com
Sent:	Today
To:	info@hotelcentral.com
Subject:	Reservation request for 19-22 July

Dear Hotel Central,

I would like to reserve a room for 2 people for 3 nights, arriving 19 July and departing 22 July. If possible, I would like a quiet room with a double bed and a bathroom inside the room.

Please let me know if you have a room available and the price.

Thank you!
Rick Steves

for smaller family-run places. Be warned that cancellation policies can be strict; read the fine print or ask about these before you book. Internet deals may require prepayment, with no refunds for cancellations.

Reconfirming a Reservation: Always call to reconfirm your room reservation a few days in advance. For smaller hotels and B&Bs, I call again on my day of arrival to tell my host what time I expect to get there (especially important if arriving late—after 17:00).

Phoning: For tips on how to call hotels overseas, see page 735.

be in a nearby shared washhouse. Because locals typically move in for a week or two, many campground huts are booked for summer long in advance. You can book these ahead as well, or try your chances on the road.

Eating

When restaurant-hunting, choose a spot filled with locals, not tourists. Venturing even a block or two off the main drag leads to higher-quality food for less than half the price of the tourist-oriented places. Locals eat better at lower-rent locales.

Most Scandinavian nations have one inedible dish

that is cherished with a perverse but patriotic sentimentality. These dishes, which often originated during a famine, now remind the young of their ancestors' suffering. Norway's penitential food, lutefisk (dried cod marinated for days in lye and water), is used for Christmas and for jokes.

BREAKFAST

Hotel breakfasts are a huge and filling buffet, generally included but occasionally a $12-or-so option. They feature fruit, cereal, and various milks (look for words like *skummet* for skim, *lett* for low-fat, *sød* or *hel* for whole, *filmjölk* for buttermilk). Grab a drinkable yogurt and go local by pouring it in the bowl and sprinkling your cereal over it. The great selection of breads and crackers comes with jam, butter *(smør)*, margarine (same word), and cheese *(ost)*. And you'll get cold cuts *(pålegg)*, pickled herring *(sursild)*, caviar paste (in a squeeze tube), and boiled eggs (egg or *æg*—*bløt* is soft-boiled, *kokt* is hard-boiled); use the plastic egg cups and small spoons provided to eat your soft-boiled egg Scandinavian-style.

The brown cheese with the texture of earwax and a slightly sweet taste is called *geitost* ("goat cheese") or *brunost* ("brown cheese"). Popular in Norway, it's not really a cheese—it's made from boiled-down, slightly sweetened whey—and often contains a blend of goat and cow's milk. Try to develop a taste for this odd but enjoyable dairy product. Swedes prefer a spreadable variety called *messmör*.

For beverages, it's orange juice (the word for orange is *appelsin*, so OJ is AJ) and coffee or tea. Coffee addicts can buy a thermos and get it filled in most hotels and hostels for around $5. While it's bad form to take freebies from the breakfast buffet to eat later, many hotels will provide you with wax paper and a plastic bag to pack yourself a lunch, legitimately, for $7-8. Ask for a *matpakke* (packed lunch).

If you skip your hotel's breakfast, you can visit a bakery to get a sandwich and cup of coffee. Bakeries have wonderful inexpensive pastries. The only cheap breakfast is the one you make yourself. Many simple accommodations provide kitchenettes or at least coffeepots.

LUNCH

Many restaurants offer cheap daily lunch specials *(dagens rett)* and buffets for office workers. Scandinavians, not big on lunch, often

just grab a sandwich *(smørrebrød)* and a cup of coffee at their work desk.

Especially in Denmark, you'll find *smørrebrød* shops turning sandwiches into an art form. These open-face delights taste as good as they look. My favorite is the one piled high with shrimp *(reker* or *rejer)*. The roast beef is good, too. Shops will wrap sandwiches up for a perfect picnic in a nearby park.

If you want to enjoy a combination of picnics and restaurant meals on your trip, you'll save money by eating in restaurants at lunch (when there's usually a special and food is generally cheaper) and picnicking for dinner.

PICNICS

Scandinavia has colorful markets and economical supermarkets. Picnic-friendly minimarkets at gas and train stations are open late.

Samples of picnic treats: *Wasa* cracker bread (Sport is my favorite; Ideal *flatbrød* is ideal for munchies), packaged meat and cheese, brown "goat cheese" *(geitost)*, drinkable yogurt, freshly cooked or smoked fish from markets, fresh fruit and vegetables, lingonberries, squeeze tubes of mustard and sandwich spreads (shrimp, caviar), rye bread, and boxes of juice and milk. Grocery stores sell a cheap, light breakfast: a handy yogurt with cereal and a spoon. Most places offer cheap ready-made sandwiches. If you're bored with sandwiches, some groceries and most delis have hot chicken, salads by the portion, and picnic portables.

DINNER

The large meal of the Nordic day is an early dinner. Most Scandinavians eat dinner at home, and restaurant dinners are expensive treats. Alternate between picnic dinners (outside or in your hotel or hostel); cheap, forgettable, but filling cafeteria or fast-food dinners ($20); and atmospheric, carefully chosen restaurants popular with locals ($40 and up). One main course

PRACTICALITIES

and two salads or soups fill up two travelers without emptying their pocketbooks. If potatoes came with your main dish, most servers are happy to give you a second helping. Booze is pricey: A beer costs about $12 in Oslo. Water is served free with an understanding smile at most restaurants (though in Denmark, there is a charge for water if you don't order another beverage).

In Scandinavia, a $40 meal in a restaurant is not that much more than a $30 American meal, since tax and tip are included in the menu price.

SMÖRGÅSBORD

The *smörgåsbord* (known in Denmark and Norway as the *store koldt bord*) is a Scandinavian culinary tradition. Though locals reserve the *smörgåsbord* for festive times such as the Christmas season, anyone can dig into this all-you-can-eat buffet any time of year at certain hotels and on overnight ferries. While the word originally referred to a spread of cold cuts, the *smörgåsbords* you'll find usually include hot dishes, too.

Seek out a *smörgåsbord* at least once during your trip, just for the high of seeing so much wholesome Nordic food spread out in front of you. Good *smörgåsbord* opportunities covered in this book are at the Grand Hotel in Stockholm; on the overnight boats between Stockholm and Helsinki or Copenhagen and Oslo; and at Kviknes Hotel in the Norwegian fjordside town of Balestrand.

Follow these simple steps to enjoy a *smaklig* (tasty) *smörgåsbord*:

1. Browse the buffet before you begin, so you can budget your stomach space. Think of the *smörgåsbord* as a five- or six-course meal.

2. Don't overload your plate. Instead, make several trips, taking a fresh plate and cutlery each time. To signal the waiter that you're finished with each round, lay your fork and knife side-by-side on the plate. If you're getting up but are not finished with your plate, place your fork and knife in the shape of an *X* on the plate.

3. Begin with the herring dishes, along with boiled potatoes and *knäckebröd* (Swedish crisp bread).

4. Next, sample the other fish dishes (warm and cold) and more potatoes. *Gravlax* is salt-cured salmon flavored with dill, served along with a sweet mustard sauce *(gravlax senap)*.

5. Move on to salads, egg dishes, and various cold cuts.

6. Now for the meat dishes—it's meatball time! Pour on some gravy as well as a spoonful of lingonberry sauce, and have more po-

tatoes. Reindeer and other roast meats and poultry may also tempt you.

7. Still hungry? Make a point to sample the Nordic cheeses—try creamy Havarti, mild Castello (a soft blue cheese), and in Norwegian buffets, goat cheese. Sample the delicious seasonal fruits and *franskbrød* white bread. And there are racks of traditional desserts, cakes, and custards (see "Dessert," later). Cap the meal with coffee.

Smaklig måltid! Enjoy your meal!

DRINKING

Purchasing heavily taxed wine, beer, and spirits in Scandinavia can put a dent in your vacation budget. In Sweden and Norway, spirits, wine, and strong beer (more than 3.5 percent alcohol) are sold in state-run liquor stores: Systembolaget in Sweden, and Vinmonopolet in Norway. Buying a beer or glass of wine in a bar or restaurant in Sweden or Norway is particularly expensive. Therefore, many Scandinavians will have a drink or a glass of wine at home (or in their hotel room) before going out, then limit themselves to one or two glasses at the restaurant. If taking an overnight cruise during your trip, you can get a good deal on a bottle of wine or spirits in the onboard duty-free shop. Liquor laws are much more relaxed in Denmark, where you can buy wine, beer, and spirits at any supermarket or corner store. Prices are a bit lower as well. Public drinking is acceptable in Denmark, while it is illegal (although often done) in Norway and Sweden. Throughout Scandinavia, drinking and driving is not tolerated.

Some local specialties are *akvavit*, a strong, vodka-like spirit distilled from potatoes and flavored with anise, caraway, or other herbs and spices—then drunk ice-cold (common in Norway, Sweden, and Denmark). *Lakka* is a syrupy-sweet liqueur made from cloudberries, the small orange berries grown in the Arctic (popular in Norway, Sweden, and Finland). *Salmiakka* is a nearly black licorice-flavored liqueur (Finland, Norway, and Denmark). *Gammel Dansk* can be described as Danish bitters for the adventurous (Denmark only).

DESSERT

Scandinavians love sweets. A meal is not complete without a little treat and a cup of coffee at the end. Bakeries *(konditori)* fill their window cases with all varieties of cakes, tarts, cookies, and pastries. The most popular ingredients are marzipan, almonds, hazelnuts, chocolate, and fresh berries. Many cakes are covered with entire sheets of solid marzipan. To find the neighborhood bakery, just look for a golden pretzel hanging above the door or windows.

Scandinavian chocolate is some of the best in Europe. In Denmark, seek out Anthon Berg's dark chocolate and marzipan treats, as well as Toms' chocolate-covered caramels (Toms Guld are the best). Sweden's biggest chocolate producer, Maribou, makes huge bars of solid milk chocolate, as well as some with dried fruits or nuts. *Daim* are milk chocolate-covered hard toffees, sold in a variety of sizes, from large bars to bite-size pieces, all in bright-red wrappers. The Freia company, Norway's chocolate goddess (named for the Norse goddess Freya), makes a wonderful assortment of delights, from *Et lite stykke Norge* ("A little piece of Norway"—bars of creamy milk chocolate wrapped in pale-yellow paper) and *Smil* (chocolate-covered soft caramels sold in rolls) to *Firkløver* (bars of milk chocolate with hazelnuts). For those who can't decide on one type, the company sells bags of assorted chocolates called *Twist* and red gift boxes of chocolates called *Kong Haakon,* named after Norway's first king.

While chocolate rules, licorice and gummy candies are also popular. Black licorice *(lakrits)* is at its best here, except for *salt lakrits* (salty licorice), which is not for the timid. Black licorice flavors everything from ice cream to chewing gum to liqueur (see "Drinking," earlier). Throughout Scandinavia, you'll find stores selling all varieties of candy in bulk. Fill your bag with a variety of candies and pay by the gram. Look around at the customers in these stores...they aren't all children.

Communicating

"How can I stay connected in Europe?"—by phone and online—may be the most common question I hear from travelers. You have three basic options:

1. "Roam" with your US mobile device. This is the easiest option, but likely the most expensive. It works best for people who won't be making very many calls, and who value the convenience of sticking with what's familiar (and their own phone number). In recent years, as data roaming fees have dropped and free Wi-Fi has become easier to find, the majority of travelers are finding this to be the best all-around option.

2. Use an unlocked mobile phone with European SIM

cards. This is a much more affordable option if you'll be making lots of calls, since it gives you 24/7 access to low European rates. Although remarkably cheap, this option does require a bit of shopping around for the right phone and a prepaid SIM card. Savvy travelers who routinely buy European SIM cards swear by this tactic.

3. Use public phones, and get online with your hotel's guest computer and/or at Internet cafés. These options work particularly well for travelers who simply don't want to hassle with the technology, or want to be (mostly) untethered from their home life while on the road.

Each of these options is explained in greater detail in the following pages. Mixing and matching works well. For example, I routinely bring along my smartphone for Internet chores and Skyping on Wi-Fi, but also carry an unlocked phone and buy SIM cards for affordable calls on the go.

For an even more in-depth explanation of this complicated topic, see www.ricksteves.com/phoning.

How to Dial

Many Americans are intimidated by dialing European phone numbers. You needn't be. It's simple, once you break the code.

Dialing Within Scandinavia

The following instructions apply to dialing from a landline (such as a pay phone or your hotel-room phone) or from a Scandinavian mobile phone. If you're roaming with a US phone number, follow the "Dialing Internationally" directions described later.

Denmark, Estonia, and **Norway** use a direct-dial system (no area codes). To call anywhere within one of these countries, just dial the number. For example, the number of one of my recommended Copenhagen hotels is 33 13 19 13. To call the hotel from anywhere in Denmark (including Copenhagen), simply dial 33 13 19 13.

Sweden and **Finland,** on the other hand, use area codes. To make domestic calls anywhere within these countries, punch in just the phone number if you're dialing locally, and add the area code if calling long distance. For example, Stockholm's area code is 08, and the number of one of my recommended Stockholm hotels is 723-7250. To call the hotel within Stockholm, just dial 723-7250. To call it from Kalmar (in southeast Sweden), dial 08/723-7250. Be aware, however, that if you're calling a mobile or toll-free number, you'll need to dial the whole number, regardless of where you're calling from.

Hurdling the Language Barrier

In Scandinavia, English is all you need. These days every well-educated Scandinavian seems to speak English. Still, knowing the key words in the language of the country you are visiting is good style and helpful.

Each country has its own language. Danish, Norwegian, and Swedish are so closely related that locals can laugh at each other's TV comedies. The languages are similar to English but with a few extra letters (Æ, Ø, Ö, Å, Ä). These letters barely affect pronunciation, but do affect alphabetizing. If you can't find, say, Årjäng in a map index, look after Z. Finnish and Estonian are vastly different from the other Scandinavian languages and English; in fact, Finnish has more in common with Hungarian than with Swedish (see page 581).

Here are a few words you'll see and hear a lot (these are all Norwegian; the Danish and Swedish versions differ slightly): *hei* (hi), *takk* (thanks), *gammel* (old), *lille* (small), *stor* (big), *slott* (palace), *fart* (trip), *centrum* (center), *gate* (street), *øl* (beer), *forbudt* (not allowed), and *udsalg*, *salg*, or *rea* (sale). For more, see the survival phrases at the end of each country introduction. Give it your best shot. The locals will appreciate your efforts.

Dialing Internationally to or from Scandinavia

Always start with the **international access code** (011 if you're calling from the US or Canada, 00 if you're calling from Europe). If you're dialing from a mobile phone, simply insert a + instead (by holding the 0 key).

Dial the **country code** of the country you're calling (45 for Denmark, 47 for Norway, 46 for Sweden, 358 for Finland, 372 for Estonia, or 1 for the US or Canada).

Then dial the area code (if applicable) and the local number, keeping in mind that calling many countries requires dropping the initial zero of the area code or local number. The European calling chart lists specifics per country.

Calling from the US to direct-dial countries (Denmark, Estonia, and Norway): To call the Copenhagen hotel from the US, dial 011 (US access code), 45 (Denmark's country code), then 33 13 19 13 (the hotel's local number).

Calling from the US to area-code countries (Sweden and Finland): To call the Stockholm hotel from the US, dial 011, 46 (Sweden's country code), 8 (Stockholm's area code minus the initial zero), then 723-7250 (local number).

Calling from any European country to the US: To call my office in Edmonds, Washington, from anywhere in Europe, I dial

00 (Europe's access code), 1 (US country code), 425 (Edmonds' area code), and 771-8303.

More Dialing Tips

The chart on the next page shows you how to dial per country. For online instructions, see www.countrycallingcodes.com or www.howtocallabroad.com.

Remember, if you're using a mobile phone, dial as if you're in that phone's country of origin. So, when roaming with your US phone number in Scandinavia, dial as if you're calling from the US. But if you're using a European SIM card, dial as you would from that European country.

Note that calls to a European mobile phone are substantially more expensive than calls to a fixed line. Off-hour calls are generally cheaper.

Don't be surprised that Scandinavian phone numbers may vary in length; for instance, a hotel can have a six-digit phone number and an eight-digit fax number.

USING YOUR SMARTPHONE IN EUROPE

Even in this age of email, texting, and near-universal Internet access, smart travelers still use the telephone. I call TIs to smooth out sightseeing plans, hotels to get driving directions, museums to confirm tour schedules, restaurants to check open hours or to book a table, and so on.

Most people enjoy the convenience of bringing their own smartphone. Horror stories about sky-high roaming fees are dated and exaggerated, and major service providers work hard to avoid surprising you with an exorbitant bill. With a little planning, you can use your phone—for voice calls, messaging, and Internet access—without breaking the bank.

Start by figuring out whether your phone works in Europe. Most phones purchased through AT&T and T-Mobile (which use the same technology as Europe) work abroad, while only some phones from Verizon or Sprint do—check your operating manual (look for "tri-band," "quad-band," or "GSM"). If you're not sure, ask your service provider.

Roaming Costs

"Roaming" with your phone—that is, using it outside its home region, such as in Europe—generally comes with extra charges, whether you are making voice calls, sending texts, or reading your email. The fees listed here are for the three major American providers—Verizon, AT&T, and T-Mobile; Sprint's roaming rates tend to be much higher. But policies change fast, so get the latest details

European Calling Chart

Just smile and dial, using this key:
AC = Area Code, LN = Local Number.

European Country	Calling long distance within ...	Calling from the US or Canada to ...	Calling from a European country to ...
Austria	AC + LN	011 + 43 + AC (without initial zero) + LN	00 + 43 + AC (without initial zero) + LN
Belgium	LN	011 + 32 + LN (without initial zero)	00 + 32 + LN (without initial zero)
Bosnia-Herzegovina	AC + LN	011 + 387 + AC (without initial zero) + LN	00 + 387 + AC (without initial zero) + LN
Croatia	AC + LN	011 + 385 + AC (without initial zero) + LN	00 + 385 + AC (without initial zero) + LN
Czech Republic	LN	011 + 420 + LN	00 + 420 + LN
Denmark	LN	011 + 45 + LN	00 + 45 + LN
Estonia	LN	011 + 372 + LN	00 + 372 + LN
Finland	AC + LN	011 + 358 + AC (without initial zero) + LN	00 + 358 + AC (without initial zero) + LN
France	LN	011 + 33 + LN (without initial zero)	00 + 33 + LN (without initial zero)
Germany	AC + LN	011 + 49 + AC (without initial zero) + LN	00 + 49 + AC (without initial zero) + LN
Gibraltar	LN	011 + 350 + LN	00 + 350 + LN
Great Britain & N. Ireland	AC + LN	011 + 44 + AC (without initial zero) + LN	00 + 44 + AC (without initial zero) + LN
Greece	LN	011 + 30 + LN	00 + 30 + LN
Hungary	06 + AC + LN	011 + 36 + AC + LN	00 + 36 + AC + LN
Ireland	AC + LN	011 + 353 + AC (without initial zero) + LN	00 + 353 + AC (without initial zero) + LN
Italy	LN	011 + 39 + LN	00 + 39 + LN

European Country	Calling long distance within ...	Calling from the US or Canada to ...	Calling from a European country to ...
Latvia	LN	011 + 371 + LN	00 + 371 + LN
Montenegro	AC + LN	011 + 382 + AC (without initial zero) + LN	00 + 382 + AC (without initial zero) + LN
Morocco	LN	011 + 212 + LN (without initial zero)	00 + 212 + LN (without initial zero)
Netherlands	AC + LN	011 + 31 + AC (without initial zero) + LN	00 + 31 + AC (without initial zero) + LN
Norway	LN	011 + 47 + LN	00 + 47 + LN
Poland	LN	011 + 48 + LN	00 + 48 + LN
Portugal	LN	011 + 351 + LN	00 + 351 + LN
Russia	8 + AC + LN	011 + 7 + AC + LN	00 + 7 + AC + LN
Slovakia	AC + LN	011 + 421 + AC (without initial zero) + LN	00 + 421 + AC (without initial zero) + LN
Slovenia	AC + LN	011 + 386 + AC (without initial zero) + LN	00 + 386 + AC (without initial zero) + LN
Spain	LN	011 + 34 + LN	00 + 34 + LN
Sweden	AC + LN	011 + 46 + AC (without initial zero) + LN	00 + 46 + AC (without initial zero) + LN
Switzerland	LN	011 + 41 + LN (without initial zero)	00 + 41 + LN (without initial zero)
Turkey	AC (if there's no initial zero, add one) + LN	011 + 90 + AC (without initial zero) + LN	00 + 90 + AC (without initial zero) + LN

- The instructions above apply whether you're calling to or from a European landline or mobile phone.

- If calling from any mobile phone, you can replace the international access code with "+" (press and hold 0 to insert it).

- The international access code is 011 if you're calling from the US or Canada.

- To call the US or Canada from Europe, dial 00, then 1 (country code for US and Canada), then the area code and number. In short, 00 + 1 + AC + LN = Hi, Mom!

before your trip. For example, as of mid-2014, T-Mobile waived voice, texting, and data roaming fees for some plans.

Voice calls are the most expensive. Most US providers charge from $1.29 to $1.99 per minute to make or receive calls in Europe. (As you cross each border, you'll typically get a text message explaining the rates in the new country.) If you plan to make multiple calls, look into a global calling plan to lower the per-minute cost, or buy a package of minutes at a discounted price (such as 30 minutes for $30). Note that you'll be charged for incoming calls whether or not you answer them; to save money ask your friends to stay in contact by texting, and to call you only in case of an emergency.

Text messaging costs 20 to 50 cents per text. To cut that cost, you could sign up for an international messaging plan (for example, $10 for 100 texts). Or consider apps that let you text for free (iMessage for Apple, Google Hangouts for Android, or WhatsApp for any device); however, these require you to use Wi-Fi or data roaming. Be aware that Europeans use the term "SMS" ("short message service") to describe text messaging.

Data roaming means accessing data services via a cellular network other than your home carrier's. Prices have dropped dramatically in recent years, making this an affordable way for travelers to bridge gaps between Wi-Fi hotspots. You'll pay far less if you set up an international data roaming plan. Most providers charge $25-30 for 100-120 megabytes of data. That's plenty for basic Internet tasks—100 megabytes lets you view 100 websites or send/receive 1,000 text-based emails, but you'll burn through that amount quickly by streaming videos or music. If your data use exceeds your plan amount, most providers will automatically kick in an additional 100- or 120-megabyte block for the same price. (For more, see "Using Wi-Fi and Data Roaming," later.)

Setting Up (or Disabling) International Service

With most service providers, international roaming (voice, text, and data) is disabled on your account unless you activate it. Before your trip, call your provider (or navigate their website), and cover the following topics:

- Confirm that your phone will work in Europe.
- Verify global roaming rates for voice calls, text messaging, and data.
- Tell them which of those services you'd like to activate.
- Consider add-on plans to bring down the cost of international calls, texts, or data roaming.

When you get home from Europe, be sure to cancel any add-on plans that you activated for your trip.

Some people would rather use their smartphone exclusively on Wi-Fi, and not worry about either voice or data charges. If that's you, call your provider to be sure that international roaming options are deactivated on your account. To be double-sure, put your phone in "airplane mode," then turn your Wi-Fi back on.

Using Wi-Fi and Data Roaming

A good approach is to use free Wi-Fi wherever possible, and fill in the gaps with data roaming.

Wi-Fi is readily available throughout Europe. At accommodations, access is usually free, but you may have to pay a fee, especially at expensive hotels. At hotels with thick walls, the Wi-Fi signal from the lobby may not reach every room. If Wi-Fi is important to you, ask about it when you book—and be specific ("In the rooms?"). Get the password and network name at the front desk when you check in.

When you're out and about, your best bet for finding free Wi-Fi is often at a café. They'll usually tell you the password if you buy something. Or you can stroll down a café-lined street, smartphone in hand, checking for unsecured networks every few steps until you find one that works. Some towns have free public Wi-Fi in highly trafficked parks or piazzas. You may have to register before using it, or get a password at the TI.

Data roaming is handy when you can't find Wi-Fi. Because you'll pay by the megabyte (explained earlier), it's best to limit how much data you use. Save bandwidth-gobbling tasks like Skyping, watching videos, or downloading apps or emails with large attachments until you're on Wi-Fi. Switch your phone's email settings from "push" to "fetch." This means that you can choose to "fetch" (download) your messages when you're on Wi-Fi rather than having them continuously "pushed" to your device. And be aware of apps—such as news, weather, and sports tickers—that automatically update. Check your phone's settings to be sure that none of your apps are set to "use cellular data."

I like the safeguard of manually turning off data roaming on my phone whenever I'm not actively using it. To turn off data and voice roaming, look in your phone's settings menu—try checking under "cellular" or "network," or ask your service provider how to do it. If you need to get online but can't find Wi-Fi, simply turn on data roaming long enough for the task at hand, then turn it off again.

Figure out how to keep track of how much data you've used (in your phone's menu, look for "cellular data usage"; you may have to reset the counter at the start of your trip). Some companies automatically send you a text message warning if you approach or exceed your limit.

There's yet another option: If you're traveling with an unlocked smartphone (explained later), you can buy a SIM card that also

Internet Calling

To make totally free voice and video calls over the Internet, all you need are a smartphone, tablet, or laptop; a strong Wi-Fi signal; and an account with one of the major Internet calling providers: Skype (www.skype.com), FaceTime (preloaded on most Apple devices), or Google+ Hangouts (www.google.com/hangouts). If the Wi-Fi signal isn't strong enough for video, try an audio-only call. Or...wait for your next hotel. Many Internet calling programs also work for making calls from your computer to telephones worldwide for a very reasonable fee—generally just a few cents per minute (you'll have to buy some credit before you make your first call).

includes data; this can be far cheaper than data roaming through your home provider.

USING EUROPEAN SIM CARDS

While using your American phone in Europe is easy, it's not always cheap. And unreliable Wi-Fi can make keeping in touch frustrating. If you're reasonably technology-savvy, and would like to have the option of making lots of affordable calls, it's worth getting comfortable with European SIM cards.

Here's the basic idea: With an unlocked phone (which works with different carriers; see below), get a SIM card—the microchip that stores data about your phone—once you get to Europe. Slip in the SIM, turn on the phone, and bingo! You've got a European phone number (and access to cheaper European rates).

Getting an Unlocked Phone

Your basic options are getting your existing phone unlocked, or buying a phone (either at home or in Europe).

Some phones are electronically "locked" so that you can't switch SIM cards (keeping you loyal to your carrier). But in some circumstances it's possible to unlock your phone—allowing you to replace the original SIM card with one that will work with a European provider. Note that some US carriers are beginning to offer phones/tablets whose SIM card can't be swapped out in the US but will accept a European SIM without any unlocking process.

You may already have an old, unused mobile phone in a drawer somewhere. Call your service provider and ask if they'll send you the unlock code. Otherwise, you can buy one: Search an online shopping site for an "unlocked quad-band phone," or buy one at a mobile-phone shop in Europe. Either way, a basic model typically costs $40 or less.

Buying and Using SIM Cards

Once you have an unlocked phone, you'll need to buy a SIM card (note that a smaller variation called "micro-SIM" or "nano-SIM"—used in most iPhones—is less widely available.)

SIM cards are sold at mobile-phone shops, department-store electronics counters, and newsstands for $5–10, and usually include about that much prepaid calling credit (making the card itself virtually free). Because SIM cards are prepaid, there's no contract and no commitment; I routinely buy one even if I'm in a country for only a few days.

In Sweden, Finland, and Estonia, buying a SIM card is as easy as buying a pack of gum. However, an increasing number of countries—including Norway and Denmark—require you to register the SIM card with your passport (an antiterrorism measure). This takes only a few minutes longer: The shop clerk will ask you to fill out a form, then submit it to the service provider. Sometimes you can register your own SIM card online. Either way, an hour or two after submitting the information, you'll get a text welcoming you to that network.

When using a SIM card in its home country, it's free to receive calls and texts, and it's cheap to make calls—domestic calls average 20 cents per minute. You can also use SIM cards to call the US—sometimes very affordably (Lebara and Lycamobile, which operate in multiple European countries, let you call a US number for less than 10 cents a minute). I've also had good luck with Telenor SIM cards in Norway and Comviq cards in Sweden. Rates are higher if you're roaming in another country. But if you bought the SIM card within the European Union, roaming fees are capped no matter where you travel throughout the EU (about 25 cents/minute to make calls, 7 cents/minute to receive calls, and 8 cents for a text message). Keep in mind, though, that Norway is not part of the EU.

While you can buy SIM cards just about anywhere, I like to seek out a mobile-phone shop, where an English-speaking clerk can help explain my options, get my SIM card inserted and set up, and show me how to use it. When you buy your SIM card, ask about rates for domestic and international calls and texting, and about roaming fees. Also find out how to check your credit balance (usually you'll key in a few digits and hit "Send"). You can top up your credit at any newsstand, tobacco shop, mobile-phone shop, or many other businesses (look for the SIM card's logo in the window).

To insert your SIM card into the phone, locate the slot, which is usually on the side of the phone or behind the battery. Turning on the phone, you'll be prompted to enter the "SIM PIN" (a code number that came with your card).

If you have an unlocked smartphone, you can look for a European SIM card that covers both voice and data. This is often much cheaper than paying for data roaming through your home provider.

LANDLINE TELEPHONES AND INTERNET CAFÉS
If you prefer to travel without a smartphone or tablet, you can still stay in touch using landline telephones, hotel guest computers, and Internet cafés.

Landline Telephones
Phones in your **hotel room** can be great for local calls and for calls using cheap international phone cards (described in the sidebar). Many hotels charge a fee for local and "toll-free" as well as long-distance or international calls—always ask for the rates before you dial. Since you'll never be charged for receiving calls, it can be more affordable to have someone from the US call you in your room.

While **public pay phones** are on the endangered species list, you'll still see them in post offices and train stations. Pay phones generally come with multilingual instructions. Most public phones work with insertable phone cards (described in the sidebar).

You'll see many cheap **call shops** that advertise low rates to faraway lands, often in train-station neighborhoods. While these target immigrants who want to call home cheaply, tourists can use them, too. Before making your call, be completely clear on the rates.

Internet Cafés and Public Internet Terminals
Finding public Internet terminals in Europe is no problem. Many hotels have a computer in the lobby for guests to use. Otherwise, head for an Internet café, or ask the TI or your hotelier for the nearest place to access the Internet.

European computers typically use non-American keyboards. A few letters are switched around, and command keys are labeled in the local language. Many European keyboards have an "Alt Gr" key (for "Alternate Graphics") to the right of the space bar; press this to insert the extra symbol that appears on some keys. Europeans have different names for, and different ways to type, the @ symbol. If you can't locate a special character (such as the @ symbol), simply copy it from a Web page and paste it into your email message.

Types of Telephone Cards

Europe uses two different types of telephone cards. Both types are sold at post offices, newsstands, street kiosks, tobacco shops, and train stations.

Insertable Phone Cards: These cards can only be used at pay phones: Simply take the phone off the hook, insert the card, wait for a dial tone, and dial away. The phone displays your credit ticking down as you talk. Each European country has its own insertable phone card—so your Swedish card won't work in a Danish phone.

International Phone Cards: These prepaid cards can be used to make inexpensive calls—within Europe, or to the US, for pennies a minute—from nearly any phone, including the one in your hotel room. The cards come with a toll-free number and a scratch-to-reveal PIN code. If the voice prompts aren't in English, experiment: Dial your code, followed by the pound sign (#), then the phone number, then pound again, and so on, until it works. Sometimes the star (*) key is used instead of the pound sign.

Most merchants promise that the cards work throughout Scandinavia (cards are generally printed with local access numbers for each country), but often they don't work in neighboring countries, leaving you stuck with extra minutes that you can't use. (It can be difficult to find international phone cards in Finland and they aren't available in Estonia, which has no public pay phones.)

Internet Security

Whether you're accessing the Internet with your own device or at a public terminal, using a shared network or computer comes with the potential for increased security risks. Ask the hotel or café for the specific name of their Wi-Fi network, and make sure you log on to that exact one; hackers sometimes create a bogus hotspot with a similar or vague name (such as "Hotel Europa Free Wi-Fi"). It's better if a network uses a password (especially a hard-to-guess one) rather than being open to the world.

While traveling, you may want to check your online banking or credit-card statements, or to take care of other personal-finance chores, but Internet security experts advise against accessing these sites entirely while traveling. Even if you're using your own computer at a password-protected hotspot, any hacker who's logged on to the same network can see what you're up to. If you need to log on to a banking website, try to do so on a hard-wired connection (i.e., using an Ethernet cable in your hotel room), or if that's not possible, use a secure banking app on a cellular telephone connection.

If using a credit card online, make sure that the site is secure.

Most browsers display a little padlock icon, and the URL begins with *https* instead of *http*. Never send a credit-card number over a website that doesn't begin with *https*.

If you're not convinced a connection is secure, avoid accessing any sites (such as your bank's) that could be vulnerable to fraud.

MAIL

You can mail one package per day to yourself worth up to $200 duty-free from Europe to the US (mark it "personal purchases"). If you're sending a gift to someone, mark it "unsolicited gift." For details, visit www.cbp.gov and search for "Know Before You Go."

The postal service works fine throughout Scandinavia, but for quick transatlantic delivery (in either direction), consider services such as DHL (www.dhl.com). You can get stamps at the neighborhood post office, newsstands within fancy hotels, and some minimarts and card shops.

Transportation

Copenhagen is usually the most direct and least expensive Scandinavian capital to fly into from the US (Icelandair serves Copenhagen as well as Stockholm, Oslo, and Helsinki). Copenhagen is also Europe's gateway to Scandinavia from points south. There are often cheaper flights from the US into Frankfurt and Amsterdam than into Copenhagen, but it's a long, rather dull, one-day drive (with a 45-minute, $90-per-car ferry crossing at Puttgarden, Germany—www.scandlines.dk). By train, Copenhagen is an easy overnight ride from Cologne or Frankfurt. The base ticket price ($200 or more) is covered if you have a Global Pass or a rail pass covering the particular countries. Another option is flying into London and then hopping to Copenhagen on a low-cost, no-frills airline, such as easyJet or Ryanair.

For transportation within Scandinavia, consider these factors: Cars are best for three or more traveling together (especially families with small kids), those packing heavy, and those scouring the countryside. Trains, buses, and boats are best for solo travelers, blitz tourists, and city-to-city travelers, those with an ambitious, multi-country itinerary; and those who don't want to drive in Europe. While a car gives you more freedom, trains, buses, and boats zip you effortlessly and scenically from city to city, usually dropping you in the center, often near a TI. Cars are an expensive headache in places like Copenhagen and Stockholm.

TRAINS

With a few exceptions, trains cover my recommended Scandinavian destinations wonderfully.

Schedules and Tickets: Pick up train schedules from stations as you go. While most information is given both in the country's language and in English, it's good to know the word for "delayed"—*forsinket* in Danish and Norwegian, and *försenad* in Swedish.

To study ahead online, check www.bahn.com (Germany's excellent Europe-wide timetable). Local train companies also have their own sites with fare and timetable information, and even online booking in English; see www.dsb.dk or www.rejseplanen.dk (Denmark), www.nsb.no (Norway), www.sj.se (Sweden), www.vr.fi (Finland), and www.gorail.ee (Estonia).

Rail Passes: One of the great Nordic bargains, the Eurail Scandinavia pass is your best rail pass deal for a trip limited to Scandinavia. Although Eurail Scandinavia passes are available only for second-class seats, Scandinavian second class is plenty comfortable. Some trains, including those that cover part of the popular Norway in a Nutshell route (see page 289), do not offer first

Railpasses

Prices listed are for 2014 and are subject to change. For the latest prices, details, and train schedules (and easy online ordering), see www.ricksteves.com/rail.

Note that youth prices apply to those under age 26. Some two-country combinations are also available.

SCANDINAVIA PASS

	Individual 2nd Cl.	Saver 2nd Cl.	Youth 2nd Cl.
4 days in 2 months	$372	$317	$383
5 days in 2 months	411	350	309
6 days in 2 months	469	399	352
8 days in 2 months	517	440	389
10 days in 2 months	575	489	432

Covers Denmark, Norway, Sweden, and Finland. Saver price per person for two or more traveling together. Kids 4–11 half adult or saver price. Kids under 4 free.

FINLAND PASS

	1st Cl.	2nd Cl.
3 days in 1 month	$289	$196
5 days in 1 month	384	259
10 days in 1 month	518	349

Children 6-16 half price, under 6 free.

Map key:

Approximate point-to-point one-way standard-class fares in US dollars. First class costs 50 percent more. Add up fares for your itinerary to see whether a railpass will save you money.

DENMARK PASS

	Adult 1st Cl.	Adult 2nd Cl.	Youth 2nd Cl.
3 days in 1 month	$241	$158	$120
7 days in 1 month	331	217	164

Kids 4-11 half adult or saver price. Kids under 4 free.

NORWAY PASS

	Individual 2nd Cl.	Saver 2nd Cl.	Youth 2nd Cl.
3 days in 1 month	$288	$245	$217
4 days in 1 month	311	265	234
5 days in 1 month	344	293	259
6 days in 1 month	391	333	294
8 days in 1 month	434	369	326

Saver price per person for two or more traveling together. Kids 4–15 half adult or saver price. Kids under 4 free.

SWEDEN PASS

	Individual 1st Cl.	Saver 1st Cl.	Individual 2nd Cl.	Saver 2nd Cl.	Youth 2nd Cl.
3 days in 1 month	$374	$319	$289	$246	$218
4 days in 1 month	401	341	310	264	233
5 days in 1 month	445	379	344	293	259
6 days in 1 month	504	429	389	331	293
8 days in 1 month	562	478	433	369	326

Saver price per person for two or more traveling together. Kids 4–11 half adult or saver price. Kids under 4 free.

SELECTPASS

This pass covers travel in three adjacent countries. Please visit **www.ricksteves.com/rail** for four- and five-country options.

	Individual 1st Class	Saver 1st Class	Youth 2nd Class
5 days in 2 months	$528	$450	$345
6 days in 2 months	583	496	381
8 days in 2 months	688	585	449
10 days in 2 months	797	679	520

"Saver" prices are per person for two or more people traveling together. Kids 4–11 pay half of adult individual or Saver fare; under 4 free.

class. For options and prices, see the rail pass chart in this chapter and www.ricksteves.com/rail.

If your trip extends south of Scandinavia, consider the flexible Select Pass, which allows you to choose four adjacent countries connected by land or ferry (for instance, Germany-Denmark-Sweden-Finland). A more expensive Global Pass is a good value only for those spending more time traveling throughout Europe. A three-week first-class Global Pass costs about $950 (if you travel with a companion, you'll save about 15 percent apiece with a Global saverpass).

Rail passes give you discounts on some boat tickets (such as Stockholm to Helsinki) and cover almost all trains in the region (though you'll need 50-kr reservations for long rides and express trains, plus a 220-kr supplement for Norway's Myrdal-Flåm ride—part of the Norway in a Nutshell route). If you'll be taking a popular train on a busy day and want to be assured of having a seat, a reservation can be a good investment even if it's not required.

For more detailed advice on figuring out the smartest rail pass options for your train trip, visit the Trains & Rail Passes section of my website at www.ricksteves.com/rail.

BUSES

Don't overlook long-distance buses, which are usually slower but have considerably cheaper and more predictable fares than trains. (In Denmark, however, the train system is excellent and nearly always the better option.) On certain routes, such as between Stockholm and Oslo, the bus is cheaper and only slightly slower than the train. Scandinavia's big bus carriers are Norway's Nor-Way Bussekspress (www.nor-way.no), Denmark's public buses (www.rejseplanen.dk), Sweden's Swebus (www.swebusexpress.se), and Finland's Matkahuolto (www.matkahuolto.fi). Estonia has several carriers, of which Lux Express is the largest (www.luxexpress.ee).

BOATS

Boats are romantic, scenic, and sometimes the most efficient—or only—way to link destinations in coastal Scandinavia. But boats can often be more expensive than other options, although some routes may be covered or discounted if you have a rail pass. Note that short-distance ferries may take only cash, not credit cards.

Advance reservations are recommended for overnight boats, especially in summer or on weekends. The main links are Oslo to Copenhagen (www.dfdsseaways.com), Stockholm to Helsinki (www.vikingline.fi and www.tallinksilja.com), and Stockholm to Tallinn (www.tallinksilja.com).

Several companies speed between Helsinki and Tallinn in 2-3 hours (see page 697). Other worthwhile routes connect Norway and Denmark (Kristiansand and Hirtshals several times daily, Stavanger and Hirtshals by overnight boat; see page 416, www.fjordline.com and www.colorline.com). Ferries are essential for hopping between the mainland and Scandinavia's many islands, such as Ærø in central Denmark (drivers should reserve in advance for weekends and summer, www.aeroe-ferry.dk), or Stockholm's archipelago. Boats are both a necessary and spectacular way to travel through Norway's fjords or along its coast (www.fjordtours.no, www.fjord1.no, and www.tide.no). Bergen, in Norway, is a departure point for boats to the Arctic (www.hurtigruten.com).

RENTING A CAR

The minimum age to rent a car varies by country and rental company (you must be 21 in Denmark and Estonia, and 19 in Sweden, Norway, and Finland). Drivers under the age of 25 may incur a young-driver surcharge, and some rental companies do not rent to anyone 75 and over. If you're considered too young or old, look into leasing (covered later), which has less-stringent age restrictions.

Research car rentals before you go. It's cheaper to arrange most car rentals from the US. Call several companies or look online to compare rates.

Most of the major US rental agencies (including Avis, Budget, Hertz, and Thrifty) have offices throughout Europe. Also consider the two major Europe-based agencies, Europcar and Sixt. It can be cheaper to use a consolidator, such as Auto Europe/Kemwel (www.autoeurope.com) or Europe by Car (www.europebycar.com), which compares rates at several companies to get you the best deal—but because you're working with a middleman, it's especially important to ask in advance about add-on fees and restrictions.

Regardless of the car-rental company you choose, always read the fine print carefully for add-on charges—such as expensive one-way drop-off fees, airport surcharges, or mandatory insurance policies—that aren't included in the "total price." You may need to query rental agents pointedly to find out your actual cost.

For the best deal, rent by the week with unlimited mileage. To save money on fuel, ask for a diesel car. I normally rent the smallest, least-expensive model with a stick shift (generally much cheaper than an automatic). Almost all rentals are manual by default, so if you need an automatic, you must request one in advance; be aware that these cars are usually larger models (not as maneuverable on narrow, winding roads).

Figure on paying about $300 for a one-week rental. Allow extra for supplemental insurance, fuel, tolls, and parking. For trips of three weeks or more, look into leasing; you'll save money on insurance and taxes. Be warned that international trips—say, picking up in Copenhagen and dropping off in Oslo—can be expensive (it depends partly on distance).

As a rule, always tell your car-rental company up front exactly which countries you'll be entering. Some companies levy extra insurance fees for trips taken in certain countries with certain types of cars (such as BMWs, Mercedes, and convertibles). Double-check with your rental agent that you have all the documentation you need before you drive off.

Big companies have offices in most cities; ask whether they can pick you up at your hotel. Small local rental companies can be cheaper but aren't as flexible.

Compare pickup costs (downtown can be less expensive than the airport) and explore drop-off options. Always check the hours of the location you choose: Many rental offices close from midday Saturday until Monday morning and, in smaller towns, at lunchtime.

When selecting a location, don't trust the agency's description of "downtown" or "city center." In some cases, a "downtown" branch can be on the outskirts of the city—a long, costly taxi ride from the center. Before choosing, plug the addresses into a mapping website. You may find that the "train station" location is handier. But returning a car at a big-city train station or downtown agency can be tricky; get precise details on the car drop-off location and hours, and allow ample time to find it.

When you pick up the rental car, check it thoroughly and make sure any damage is noted on your rental agreement. Find out how your car's lights, turn signals, wipers, radio, and fuel cap function, and know what kind of fuel the car takes (diesel vs. unleaded). When you return the car, make sure the agent verifies its condition with you. Some drivers take pictures of the returned vehicle as proof of its condition.

In some cases, I prefer to connect long distances by train or bus, then rent cars for a day or two where they're most useful (I've noted these places throughout this book).

Navigation Options

When renting a car in Europe, you have several alternatives for your digital navigator: Use your smartphone's online mapping app, download an offline map app, rent a GPS device with your rental car, or bring your own GPS device from home.

Online mapping apps used to be prohibitively expensive for overseas travelers—but that was before most carriers started offering affordable international data plans. If you're already getting a data plan for your trip, this is probably the way to go (see "Using Your Smartphone in Europe," earlier).

A number of well-designed apps allow you much of the convenience of online maps without any costly demands on your data plan. City Maps 2Go is one of the most popular of these; OffMaps, Google Maps, and Navfree also all offer good, zoomable offline maps for much of Europe (some are better for driving, while others are better for navigating cities).

Some drivers prefer using a dedicated GPS unit—not only to avoid the data-roaming fees, but because a stand-alone GPS can be easier to operate (important if you're driving solo). The major downside: It's expensive—around $10-30 per day. Your car's GPS unit may only come loaded with maps for its home country—if you need additional maps, ask. Make sure your device's language is set to English before you drive off. If you have a portable GPS device at home, you can take that instead. Many American GPS devices come loaded with US maps only—you'll need to buy and download European maps before your trip. This option is far less expensive than renting.

Car Insurance Options

When you rent a car, you are liable for a very high deductible, sometimes equal to the entire value of the car. Limit your financial risk with one of these options: Buy Collision Damage Waiver (CDW) coverage from the car-rental company, get coverage through your

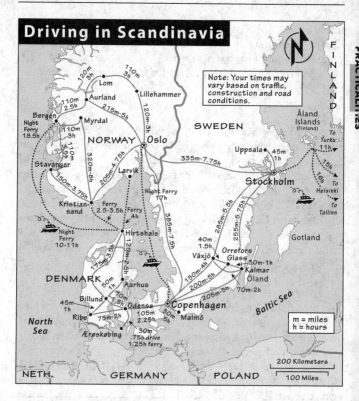

Driving in Scandinavia

Note: Your times may vary based on traffic, construction and road conditions.

m = miles
h = hours

200 Kilometers
100 Miles

credit card (free, if your card automatically includes zero-deductible coverage), or get collision insurance as part of a larger travel-insurance policy.

CDW includes a very high deductible (typically $1,000-1,500). Though each rental company has its own variation, basic CDW costs $10-30 a day (figure roughly 30 percent extra) and reduces your liability, but does not eliminate it. When you pick up the car, you'll be offered the chance to "buy down" the basic deductible to zero (for an additional $10-30/day; this is sometimes called "super CDW" or "zero-deductible coverage").

If you opt for **credit-card coverage,** there's a catch. You'll technically have to decline all coverage offered by the car-rental company, which means they can place a hold on your card (which can be up to the full value of the car). In case of damage, it can be time-consuming to resolve the charges with your credit-card company. Before you decide on this option, quiz your credit-card company about how it works.

If you're already purchasing a **travel-insurance policy** for your trip, adding collision coverage is an option. For example, Travel Guard (www.travelguard.com) sells affordable renter's collision insurance as an add-on to its other policies; it's valid everywhere in Europe except the Republic of Ireland, and some Italian car-rental companies refuse to honor it, as it doesn't cover you in case of theft.

For more on car-rental insurance, see www.ricksteves.com/cdw.

Leasing

For trips of three weeks or more, consider leasing (which automatically includes zero-deductible collision and theft insurance). By technically buying and then selling back the car, you save lots of money on tax and insurance. Leasing provides you a brand-new car with unlimited mileage and a 24-hour emergency assistance program. You can lease for as few as 21 days to as long as five and a half months. Car leases must be arranged from the US, and cars must be picked up and dropped off outside Scandinavia. One of many companies offering affordable lease packages is Europe by Car (www.europebycar.com).

Driving

Except for the dangers posed by scenic distractions and moose crossings, Scandinavia is a great place to drive. But never drink and drive—even one drink can get a driver into serious trouble.

Road Rules: Seat belts are mandatory, and children too small to be secure in seatbelts (generally, under 4.5 feet) need a child-safety seat. Be aware of typical European road rules; for example, many countries require headlights to be turned on at all times, and it's generally illegal to drive while using your mobile phone without a hands-free headset. In Europe, you're not allowed to turn right on a red light, unless there is a sign or signal specifically authorizing it, and on expressways it's illegal to pass drivers on the right. Ask your car-rental company about these rules, or check the US State Department website (www.travel.state.gov; search for your country in the "Learn

STOP **AND LEARN THESE ROAD SIGNS**

- **50** — Speed Limit (km/hr)
- Yield
- No Passing
- End of No Passing Zone
- One Way
- Intersection
- Main Road
- Expressway
- Danger
- No Entry
- Cars Prohibited
- All Vehicles Prohibited
- No Through Road
- Restrictions No Longer Apply
- Yield to Oncoming Traffic
- No Stopping
- Parking
- No Parking
- Customs
- Peace

about your destination" box, then click on "Travel and Transportation").

Fuel: Gas is expensive—often more than $8 per gallon. US credit and debit cards likely won't work at pay-at-the-pump stations, but are generally accepted (with a PIN code) at staffed stations. Carry cash just in case. Diesel rental cars are common; make sure you know what type of fuel your car takes before you fill up.

On the Road: Roads are good (though nerve-rackingly skinny in western Norway). Bikes tend to whiz by close and quiet in cities, so be on guard. In the countryside, traffic is generally sparse, and drivers are civil. Signs and road maps are excellent. Local road etiquette is similar to that in the US. There are plenty of good facilities, gas stations, and scenic rest stops. Snow is a serious problem off-season in the mountains.

Tolls: You'll encounter one-way tolls of €20-45 on major bridges including the Øresund Bridge between Sweden and Denmark, the Svinesund Bridge between Sweden and Norway, and the Storebælt Bridge between the Danish islands of Zealand and Funen. Cities such as Oslo, Bergen, and Stockholm charge tolls for entering the city center.

To minimize tolls in Norway, register as a visitor at www. autopass.no. By prepaying a lump sum with your credit card and specifying when you'll be on the road, you won't need to buy a sticker or pay manually at toll plazas; you can even register up to 14 days after you've driven through your first toll point. Any remaining balance will be credited back to your card three months later.

Parking: Parking on the street is a headache only in major cities, where expensive garages are safe and plentiful. Denmark uses a parking windshield-clock disk (free at TIs, post offices, and newsstands; set it when you arrive and be back before your posted time limit is up). Even in the Nordic countries, thieves break into cars. Park carefully, use the trunk, and show no valuables.

Signage: As you navigate, you'll find town signs followed by the letters *N, S, Ø* (Ö in Sweden), *V,* or *C.* These stand for north *(nord)*, south *(syd)*, east *(øst)*, west *(vest)*, and center *(centrum)*, respectively; understanding them will save you lots of wrong turns. Due to recent changes, some maps have the wrong road numbers. It's safest to navigate by town names.

FLIGHTS

This book covers far-flung destinations separated by vast stretches of mountains and water. While boats and trains are more romantic, cheap flights can provide an affordable and efficient way to connect the dots on a Scandinavian itinerary.

The best comparison search engine for both international and intra-European flights is www.kayak.com. For inexpensive flights within Europe, try www.skyscanner.com or www.hipmunk.com; for inexpensive international flights, try www.vayama.com.

Flying to Europe: Start looking for international flights four to five months before your trip, especially for peak-season travel. Off-season tickets can be purchased a month or so in advance. Depending on your itinerary, it can be efficient to fly into one city and out of another. If your flight requires a connection in Europe, see our hints on navigating Europe's top hub airports at www. ricksteves.com/hub-airports.

Flying within Europe: If you're considering a train ride that's more than five hours long, a flight may save you both time and money. When comparing your options, factor in the time it takes to get to the airport and how early you'll need to arrive to check in.

SAS, the region's dominant airline, operates a low-cost Finnish subsidiary called Blue1 (hubs in Helsinki and Stockholm, www.blue1.com) and is affiliated with Oslo-based Widerøe Air (www.wideroe.no). Other options are Norwegian Airlines (hubs in Oslo and Bergen, www.norwegian.no); the Denmark-based Cimber Sterling (specializes in connecting Scandinavian capitals such as Oslo and Copenhagen with sunny destinations in southern Europe, www.cimber.com); and Tallinn-based Estonian Air (www. estonian-air.com). Well-known cheapo airlines easyJet (www. easyjet.com) and Ryanair (www.ryanair.com) fly into Scandinavia.

Be aware of the potential drawbacks of flying on the cheap: nonrefundable and nonchangeable tickets, minimal or nonexistent customer service, treks to airports far outside town, and stingy baggage allowances with steep overage fees. If you're traveling with lots of luggage, a cheap flight can quickly become a bad deal. To avoid unpleasant surprises, read the small print before you book.

Resources

RESOURCES FROM RICK STEVES

Rick Steves Scandinavia is one of many books in my series on European travel, which includes country guidebooks, city guidebooks (Rome, Florence, Paris, London, etc.), Snapshot guides (excerpted chapters from my country guides), Pocket Guides (full-color little books on big cities), and my budget-travel skills handbook, *Rick Steves Europe Through the Back Door*. Most of my titles are available as ebooks. My phrase books—for German, French, Italian, Spanish, and Portu-

Begin Your Trip at
www.RickSteves.com

My **website** is *the* place to explore Europe. You'll find thousands of fun articles, videos, photos, and radio interviews on European destinations; money-saving tips for planning your dream trip; monthly travel news; my travel talks and travel blog; my latest guidebook updates (www.ricksteves.com/update); and my free Rick Steves Audio Europe app. You can also follow me on Facebook and Twitter.

Our **Travel Forum** is an immense, yet well-groomed collection of message boards, where our travel-savvy community answers questions and shares their personal travel experiences (www.ricksteves.com/forums).

Our **online Travel Store** offers travel bags and accessories that I've designed specifically to help you travel smarter and lighter. These include my popular bags (roll-aboard and backpack versions), money belts, totes, toiletries kits, adapters, other accessories, and a wide selection of guidebooks, planning maps, and DVDs.

Choosing the right **rail pass** for your trip—amid hundreds of options—can drive you nutty. Our website will help you find the perfect fit for your itinerary and your budget: We offer easy, one-stop shopping for rail passes, seat reservations, and point-to-point tickets.

Want to travel with greater efficiency and less stress? We organize **tours** with more than three dozen itineraries and more than 800 departures reaching the best destinations in this book...and beyond. Our 14-day Best of Scandinavia tour features the big-city highlights of Stockholm, Copenhagen, and Oslo as well as quieter Nordic nooks such as the Danish island of Æroskobing and a scenic cruise through the fjords; we also offer a nine-day tour of Tallinn, Helsinki, and St. Petersburg. You'll enjoy great guides, a fun bunch of travel partners (with small groups of 24 to 28 travelers), and plenty of room to spread out in a big, comfy bus when touring between towns. You'll find European adventures to fit every vacation length. For all the details, and to get our Tour Catalog and a free Rick Steves Tour Experience DVD (filmed on location during an actual tour), visit www.ricksteves.com or call us at 425/608-4217.

guese—are practical and budget-oriented. My other books include *Northern European Cruise Ports* and *Mediterranean Cruise Ports* (how to make the most of your time in port), *Europe 101* (a crash course on art and history designed for travelers), and *Travel as a Political Act* (a travelogue sprinkled with advice for bringing home a global perspective). A more complete list of my titles appears near the end of this book.

PRACTICALITIES

Video: My public television series, *Rick Steves' Europe*, covers European destinations in 100 shows, with six episodes on Scandinavia. To watch full episodes online for free, see www.ricksteves.com/tv. Or to raise your travel I.Q. with video versions of our popular classes, such as Northern European Cruise Ports, see www.ricksteves.com/travel-talks.

Audio: My weekly public radio show, *Travel with Rick Steves*, features interviews with travel experts from around the world. All of this audio content is available for free at Rick Steves Audio Europe, an extensive online library organized by destination. Choose whatever interests you, and download it via the free Rick Steves Audio Europe app, www.ricksteves.com/audioeurope, iTunes, or Google Play.

MAPS

The black-and-white maps in this book are concise and simple, designed to help you locate recommended places and get to local TIs, where you can pick up more in-depth maps of cities and regions (usually free). Better maps are sold at newsstands and bookstores. Before you buy a map, look at it to be sure it has the level of detail you want. Map apps for your smartphone or tablet are also handy (see "Navigation Options," earlier).

Train travelers can use a simple rail map (such as the one that comes with your train pass). But drivers shouldn't skimp on maps—get one good overall road map for Scandinavia (either the Michelin *Scandinavia* or the Kummerly & Frey *Southern Scandinavia* 1:1,000,000 edition). The Collins Road Atlas is also good. The only detailed map worth considering is the *Southern Norway-North* (*Sør Norge-nord*, 1:325,000) by Cappelens Kart (about €30 in Scandinavian bookstores).

RECOMMENDED BOOKS AND MOVIES

To learn about Scandinavia past and present, check out a few of these books and films.

General Scandinavia

A History of Scandinavia: Norway, Sweden, Denmark, Finland, and Iceland (T. K. Derry, 1979). This comprehensive tome weaves together the history of these five countries.

Scandinavia Since 1500 (Byron J. Nordstrom, 2000). Nordstrom presents a readable account of the region's history.

Scandinavian Folk and Fairy Tales (Claire Booss, 1988). This collection of Scandinavian folklore includes illustrations by local artists.

The Vikings (Else Roesdahl, 1987). Roesdahl offers a Scandinavian perspective on this complex Nordic society.

Denmark
Books

Conquered, Not Defeated (Peter Tveskov, 2003). Tveskov combines historical fact with childhood memories of Denmark under German occupation in World War II.

The Fairy Tale of My Life (Hans Christian Andersen, 1975). Andersen's autobiography chronicles everything from his impoverished childhood to encounters with other literary greats.

Hans Christian Andersen: A New Life (Jens Andersen, 2003). The author reveals new dimensions to the man behind many famous childhood stories.

The Little Mermaid (Hans Christian Andersen, 1837). This charming story about a mermaid selling her soul to become a human doesn't end quite as happily in Andersen's original tale as it does in Disney's world. Other beloved stories by the Danish-born Andersen include *The Little Match Girl*, *The Princess and the Pea*, and *The Steadfast Tin Soldier*.

Music and Silence (Rose Tremain, 1999). Tremain captures Denmark in the 17th century through the eyes of a lute player at court.

Smilla's Sense of Snow (Peter Høeg, 1992). In this thriller set in snowy Copenhagen, Smilla looks into the murder of her six-year-old neighbor (later adapted as a 1997 movie starring Julia Ormond).

We, the Drowned (Carsten Jensen, 2010). This novel covers the wars and adventures of the seafaring men of the port town of Marstel—and the angst of the families they leave behind.

Winter's Tale (Isak Dinesen, 1942). Best known for her memoir *Out of Africa*, Isak Dinesen (a.k.a. Karen Blixen) set most of these short stories in her homeland of Denmark.

Film and Television

Babette's Feast (1987). This Oscar winner for Best Foreign Language Film, about a Frenchwoman taking refuge in rural 19th-century Denmark, is the original foodie movie (based on the novel by Isak Dinesen).

Borgen (2010-). In this dramatic political TV series, principal character Birgitte Nyborg juggles her ambitions as the first female prime minister of Denmark with her responsibilities as a wife and mother.

The Bridge (Danish: *Broen;* Swedish: *Bron;* 2011-). This crime drama, a coproduction of Swedish and Danish TV, follows the cases and personal lives of a brilliant but obsessive-compulsive Swedish detective and her empathetic Danish collaborator.

Italian for Beginners (2000). Thirtysomethings learn Italian in hopes of finding romance in a small Danish town.

Pelle the Conqueror (1988). A Swedish father and son emigrate to Denmark in the 19th century and work to build a new life in this film based on the 1976 book by Martin Andersen Nexø (winner of the 1989 Oscar for Best Foreign Language Film).

Estonia
Books

The Czar's Madman (Jaan Kross, 1992). Accused of insanity, a nobleman from the Livonian region of Estonia is subsequently monitored and scrutinized by his family.

Treading Air (Jaan Kross, 1998). This novel follows the life of protagonist Ullo Paerand, from the 1920s through the Soviet occupation of Estonia.

Truth and Justice (Anton Hansen Tammsaare, 1926). In one of the cornerstones of Estonian literature, Tammsaare draws from his own life to describe Estonia's evolution into an independent state.

Film

Autumn Ball (2007). Based on the novel by Mati Unt, this film explores the isolation of six disparate people living in a Soviet-era apartment complex.

The Singing Revolution (2006). This documentary follows the evolution of Estonian music as a form of peaceful protest and symbol of patriotism.

Spring (1969). Set in a small town boarding school, this coming-of-age story is an Estonian classic.

Tangerines (2013). In this Golden Globe-nominated film, a man in a small village must care for wounded victims during the 1992 war in Abkhazik, Georgia.

Finland
Books

The Adventurer (Mika Waltari, 1950). An orphan drifts through historical events in Europe during the Middle Ages.

Kalevala (Elias Lönnrot, 1835). Regarded as Finland's national epic, *Kalevala* is a compilation of Karelian and Finnish oral folklore and poetry.

My Childhood (Toivo Pekkanen, 1966). Toivo Pekkanen chronicles his family's working-class life in early-20th-century Finland.

Purge (Sofi Oksanen, 2010). Finnish author Sofi Oskanen explores the Soviet occupation of Estonia and postwar suffering in this powerful novel about two women who reconcile their violent pasts.

Seven Brothers (Aleksis Kivi, 1870). In this Finnish classic, young brothers must learn to work hard and become productive members of society.

The Unknown Soldier (Väinö Linna, 1957). This iconic Finnish book candidly captures native soldiers' responses to World War II by delving into each character's psyche.

Film

Hellsinki (2009). Two criminals get caught up in a neighborhood black-market liquor business in 1960s Finland.

The Man Without a Past (2002). In this Academy Award-nominated film, a man is beaten up shortly after arriving in Helsinki, loses his memory, and must start his life anew.

Mother of Mine (2005). A young Finnish boy is evacuated to Sweden during World War II.

Road North (2012). An estranged father and son reunite for a road trip to northern Finland.

Uuno Turhapuro (1973-2006). Many Finnish politicians and celebrities make appearances throughout these 19 classic Finnish comedies about good-for-nothing Uuno, who disrupts and undermines his father-in-law in outlandish situations.

Norway
Books

Beatles (Lars Saabye Christensen, 1984). Four Beatles fans grow up in Oslo in the '60s and '70s.

A Doll's House (Henrik Ibsen, 1879). Ibsen's controversial play questions marriage norms and the role of women in a 19th-century man's world. (Ibsen explores similar themes in *Hedda Gabler*.)

Growth of the Soil (Knut Hamsun, 1917). This epic tale of a man living in back-country Norway won the Nobel Prize in Literature.

The Ice Palace (Tarjei Vesaas, 1993). Two young girls become unlikely friends—until a tragic disappearance shatters one of their lives.

Into the Ice: The History of Norway and the Polar Regions (Einar-Arne Drivenes and Harald Day Jolle, 2006). This comprehensive overview details expeditions, research, and the history of the polar region from the 19th century to the present.

Kon-Tiki (Thor Heyerdahl, 1948). Heyerdahl chronicles his historic 1947 journey from Peru to Polynesia on a balsa-wood raft. Norwegian filmmakers have catalogued his exploits in two films called *Kon-Tiki:* an Academy-Award-winning documentary (1950) and a blockbuster historical drama that was nominated for an Oscar for Best Foreign Language Film (2012).

Kristin Lavransdatter (Sigrid Undset, 1920-1923). This trilogy (also a 1995 movie) focuses on the life of a Norwegian woman in the 14th century.

My Struggle (Karl Ove Knausgaard, 2012). This six-part autobiography of a father and writer from Oslo is hugely popular in Norway and is quickly gaining worldwide recognition.

Out Stealing Horses (Per Patterson, 2005). A widower in remote Norway meets a neighbor who stirs up memories of a pivotal day in 1948.

Sophie's World (Jostein Gaarder, 1994). A 14-year-old Norwegian girl becomes embroiled in a metaphysical mystery wrapped in the history of philosophy.

Film and Television

Cool & Crazy (2001). In this uplifting documentary, a group of Norwegian men find companionship and success when they join an all-male choir.

Elling (2001). After his mother passes away, an autistic man—with a new oddball roommate—struggles to function in society.

Insomnia (1997). The midnight sun plays a role in this Norwegian thriller about a police detective investigating a small-town murder.

The Kautokeino Rebellion (2008). Based on the true events of 1852, the Sami people of Norway revolt against their exploitation by Norwegian authorities.

Lilyhammer (2012-). This Netflix original series follows a *Sopranos*-style New York mobster who, under the witness protection program, relocates to Lillehammer and must adjust to Norwegian living.

Max Manus (2008). Based on real events in the life of WWII resistance fighter Max Manus, this film traces the exploits of Manus and his comrades in Oslo during the Nazi occupation of Norway.

Pathfinder (1987). Around 1000 A.D., a boy in Lapland must survive and fight against other Norse tribes.

Song of Norway (1970). This musical is based on the life of Norwegian composer Edvard Grieg.

Trollhunter (2010). Trolls wreak havoc in modern-day Norway in this fun fantasy/thriller that explains the real purpose of those power lines in the Norwegian mountains.

Vikings (2013-). This History Channel series centers on the adventures of mythological Viking Ragnar Lothbrok as he rises to become one of the most renowned Norse heroes.

Sweden
Books

Faceless Killers (Henning Mankell, 1990). This is the first of 10 mysteries featuring inspector Kurt Wallander.

The Girl with the Dragon Tattoo (Stieg Larsson, 2005). The first book in Larsson's *Millennium* trilogy, about a punky computer hacker and a disgraced journalist, put Swedish crime fiction on the map. The Swedish film versions of these books (with Noomi Rapace as Lisbeth) are as compelling as the novels. Hollywood released its own version of *The Girl with the Dragon Tattoo* in 2011, starring Daniel Craig and Rooney Mara.

Hanna's Daughters (Marianne Fredriksson, 1994). This moving novel follows the lives of three remarkable Swedish women from the 1870s through World War II.

Pippi Longstocking (Astrid Lindgren, 1945). Kids of all ages love reading about the adventures of the strong-willed and unconventional nine-year-old living in Sweden.

The Red Room (August Strindberg, 1879). This biting satire on Stockholm society made Strindberg a literary giant.

Sweden: The Nation's History (Franklin D. Scott, 1988). Scott provides a comprehensive overview of the history of the Swedish people from feudalism to democracy.

The Wonderful Adventures of Nils (Selma Lagerlöf, 1906). In this fantastical children's novel (winner of the Nobel Prize for Literature), Nils loves nothing more than eating, sleeping, and tormenting animals—at least until he is shrunken down to their size.

Film and Television

As It Is in Heaven (2004). A famous conductor returns to his village in Sweden, where he finds love and the key to happiness.

Dalecarlians (2005). After living in Stockholm, Mia returns home to her small village and must adjust to the life she left behind.

The Emigrants (1971). A Swedish family faces a rough transition as they move from Sweden to Minnesota in this film starring Max von Sydow and Liv Ullmann (based on the novels by Vilhelm Moberg). The sequel *The New Land* (1972) continues the family's journey.

Let the Right One In (2008). In this Swedish romantic horror film, a lonely boy finds friendship with a vampire girl.

My Life as a Dog (1985). This bittersweet tale from director Lasse Hallström focuses on a young boy in 1950s Sweden.

The Seventh Seal (1957). In this Ingmar Bergman film (set in Sweden during the Black Death), a knight questions the meaning of life. Other masterpieces from the Oscar-winning Swedish director include *Smiles of a Summer Night* (1955), a turn-of-the-century frolic, and *Fanny & Alexander* (1983), about two children overcoming their father's death.

Together (2000). This satirical view of socialist values is set in a 1970s Stockholm commune.

Wallander (2005-2013). Based on the characters in Henning Mankell's Kurt Wallander detective novels, this Swedish crime series is a study in the Scandinavian temperament and culture.

Welcome to Sweden (2014-). In this NBC comedy series starring Greg Poehler (who coproduces the show with his sister Amy), an American accountant follows his girlfriend back to her home in Stockholm, where he embarks on crazy adventures with her quirky family.

APPENDIX

Contents

Useful Contacts

Emergency Needs

In all the countries in this book, dial 112 for medical or other emergencies. For police, dial 112 everywhere except Estonia (dial 110).

US Embassies

Embassies are located in all the capital cities.

In Denmark: Dag Hammarskjölds Allé 24, Copenhagen, passport services by appointment, info tel. 33 41 71 00 (Mon-Fri 14:00-16:00), emergency tel. 33 41 74 00, http://denmark.usembassy.gov

In Estonia: Kentmanni 20, Tallinn, passport services Mon-Fri 9:00-12:00 & 14:00-17:00, tel. 668-8128, emergency tel. 509-2129, http://estonia.usembassy.gov

In Finland: Itäinen Puistotie 14B, Helsinki, passport services by appointment, info tel. 40/140-5957 (Mon-Thu 14:00-16:00), emergency tel. 09/616-250, http://finland.usembassy.gov

In Norway: Henrik Ibsens Gate 48, Oslo, passport services by appointment, info tel. 21 30 85 58 (Mon-Fri 15:00-16:30), emergency tel. 21 30 85 40, http://norway.usembassy.gov

In Sweden: Dag Hammarskjölds Väg 31, Stockholm, passport services by appointment, info tel. 08/783-4375 (Mon-Tue and

Thu 13:00-14:00), emergency tel. 08/783-5300, http://stockholm.
usembassy.gov

Canadian Embassies

In Denmark: Kristen Bernikowsgade 1, Copenhagen, passport
services Mon-Fri 8:30-12:00 & 13:00-16:30, tel. 33 48 32 00,
www.canada.dk

In Estonia: Toomkooli 13, Tallinn, passport services Mon-Fri
8:30-17:00, tel. 627-3311, www.canada.ee

In Finland: Pohjoisesplanadi 25B, Helsinki, passport services
Mon-Fri by appointment only, tel. 09/228-530, www.canada.fi

In Norway: Wergelandsveien 7, Oslo, passport services Mon-Fri
8:30-12:30, tel. 22 99 53 00, www.canada.no

In Sweden: Klarabergsgatan 23, Stockholm, passport services
Mon-Fri 9:00-12:00, tel. 08/453-3000, www.canadaemb.se

Holidays and Festivals

This list includes selected festivals in major cities, plus national
holidays observed throughout Scandinavia. Many sights and banks
close down on national holidays—keep this in mind when planning your itinerary. Before planning a trip around a festival, verify its dates by checking the festival's website or TI sites (www.
goscandinavia.com; for Estonia, check www.visitestonia.com).

Jan 1	New Year's Day
Jan 6	Epiphany, Sweden and Finland
Feb	Vinterjazz, winter jazz festival (www.jazz.dk), Denmark
Feb 24	National Day, Estonia
Good Friday	April 3 in 2015, March 25 in 2016
Easter	April 5 in 2015, March 27 in 2016
April 30	Walpurgis Night (bonfires, choirs), Sweden and Finland
May 1	Labor Day (parades, some closures)
Common Prayer Day	May 1 in 2015, April 22 in 2016, Denmark (businesses closed)
Early-Mid-May	MaiJazz (international jazz festival, www.maijazz.no), Stavanger, Norway
Ascension Day	May 14 in 2015, May 5 in 2016
May 15	St. Hallvard's Day (theater, concerts), Oslo
May 17	Constitution Day (parades, closures), Norway

Whitsunday and Whitmonday	May 24-25 in 2015, May 15-16 in 2016
Late May-Early June	Bergen International Festival (concerts, ballet, opera, theater; www.fib.no)
Late May-Early June	Old Town Days (music and parades; http://vanalinnapaevad.ee), Tallinn
May-June	Medieval Festival ("Middelalderfestival," www.oslomiddelalderfestival.org), Oslo
June 5	Constitution Day (businesses closed), Denmark
June 6	National Day (parades), Sweden
Early June	Archipelago Boat Day (steamboat parade, (www.skargardstrafikanten.se), Stockholm
Early June	Taste of Stockholm (outdoor food vendors; www.smakapastockholm.se)
Mid-June	Norwegian Wood Rock Music Festival (www.norwegianwood.no), Oslo
Mid-June	Bergenfest (rock, pop, hip-hop, and folk music; www.bergenfest.no), Bergen, Norway
Mid-June-Mid-Aug	Fløyen Concert Festival (classical music, www.floyenfolk.no), Bergen, Norway
Mid-June-Mid-Aug	Grieg in Bergen Festival (summer-long concert series; www.grieginbergen.com), Bergen, Norway
June 23	Victory Day, Estonia (celebrates decisive 1919 battle in Estonia's War of Independence)
June 23	Sankthansaften (St. John's Eve, midsummer festival, Norway and Denmark)
Late June	Midsummer Eve and Midsummer Day (celebrations, bonfires), Scandinavia
July 4	Fourth of July festivities, Stockholm
Late June-Early July	Roskilde Festival (music and culture, www.roskilde-festival.dk), Roskilde, Denmark
Early July-Late Aug	Savonlinna Opera Festival (www.operafestival.fi), Savonlinna, Finland
Mid-July	Copenhagen Jazz Festival (www.jazz.dk)
Mid-Late July	International Jazz Festival (www.jazzfest.dk), Aarhus, Denmark
Late July	Food Festival ("Gladmat," www.gladmat.no), Stavanger, Norway
Late July-Mid-Aug	Hans Christian Andersen Festival (www.hcandersenfestspil.dk), Odense, Denmark

Mid-Aug	International Chamber Music Festival (www.icmf.no), Stavanger, Norway
Mid-Aug	Chamber Music Festival (www.oslokammermusikkfestival.no), Oslo
Mid-Aug	Jazz Festival (www.oslojazz.no), Oslo
Mid-Late Aug	Helsinki Festival (music, dance, film, theater; www.helsinkifestival.fi)
August 20	Day of Restoration of Independence (celebrates Estonia's 1991 independence), Estonia
Late Aug-Sept	Aarhus Festival (music, dance, theater; www.aarhusfestuge.dk), Aarhus, Denmark
Mid-Sept	Ultima Contemporary Music Festival (www.ultima.no), Oslo
Mid-Oct	DølaJazz Festival (www.dolajazz.no), Lillehammer, Norway
Mid-Oct	Stockholm Jazz Festival (www.stockholm-jazz.com)
Mid-Nov-Early Jan	Christmas Fair (Tivoli Garden), Copenhagen
Dec 6	Independence Day (candlelit windows), Finland
Dec 10	Nobel Peace Prize Award Ceremony, Oslo and Stockholm
Dec 13	St. Lucia Day (festival of lights), Sweden, Norway, and parts of Finland
Dec 25	Christmas
Dec 26	Boxing Day

Conversions and Climate

NUMBERS AND STUMBLERS

- Europeans write a few of their numbers differently than we do. 1 = 1, 4 = 4, 7 = 7.
- In Europe, dates appear as day/month/year, so Christmas 2016 is 25/12/2016.
- Commas are decimal points and decimals commas. A dollar and a half is $1,50, one thousand is 1.000, and there are 5.280 feet in a mile.
- When counting with fingers, start with your thumb. If you hold up your first finger to request one item, you'll probably get two.
- What Americans call the second floor of a building is the first floor in Europe.

- Scandinavians number their weeks. Instead of saying, "Spring break is the third week in March," they'd say, "Spring break is week 12."
- On escalators and moving sidewalks, Europeans keep the left "lane" open for passing. Keep to the right.

METRIC CONVERSIONS

A kilogram is 2.2 pounds, and l liter is about a quart, or almost four to a gallon. A kilometer is six-tenths of a mile. I figure kilometers to miles by cutting them in half and adding back 10 percent of the original (120 km: 60 + 12 = 72 miles, 300 km: 150 + 30 = 180 miles).

1 foot = 0.3 meter	1 square yard = 0.8 square meter
1 yard = 0.9 meter	1 square mile = 2.6 square kilometers
1 mile = 1.6 kilometers	1 ounce = 28 grams
1 centimeter = 0.4 inch	1 quart = 0.95 liter
1 meter = 39.4 inches	1 kilogram = 2.2 pounds
1 kilometer = 0.62 mile	32°F = 0°C

CLOTHING SIZES

When shopping for clothing, use these US-to-European comparisons as general guidelines (but note that no conversion is perfect).

- Women's dresses and blouses: Add 30
  (US size 10 = European size 40)
- Men's suits and jackets: Add 10
  (US size 40 regular = European size 50)
- Men's shirts: Multiply by 2 and add about 8
  (US size 15 collar = European size 38)
- Women's shoes: Add about 30
  (US size 8 = European size 38-39)
- Men's shoes: Add 32-34
  (US size 9 = European size 41; US size 11 = European size 45)

SCANDINAVIA'S CLIMATE

First line, average daily high; second line, average daily low; third line, average days without rain. For more detailed weather statistics for destinations in this book (as well as the rest of the world), check www.wunderground.com.

	J	F	M	A	M	J	J	A	S	O	N	D
DENMARK • Copenhagen												
	37°	37°	42°	51°	60°	66°	70°	69°	64°	55°	46°	41°
	29°	28°	31°	37°	45°	51°	56°	56°	51°	44°	38°	33°
	14	15	19	18	20	18	17	16	14	14	11	12
ESTONIA • Tallinn												
	25°	25°	32°	45°	57°	66°	68°	66°	59°	50°	37°	30°
	14°	12°	19°	32°	41°	50°	54°	52°	48°	39°	30°	19°
	12	12	18	19	19	20	18	16	14	14	12	12
FINLAND • Helsinki												
	26°	25°	32°	44°	56°	66°	71°	68°	59°	47°	37°	31°
	17°	15°	20°	30°	40°	49°	55°	53°	46°	37°	30°	23°
	11	10	17	17	19	17	17	16	16	13	11	11
NORWAY • Oslo												
	28°	30°	39°	50°	61°	68°	72°	70°	60°	48°	38°	32°
	19°	19°	25°	34°	43°	50°	55°	53°	46°	38°	31°	25°
	16	16	22	19	21	17	16	17	16	17	14	14
SWEDEN • Stockholm												
	30°	30°	37°	47°	58°	67°	71°	68°	60°	49°	40°	35°
	26°	25°	29°	37°	45°	53°	57°	56°	50°	43°	37°	32°
	15	14	21	19	20	17	18	17	16	16	14	14

FAHRENHEIT AND CELSIUS CONVERSION

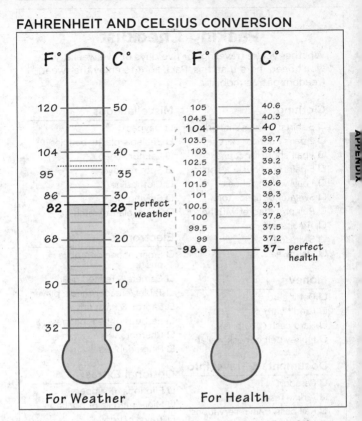

For Weather   For Health

Scandinavia takes its temperature using the Celsius scale, while we opt for Fahrenheit. For a rough conversion from Celsius to Fahrenheit, double the number and add 30. For weather, remember that 28°C is 82°F—perfect. For health, 37°C is just right. At a launderette, 30°C is cold, 40°C is warm (usually the default setting), 60°C is hot, and 95°C is boiling.

Packing Checklist

Whether you're traveling for five days or five weeks, you won't need more than this. Pack light to enjoy the sweet freedom of true mobility.

Clothing

❏ 5 shirts: long- & short-sleeve
❏ 2 pairs pants or skirt
❏ 1 pair shorts or capris
❏ 5 pairs underwear & socks
❏ 1 pair walking shoes
❏ Sweater or fleece top
❏ Rainproof jacket with hood
❏ Tie or scarf
❏ Swimsuit
❏ Sleepwear

Money

❏ Debit card
❏ Credit card(s)
❏ Hard cash ($20 bills)
❏ Money belt or neck wallet

Documents & Travel Info

❏ Passport
❏ Airline reservations
❏ Rail pass/train reservations
❏ Car-rental voucher
❏ Driver's license
❏ Student ID, hostel card, etc.
❏ Photocopies of all the above
❏ Hotel confirmations
❏ Insurance details
❏ Guidebooks & maps
❏ Notepad & pen
❏ Journal

Toiletries Kit

❏ Toiletries
❏ Medicines & vitamins
❏ First-aid kit
❏ Glasses/contacts/sunglasses (with prescriptions)
❏ Earplugs
❏ Packet of tissues (for WC)

Miscellaneous

❏ Daypack
❏ Sealable plastic baggies
❏ Laundry soap
❏ Spot remover
❏ Clothesline
❏ Sewing kit
❏ Travel alarm/watch

Electronics

❏ Smartphone or mobile phone
❏ Camera & related gear
❏ Tablet/ereader/media player
❏ Laptop & flash drive
❏ Earbuds or headphones
❏ Chargers
❏ Plug adapters

Optional Extras

❏ Flipflops or slippers
❏ Mini-umbrella or poncho
❏ Travel hairdryer
❏ Belt
❏ Hat (for sun or cold)
❏ Picnic supplies
❏ Water bottle
❏ Fold-up tote bag
❏ Small flashlight
❏ Small binoculars
❏ Insect repellent
❏ Small towel or washcloth
❏ Inflatable pillow
❏ Some duct tape (for repairs)
❏ Tiny lock
❏ Address list (to mail postcards)
❏ Postcards/photos from home
❏ Extra passport photos
❏ Good book

INDEX

MAP INDEX

Explore Europe

At ricksteves.com you can browse through thousands of articles, videos, photos and radio interviews, plus find a wealth of money-saving travel tips for planning your dream trip. And with our mobile-friendly website, you can easily access all this great travel information anywhere you go.

TV Shows

Preview the places you'll visit by watching entire half-hour episodes of Rick Steves' Europe (choose from all 100 shows) on-demand, for free.

your travel dreams into affordable reality

Radio Interviews

Enjoy ready access to Rick's vast library of radio interviews covering travel

tips and cultural insights that relate specifically to your Europe travel plans.

Travel Forums

Learn, ask, share! Our online community of savvy travelers is a great resource for first-time travelers to Europe, as well as seasoned pros. You'll find forums on each country, plus travel tips and restaurant/hotel reviews. You can even ask one of our well-traveled staff to chime in with an opinion.

Travel News

Subscribe to our free Travel News e-newsletter, and get monthly updates from Rick on what's happening in Europe.

Rick's Free Travel App

Gear up for your next adventure at ricksteves.com

Light Luggage

Pack light and right with Rick Steves' affordable, custom-designed rolling carry-on bags, backpacks, day packs and shoulder bags.

Accessories

From packing cubes to moneybelts and beyond, Rick has personally selected the travel goodies that will help your trip go smoother.

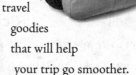

Shop at ricksteves.com

Save time and energy

This guidebook is your independent-travel toolkit. But for all it delivers, it's still up to you to devote the time and energy it takes to manage the preparation and logistics that are essential for a happy trip. If that's a hassle, there's a solution.

Rick Steves Tours

A Rick Steves tour takes you to Europe's most interesting places with great

with minimum stress

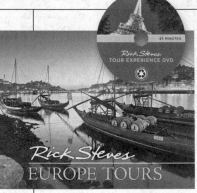

guides and small groups of 28 or less. We follow Rick's favorite itineraries, ride in comfy buses, stay in family-run hotels, and bring you intimately close to the Europe you've traveled so far to see. Most importantly, we take away the logistical headaches so you can focus on the fun.

customers—along with us on 40 different itineraries, from Ireland to Italy to Istanbul. Is a Rick Steves tour the right fit for your travel dreams? Find out at ricksteves.com, where you can also get Rick's latest tour catalog and free Tour Experience DVD.

Join the fun

This year we'll take 18,000 free-spirited travelers— nearly half of them repeat

Europe is best experienced with happy travel partners. We hope you can join us.

See our itineraries at ricksteves.com

Rick Steves

Maximize your travel skills
with a good guidebook.

Credits

RESEARCHERS
To help update this book, Rick relied on...

Glenn Eriksen

Glenn, the son of Norwegian immigrants, is a Rick Steves guidebook editor who researched Norway and Denmark for this book. In these lands flowing with coffee, pastry, cheese, and herring, he explored bustling cities, lovely countrysides, tidy villages, and spectacular fjords. Though he feels perfectly at home in Scandinavia, Glenn lives in Seattle.

Cameron Hewitt

Cameron writes and edits guidebooks for Rick Steves, specializing in Eastern Europe. For this book, he island-hopped through Stockholm, prowled the cobbles of Tallinn, and went on a design-store shopping spree in Helsinki—all while fighting insomnia in the land of the midnight sun. When he's not traveling, Cameron lives in Seattle with his wife, Shawna.

CONTRIBUTOR
Gene Openshaw

Gene is the co-author of a dozen Rick Steves books. For this book, he wrote material on Europe's art, history, and contemporary culture. When not traveling, Gene enjoys composing music, recovering from his 1973 trip to Europe with Rick, and living everyday life with his daughter.

ACKNOWLEDGMENTS
Thanks to Thor, Hanne, Geir, Hege, and Kari-Anne, our Norwegian family. Special thanks to Jane Klausen for her expertise in all things Danish. Thanks to these translators for their help with the survival phrases: Marita Bergman, Unni-Marie Kvikne, Mati Rummessen, and Christina Snellman. And in loving memory of Berit Kristiansen, whose house was my house for 20 years of Norwegian travel.

Avalon Travel
a member of the Perseus Books Group
1700 Fourth Street
Berkeley, CA 94710

Text © 2015 by Rick Steves' Europe, Inc. All rights reserved.
Cover © 2015 by Avalon Travel. All rights reserved.
Maps © 2015 by Rick Steves' Europe, Inc. All rights reserved.
Printed in Canada by Friesens. Second printing March 2016.

ISBN 978-1-63121-058-7
ISSN 1084-7206
14th Edition

For the latest on Rick's lectures, guidebooks, tours, public radio show, and public television series, contact Rick Steves' Europe, 130 Fourth Avenue North, Edmonds, WA 98020, 425/771-8303, www.ricksteves.com, rick@ricksteves.com.

Rick Steves' Europe

Managing Editor: Risa Laib
Editorial & Production Manager: Jennifer Madison Davis
Editors: Glenn Eriksen, Tom Griffin, Cameron Hewitt, Suzanne Kotz, Cathy Lu, Carrie Shepherd
Editorial & Production Assistant: Jessica Shaw
Editorial Intern: Stacie Larsen
Researchers: Glenn Eriksen, Cameron Hewitt
Maps & Graphics: David C. Hoerlein, Sandra Hundacker, Lauren Mills, Mary Rostad

Avalon Travel

Senior Editor & Series Manager: Madhu Prasher
Editor: Jamie Andrade
Associate Editor: Maggie Ryan
Copy Editor: Patrick Collins
Proofreader: Jennifer Malnick
Indexer: Beatrice Wikander
Production & Typesetting: Tabitha Lahr, Rue Flaherty
Cover Design: Kimberly Glyder Design
Maps & Graphics: Kat Bennett, Mike Morgenfeld
Photo Credits
Front Cover: Norway, Western Fjords, Bergen, Hardangerfjorden © Peter Adams/Getty Images
Title Page: Copenhagen, Denmark © Rick Steves
Full-page Pages: p. 17, Viking Prows, Oslo, Norway; p. 25, Copenhagen's Nøjbroplads, Denmark; p. 205, Sognefjord, Norway; p. 423, Archipelago, Sweden; p. 577, Helsinki, Finland; p. 643, Tallinn, Estonia
Additional Photography: Dominic Arizona Bonuccelli, Tom Griffin, Sonja Groset, Cameron Hewitt, David C. Hoerlein, Lauren Mills, Moesgaard Museum, Rick Steves, Ian Watson, Chris Werner (photos are used by permission and are the property of the original copyright owners).